A SHIPYARD IN MAINE

A Shipyard in Maine

Percy & Small and the
Great Schooners

Ralph Linwood Snow

Captain Douglas K. Lee

Tilbury House, Publishers
Gardiner, Maine

Maine Maritime Museum
Bath, Maine

Tilbury House, Publishers
132 Water Street, Gardiner, Maine 04345
800-582-1899

Maine Maritime Museum
243 Washington Street, Bath, Maine 04530
207-443-1316

First printing: February, 1999

10 9 8 7 6 5 4 3 2 1

Library of Congress Cataloging-in-Publication Data:
Snow, Ralph Linwood, 1934–
A shipyard in Maine : Percy & Small and the great
schooners / Ralph Linwood Snow, Douglas K. Lee.
p.   cm
ISBN 0-88448-193-X (alk. paper)
1. Percy & Small—History.   2. Shipyards—Maine—
Bath—History.   3. Shipbuilding industry—Maine—
Bath—History. I. Lee, Douglas K., 1946–   . II. Title.
VM301.P43S66   1999
338.7'62382'009741—dc21   98-31176
                                 CIP

Text and jacket designed on Crummett Mountain by
    Edith Allard, Somerville, ME
Layout: Nina Medina, Basil Hill Graphics, Somerville, ME
Editorial and production: Jennifer Buckley Elliott and
    Barbara Diamond
Color scans, B&W scans, and film: Integrated Com-
    position Systems, Spokane, WA
Text printing and binding: Quebecor, Kingsport, TN
Jacket film and printing: The John P. Pow Co., South
    Boston, MA

Frontispiece caption: The five-master GRACE A. MARTIN
"smokes" into the Kennebec River from Percy & Small on
a warm and sunny 16 July 1904. Despite the large crowd
of fashionably attired observers—on shore and aboard—
the shipyard is obviously a place of serious business with its
stacks of ship timber, staging, a huge pile of sawdust/chips,
and the frame of the six-master RUTH E. MERRILL taking
shape on the north building ways.
Courtesy of Maine Maritime Museum

Contents

Dedication

He pioneered the serious study of the last generation of large, wooden sailing vessels to serve in America's merchant marine and the trades in which they engaged. The resulting book published a half century ago, *The Great Coal Schooners of New England, 1870–1909*, has easily weathered the test of time as an articulate, thoroughly researched, and carefully documented study in the best traditions of scholarship.

Captain Parker—"Lew" to his friends and colleagues—pursued an active career in the U. S. Coast Guard from World War II through the early 1970s which included combat service in the Pacific, weather patrols in the Atlantic, and command of the 255-foot cutter Owasco. However busy his Coast Guard duties kept him, Lew still found time to seek out and interview many of those who were participants in the last act of American merchant sail. He also, fortuitously, rescued many of the records and photographs of that past from otherwise certain destruction.

Since his retirement from the Coast Guard, Captain Parker has remained fully involved in the maritime history field, delivering papers at conferences and symposia in the U. S. and abroad on such diverse subjects as the Kennebec River ice trade and the River Plate trade. He has written articles for journals and periodicals, and has been a contributor to the Conway *History of the Ship* series. In his spare time, he has served as a longtime and highly valued trustee of Maine Maritime Museum.

Lew has opened his archive, his memories, his meticulous notes, his voluminous image files, and his home to the authors without hesitation and without stint. He has spent uncounted hours with us discussing schooners in general, the great schooners in particular, and those who were involved with them. He has delighted in our discoveries and mourned with us when leads have run into dead ends. He has been our mentor, a generous friend, and an unwavering colleague. Simply put, this book could never have been written without him.

Ralph Linwood Snow
Captain Douglas K. Lee

Foreword

This is a book that I have long desired to see written, and I expect it was also a priority of Maine Maritime Museum, since for a number of years the museum has been located at the old Percy & Small shipyard in Bath, Maine. Alone of all the many builders of large wooden sailing vessels, Percy & Small still looks much as it did when Bath's last big schooner was launched in 1920, its major structures still miraculously surviving periods of neglect and change. In its quarter century of operation, Percy & Small built forty-one big schooners, sixteen of which were for their own managing ownership. Most noteworthy of them all was the six-master WYOMING, the largest wooden merchant sailing vessel ever built. Maine Maritime Museum could have found no more appropriate a home than this historic shipyard. The Percy & Small story survives through a serendipitous series of events.

My own interest in maritime history is long-standing and broad, encompassing both sail and steam. During my early boyhood in Halifax, Nova Scotia, my father delighted me by taking me aboard transatlantic liners. An especially vivid recollection was the thrill of watching BLUENOSE cross the finish line well ahead of the Gloucesterman ELSIE in the final race of the 1921 International Fisherman's Race. The following day, a Sunday, my joy was complete when my father took me aboard BLUENOSE. From the forecastle companionway, down which I peeked, there arose a robust and pleasing aroma of pipe smoke and Demerara rum, a fondness for which has never left me. A move to

Boston in 1922 by no means abated my enthusiasm for the maritime scene. I was an avid reader of the column-long shipping news of the *Boston Herald* and learned much therefrom of the trading patterns of steamers and schooners. In 1927, armed with my first Kodak Brownie, I was taken to Nantasket to go aboard the West Coast five-master NANCY, which had dragged ashore there the previous winter. She seemed little damaged, but low freights offered little incentive to incur the expense of salvage. I think it cost twenty-five cents to board her, and it was most certainly a bargain for this schooner-struck youngster. Frequent trips on coastal steamers to Saint John (New Brunswick), Yarmouth (Nova Scotia), New York, and Norfolk afforded tantalizing glimpses of schooners at sea, but there were no opportunities to go aboard them. A move to New York came at an age when I was old enough to ride the ferries on Saturdays by myself, to photograph the departing liners. This routine was soon extended to rambles along the Brooklyn waterfront from the Brooklyn Bridge to the Atlantic and Erie Basins and the Bush Terminal. Occasionally I would see a schooner at anchor on Red Hook flats, but they were frustratingly inaccessible. I read marine books voraciously, learning much about British tea and wool clippers from the works of Basil Lubbock, and the Australian grain racers from Alan Villiers's fine writings. But nowhere did I find anything to satisfy my curiosity about the dwindling fleet of schooners that still plied our own coastal waters.

My Saturday excursions to New York Harbor

commenced with a short rail journey from our suburban home in northern New Jersey to the Erie Railroad station and ferry terminal in Jersey City. Before entering the yard, the train passed through a tunnel and after it emerged, there were a few seconds when it was possible to see the Delaware, Lackawanna & Western Railroad's coal dock in Hoboken. At rare intervals, my heart would be gladdened by the sight of three or four topmasts of a schooner loading anthracite for eastern Maine or the Maritime Provinces, and my plan of the day would be scrapped forthwith as I veered course on jaunts that led me to visit about two dozen working schooners, some of them several times, during the five years preceding Pearl Harbor. Among them was the last East Coast five-master, EDNA HOYT, while she was discharging what was unquestionably the last cargo of bituminous coal brought to Boston from Hampton Roads in a schooner. Others included the big four-masters HERBERT L. RAWDING and HELEN BARNET GRING; only one Percy & Small-built schooner, the ANNIE C. ROSS; down to a handful of smaller Nova Scotian schooners.

The ROSS was a handsome vessel, although a bit past her prime. She will always be remembered as the inspiration for John A. Noble's remarkable series of lithographs, *Schooner's Progress*, and for Frederick F. Kaiser's fond reminiscences of his voyages in her, told in his book *Built on Honor, Sailed with Skill*. After my sole visit to her in the headwaters of Newtown Creek on a torrid August day, I sought a vantage point from which to photograph her. Nearby, I found a small oil terminal, devoid of fence or watchman, and I inched my way out on two six-inch pipes for a distance of forty feet to a clump of piling to which oil barges were secured when making their deliveries. Beneath me were the miasmal waters of the creek, ripe with the scent of raw sewage, marsh gas, and oil slick. The Lord was with me and I got my picture. Had I fallen in, I wouldn't have been worth saving.

During the summer of 1936, between my sophomore and junior years at Dartmouth College, I was determined to go to sea in a steamer to see a bit of the world, but because of the depression and mili-

tant unionism, I stood not a chance. At that point it struck me that there would be few more opportunities to make a trip or two in coasting schooners, and after two or three disappointments, I had the good fortune to persuade Captain John J. Taylor of the big Parrsboro, Nova Scotia, tern (three-masted) schooner T. K. BENTLEY to let me go in her for a round trip from New York to Saint John, New Brunswick, with coal, then back to New York with spruce piling from the Minas Basin. Wages I had none. In fact, I paid the princely sum of five dollars a week for my board, occupied a very decent spare stateroom aft, and ate in the cabin. I had no duties but tried to be as helpful as possible and was free to photograph the good old vessel alow and aloft. For several hours each day, the "Old Man" took the wheel so that one of the three sailors could be more useful in cleaning, painting, or sailorizing, and I often kept him company, for he was a good conversationalist and I learned much from him. The mate, Asher Knowlton, was a genuine shellback who ran away to sea in the 1870s, not returning to his Nova Scotia family until some four years later, the proud possessor of a mate's certificate. He averred that the finest ship in which he had ever served was the clipper BRENDA with contract labor and gunny sacks from Calcutta to Trinidad. He had commanded a number of tern schooners in the Parrsboro fleet, but the shrinkage of the fleet and his advanced age had left him no option but to sail as mate. In such company, my eight-day passage to Saint John passed too quickly. The coal cargo took a week to discharge, after which we were favored by a perfect day to romp up the Bay of Fundy impelled by a strong, fair, southwest breeze. We anchored at Spencer Island over a weekend, and early on Monday morning we towed around to Advocate Harbour, the village in which the BENTLEY had been built in 1920. Here, we lay in the Lubber Hole, snuggled up against a natural breakwater of stones. Within three hours after high water, the vessel was grounded out and it was possible to walk the half mile to town. The schooner's bow ports were opened and fitted with spile chutes. Each time the tide returned, our underdeck cargo of 50- or 60-foot sticks of spruce piling, made up in rafts, was towed out by a motor boat and positioned ahead of the spile chutes, up which they could be hauled into the hold by the vessel's gasoline hoisting engine. A week or more passed filling the hold. Captain John had gone home to Parrsboro, leaving the loading to the mate and the stevedore, but now and then he would come down before noon with his son Morley, and we often enjoyed a large bottle of Dow's Ale apiece before lunch. I was overwhelmed by the kindness of the good people of Advocate Harbour and have fond memories of evenings yarning with Captain Brad Morris, the long-retired master of the four-masted barkentine ENSENADA. Just before we were to take on the deck load, this idyllic time was shattered by news of my mother's serious illness, and my newfound friends drove me to Parrsboro to wish me Godspeed on the first leg of my homeward journey.

The following summer I made another trip in the T. K. BENTLEY, coal-laden, from South Amboy to Saint John. Thereafter, I was made welcome aboard her whenever she was in New York, often having a meal or spending the night in my old room. I would be hard pressed to recall any experience in my long life that has given me more pleasure than my days in the BENTLEY with Captain Taylor as friend and mentor.

On my way back to college after Christmas vacation in 1936–37, I first beheld the Stebbins marine photographs at the Society for the Preservation of New England Antiquities in Boston. I was fascinated by the views of a number of handsome, white five-masted schooners, the names of which all terminated with the surname "Palmer." Why, I wondered, were these vessels built, and what was their trade? It was with incredulity that I soon learned that these graceful vessels were built primarily to carry bituminous coal from Norfolk, Newport News, Baltimore, and Philadelphia to power New England industry during the first decade of this century. It was the last anachronistic challenge of centuries of wooden shipbuilding against the inevitable technical advantages of steam and steel. Percy & Small took the lead and led it to a spectacular finale. I was fascinated by this story and, concentrating on the Palmer fleet, I sought to explain why it had occurred.

In the autumn of 1938, I commenced work for a master's degree in history at Columbia University under the guidance of Professor J. Bartlet Brebner, specializing in the congenial field of Canadian-American relations. Scarcely a month into my studies, I was lured away one afternoon to the malodorous headwaters of Newtown Creek in the Maspeth section of Brooklyn. There lay the four-master ALBERT F. PAUL, discharging spruce lumber from Sheet Harbor, Nova Scotia. The mate, William H. Davis, bade me welcome, and, as was my custom, I asked him if he remembered the Palmer fleet. He laughed and replied, "I guess I ought to! I had command of two of them, the MAUDE PALMER and the REBECCA PALMER," and he was obviously delighted to talk about them. Many times that fall and winter, while the PAUL lay idle awaiting a charter, I visited her to talk with Will and her master, Captain Robert O. Jones. I always came armed with a list of written questions about various aspects of design, seamanship, and business practices that governed the big coal schooners, as well as the personalities involved in management and labor. We would have a bite of supper served by the black cook, after which we would light up the cigars I had brought with me, then Will Davis would adjust his battered glasses, take my list of questions, and proceed to give me thorough, carefully considered answers. I have met a goodly number of men who sailed big schooners, but I can think of none who could have stuck to the matter at hand as well as did Will Davis.

I reported my extracurricular activities to Professor Brebner, and he most graciously consented to let me do my master's essay on the great coal schooners. He avowed ignorance of maritime history and suggested that I seek guidance from Professor Robert G. Albion at Princeton.

Bob Albion and I found a great deal in common and our friendship was to endure for the rest of his life. It was essential, he told me, that I should spend the week between semesters in Boston, Portland, and Bath, and he gave me a number of very good leads. In the Boston Custom House, I found records of the owners of shares in a number of the Palmer schooners, including the PAUL PALMER. Miss Decrow, successor to her father in running Boston's venerable ship chandlery, James Bliss & Company, insisted that I should meet Charles S. Morgan, who became the best of friends; we shared a deep interest in schooners until his untimely death some fifty years later. In Bath—my first visit to the City of Ships—I was warmly received by Mark Hennessy, whose *Sewall Ships of Steel* I had just read with great pleasure. Upon returning to New York, I reported my findings to Alfred W. Paine, proprietor of a most delightful shop of "Books Relating to Salt Water." He looked at the list of owners of the PAUL PALMER, swung around in his chair, and pulled out his Harvard directory, saying, "Paul Palmer was at Harvard about my time. He is living in Fort Lauderdale now." Paul, son of William F. Palmer, manager of the Palmer fleet, responded with enthusiasm to my letter and supplied me with information on the earnings of the Palmer schooners, an essential ingredient to my essay on the coal schooners. A much later visit to Florida revealed the richness of the Palmer fleet papers, which Paul had saved. Outstanding in importance were the letter books of William F. Palmer's outgoing correspondence, drawings, contracts, and photographs. I was most anxious that this collection should come to Maine Maritime Museum, and so it came to pass after Paul's death, thanks largely to the good offices of Captains Douglas and Linda Lee and Morrison Bump. The Palmer letters to Percy & Small have added no little spice to this fine book.

My master's essay achieved its purpose in 1940, but there seemed little prospect of earning a living teaching history. Once again Freddy Paine proved of inestimable service by suggesting that I investigate the newly established but little publicized Coast Guard Reserve. It was the turning point in my life, leading to a commission in the regular establishment after the war and to twenty-eight happy years of service. For several months in 1946, while on terminal leave and awaiting a recall to active duty in weather patrol cutters, I lived in Mystic, Connecticut, absorbing maritime history from that wonderful man, Carl Cutler, curator of what was soon to become Mystic Seaport Museum, and it was he who made possible the museum's publication of my book, *The Great Coal Schooners of New England, 1870–1909.*

My friendships with like-minded individuals, including Andy Nesdall, Giles Tod, Mike Costagliola, and Charlie Morgan, gave me much pleasure and fueled my investigations. Over the next ten years, the greater part of my leaves was spent on the coast of Maine, seeking to learn more about the big schooners and the men who built and sailed them. Fortunately, there were still a goodly number of men and women living who had participated in the last days of merchant sail, and almost always they were glad to share their recollections and memorabilia with me.

It was a particularly fortunate day in the autumn of 1954 when I first called on Captain Sam Percy's gracious daughter, Eleanor Irish. She had already chanced to read my book, and it was obvious that it had rekindled a strong interest in her father's career as a shipmaster, shipbuilder, and ship owner. It was soon apparent from our conversation that the great bulk of Percy & Small's business records had long since been discarded. She was, however, having her father's house, vacant since her mother's death, cleaned out to be sold. There were, she told me, some papers on the kitchen floor which would soon be on the way to the dump unless I thought them worth saving. They proved, indeed, to be a treasure-trove. They included the journal or day book covering the first fourteen years of Percy & Small's existence, contracts and specifications for building vessels, blueprints, and the original bills detailing the costs of nearly all of their vessels. I am happy to have been the agent for the survival of these records, and their skillful use by author Lin Snow will be apparent to the fortunate readers of this wonderful book.

CAPTAIN W. J. LEWIS PARKER, USCG, RET.
CAMDEN, MAINE

Preface

The great schooners—four-, five-, six-, and seven-masted schooners—have received relatively little attention in scholarly or popular histories although their era extended over four decades (1879–1921), far longer than the American clipper ship era (circa 1845–60) upon which oceans of ink have been expended. The great schooners not only enjoyed an edge in longevity, but as a class they contributed far more to the prosperity of the nation than did the clippers.

Between 1879 and 1921 approximately 526 great schooners were built along the Atlantic and Gulf coasts, all but three of traditional wooden construction. Three-quarters of these schooners were built in Maine shipyards. Most were engaged in the unromantic but critical task of hauling coal to fuel the burgeoning industries in the northeastern United States, an example of a traditional and low-tech industry—operating wooden sailing vessels—supporting the growth of a high-tech industry, the conversion of fossil fuel into various useful forms of energy.

Percy & Small, one of the Maine firms that built and operated great schooners, and one of the last of a long line of wooden shipyards that had made the name of Bath synonymous with wooden shipbuilding, established a unique record during its active career. It built nineteen four-masters (4 percent of all those built on the Atlantic/Gulf Coasts); fifteen five-masters (27 percent of all those built on the Atlantic/Gulf Coasts); and seven six-masters (70 percent of all those built on the Atlantic/Gulf Coasts). While achieving this production record, the firm also pushed the boundaries of traditional wooden ship design and ship construction to their maximum limits just as the curtain rang down on five hundred years of commercial, oceangoing, plank-on-frame wooden shipbuilding.

The history of Percy & Small is a story worth telling. It is also a story unusually well documented for a commercial operation. The shipyard that closed out the age of commercial wooden shipbuilding remains basically intact; and one of the great schooners built there survived in sufficiently good condition and long enough to have her structure and construction thoroughly recorded with tape measure, camera, and sketch pad by Douglas and Linda Lee. But there is far more than just the bodies, so to speak.

Captain W. J. Lewis Parker, USCG, Ret., author of the pioneering study *The Great Coal Schooners of New England, 1870–1909*, has consistently encouraged the authors and provided the benefit of his encyclopedic knowledge concerning Atlantic Coast schooners and the schooner trades in general. He has also generously opened his extensive collection of documents and photographs relating to Percy & Small, many rescued by him from the brink of destruction five decades ago, and made available his detailed notes of interviews with a number of persons involved in the history of that firm.

Maine Maritime Museum has also proved to be a rich source of information concerning Percy & Small and their schooners. Thanks to Librarian Nathan Lipfert and Archivist Elizabeth Singer Maule, the authors were able to thoroughly canvass the museum's archival and photo collections and, with their assistance, uncover many significant items.

We are particularly indebted to the museum and the thirty generous donors who financed the purchase of the William F. Palmer papers from the Palmer grandchildren in 1993. Palmer's letter books have been particularly valuable in illuminating the activities of the Atlantic Carriers' Association as well as the day-to-day trials and tribulations confronted by the coal schooner operators.

Photographs have been an essential part of our research on Percy & Small from the very beginning. Pictures have revealed vessel design and construction details and techniques. They also document the evolution of the shipyard, the travels of the schooners, and frequently their ultimate fate. In all, we examined well over five hundred photographs that have some bearing on Percy & Small, far more than we could include in this book.

Where possible, our photo credits identify the person who took the photograph. The observant reader will notice the frequent attribution: Stinson Brothers Photo. Ernest and Frank Stinson were young brothers much taken with the hobby of photography at the turn of the century. Percy & Small was literally in their front yard, so when free time permitted, often on Sundays, they took their simple box camera around the neighborhood snapping interesting scenes, many found in and around the shipyard. They were joined over the years by other amateur and professional photographers, many now unknown, who have contributed to the photographic record of Percy & Small.

A few words about the plans of specific Percy & Small schooners reproduced in this book: As noted in the text, Percy & Small did not use detailed paper plans to build their schooners. Douglas Lee has based these plans on extensive research that has involved the following: photos; published descriptions often found in launching accounts; registered dimensions as printed in the annual *List of Merchant Vessels of the United States* and in the *Record of American and Foreign Shipping;* the builder's half models; construction data from the American Bureau of Shipping surveyor's notebooks, building invoices, and insurance reports; and a handful of rigging and sail plans and other drawings. Several lines drawings and a nearly complete set of plans based on a Percy & Small World War I era four-masted schooner have also proved very useful.

The most useful single source of information for the plans has been the hulk of the five-masted CORA F. CRESSY, now slowly disintegrating at Bremen, Maine. Direct examination, measurements, and photographs taken of the actual vessel from the 1930s through the 1990s have been a primary source of information used in developing a detailed set of plans of that schooner. The examination of her huge hull also expanded our knowledge of how Percy & Small built all their schooners.

We wish to thank each and all of the people—their names can be found in the acknowledgments—who have assisted us in this project over the years. Without their unqualified support this work would be sadly diminished. We also wish to thank Linda J. Lee and Christie Snow, our long-suffering wives, who have lived with Percy & Small for nearly as long as that firm was active in business.

RALPH LINWOOD SNOW
DOUGLAS K. LEE
AUGUST 1998

Acknowledgments

The authors have been blessed by a large number of people and institutions who have assisted in one way or another with the completion of this work. Ideas, photos, and information were just a few of the ways those named below have helped us during the long course of this project going back to the 1970s. They have encouraged and prodded us, and in some cases have generously helped underwrite expenses by contributing to Maine Maritime Museum for the purchase of the critical Palmer Collection and/or the publication costs. An amazing number of people were involved in all of the above.

Several organizations rendered important assistance during the course of this project. They are listed below, along with the names of the staff persons directly involved in responding thoroughly and graciously to our persistent requests.

Bath Historical Society: Nathan Lipfert, President.

Maine Historic Preservation Commission: Earle Shettleworth, Director.

Maine Maritime Museum: Nathan Lipfert, Tom Wilcox, Elizabeth Maule, Robert L. Webb, Richard "Frenchy" DeVynck, Darren Poupore.

Mystic Seaport Museum: William Peterson, Captain Francis E. "Biff" Bowker, Marifrancis Trivelli.

National Archives, Washington, DC: Angie S. VanDereedt.

Patten Free Library, Bath: Denise Larson.

Penobscot Marine Museum: Renny M. Stackpole, Director.

Wyoming State Museum: Tim White, Curator, Historic Governor's Mansion.

A large number of Maine people have lent a direct hand in one capacity or another over the years including:

Kathy Brandes, William H. Bunting, Dr. Charles E. Burden, Richard O. Card, Edward Coffin, Robert Colfer, Captain John Foss, Terrance E. Geaghan, Frank A. Givin, Captain Edward Glaser, Henry Keene, David Kenney, Norman Kenney, Howard W. Kirkpatrick, Sam Manning, Kenneth R. Martin, Mae McCabe (Mrs. Willard McCabe), James McGuiggan, Captain Steve Pagels, Captain W. J. Lewis Parker, James S. Rockefeller, Robert Schultze, Donald N. Small, Jr., Margaret Small (Mrs. Donald N. Small, Sr.), Philip Chadwick Foster Smith, Bertram G. Snow, Dr. Richard I. Snow, James Stevens, Earl R. Warren, Jean Webber.

Not to be outdone by those fortunate to be resident in the Pine Tree State, outlanders from as far away as Germany, England, Wyoming, and Washington State have also pitched in enthusiastically:

Charles Barth, Morrison Bump, John S. Carter, Robert H. I. Goddard, Dr. Basil Greenhill, Evelyn Hannaren, Gail Hilston and Shelley McCleary Trumbull (granddaughters of Lena Brooks McCleary and great-granddaughters of Governor Bryant B. Brooks), Captain Harold Huycke, Fred F. Kaiser, Kenneth Kramer, Dr. Jürgen Meyer, Paul C. Morris, Andrew Nesdall, William P. Quinn, Virginia Wood, Charlotte Zahn.

As this project had its origins back in the early 1970s, many of those who contributed to our knowledge about wooden shipbuilding in general, Percy & Small in particular, and the great schooners have passed away. These include:

Samuel Barnes, Henry Bohndell, Charles A. Coombs, Captain Stinson Davis, William T. Donnell, John F. Eaton, Jay Hannah, John F. Leavitt, Maynard D. Lee, Willard McCabe, Charles S. Morgan, Gerald A. Morris, John G. Morse, Jr., Raleigh G. Osier, Homer Potter, Thomas P. Robson, Charles F. Sayle, Loyall F. Sewall, Jr., Donald A. Small, Sr., Raymond A. Small, Mr. and Mrs. L. M. C. Smith, Jack Sturtevant, Giles M. S. Tod, Bernard T. Zahn, Mrs. Nancy Zahn.

Maine Maritime Museum and the authors are also grateful for the generous financial support that allowed this project to reach fruition. The first challenge was to raise the money required to purchase the Palmer Collection from the heirs of William F. Palmer. The Palmer letters proved particularly useful in casting light on a number of issues revolving about the big schooner business. Contributors to the fund to purchase the collection include:

J. Aron Foundation, Morrison Bump and Leah Sprague, William H. Bunting, Dr. Charles E. Burden, Richard O. Card, Edward W. Coffin, Nancy and Crispin Connery, Terry and Jocelyn Geaghan, Frank A. Givin, Sally Graves, Cyrus Hamlin, Ned and Kathy Harding, Jim and Ann Hunt, Henry and Jane Keene, Kenneth Kramer, Douglas and Linda Lee, Harold Lister, Kenneth R. Martin, Seymour Mintz, Andy and Sarah Nesdall, Betty Noyce, W. J. Lewis and Frances Parker, John H. and Mary Reevy, John Ross, P. C. F. Smith, Ralph Linwood Snow, Jim Stevens, Ronald and Cora Tarbox, Henry and Ingrid Thomas, Howard Whalin, Colonel Roger Willock, USMC, (Ret.).

Maine Maritime Museum got its start in the 1960s as an organization to underwrite the research, writing, and publication of the maritime history of Bath and the Kennebec region. Through the generous support of many people, William Avery Baker's award-winning *Maritime History of Bath, Maine, and the Kennebec River Region* was published in 1973. Since that time several more publications have followed, each relying upon contributions to meet the sizable investment publishing requires. The Percy & Small history is no exception and has been made possible by the generosity of:

Mr. and Mrs. Thomas M. Bartlett, Morrison Bump, William H. Bunting, Dr. Charles E. Burden, Richard O. Card, Mr. and Mrs. E. Barton Chapin, Mr. and Mrs. Harry A. Crooker, Mr. and Mrs. Terrance Geaghan, Frank A. Givin, Mr. and Mrs. Edward P. Harding, Mr. and Mrs. James W. Hunt, Mr. and Mrs. Henry R. Keene, Kenneth D. Kramer, Arthur E. Lapham, Libra Foundation, Mr. and Mrs. Roger M. Luke, Kenneth R. Martin, Elizabeth B. Noyce, Captain W. J. Lewis Parker, USCG, (Ret.), Mr. and Mrs. P. C. F. Smith, Mr. and Mrs. Henry Thomas, Mr. and Mrs. Arthur F. Williams.

To each and all, we tender our sincere thanks.

RALPH LINWOOD SNOW
CAPTAIN DOUGLAS K. LEE

A Shipyard in Maine

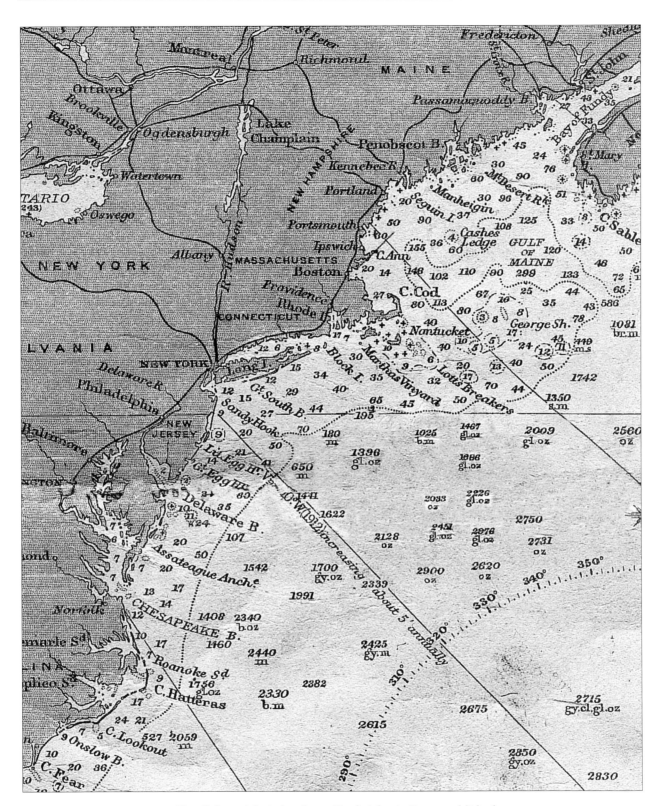

Detail from Admiralty chart, *North Atlantic Ocean*, published
30 October 1912, soundings in fathoms.

Courtesy: Captains Douglas K. and Linda J. Lee

WYOMING Launching Flyer

Courtesy: Captain W. J. Lewis Parker, USCG, Ret.

Sustaining Tradition

A NOTABLE EVENT: 1909

It was the quiet after the storm in Bath on this fifteenth day of December. Nonetheless, there was a sense of anticipation in the air as the community set out to mark an important milestone in its long history of shipbuilding, albeit twenty-four hours late thanks to an intense, fast-moving gale that had lashed the Maine coast the previous day.

Bath's merchants—ever optimistic—long planned to piggyback a big sales promotion on the history-making maritime event as a way to attract additional business just as the Christmas season racheted up. The Bath Marine Band was hired to entertain the anticipated crowds with stirring martial tunes at Sagadahoc Square in downtown Bath—the point where most visitors arriving on the Boothbay steamer, the cross-river passenger ferry, Maine Central railroad cars, and the Lewiston, Augusta, & Waterville interurban electric cars converged to board the local street railway. Retail stores throughout the downtown area sprouted placards offering unbelievable bargains to the anticipated throngs. And flyers printed by the Times Press of Bath were broadcast throughout midcoast and southern Maine in hopes of making those anticipated throngs a profitable reality.

"Ship Launching At Bath," they proclaimed. "The largest sailing vessel in the world will be launched at Percy & Small's Shipyard. Did you ever visit Bath? Ever see a big launching? This is your chance. Be sure and see both. Get transfer at Bath to Percy & Small's shipyard on the local car line."[1]

The cynosure of all this attention loomed tall over the buildings at Percy & Small's south end shipyard and the surrounding homes. WYOMING! Like her namesake, big. From keel to mast truck she was taller than a seventeen-story building. Her great black hull stretched for 350 feet overall, and if you insisted on counting her jibboom thrusting out to Washington Street and her spanker boom overhanging the Kennebec River, she checked in at 450 feet. Her wooden hull would, the builders confidently asserted, carry over 6,000 tons of coal.

The construction of that hull consumed in excess of 2,400 tons of longleaf yellow pine, 700 tons of white oak, and 300 tons of iron and steel for fittings, fastenings, and strapping.[2] Her six lower masts were 123-foot Douglas-fir sticks that had begun life as seedlings long before Lewis and Clark completed their epic journey of discovery or the United States even existed in fancy or in fact. Twelve thousand yards of heavy cotton duck had been cut and sewn into sails for the six-masted giant. And her massive battleship-sized ground tackle, comprised of 240 fathoms of anchor chain and two cast-steel stockless patent anchors, tipped the scales at 60 tons.[3]

As big as she was, WYOMING was not the largest sailing vessel in the world, as the Bath merchants proclaimed, but she was the largest *wooden* sailing vessel.[4]

Curiously, Bath was a city where shipbuilding had taken a decidedly high-tech turn in the previous two decades. Its modern, up-to-date steel shipyard—the Bath Iron Works—actually began shipbuilding four years before Percy & Small was organized, and was acknowledged to be on the cutting-edge of steam propulsion. The Iron Works had recently delivered the second steam turbine-powered commercial vessel in the U.S.—SS CAMDEN—in 1907, the U. S. Navy's first steam turbine-powered warship—cruiser USS CHESTER—in 1908, and—in this very year—its fastest ships, the navy's first turbine-powered destroyers FLUSSER and REID.

This day, however, was a celebration of the launching of a wooden sailing vessel—long a Bath and Maine specialty—and to honor Percy & Small, the builders and managing owners of the giant craft. Organized sixteen years earlier, the firm had become widely recognized for its ability to sustain Bath's

Launching Day: WYOMING
N. E. Card/Rollins Photo, courtesy of Richard Card

traditional wooden shipbuilding and merchant shipping industry in the face of the challenge of modern steel and steam technology and the flight of capital from America's merchant marine. With WYOMING, Percy & Small sought to bring the wooden sailing vessel to its highest level of efficiency and profitability—all this in the decidedly unromantic, but economically crucial trade of carrying coal from the mid-Atlantic region to the coastal ports of the northeastern United States.

The fliers spread far and wide by Bath's merchants did their job well. A goodly crowd journeyed to Bath to watch the giant slide and to pick up a few Christmas bargains. The purser aboard the Boothbay boat reported a hundred more passengers than normal this late in the season.[5] The steam cars and electrics did their jobs as well, bringing in thousands of visitors. To keep traffic flowing smoothly, the Lewiston, Augusta & Waterville Street Railway sent chief superintendent W. G. Bowie to Bath to oversee the movement of the public from downtown to the south end aboard five special cars running between Sagadahoc Square and the shipyard. Additional specials were run from Brunswick to accommodate the anticipated surge of visitors from neighboring towns to the westward.[6]

By late morning, crowds began collecting at Percy & Small's shipyard. Young Johnny Eaton, stepson of shipyard joiner and boatbuilder (and Percy & Small landlord) Harry Stinson, and stepgrandson of John Stinson, a longtime Percy & Small employee, kept a wary eye out for the bane of all Bath school children, truant officer-cum-drum major Eddie Emmons. Even though local schools planned to close for the day before the scheduled 1:00 P.M. launching, young Johnny made the executive decision to start his half-holiday a half day early so that he could watch the launching preparations.

By virtue of his close proximity to the shipyard—Percy & Small stored much of their timber in his family's front yard, and their office occupied the southeast corner of the Stinson house lot directly across Washington Street from the shipyard—young Johnny knew all the best places of concealment as well as most of the men who worked with his father and

grandfather. It was a lovely place to play, offering ready-made forts of stacked timber, bustling activity, Mr. Totman's teams of big draft horses, and loud, dangerous, fascinating machines.[7]

If Master Eaton was trying to avoid the eagle-eyed truant officer, Master Donald Small was attempting to avoid the notice of his contemporaries. Reluctantly in tow of his mother, Martha P. Small, and father, junior Percy & Small partner Frank Small, young Donald was part of the official party representing the builders and managing owners of WYOMING. That honor, however, cut little ice with him. His mother, the stylish Martha, had dressed him in a velvet "Little Lord Fauntleroy" suit designed to make mothers swoon with joy and sons shrivel in utter mortification. More than six decades later, Donald Small still remembered the launching of the world's largest wooden sailing vessel—a tribute to his father and Captain Percy's business skills and faith in an uncertain future—as one of the worst experiences of his life.[8]

As crowds of the curious began gathering at the cluttered shipyard, arriving on foot or via "the cars," there was plenty at Percy & Small to occupy their attention. Two schooners lay alongside undergoing routine repairs. The MARTHA P. SMALL, named for young Donald's mother, was berthed at the south end of the shipyard while the BAKER PALMER, docked at the adjoining Donnell shipyard, had arrived under tow in the teeth of yesterday's storm. Crews of ship carpenters and caulkers from Percy & Small swarmed over both schooners, the sound of their tools adding an air of industry to the festive shipyard.

But the focal point for most visitors was WYOMING, dressed with colorful flags. Before the big moment arrived, hundreds of invited guests would make their cautious way up the long, seemingly insubstantial boarding ramp to the giant schooner's main deck. There, official hosts Frank Small and Captain Angus McLeod greeted the newcomers and offered each the freedom to roam at will to inspect this marvelous new creation, Percy & Small's pride and joy.

Captain Samuel Percy, senior partner and founder of the firm, took up his traditional position in the shipyard, welcoming invited guests and the general public. He also joined Master Builder Miles M. Merry in keeping a close eye on the activities of the launching gang and the spectators—the latter being prone to occasionally placing themselves in harm's way for the sake of an unparalleled vista when the giant was launched.

For all of his genial demeanor, Captain Percy could not help but feel some trepidation. WYOMING represented a huge investment, one that had been initiated well over a year earlier. But the optimism expressed then about the future economic prospects of the sailing coastwise collier fleet was rapidly diminishing in the face of competition from steam colliers and tug-barge lines as freight rates fell. It remained to be seen whether the enormous schooner would justify the faith of her builders and managing owners, and her shareholders. But for this day at least, Captain Sam would hide his concerns and bask in the glory of the moment. The firm had, after all, survived and prospered for over fifteen years, in bad times as well as good, even in the face of the general decline of the American merchant marine and the specific decline of the wooden shipbuilding industry.

Captain Sam greeted the multitude of guests invited aboard for the launching: shipmasters active and retired, P&S subcontractors, investors and their families, prospective investors, and politicians. Seen in the crowd were Mrs. Bryant B. Brooks (first lady of Wyoming) and daughter Lena—the latter serving as sponsor; brother-in-law/uncle John Brooks, New York businessman and promoter; Eleazer Clark, freewheeling boss of the firm J. S. Winslow & Co. of Portland, Percy & Small's best customer for new vessels and close ally in the shipping business; and a variety of active and retired sea captains, including Captain and Mrs. L. B. Clark, Captain Mitchell Reed, Captain Sam Skolfield, and Captain and Mrs. Fessenden Chase, just to name a few.

Chef Joseph Begin, who saw to it that the Bath Elks were well fed, had received the assignment to serve the traditional buffet lunch aboard WYOMING after the launching. His crew of waiters and assistants had hustled buckets of chicken and lobster salad to the galley and fired the range to prepare coffee and tea for the onboard guests.

As Begin and his minions labored to prepare the forthcoming repast, the growing number of onboard guests had the opportunity to tour the big schooner, oohing and aahing over the "commodious, comfortable, and cosy quarters not only for the officers but for the sailors as well." The stock elderly seadog—there always appeared to be at least one at every launching—was sought out by a reporter to make a pithy comment: "The forecastle accommodations are as good as those in the cabin used to be when I went to sea." In all fairness, however, the quarters in the main cabin were a bit more luxurious, being finished in quartered oak, mahogany, and birdseye maple and outfitted with plush-covered furniture.[9]

Somewhere on the big schooner—perhaps in Captain McLeod's personal quarters—resided a punch bowl whose chemical contents were guaranteed to lay the unwary low.[10] Although Maine was "dry" and Percy & Small used only flowers to christen their own vessels, tradition still had to be served, however discreetly.

Master Builder Merry's launching crew had been preparing for the big day for the past two weeks. Once the caulkers and painters finished the bottom, the heavy timber groundways were installed on the permanent bed logs underpinning the building slip, extending a short distance out into the river. Under the vessel and on top of the groundways greased with tallow and cottonseed, the carpenters installed the sliding ways—two layers of timber separated by a filling composed of the thin edge of a series of tapered oak wedges. The cradle and hull packing was then built on top of the sliding ways and fitted snugly under WYOMING's hull; in effect, the schooner now sat on a big sled perched on inclined greased tracks.

The only thing that kept her from sliding was the series of red oak keel blocks set on heavy timber cribwork and extending from stern to bow, supporting virtually the entire weight of the vessel. A multitude of spruce shores kept the vessel upright.

To launch her, the crew first drove the wedge "filling" into the sliding way "sandwich" in an orderly progression along both sides of the vessel, working forward from the stern. When this was accomplished, a substantial portion of the schooner's weight had been shifted from the keel blocks to the cradle and sliding ways/ground ways, at the same time firmly marrying the hull and cradle to the sliding ways. As the crew wedging up moved up the cradle, another gang kept pace knocking out the shores. Soon, just the keel blocks remained holding the schooner in place.

Percy & Small did not rely upon any form of "trigger" release to start the vessel down the ways, so the final stage in the launching sequence could get more than a little dramatic. A crew of men would begin to methodically split out the keel blocks, moving from the stern toward the bow, swinging their axes and mauls in the gloomy, cramped space under the vessel, gradually transferring the rest of the schooner's weight to the greased sliding ways.

Miles Merry figured from his long experience that it would take his crew about thirty minutes to split out all but the last few blocks before the big schooner began to move. With local slack high water coming at 1:00 P.M., Merry planned to start his men splitting-out the blocks at 12:30 P.M. And because launching was an inexact science, the invited guests were advised to be on board the vessel before that time if they wanted to ride the schooner down the ways.

Late-arriving VIPs were hustled aboard so the ship's gangway could be hoisted clear of the ramps and staging. The schooner's engineer checked the pressure of the steam in his donkey boiler, and other shipyard employees checked the snubbing cables that would jerk the cradle from under WYOMING when she was clear of the launching ways.

Then the crew of doughty carpenters moved under the cradle at the stern with razor-sharp axes and heavy mauls. Captain Percy and Miles Merry, with an authority that forestalled challenges, cleared the area immediately around the schooner as the sounds of

WYOMING sponsor Lena Brooks, attired in her launching finery.
Courtesy: Granddaughters Shelley McCleary Trumbull and Gail Hilston

keel blocks being split out echoed from under the vessel. On deck, the official launching party—Lena Brooks with an armful of roses, carnations, and asparagus fern, accompanied by her mother, Eleanor Percy, and Captain and Mrs. McLeod—took their places at the very bow of WYOMING.

At 12:45 P.M., the Bath Marine Band members were ensconced in a local trolley bound from Sagadahoc Square to Percy & Small, where they were to send off the big schooner with a rousing fanfare. They were not alone; many would-be spectators for the launching were also on that car or making their way to the shipyard by foot, buggy, or in one of those new-fangled automobiles. Perhaps the lure of downtown sales had been too overwhelming!

At the shipyard at 12:45 P.M., long before the forwardmost keel blocks were reached, the remaining blocks began to creak and crack ominously as the combination of gravity, 4,000-plus tons of impatient schooner, and well-greased inclined ways began to take over. Scrambling forward toward the bow of the big schooner and daylight, the carpenters soon found themselves leaping over rolling blocks and cribbing in a desperate effort to get clear. Then the daylight appeared as WYOMING passed over their heads with a sigh bound for the Kennebec River. Lena Brooks, Dana Hall student and Wyoming cowgirl, "... dressed in a very stylish green rajah suit ..." pronounced the traditional blessing, "I christen thee WYOMING," scattering the bouquet over the bow, the fluttering flowers and ferns marking the mighty schooner's passage to her future home.

The forward end of the cradle left a smoking trail as it dropped off the end of the ways, the vessel appearing to politely curtsy to the throng as she dipped her bow. Steam whistles screeched and the crowd cheered; little boys—and not-so-little boys—

scrambled across the now-empty ways to retrieve the scattered flowers to sell as souvenirs to the assembled crowds.

On Captain McLeod's command the port anchor was let go, the chain thundering out of the hawsepipe, to secure WYOMING in midstream. Then the estimated crowd of 250 aboard for the launching was summoned by Chef Begin to enjoy an elegant lunch and to continue inspecting the giant in all her fresh-painted glory—some perhaps sampling a second round of the notorious punch. The tugs SEGUIN and CHARLIE LAWRENCE moved out from the waterfront to prepare for her return to Percy & Small's main fitting-out pier, and at 3:00 P.M. the big schooner was docked, the gangway set in place, and the privileged guests began to depart, the Brooks party heading to the railway depot to take the four o'clock train for Boston and points west.[11]

Before the day ended, the *Bath Times* was on the street with an editorial praising Percy & Small and the firm's alliance with western capital:[12]

We congratulate her progressive builders not only upon the production of such a notable addition to the merchant fleet of the nation, but also upon their success in interesting the people of a Rocky Mountain State in the Merchant Marine, a happy achievement of which the name WYOMING is the sign and expression. We know of no more effective way to break down the Western indifference to national shipping than to enroll a sufficient number of Westerners among the owners of the fleet.

WYOMING spent a few more days at Percy & Small's shipyard before tugs, officers, crew, and a young military cadet named Brooks—along for the ride—took her to open water and a career that lasted over fourteen years. She routinely carried 6,000 tons of coal from Virginia ports to Boston and Portland over the next several years. Then the effects of World War I directed her into new channels—offshore voyages to Europe and South America—under new owners. When peace returned, she went back to her old trade as a coastwise collier, but times turned hard and competition cutthroat. Sold again—her last owners were based in Maine—she eked out a living until a bitter, late-winter northeaster caught her on Nantucket's deadly shoals. There she died, the largest of all wooden sailing vessels to ever carry cargo and the greatest of the great schooners, Percy & Small's WYOMING.

PLANK-ON-FRAME BUILT AND SCHOONER RIGGED

Although many who participated in the pageantry surrounding the launching of WYOMING knew that times and technology were changing, few even remotely sensed the true significance of the fifteenth day of December 1909. The technology that produced the mighty WYOMING, a wooden shipbuilding technology that traced its origins back to the early Middle Ages, achieved its apogee with the big schooner built at Percy & Small. To be sure, more wooden sailing vessels would be built—by Percy & Small and others—before the industry all but vanished just over a decade later, but none would achieve the size, capacity, and efficiency of WYOMING. The fact of the matter was that WYOMING and the hundreds of four-, five-, and six-masted schooners built since the 1880s placed the cap on what is described by academics as the non-edge-joined, fully skeletal shipbuilding tradition. For the sake of brevity, we shall call it plank-on-frame shipbuilding.[13]

Since the ancestors of man became capable of joining two concepts together, enabling them to cross some creek, stream, or river by straddling a log and paddling, they—ancestors and man—have been busy attempting to make this mode of transportation more efficient. By the end of the first millennium (Common Era), a well-established wooden shipbuilding technology with variables reflecting local circumstances and materials existed throughout the maritime and riverine world. It was a technology largely based on the principle of shell-built, edge-joined vessels—

the direct ancestors of traditional wooden small craft.[14]

Simply put, the shell-built, edge-joined technology involved building the outside of the craft—the shell—first, and applying the internal frame after the shell was partially or fully completed. This technique involved the builders—the shipwrights—directly in the shape of the vessel as they worked and installed each shell piece. Overlapping planks—lapstrakes—were carefully fitted and fastened together or joined edge-to-edge by tenons, providing the bulk of the strength of the total structure. Only when the shell was at least partially completed were the frames, shaped to conform to the pre-existing shell, put in place and fastened to the shell.

A large number of edge-joined types of vessels evolved over the millennia, many such as the Greco-Roman ships, long ships, knarrs, cogs, and hulcks capable of open water voyages. But the inherent limitations of the edge-joined, shell-first technology—limited growth potential, relatively heavy consumption of high quality timber, and a disproportionate reliance on highly skilled labor—ultimately encouraged the development of the plank on frame vessel.

It appears to have evolved from the shell-first vessels in the Mediterranean, with the Contarina ship in the Po River delta being the earliest example of a full-blown frame-built ship so far uncovered, dating from the late thirteenth to early fourteenth centuries.[15] This dating suggests that the technology was fully developed earlier, placing its origins back perhaps to the beginning of the second millennium (C.E.). But as the shipbuilders around the Mediterranean developed and refined the new technique of plank-on-frame construction, their counterparts in western Europe, the British Isles, and along the Baltic and Scandinavian peninsula continued to push the older, skin-first technique to its practical limits for nearly two more centuries.

The very slow extension of the new shipbuilding technology beyond the Mediterranean world was more a reflection of the complex revolution necessary to make the transition to the plank-on-frame technology than sheer obstinacy. The new technology supplanted the traditional method of shaping the vessel by trial and error and replaced it with the necessity of conceptualizing the hull form before construction: in effect, it separated the functions of design and construction. An entirely new mindset, as well as a new construction sequence, had to be developed.

The advantages of the new technology, however, overcame the drag of past technology: larger, stronger, more capacious, and more seaworthy vessels could be built; the designer and builder had more flexibility in the choice of hull forms without increasing the materials and labor bill; and the plank-on-frame vessel was less demanding in terms of shipwright time and skill.[16]

The historical impact of the new technology cannot be denied. The plank-on-frame hulls, coupled with the evolving ship rig, made extended voyaging for exploration, trade, and the projection of national power to the ends of the earth a reality. Within three centuries the entire world was changed forever. Basil Greenhill summed it up best when he wrote that plank-on-frame shipbuilding ". . . is one of the great achievements in the history of European (and, at one remove, of North American) man."[17]

WYOMING, built in the plank-on-frame tradition, was a part of that great historical process representing, as she did, its highest point of development. Yet in terms of her rig—the characteristic arrangement of masts, rigging, and sails that propel and classify a sailing vessel (ship, bark, brig, schooner, etc.)—WYOMING came from a much younger and humbler tradition.

It was the squaresail ship rig that conquered the oceans of the world between the fifteenth and eighteenth centuries. But it was the schooner rig that extended the economic viability of the wooden sailing vessel well into the twentieth century. Its probable origins can be traced back to the Dutch, evolving from what was essentially a small boat rig of the early seventeenth century, although there is some debate on this subject.[18] Easily identifiable in its fully developed form by the fore-and-aft arrangement of principal sails, both gaff-headed, with the foresail being smaller than the mainsail, the two-masted schooner became the transportation mainstay along the North American coast by the late eighteenth century.

The schooner that developed in the American colonies had, by mid eighteenth century, a square topsail and, perhaps, a square topgallant sail. Curiously, a rig that had not achieved wide use in Great Britain up until this time became more popular among British shipbuilders and coastwise shipowners as examples of the topsail schooner rig began appearing in British ports on trading voyages from the North American colonies or were acquired by the Royal Navy. The reborn schooner in Britain remained a topsail schooner until the end, while its North American counterpart—with a few notable exceptions—became an out-and-out fore-and-after, discarding the square topsails during the first half of the nineteenth century. The differentiation appears more a product of final use—the American schooners being largely employed coastwise, where squaresails were a hindrance, and their British counterparts being employed in trades where such sails' usefulness outweighed the additional complexity and expense.

The schooner was the most numerous and important rig type in North America by the beginning of the nineteenth century.[19] It was inexpensive to build in a society where capital resources were limited. It was a rig that worked well to windward, a highly desirable characteristic in vessels usually engaged in coastwise trade along the Atlantic Seaboard. It was a rig that was economical in terms of the manpower necessary to handle it, a factor especially important in a region that suffered from a chronic labor shortage thanks to the proximity of the much-promoted frontier. And it was a rig that handled particularly well in a region that demanded agile handling.[20] The coasting schooner (two-masted schooner is redundant) was a small vessel, only occasionally exceeding 100 tons, but it proved capable of changing that image during the nineteenth and early twentieth centuries thanks to its great potential for growth.

And it did grow during the first half of the nineteenth century, albeit slowly. Growth brought with it three-masted schooners, the additional mast serving to keep the sails to manageable sizes. The first identified three-masted schooners appear, however, to have been built more for speed than manageability—an important consideration during the wars that wracked the first fifteen years of the century. They disappeared shortly after the Treaty of Ghent of 1815, apparently unprofitable in a more pedestrian peacetime world. A dozen years later, the 380-ton POCAHONTAS was built in Matthews County, Virginia. She was quickly followed by a brief flurry of three-master building activity in Maine. By the 1850s the type had become pretty well standardized: masts of nearly equal height and no yards crossed on the foremast, with the largest three-master having a carrying capacity of about 500 tons.[21]

Schooners continued to fill the unromantic but essential role of trucker, hauling cargoes of lumber, cordwood, lime, foodstuffs, and virtually everything manufactured between the major seaport cities and the outlying ports, from the Bay of Fundy to the Gulf of Mexico. Some carried passengers before being displaced by the coastal steamers and, subsequently, the railroads. Others made voyages to the West Indies and even offshore. A case in point are the voyages of three-masted ISLAND CITY, built at East Boston in 1871. This peripatetic "coaster" made voyages to Egypt, Germany, Italy, Sweden, Argentina, Constantinople, Australia, Portugal, and Spain as well as more routine trips between U.S. ports of call before she was ten years old.[22]

It was in the post-Civil War era that schooner growth really took off, however. And the impetus behind that growth lay with coal—the principal fuel of America's industrial revolution—underpinned by advances in sail, rigging, and auxiliary power technology.

COAL, COASTERS, AND WOODEN SHIPBUILDERS

Created over the eons from the peat-like remains of prehistoric forests which have been subjected to great pressure and heat, coal's combination of fixed carbon and volatile matter—hydrocarbons and other gases—provided a fuel with a high heat value that varied with the type of coal.[23] More important, coal produced far more heat per pound than North America's basic fuel, wood, and enormous reserves were identified, particularly in the Appalachian Mountains.

By mid-century, the great hardwood forests that had clad the landscape of eastern North America in the seventeenth century were seriously depleted, especially in the way of more heavily settled regions. Coal, therefore, was an alternative fuel potentially available for large scale use for heating and industrial purposes once the technology and infrastructure for mining, transporting, distributing, and burning it was in place.

Coal had, in fact, been in play commercially for coastwise shipping since the 1790s. The first coal mine in the new nation, near Richmond, Virginia, began shipping bituminous coal in 1798 to Philadelphia, New York, and Boston, probably for the use of blacksmiths.[24] It is important to note here that the shipping of what can be described as a bulk cargo required access to waterborne transportation as land transport was, at best, chancy and expensive and, at worst, impossible.[25] Early in the nineteenth century, New England's focus on the southern bituminous trade was replaced by the pressure of northern Pennsylvania anthracite. Once grates had been designed and manufactured that would burn the hard coals reliably, demand in the northeastern states increased dramatically with 350,000 tons of anthracite being shipped from Philadelphia by 1837, nearly ten times as much as shipped ten years earlier.[26] Unfortunately for the anthracite industry, although its product was essentially smokeless, it produced less heat per pound than bituminous, was unsuitable for producing illuminating gas—a market that expanded rapidly shortly before the Civil War—and was found in far less abundance than the soft coal.

The American Civil War was an enormous watershed. The demands of the war machine led to unprecedented capital investment in industry. And as waterpower sources were already developed to the limit, steam power was the shining alternative. However, steam was best produced by semi-bituminous (really super-bituminous) coal. And this coal was mined in the Cumberland district of Western Maryland, then shipped via the Baltimore & Ohio Railroad to Baltimore, or via the Chesapeake & Ohio Canal to Alexandria, Virginia, where it was then transshipped via coastwise schooners bound to New York, New Haven, and Down East to Providence, Boston, Portsmouth, Portland, and Penobscot Bay. But the flow of coal on these routes was constantly interrupted by military action throughout the war, forcing the price of bituminous delivered at New York in 1864 up to $7.68 per ton, fully a dollar higher than the formerly more expensive anthracite.[27] Another route, developed shortly before the war by the Pennsylvania Railroad, connected the coal fields around Pittsburg to the tidewater at Philadelphia. It made up some of the loss of production from the western Maryland mines.

The war interrupted supplies of the valuable fuel, but it underlined its importance, a fact not lost on the coal mine owners. Production accelerated rapidly after the war, and bituminous output overtook anthracite production during the first half of the 1870s. With its superior steam-generating power recognized, bituminous coal production became a reflection of America's industrial development during the last half of the century, tied, as it was, to the steam engine. Nowhere was this more evident than in the railroad business. The Maine Central Railroad, which purchased approximately 48,000 cords of wood to fuel its engines in 1872, consumed 168,903 tons of bituminous coal to keep its fleet of 156 locomotives on the move in 1900.[28]

During the 1880s, two other developments furthered the large-scale production and consumption of coal. From the consumption angle, Thomas Alva Edison introduced electrical power production (direct current) in New York City in 1882, and Nikola Tesla's research in alternating current laid the foundation for today's electrical generating/distribution system. In the late 1880s electric street railways began springing up in urban areas across the country, following Frank Julian Sprague's commercially successful Richmond, Virginia, project in 1887. By 1893 over 250 electric street railways had been incorporated throughout the country—including one in Bath, Maine—and 7,200 miles of track were electrified. The production of electricity for lighting, motors, and transportation required steam coal in huge quantities, since most early electrical generation used steam engine-driven dynamos.

The second development substantially expanded the supply of bituminous coal, reduced its cost, and established Norfolk and Newport News, Virginia, as the major coal-shipping ports of the United States. The rich coal fields of West Virginia lay largely untapped for lack of a rail connection to markets in the Northeast. In 1881 the Chesapeake & Ohio Railroad completed the link between some of the West Virginian coal fields, Richmond, and then down the James River peninsula to the drowsy village of Newport News on Hampton Roads. Two years later, the Norfolk & Western Railroad pushed its New River line into the heart of the Pocahontas district. The first carload of West Virginian coal arrived at Norfolk on 17 March 1883 to much celebration; by 1885 bituminous coal was that city's chief export.[29]

The connection of the rich West Virginia coalfields to Virginia tidewater by rail reflected the important role played by coastwise shipping in the bulk trades. Although railroads were a major user of coal to fuel their engines, it was far more economical to ship the coal by sea, where possible, to ports east of the Hudson River and then tranship it—largely by rail—to the final consumers.[30] New Haven, New London, Providence, Boston, Portsmouth, Portland, Bath, and Searsport served as New England's principal distribution centers for the seaborne coal trade, with waterfront "coal pockets" serving as visible monuments to the new age.

So the coal flowed in ever increasing quantities from the coal mines in the mid-Atlantic states to the sea and then northeastward to New England's coal ports. Deliveries to Boston, the leading New England discharging port, illustrate the growth of the trade:[31]

1864—   516,665 tons
1874—1,125,516 tons
1884—2,197,864 tons
1894—3,151,482 tons
1909—5,201,670 tons

WOOD AND SAIL VS. STEEL AND STEAM

The demand for tonnage to carry coal gave Maine's flagging wooden shipbuilding industry a much-needed boost. The Panic of 1857, followed by the Civil War, had seen investment in American merchant shipping decline drastically. That decline was mirrored by the contraction of the wooden shipbuilding industry. Most of the shipyards south of Boston, saddled with high overhead and labor costs, closed down in the face of declining orders and the competition from shipbuilders in the Northeast, particularly in Maine. The latter builders, benefiting from a highly skilled but lower paid labor force and far lower overhead costs were, in many cases, able to hold their own or even expand production in the two decades after the war. For example, in 1881–82 Bath shipbuilders outdid themselves by producing more tonnage than during the halcyon days of the early 1850s, when the American merchant marine and shipbuilding industry came close to world dominance.

Nonetheless, there were those shipbuilders on the Kennebec who issued Cassandra-like warnings concerning the future of wooden sailing vessels. William Rogers, the dean of Bath shipbuilders, warned in 1881 that "wooden ships must give way to iron vessels; it [is] bound to come as we live in a world of improvements. The time [is] not far distant when a wooden vessel [will] cost as much as an iron one, and then Bath must build iron vessels or none at all."[32]

Charles V. Minott, Jr., of Phippsburg occupied a much different position in his Kennebec River town. The Bowdoin-educated (Class of '91) son of a Phippsburg shipbuilder, young Minott had dreamed of becoming an engineer. But father and fate dictated otherwise, and he linked his fortunes with wooden shipbuilding and wooden vessels until he sold the remnants of the Minott fleet in 1917. In a rather poignant letter in 1892 reflecting his own dilemma, he wrote: "I do not wish to give the impression that I think wooden shipbuilding is over . . . but what I do believe and hold as an opinion . . . is that he who in his youth now binds himself down to a wooden ship-yard, will, if he lives 25 years, find himself 'one of the has beens.'"[33] Two years later, his father built America's last wooden, full-rigged ship.

When Captain Sam Percy and Frank Small combined their talents and capital in 1893–94, their chosen field of business was being swept by fundamental changes in the capitalization, construction, and propulsion of vessels. These changes, gathering force since the early nineteenth century and threatening the very existence of the tradition-based industries of wooden shipbuilding and wind-driven waterborne commerce, are what Rogers and Minott saw as leading inevitably to the end of wooden merchant sail and the many centuries of the plank-on-frame tradition.

Maritime industries have, historically, been resistant to change; the tried and proven, regardless of its shortcomings, is much preferred to the new and experimental. This resistance to change is not solely a reflection of curmudgeonly contrariness, but also takes into account the potential for both human and financial loss due to ill-considered experiments in an already high-risk operating environment. It is no coincidence that the person largely responsible for the GREAT WESTERN, GREAT BRITAIN, and GREAT EASTERN, the vessels which were the precursors to the steel and steam ships of the twentieth century, was engineer Isambard K. Brunel, rather than a shipbuilder or traditional ship designer. Conservatism notwithstanding, some shipbuilders and investors in Britain tackled the new technologies—as much because of the growing shortage of quality shipbuilding timber in Great Britain as for the thrill of being on the cutting edge—overcoming their limitations one by one, until the wooden sailing vessel began disappearing from the world's sea lanes and steam propulsion went from novelty to serious competitor of sail on the ocean's highways. Yet this technological change received relatively little attention among the movers and shakers of American industry.

The American Civil War refocused national energies and investment in an unprecedented concentration upon internal development. The rapidly expanding rail system subsidized by enormous land grants, a population boom fed by a veritable flood of immigration, and a highly protected and expanding industrial base forged in America's "Great War" drew American investors away from the antebellum merchant marine that found itself with a shrinking slice of the investment pie and a declining share of political clout in the halls of national government.

Limited capital, high prices engendered by tariff-protected steel makers, and the high initial cost of building and operating a modern industrial plant capable of building steel steamships, coupled with their limited market potential, discouraged rapid growth of the new technology. Most of the American steel shipyards developed in the late nineteenth century were in direct response to the growth of the American steel navy rather than any overwhelming demand for oceangoing merchant vessels. Without a system of construction and operating subsidies, American shipowners found it difficult to profitably compete with heavily subsidized British and other foreign-built steel vessels.

The American maritime industries were not without some government protection, however. Shipbuilders were assured of little or no competition from foreign-built vessels brought under the American flag, thanks to laws that severely limited the amount of coastal trade in which they could engage. The ship operators, in turn, also enjoyed the protection of laws that barred foreign-flag vessels from the U.S. coastal trade, which encompassed a huge area.[34] An 11,000–12,000-mile voyage from New York to San Francisco or Puget Sound was an intercoastal voyage—albeit a long and stormy one around Cape Horn—not to mention contiguous passages along both east and west coasts. This provided many opportunities for vessel operators to find shipping charters that were denied them in foreign trade.

But it was the adoption of bituminous coal as the fuel of industry in the Northeast that preserved and even expanded America's sailing merchant fleet in the post-Civil War era, even as American tonnage in foreign trade declined.

Bath's shipyards produced 34,304 tons of merchant

sailing vessels in 1881. Over 60 percent of that tonnage crossed yards on one or more masts and was clearly destined for deepwater service, including the California grain trade. The balance of the production was made up of thirty-one schooners, averaging 420 tons each. Nine years later, in 1890, Bath shipbuilders built 30,191 tons of sailing vessels but only about 30 percent of the tonnage was square-rigged. The balance—20,886 tons—consisted of schooners averaging 696 tons each. The last square-rigged wooden vessels from Bath's shipyards sailed from the Kennebec in 1892, OLYMPIC and the huge Sewall-built ROANOKE; the last wooden, full-rigged ship built in the U.S.—ARYAN—was launched the following year at Phippsburg. One year later Arthur Sewall & Company became the only builder of steel square-riggers in the United States.

The shift reflected two major developments in the 1880s. The first was the marginalization of American square-rigged wooden vessels in the Cape Horn trades following substantial insurance rate increases by Lloyds in the early 1880s on wooden ships and the general decline in freight rates. This brought the production of the big Down Easters virtually to a halt.

The second development was the rapid growth in coal shipments from the coal ports to New England and the need for tonnage to meet the demand. The net effect was the supplanting of the Down Easter by the schooner in Bath's and Maine's shipyards.

The three-masted schooner, reaching the practical limit in the size of its sails, gave birth to the four-masted schooner, soon to be characterized, along with her five- and six-masted offspring, as the "great schooners." In 1880 Bath's Goss & Sawyer-built WILLIAM L. WHITE became the first purpose-built great schooner on the Atlantic coast.[35] By the end of the decade, Bath shipyards had turned out thirty-five four-masters. But the demand didn't slack off; local builders launched eleven in 1890, a year that saw a total of forty-one four-masters completed by East Coast wooden shipbuilders.[36] By the time production ceased in 1921, 459 of the popular four-masted schooners had been completed. Ranging up to 2,047 gross tons, they are considered by many authorities as the most handsome and versatile of the great schooners.[37]

Ironically, the great schooners relied on some of the same technology that doomed them in the end—steam—but enabled them to achieve economies in operation unheard of previously.[38] Without the steam hoisting engine, the big schooners would have been virtually impossible to operate. It allowed small crews to hoist and handle the heavy sails with relative ease; it could raise the massive ground tackle that became the trademark of the great schooners and essential to their survival; steam-driven pumps were also an imperative necessity for the long and frequently leaky schooner hulls; and steam provided warmth in the form of steam heat and, in later years, illumination in the form of electric lights. In short, without the assistance provided by steam-driven machinery, the age of the great schooners would never have dawned.

Taking advantage of technical developments in auxiliary machinery, the economies of scale, an in-place infrastructure developed to support wooden shipbuilding, and a reservoir of mechanical and business skills, Maine businessmen met market demand by financing, building, and managing larger and larger schooner-rigged wooden sailing vessels. Even in the face of the competitive challenges of steel, steam, and well-financed corporations, entrepreneurs such as Captain Samuel R. Percy and Frank A. Small were able to profitably extend the economic working life of plank-on-frame wooden sailing vessels for another generation thanks to their determination and thorough grounding in the ways of the sailing ship business.

A THOROUGH GROUNDING

Captain Samuel R. Percy was master of the big three-masted schooner HENRY P. MASON when he received a summons to return posthaste to Bath early in March 1893 as his vessel lay at Salem, Massachusetts, unloading coal.[39] The MASON's managing owner and Percy's stepfather, George M. Adams, lay dying at his Bath home. When the captain left his schooner for the melancholy trip to Bath, he left behind a seagoing career that dated back to 1875, when he had shipped as an eighteen-year-old "boy" aboard the Bath-built square-rigger M. P. GRACE.[40]

The posthumous son of Captain Samuel Rogers Percy, who had died of yellow fever at Santiago de Cuba while commanding the bark BYRON, young Percy grew up in his native Phippsburg, at Parker's Head, a few miles south of Bath. At the age of eleven he acquired a stepfather and an important influence on his life when his mother married widower George M. Adams, a well-known Bath shipbuilder. With this marriage, young Sam and his mother moved to Bath to George Adams's big house on the corner of Washington and Union streets. Here he attended Bath schools until he reached the age of sixteen.

As was common with most of his contemporaries, young Percy then left formal education behind and proceeded to acquire the training that would stand him in good stead for years to come. Sizable and strong for his age, Percy first worked in the big Treat & Lang steam sawmill, probably as a "gofer," given his inexperience and strength. Then he did a three-year stint in shipyards, first at his stepfather's operation—Adams & Hitchcock—and then at Hagan & Thurlow's. By the time he was eighteen, Sam had a basic education in timber processing and wooden shipbuilding.

He decided to go to sea in 1875. Although a little old to start a sea career—most Bath shipmasters got their start around the age of sixteen—Percy learned fast and rose fast. For seven years he sailed on Cape

Captain Samuel Rogers Percy (1856–1940), Cape Horner and schooner captain, about 1890.

Courtesy: Maine Maritime Museum

Horners, including the M. P. GRACE, ORACLE, BOHEMIA, STANDARD, and ENOS SOULE, not to mention a brief stint in West Coast steamers. By the time he was twenty-three, he was second mate in the full-rigged ship STANDARD—built in Phippsburg—and three years later he was chief mate in the Freeport ship ENOS SOULE, under Captain Claude M. Lawrence. The latter, a notorious penny-pincher and baiter of his mates, was in need of a chief mate when he heard of the able young second mate on the STANDARD while both ships were in San Francisco. Captain Ellis Percy of the STANDARD—Percy was a common name in Phippsburg—was more than willing to see his second mate and kinsman get another step up the ladder to command and agreed to let him go. Lawrence, however, expected the neophyte first mate to serve on the ENOS SOULE at lower-than-average wages, given his lack of experience. Percy stood his ground: if he was good enough to be hired as chief mate, he was entitled to a chief mate's pay. Captain Lawrence backed down. But soon after the SOULE put to sea, there was another confrontation between the captain and his chief mate.

Lawrence did not like his men kept aloft after the afternoon watch for any reason except to handle sail. Yet one day when he came on deck after his deadline hour, he found two men from young Percy's watch still aloft, sending down gear that they had been using during the afternoon watch in the main-top rigging. The captain bellowed at the men to come down immediately, pointedly ignoring Percy standing on deck nearby. The mate joined the captain and suggested quietly that if Lawrence wished to correct or overide Percy, he had that privilege, but never in front of the men. Whereupon the captain threatened to send the upstart mate to his room.

"Best thing you could do," Percy is reported to have rejoined. "There can't be two [chief] mates on this ship. If you want to be captain and [chief] mate, best thing is to let the other get out of the way."[41] Lawrence backed down again, having met his match in Sam Percy, who refused to be buffaloed or intimidated. They sailed together for three years, and their relationship remained consistently friendly if occasionally thorny.

In 1882 stepfather George Adams offered Chief Mate Sam the command of the Adams & Hitchcock three-masted schooner NORMANDY, built in 1878. It was an opportunity that Percy couldn't refuse: his own command and the opportunity to spend more time with his bride of two years, the former Lucy Tobey. So, after seven years in deepwater sail that encompassed such varied delights as ten Cape Horn passages, lying three months in the Chincha Islands to load guano aboard the Houghton's BOHEMIA, and a knife fight with a crewman that left his back permanently scarred, he bid goodbye to square-riggers and joined Adams & Hitchcock's fleet of schooners as a shipmaster.

In 1884 Captain Percy moved to the command of the brand new tern (three-masted) schooner HENRY P. MASON, the last addition to the Adams & Hitchcock fleet. During that year Samuel P. Hitchcock, his stepfather's longtime friend, fellow shipwright, partner, and (more recently) shipbuilding side of the partnership, died at fifty years of age. The firm continued

Schooner HENRY P. MASON anchored in the Kennebec River on her launching day, 12 June 1884. The original of this photo hung for many years in Captain Percy's home.
Courtesy: Captain W. J. Lewis Parker, USCG, Ret.

under the old name, but Adams would build no more vessels himself, concentrating instead on managing the fleet and grooming young Percy for bigger and better things.[42]

Although Captain Percy had given up the dubious pleasures of Cape Horn voyages, his seafaring career was not limited to short coastwise passages or a lack of excitement. And now he could look forward to being accompanied by Mrs. Percy and young daughter Eleanor.

Two such voyages took the Percys and the MASON to the Argentine with lumber, specifically to Rosario on the Rio Parana. Here, mother and daughter experienced a pampero with "dust thick as a fog" and big hailstones. At sunset, clouds of mosquitoes that placed the Maine variety into a strictly amateur class drove mother and daughter into their bunks under mosquito netting, as the schooner worked her way up the winding, sluggish Rio Parana through thousands of acres of marshes. On both the upstream and downstream trips, the big three-master occasionally grounded on soft mud banks or drifted lazily downstream—bow first, then stern first. At Rosario, it was found necessary to place rat guards on anchor chains and mooring lines, not to keep out the ubiquitous rodents, but to repel rope-crawling snakes.[43]

But it was a trip to the aspiring Texas port of Velasco that made a far greater impression on the Percys. Carrying granite for jetties at the entrance to this up-and-coming community at the mouth of the Brazos River, the MASON was hailed as the largest vessel to ever visit the town. A group of Velasco boosters even serenaded family and crew, presenting Captain Percy with a chest of sterling silver flatware inscribed "Capt. S. R. Percy . . . from his Velasco friends,

1892." Young Eleanor enjoyed her first fifteen minutes of fame when she and the mayor's daughter were selected to turn on the community's first electric lights—Eleanor throwing the switch for the light in the hotel cupola and the mayor's daughter turning on the street lights. To cap the event, the two generators at the power plant were named for the two girls. Captain Percy was sufficiently impressed by the booster spirit of the community that he subsequently purchased land there. It was not one of his most profitable ventures.[44]

The Velasco voyage was the last that the family took together. Enroute to the Texas port, the MASON had encountered severe weather. Unable to stay in their bunks due to the schooner's gyrations, mother and daughter tried to get as much sleep as they could on the cabin floor, jammed between bolted-down furniture. Even this desperate measure was undone when Mrs. Percy's big treadle sewing machine broke loose during a particularly violent plunge and went crashing across the cabin. Henceforth, Mrs. Percy and Eleanor stayed home when the captain set sail.[45] It would not be long, however, before Sam Percy's seafaring career came to an end and he would join them there.

AN END AND A BEGINNING

George Adams died on Saturday, the eleventh of March, 1893, two days after Captain Sam Percy arrived home by train from Salem in response to the urgent summons. Husband, stepfather, senior partner of a widely respected firm, and managing owner of a fleet of ten schooners totaling 6,520 tons, Adams had achieved much in his lifetime.[46]

Starting as a ship carpenter in the shipyard operated by his father James and uncle David Adams on the Sheepscot tidewater north of Boothbay's Adams Pond, George M. Adams built his first ship as a master carpenter in 1844 at the age of twenty-five in Edgecomb.[47] He next appears on the master carpenter's certificate for the ship YORKTOWN, built at Parker's Head in 1849. From there, he moved to Bath, capital of Maine's wooden shipbuilding industry.

There were plenty of opportunities available here for an ambitious and skilled young man, and George was not long in finding them. He spent a decade working for William Rogers, one of Bath's most durable shipbuilders. Then, with Samuel P. Hitchcock as partner, the two negotiated a deal with J. Parker Morse to build vessels for Morse's fleet. They would provide the labor and supervise the construction of the Morse vessels while J. Parker Morse provided the shipyard and the materials. By all accounts it was a successful arrangement, with ten vessels—nine ships and one tug totaling 10,458 tons—being built between 1860–71.[48] According to one story, they were so successful that Parker Morse's brother Alden accosted George Adams at the shipyard one day and complained: "George, you're making $40 a ton on this vessel." Adams's instant response: "Alden, it's none of your _____ _____ business if I am making $100 a ton."[49] End of discussion.

The Adams-Hitchcock partnership began building for their own management in 1872, starting with the three-masted schooner HENRY H. FISK of 239 tons. At the time of Hitchcock's death in 1884, they had completed fourteen vessels for their own account, all but one—the bark EDWIN REED—being three-masted schooners.

In 1877 the partners hired Elwell S. Crosby as clerk and bookkeeper. Crosby arrived in Bath in 1873 from his native Arrowsic with forty cents in his pocket and the desperate need for a job. Prior to his employment by Adams & Hitchcock, young Crosby tried his hand at cabinetmaking, cordage-making, working at a fruit store, and driving a team of oxen at a local shipyard.[50] After Hitchcock's death, Crosby's connection with the firm changed as he became more than an employee but less than a full partner.

In addition to his association with Adams & Hitchcock, Crosby purchased an insurance business in partnership with Zina Blair in 1878, apparently handling the insurance business on the side; ten years later, he acquired the George Fisher Agency. He also got into shipbuilding, leasing the Reed yard in the south end—we'll hear again of the Reed yard in subsequent chapters—building the four-masted FRANK T. STINSON in 1887 and the three-master FANNIE J. BARTLETT in 1888. George Adams was the managing owner of both of these schooners, which suggests that the ambitious Crosby was being bankrolled by his former boss and mentor and that Crosby had moved from being employee to junior partner.

The younger man subsequently shifted his operations to Bath's north end at John Patten & Son's yard, building five three- and four-masters, four for his own account between 1889–91. Although Adams owned a $2/64$ share in each of Crosby's subsequent four-masters, the younger man was the managing owner.

With George Adams's death, Elwell Crosby's and Captain Sam Percy's paths crossed in an unusual way. While Adams's last will and testament distributed his estate valued in excess of $60,000 (over $1,000,000 in 1998) among family members, it did not directly address his role as *managing* owner of ten schooners.[51] This required the action of all the shareholders of each vessel, who would vote to select one of their number as the new manager of the vessel. In any event, Captain Percy and Elwell Crosby presented themselves to the shareholders as candidates for the job. Until a decision was reached, however, Captain Fessenden Chase, an old friend of Adams's, stood in as temporary manager.

When the vote was taken, the shareholders in the various schooners were deadlocked between the two candidates. What to do? Both candidates agreed that arbitration was the only course, each selecting a representative who would, in turn, pick a third party to make the final decision. Crosby nominated Reuben Hunt, sawmill owner and occasional shipbuilder in the Winnegance section of Bath; Percy picked James B. Drake, one of Bath's most experienced ship brokers. Hunt and Drake then selected Captain John R. Kelley to make the award.

No man in Bath was more respected than the sixty-five-year-old retired shipmaster. In command of vessels for thirty-two years, including four big John Patten & Son Down Easters—NIMBUS, ASTORIA, FLORENCE, and TACOMA—Kelley's worst accident at sea had been the loss of TACOMA's fore-topmast, and that on his last voyage. Once ashore, Captain Kelley didn't retire to the porch rocking chair. He became a manager of sailing vessels and, subsequently, a founder and first president of Kelley, Spear Co., the firm that would build the last large, wooden-hulled vessel in Bath.

His decision in the Adams & Hitchcock case was Solomonaic: Sam Percy would manage six three-masters, representing 56 percent of the tonnage. Crosby, in turn, would manage 44 percent of the tonnage. That disparity was balanced out by the fact that the Percy tonnage was, on average, older than the tonnage assigned to Crosby. Percy would, henceforth, manage schooners NORMANDY, CARRIE A. NORTON, S. P. HITCHCOCK, GEORGE M. ADAMS, CELINA, and HENRY P. MASON. Elwell Crosby, in turn, received control of the THOMAS W. HYDE, B. R. WOODSIDE, FRANK T. STINSON, and FANNIE J. BARTLETT.[52]

PERCY & SMALL: MANAGING OWNERS

It was not the best of times for Captain Percy to be embarking on a new venture. In late 1890 the great British banking house of Baring Brothers failed—for the first time—setting off a chain of events that led to financial panic on Wall Street and the virtual collapse of the American economy during 1893. By the end of that year—the same time Percy & Small was founded—491 banks and over 15,000 commercial institutions had failed. Unemployment was endemic across the nation and labor strife culminated in the bitter Pullman Strike during the summer. Twenty-five percent of the value of stocks evaporated overnight, and the national economy would linger in the gloom of depression for four years. Only one financial disaster in American history has had a greater impact: the Crash of 1929 and the subsequent Great Depression.

Arthur Sewall, "the Merchant Prince," head of one of America's major maritime dynasties, and president of the Bath National Bank, wrote, "The outlook for the future is very pessimistic. Conditions at present are very discouraging, but I have confidence, as I always have had in periods of depression in the past, that the turn will surely come."[53] Sewall may have been whistling in the dark; his firm was building the first steel square-rigger in the country, DIRIGO, which represented no small investment in an uncertain future.[54]

The *New York Maritime Register*, the maritime industry's principal journal, stated: "1893 [was] the worst year the commercial world has passed through . . . thank goodness it is past." As events were to prove, it was a premature sigh of relief. In fact, historians working from the vantage point of hindsight see the period in even starker terms. "This year, 1894, . . . was the darkest that Americans had known for thirty years. Everything seemed to conspire to convince the people that democracy was a failure. Prices and wages hit rock-bottom and there seemed to be no market for anything."[55]

Nowhere was this better illustrated than in the production from Bath's shipyards. The combined output—all commercial and private vessels, sail or steam—in 1890 was 32,183 tons. This had slipped by over a third to 20,616 tons in 1892, and collapsed the next year as the output sagged to 7,825 tons. Although shipbuilding showed modest improvement over the next three years with deliveries reaching 16,607 tons in 1896, it then plunged to a decade low of 6,868 tons in 1897 before again recovering rapidly over the last three years of the century, when it finally topped the figure for 1890.

In this decidedly uncheerful environment, Captain Percy was faced with some important decisions concerning his own future, as well as that of the fleet of three-masters he now managed. Should he seek out a partner, one with complementary skills and the will-

Frank Albion Small (1865–1917), the capable business manager and junior partner of Percy & Small. This photo was taken about 1911 when Small was mayor of Bath.

Courtesy: Maine Maritime Museum

ingness to invest substantial sums in coastwise shipping? Should he expand his fleet by purchasing or building additional vessels? If building additional vessels, should he contract construction to an existing shipbuilder, or should he undertake to be his own shipbuilder?

It is probable that Sam Percy explored these questions with several people active in Bath's shipping circles who were formerly close to his stepfather.[56] Unquestionably one of those consulted was Captain John R. Kelley. If so, his advice was direct: find a partner who is detail-oriented and understands the intricacies of the shipping business in general and the coal trade in particular. One can be certain that the top person on Kelley's list was his own assistant and bookkeeper, Frank A. Small.

Small, youngest son of Captain Joseph Small, was a graduate of Bath High School. His business career commenced in the office of James B. Drake where, for six years, he learned the shipping business from the ground up. He then entered the employ of Captain John R. Kelley. By 1893 the twenty-eight-year-old bachelor businessman had earned a reputation for being thoroughly conversant with the coastwise shipping business, attentive to detail, and ambitious.

With Sam Percy's ample hands-on experience with shipbuilding and the actual operation of coastwise schooners, he needed—and got—a partner who could organize, understand, and manage the myriad financial and chartering details of the business. Sam Percy chose wisely, teaming the up-front extrovert with the methodical, precise, well-versed administrator. By the end of 1893, Captain Sam Percy and Frank Small had all but signed a partnership agreement that blended the talents of shipbuilder and seaman with detail man.[57] It was a good fit. The partnership would endure and prosper for nearly a quarter century.

Tradition still dominated the shipping business as it related to the sailing vessel at the end of the nineteenth century, and Percy & Small was content to accept the traditional system as its own. The Adams–Hitchcock house flag was adapted by substituting a white "P–S" on the navy blue field for the original "A–H." The partners also took over the second-floor office suite that had formerly been occupied by Adams & Hitchcock over the Lincoln Bank. Located at 52 Front Street on the busy corner with Centre Street, the office was soon redecorated and, incidentally, acquired the reputation among Bath's maritime fraternity as "Sailor's Snug Harbor."[58] Here, retired shipmasters, shipbuilders, and shipping brokers gathered almost daily to tell sea stories, discuss the current and future state of the shipping business, and—no doubt—distract Captain Percy and Frank Small from their duties.

Nowhere was the new firm more traditional than in its organization and method of doing business. The partners raised capital from investors which, when combined with their own capital, permitted the construction from time to time of new vessels. The firm's financial rewards were derived from fees for arranging and overseeing vessel construction, a percentage of each vessel's gross freight for arranging charters, a small management fee also based on a percentage of the gross freight, and the firm's pro rata share of the net profits from each vessel. The financial interest of other investors encompassed only the specific schooners in which they owned shares, and not the business itself.

Although Percy & Small came into existence with what appeared to be a ready-made fleet of vessels, Captain Percy was technically their sole managing owner. Frank Small never owned any shares in the former Adams–Hitchcock schooners and they never flew the P&S house flag.[59] Small, on the other hand, was all but managing owner of the three-master MARY B. OLYS, built in 1891. Originally handled by Swanton & Jameson, the schooner was turned over to Small's management skills in late 1893, following the bankruptcy of the former management team.[60]

As a practical matter, the principal objective of the partnership was to jointly build and manage a new fleet of schooners. Partners Percy & Small set out to do this immediately, undeterred by the worst financial crisis the American nation had yet faced. Nor were they to be put off by challenges proffered by steel and steam, or the warnings of two of the shipbuilding community, William Rogers and Charles V. Minott, Jr., concerning the future of wooden shipbuilding.

The ink had barely dried on their partnership agreement before an order was placed with Fred W. Rideout for model, moulds, deck plan, and midship section plan for a 1,500-ton schooner.[61] All the new partners now had to do was find investors and a shipyard. The latter they leased for $400 per year from C. W. Morse; it was the same shipyard where Adams & Hitchcock had built ships for J. Parker Morse three decades earlier.[62] The former presented Percy & Small with its first major challenge.

To be managing owners, Percy & Small first had to organize enough capital in the form of shares to build and equip a vessel. Some of that capital was their own, more came from family, friends, business associates, subcontractors, and small investors within the Bath and Maine community. A growing portion of the total was drawn from out-of-state investors.

Each vessel was financed individually through the traditional method of "taking up shares." Customarily the share was regarded as $1/64$, but investors in schooner property sometimes took as little as $1/256$, as the size and cost of the schooners grew to the point where a single share represented a major investment. A sixty-fourth of Percy & Small's first schooner represented an investment of $1,007.78 in 1894 (+/- $18,000 in 1998). Fifteen years later, $1/64$ of the WYOMING cost the investor approximately $2,600 (+/- $40,000 in 1998).[63]

It was not just the cost of a new vessel that encouraged spreading the investment among a number of owners. Ownership in seagoing vessels represented a venture with a moderate to high degree of risk, and not just from the normal economic fluctuations that marked the nineteenth century or the normal wear and tear that afflicts all machines. The vessels operated in a high-risk environment where carelessness, chance, nature, or human *hubris*—singularly or in combination—could render the investment worthless in moments. Given the potential for total loss, it behooved the prudent investor to spread his or her investment dollars over the largest number of vessels possible. Then, if a vessel was lost or put out of service, the small investor was not apt to lose his financial shirt.

Why, then, would any sensible, conservative investor wish to risk money on a coastwise sailing vessel, given the physical and technological risks? First, there was the "devil you know" syndrome. You invested your money with your neighbors within your community, possibly friends and schoolmates of old, and certainly someone of whom you had personal knowledge of their character and ability. This was not some business entity physically far removed and led by some mythic colossus of industry or high finance.

Second, it was the type of business with which most local investors were quite familiar, because it was the meat and drink of the community. The local newspapers published regular columns on the shipping business, including the activities of locally owned/managed vessels, recent charters, and other shipping news of interest to the investor. The risks of navigation and storm and the fluctuations of the seaborne freight market were well known in Bath, as was the potential for profit.

And finally, there is a sense of empowerment translated into physical reality. You owned a real piece of a real vessel—even if it was a $1/256$ piece—that you could see and touch. You possessed official documentation of that fact, signed by U.S. Customs officials.[64] And you received regular financial statements on *your* vessel's performance (with, hopefully, a tidy check), detailing her activities since the last statement. As an investor in a new vessel, you received an invitation to come aboard for the launching of the new schooner with the other owners and invited guests. If you were so inclined, you could even arrange to sail aboard "your" schooner in one of the guest cabins reserved for the owners, preferably in the summer. This conveyed a far different sense of involvement than owning shares of the same value in some remote corporation where ownership was far more abstract and diluted.

The shareholders in a schooner had some say in who managed the vessel—sometimes called the ship's husband—especially if the original managing ownership was dissolved or terminated by death. This was a limited right in practice, however, because managing owners could protect themselves against unfriendly "takeovers" by holding enough shares in the vessel to effectively control a majority of the ownership. With Percy & Small's first schooner, for example, the partners initially held $39/128$, and the captain held an additional $16/128$, 43 percent of all the shares. The rest of the shares were spread among thirty-three owners.[65] It was highly unlikely that an individual investor or group of investors would be able to challenge Percy & Small's management of the vessel, even if there were grounds for accusing the management of gross incompetence (which there decidedly were not). Another approach managing owners used to secure their continued management rights to a vessel was through a trust agreement. This effectively removed the shareholders' right to vote in a new management team without the consent of the old, and gave the existing management an effective veto on the sale of shares by current shareholders to new owners, unless the prospective buyers agreed to accept the existing management. Percy & Small appears to have used this approach occasionally, but it was the Palmer fleet of Boston where the trust arrangement was most common.[66] The most effective means for the managing owners to retain operational control over a vessel was to scrupulously carry out their fiduciary and management responsibilities.

Although Sam Percy and Frank Small were well known individually within Bath's maritime circles, they were a new combination and, as yet, untried. They lacked a track record and were up against the natural reluctance to invest in new ventures at the height of a financial depression. Nonetheless, the new partners went forth and buttonholed Bath's business community.

Some were obvious targets. Shipbuilding subcontractors (blacksmiths, riggers, fasteners, joiners, etc.) depended on shipbuilding to survive and prosper. By investing in a prospective schooner, they materially underwrote its construction, assured work and profit in the short term, and through shares held in the new vessel could look forward to a long string of dividends in the future. The same considerations also played a role when it came to local firms engaged in supplying materials to shipbuilders. Together, the two groups underwrote ^{28}/128 of the vessel's shares, while family and friends took up ^{8}/128 of the shares. The schooner's namesake, Charles P. Notman, and his brother also took ^{8}/128, and the former's New York ship brokerage firm, James W. Elwell & Company, kicked in for an additional ^{10}/128. Of the balance, ^{19}/128 was held by miscellaneous parties whose exact connection with P&S has not been identified. This, however, constituted only 57 percent of the total shares.[67]

As was the custom with most of Maine's shipping houses, Percy & Small required their shipmasters to take a substantial share of the ownership in vessels they commanded. This was believed to encourage enthusiastic diligence tempered by reasonable caution on the part of the captains. It required a hefty investment, often accomplished through loans.

Captain Lincoln W. Jewett was selected by the partners to command the new schooner. Captain "Linc," as he was known on many a waterfront, was required to take ^{16}/128 of the schooner, requiring an ante of $8,062.16 (+/- $144,000 in 1998). For this very substantial commitment, the captain could expect to receive $40.00 per month wages (+/- $715.00 in 1998), plus the dividends on his vessel shares and a 5 percent commission (primage) on the gross freight.

Primage was the key source of income for many of the shipmasters at this time, although some canny managing owners eliminated this provision during the war years, paying high wages instead.

With the depression scaring off investors, Sam Percy and Frank Small really had to dig deep into their own pockets if the big schooner was to be built. Together, they took ^{39}/128, representing $19,651.71 (+/- $350,000 in 1998), which required very heavy borrowing with its accompanying interest and insurance premiums to cover shares serving as security against the loans.[68] Yet they were able to sell ^{17}/128 of their shares within a year, reducing debt and improving their cash position, as the NOTMAN soon proved to be a prodigious cash cow.[69]

Captain Percy turned to Fred W. Rideout for the design of the proposed new schooner. Former assistant to the nationally famous ship designer William Pattee, who has been credited with designing over seven hundred sailing ships and steamships, Rideout worked closely with Pattee and his own father, Johnson Rideout, who was Pattee's partner.[70] Following Pattee's death in 1892, Johnson Rideout made Frederick a full partner in the firm in 1893 and then retired. Coincidentally, Johnson Rideout was a full-fledged, card-carrying member of the "Sailor's Snug Harbor" club that met every morning at the offices of Percy & Small.

Fred Rideout produced the half model and frame patterns (called moulds) for a moderately large four-masted schooner measuring approximately 1,500 gross register tons with a payload capacity of 2,400 tons.[71] A big schooner for her day, with a registered length of 219.3 feet, #1's design did not push the schooner design envelope; with her long poop, short well deck forward of the mainmast, and forecastle deck (called topgallant forecastle deck), her profile could be that of any number of Maine-built four-masted schooners.

Her frame of mixed hardwood and hackmatack was not the white oak preferred by underwriters and surveyors, but it had the dual advantages of being near at hand in the forests of southern Aroostook County in Maine and relatively inexpensive. The 270 tons of hardwood and "hack" needed to be on hand in the shipyard at the earliest possible moment if construction was to be completed by late summer or early fall, so the order and the moulds were dispatched to timber merchants Lewis & Littlefield before the first of the year.[72] Another order was placed with Morse & Co. for 455,708 board feet of the southern longleaf yellow pine (hard pine) that would make up the new schooner's internal structure including deck beams, keelsons, internal planking (ceiling), and external planking. Meanwhile, as Percy & Small awaited the arrival of the heavy timber, Sam Percy scoured the local—and for the most part idle—shipyards for the necessary timber not included in the original orders.

The new schooner was built under survey by the American Shipmasters Association—since 1898 known as the American Bureau of Shipping (ABS)—a classification society that prescribed standards for construction, materials, and structural strength of wooden and steel vessels. Patterned after far older organizations such as Lloyd's Register of British and Foreign Shipping and Bureau Veritas, the ABS inspects vessels during construction and, in accordance with standards developed for materials, scantlings, fastenings, workmanship, etc., incorporated in the vessel, assigns it a class such as 1A and a class life in years. While Percy & Small were not required to build this, or any vessel, to any classification society's requirements, marine insurance underwriters relied upon vessel classifications to set premium rates. Thus a vessel with a 1A class received better rates than a

The CHARLES P. NOTMAN poses for her first formal portrait afloat. Her subsequent success underwrote the expansion of Percy & Small's fleet for the next six years.

Courtesy: Maine Maritime Museum

vessel classed as 2A or lower. In the case of P&S Hull #1, the ABS awarded a class of 1A for thirteen years, the lowest time any vessel built by the firm ever received.[73]

The American Shipmasters Association did not wash its hands of the new vessel once she took to the water. All significant damage had to be reported and was subject to a surveyor's scrutiny and recommendations, and repair work was carried out under survey, as well. In addition, the vessel was required to undergo a half-time survey, at which time the surveyor often made what amounted to binding recommendations for necessary repairs if the vessel was to maintain its class. Assuming the vessel survived to reach the end of its original class life, it was then subjected to a thorough full-time survey that involved removal of random hull and ceiling planking to determine the condition of the underlying structure, a careful inspection of caulking, machinery, and general vessel condition. Those vessels in good condition or with repairable deficiencies could get their class continued for a stated period of time.

Horatio N. Douglas was selected to be the master builder for the new schooner. As such, he would directly supervise the Percy & Small-employed ship carpenters and the various subcontractors. For his expertise and services, Douglas received $619 (+/- $11,000 in 1998). At age fifty, he had a wide breadth of experience. Caught up in the fires of patriotic fervor that swept Maine in 1861, he enlisted in the Union Army and served throughout the entire war. Returning to Bath, he apprenticed himself to Captain Guy C. Goss, the senior partner of the massively productive but ill-fated shipbuilding firm of Goss & Sawyer and Goss, Sawyer, & Packard (we will meet a number of the men involved with Percy & Small who were alumni of the Goss firm). When that firm was reorganized as the New England Company, Douglas became its senior master builder. During the mid-1890s, another lull in contracts at the New England yard provided the veteran soldier and shipbuilder with enough time to do a bit of free-lancing for Percy & Small, and he supervised the construction of their first four schooners.[74]

Among the subcontractors were several who would become fixtures in later years in Percy & Small's shipbuilding business: Fred B. Scott, joiner; Leonard Gibson, blacksmith; Charles S. Colby, fastener; Frank A. Palmer, rigger; and Charles Oliver, caulker. Each brought with him a team of highly skilled employees who practiced their arcane arts at a number of shipyards, thus avoiding some of the uncertainty that accompanied employment in the highly cyclical shipbuilding business.

On 29 August 1894, Percy & Small launched the 1,518-gross ton (GRT) CHARLES P. NOTMAN, a small down payment on the 78,626 gross tons of wooden vessels they would deliver over the next quarter century. But the lack of prescience among Bath's newspapers was never more obvious than on this day, when the *Enterprise* awarded the event four column inches at a time when the local press was bemoaning the miserable economy and the poor state of Bath's shipbuilding business.[75] By 1909 Percy & Small had really captured the attention of the local press.

---

[1] Flyer: "Ship Launching at Bath." Captain W. J. Lewis Parker Collection; hereafter cited as Parker Collection.

[2] *Bath Daily Times*, Supplement, September 1916. Hereafter cited as *BT*.

[3] *BT*, November 11, December 14, 1909.

[4] The German-built steel five-masted, full-rigged ship PREUSSEN holds the largest square-rigged vessel honors, and the American-built seven-masted steel schooner THOMAS W. LAWSON was the largest sailing vessel ever built. It is often claimed that the wooden American-built GREAT REPUBLIC holds the palm as the largest wooden sailing vessel, but there are a number of authorities who dispute this claim. The GREAT REPUBLIC never carried cargo as built, being a victim of fire before clearing port. Cut down and rebuilt, she sailed for nearly nineteen years, but her new tonnage measurements as rebuilt were drastically changed, especially breadth, suggesting to the late Professor John Lyman that there had been a serious error when she was first admeasured before the fire. See: *Log Chips*, v. I, no. 3 (11/1948), p. 28.

[5] *Bath Independent*, 12/18/1909. Hereafter cited as *BI*.

[6] *BT*, 12/15/1909.

A SHIPYARD IN MAINE

24

[7] *John F. Eaton Reminiscences*, 1/15/1979. Tape #79-T-1, Maine Maritime Museum.

[8] Personal conversation between Donald Small and Ralph Linwood Snow, September 1972.

[9] *BT*, 12/15/1909.

[10] That authority on all things maritime, William F. Palmer, noted over the years the availability of "punch" at Percy & Small launchings. See: Palmer Letter Book 11/1905–3/12/1906, WFP to Dr. J. M. Hills, 12/5/1905: "We had a beautiful launching down in Bath, and the launching fluid embalmed the usual number." In a letter to Maria Davis, Palmer wrote, "Eben simply must come to the launching. There will be nothing used but flowers, but you may tell him that the launching may not be exactly dry as far as the after cabin is concerned." WFP to Miss Maria Davis, 10/23/1905, Palmer Letter Book 7/1905–10/1905. William F. Palmer Fleet Collection, MS-50, Maine Maritime Museum. Hereafter cited as Palmer Collection.

[11] *BT*, 12/15/1909; *BI*, 12/18/1909. The latter account of the launching is more detailed. One old shipmaster, when invited to partake of the buffet, replied: "Don't bother me about eating. I am having too good a time looking over this craft. That is far better than any grub you have aboard." *BT*, 12/16/1909.

[12] *BT*, 12/15/1909.

[13] Basil Greenhill, *Archaeology of the Boat*. Middletown, CT: Wesleyan University Press, 1976, p. 300. Hereafter cited as Greenhill, *Archaeology*.

[14] *Ibid.*; also see Robert Gardiner, ed. *The Earliest Ships: The Evolution of Boats into Ships*. London: Conway Maritime Press, 1996.

[15] John H. Pryor, "The Mediterranean Round Ship," in *Cogs, Caravels and Galleons: The Sailing Ship 1000–1650*, Robert Gardiner, ed. London: Conway Maritime Press, 1994, pp. 62–63.

[16] For a detailed discussion of the evolution of the plank-on-frame vessels read: *Cogs, Caravels and Galleons: The Sailing Ship 1000–1650*, especially the Introduction, "The Cog as Cargo Carrier" and "The Mediterranean Round Ship."

[17] Greenhill, *Archaeology*, p. 288.

[18] Basil Greenhill and Samuel Manning, *The Schooner Bertha L. Downs*. London: Conway Maritime Press, 1995, p. 8. Hereafter cited as Greenhill and Manning, *Schooner*. Greenhill believes that the topsail schooner and fore-and-aft schooner rigs had different origins but cross-fertilized each other. David R. MacGregor, *The Schooner: Its Design and Development from 1600 to the Present*. London: Chatham Publishing, 1997, pp. 13–20. MacGregor suggests that the two shared common ancestry.

[19] Howard I. Chapelle, *The History of the American Sailing Ship*. New York: W. W. Norton, 1935, p. 219.

[20] Greenhill and Manning, *Schooner*, pp. 7–8.

[21] Charles S. Morgan, "New England Coasting Schooners," *American Neptune*, v. XXIII, no. 1, pp. 7–8. Hereafter cited as Morgan, "Coasting Schooners." Curiously, Bath—the schooner-building capital of the world by the end of the century—did not build its first three-master until 1868. This probably reflects the fact that its many building ways were occupied by the then much larger, more prestigious, and more profitable full-riggers that had become the city's trademark.

[22] *Ibid.*, pp. 5–21.

[23] The U.S. Geological Survey ranked American-produced coals as follows (type/heat value in BTUs per pound): lignite—7,400; sub-bituminous—9,720; low-rank bituminous—12,880; medium-rank bituminous—13,880; high-rank bituminous—15,160; low-rank semi-bituminous—15,480; high-rank semi-bituminous—15,360; semi-anthracite—14,880; anthracite—14,440. See *Marine Steam*. New York: Babcock & Wilcox Company, 1928, pp. 143–47.

[24] W. J. Lewis Parker, *The Great Coal Schooners of New England, 1870–1909*. Mystic, CT: Marine Historical Association, 1948, p. 15. Hereafter cited as Parker, *Coal Schooners*.

[25] A classic case of the problems of transporting bulk cargoes in the new Republic was dramatized in the so-called "Whiskey Insurrection" in western Pennsylvania. Because land transport was unreliable and expensive, farmers in the region converted their abundant grain crops to whisky, a far more transportable product, with a high value-added quotient. The Federal Government taxed the product and the farmers rebelled in 1794.

[26] Parker, *Coal Schooners*, p. 16.

[27] *Ibid.*, p. 18.

[28] W. H. Bunting, *A Day's Work: A Sampler of Historic Maine Photographs, 1860–1920, Part I*. Gardiner, ME: Tilbury House, 1997, pp. 108, 216.

[29] Parker, *Coal Schooners*, p. 18.

[30] In 1900 Boston received 4,064,100 tons of coal by sea. (*Fifteenth Annual Report of the Boston Chamber of Commerce in the Year Ending December 31, 1900, Boston, 1901*, p. 226.) If this coal had been shipped to Boston by rail, it would have required approximately 271,000 carloads passing through the New England rail net at the rate of 750 gondola cars per day each way in trains that totaled altogether over ten miles in length—all this on a rail network already heavily utilized.

[31] J. G. B. Hutchins, *The American Maritime Industries and Public Policy, 1789–1914*. Cambridge, MA: Harvard University Press, 1941, p. 546. Hutchins noted that Boston received only 77,024 tons by rail in 1905.

[32] *Bath Sentinel*, May 12, 1881. Hereafter cited as *BS*.

Rogers delivered his last vessel in 1902.

[33] Transcription in Personal Research Files, Parker Collection. Original letter in collection of Ada Y. Haggett.

[34] U.S. Code Title 46, Sec. 290: R.S. 4347, Feb. 17, 1893, Sec. 1.

[35] At least three four-masted schooners preceded the WHITE, converted from various pre-existing hulls. ELIZA, ex-OSCEOLA, was converted from a former Civil War gunboat in 1868; WEYBOSSET was converted from a steamer in 1879; on the Pacific coast, the VICTORIA was rebuilt from a barge in 1863 (per *Log Chips*, July, 1949). William H. Bunting—historian, cattleman, and bulldozer operator extraordinaire—has proposed another possibility, the Portland (ME)-built E. D. SIDBURY of 1879 as the *first* purpose-built four-master, per an account in the *Industrial Journal*.

[36] Morgan, "Coasting Schooners," p. 13.

[37] Greenhill and Manning, *Schooner*, p. 11.

[38] The first schooner equipped with a steam hoisting engine was the Taunton-owned tern CHARLES A. BRIGGS, built by Bath's Goss & Sawyer in 1879. See: Parker, *Coal Schooners*, footnote 24, p. 107, and William Avery Baker, *Maritime History of Bath Maine and the Kennebec River Region*. Bath, ME: Marine Research Society, 1973, II, p. 573. Hereafter cited as Baker, I (or subsequent volume numbers).

[39] Samuel R. Percy file, 15/1, Mark W. Hennessy Research Papers, MS-53, Maine Maritime Museum: hereafter cited as MWHRP. Percy left the MASON on 9 March, his stepfather died two days later.

[40] Data concerning SRP background drawn from following sources: *Log Chips*, v. III, no. 7, October 1953, pp. 74–75; Samuel R. Percy file, 15/1, MWHRP; *BT*, 2/21/1901, and *BT*, 10/4/1940, obituary; Baker, II, pp. 690–91.

[41] Masters and Mates File, 15/7, MWHRP.

[42] *Bath Anvil*, 3/21/1908. Hereafter cited as BA.

[43] Notes of interview with Mrs. Eleanor Percy Irish, 24 October 1954, Personal Research Files, Parker Collection.

[44] *Ibid.* Velasco has since lost its identity as a town and is now a state park near Freeport.

[45] Eleanor A. Percy Irish File, 2/19, MWHRP.

[46] There has been some confusion concerning the division of the fleet. Captain John R. Kelley took into account a total of ten vessels including seven for which Adams & Hitchcock was listed as managing owner, one for which S. P. Hitchcock was listed as managing owner, and two with Crosby as master carpenter and Adams as managing owner.

[47] James P. Stevens, *Reminiscences of a Boothbay Shipbuilder*. Boothbay, ME: Boothbay Region Historical Society, 1993, p. 64.

[48] BA, 3/21/1908; Baker, I, pp. 537–39. Baker presents circumstantial evidence that Adams & Hitchcock also built the Morse ship NIAGARA in 1859 and probably two tugs, as well. Morse signed all the carpenter certificates.

[49] *BA*, 3/21/1908.

[50] Baker, II, p. 630; and *BI*, 10/8/1931, obituary.

[51] "Estate Inventory," George M. Adams Probate File, Sagadahoc County Court of Probate, Bath, ME.

[52] *BT*, 4/28/1893. Crosby later created a tempest in a teapot among some shareholders of his vessels when it was announced that he was selling his managerial interest to J. S. Winslow & Co. in Portland without their prior approval. See: *BT*, 5/8, 10, 11/1897.

[53] Bath National Bank, *Our First Hundred Years*. Bath, ME, 1955, p. 57.

[54] Dirigo is Maine's state motto, Latin for "I Lead."

[55] *New York Maritime Register*, 1 January 1894; hereafter cited as *NYMR*; and Samuel Eliot Morison and Henry Steele Commager, *The Growth of the American Republic*, 3d ed., New York, 1942, v. II, p. 254.

[56] Among those who regularly visited the offices of Percy & Small in later years were Captain Kelley, Captain Fessenden Chase, and Johnson Rideout. All three also invested in subsequent Percy & Small schooners.

[57] Maine Central Railroad Waybills, Construction Bill File, P&S Schooner #1, Parker Collection. The earliest waybill, dated 12/18/1893, is directed to "Capt. Sam'l Percy"; another bill, order dated Jan. 11, 1894, for stationery, is the earliest addressed to Percy & Small; however, it is apparent from the timing of model, moulds, and plans and the subsequent delivery of the frames, that the process was in train *before* the end of 1893.

[58] *BI*, 1/6/1894; Captain Kelley spent so much time there, the newspaper assumed he shared the office with Captain Percy.

[59] Evidence suggests that although Sam Percy was technically managing owner of the former Adams & Hitchcock vessels, Frank Small probably handled their day-to-day business. P&S purchased a few shares in these vessels from time to time, but treated them as any other investment in vessels managed by others. By 1905 all these schooners were gone—sold or lost. See: *P&S Journal*, MS-157, Maine Maritime Museum, hereafter cited as *PSJ*; *City of Bath Ship Books*, (1905) MS-46, Maine Maritime Museum, hereafter cited as *BSB* (year); and P&S Trial Balances, Parker Collection.

[60] MARY B. OLYS Account Book, A-142, on loan to Maine Maritime Museum. William B. Olys of Boston was listed as her managing owner, but he contracted out the most onerous of those chores to others. Aside from Frank Small's ¹/64, the firm also acquired a share or two in the OLYS at the turn of the century.

[61] Construction Bill File, Schooner #1, Parker

Collection; Rideout probably made the model and moulds in December of 1893. He received $147.65 for his design services per bill dated 8/13/1894, but 270 tons of hardwood and hackmatack for the frame appear on a bill from Lewis & Littlefield dated 3/13/1894, and the shipment was receipted at the Bath railway depot as having arrived from Wytopitlock, Maine, between 2/23–3/9/1894. The moulds arrived back from Littlefield on 3/8/1894. The dates suggest the moulds were shipped to Littlefield about the first of the year, and that he was in the woods getting out the frame shortly thereafter.

[62] "To Use of Yard and Tools," Morse & Co., 9/11/1894, Construction Bill File, Schooner #1, Parker Collection.

[63] *PSJ*, pp. 3–4; Hull # 30 [WYOMING] Summary Cost Account, Parker Collection. The cost account lists cost for materials, equipment, and labor at $149,735.88. This does not include P&S's traditional charges for use of shipyard and tools and their customary $2 per gross ton fee for building a vessel for their own account.

[64] Certification of Ownership of $1/128$ of the Schooner DUSTIN G. CRESSY, dated July 16, 1912, James H. Cameron Papers, MS-89, Maine Maritime Museum.

[65] Owners, Schooner #1, *PSJ*, pp. 3–4.

[66] Agreement Constituting Percy & Small of Bath, State of Maine Trustees of Certain Schooner Property, SM 02/06, Maine Maritime Museum. The preamble describes the agreement as being ". . . for the purpose of mutual pro-

tection of said property from the depredations of speculators . . . ."

[67] Owners, Schooner #1, *PSJ*, pp. 3–4.

[68] *Ibid.*, p. 6. Entries for 1/31/1895 show the firm to have notes outstanding of at least $11,296.39 (+/- $202,205 in 1998).

[69] CHARLES P. NOTMAN Earnings, Personal Research Files, Parker Collection. *PSJ*, Earnings CHARLES P. NOTMAN. For some reason the first six dividends paid by the NOTMAN do not appear in *PSJ*.

[70] Baker, II, pp. 785–88.

[71] When referring to a vessel's tonnage, the author uses gross register tons, a measurement of volume (100 cu. ft. = 1 ton), also called measurement tonnage. Deadweight tonnage, or burthen, refers to the payload capacity of the vessel calculated in long tons of 2,240 pounds. Displacement tonnage is the weight of the water displaced by the vessel in long tons.

[72] *BI*, 1/6/1894: "As the men are now well under way cutting the frame for Capt. Samuel Percy's . . . schooner . . . ."

[73] The usual period for a first-class vessel was fifteen years, but the extensive use of mixed hardwoods for floor timbers and keel rather than the higher rated white oak apparently reduced it by two years in the opinion of the surveyor.

[74] *BT*, 9/12/1927, obituary.

[75] *Bath Enterprise*, 9/1/1894; hereafter cited as *BE*.

Building the Foundation: 1894-1899

MAKING A GOOD START

I t was no small achievement in 1894 for the new business partnership of Percy & Small to successfully raise the necessary capital to build a big four-master while the nation languished in the depths of a major depression. The next big test was whether they could make the schooner CHARLES P. NOTMAN pay dividends sufficient to justify the original investment. In this endeavor they had the assistance of one of the most colorful and, as it turned out, able captains in the Atlantic coasting trade.

Lincoln Webb Jewett was a Maine original. He was born in 1855 on Westport Island to Captain James and Elvira Jewett. Among "Linc's" several siblings were two considerably older brothers, Captain Amos and E. F., and a twin sister, Aramed. At the age of seven he accompanied his parents to sea for the first time and, seven years later, young Linc shipped aboard a fishing schooner, commencing a forty-year sea career.

Unlike Captain Sam Percy, however, Linc never went into the deepwater trades, concentrating his activities instead on the fisheries and then coasting. Although the maritime pecking order tended to place coasting and fishing sailors below those sailing deep-water, especially the Cape Horn trades, the former needed skills of the highest order (and nerves to match) to survive the hazards endemic to sailing along America's eastern seaboard. Captain Lincoln Webb Jewett possessed these skills in spades when he was tapped by Captain Percy for command of the firm's first schooner.

By then Captain Jewett, a full-fledged member of the select and demanding fraternity of coastwise skippers, had established his *bona fides* in the fast mackerel seiner ELSIE M. SMITH, the big two-masted coaster GRACE WEBSTER, followed in 1890 by the 414-ton tern schooner CUMBERLAND. During the several years after Captain Linc left fishing schooners to pursue the coasting trade, and before he assumed command of Percy & Small's first schooner, it is highly likely that he had crossed paths with Sam Percy more than once.

Aside from the obvious skills required for the job—ability to command, sail and vessel handling, navigation, knowledge of the rules of the road and weather signs—a highly successful coaster captain in that age before electronics needed an intuitive sense of weather and position: a unique combination of psychic qualities imitating modern weather satellites and the global positioning system. But even that could often prove inadequate if the captain didn't know, in the parlance of the poker player, when to raise, when to hold, and when to fold.

Captain Amos Jewett, master of the schooner ERNESTINE and Linc's much older brother and self-proclaimed teacher, once said of him: "That kid brother of mine will go out in any sort of weather. When his vessel is ready for sea, he is ready, and he will come through weather that timid skippers call impossible. He isn't a 'daredevil,' as they call him; he has wonderful judgment, knows what is under his feet, and what is aloft—he knows just how far he can go—and he knows when to stop."[1]

These were essential qualities, especially in the coal trade where the financial success of a coal schooner was directly in proportion to the amount of tonnage hauled from loading ports to discharging ports over a period of time. Although the prevailing winds along the Atlantic seaboard are southwesterly and northwesterly, this constitutes an average situation. Frequently, especially during the months of November through April (the period of greatest coal demand and highest cargo rates), the coast is repeatedly wracked by bitter easterly gales, blinding snow, and freezing spray. And when these winter gales lashed the coast, the coal schooners huddled in any lee they could find—inside the Virginia and Delaware Capes, at Vineyard Haven, Monomoy Point—or, in desperation, placed their faith on their massive ground tackle by anchoring in locations exposed to the full force of wind, wave, and current.

When the storm blew itself out and the winds once again became fair, the mad scramble began as the schooners raised sail and anchors and got underway. Operating on the principle of first to report—first to come alongside (the maritime equivalent of first come, first served)—a large fleet of schooners arriving at Boston, Portland, or the loading ports quickly pro-

Captain Lincoln "Linc" Jewett (1854–1929), who possessed a self-confident, steely gaze, was a consummate navigator of coastal waters. He was the firm's senior captain from 1894 until he retired in 1910.

Courtesy: Maine Maritime Museum

duced a backlog of waiting vessels, frustrated skippers, grumbling managing owners, and time-consuming and expensive delays for the laggards. But the master of the CHARLES P. NOTMAN, Linc Jewett, proved time and again that he could push through when most captains sought shelter.

Long before he paced the quarterdeck of a big coal schooner he had demonstrated his lack of fear of bad weather. While in command of a fishing schooner in his early years, Captain Jewett once blew into Portland during a winter gale expecting to find a good market for his fish thanks to several days of stormy weather and the fact that most of the fishing fleet had remained huddled in port. The local fish dealers, however, tried to gang up on the young, inexperienced skipper by mutually agreeing to fix a low price for his load of fish and then dividing the catch among themselves. The plan didn't work. Getting underway in the howling blizzard, warmed only by a few comments on the character of Portland fish dealers, Jewett sailed for Gloucester, where he received a premium price for his fish from the more appreciative Massachusetts dealers.

Years later, with the NOTMAN under his command, Jewett demonstrated that age and experience had not slowed him down or dulled his edge. A serious coal shortage had developed in Portland after a spell of bad weather. A fleet of fourteen schooners loaded with coal was finally able to get away from the coal ports, the NOTMAN and Jewett among them. But the bad weather returned as they passed the Delaware Capes and turned into a furious northeast blizzard as they approached the Nantucket shoals. The other captains sought secure anchorages to ride out the gale. The marine reporter at Vineyard Haven methodically sent his telegraph reports to Boston announcing, one after another, the arrival of thirteen schooners at the anchorage. Then he reported: "Passed, schooner

CHARLES P. NOTMAN, Jewett, Newport News for Portland." Passed? Was Linc Jewett crazy?

As a fox. He crossed the shoal-strewn maze of Nantucket Sound as the gale shifted into the southeast and laid a course for Portland Head, where he materialized out of the snow with all sail set the next afternoon. Sailing up the harbor, he rounded up in front of the empty coal berths and docked her without the aid of a single tug. Two days later, after a quick discharge, Jewett and the NOTMAN were running south past Cape Cod when he passed the rest of the fleet straggling north. No doubt he offered his fellow coal schooner skippers a few observations via signal hoists commenting, as one Boston writer put it, "on fast passages, loafing in harbors, and getting 'round in the world generally."[2]

Linc Jewett didn't reserve his hard driving for foul weather. Charles M. Harford of South Portland once accompanied the captain and his beloved NOTMAN as a passenger in December 1899. Here are extracts from his letters home:

We sailed from Portland on Wednesday morning at ten A.M. and run out into a heavy sea and almost head wind; that night at twelve o'clock we ran abreast of Highland Light with every rag of sail on. The wind had hauled so that we went over the South Channel instead of going over the Shoals. Thursday morning found us a great distance at sea, about off Nantucket. All day the wind was light, south-southwest, and in the afternoon we were becalmed for two hours, with only a lazy roll and as warm as summer. At six P.M. the wind hauled and gave us a brush in which we bowled along at the rate of fifteen knots. Friday morning the wind was northwest, and blowing at least fifty miles an hour, and we took in the flying jib and reefed the spanker. I am told that this is the third time she has been reefed since she was built in 1894.

It was fun to see Captain Link watch her. You would not wonder at his always coming in first if you could see him watch every chance to crowd on more sail. We passed quite a number of large four-masters and a big, red-funnelled steamer. She was going dead into the wind and

every sea was breaking over her. Saturday morning we were abreast of Hog Island Light, Delaware, and made the Capes [Virginia] about noon. We passed everything we came up to and left them far astern. The last land we saw until now was Cape Elizabeth [Maine] and until this Saturday morning we saw but very little shipping, though during the day we overhauled lots of them . . . . Later. We arrived at Norfolk at three o'clock . . . .[3]

Jewett was not only a sail carrier but an uncannily accurate dead-reckoning navigator as well, a particularly desirable quality when transiting the shoal and ledge-strewn route between the southern coal ports and New England's coal pockets in poor visibility. On one occasion Jewett and the NOTMAN, in company with the JOHN F. RANDALL, Captain Crocker, raced around Cape Cod in a snowstorm, bound for Portland. With no bearings and in poor visibility, Jewett led the way for ninety miles using only his calculations for wind, tide, and current to set the compass course for the buoy marking the offshore end of the Portland channel. The RANDALL rounded up off Cape Elizabeth and anchored rather than risk missing the channel in the poor visibility, but Captain Linc drove on, literally running down the buoy that he had laid a course for while off Cape Cod.[4]

It was a good thing Linc Jewett wasn't accident prone, although he had his fair share of near misses. One nearly cost him his life and involved a rather odd maritime accident. Another cost him the NOTMAN. And the third, related in Chapter 3, almost sank the first six-masted schooner on the East Coast and cost Linc, Percy & Small, and the other owners of the big ELEANOR A. PERCY dearly.

The NOTMAN and Jewett had arrived in Portland in early July 1899 after an uneventful passage. The captain decided to go to Bath to confer with Percy & Small, possibly to discuss a new schooner, then he planned to visit his eighty-four-year-old mother at Westport Island. Completing his business in Bath on the morning of 11 July, Jewett boarded his craft, a two-wheeled road cart powered by a young, nervous horse, for the journey to Westport. But first, he, cart and horse had to cross the Kennebec from Bath to

Sagadahoc Ferry on the Woolwich shore aboard the steam ferry UNION.

The horse became decidedly agitated as the sidewheeler UNION thrashed her way across the Kennebec—so much so, that the crewmen were required to stop the ferry in midstream and throw the horse to the deck in order to restrain it, since there were no gates or chains at the ends of the ferry to prevent the horse from bolting overboard. A crewman pointed out to Captain Jewett a series of ringbolts available for fastening horses, but the good Captain assured the ferry crewman that he—a man who challenged wind and wave for a living—was more than a match for a skittish horse and didn't need ringbolts to do a man's job. He was wrong.

As the ferry approached the slip on the Woolwich side, the reversing paddlewheels and shrieking steam whistle panicked the horse again. With Linc Jewett clinging to its bridle in a futile attempt to control it, the horse bolted through the gateless bow and plunged into the water accompanied by Captain Jewett and the two-wheeled cart.

The excitement at that moment is not hard to imagine: the ferry heading into the slip where horse, cart, and owner have just tumbled; horse and man struggling in the turbulent currents generated by the thrashing paddlewheels within the confines of the slip as the ferry bore down upon them; and, finally, crew and passengers desperately trying to effect a rescue.

Captain Jewett, soggy and battered by the experience, was retrieved from the turbulent waters by passenger Clarence Carleton. The horse was freed from the cart and dragged ashore but drowned before he could be removed from the water. Captain Jewett later observed that he wouldn't have repeated that adventure for all the horses in the world.[5]

Captain Linc Jewett obviously thought driving a big four-master through stormy seas and low visibility was far safer than taking the Bath-Woolwich ferry with his horse and cart. But he wasn't entirely correct, as events in the early morning hours of 11 June 1900 were to prove.

Enroute north with 2,400 tons of coal aboard the ever-reliable NOTMAN, Captain Linc and his wife Annie Tarbox Jewett were on what was planned to be their last trip on the schooner that had contributed much to their present prosperity; the good captain had arranged to sell his shares in the vessel and purchase the master's interest in Percy & Small's newest and largest project, the six-master-to-be, ELEANOR A. PERCY. But the NOTMAN never arrived at her destination, although the twelve souls on board did come ashore at New York.[6]

Proceeding in a heavy fog on a compass course of NE-by-E in a light breeze at 3:54 A.M., the NOTMAN was dutifully sounding her mechanical foghorn with pauses to listen for other fog signals when the watch on deck heard a steamer whistle close aboard. Immediately the watch again sounded the foghorn and rang the ship's bell, but it was too late. But let Captain Jewett tell the story:

> A big black hull bore down upon us and her bow crashed into us cutting us down to the water's edge. She turned out to be the COLORADO. She was steering east southeast.
>
> The liner was making about seven knots. The schooner was making two knots. As a sailing vessel the schooner had the right of way. All our canvass [sic] was set. The steamer struck us abaft the mizzen and just forward of the jigger mast, almost at right angles, punching a big V-shaped hole, three feet wide at the top and six feet deep. The captain of the steamer held her close up to that big hole and gave us a chance to save ourselves. If he had backed out the water would have rushed in and filled the schooner before a life could have been saved.
>
> My wife jumped to the steamer's rail where she was caught by the sailors on the steamer. Then I ordered all hands to lower our big boat [yawlboat] which hung from the davits over the stern. I only saved my chronometers. We had no time to save our clothing. The sea was smooth but there was quite a ground swell.[7]

The NOTMAN sank in sixteen minutes, underlining the vulnerability of the big, heavily laden coal schooners following massive hull damage.

There is a little more to the story than Captain Jewett reported. COLORADO lowered a lifeboat immediately after the collision under the command of the steamer's chief mate. When it came alongside, Mrs. Jewett refused to board it unless accompanied by the captain. He was, however, engaged in getting the yawl boat lowered and then ducked below to retrieve his expensive chronometers. Mrs. Jewett was then passed up to the deck of the steamer, becoming hysterical when she discovered her husband had not followed her.

There was one more moment of drama to be played out before the NOTMAN disappeared beneath the waves. The crew and the mate had boarded the yawl boat when Jewett returned to the cabin. While he was below, some crewmen moved to cut the boat's painter for fear the sinking schooner would drag them down when she went. But the mate threatened to shoot anyone who touched the painter until the captain was safely aboard the boat.[8]

Ten days later, Jewett arrived in Bath with Mrs. Jewett after a six-hour trip from Portland in the last surviving piece of the late, lamented schooner—the twenty-four-foot yawl boat. After spending the day explaining how his vessel was run down, he no doubt toured his new schooner, which was nearing the 50 percent completion mark.[9]

Any post-mortem on the NOTMAN's career could only conclude that she had been Percy & Small's little gold mine, especially after the Mallory Line, owners of COLORADO, paid Percy & Small $49,250 (+/- $760,000 in 1998) for the sunken schooner.[10] After deducting final expenses, including crew and captain's claims for personal property lost in the sinking, Percy & Small distributed a final payment of $705.10 (+/- $10,900 in 1998) per $1/64$ to the vessel's owners. This payment brought the NOTMAN's total return for a $1,007.77 original investment to $1,963.79, or 195 percent, in just six years.[11] With an average annual return over the life of the vessel of 15.8 percent and an annual earning rate of 10.8 percent after deducting 5 percent for depreciation, the NOTMAN chalked up an excellent performance for the new firm, especially in the face of the economy's slow recovery from the 1893–97 depression.

The glorious, if all too brief, career of the NOTMAN underlined the importance of selecting the right person as master. A first-class captain's drive and ability could overcome much, if not all, of the existing disadvantages of market and weather while avoiding many of the expensive perils of the coal trade such as long delays and physical damage to the vessel. As evidence of the NOTMAN's success was recorded in the firm's ledger and made manifest in shareholder's statements, Percy & Small began the process all over again of soliciting investors for their next vessels.

THREE OF A KIND

Having proven that they could successfully build a schooner and operate the vessel at a profit, Captain Percy and Frank Small raised their sights with the goal of further expanding their fleet. They would succeed. Within two years of launching the NOTMAN, two more schooners joined the fleet, more than tripling the firm's cargo capacity.

Less than six weeks after the NOTMAN took to the Kennebec in August 1894, the Bath rumor mill had Percy & Small preparing to build their next schooner at the Morse shipyard. The report was denied by the firm, which disclaimed any plan to undertake to build another schooner "this winter, at least."[12] Yet within two months, Horatio Douglas and his crew stretched the birch keel of Percy & Small Schooner #2, a new model from Fred Rideout that measured slightly larger than the NOTMAN.[13]

Given the state of the economy in late 1894, it is surprising that Percy & Small were able to raise the capital necessary to build a schooner so quickly after completing their first. However, they were compelled to take an even larger ownership position in the vessel than had been required for the NOTMAN, taking $49/128$ and once again assuming a fairly heavy load of debt with its concomitant interest. But this was balanced out to some extent by the sale of nearly a quarter of their shares in the NOTMAN, no doubt at a good price, given that schooner's good earnings record to date.[14]

Progress on their Hull #2 was very slow, suggesting

that beyond laying the keel, the builders had no plans to push construction during the depths of winter. The delay also provided them with the opportunity to further monitor the financial performance of the NOTMAN, as well as more time to round up additional investors in the new vessel.

During the fall and winter of 1894-95, Jewett and the NOTMAN racked up a series of profitable voyages producing six dividend payments totaling $108.59 per $1/64$ (+/- $1,945.00 in 1998), a healthy return of 11 percent in just nine months![15] The figures coming from the NOTMAN certainly encouraged Percy & Small to push ahead with their next schooner, even if capital was still as difficult to raise as the previous year's. Nonetheless, 77 percent of the new vessel's shares were subscribed by the original investors in the NOTMAN, a resounding vote of confidence in Captain Sam Percy and Frank Small.[16]

As with the NOTMAN, the new schooner's investors included a substantial number of people and firms, such as suppliers or subcontractors, who benefited directly from her construction. At least 30 percent of the total shares were in this class, not including the managing owners and builders, Percy & Small. The largest single investor besides Percy & Small ($49/128$) and the captain-designate ($6/128$) was William H. Clifford, Bath's most prominent sailmaker. One of the largest shareholders in vessels in Maine, Clifford began learning the sailmaking trade in his father's loft, Clifford & Lambert, on Bath's Commercial Street, before the Civil War.[17] Eventually he took over the sail loft in partnership with Levi Totman and upon his partner's death, became the sole proprietor of the business.

Clifford routinely invested in every vessel for which he had the sailmaking contract, taking shares in lieu of cash as part payment for the sails. When the NOTMAN was built, Clifford was down for $5/128$ shares—a $2,519 investment (+/- $45,100 in 1998).[18] When Percy & Small began raising capital for Schooner #2, William Clifford underwrote $6/128$ of the new schooner and persuaded his brother-in-law, Sewall J. Watson, to take up an additional $2/128$ for a combined investment of $4,170.24 (+/- $75,000 in 1998).[19] For this demonstrated commitment to

Percy & Small's future, Schooner #2 was named WILLIAM H. CLIFFORD in honor of the venerable sailmaker.

Naming vessels was an exercise driven largely by economics in the late-nineteenth-century shipping business, although it had not always been that way. Bath's largest pre-Civil War merchant fleet, managed by George F., Captain John, and Captain James F. Patten is a case in point. Of the forty-four vessels—predominantly full-rigged ships—built for their own account between 1821 and 1860, eight were named for living persons—mostly family; twenty-one were named for places; two for explorers; five for various human qualities; and eight names were from classical or other sources.[20] By the 1850s, ship-naming achieved new heights with the advent of the clippers. Names that suggested speed, beauty, and patriotic sentiments were particularly popular: FLYING FISH, FLYING CLOUD, STAG HOUND, LIGHTNING, RAINBOW, SOVEREIGN OF THE SEAS, ANDREW JACKSON, YOUNG AMERICA, and GREAT REPUBLIC. But the Clipper Age was short, barely a decade, and the Panic of 1857 and the subsequent American Civil War did much to deflate the heady optimism that had characterized the American merchant marine's drive for the top.

Poetic fancy and classic allusions were increasingly supplanted by hard, practical, economic calculations when it came to naming vessels in the postwar decades. A few operators such as Bath's Houghton dynasty resisted the pressures, persisting to the end in naming their vessels after places ending in the letter *a*.[21] By way of contrast, the Sewalls of Bath tried to balance the more traditional naming customs by recognizing the practical economic importance of stroking the self-esteem of potential investors. Of the forty-nine square-riggers and schooners built by that firm between 1866–92, twenty were named for living people, and the balance was spread across the spectrum of place, history, character, and trade. When Arthur Sewall & Company made their last effort to perpetuate the great wooden Cape Horners with the "Big Four," they were named after rivers in the mid-Atlantic states with Native American names that had played an important role in the nation's history.[22]

Percy & Small didn't invent the ego-stroking (and pocketbook-opening) practice of naming vessels after living people, especially people who had some strong economic ties to the vessels, but they adopted it as their own. Altogether, the firm would build sixteen schooners for their own fleet. Two were named by the firm's principals—Sam Percy to honor his daughter and Frank Small to honor his wife. One was named for a state, but a state that had become important as a source of real and potential investment. One honored the firm's highly respected master builder, who also invested in the vessel. The rest reflected the need to go forth into the marketplace and raise capital, a need that took the firm and its agents from Bath to the New York, Boston, and Portland waterfronts, and then on to the Hudson River Valley around Albany, and the semi-arid cattle country of central Wyoming.

Percy & Small named only a few vessels for local residents, underlining the growing need to import capital if the firm was going to expand its fleet. Of all the vessels built for their own account, only five were named for Bath natives or residents. The importance of outside investment was further emphasized as Percy & Small sought capital to build the CLIFFORD. Among those who subscribed for shares in the vessel ($^{1}/64$) was Boston teamster Myron D. Cressy. When the books closed on the Percy & Small fleet over two decades later, no fewer than four schooners flying the blue and white P&S house flag carried the Cressy surname.[23]

The business of names and finance notwithstanding, the WILLIAM H. CLIFFORD went overboard from the Morse shipyard on 6 August 1895 at 12:56 P.M., christened by Mrs. Frank A. Small in a well-attended launching. The CLIFFORD, virtually ready for sea, was the focus of much enthusiastic comment from the shipping community and the general public. Described as "a perfect beauty," the new four-master was the recipient of a nearly nine-column-inch story in the *Bath Independent*, twice what the same newspaper had awarded to the new schooner's predecessor, the NOTMAN, launched just a year earlier.[24]

Slightly longer and beamier than the NOTMAN, the CLIFFORD's model offered an important plus: she increased her carrying capacity (deadweight tonnage,

abbreviated as DWT) by 10 percent with only a 5 percent increase in her measurement tonnage (GRT). All else being equal, that 10 percent increase was significant for all shareholders, but particularly so for the captain, who received primage for his services in addition to a small salary. Primage was a payment to the captain based on a percentage of the gross freight—Percy & Small customarily paid 5 percent—received for each cargo, straight off the top. In contrast, dividends were made up of the remaining proceeds from a cargo after all expenses were deducted.

A simple hypothetical case underlines the significance of the increase in capacity. The NOTMAN carried 2,400 tons of coal and the CLIFFORD carried 2,650 tons.[25] If the two vessels made the same number of trips carrying maximum cargo during the same period at the same rates, the CLIFFORD's primage payments would be 10 percent greater. If their operating expenses were the same, the dividends would also give the 10 percent edge to the larger schooner in total dividends. The earnings rate gap—net of depreciation—would, however, be reduced for the larger schooner, thanks to her greater initial cost per $^{1}/64$.[26]

Captain William F. Harding, the CLIFFORD's first master, was vitally interested in his vessel's capacity edge over the NOTMAN's. A Cape Codder from Chatham, where Hardings were more numerous than gulls on a fish pier, Percy & Small's newest master had won his first command in 1881 at the age of twenty-two. Now in his mid-thirties, Harding would work the rest of his life under the blue and white house flag of Percy & Small, becoming the master of no fewer than four separate schooners before dying of heart disease in 1910.

Harding's apparent restlessness was spurred on more by his search for economic success than by a search for the perfect schooner. In his case, primage was the principal concern, and he sought commands that had ever-increasing cargo capacity and, therefore, greater earning potential.[27] Aside from his financial ambitions, Harding's career appears to have been one of competence, if not brilliance, interrupted by only a few of the many perils that lay strewn across the routes of the great schooners.

Comparing the earnings of the CLIFFORD under

Harding with those of the NOTMAN under Jewett for the same thirty-nine-month period (1 October, 1895–31 December 1898), however, is instructive. In contrast with the hypothetical model, the smaller schooner did better overall, even with her smaller capacity, ringing up dividends totaling $593.48 per $1/64$ (+/- $10,600 in 1998) against the CLIFFORD's $538.08 per $1/64$ (+/-$ 9,600 in 1998). Only during 1898 did Harding and the CLIFFORD do better than Jewett and the NOTMAN, bringing in $265.90 (+/- $4,800 in 1998) versus $192.60 (+/- $3,450 in 1998) for the latter. The most significant year was 1897,

when the NOTMAN paid $177.87 (+/- $3,200 in 1998) and the CLIFFORD paid only $50.94 (+/- $900 in 1998) per $1/64$.[28]

It is useful, however, to know what lay behind some of these figures. For example, the CLIFFORD's poor performance in 1897 can be traced to a single phosphate rock charter between Punta Gorda on Florida's west coast and Baltimore.

Phosphate rock, an important ingredient in commercial fertilizer, was a cargo that was notoriously hard on the big wooden schooners. Heavy and dense—it weighed more per cubic foot than coal—a

The WILLIAM H. CLIFFORD takes to the Kennebec with a rush in early August 1895 under the watchful eyes of the stylishly clad spectators ashore. Some of the fortunate guests aboard the new schooner for the launching have a particularly interesting view of the event from the mizzen and spanker crosstrees. Note also the schooner's large stock anchors hanging from the catheads, ready for instant service with the swing of a large maul.

Courtesy: Maine Maritime Museum

full cargo loaded conventionally concentrated the weight of cargo so low in the hull that the vessel was in danger of developing a quick, snapping motion that could roll the spars out. To combat this tendency, a special platform was erected on top of the keelson for the cargo of rock. This effectively raised the center of gravity of the cargo, damping the rolling motion. It also had the added benefit of keeping the water-absorbent rock well clear of any water in the bilges.

Aside from all the work and care necessary to load phosphate rock, Punta Gorda was no paradise, either. Located on Charlotte Harbor, the channels were shoal, a danger to large, heavily laden schooners, and Florida's west coast was vulnerable to hurricanes and hot, miserably humid summers. All in all, phosphate rock was not most shipmasters' favorite cargo but the freight money was good—$2.00 per ton—especially when coal charters were hard to come by.

Loaded with rock, the CLIFFORD sailed from Punta Gorda on 30 January 1897, only to run hard aground in the Boca Grande Pass. Efforts to pull the schooner off were not successful, and it became evident to Captain Harding that the only course was to lighten ship. This required several days to remove 400–500 tons of cargo to lighters and, once free, to reload and stow the rock.[29] Although no damage was apparent after the ship was hauled off, the American Shipmasters Association routinely required vessels that had grounded to be drydocked to undergo a survey. As there were no facilities to haul out the schooner in the area and no visible signs of serious damage, the CLIFFORD was allowed to proceed to Baltimore where such facilities existed.

The CLIFFORD was finally drydocked at Baltimore's Columbian Iron Works on 1 April. Inspection revealed that a portion of her keel needed to be replaced, and a number of seams needed to be recaulked.[30] While these did not constitute major repairs, the time the CLIFFORD was not in service while first getting free and reloading, and then undergoing repairs, cut deeply into her earning potential for 1897. Include the expense of lightering and reloading cargo, tugs, and repair work, and it is not surprising that several dividends were passed in order to pay the bills.[31]

The CLIFFORD's superior dividend performance in 1898—her best year ever under the P&S flag—was, in part, because of the selfsame phosphate rock trade. The declaration of war on Spain (20 April 1898) brought a lively demand for shipping. Percy & Small negotiated a government charter for the CLIFFORD to carry coal to Tampa Bay—the forward operating and logistics base for American forces in and around Cuba—at $2.00 per ton, discharged (unloaded at no expense to the vessel). Frank Small was also able to negotiate a return charter, Port Tampa to New York, with phosphate rock.

When Harding and the schooner arrived at Port Tampa, they found the port facilities more overwhelmed than usual by the military and naval demands placed by U. S. operations in and around Cuba, resulting in long delays in discharging the coal and then loading the phosphate rock. In all, the CLIFFORD and Captain Harding were detained at Tampa Bay during the height of the hurricane and fever season for over two months.

Fortunately, charter parties contained clauses called demurrage which indemnified a vessel against unreasonable delays in loading and discharging. Upon the expiration of the specified number of "lay days" (the period in which the cargo was to be loaded or unloaded), the charterers were obligated to pay the vessel a daily rate of demurrage which approximated the daily earning capacity of the vessel. In this case, Percy & Small not only collected freight in excess of $9,600 (+/- $170,000 in 1998) but an additional $1,700 (+/- $30,000 in 1998) in demurrage payments.[32] Captain Harding lost thirty pounds during his long, enforced stay at Tampa Bay, but he pocketed well over $500 in primage (+/- $9,000 in 1998) in addition to his wages and dividends. It was a fair exchange.

William Harding left the CLIFFORD in 1899 to assume command of Percy & Small's first five-master, the M. D. CRESSY. The CLIFFORD sailed on—and on and on and on—for her managing owners before being sold in 1916 in the great fleet sell-off of 1916–17. She never again equaled her earnings of 1898 but continued to return modest to good dividends year after year. Her sale price of $70,000 in 1916, when adjusted for inflation, returned 65 percent of original capital cost. Add that to her known earnings through early 1908—199 percent of original cost—and one can see that Percy & Small's most senior vessel more than looked after her managing owners' financial interests.[33] Nineteen months after the sale, the CLIFFORD was sunk by a German U-boat six hundred miles off the coast of France.

By the time the U-boat sank the CLIFFORD, her larger, younger sister, the S. P. BLACKBURN, had foundered nearly four years earlier. Launched on 24 June 1896, the BLACKBURN assumed the mantle of largest vessel in the P&S fleet and the second largest four-master yet built at Bath.

Samuel P. Blackburn was a Bath boy and Sam Percy's cousin who had made his way to success in the big city—three cities, in fact. After leaving Bath, Blackburn developed a veritable chain of waterfront ship chandleries in Philadelphia, New York, and Boston. Given his reliance on the shipping business, Blackburn understandably maintained close capital investment ties with his hometown shipping entrepreneurs. He was a consistent investor in Percy & Small vessels from the very beginning, taking $^1/_{64}$ in the NOTMAN, $^2/_{64}$ in the CLIFFORD, and another $^2/_{64}$ in his namesake when the subscription was opened.[34]

One less than common feature in the ownership pattern was the large share ostensibly taken by Captain Alexander Ross, the new schooner's first captain. He is recorded in the *P&S Journal* as being down for no less than $^{22}/_{64}$ of the vessel, which represented a huge investment for the mid-1890s, coming in at $24,689.06 (+/- $440,000 in 1998). Ross, however, had rounded up what amounted to a syndicate of investors who pooled their resources to acquire the equivalent of $^{14.6}/_{64}$ of Ross's $^{22}/_{64}$ share of the vessel. It is not clear whether the good captain organized these investors through a trust arrangement with himself as trustee, or how it was handled. Two members of the syndicate, C. A. Davis and J. F. Davis, had been masters and managing owners of schooners subsequently under Ross's command.

Alexander Ross was a native of Somerset, Massachusetts, on the Taunton River, an important center of the bituminous coal trade into the mid-

1890s. The Davises mentioned above were fellow natives of Somerset and operators of a fleet of schooners that included three-masters, four-masters, and one five-masted schooner.[35] It was in their vessels that Ross learned his trade, rising to command of their three-master WILLIAM P. HOOD in 1887 and then the four-master BENJAMIN F. POOLE, before moving on to take command of the brand-new BLACKBURN in 1896.

As master of the big four-master, Ross established a solid record of performance. With the exception of a collision with the schooner FRED GOWER, later determined to be the fault of that schooner, the BLACKBURN enjoyed a relatively trouble-free career and a 65 percent return on her original cost in her four years under Ross's command.[36]

In 1900 Ross went on to command the big five-master HELEN W. MARTIN, and in 1910 he took over the six-master ELEANOR A. PERCY from the retiring Linc Jewett. He would stay with the PERCY until she was sold in December of 1915. His eighteen continuous years of service under the Percy & Small house flag were unchallenged by any other captain.

The BLACKBURN, launched with considerable pomp and ceremony on 24 June 1896 (thanks to Captain Percy's sense of public relations and fraternal ties), was declared an instant success. Percy, a Mason heart and core, arranged for Bath's Dunlap Commandery of the Knights Templar, joined by their fellow Knights Templar from the DeWitt Clinton Commandery from Portsmouth, New Hampshire, to parade to the shipyard accompanied by two bands and attired in their bright regalia, waving plumes, and glittering swords. With all this pomp and circumstance, there were no launching problems as the biggest schooner yet built by the young firm took to the Kennebec accompanied by the cheers of all present.[37] It was a glorious event and heavily publicized, a point that did not escape Captain Percy's eagle eye. Subsequent launchings by this firm would be awarded far more column inches in the press, with the accompanying public recognition. Sam Percy not only knew the value of a good earnings record for P&S schooners, he had developed a taste for, and a sense of the value of, a little "show biz."

Meanwhile, he and junior partner Frank Small had one more problem to resolve. Their lease of the Parker Morse shipyard had come to an end, and the shipyard had been sold to General Thomas W. Hyde, president and principal owner of the Bath Iron Works. He was planning to spin off Bath Iron Works' deck machinery manufacturing into a new company—Hyde Windlass—and focus the Iron Works on shipbuilding.[38]

OPTIONS AND CHOICES

In the thirty-odd months since they had formed their partnership, Sam Percy and Frank Small concentrated their capital investments on vessel property rather than shoreside real estate and a shipbuilding plant. With the loss of the minimally equipped Morse Shipyard and its moderate rent to the expanding Hyde industrial empire, the partners needed to re-examine the premises that had underpinned their success to date.

First, they could continue as in the past to build only for their own account. As so-called captive shipyards required little in the way of up-to-date equipment, almost any idle shipyard in Bath—and there were several in town—could fill the bill. Most of these shipyards had been inactive for considerable lengths of time, however, and would require additional investment to make them even marginally efficient.

A second course would be to contract out all future shipbuilding to a commercial shipbuilder. There were three such shipyards in Bath: one operated by Bath's senior shipbuilder, William Rogers; Kelley, Spear, headed by Percy & Small mentor John R. Kelley; and the New England Company, an increasingly pale shadow of the famous Goss, Sawyer, & Packard shipyard. To contract out new vessels would certainly reduce the capital diversification necessary to acquire, maintain, and operate a shoreside facility, especially one intended for only occasional use. But it also meant loss of control over the shipbuilding process, contracts and specifications notwithstanding, and the reality that any profit that might be earned building vessels was going to accrue to the commercial shipyard rather than to the partnership.[39] Given Captain Percy's background and successful experience building the P&S fleet's first three schooners, it is not likely that this was a very serious consideration.

Another option may well have occurred to Sam Percy: establish a shipyard that specialized in building large schooners both for the firm and under contract to other schooner operators. Such an operation would need to be well-equipped with labor-saving machinery if it was to be capable of competing with the other commercial wooden shipyards in Bath, Belfast, Camden, Phippsburg, Rockland, and Thomaston. But the additional capital investment required to outfit such a plant could well be offset by efficiencies of scale and profits from contract shipbuilding work and do-it-yourself maintenance and repairwork.

For the moment, however, such a move was out of the question. Percy & Small's capital was totally tied up in its three schooners, and the firm was already carrying a substantial debt load.[40]

The first clue of P&S's intentions was a rumor floating around town that the firm had just negotiated the purchase from William T. Donnell of the old Daniel Orrin Blaisdell shipyard (idle since 1880) in Bath's south end. When approached by the reporter from the *Bath Enterprise*, Frank Small denied the story. Percy & Small might lease the shipyard to store materials and make repairs on vessels, but there was very little likelihood of a new schooner being built there in the near future. Where would a P&S schooner be built, then, queried the reporter? "It may be the Blaisdell yard and it may not," Small replied.[41] On 26 September 1896, the deed from William T. Donnell to Percy & Small, conveying what was known as the Orrin Blaisdell Shipyard property was filed at the Sagadahoc County Courthouse.[42] Percy & Small had taken the first step toward making shipbuilding the equal, if not the superior, of the shipping business in their order of priorities.

Percy & Small may have purchased the Daniel Orrin Blaisdell shipyard property, but they acquired only the ghost of a shipyard past.

Blaisdell, who began his career as a sparmaker in Bath before striking out on his own as a shipbuilder, focused his efforts in the shipbuilding city's south end. He first leased the old Berry & Richardson yard opposite Pleasant Street, where he built the 62-gross-ton fishing schooner MERCY A. HOWSE in 1861 at the ripe old age of twenty-eight.[43] Then he moved to the Hall & Snow shipyard just south of Weeks Street, building two barks delivered in 1863 and 1866.

But however minimal the outlay for their rent may have been, leased shipyards had disadvantages. For the most part they were poorly equipped, lacking the most basic labor-saving machinery, and their limited facilities were often the victims of neglect. A go-getter like D. O. Blaisdell would begrudge capital outlays to upgrade and update a shipyard not his own. The solution: buy and develop his own.

There was a property just south of Marshall Street on the east side of Washington Street—not far from its southern end—that attracted his attention, and it was for sale. The gradient to water was optimum for launching vessels, and the water was deep immediately offshore—except for one frequently forgotten ledge. The property was also in a neighborhood of shipyards: a hundred yards north was the former Hitchcock Shipyard, soon operated by the partnership of G. G. Deering and William T. Donnell—the latter being a Hitchcock son-in-law; and a hundred yards to the south lay the former Arnold & Company yard that was later acquired by the firm of Chapman & Flint and its shipbuilding manager John McDonald.

Blaisdell took the plunge in 1867. The property, a

The last schooner built at the Parker Morse shipyard—soon to become the Hyde Windlass Company—the S. P. BLACKBURN is anchored in mid-stream following her launching and awaits a tug to return her to the dock. Meanwhile, the invited guests are socializing and partaking of the launching buffet.
Courtesy: Captain W. J. Lewis Parker, USCG, Ret.

The W. H. OLER of 1880 was the last of fifteen vessels launched by Daniel Orrin Blaisdell, the first shipbuilder to occupy the site that subsequently became the Percy & Small shipyard.
Courtesy: Captains Douglas K. and Linda J. Lee

rectangle measuring approximately 195 feet on the short side on muddy Washington Street and 500 feet to the water, was spacious enough to be developed into a small, but well-equipped shipyard over the next several years. Blaisdell never suspected that in this city of wooden sailing vessels, its last big commercial sailing vessel would subsequently be built on this property.[44]

Over the course of the next thirteen years, Blaisdell built fifteen vessels—eleven schooners, one barkentine, two barks, and one ship. Included among the schooners were the first three-masters built in Bath, the ADDIE BLAISDELL (1868) and MAGGIE A. FISKE (1869). While not a real challenge to the "ship factory" of Goss, Sawyer & Packard at Bath's north end, Blaisdell's enterprise required a moderate degree of investment in labor-saving machinery. In 1874 he built a steam-powered mill that housed "planers and jigsaws"; he added other buildings as well, including housing and storage buildings. However, the shipyard had space for only one set of

building ways, limiting its production.

Did the mature but still relatively young shipbuilder have ideas for further expansion, challenging the "big guys" in Bath shipbuilding? We shall never know. He died in 1880 just days after launching Blaisdell Hull #15, the three-masted schooner W. H. OLER. He was only forty-seven years old.

The Blaisdell shipyard was soon purchased by another Bath entrepreneur, Robert Goddard. Formerly the operator of a small foundry producing castings for shipbuilders—his first foundry had been located at the old Hall, Snow & Company shipyard where, sometime later, Blaisdell laid the foundation for his reputation as shipbuilder—Goddard moved into the ice business and real estate development, concentrating his efforts in Bath's south end.[45] His name is perpetuated to this day by Goddard Street, off Marshall Street, and Goddard Pond at the junction of Marshall Street with High Street.

That pond—now a recreation department facility

"... fine building nearly new, large enough for the construction of large yachts under cover . . . ." So read the advertisement announcing the auction of the former Blaisdell shipyard property in 1890. Indeed, a yacht was built here by John McDonald, the FLEUR DE LYS, launched during the summer of 1890.

Courtesy: Maine Maritime Museum

which is dry in summer and flooded in winter for ice skating—was the source of the ice that was then stored in a large icehouse on its shore. With the purchase of the idle Blaisdell shipyard, south Bath's "ice king" acquired rental houses, a building that was soon converted into additional ice storage, and a wharf for the convenient shipping of ice to points south.[46] This arrangement lasted for only a decade before Goddard placed the former shipyard property on the market again, but not before another vessel was launched from its long-idle ways. John McDonald had needed space in his own shipyard for a large square-rigger and moved the construction of the 91-GRT schooner-yacht FLEUR DE LYS to the former Blaisdell facility.

The 10 September 1890 edition of the *Bath Times* carried the following advertisement:

On Wednesday, September 17th, 1890 at 10 o'clock, A.M., on the premises, if not previously disposed of at private sale, we shall sell the well known shipyard formerly occupied by the late Orrin Blaisdell. This is without question one of the best yards for shipbuilding in this city, being about 195 feet on Washington Street, and 500 feet deep. On this property is a large machine shop with engine and boilers, shafting and pulleys all in running order, fine building nearly new, large enough for the construction of large yachts under cover, two dwelling houses, also a good wharf large enough for any kind of a vessel to lie to and in fine condition.

—David Owen Foye & Co, Auctioneers.[47]

The advertisement is revealing. It mentions the large "machine shop with engine and boilers, shafting and pulleys," but fails to mention the planers and jigsaws that once occupied the building. In the time between Blaisdell's death and the auction, the shipyard's timber processing machinery had been disposed of, but the steam engine and power transmission equipment remained in place.

The building is described as "fine," and "nearly new." Even allowing for realtor hyperbole this description was overly optimistic if the one known photograph of the structure is any indication. Probably taken in the early 1890s, the photo shows a building in an advanced state of decrepitude, sagging badly, windows broken or sashes gone completely. One incongruous note is the lean-to shed at the left end of the building. The shed stands straight and true in contrast with the main structure, and a close examination reveals that a portion of the clapboarded siding had been recently replaced, perhaps as part of the brief rental arrangement with John McDonald. It is probable that this shed contained the steam stationary engine and boiler described in the auction advertisement.[48]

William T. Donnell purchased the Goddard property, formerly the Blaisdell shipyard, in 1890. Along with the ex-icehouse and machine shop, he acquired two rental houses—one-and-one-half-story and two-story—a wharf, and almost two and one-half acres of land running from Washington Street to the Kennebec. What the old shipbuilder's plans for the property were, we have no way of knowing. He and his former partner, G. G. Deering, had gone their separate ways three years earlier but Donnell continued to build a schooner a year for his own account from the former Deering & Donnell shipyard.

About 1893 he sold abutter Charles E. Hyde a swath of land from the former Blaisdell–Goddard property—about 90 feet wide on Washington Street by 263 feet deep—leaving a peculiar but explainable jog in the south boundary of the property. Hyde may have wanted the entire swath from Washington Street to the Kennebec, but one of the attributes that made this a shipyard property was the wharf. It was located on the extreme southeastern edge of the land on the river. To sell Hyde a strip from street to river would effectively separate the wharf from a potential shipbuilding property, reducing its value. So Donnell did the next best thing: he sold Hyde a strip from the street to the beginning of a prominent ledge, giving the latter a much expanded front yard without seriously detracting from the property's shipyard potential.

Donnell also eliminated the so-called icehouse during the course of his ownership of the property. The building had experienced a minor fire in the vicinity of the chimney during McDonald's brief tenure, and was generally run down, even before it was purchased by Donnell.[49] Whether he salvaged the steam stationary engine, boilers, and shaft and pulley system for his own shipyard, or sold it all to someone else is not known. But it is certain that he tore down the icehouse (ex-machine shop) before this property was sold in 1896. Percy & Small bought, therefore, the shipbuilding tradition along with two tenements and some waterfront real estate. The shipbuilding plant, however, would need to be built virtually from scratch. This was accomplished over the next five years.

A NEW SHIPYARD: PHASE I

Percy & Small were confronted with two essential problems in the summer of 1896. First, their efforts to develop a fleet of coal schooners—three in three years—during a serious depression had placed a serious strain on finances. Second, the Morses' decision to sell their shipyard to Hyde Windlass effec-tively removed Percy & Small's base of operations on the waterfront.

Purchasing the remains—bare bones, more appropriately—of the former Blaisdell shipyard put them back on the waterfront, although it wasn't too clear from Frank Small's statement whether they had decided what they really wanted to do on that waterfront.[50]

But for an estimated $1,500–$1,800 (+/- $26,000–$32,000 in 1998), they succeeded in purchasing just over one and one-half acres with 105 feet of street frontage, roughly 200 feet of river frontage and a wharf, and two rental houses.[51]

That they planned to do something was evident even before the deed was recorded at the Sagadahoc County Registry of Deeds. The *Bath Enterprise* announced that Percy & Small were building a blacksmith shop and rigging loft at the former Blaisdell shipyard.[52] The new building, measuring approximately 84 feet by 26 feet, was set back about 60 feet from Washington Street, behind one of the houses, hard against the property's south boundary with Charles E. Hyde. In fact, it may have been set too hard against the boundary. The following August, Hyde deeded Percy & Small a two-foot strip in exchange ". . . for another piece of land this day deeded to me by said Percy & Small"[53]—all of which suggests that the south boundary was not clearly marked and the blacksmith shop inadvertently enroached on Hyde's land.

The fact that Percy & Small chose to erect a blacksmith shop as their first building (although also called a rigging loft initially, there is no evidence that the building was ever used as such) speaks volumes about the important role this trade played in wooden shipbuilding, not to mention the special relationship that existed between Percy & Small and some of their subcontractors, not the least of whom was Leonard H. Gibson, boss blacksmith.

Known as "Len," Gibson learned the blacksmithing trade as a very young man and practiced the trade in the Bath shipyards for some forty-five years before illness compelled him to retire in 1916 to a life of reading—classical literature, science, and history—at his home at 1082 High Street.[54] By the time he had reached his mid-thirties, Gibson was the foreman blacksmith at two Bath shipyards at the same time, first at the Arthur Sewall & Co. plant at 411 Front Street, where he supervised the production of the extensive ironwork for the ten steel sailing vessels built by that firm between 1893–1903. Then, in 1894, he took on the same position with the fledgling firm of Percy & Small when it began construction of the NOTMAN in the Morse yard.[55] For the next twenty-two years, Gibson held sway over all the ironwork that went into each Percy & Small schooner—from mastbands to hatch irons and drifts to davits.

Gibson was a Percy & Small subcontractor,

Percy & Small Plan: 1896–99

D. K. Lee & R. L. Snow, 1997

In one of the earliest known views of the Percy & Small shipyard, the firm's first shop building—the 1897 blacksmith shop—shares the picture with the schooner M. D. Cressy—the firm's first five-masted schooner. Trolleycar tracks and the overhead wire are visible in the foreground.

Courtesy: Maine Maritime Museum

responsible for the fabrication of ironwork for the firm. He employed his own gang—their numbers depending on the workload—and was responsible for paying them. The shipyard, in turn, provided the materials to be worked and paid him an agreed amount per gross ton on new construction and a flat fee per man-hour for repairwork.[56] In addition, Percy & Small provided the physical space for the blacksmiths, equipping it with all the necessary heavy equipment—forges, bellows, anvils, etc.—everything except each man's personal tools. Gibson, who exercised the shipbuilder's prerogative of taking shares in vessels he worked on in lieu of some of the cash, also

became Percy & Small's leading subcontractor shareholder.[57]

It was no surprise that the shipyard's smiths had plenty of work, given that a typical schooner the size of the NOTMAN or CLIFFORD required many tons of custom iron fittings that first had to be fabricated from flat, round, and bar stock in the shipyard's blacksmith shop before going to Wilbur Oliver's Bath Galvanizing Works.[58] There was even more work, in fact, since other vessels called at the partners' shipyard for repairs, often requiring the talents of a blacksmith.[59]

In appearance, the new shop's south elevation

looked almost like a residence except for the prominent clerestory adorning its roof line. For three-quarters of its length, the building was a one-and-a-half-story structure—perhaps giving rise to its original description as a blacksmith shop and rigging loft—but the eastern-most 20-foot section was only one story, resulting in a clear break in the ridgeline. The interior of the building was decidedly unhome-like, starting with the floor, much of which was hard-packed clay, hence fireproof. The interior was unfinished, all the walls being nothing more than studs and sheathing. The building's specific layout changed over the years with the addition or replacement of equipment, but the basic configuration remained the same. The western portion always housed the forges and anvils, while along the south wall could be found the drill press and sharpening stones. The eastern end contained a scrapwood-fired boiler providing steam for the steam box and a twenty-four-hour-a-day heat source in season. Here also was located the only hydrant in the shipyard with a single faucet for keeping the quenching barrels topped off in the smithy itself, and for use by shipyard employees. Five hundred feet of fire hose rounded out the installation and provided the potentially flammable plant with its second line of defense against combustion.[60]

It was not until June of 1897 that the blacksmith shop was joined by another purpose-built shop building at the shipyard. This was the joiner shop, first mentioned the previous summer but delayed until the firm had nailed down—and commenced—construction on another schooner.[61] Simply put, further devel-

opment of the shipyard had been put on hold until enough work and improved cash flow would justify the additional expense. These conditions were met when Percy & Small reached an agreement with J. S. Winslow & Company of Portland, one of the largest coastwise shipping firms in the East, to build them an enlarged and improved version of the CHARLES P. NOTMAN.

As with the blacksmith shop, the new joiner shop was set back approximately 60 feet from Washington Street but hard against the shipyard's north boundary. As before, the setback was to accommodate one of the pre-existing houses on the property. The newest shop was a neat, white, two-and-one-half-story, clap-boarded frame building set on posts and measuring 30 feet wide by 45 feet long. There is no definitive record of the early interior layout of the building or of the machinery installed. However, the only known photo of the building in its original location shows an enormous pile of treenail blanks stacked against its south side, and a brief news item notes that the firm installed a 5-HP electric motor in the building ". . . to run the treenail machine and [it] will also furnish power for the joiner shop."[62]

The joiner shop—and probably the blacksmith shop, as well—was not a heavily built structure intended for big machinery. Balloon framed with the studs running in one piece from the sill to the plate, it can best be described as a light-duty industrial building. Nonetheless, today it is the oldest surviving structure in the shipyard, having survived the vicissitudes of fire and neglect to reach the century mark.

J. S. WINSLOW & COMPANY: A NEW OPTION?

Percy & Small built three schooners for their own account in the thirty months between forming the partnership and the early summer of 1896. Then their pace of new construction ground to a stop. In fact, Bath shipbuilding, which declined sharply with the 1893 panic and then recovered somewhat by 1896, sagged to its lowest level of the decade in 1897.[63] Sam Percy and Frank Small were not alone in their reluctance to build additional schooners even as their own schooners were making good money.[64]

Enter J. S. Winslow & Company of Portland, Maine, established in 1861 by Captain Jacob S. Winslow, known along the waterfront as the "bare-foot captain" and originally from the Down East village of Pembroke, within hailing distance of Passamaquoddy Bay. The "Company" in J. S. Winslow & Company was another native of Pembroke, Henry P. Dewey. Their firm eventually operated the largest fleet of sailing vessels on the East Coast. Originally engaged principally in the West

Indian and deepwater trades, Captain Winslow built a fleet of brigs, barks, and full-rigged ships at shipyards in East Deering and his hometown of Pembroke. In 1880 Captain Jacob turned to William Rogers at Bath to build a few barkentines, followed nine years later by large schooners as the Winslow fleet shifted its emphasis to the coastwise coal trade.

By the time we run into the Winslow operation, Captain Jacob is semi-retired, and the basic responsibility for the firm's affairs are in the hands of Eleazer W. Clark, the ambitious and capable brother-in-law of the founder of the firm.[65] He, too, hailed from Pembroke and, in keeping with Maine's tradition of looking after one's own, was introduced into the Portland business community by fellow Pembrokians Henry Dewey and Henry F. Merrill, treasurer of Randall & McAllister (the city's major coal distributor) and an important owner in coal schooners. Before long, Captain Winslow found a place in his firm for the hometown boy and brother of his second wife Melvinia.[66]

In 1897 Clark, no doubt looking for the most advantageous deal, negotiated with Percy & Small for the firm's next schooner, turning J. S. Winslow & Company's back on its longtime but increasingly contentious supplier of new vessels, William Rogers.[67] It is likely, however, that the dean of Bath shipbuilders was not interested in the terms of the proposed shipbuilding contract. For Percy & Small, however, it was a harbinger of good things to come: J. S. Winslow & Company became a substantial and profitable customer for new vessels and ship repairs over the next two decades.

According to William A. Baker:

As sole manager of the firm, Eleazer W. Clark entered into an agreement with Percy & Small whereby the partners furnished the yard, the workmen, and the supervision. All the material used in the construction of the schooners was supplied by J. S. Winslow & Company. This firm bought the southern pine lumber, and being ship brokers, chartered the vessels to carry it to Bath. The firm's store furnished all the wire rigging, manila cordage, galvanized iron, and

duck for the sails which were cut in the loft on Portland Pier owned by Captain Lester Clark, Eleazer's brother.[68]

If this arrangement sounds familiar, it is. A similar shipbuilding deal had been worked out by J. Parker Morse and Percy & Small's predecessor firm of Adams & Hitchcock. However, Baker has overstated the amount of involvement on the part of J. S. Winslow & Company in supplying materials.

The building accounts and statements have not survived for Schooner #4, but those for some of the subsequent schooners built for J. S. Winslow have.[69] According to these statements, ship timber for Winslow vessels was purchased through Percy & Small's usual suppliers, including James B. Drake. They also show that most of the other materials going into these vessels were purchased on a price and availability basis from largely the same circle of suppliers that Percy & Small normally used for its own vessels.

Nonetheless, J. S. Winslow did get its share of business for chandlery, sailcloth, anchors, chain, and some of the vessels' outfits. But in only one case did the Portland firm clearly provide the steel and iron for a vessel (Hull #15). In all, it appears that between six and eight percent of the total cost of vessels built by Percy & Small for Winslow was returned to the latter firm for materials and supplies.[70]

It should be noted that this was not an unusual practice, especially as competition for building a declining number of schooners became more intense among the surviving shipbuilders. The prospective managing owner of a vessel was not averse to strengthening his bottom line by running some of the purchasing for a new vessel through his books. And as investors in new schooners were frequently found among the maritime business community, it was also considered good policy to patronize suppliers who were actual or potential investors in the vessel.

Finally, the prospective managing owner often expected the chosen shipbuilder to take shares in the new vessel. This reduced the need to raise hard cash during the construction of the vessel, and the builder could market his shares among his circle of business acquaintances at his convenience to convert equity to cash. This was certainly the case in the developing relationship between Percy & Small and J. S. Winslow & Company. The surviving records show that Percy & Small took between 9 and 22 percent of the shares in each Winslow vessel built by them.[71] However, the Bath firm turned these shares over in a short time. For example, in 1908 after having built and delivered no fewer than eight schooners to the Portland company over the previous decade and taken shares in each, Percy & Small owned nary a share in any Winslow schooners.[72]

SCHOONER #4: ALICE E. CLARK

It is impossible now to date the contract between J. S. Winslow & Company and Percy & Small that produced the ALICE E. CLARK. Nor do we know the terms of the agreement except what can be drawn from circumstantial evidence: the new schooner was to be an enlarged and improved CHARLES P. NOTMAN, using the same model and moulds.[73] It was to be fitted with wire standing rigging, but unlike the NOTMAN (but like the BLACKBURN), the rigging was set up with modern rigging-screws (turnbuckles) rather than the traditional deadeyes and lanyards.

Additionally, there were a number of detail improvements that reflected both Percy & Small's cumulative experience with their first three schooners and the desires of J. S. Winslow & Company and the designated skipper—and Eleazer's brother—Captain Leslie Clark. The after house acquired a skylight over the forward cabin (dining room), and a coach house replaced the more traditional companionway slide on the galley house. But the most important change was to move the Adair pump (bilge pump) from its traditional location abaft the mainmast on the raised poop, a location that necessitated operating the pump by hand (it wasn't called the "Liverpool Hurdy-Gurdy" on square-riggers for nothing) or rigging a clumsy and dangerous arrangement for the messenger chain between the pump and the steam hoister in the forward house. The pump was relocated to the after side of the forward house, convenient to the steam hoister.[74] Finally, the vessel was to cost approximately $65,000 (+/- $1.16 million in 1998).[75]

The agreement to build this schooner was probably signed in early winter to facilitate getting out the frame of hardwood and hackmatack from Maine's North Woods. The best time to cut the maple, birch, and hackmatack was during the depths of winter when the sap was down (reducing the likelihood of decay) and the trees—often found in swampy areas—were most accessible to the loggers and their teams.[76]

The first cryptic reference to the vessel in the Bath newspapers appears on 26 March 1897: "the frame for the [Percy &] Small four master is being put together."[77] More than a month passes, and then another newspaper reports that the crew at Percy & Small are getting things ready to lay the keel of the new vessel.[78] But progress was really slow because six weeks *later*, the *Bath Times,* which first hinted at the new schooner in March, notes that: "Percy & Small *will shortly* commence operations in their new yard at the South End . . . ."[79] So why did it take virtually three months after the preliminary announcement that work had begun on the new schooner for the work to actually begin?

The answer to that question will never be known absolutely, but some conclusions can be drawn from the reports. First, Percy & Small were collecting and organizing the frame timber arriving by rail from Wytopitlock. Second, the shipyard was in the process of building the new joiner shop. And, finally, it was likely that Percy & Small were also rebuilding D. O. Blaisdell's original slipway—idle for all practical purposes for seventeen years—replacing rotten timbers and extending the bedlog foundation that supported new vessels as they were assembled on the building ways.[80] Given all of this activity in a small area, it is not surprising that reporters and editors may have confused work involving construction of the new joiner shop or refurbishing the building slip with the laying of the keel of the new schooner.

In mid-June the actual work on the schooner got underway as the shipyard workers stretched the keel.

Within a month, the ship carpenters began the painstaking process of assembling and setting up the frames. Coincidently, the new, white-painted joiner shop—"airy, convenient"—neared completion. Six weeks later, in late August, the schooner was half in frame as the work moved steadily, if not rapidly, forward.[81]

Captain Leslie Clark, the captain-designate of the new craft, moved to Bath with his wife in October to represent J. S. Winslow & Company as construction headed down the home stretch. Big, rough, and hearty, Clark was seen by some as challenger to Linc Jewett's reign as "King of the Coaster Captains," especially as he would be sailing a schooner that was an improved version of Jewett's own tried and true NOTMAN. However, despite a number of very creditable passages, Clark lacked the color of the charismatic Jewett and failed to dethrone him.

The ALICE E. CLARK—named for the captain's wife—was launched on Monday, 24 January 1898 at 1:24 P.M. She was the first vessel to take to the water in Bath that new year. A big turnout materialized for the event despite a heavy snowstorm over the weekend that stalled Bath's electric street railway cars and caused delays on the Maine Central. A particularly big crowd of Portland businessmen, luminaries, and maritime types and their families joined Captain Jacob Winslow, his wife, the Misses Philena, Grace, and Elizabeth Winslow, and Captain and Mrs. Clark for the launching aboard the flag-bedecked schooner. The latter couple had moved aboard their new home four days earlier and were well settled in, enjoying their steam-heated quarters finished in quartered oak, sycamore, and walnut with black and gold trim.[82]

The launching party aboard the CLARK watched as Miss Elizabeth Winslow deftly whacked the ribbon-wrapped bottle of American champagne across the knighthead bitts, pronouncing the traditional litany "I christen thee . . . ." as the vessel began her slide to the river. Maine temperance laws notwithstanding, J. S. Winslow vessels were always baptized with champagne rather than flowers.

The traditional buffet was served to the guests as the vessel lay in the stream, but the new schooner was not returned to her builder's dock as the event wound down. The tug ADELIA moved her to Woodward's wharf near the railway station where the Portland guests could conveniently board the afternoon train for home. Then Captain Clark ordered the gangway hoisted aboard, the mooring lines cast off, and the CLARK and ADELIA proceeded downriver to the open sea at 3:45 P.M. to the rousing cheers of her former guests. At 5:25 P.M., the ADELIA cast off the towline just west of Seguin Island, and the ALICE E. CLARK laid off on a port tack, sails filled, bound for Norfolk.[83]

For the next eleven-plus years the CLARK enjoyed a generally profitable career, free from many of the problems that often plagued other vessels. With the exception of a minor collision with a lightship in 1905 and a fire set by the ship's steward to cover a theft in 1908, the schooner's career was unblemished.[84] In fact, the CLARK was even involved in rescuing twenty-two passengers and crew of the steamer CROATAN, which had burned and sunk about eighteen miles north of Cape Charles. Most of those rescued had been in the water for more than an hour when Captain Les Clark arrived on the scene, hove to, and put a boat over to pick them up.[85]

All this good fortune came to an end on 1 July 1909. Bound for Bangor under the command of Captain L. McDonald with 2,717 tons of coal, the ALICE E. CLARK struck Coombs Ledge off Islesboro in East Penobscot Bay. According to McDonald's account, the flood tide was setting strongly to the west and he had therefore set his course (NE-by-E) accordingly to avoid the submerged ledges that project from Islesboro's eastern shore. Somehow the captain and his crew lost sight of the Coombs Ledge buoy (he claimed there was haze low on the water), and when they did locate it they were about to pass it on their starboard rather than port side. Although the captain and helmsman put the helm up and the CLARK began to fall off to leeward, it was too little, too late. One-half a ship length past the buoy, the CLARK struck bow-on with a barely perceptible thump. Although the schooner had very little way on, the combination of her 2,717 tons of coal and what little speed she was carrying was enough to punch a hole in her planking near the keel.

It must have been a big hole. Even with her pumps running, the CLARK began to settle by the stern as her bow remained impaled on the submerged ledge. Captain and crew started to take in sails and salvage cabin contents. Before the sails were completely lowered—in what appears to be the age-old tradition that when it rains, it pours—a sudden squall from the northwest struck the vessel, twisting her stern around as she settled to the bottom. Lying with her bow partially above water and her stern completely under water at high tide, the schooner looked to be a good candidate for salvage.

The CLARK was soon sold by J. S. Winslow to the Pendleton Brothers of New York and Penobscot Bay. That firm had a reputation for picking up maritime basket cases cheap, refurbishing them, and squeezing a few profitable years of service from their weary hulls. The Pendletons conducted extensive salvage operations on the CLARK, removing equipment and sails and an estimated 2,000 tons of coal. Thus lightened, the Pendletons hoped to float her with two large pontoons sunk on both sides of the vessel, then connected with chains under the schooner's keel. When all was ready, the pontoons would be pumped dry, lifting the soggy wreck off the bottom. A temporary patch could then be applied to the fatal hole, and the vessel would be pumped dry, ready to be towed to the nearest dry-dock to be hauled and thoroughly repaired.[86]

Despite one totally erroneous story that had the half-submerged schooner afloat once again, and after spending $10,000 (+/- $150,000 in 1998), the Pendletons' ambitious plans and the largest salvage effort to that time in Penobscot Bay came to naught.[87] The ALICE E. CLARK had reached her final resting place.

The ALICE E. CLARK was the first schooner Percy & Small built for other owners. She served
J. S. Winslow & Co. well for over eleven years until Captain McDonald passed on the wrong side
of a buoy and struck Coombs Ledge off Islesboro in East Penobscot Bay. The missed buoy is visible
to the right of the schooner. Subsequent salvage efforts failed.

John I. Snow Photo, courtesy of Captains Douglas K. and Linda J. Lee

By 1898 America was finally propelled out of the 1893 depression by the "splendid little war" with Spain, fought ostensibly for Cuban independence. There was a revival in the wooden shipbuilding industry in Maine, although the bulk of the initial orders in Bath went to building the great schooner's most persistent challengers for the coastwise coal trade, barges towed by seagoing tugs.

Moreover, after a decade-long pause, construction began on the second East Coast five-masted schooner, the NATHANIEL T. PALMER.[88] At 2,440 tons, the PALMER was clearly the largest schooner anywhere in the world when launched. She represented the aspirations of her builder and namesake, son of a prominent Bath family, to become a major player at both ends of the schooner business—building and managing.

Nathaniel Palmer, son of Augustus and brother of rigger Frank A. Palmer, went into business the same year as Percy & Small. During the course of the next five years, Palmer outbuilt the rest of Bath's schooner builders, turning out five four-masters and the one five-master totaling 10,298 gross tons, all for his own account. It was a virtuoso performance for a man who designed, built, and managed his own fleet of great schooners, including the largest four-masted schooner built to that time (FRANK A. PALMER, 1897, 2,014 gross tons) and, briefly, the largest five-master.[89] Unfortunately, Palmer's ambition blinded him to certain economic realities: he was broke.

The end came after the Bath tax collector submitted his bill and Palmer couldn't pay. There was talk about political enemies, but Palmer simply couldn't pay his taxes. In the end, he sold the management interest to J. S. Winslow & Company, thus closing out the career of the "other Palmer."[90]

Palmer's brief and bitter experience with five-masters did not deter others from following quickly in his footsteps. Before 1899 ended, five additional five-masters were launched from Maine shipyards, and these were followed over the next two decades by forty-six more, fully 95 percent of all five-masters built on the East Coast.

So, why was there a decade time-lapse between the first five-masted schooner and its fellows? In 1888 the first Atlantic five-master, GOV. AMES, left the ways at the Leverett Storer shipyard in Waldoboro.[91] Unfortunately her first voyage, coupled with an unanticipated cost overrun for construction, nearly sank her owners financially. Designed by Albert Winslow of Taunton, Massachusetts, and built through the efforts of Captain Cornelius Davis of Somerset—the same who mentored Captain Alexander Ross—the five-master was briefly the wonder of the Western world until she shed all her masts on her maiden voyage.[92] Then she became the laughing stock.

Remasted and rerigged at no small cost, the AMES went back onto the sea's highways.[93] Declining coal freights in the Eastern coal trade, the expectation of better business, and even the possible sale of the vessel on the West Coast led the owners to send the AMES from Baltimore to San Francisco in 1890 in 143 days with a light cargo of 2,070 tons of coal for ballast. She was the only five-master to successfully weather Cape Horn in a westward passage, although her captain evinced no interest in repeating the experience. The passage did a lot to restore the GOV. AMES's rather tattered reputation.

During the next four years she was chiefly employed hauling coal from Nanaimo, British Columbia, and Seattle to San Francisco. This routine was broken with a passage to Redondo Beach, California, with a cargo of Puget Sound lumber and then a long passage to Australia with another load of lumber. She then carried a cargo of coal from Australia to Hawaii before returning to the West Coast. Shortly thereafter, the AMES loaded another cargo of Puget Sound lumber and sailed for Liverpool. She made a stately passage of 168 days without serious incident, returning to Newport News in August 1894 to resume her place in the New England coal trade with her reputation reestablished.[94]

The dismasting of the AMES, and the loss of two big four-masters at about the same time which had also shed their spars, led to a lengthy discussion in maritime circles about the viability of the great schooners.[95] The *New York Maritime Register* drew a bead on the subject in two editorials that invited response. In the first, the writer spoke glowingly of the revival of wooden shipbuilding thanks to the big schooners whose qualities—ease of handling, economy of operation, and cargo capacity—made them adaptable to almost any trade. Nonetheless, there was a downside, the writer averred. There was a growing perception that the five-master and large four-masters were oversparred and less seaworthy than their smaller cohorts.[96]

A week later, the writer of "Big Schooners" noted that the four- and five-masters had definitely extended the career of wooden sailing vessels *but* " . . . they are not the ideal sailing vessel that has long been believed. Their rig, admirable as it is and the cause of so much rejoicing among builders of wooden vessels, is now being regarded with suspicion."[97] The writer saw two problems with the big schooners' rigs: the staying of the masts was inadequate, and the vessels tended to get out of control in heavy weather.

That position was quickly seconded in a letter to the editors, signed "Ex-Second Mate," which agreed the staying of masts was inadequate and added another complaint: the big schooners were under manned. Moreover, while the much vaunted steam donkey engine was perfectly fine for hoisting sail and anchors, until the owners could get it to take in and furl sails the big schooners should not be allowed to sail shorthanded.[98] Other letters stressed much the same point as the Ex-Second Mate's.

Two of Bath's most respected shipbuilders joined in the discussion. John McDonald, who brought to bear forty years' experience as a shipbuilder, opined that the schooner rig was unsuitable for vessels over a thousand tons because the long masts of such a vessel placed an abnormal strain on the standing rigging. William Rogers shared this view, although a decade later he would build a schooner considerably larger than that figure.[99] In the end, this sudden notoriety of the schooner rig compelled improvements, and the frequency of catastrophic dismastings declined substantially in the following years.

Just over a year after the original discussion in the columns of the *New York Maritime Register*, the paper observed, "Our shipbuilders, however, seem to have fallen out with the brig or bark rigs, and to have fastened their faith to . . . four- and five-masted schooners. The latter have not been letting their masts go overboard so much lately, and doubtless a better way has been found for securing them, to the manifest advantage of shipowner and underwriter."[100] And it was those self-same underwriters who may have made the largest contribution to the resolution of the early great schooners' habit of shedding their rig. An obscure item in the 22 January 1890 *New York Maritime Register* noted, "marine underwriters are very stiff in their premium rates upon schooners of 1,000 tons burthen (deadweight) and over. Their increase of premiums will do much to secure an improvement in the rig of these vessels." It is an old adage in business that the most effective means of promoting change is to provide a compelling economic reason to change.

SCHOONER #5: M. D. CRESSY

Percy & Small joined the ranks of shipbuilders producing five-masters in 1899 with the launching of their M. D. CRESSY. This vessel introduced three new elements into the Percy & Small equation. It was the firm's first five-masted schooner (over the next two decades they would deliver no fewer than 25 percent of all the East Coast-built five-masters) and the first to exceed 2,000 gross tons; it introduced a new figure into ownership's inner circle; and it saw a new character assume the role of Percy & Small master builder.

The firm appeared to hesitate for some time, however, before committing itself to making Schooner #5 something more than the largest four-master. The keel for the new schooner was laid down during July 1898 under the impetus of war-inflated freight rates.[101] Yet the local press did not cease calling it a four-master until November of that year, when the papers announced it would be a five-master.[102] This suggests that Percy & Small's front office thought long and hard about the masting of their new schooner. Surely, the misgivings expressed at the beginning of the decade were recalled. And as there was still only one working five-master on the coast, perhaps Sam Percy and Frank Small inquired of Captain Alex Ross what he might have heard from his friends from Somerset on how things were doing with the GOV. AMES since she returned East.[103] Then, of course, there was Frank A. Palmer who had rigged his brother's big schooner, making him the only man in Bath and the second in the world to have rigged a new five-masted East Coast schooner.[104]

What they would have learned, if they did not already know it, was that there were several steps one could take in rigging big schooners that would virtually guarantee they would keep their spars firmly in place. The combination of wire standing rigging—with long splices—and rigging screws was an important step forward. Setting up the shrouds and backstays with the proper amount of tension became infinitely easier, especially as schooners grew in size

Myron D. Cressy invested heavily in Percy & Small schooners over the years. Before the firm folded its shipping business, four schooners were named for members of this successful Boston teamster's family.

Courtesy: Maine Maritime Museum

and their masts became longer and heavier. Improvements in staying also included cap shrouds—leading from foremast mast cap to chainplates just abaft the catheads, port and starboard, and crown shrouds—from the crown (halfway up) of the foretopmast to the same location. (Bath rigger Frank Palmer referred to the latter as "Fools Stays"—perhaps an indication of what he thought of them.) Finally, Maine shipbuilders began adopting the practice of increasing the rake of the masts in small increments from foremast to spankermast. This had the effect of leading the

shrouds progressively farther aft on each mast and provided better staying against shocks caused by head-on collision, grounding, or even shouldering into large waves.

In the end, one suspects that the final determinant for Percy & Small was the potential area of the spanker sail on a four-master compared to that of a same-sized five-master. Captain Percy, experienced mariner and schooner captain that he was, knew the potential for disaster represented by an unintended jibe when running before the wind. The larger the sail, the greater the shock. Add to this formula a long, heavy spanker boom and gaff, and you have a recipe for potential disaster. It behooved those who built ever-larger schooners to keep the size of sails within controllable limits, even if it meant adding another mast. This was a replay of the same phenomenon that had led to the introduction of the WILLIAM L. WHITE, the first of the four-masters.

Myron D. Cressy, whom we met in the previous chapter, was a Boston teamster whose business was headquartered on Long Wharf next to the United Fruit Company. Although he did not possess strong personal ties to Bath as did the namesakes of Percy & Small's first three vessels, Cressy established a close relationship with Sam Percy and Frank Small and became a consistent and heavy investor in their vessels starting with the WILLIAM H. CLIFFORD. In the end, the Percy & Small partners named four of their vessels for members of Cressy's family in recognition of his personal investment in

Launching day, 11 May 1899. The M. D. Cressy occupies center stage with the blacksmith shop visible on the right and the joiner shop (later paint and treenail shop) in its original position on the left.

Courtesy: Robert Colfer

Percy & Small schooners and the other Boston area investors he brought into the fold.

For Master Builder Willard Avery Hodgkins, the M. D. CRESSY offered both a new start in his career and the biggest vessel he had yet undertaken to build. He was brought onboard at Percy & Small's new shipyard to replace Horatio N. Douglas who, with the resurgence of the wooden shipbuilding business, had returned full-time to his beloved New England Company.

Hodgkins, born in Jefferson, Maine, in 1844, spent most of his life in Bath and followed his father Asa Hodgkins into the shipyards while still a boy. Prior to his move to Percy & Small, he was employed as master builder by Thomas Hagan and William T. Donnell and was credited with fifty vessels.[105] He may, in fact, have worked for both shipbuilders during 1887, building the F. G. FRENCH (184 GRT) for Hagan and the four-master KATIE J. BARRETT (964 GRT) for Donnell. The last and largest schooner he built for Donnell was the ALICE M. COLBURN (1,603 GRT) in 1896. For a brief span of time (1888-89) both Hodgkins, Asa and young Willard, were simultaneously active as master builders in Bath.[106]

By late July 1898, workmen at Percy & Small began stretching the new schooner's keel under the close supervision of Master Builder Hodgkins. Aside from size, the CRESSY shared a close family resemblance with Percy & Small's previous four schooners, including the long poop that was becoming the most visible characteristic of the great schooners. The resemblance was more than just skin deep for the CRESSY was probably built from the WILLIAM H. CLIFFORD model, so she offered little or nothing in the way of innovation in terms of construction and form. This was in definite contrast to the HENRY O. BARRETT, built by G. G. Deering and launched a few days after the CRESSY. The BARRETT sported a flush-deck configuration which was unusual but not unique. What really set her aside was the omission of hanging knees fitted between the deck beams and frames. In their place Deering had massive, longitudinal timbers called shelves bolted under the deck beams and running down the full length of the vessel on each side. Additional heavy longitudinals called

clamps supported the shelf timbers and tied frame timbers, deck beams, and shelves into a single structure. A schooner so fitted was said to be built with "shelves and clamps," a construction innovation that improved longitudinal strength—an important factor as hull length increased—although some builders were not convinced that shelves and clamps were as effective in resisting wracking forces upon the hull as the traditional hanging knees.[107]

The CRESSY did possess one innovation, however, which was soon adopted throughout the industry. She was outfitted with a 3,000-pound stockless anchor in place of one of the traditional stock anchors. The stockless anchor was introduced in the 1850s but enjoyed only minimal acceptance until the 1870s, when its use aboard steam vessels spread steadily. And, as we have noted, the century was coming to an end when it was first used aboard a sailing vessel. The adoption of the stockless anchor was a natural step in the march to make the operation of the great schooners more efficient (read: smaller crew).

The traditional stock anchor possessed good holding power but was difficult to handle and stow securely. Once the anchor was raised clear of the water on vessels going offshore, a "fish hook" on a long pendant was dropped over the bow and hooked into the ring of the anchor. The Spanish burton anchor tackle, permanently secured to the foremast head, was hooked on and the "hands" hoisted away, bringing the anchor onto the forecastle head where it was secured until the vessel came on soundings again.

On coastwise passages, the same Spanish burton anchor tackle was used and the anchor was hoisted out—with the assistance of the hoisting engine—and hung by the anchor ring from the anchor stopper mounted near the outboard end of the cathead. If the captain anticipated using the anchor because of changing winds or tides, he could leave the anchor hanging from the cathead, ready for deployment with the blow of a maul to release the stopper mechanism. If, however, the captain didn't feel the need to leave the anchor ready for instant use, he could have the crew reset the fish tackle once the anchor was hung from the cathead in order to hoist one fluke high enough to rest in the billboard atop the rail, where it was then lashed

Anchored in the Kennebec following her launching, the
M. D. CRESSY was the first of fifteen five-masters built by Percy &
Small over the next two decades. Despite significant structural
problems, the CRESSY proved to be a profitable investment.

Courtesy: Robert Colfer

down by the chain shank painter—called "fishing the anchor."[108]

Leaving the anchor hanging from the cathead (catting the anchor), unless its use in the immediate future was likely, was not a wise move: a big anchor swinging from the cathead, however short the tether, could inflict considerable damage on a vessel's bow, especially in a heavy sea. A "fished anchor" was almost instantly ready for use—release the shank painter and trip the anchor stopper and over it went with a huge splash and the roar of the chain in the hawsepipe. Coasting schooners of all sizes normally catted or

fished their anchors to have them available for instant—and often frequent—use as changing currents and winds, nearby shoals, and maritime traffic entered the navigation equation. Nonetheless, handling the big stock anchors with a small crew on the crowded, open, and often wet topgallant forecastle deck in a heavy swell or breaking seas remained a dangerous and difficult operation—for crew and vessel—even though the steam hoister had eased the physical labor.

By way of contrast, the stockless anchor was designed to be drawn up by its shank into the hawsepipe. Thus housed, its movable flukes drawn tight against a metal plate secured to the hull around the hawsepipe, the stockless anchor remained held securely in place by the riding stopper and windlass brake until needed. It vastly simplified the entire operation, not to mention making it appreciably safer.

While the stockless anchor gained rapid acceptance for its ease of handling, the spirit of conservatism still permeated the maritime community and the traditional stock anchor was retained as one-half of the ground tackle outfit for a few more years. The Percy & Small-built WILLIAM C. CARNEGIE became the first of the great schooners equipped solely with stockless anchors in 1900. The caution was, to a degree, justified. It was quickly discovered that the stockless anchor's holding power was not equal to that of the stock anchor. In compensation, firms such as Percy & Small equipped their vessels with larger, heavier stockless anchors until the great schooners carried some of the heaviest ground tackle installed on any vessel anywhere. Three years after the 2,114-GRT M. D. CRESSY took to the Kennebec with her 3,000-pound stockless anchor, Percy & Small built the CORA F. CRESSY. That 2,499-ton five-master was equipped with an 8,200-pound stockless anchor along with a 6,200-pound stock anchor.[109]

The M. D. CRESSY was launched on 11 May 1899 with great fanfare, an increasingly important feature of Percy & Small launchings. Miss Mabel Harding, sister of the redoubtable captain—William F. Harding, formerly of the WILLIAM H. CLIFFORD— did the christening honors as two hundred invited guests rode the new vessel down the ways into the river. More than thirty of the guests were Boston business associates of the schooner's namesake and had accompanied him to Bath on a chartered Pullman car

from Boston. Before the launching, the Cressy party presented Captain Harding with a large national ensign and the ship's burgee.

After the usual catered luncheon and launching punch, the CRESSY was returned to the dock with the assembled guests offering rousing cheers for the builders, Captain Harding, Miss Mabel Harding, and the estimable Mr. Cressy. Seventy of the launching party, including Captain Sam and Frank Small, the Cressy guests, and other assorted bigwigs adjourned to the New Meadows Inn for a $3-a-plate (+/- $45 in 1998) banquet tendered by Mr. Cressy and Captain Harding.[110]

The local press pronounced the day's events to be an unalloyed success and the new five-master as good as any vessel ever built. But for all of the local booster spirit, events leading to this day and coming long after contained two very important lessons.

The first lesson already perceived was that the new Percy & Small shipyard was inadequate to the task of building the larger and larger schooners that the coal shipping business now appeared to demand. Before the year ended, Percy & Small commenced a major upgrade of the shipyard that firmly placed it in the ranks of major wooden shipbuilders.

But the second lesson would take a little while to make itself manifest, and the M. D. CRESSY was one of its messengers. If great schooners were to continue to be built larger and larger, more attention needed to be paid to their structural integrity. Although she lasted longer than the average five-master, the M. D. "Doctor" CRESSY was plagued throughout her career with structural problems that necessitated doctoring in the form of major longitudinal reinforcement of the hull by the time she was six years old.

---

[1] BT, 10/20/1905.

[2] BT, 4/15/1903.

[3] BT, 12/20/1899.

[4] BE, 3/25/1899. Reprinted from the Portland Argus.

[5] BE, 7/15/1899. Captain Jewett later sued the ferry for $600 (+/- $10,000 in 1998), BT, 12/2/1899; the judge later declared both parties to be at fault, Jewett because he failed to use the ringbolts to restrain his horse and the ferry

company for failing to provide safety gates or chains across the open ends of the ferry. He awarded Jewett $300, one-half his claimed loss; BT, 3/21, 22/1900.

[6] BT, 6/12/1900. Including the captain, mate, steward, and engineer there were nine in the crew, plus Mrs. Jewett and the wife and son of the steward.

[7] Ibid.

[8] Ibid.

[9] *BT*, 6/22/1900. One unanswered question is the fate of the NOTMAN's yawl boat. Did it end up aboard the schooner being built for Jewett, or aboard one of the others under construction or on order at Percy & Small?

[10] *BT*, 9/18/1900. The payment represented the depreciated value of the NOTMAN, i.e., construction cost less 5 percent per year.

[11] The figures on the NOTMAN's earnings come from Personal Research Files, Parker Collection, *PSJ*, and *BT*, 6/12/1900; *PSJ* does not include the first six dividends which Captain Parker subsequently estimated totaled $60. However, an article on the loss in *BT* reported that until her sinking she had paid a total of $80,556 in dividends (Statements 1–58), which places the first six dividends total at $108.59, a figure consistent with her subsequent earnings.

[12] *BE*, 10/17/1894.

[13] Denny M. Humphreys Survey Notebook #14 (1893–94), MS-8, MMM, hereafter cited as DMHSN. Humphreys notes keel laid "Dec 1 94" but the *BE* reported on 12/8/1894: "Percy and Small are getting the timbers out for a big four-masted schooner that they will build at once."

[14] *PSJ*, p. 22; *BSB* (1896), MS-46, MMM. The latter is the city tax collector's record of vessel shares owned by residents, year by year, giving name of owner, name of vessel, shares owned, etc.

[15] See footnote 11.

[16] *PSJ*, p. 16. Percentage includes the captain's shares.

[17] *Bath Independent and Enterprise*, 5/4/1904, obituary. Hereafter cited as *I&E*.

[18] *PSJ*, p. 3.

[19] *Ibid.*, p. 16.

[20] Martin, Kenneth R. and Ralph Linwood Snow, *The Pattens of Bath: A Seagoing Dynasty*. Bath, ME: Maine Maritime Museum/Patten Free Library, 1996, pp. 161–67.

[21] The Houghton's built thirteen ships for their fleet between 1866 and 1891, ranging from CHINA to PARTHIA.

[22] Sewall vessel names ranged from the grain series—GRANGER, HARVESTER, REAPER, THRASHER—to the Big Four: RAPPAHANOCK, SHENANDOAH, SUSQUEHANNA, and ROANOKE.

[23] Located on Long Wharf next to the United Fruit Company, the firm flourished and went into general trucking; their green trucks with gold trim and red wheels were a fixture around the Boston waterfront down to mid-century. One of the Cressy sons, Carl, was still alive in the late 1980s.

[24] *BI*, 8/10/1895.

[25] Survey: WILLIAM H. CLIFFORD, 6/16/1896, Boston Marine Insurance Co., Parker Collection.

[26] Capital costs: NOTMAN—$42.49 per GRT; CLIFFORD—$41.89 per GRT.

[27] Harding's four P&S commands included the CLIFFORD with 2,650 DWT capacity, the M. D. CRESSY with 3,200 DWT capacity, the CORA F. CRESSY with 3,850 DWT capacity, and the GRACE A. MARTIN with 5,000 DWT capacity. Harding would almost double his primage take-home pay while on the MARTIN, all things being equal, over what he could expect on the CLIFFORD.

[28] *PSJ*, various entries for the NOTMAN and the CLIFFORD, 1895–98.

[29] *NYMR*, 2/10/1897.

[30] *BE*, 4/3/1897.

[31] The CLIFFORD paid no dividends between 12/15/1896 and 10/26/1897. In the same period the NOTMAN paid eleven dividends. *PSJ*, various entries.

[32] *BT*, 6/8 and 9/7/1898.

[33] *PSJ*, various entries. The sale price was found in a Boston Marine Insurance Co. report by T. J. Faithwaite, dated 3/11/1916, Personal Research Files, Parker Collection. P&S owned $19/128$ at the time of her sale per *BSB*, 1915.

[34] *PSJ*, pp. 16, 30; $1/64$ in the CLIFFORD and later in the BLACKBURN were placed in his wife's name.

[35] Parker, *Coal Schooners*, pp. 37–39. Cornelius A. Davis was the managing owner and first captain of the GOV. AMES, the first five-master.

[36] *BT*, 2/28/1898; *PSJ*, various entries.

[37] *BE*, 6/24/1896; *BT*, 6/25/1896; *BI*, 6/27/1896.

[38] Ralph Linwood Snow, *The Bath Iron Works: The First Hundred Years*. Bath, ME: Maine Maritime Museum, 1987, pp. 108–09.

[39] William F. Palmer of Boston was managing owner of one of the most successful coal fleets during the first decade of the twentieth century. He often complained about his problems with contract shipyards. Nevertheless, he also rejected out-of-hand offers of idle shipyards for sale or lease, and his few experiences involving the actual construction of schooners—JANE PALMER, HARWOOD PALMER, and SINGLETON PALMER—were enormously demanding of time and energy at the expense of the Palmer fleet operations. Palmer Collection.

[40] The firm had outstanding notes totaling $34,500 (+/- $615,000 in 1998) in May 1896. *PSJ*, p. 22.

[41] *BE*, 7/15/1896.

[42] William T. Donnell to Percy & Small, Sagadahoc County Registry of Deeds, Book 88, p. 492. Hereafter cited as SCRD.

[43] Baker, I, pp. 518–19.

[44] CECILIA COHEN, 1,102 GRT, launched 2/9/1920.

[45] *BT*, 8/5/1910, obituary.

[46] Property Description Cards, Assessor's Office, City of Bath. Described at the time of sale as: "land, tenement houses, wharves, and ice house on east side of Washington Street." It was valued at $2,800.

[47] *BT*, 9/10/1890.

[48] The photo was taken from the knoll between the current location of the Percy & Small pitch oven and the caulker's shop looking northwest. The only evidence for

dating the photo comes from the tax assessor records. When the property was sold in 1890, the records mention an icehouse along with tenements and a wharf. When Percy & Small purchased the property in 1896, the icehouse was no longer mentioned. In addition, the assessment changed substantially between 1893 and 1894, from $2,800 for land and buildings to $1,800 for same. Part of this reduction, $500 worth to be exact, can be accounted for by the sale of a strip of the land—+/- 91 feet by 263 feet—to the south abutter, Charles E. Hyde. His assessment rose by $500, the valuation placed on the land. That leaves $500 of the old Blaisdell property assessment reduction unaccounted for, and it must represent the elimination of the so-called icehouse *cum* machine shop which was no longer in evidence in 1896.

[49] *BT*, 7/17/1890.

[50] *BE*, 7/15/1896.

[51] The actual price is not known, but given the tax-appraised value of $1,800 in 1894 (Property Cards, Tax Assessor's Office, City of Bath) and the firm's subsequent placing of a $1,500 mortgage on the property (Percy & Small to People's Safe Deposit, 6/23/1898, SCRD, Book 89, p. 448), the estimated $1,500–$1,800 is definitely within the ballpark.

[52] *BE*, 8/8/1896.

[53] SCRD, Book 93, p. 142. The deed does not specify the land provided by Percy & Small as its share of the swap.

[54] *BT*, 10/11/1920, obituary. Gibson returned to shipsmithing about 1917–18, becoming the foreman blacksmith at Bath Iron Works. *Bath City Directory*, 1919.

[55] *Bath City Directory*, 1902 and 1905–06. His work place is listed as 411 Front Street.

[56] *PSJ*, pp. 1–3. Earliest entries show Gibson receiving $.40 per hour for repairwork and $.82 per ton for new construction. P&S charged the most for blacksmith time for repairwork getting $.50 per hour for the smithy's time as opposed to $.275 per hour for joiners, and $.225 per hour for ship carpenters (*PSJ*, p. 2). By 1902 Gibson was charging $.70 per hour for blacksmith labor but was still receiving $.82 per ton for new construction.

[57] *BSB*, various years. In 1913 Gibson owned $13/128$ shares in six P&S schooners and his wife held an additional $6/128$; none of the other subcontractors came close to the Gibsons, with rigger Frank A. Palmer being the next highest with $8/128$ shares in various P&S vessels.

[58] Construction Statements: CHARLES P. NOTMAN, Parker Collection. A lot more iron was purchased and processed through the blacksmith shop but was not galvanized. This included tons of iron used for the long driftbolts (used for fastening big timbers together) that needed to be cut to length and pointed by the smiths. See: *BS*, 5/2/1889, re: bolt-cutting machine at Morse yard.

[59] *PSJ*, p. 1. One of the earliest entries in the journal, Gibson soon becomes one of the most frequently identified entries thereafter.

[60] Much of the information on interior layout and equipment in shipyard shops comes from tape-recorded interviews with four former Percy & Small employees. These include Charles A. Coombs (MMM Tapes #68-T-1,2,3), Raleigh Osier (MMM Tapes #72-T-2,3), Thomas Robson (MMM Tapes #72-T-5,6), and Samuel Barnes (RLS Notes). Also of use were the taped reminiscences of William Donnell (MMM Tape #72-T-1) and Homer Potter (MMM Tape #72-T-4).

[61] *BE*, 6/9/1897; BI, 8/22/1896. Hull #4 was probably laid down during June 1897, but preliminary work went back to March of that year. See: *BT*, 3/26/1897.

[62] *BT*, 11/1/1897.

[63] Bath's wooden shipyards turned out 13,187 gross tons (sail and steam) in 1892, 7,825 gross tons in 1893, and only 5,116 gross tons in 1897.

[64] The cumulative net earnings per $1/64$ for their three vessels totaled $581.66, 18 percent of the total cost per $1/64$, by the end of 1896.

[65] *BT*, 5/10/1902, obituary. Winslow's second wife was Eleazer Clark's sister. They had three daughters.

[66] Notes of Meeting with Henry F. Merrill, 1950, Personal Research Files, Parker Collection.

[67] William F. Palmer, who had a high regard for himself, had a low regard for Rogers after building two schooners there. Palmer may have been put off by dealing with someone as opinionated as himself. See: W. F. Palmer to W. H. Reed, 8/5/1903, Palmer Letter Book 6/03–5/04, Palmer Collection.

[68] Baker, II, p. 692.

[69] Construction Statements: Hulls #12, 15, 19, and 24, Parker Collection.

[70] Percy & Small did not abandon old suppliers. Although Eleazer Clark's brother ultimately ran a sail loft in Portland, P&S did not contract with him to make sails for their vessels until after the death of William Clifford.

[71] Construction Statements: Hulls #12, 15, 19, and 24, Parker Collection.

[72] Captain Percy privately owned shares in various Winslow schooners along with shares in others divided amongst various managing owners. Goss, Sawyer & Packard, Bath's largest wooden shipbuilding firm, failed in the 1880s in part because it had too great a financial interest in the ships it built for other owners. This was well known in Bath and to Sam Percy and Frank Small.

[73] The CLARK's registered length was 8.1 feet greater than the NOTMAN's. This was obtained by increasing the distance between frame centers one-half inch per frame ($33 1/2$ inches to 34 inches) and, probably, adding additional frames amidships. See: DMHSN, "Schooner ALICE E. CLARK."

[74] Percy & Small's CLIFFORD and BLACKBURN subsequently had their Adair pumps shifted to the same location as on the CLARK.

[75] *BT*, 1/24/1898 and BI, 1/29/1898, launching accounts; *BT*, 12/10/1897, cost.

[76] Maple used for shipbuilding was the sugar maple (also called rock or hard maple) *Acer saccharum*; yellow birch, *Betula alleghaniensis*, was also commonly used for hardwood frames, especially for floor timbers; hackmatack or tamarack, *Larix laricina*, was used for the top timbers in the frames because of its strength, resistance to rot, and relative lightness. White oak, preferred by the underwriters, was pretty well logged off in Maine by the end of the century and so was brought in principally from Maryland and Virginia.

[77] *BT*, 3/26/1897.

[78] *BE*, 5/1/1897.

[79] *BT*, 6/10/1897; emphasis added.

[80] The old slipway layout was probably too short to accommodate the big four-master ALICE E. CLARK, even if the bed logs had survived intact after seventeen years of neglect.

[81] *BE*, 7/10 and 8/26/1897.

[82] *BT*, 1/24/1898; *BI*, 1/29/1898.

[83] *BT*, 1/25/1898.

[84] *BT*, 1/13/1905 and 4/22/1908.

[85] *BT*, 11/5/1898.

[86] *BT*, 11/10/1909.

[87] *BT*, 11/12, 16/1909.

[88] The first American five-master—DAVID DOWS—was built in Toledo, Ohio, for service on the Great Lakes in 1881.

[89] *BT*, 10/30/1917. The FRANK A. PALMER lost its laurels as largest four-master in 1906 to NORTHLAND, 2,047 GRT, built by Cobb-Butler in Rockland.

[90] Curiously, J. S. Winslow & Company subsequently bought the management interest in the William F. Palmer fleet as well in 1910, thus absorbing both Palmer fleets.

[91] GOV. AMES was the official name on her registry. By using an abbreviation, the managing owners could save money on telegrams.

[92] One theory concerning the dismasting is that the rigger made some splices in the standing rigging too short, allowing them to pull out while under strain.

[93] Earnings Accounts #1, #2, Schooner GOV. AMES, Parker Collection. The records indicate that the cost of salvage, remasting and rerigging the schooner came to $15,833.36 (+/- $270,000 in 1998). Additional charges of $7,253.44 (+/- $123,300 in 1998) were levied for construction cost overruns.

[94] Captain W. J. Lewis Parker, USCG (Ret.), "The GOV. AMES, Maine's First Five-Masted Schooner," *Down East*, July 1970. She was lost on Thimble Shoals, 13 December 1909. There was one survivor.

[95] T. A. LAMBERT, 1,630 GRT, 1887–88, and MILLIE G. BOWNE, 1,680 GRT, 1889–89.

[96] *NYMR*, Editorial, 1/8/1890.

[97] *NYMR*, Editorial, 1/15/1890.

[98] *NYMR*, 2/5/1890.

[99] Baker, II, pp. 797–98.

[100] *NYMR*, 2/25/1891.

[101] Nathaniel Palmer suspended work on his five-master laid down in 1897, probably for financial reasons. He resumed work on it after chartering his fleet of five four-masters to the government at high rates to haul coal for the U.S. Navy to Florida.

[102] *BI*, 11/5/1898.

[103] NATHANIEL T. PALMER did not enter service until early 1899.

[104] Christian Henry Bohndel rigged the AMES when she was new. The next vessel he rigged, the AUGUSTUS WELT, had the heaviest rigging yet installed on a schooner. She lasted for a very long time.

[105] *BI*, 5/13/1899.

[106] *BT*, 2/4/1931, obituary.

[107] Baker, II, p. 801; *BI*, 5/13/1899.

[108] John F. Leavitt, *Wake of the Coasters*. Marine Historical Association/Wesleyan University Press, 1970, pp. 29-31.

[109] *BT*, 4/12/1902.

[110] *BT*, 5/11, 12/1899; *BI*, 5/13/1899.

THREE

Creating a Niche

A DECADE AT THE TOP

The resurgence of wooden shipbuilding that began with the Spanish-American War offered Percy & Small an opportunity to further expand their horizons by placing shipbuilding on an equal footing with the shipping side of the business. This they opted to do, investing substantially in the former Blaisdell shipyard throughout the decade in order to create a shipbuilding plant capable of efficiently, and profitably, building the larger classes of schooners Percy & Small targeted as their speciality. It was a wise move.

The first decade of the twentieth century was, for Percy & Small, to become the zenith of their shipbuilding business as it came to dominate the traditional wooden shipbuilding industry on the Atlantic Coast. By the time 1910 dawned, Percy & Small had produced 58,467 GRT of shipping, averaging 5,847 gross tons per year, four times as much tonnage per year as they built during their first six years in business. Although they underlined their commitment to their own shipping business by adding 23,270 GRT to their own fleet during the decade, J. S. Winslow & Company and a new client, William F. Palmer, purchased fully 60 percent of the shipyard's total output.

SHIPYARD DEVELOPMENTS: 1899–1909

When the M. D. CRESSY took to the Kennebec and was duly celebrated as Percy & Small's first five-master and their largest vessel yet, few in Bath realized that there was more to come. Before the year of 1899 ended, the firm had commitments in hand for over 8,000 tons of new construction for delivery during the next year.[1]

But there was an obstacle in Percy & Small's way, especially since shipbuilding began to acquire the sta-tus of a major profit center for the firm. The shipyard was dismally lacking in the most essential elements if it was to become a major player building the great schooners. The financially brave, if deliberate, development of Percy & Small's recently acquired shipyard would serve as a shipbuilding chokepoint until something more was done.

First, if the firm's shipbuilding arm was going to be competitive in the great schooner market, it needed to improve its ability to efficiently process the heavy timber that was part and parcel of wooden shipbuilding. The year-old joiner shop hardly qualified on that account with only a 5-HP electric motor available to power machinery, and if Percy & Small planned to process big timbers with efficient, modern machinery, it was going to have to construct a mill building capable of handling the timber as well as the weight and vibration of the machinery.

Now that was a problem: Not enough space to put a building of that size on the shipyard property along with the existing buildings and accommodate a vessel as big, or bigger, than the just-launched M. D. CRESSY—especially since some vessels on Percy & Small's "to do" and "might do" lists were bigger than their first five-master!

The solution was pure Maine, where the motto: "use it up, wear it out, make it do, or do without" was probably more thoroughly observed than the Ten Commandments. Percy & Small sold the two houses fronting on Washington Street to Sam Percy's brother-in-law, Fred Tobey, for $300 (+/- $5,300 in 1998).[2] Tobey had the houses moved off the shipyard property to a lot owned by his mother on the northwest corner of Marshall and Middle Streets (see map, p. 68), less than a block away.[3] Fortunately for Tobey, the local officials were not concerned about setbacks from the public ways and lot lines as long as the building was within the property boundaries. Within two years the former shipyard "tenements" were repurchased by Percy & Small and moved once again.

Frank Wildes, who had the contract to move the newly purchased Tobey houses, was also hired by Sam Percy. Once he moved the Tobey houses out of the shipyard—uphill—to their new location, Wildes turned his attention to the shipyard's joiner shop. He moved this building diagonally across the yard to the space just vacated by one of the houses.[4] Not only did Wildes move the building to its new location, he rotated it 180 degrees in the process.[5] This placed the building on the southwest corner of the property, facing onto Washington Street where it assumed a new persona as the paint and treenail shop.

In the space vacated by the second house and the former joiner shop, Sam Percy ordered the construction of a new mill building. It was to be a substantial industrial structure measuring 40 feet wide by 75 feet deep with two floors totaling 6,000 square feet. The Washington Street end was set back only a few feet from the road and trolley tracks (a situation that led on one occasion to a rather bizarre accident). At this end, the first floor was slightly above ground level. As the shipyard property fell away from the road as it approached the river, the first floor at the rear of the building was nearly eight feet above the ground. While this created some timber-handling problems for the mill, it also created a convenient "daylight basement" area with ground-level access on the shipyard side that was used for storage and the housing of the mill's big electric motors.

The first, or mill, floor offered a clear-span work space measuring 40 feet by 75 feet. The shipyard end was open with a timber ramp descending to ground level, flanked by two wooden trestles extending out 15 to 18 feet into the shipyard at floor level. In severe weather this end could be closed off with heavy canvas weather curtains. At the other end, the street side was lined with awning doors that could be opened or closed from inside the building by a system of ropes and pulleys. Along the first floor's north wall, hard against the property line of the adjoining Powers homestead, was a row of windows to provide a natural supplement to the none-too-bright electric lights that hung from the overhead. The south wall had a few low awning doors, along with a few windows, opening onto the roadway between the mill and the newly redesignated paint and treenail shop. The awning doors facilitated clearing out the prodigious quantities of sawdust and wood chips that were generated during the course of the sawing and planing operations that took place on this floor.

The second floor, designated as the joiner shop, had the same dimensions as the first floor but lacked the clear span due to the system of roof trusses and tie rods that supported the 8- by 10-inch crossbeams that carried the shop floor joists. The joiner shop had windows on all sides as well as skylights to take advantage of natural lighting. The only access to the floor was via an outside stairway and sliding door on the south side. The exterior of the building was clapboarded and painted white.

The 8- by 10-inch post-and-beam construction, along with the liberal use of ship's knees, defined the mill and joiner shop's industrial nature. The building was intended to contain and support heavy machinery. The mill floor housed three pieces of heavy machinery purchased from the Winnegance sawmill of the late Reuben S. Hunt, who just a few years earlier had been involved in the division of George Adams's fleet of schooners.[6]

A right-hand circular sawmill with a 42-inch blade was installed on the north side of the building.[7] This outfit was equipped with a 43-foot timber carriage whose track extended out of the east side of the building on one of the two trestles. It was this particular piece of machinery that once took on a passing trolley car. In May 1906, Car #21 of the local street railway was cruising past the shipyard just as the saw carriage carrying a long piece of timber completed its pass through the whirling saw blade and reached the end of its track at the west end of the mill. The timber extended a few feet beyond the saw carriage and projected out of the building and into the trolley

track right-of-way. Ka-thump! Trolley meets timber. No serious damage was done, but it gave Bath's humorists—real or imagined—plenty of fodder.[8]

The sawmill was an important addition to the shipyard's capabilities. Percy & Small could now resaw the four-sided balks of timber brought by schooner and rail from the South and even the West Coast into the necessary dimensions. The sawmill could also process local logs into the huge quantities of staging plank, cribbing, keel blocks, and other timbers that were consumed in shipbuilding.[9]

The machine that found a place on the south side of the mill floor was an impressive piece called a Daniels planer. Designed "to true out, square up, and bevel with the utmost precision hard and soft wood, any length or width," the planer was also useful for surfacing irregularly shaped pieces such as ship knees.[10] Unlike conventional planers, the Daniels type allowed the operator to independently control the direction and speed of the timber—dogged-down on a track-mounted planer table—through the blades. The open planer head housed the blade

The shipyard after completion of the 1899 expansion. The new mill (center), paint and treenail shop (right) in its new and final location, and blacksmith shop (right rear) constituted the core of the shipyard's structures. Behind the mill, the frame of the massive ELEANOR A. PERCY is taking shape, and in the foreground the firm is storing ship timbers on land leased from the Stinson family. The Powers house and barn are visible on the left of the mill.

Stinson Brothers Photo, courtesy of Bath Historical Society

assembly mounted on a vertically adjustable frame along with the belt-drive power take-off wheels and clutches and table control levers. The blade assembly was composed of a heavy vertical shaft with a two-foot arm mounted on the lower end. The planer blades were mounted at the ends of the arm which rotated at high speed in the horizontal plane. They were capable of shaving through two inches of wood on each pass. Percy & Small's planer came with a 43-foot table and a 93-foot bed made of iron or steel I-beams that weighed between five and six tons.[11] There were other Daniels planers at work in Bath, but only one was larger than the one at Percy & Small.[12] Large, noisy, and violent, it shaved off large curls of wood with such violence that they literally "chip blasted" some of the building's structural timbers smooth, and the vertical planing head structure had to be partially screened with heavy curtains made from old sail canvas in order to protect the operator and other men working on the floor from the flying chips.

The third piece of machinery installed on the mill floor was designed to saw continuously changing bevels where needed in frame futtocks and floor timbers. Often referred to as a jigsaw—the blade had a reciprocating action rather than moving continuously in one direction like a bandsaw—this was not a tool found in the ordinary home woodworking shop. The entire blade assembly was mounted on a toothed, circular iron ring that could be rotated through a considerable arc on both sides of vertical. This arrangement was a major improvement over the method of tilting the saw table to make bevel cuts, especially when working with large, heavy frame stock, because the movement of the stock through the blade could be more accurately controlled.

The second floor of the mill building housed the joiner shop, presided over by only two foreman joiners during the shipyard's active years—Fred B. Scott and Charles A. Coombs. The woodworking machinery layout on this floor changed over the years as old equipment was retired and new was added, but the inventory remained basically the same: bandsaw, molding machine, table saw, jointer, thickness planer, mortise and tenon machine, and a long-bed lathe.[13]

A full-length workbench occupied the west wall overlooking the street, and a shorter workbench was installed in the southeast corner for saw sharpener Lincoln Barnes. A pot-bellied woodstove provided what can only be described as inadequate heat during the long and frequently bitter-cold Maine winters, but the joiners could at least warm their hands occasionally, which was more than the men in the open-ended mill below could do. Another "convenience" was a crude urinal attached to the north wall. Given the distance to the shipyard privy perched over the river—not to mention its lack of ambience, especially during the winter—this was a real time-saver.

The lumber turned into the fancy and not-so-fancy paneling found in the great schooner deckhouses entered the shop via a chute from the mill below. Once the sectional panels which made up much of the cabin paneling, especially in the after house, were completed, they were carried down the outside stairs over to the painters located on the second floor of the former joiner shop for finishing.

Powered machinery had been introduced into some American shipyards in the 1840s–1850s, but the first shipbuilder to introduce such an innovation to Bath was Captain Guy C. Goss in 1869. At that time he purchased the machinery of the bankrupt Donald McKay shipyard in East Boston for use in the burgeoning Goss, Sawyer & Packard shipbuilding plant in Bath's north end.[14] Driven by a stationary steam engine through a system of shafts and belts, the machinery brought about substantial improvements in efficiency.

Prior to this time, Bath shipbuilders had not been totally dependent upon such age-old, but labor-intensive, techniques as hand-hewn timbers or planking and decking sawn with man-powered pitsaws. They were able to look to a series of tidal mills at Winnegance just south of Percy & Small for some of their sawing needs, and to Bath's first steam sawmill that went on line at Trufant Point in 1821. Nonetheless, these mills and their successors provided the local shipbuilders with planking, decking, and sawn timbers more economically than was possible by traditional handworked means.

By the 1870s–1880s, many of the active Bath shipyards, large and small, were operating some type of steam-powered machinery, including Percy & Small's Blaisdell predecessor. The shift to in-house timber processing—never complete by any means—gave the shipbuilders more flexibility as well as greater control over the process. But there were difficulties with the system. When the shipyard was operating, it was necessary to keep the boiler fired twenty-four hours a day and employ a stationary steam engineer to operate and maintain the system.

Life became simpler with the introduction of electricity to Bath and its shipyards. The Bath Electric Light and Power Company, organized in 1887, initially focused its efforts on street lighting in the form of carbon arc lamps and had few private customers. About 1890 the electric company absorbed the old gas company and became Bath Gas and Electric Company. It then began a serious effort to sell its electricity to businesses, industrial firms, and the homeowners throughout the city—a program that began to show results by the mid-1890s. Kelley, Spear became the first shipyard to adopt electricity in 1895, followed closely by Percy & Small early in 1896. The latter installed a 5-HP electric motor in the blacksmith shop at the Morse yard to operate the bolt cutters, a drill press, and circular sharpening stones.[15] The local high-tech firm—Bath Iron Works—shifted over entirely from steam- to electric-powered machinery later the same year.

When Percy & Small began setting up their new shipyard, electricity was the power of choice. They brought the motor originally installed at the Morse shipyard's blacksmith shop and set it up in the new joiner shop to operate the treenail machine, while the

The McNutt patent portable bevel jigsaw mill was similar to the big bevel jigsaw installed on the main floor of Percy & Small's new mill.

Courtesy: Maine Maritime Museum

new blacksmith shop got a 10-HP motor to operate the equipment there.[16]

The new mill, with all of its machinery, needed something more than a 10-HP motor. In fact, the two 40-HP motors originally installed in November 1899 soon proved inadequate to the task, and one was quickly replaced by a 90-HP model. That motor—and its 100-HP successor—powered the machinery on the mill floor and became a legend in its own time among the residents of Bath's south end.

The local electric company had oversold the virtues of electric power, and during peak use, demand began to exceed supply even though the company had invested heavily in new generating capacity. The end result became apparent when sudden heavy loads came on the line. One elderly lady recalled years later that, as a young girl, she would be in the kitchen with her mother getting ready for school at 7:00 A.M. when the kitchen lights would dim to a dull red glow. Her mother's standard reaction would be: "There they go starting the mill at Percy & Small."[17] When the mill-wright threw the switch to turn on the big motor, the load on the line was so great that all the lights in the south end dimmed and already running motors slowed dramatically until Percy & Small's 90-HP monster (and its 100-HP successor) got up to speed.

Dimming lights notwithstanding, electric power possessed two distinct advantages: it was available on demand, and it required little in the way of maintenance and personnel. The system could be brought on line from a cold start in a few minutes, and there was no steam boiler with its associated equipment that required constant supervision and maintenance. The entire system could be shut down during the lunch hour and brought immediately back to full operation when the whistle blew calling the men back to work.

Percy & Small's commitment to electric power never waivered. Their shipyard boasted of a total of 145 HP in 1903, second only to the city's largest industrial establishment, Bath Iron Works.[18] By 1909, as WYOMING took shape on the ways, the yard's electric motor output had risen to 185 HP.[19]

Getting the power from motor to machine required an elaborate system of steel shafts, shaft hangers and bearings, belt wheels, and leather belts. With the mill's two electric motors in the daylight basement and the machinery to be driven on the two floors above, the system in Percy & Small's mill was particularly elaborate. The larger motor supplied the motive force to the three big pieces of machinery on the mill floor, and the smaller motor drove the machinery in the joiner shop. Even today, it is relatively easy to reconstruct the layout of the jackshaft system in the old mill thanks to the marks left by shaft hangers and belt openings.

When one of the motors was operating, its particular transmission system throughout the building was also turning—shafts rumbling and belts slapping. However, each piece of machinery was independently isolated from the system just as the drive wheels of a car are when the transmission is in neutral. When an operator needed to start his machine, he engaged the clutch mechanism which shifted the belt that came from the transmission shaft and pulley from his machine's idler pulley to its drive pulley.[20]

The specific torque and revolutions-per-minute needs of each machine were dealt with by the use of carefully sized power take-off pulleys on the line shafts and drive pulleys on the machines. The Daniel planer's cutting head, for example, needed to rotate at a very high speed, but the planing table carrying the heavy timber through the rotating blades needed power, not speed.[21] If the transmission line shaft was turning at 100 RPM and the planer cutting head needed to turn at 1,000 RPM, the line shaft pulley would need to be ten times the diameter of the drive pulley on the planer. On the other hand, if the plan-

ing table drive mechanism needed only 10 RPM, its drive pulley would need to be ten times the diameter of the take-off pulley on the transmission shaft.

Not surprisingly, the construction of the mill overshadowed two other building projects the partners carried out in the same time frame. A small 20- by 20-foot, clapboarded shop building was also completed in 1899 down near the river on the shipyard's south line. This shop was where the caulking gang stored its gear along with bales of oakum and cotton. It was also a good place for the men to do important "rainy day jobs" such as spinning oakum into the hanks used during caulking; the shop's ambience was assisted by the cheery warmth of a pot-bellied stove and the fragrance of pitch. From the steps of this neat little building Charles H. Oliver, the boss caulker and independent contractor, could keep a judicious eye on his crews at work caulking new vessels and recaulking the old.

Percy & Small also negotiated a land deal at this time with their neighbor—and employee—across Washington Street from the shipyard. Harry Stinson worked at Percy & Small's shipyard at the south end until his death in 1916. A skilled joiner, he also contracted to build several yawl boats for various schooners during the same period. He had purchased the house and approximately one acre of land bounded on the west by Middle Street, north by Marshall Street, and on the east by Washington Street in 1892.[22] Although the Stinson house faced onto Washington Street, it was actually set much closer to Middle Street at its rear. This left a spacious front yard that overlooked Percy & Small's new mill.

It was a potential godsend to the cramped-for-space shipbuilders. And, happily, Stinson was willing to lease his front yard rather than sell it, saving the firm an immediate capital outlay.[23]

Percy & Small then converted more than half of their leasehold into lumber and timber storage. In the spring of 1900, the partners also built a small but well-equipped office for the shipyard on the leasehold's southeast corner. The construction of the office recognized the growing complexity and volume of their shipbuilding business, and the need to place the administrative and purchasing functions of shipbuilding close by the shipyard, rather than keeping them at the downtown office.

The improvements were not cheap. The mill and its equipment constituted the principal investment in shoreside facilities for Percy & Small. It cost them $7,006.74 (+/- $108,000 in 1998), and that did not include the cost of moving the "old" joiner shop.[24] But it became quickly evident that this was money well spent.

BIG-TIME SHIPBUILDING

The impetus behind the extensive and expensive upgrading of the shipyard was a rapidly growing backlog of orders for big—very big—schooners unleashed by the surging economy. Even as the M. D. CRESSY smoked down the ways into the Kennebec, Percy & Small were preparing to lay the keel of another five-master as soon as the building ways were cleared and new keel blocks could be set. Schooner #6, destined to become the HELEN W. MARTIN, was a slightly enlarged version of the just-launched M. D. CRESSY.

And waiting in the wings was Schooner #7 whose planned construction was hinted at in March of the previous year, before work on the CRESSY even began. Hull #7 was not just another schooner, incrementally larger than her predecessors. Intended for Percy & Small's own account, she was to be a six-masted, 3,000-ton giantess.[25] Hull #7, more than anything else, lay behind the shipyard's extensive upgrading during the second half of 1899 and early 1900. Until that work was completed, however, and the MARTIN finally vacated the single building slip, that project was on hold.

The construction of the MARTIN was plagued by delays. Even though the shipyard carpenters stretched her keel and completed the fabrication and erection of all frames by late July (1899), the suppliers of the hard pine (longleaf yellow pine) were late making their deliveries.[26] That delay was compounded by the work in the shipyard involving the removal of the two houses and the relocation and reorientation of the old joiner shop by contractor Wildes.

As the work on the MARTIN and the new mill and joiner shop proceeded simultaneously through the fall, the latter contributed nothing to the progress on the former. In fact, much of the work subsequently done at the shipyard in the modern mill was contracted out for Schooner #6. Most of the prefabricated joinerwork was done at Passmore's shop on Commercial Street, and all the decking was planed at Richardson's mill at Winnegance.[27] Unfortunately, the construction accounts for the MARTIN have not survived, but it is possible that operations involving the sawing and planing of large timbers were done at the nearby Donnell shipyard's steam mill, which had been idle for three years.

However it was done, the work on the schooner moved ahead slowly. In December, #6 came to be known as the HELEN W. MARTIN, whose namesake resided in Gloversville, New York. Gloversville—halfway between Schenectady and Utica in the Mohawk Valley—was pretty far removed from the haunts of the great schooners, but was not far from those of Osceola Cahill, a traveling salesman for the Farley & Harvey Company of Boston.[28] Cahill, who detested his first name and always used the contraction "Ocea," sold a line of damasks, dress goods, and silks to department and dry goods stores from Albany to Buffalo. Handsome, with large brown eyes and curly brown hair, Ocea possessed the best virtues of his calling: he was genial, humorous, kindly, honorable, socially adept, and made legions of friends (and kept them) wherever he went.[29] And he could sell.

While one might think that coal schooners might be a little removed from the cognizance of a dry goods "drummer," Ocea was in fact a Bath boy born and bred. Moreover, his brother Charles Cahill was the jolly and accommodating host of the New Meadows Inn where many a Percy & Small shareholder partook of that hostelry's famous shore dinners at banquets celebrating the latest launching.

Exactly how the Percy & Small–Cahill connection

came about is lost in the mists of time, but come about it did, to the great advantage of both parties. In return for selling shares in Percy & Small schooners, Ocea received a 2.5 percent commission. He started with Schooner #6.[30]

One of his best customers and best friends was John Martin, senior partner in Gloversville's Martin & Naylor Department Store. Mr. Martin was convinced to take a substantial interest in the second Percy & Small five-master, sufficient to extend to him the privilege of naming it after his eldest daughter. Others in the Gloversville area were also encouraged to invest in the new vessel.[31]

It worked. Martin found himself doing the same thing for daughter number two a few years later. In the meantime, a number of others along Cahill's route appeared as more modest investors as various P&S

schooners went down the ways. Robert P. Murphy and John Brooks were two of those swept up in the Cahill net and would subsequently have something to do with future schooner names.

Murphy ran two hotels, one in Albany and one in New York City, that catered to the more respectable "drummer" trade. Along with Martin, he came to be a steady investor in Percy & Small schooners. Eventually he would have a small—for Percy & Small—four-master named for him, Schooner #23. But it was John Brooks, as we shall see in Chapter 8, who gave the partners access to capital west of the Mississippi and the Great Plains.

All in all, Ocea Cahill had a considerable impact on the funding of Percy & Small vessels for the decade beginning in 1899. Unfortunately he did not live to see WYOMING, in part a product of his contacts. He

The HELEN W. MARTIN takes to the Kennebec as spectators crowd the knoll upon which the shipyard's oakum shop sits (right). From the vantage point of the shop's front steps, boss caulker Charles Oliver kept an eagle eye on the progress of his "gangs" of caulkers.

Courtesy: Maine Maritime Museum

was stricken by an attack of appendicitis while tending his customers in the Mohawk Valley in August 1908 and died in a Syracuse hospital at the age of forty-eight.[32]

But that unhappy event was nearly a decade in the future when the HELEN W. MARTIN took to the waters of the Kennebec before two thousand spectators on a raw, damp day in March 1900. Once again the usual experts gave their considered opinions in the columns of the *Bath Times*. As one man expressed it, "She is as near perfection as possible."[33]

As with her near sister, the M. D. CRESSY, she broke little new ground. She shared the same long poop configuration, the use of one patent anchor (hers weighed in at 7,235 pounds, though), and the same five-masted schooner rig. As with any big schooner of her day, the MARTIN consumed large quantities of iron in her construction and rigging; 150,000 pounds went into bolts for fastening alone.

Captain Alexander Ross, formerly of the S. P. BLACKBURN, purchased the master's interest in the new schooner (he would stay with her until he succeeded Linc Jewett in the ELEANOR A. PERCY in 1910). Ross's years in the MARTIN were moderately quiet and profitable. In her first ninety-eight months of service, the schooner paid, after expenses, 80 percent of her original cost.[34] While not an earthshaking

Percy & Small Plan: 1899–1901
D. K. Lee and R. L. Snow

return, it was better than many schooners experienced in the period as competition with the tug-barges and steam colliers heated up.

The MARTIN was not exactly accident-free during the Ross years, but she avoided serious damage. Once she collided in a fog with the British steel steamer MILBRIDGE, causing the latter to limp away from the scene after suffering moderate damage.[35] Several months later, while anchored in the sound off Perth Amboy, New Jersey, she dragged her anchor and went aground on mud flats where she was embarrassingly stranded until the next high tide. But no damage was done, except to pride.

Namesake Helen Martin, her younger sister Grace, and a friend had a chance to visit Helen's schooner two years after the launching as guests of Captain Ross while the MARTIN lay at Curtis Bay, outside of Baltimore. Captain Ross met the young women in Baltimore and brought them to the schooner. Once aboard, the captain placed Helen in charge of the big vessel and all aboard her. Captain *pro tem*, Martin then ordered up a fine meal from the steward and turned to with ladylike gusto. After a long evening of dinner, touring the ship, and answering many questions as to what was what, Captain Ross had to resume command and remind the young ladies that the hour was late and they needed to turn in if they were to catch their train to

Washington and school the next day.[36] It is not known whether Miss Helen W. Martin and the HELEN W. MARTIN ever met again.

Although larger than the M. D. CRESSY, the MARTIN shared the same model and, as it turned out, many of the same structural weaknesses as her older sister. She returned to Percy & Small for extensive repairs in July 1906. The total bill, including the addition of permanent ballast, came to $8,332.06 (+/- $128,000 in 1998).[37] Although there is no detailed record of those repairs surviving today, the breakdown in the *Journal* shows expenses heavily weighted toward structural work.

After Captain Ross left the schooner in 1910, the MARTIN's career suffered a severe jolt when she grounded on Whiskey Ledge off Cape Ann and became badly strained as the tide went out and she rolled back and forth on the rocks. It was feared that she might become a total loss as she was leaking badly, requiring not only her own pumps, but the wrecking pumps aboard assisting tugboats to keep her free of water. But she was hauled off at the next high water and towed into Gloucester, where a diver put a temporary patch over the damaged portion of her hull. She then went on to her destination, unloaded her coal, and then proceeded to Bath for repairs before going into drydock.[38]

In July 1915 the MARTIN had the distinction of being the first vessel sold out of the Percy & Small fleet as part of the World War I sell-off. The price was good at the time—$60,000 (+/- $750,000 in 1998)—nearly 60 percent of her cost new, even

Osceola "Ocea" Cahill (ca. 1860–1908), dry goods salesman and Percy & Small's extraordinary schooner promoter.
Courtesy: Captain W. J. Lewis Parker, USCG, Ret.

though she was a tired fifteen years of age and beginning to show it.[39] As it turned out, however, she was due to have a few adventures that were the stuff of great sea stories.

The new owner, Irby Harris & Company of New York, chartered her to carry 5,800 bales of cotton to Archangel, Russia. It was a long voyage—forty-eight days—that took the big schooner with American flags painted on her long black hull around Norway's North Cape, past Murmansk, past the Kola Peninsula, and into the White Sea.[40] The MARTIN may have been the only great schooner to ever sail this route which, a quarter century later, constituted one of the most dangerous sea voyages in history—the Murmansk Run.

Having safely arrived, the next problem was to discharge her cotton cargo and stow a cargo of timber, saw logs, and mine shore timbers before the harbor and the White Sea froze over in October. She did get clear in good time and reportedly sailed for New York.[41]

The HELEN W. MARTIN never reached that port, if she was ever headed there. Instead, while sailing across the North Sea on 18 November, she hit a floating mine, one of the more common hazards in the war zone. Although she was heavily damaged, the MARTIN floated on her cargo of timber and logs, allowing rescue vessels to tow her to Aldeburgh on the Suffolk coast the same day. The next day she was taken in charge by a big tug and towed to Greenhithe on the Thames below London.[42]

Five months after the mine incident, the MARTIN

was put up for sale at an auction in London. When the bidding only reached £4,350 (+/- $20,000), she was withdrawn from the sale and continued to languish unrepaired for fifteen more months.[43] At last, in July 1917, the battered schooner was purchased by a Swedish concern—AB Svenska Konstgodningsoch Svavelsyrefabrikerna—based in Malmö. They renamed her FENIX, an appropriate if premature name, for there was yet one more hitch. British authorities refused to allow her to be transferred to Swedish registry or to sail for fear she might be used by the neutral Swedes to trade with the German enemy.

Finally, in August 1918, she was transferred to the Swedish flag with an interim certificate. She was then towed to Halmstad on Sweden's southwest coast where, at last, the mine damage was made good and she resumed service. Thirteen months later, she received her full Swedish registration, becoming the largest schooner to ever fly the Swedish flag.[44]

FENIX, ex-HELEN W. MARTIN, was not in good shape by 1918–19. Her long hull had developed a distinct hog years before which had not been improved by the grounding, fully loaded, off Gloucester; the long voyage to Archangel across the notoriously turbulent North Atlantic, Norwegian Sea, and Barents Sea; the shock and damage of the mine explosion; and the nearly three years of minimal maintenance while laying unrepaired at Greenhithe.

When FENIX sailed from West Hartlepool in ballast bound for Baltimore in October 1919, the buzzards came home to roost. She hadn't gone far when increasing winds caused the schooner to pitch and roll

heavily. Seams started and she began to rapidly take on water. With both the steam pumps and hand pumps working continuously, the hard-pressed crew was barely able to keep up with the leaks. Two days out, the crew and mates came aft and announced to the captain that they refused to proceed with the vessel to Baltimore until she had gone into port, been surveyed, and received the necessary repairs. She was towed into Gravesend, anchored, and a survey convened.[45]

The subsequent report revealed a vessel with considerable "keel camber"—a nice way of saying hogged—and scarfs opened in the keelson from $7/8$ inches to $3/8$ inches. Curiously, the surveyors found little sign of straining, with just a couple of places forward where the caulking appeared to be started. They had no objection to the schooner proceeding to southern Norway, Sweden, or Denmark with a cargo of coke, but they insisted if the FENIX was to continue to the States she would need to be drydocked, have her bottom caulking renewed, and be extra fastened with bolts on the keelson and along the bilge ceiling.

FENIX finally set sail from London during the first week of January 1920 with 2,150 tons of coke bound for Kalundborg, a port on the west side of the Danish island of Sjaelland. She never arrived, having gone ashore in heavy seas on 14 January three miles west of Hojens Lighthouse at the northern point of the Jutland peninsula. All hands got off in her boats and made it to shore safely, but the FENIX, ex-HELEN W. MARTIN, left her bones on the shores of the Skagerrak.[46]

A SIX-MASTER OR TWO

The M. D. CRESSY had yet to be laid down when the *New York Maritime Register* announced in March 1898: "A six-masted schooner, for the coal trade, will be built by Percy & Small. She will have a cargo capacity of 4,000 tons and will be 300 feet overall. She will cost $90,000."[47] The maritime trade paper was correct on only one point: Percy & Small planned to build a six-master. When built, the actual

six-master measured 301.6 feet on the keel, measured out at 3,401 gross tons, carried cargoes averaging over 5,500 tons, and cost $157,576.96 (+/- $2.4 million in 1998). Finally, it took two years before the six-master's keel was stretched at Percy & Small's shipyard on the banks of the Kennebec.

Fourteen months after the above premature announcement, the *New York Maritime Register*

A Schooner's Progress: #1

The decorative flag hoists, the pristine whiteness of the sails and the taut towline all suggest that the HELEN W. MARTIN is being towed out of the Kennebec River on her maiden passage in March 1900. The puff of steam coming from the hull below the foremast is from the schooner's hoisting engine which has just been used to raise the sails.

Courtesy: Maine Maritime Museum

A Schooner's Progress: #2

Aground on the mud flats of the Arthur Kill near Perth Amboy, the HELEN W. MARTIN reveals the form derived from the model of the S. P. BLACKBURN. Barely three years old, the MARTIN has yet to reveal the signs of structural weakness that plagued some of Percy & Small's earliest five-masters.

Courtesy: Paul C. Morris

A Schooner's Progress: #3

Battered by age, neglect, and a mine in the North Sea, FENIX, ex-HELEN W. MARTIN, lies at Halmstad, Sweden, awaiting extensive repairs in 1918. The mine-caused damage to her hull is faintly visible below the mainmast forward to her cutwater. Her sweeping sheer has become a distant memory.

Courtesy: Maine Maritime Museum

A Schooner's Progress: #4
The repaired FENIX, ex-HELEN W. MARTIN, lies at anchor at Malmö, Sweden, circa 1919. Built
on the Kennebec, named for the daughter of an upstate New York retail merchant, the weary
vessel had become the largest schooner ever to be registered under the Swedish flag

Courtesy: Captain W. J. Lewis Parker, USCG, Ret.

A Schooner's Progress: #5
The last voyage of the FENIX, ex-HELEN W. MARTIN, from London to Kalundborg (Denmark) with 2,150 tons of coke
came to an abrupt end near the Hojens Lighthouse on the northern tip of the Jutland peninsula in January 1920.

Courtesy: Maine Maritime Museum

announced that Holly M. Bean, shipbuilder of Camden, Maine, was to build a six-master for John G. Crowley, a major competitor of Percy & Small's in the coal shipping business.[48] Thus the stage was set for the big contest: who would lay claim to title of builder of the first six-masted schooner?

Holly Bean had been in the shipbuilding business since 1877, far longer than Sam Percy and Frank Small. In fact, by the end of 1893, Bean had produced no fewer than twenty-nine schooners, although only one exceeded 1,000 GRT. Then, in 1899, Bean joined the five-master gold rush by constructing two big ones, the 1,993-GRT JENNIE FRENCH POTTER and the 2,454-GRT JOHN B. PRESCOTT. In short, he already possessed substantial shipbuilding experience and a plant with the capability of building two vessels simultaneously.

Percy & Small certainly started out in the lead, if the *New York Maritime Register* is to be believed, but some significant hurdles had to be overcome before the project became a reality. Capital had to be raised from individual investors—lots of capital—to pay for the proposed schooner. The firm also had to address the severe shortcomings of the shipyard itself, the correction of which required additional capital. As we saw previously, Percy & Small initiated the process of upgrading their shipbuilding plant in the fall of 1899.

In September 1899 the moulds for the proposed six-master were shipped to the timber crews, although the modeling and lofting may have been completed months earlier.[49] It is safe to say, however, that Percy & Small were definitely committed by the late summer to the construction of the big schooner and that probably a significant portion of the financing was pledged if not in hand. It is an open question as to how much the Crowley announcement accelerated Percy & Small plans.

Although timber for Schooner #7 began arriving at the shipyard by January 1900, work had to wait for the MARTIN to be launched, the ways removed and stored, and new keel blocks set before construction could officially start. But there were now additional challenges confronting the firm. It had accepted another contract from J. S. Winslow & Company to deliver a big five-master by the mid-summer of 1900.[50] And with that contract came one other small

question: where was the Winslow schooner, designated Schooner #8, to be built? The building slip was occupied by #6, and once she was launched sometime in the early part of 1900, #7 would take her place. There simply was no place at the Percy & Small shipyard for another schooner.

But there was space to build #8 almost next door at the former Chapman & Flint yard—often called the John McDonald yard. It had lain idle since 1891 and lacked everything in the way of equipment and machinery. But it was only four hundred feet from the new mill, easily accessible to Percy & Small's teamsters and draft horses. Moreover, the McDonald yard had just been purchased by Gardiner G. Deering, one of Bath's longtime schooner builders. Deering and Sam Percy had engaged in a little friendly rivalry back in the days when they built schooners next to each other in the adjoining Morse and Houghton yards, but spent far more time helping each other out than competing. "Gard" Deering, who built principally for his own account, was willing to accommodate Percy & Small's need for more space and agreed to lease his newly acquired shipyard to Percy & Small through July 1900.[51] By December 1899, the hardwood frame for Schooner #8 began arriving from northern Maine.[52]

In late January, Master Builder Willard Hodgkins and Percy & Small may have felt they had bitten off more than they could chew. In their newly refurbished shipyard, a 2,265-GRT five-master (the MARTIN) was being rushed to completion for launching. Meanwhile, timber for their 3,401-GRT six-master was arriving steadily, along with the timber for the 2,663-GRT Winslow five-master they had just laid down at Deering's yard down the street. This was not the leisurely one-ship-a-year pace of the past.

It soon became even less leisurely. Charters were good and appeared to be getting better, with many schooners beginning to pay from 20 to 30 percent annually as the demand for coal in the Northeast exceeded shipping capacity.[53] Eleazer Clark, manager of J. S. Winslow & Company and a man who never passed up an opportunity to make money, wanted yet another schooner—quickly. This vessel, Schooner #9, was to be a smaller version of #8 at the Deering shipyard. So Percy & Small leased the old Reed shipyard, within a quarter mile of their yard, where Daniel O. Blaisdell once built vessels before establishing his own shipyard on their present site.[54] The wheel had now gone full turn.

The Reed yard, however, needed extensive work before it could be used: new piling had to be driven, new bed logs laid. And because it was not quite as convenient to the firm's now well-equipped shops, Percy & Small found it necessary to install some basic machinery along with a 10-HP electric motor.[55]

All of this work constituted too much responsibility for the single master builder, especially as it involved not only three different shipyards but a vessel that would, in months, become the world's largest schooner. It may also have been that Sam Percy and Willard Hodgkins were not exactly warm friends, and Captain Sam was availing himself of the opportunity to bring in a possible successor.

Miles M. Merry was one of the most experienced wooden shipbuilders in Bath and, for that matter, the entire country. He was also an authority on the construction of very large wooden ships, having been involved in the building of Sewall's "Big Four" and master builder of record on the last and largest of the quartet, and the largest wooden sailing vessel in the world at that time, ROANOKE.

Born in Damariscotta in 1844, Miles went to work at the age of twelve and moved to Bath to work in the shipyards four years later. In 1866 he became a master builder at that burgeoning nursery of shipbuilders, Goss, Sawyer & Packard when he was only twenty-two years of age.

For the next quarter century, Merry worked for Captain Goss, then moved on to William Rogers's shipyard before arriving at the Arthur Sewall

Company shipyard on Front Street. With the completion of the ROANOKE, however, the Sewall firm abandoned wooden shipbuilding altogether and Miles Merry found himself the victim of technological obsolescence. What he did during the next seven years is not clear, although it is likely that he freelanced his skills to shipyards up and down the coast. Then he came to work for Sam Percy and Frank Small. It was one of the most significant events in the history of the firm.

Schooner #7, the big six-master, and Schooner #9 at the Reed yard were assigned to Miles Merry to supervise. Hodgkins was to look after #8 at the old McDonald yard, now owned by Gard Deering. The latter project was the most important because Deering wanted his shipyard back by a certain date so that he could build his next schooner. This meant that Percy & Small had to apply maximum resources to the completion of that schooner, even at the expense of their big six-master. This was clearly evident during May and June when double crews of plankers worked feverishly on the Winslow schooner, while work on the six-master ground to a virtual halt.[56] Even so, Percy & Small were able to lay down the keel of the six-master first, beating Holly Bean's six-master by roughly two weeks.

In the end, however, Bean won the contest with the 2,970-GRT GEORGE W. WELLS, launched 14 August 1900—two months earlier than the larger Percy & Small schooner, ELEANOR A. PERCY. Not surprisingly, the time difference was roughly equal to the period construction on the PERCY had been virtually suspended to facilitate completion of #8. It was one of the few times the WELLS came out ahead of the PERCY.

A BEEHIVE OF ACTIVITY

Throughout the spring, summer, and fall, the south end neighborhood around Percy & Small hummed with activity as the firm appeared determined to build schooners in as many shipyards as it could find. At McDonald's, P&S Schooner #8 was being rushed to completion to make way for the first of Gardiner Deering's new schooners.

A new model by Fred Rideout, the Winslow schooner bid fair to become the largest vessel in the substantial fleet of Portland-based schooners. Measuring 270 feet on the keel and 289.2 feet on deck, her tonnage was calculated at 2,663 GRT. The five-master employed the popular long poop deck arrangement that characterized most great schooners along with a sweeping sheer that left many an authority on the schooner aesthetic proclaiming her the most handsome of all five-masters.[57] She certainly put a crimp in the assumption that functionality and ugly were synonymous.

The new schooner, named for William C. Carnegie, the nephew of the famous rags-to-riches steelmaker, incorporated a few innovations in her construction and outfit. She became the first of the great schooners to be equipped with two stockless anchors, each weighing 8,500 pounds. And she became the first vessel built by Percy & Small to incorporate steel strapping in order to stiffen her long hull. In her case, twenty-five steel straps—4- by ⅝-inch—ran diagonally from the upper clamps on each side to the short floor timbers.[58] The strapping was, in fact, technically mandatory according to the American Bureau of Shipping (ABS) rules on vessels whose depth-to-length and breadth-to-length ratios exceeded certain parameters, while tonnage determined the size of the straps. The ABS established the operative ratio (depth:length) to be 1:10, but permitted a certain amount of flexibility in applying the rules when the builders used larger scantlings (dimensions) for structural timbers than called for in their scantling tables.

The CARNEGIE's launching became entwined with Bath's plans for the Old Home Week celebration, a statewide promotion designed to attract emigrant Mainers back to their home turf. And no city or town in Maine could match the enthusiasm and booster spirit that fired the imaginations of the local planners. Visiting battleships, a water carnival, grand parades, balloon ascensions, and a fireworks spectacular were to be backdrops for the launching of the schooner, briefly to claim title as the largest in the world. The

A massive Old Home Week crowd has gathered in anticipation of the launching of the WILLIAM C. CARNEGIE from the McDonald/Deering shipyard just south of Percy & Small, 11 August 1900. Built in this yard because Percy & Small's single set of ways was already taken (the frame of the ELEANOR A. PERCY rises in the background at the left of the photo), the CARNEGIE's launching attracted an estimated 10,000 people on the hottest day of the year.

Courtesy: David Kenney

A group of stylish young adult spectators poses for a photo in the hot midday
sun on one of the CARNEGIE's hatch covers before the scheduled launching.
The shipyard's safety inspector has apparently missed the timber scrap with the
two spikes sticking point up in the foreground.

Stinson Brothers Photo, courtesy of Bath Historical Society

launching was an event that would attract people from far and wide who would not otherwise come to Bath, including Portland's shipping, business, and social elite, Boothbay's many friends and relatives of the prospective captain, Mitchell Reed, and perhaps even the namesake himself, nephew of the fabulously wealthy and philanthropic Andrew Carnegie. Even better was the fact that it gave Bath a shipbuilding event of stature that offset some, if not all, of the publicity emanating from rival community Camden which was gleefully trumpeting the launching of THE WORLD'S FIRST SIX-MASTER, set for 14 August.

There had to be, of course, one small problem. Sam Percy was delighted to oblige and delay the launching for several days, but it wasn't his shipyard. Owner Gard Deering was anxious to get to work on the first of two schooners he planned to build there, so the celebration planners needed his permission to delay the launching until Saturday, the 11th of August, the day the celebration in Bath was scheduled

to reach its crescendo. So the planning committee "waited upon Mr. Deering this noon and he very kindly consented . . . ." [59]

The formal schedule of events in Bath was impressive, extending over five days from Wednesday through Monday. But Saturday was *The Day*. In the morning, battleships KENTUCKY and MASSACHU-SETTS—the former billed as the "largest and most powerful"—were scheduled to arrive, steaming majestically up the Long Reach to anchor off the city's waterfront. At noon, "the largest five-masted schooner ever built," would then go overboard, followed by open houses at all the wooden and steel shipbuilding plants in Bath. Saturday's events were to conclude in the evening with a grand water carnival and marine pageant, followed by a $1,000 (+/- $15,000 in 1998) display of fireworks. [60]

"The best laid schemes o' mice an' men gang oft a-gley," and Bath's Saturday celebration was no exception. First, the Navy canceled KENTUCKY and

The reluctant WILLIAM C. CARNEGIE the day after she refused to slide. A crew of Percy & Small
workmen and Master Builder Miles M. Merry labored all day Sunday under the big schooner to ready
her for the second—and successful—attempt on 13 August.

Stinson Brothers Photo, courtesy of Bath Historical Society

MASSACHUSETTS on the grounds that, on second thought, the big KENTUCKY's draft was perilously close to the controlling depth of the Kennebec River's channel. In the end, in response to anguished wails from Bath, the battleship TEXAS of Spanish-American War fame was substituted.

Then there was the launching. The event had been well advertised throughout the state, and the celebration planners looked forward to a huge influx of visitors. They got their wish.

The weather was sunny and hot. The morning trains from Portland were crammed: J. S. Winslow, Mrs. Winslow, Miss Grace Winslow—sponsor designate—her sisters, and a huge party of Portland dignitaries arrived on the early train. After all, Master Builder Willard Hodgkins had warned one and all to

be on the scene by 11:45 A.M. if they wanted to see the giant slide.

As the morning advanced, Bath's south end took on the appearance of an enormous summer garden party as hundreds, then thousands, of spectators gathered to view the launching. Ladies attired in fashionable white summer dresses and carrying parasols, gentlemen in straw boaters, blazers, and white trousers, mixed with sailors and shipyard workers in work clothes, local urchins, and even pickpockets who knew their market well.[61] The waters off the shipyard were equally crowded as innumerable sail, steam, and rowing craft crammed with spectators joined the tug KNICKERBOCKER for the launching.

At 12:20 P.M., the TEXAS rounded Doubling Point into the Reach and was greeted by the CARNEGIE's steam whistle; the band playing for the launching struck up the "Star Spangled Banner." After the battleship passed upriver, however, the launching spectators—some ten thousand according to the *Bath Times*—began to get impatient as the scheduled launching hour receded into the distance and the big schooner just sat there.

But things were happening. In the bow of the reluctant schooner, Miss Grace Winslow was overcome by the heat. She remained bedridden for many weeks thereafter. Underneath the schooner, Willard Hodgkins and his crew labored manfully to put her over, but even with all the keel blocks split out, she refused to slide. There would be no launching, and ten thousand spectators went home dissatisfied. It was Captain Sam Percy's worst nightmare.

The failure to launch was, of course, traceable to the unusually hot weather which caused the grease to squeeze out from between the fixed ways and the sliders. Nonetheless, it was small consolation for a man who had enormous pride in his firm to see it fail so miserably before a statewide audience.

The results were immediately apparent: Willard Hodgkins never worked for Percy & Small again. In fact, his next job was in Mystic, Connecticut.[62] In the meantime, it was put about that he was ill and unable to overhaul the ways for another launching attempt,

so the task was assigned to Miles M. Merry.[63]

All day Sunday, Merry and a large crew of men labored to set everything to rights for another launching attempt. They had to wedge up the schooner and set her keel on temporary keel blocks, overhaul the fixed and sliding ways, and then rebuild the cradle and poppets. By the end of a very long day, Merry informed Percy that the launching could go ahead the next day at high tide. The captain got the word out and a sizable crowd reappeared for the event—some no doubt anticipating another disaster—including a smaller, but respectable crowd of Portland luminaries. Miss Grace did not appear to do the honors this time, and the privilege of smashing a bottle of American champagne over the bow went to her sister Elizabeth.

Wedging-up commenced at 1:00 P.M. and one-half hour later the schooner stirred, gathered way, and "went down the ways like a race horse and made a picturesque plunge and bow."[64]

Three months and thirteen days shy of the ninth anniversary of her launching, the CARNEGIE went ashore in thick weather and a gale one-half mile from the Moriches Life Saving Station on the south shore of Long Island, New York. Coal laden, she did not survive this experience, although Captain Reed and his crew did.

SCHOONER #7: ELEANOR A. PERCY

Percy & Small did not complete the first six-master (although not by much), but they did build the largest. And in the next decade, they also built the most, as the six-masted schooner became synonymous with Percy & Small.[65]

Schooner #7 was one of two vessels the partners named after members of their own families. The fact that Sam Percy was the senior in the firm no doubt secured for him the privilege to go first in selecting the appropriate name. Daughter Eleanor had already christened Percy & Small's first schooner—the CHARLES P. NOTMAN—when she was selected to be the namesake for Bath's first six-master. She would be seventeen-and-a-half years old when it was launched and was saluta-

torian of Bath High School's Class of 1902.

The statistics for her namesake were impressive, so impressive that they reigned supreme against all challenges until 1908. The ELEANOR, as she was often referred to in her home town, had a gross tonnage that measured 14 percent more than her Camden rival (3,401 vs. 2,970). From a payload point of view, the PERCY easily carried 5,500 tons, 10 percent more than her rival, the WELLS. In fact, during 1908, the PERCY once carried 6,115 tons of coal from Newport News to Boston, a load second only to that carried by her younger stablemate, WYOMING.[66]

No two schooners were ever exactly alike, even those built from the same model and moulds by the same builder. But the ELEANOR A. PERCY offers an excellent example of the great schooner in its six-masted manifestation (and to a lesser degree, its five-masted manifestation) during the first decade of the new century.[67]

The PERCY measured 323.5 feet on her main (tonnage) deck from the aft side of the rudderpost to the aft side of the stem. Her length overall, after edge of taffrail to forward side of the bow chock, extended 347 feet. Her beam was a hefty 50 feet, and registered depth of hold 24.8 feet. A little quick math shows that the depth-to-length ratio was 1:13.04, a figure that put her hull well into the region where steel strapping for reinforcing the hull was in order.

And reinforced she was, but on a different plan than the CARNEGIE. A riveted steel plate, 1 inch by 28 inches by 290 feet, was laid between the third and fourth keelsons and bolted through and through with $1^{1}/4$-inch iron every 9 inches. There was also a pair of parallel steel straps ($^{3}/4$ inch by 12 inches), 6 feet apart, let into the outside of the frame on each side and running fore and aft, forming a simple truss. Variations on this truss pattern were subsequently tried with the six-master ADDIE M. LAWRENCE and the five-master ELIZABETH PALMER, but with the strapping on the inside of the frames.

Once again, the popular long poop deck layout was employed with the break occurring just ahead of the mainmast. The 249-foot sweep of the poop was broken by six hatches and two deckhouses, with the largest being the after house measuring 29 feet by 34 feet. Both houses were set into the deck and actually rested on the main deck, 4.5 feet below.

Captain Linc Jewett and, on occasion, his wife Annie, resided in the large after house. Their cabin—at

Launched unrigged to clear the building ways, the ELEANOR A. PERCY was rigged while afloat alongside the shipyard wharf. Also visible is the neighborhood in the immediate vicinity of the shipyard. Moving from left to right on the river side of Washington Street are: the W. T. Donnell carriage house and residence; the barely visible cupola and roof of the Powers barn; the shipyard oakum shop, mill, paint and treenail shop and diagonally to its rear, the Charles E. Hyde residence. The small building immediately across Washington Street from the paint and treenail shop was the shipyard office. The house in the right center foreground was shipwright Eliakim McCabe's residence, and the faintly visible gable on the extreme right is one of the two houses Percy & Small moved up from the shipyard during the previous year. Most of the land on the river side of the street visible in the picture is now part of Maine Maritime Museum.

Stinson Brothers Photo, courtesy of Bath Historical Society

the after end of the house—was finished in oak and mahogany with a Brussels carpet on the floor. A built-in bed, large oak roll-top desk, oak bureau, oak-framed mirror, and two chairs rounded out the furnishings. Across the companionway, elegantly finished in highly varnished cypress, were the bathroom facilities, including a separate head with a water closet, and a bathroom that was equipped with a copper bathtub, sink, and medicine cabinet. Immediately ahead of the Jewetts' cabin was the after cabin (a shipboard version of the parlor) which was 13 1/2 feet square. It was furnished with a store-bought, three-piece parlor set and a box couch. Opening off the sides of the after cabin were three small guest staterooms finished in oak and cypress. The forward cabin served as the dining room (11 feet by 11.5 feet), with the first mate's stateroom on the port side, the steward's pantry on the starboard side, and the forward companionway opening off it. The house was heated by steam radiators fed from the donkey boiler in the forward house.

The midship house (15 feet by 21 feet) contained the galley, a small mess room, and the second mate's and cook's staterooms. It, too, was heated by steam radiators as well as by the large Shipmate range. The interior of the house was finished in North Carolina pine.

The forward house contained the mechanical heart of the vessel—and of all great schooners. Berths for ten seamen were crammed into one side of the 26- by 29-foot house—still called the forecastle—along with their table and benches. The other side of the house, however, contained the 52-inch (diameter) vertical boiler, a 9- by 10-inch steam hoisting engine, steam feed and circulating pumps, feed water tank, and coil condenser. The engineer's stateroom was conveniently located off the engineroom. A steam wrecking pump capable of discharging 440 gallons per minute over the side was located immediately below the forward house on a platform deck. Steam was also piped to a second, 6- by 8-inch hoisting engine abaft the driver mast (number 5) and a second wrecking pump (295 GPM) located below it on the main deck.

The hoisting engines made the raising of sail and anchors possible on these giants with their small crews. The lower sails were all 2/0 duck, the heaviest sail canvas in the world. Dry, it was backbreakingly heavy (+/-

4 ounces per square foot); wet, it was worse than trying to hoist pig lead. But with the use of strategically placed snatch blocks, halyards for each sail could be led to the clutch-controlled gypsy heads on each side of the forward deckhouse or the after hoisting engine house. A few turns of the halyard around the gypsy head, pulled taught, and up went the sail.

The forward hoisting engine could also be clutched into the #12 Hyde brake windlass (snugly ensconced under the topgallant forecastle) via a messenger chain arrangement. There was no other way that ten men could have raised one—not to mention two—four-ton anchor (plus chain) in anything approaching reasonable time. Among other things keeping the big windlass company under the topgallant forecastle deck was the crew's head, another water closet.

Before the decade ended, the newest and largest great schooners added something else to the engine-room. A steam-powered electric generator became the new standard for equipment to provide power for searchlights, navigation lights, and cabin lighting, consigning smoky kerosene lamps and lanterns to backup status. In the fullness of time, many older schooners, including the PERCY, had the generators retrofitted. Some would even acquire newfangled radio gear.[68]

When the ELEANOR A. PERCY was launched, young Eleanor christened the vessel with a bouquet of roses and pinks cast over the bow. Although a fair-sized party was aboard for the launching, the decks were cluttered with the schooner's as-yet-unstepped masts, and below decks much work remained to be completed. But the single shipbuilding ways needed to be cleared so that the next Percy & Small schooner could be laid down. The PERCY would have to be finished as she lay alongside the shipyard. She would be one of only three schooners launched by the firm that was not virtually ready for sea when she first took to the water.

Thirty-six days after launching, the ELEANOR A. PERCY—flags flying—left the shipyard with Captain Percy and five friends aboard as guests to see her off. They returned to Bath on the tugs after Captain Linc set sail near Fort Popham. As she passed Popham one local reported, "the craft had every sail up and presented a beautiful sight."[69] Bound for Baltimore or Newport News, she was unchartered but hopeful.

Her first trip with coal suggested she might not enjoy a long career of untrammeled success. Loaded with 5,514 tons of coal destined for Boston (the largest coal cargo yet consigned to that port), she made reasonable time, but then came to grief while anchored in Boston's outer harbor while awaiting a berth alongside to unload. Swinging on her anchor chain, she struck a ledge and pounded several times before the anchor was hove in and she was moved to less perilous surroundings. In the process, she lost her 8,500-pound stockless anchor due to a flawed shackle.[70] The problems didn't end there. As soon as she was unloaded, she was moved to a Boston dry-dock where an inspection of her bottom showed a loss of most of her false keel, a considerable loss to her main keel, and a number of bottom planks badly chafed where she had hit the ledge. By the time the drydocking and repairs were toted up, it is likely that she lost money on her first trip with cargo.[71]

There was more to come.

On 29 June 1901, at 10:15 P.M., 5.5 miles SSE of Cape Cod Light, the ELEANOR A. PERCY—Lincoln W. Jewett, commanding—and the GEORGE W. WELLS—Arthur Crowley, commanding—met, up close and personal. The PERCY was proceeding towards Boston with 5,500 tons of coal and the WELLS was bound to

Riggers working for Frank Palmer make a few last adjustments to the ELEANOR A. PERCY's rigging before she departs for the coal ports. While she missed being the first six-master launched in 1900, she was definitely the largest until surpassed by the Percy & Small-built EDWARD B. WINSLOW in 1908. Compare the size of the rigger standing on the martingale backstays clinging to the martingale with the size of that martingale. Two other riggers are working above him and a fourth rigger is visible partway up the main topmast. The vessel being framed is the MARTHA P. SMALL.

Courtesy: William H. Bunting

the southward, light. The winds were light and variable, probably westerly, the sky was clear, and visibility was good. Yet, the only oceangoing six-masted sailing vessels in the world attempted to cross the exact same point on the earth's surface at the identical moment. The results were predictable.

With a grinding crash the PERCY bit into the WELLS's portside abreast of her mizzenmast. Even though the PERCY was making little more than steerage way at the moment of contact, the shock was terrific. Her bow cut through the waterways, lock strakes, decking, frame futtocks, ceiling, and planking to within three feet of the WELLS's light waterline. The PERCY's jibboom and bowsprit carried away, but not before they had cut a huge chunk out of WELLS's mizzenmast. The shock of the collision also crushed the WELLS's midship deckhouse, heaved up the deck, temporarily jammed her steering gear, gave her a two-foot bulge in her starboard side, and left the flukes of the PERCY's new stockless anchor imbedded in her battered hull.

Having delivered the blow head-on, the PERCY suffered far less spectacular damage. Of course her headgear had carried away, but the most serious damage was done to her stem and bow planking. In view of the long-held concern about the ease with which the great schooners shed their masts, it should be noted that no masts or topmasts went by the board even though the WELLS's mizzenmast had a third of its diameter gouged out by the PERCY's jibboom and bowsprit.[72]

It is easy to imagine the momentary confusion, even panic, that must have swept through the crews of both schooners. But it was soon ascertained that there were, miraculously, no injuries and neither vessel was in danger of sinking. The conversation between Captains Jewett and Crowley at that point was, unfortunately, unrecorded, but they obviously discussed the collision and agreed on a course of action vis-à-vis the press. In the meantime, they devoted their energies to getting their battered vessels into Boston under sail.

Both schooners arrived in Boston Harbor Sunday morning and were soon swarming with reporters. Crowley left no doubt as to whom *he* thought was the guilty party, although he carefully avoided making any direct accusations:

We were struck on the port bow by the six-master ELEANOR A. PERCY at about 10:00 on Saturday night. Just who is to blame I do not care to say now. I did not run into anyone, as you can see by a glance at that cavern [the large hole in the port side]. We had a head wind. The PERCY had a fair wind. Further comment I do not care to make.[73]

Linc Jewett, on the other hand, placed the most charitable of assessments on the whole affair:

Accidents will happen on the best regulated ships and I suppose we must get our share, as well as the others. The whole trouble was that we did not see each other in time to get clear, that is all. I am not trying to blame anyone, for under the conditions I do not, at the present moment, know with whom the fault lies.[74]

How exactly did these two schooners fall afoul of each other in light airs and on a clear night while both were under the command of highly experienced captains? There is no definitive answer, but there are some clues that suggest the cause.

It was clear, but dark, with only starlight for illumination. The wind was light and its direction variable according to local conditions. One report has Captain Jewett below just before the collision, with the mate on deck.[75] The WELLS was sailing close-hauled, probably on a starboard tack, and the PERCY was probably on a port tack although she was in the process of tacking due to the shift in local winds.[76] In the meantime, the WELLS's course took her across the bows of the PERCY.

It is probable that whoever had control of the PERCY either did not see the WELLS (being involved in bringing the PERCY about) or seriously misjudged distance, course, and speed of the Camden-built vessel. It is even possible that the command to turn the PERCY into the wind may have been a tardy attempt to take way off the big schooner and to avoid a collision.

Captain Percy, who left for Boston as soon as he learned of the collision, soon reached his own conclusions concerning cause and fault. After reviewing the situation with Captains Jewett and Crowley, and J. G. Crowley (managing owner of the WELLS), he

Collisions at sea can ruin your whole day, but the GEORGE W. WELLS managed to survive her meeting with the ELEANOR A. PERCY off Cape Cod, if just barely. The damage does not look too severe here, but the heaved-up deck is clearly visible and the Camden-built six-master required extensive rebuilding.

Courtesy: Maine Maritime Museum

The real extent of the damage was revealed as the WELLS was repaired. Virtually the entire portside midship section down to her light waterline was replaced along with numerous deck beams, the midship house, and the mizzenmast (the replacement mizzenmast is on the pier).

Courtesy: Maine Maritime Museum

arranged for the latter's vessel to be towed to Bath to be repaired at Percy & Small's expense.

The WELLS arrived on the end of a towline on 5 July and was tied up at the leased Reed shipyard, where Percy & Small were building yet another schooner for J. S. Winslow. The wounded six-master immediately became a focal point of great interest. One curious visitor was William F. Palmer, Boston's burgeoning schooner mogul who, characteristically, offered his opinion: "I looked over the WELLS while in Bath Saturday, where they were cutting out the broken timber, and found her much worse than one would suppose. She has 13 deck beams broken off, and, altogether, she is in a bad plight."[77]

The PERCY, looking appropriately hangdog without her headgear, soon joined the crippled WELLS, docking at Percy & Small shipyard proper on 12 July after unloading her cargo in Boston. Bath now had the biggest and best tourist attraction in Maine: the two largest—and the only two oceangoing—six-masted schooners in the world gracing the city waterfront. People flocked from far and wide to see the wounded giants, often jamming the "cars" into Bath, especially on weekends.

The amount of work required to repair the WELLS and the PERCY was prodigious, especially on the former. Essentially, the shipyard carpenters under the direction of Miles M. Merry rebuilt a 30-foot-long section of the WELLS's hull from the light waterline to the poop deck. The work entailed cutting out the broken and damaged structural timbers and planking—including using a double team of horses to pull out the PERCY's broken anchor firmly lodged in the WELLS's hull—and eliminating the starboard bulge. The shipbuilders renewed the portside frames to the lower deck along with ceiling, waterways, and lock strakes, all well bolted. They removed and replaced ten main deck beams, thirteen poop deck beams, laid new decks on both, and fastened new hanging knees under each beam. A new midship house, new mizzenmast, twenty-eight strakes of planking on the port side and nine on the starboard side, not to mention rerigging and recaulking as required, rounded out the heavy work.[78]

The PERCY also got a thorough going over. Merry replaced thirty-one strakes of planking on the port

bow and thirty-two on the starboard bow that had been broken or badly scarred in the collision. A 36-foot piece of stem was also replaced, along with the bowsprit and jibboom, and two new catheads were installed. She sailed from Bath on 14 August, and the WELLS left a week later.

The financial reckoning for that little adventure was not long in coming. The total cost for repairs and towage to Bath for both vessels came to $21,126.35 (+/- $325,000 in 1998).[79] The bill for the WELLS made up 81 percent of the total cost, or $17,160.33 (+/- $264,250 in 1998).

Liability for the costs lay with the collective ownership of the PERCY in proportion to their share of the vessel. Unlike corporations where stockholder liability was limited to the value of each individual holding, traditional vessel ownership involved the notion that liability was limited only by the individual's total share of the ownership. Percy & Small were, therefore, not on the hook for the total damages, but only in proportion to their ownership—$10/64$ at the time of the collision.

The partners had two options for paying the bills. If the debt was not very large, they could choose to pay it off, along with interest, out of the vessel's earnings while the managing owners carried the debt. This was the most common method the partners used when various vessels they managed briefly fell into the red. But if the amount involved large sums, they could assess each owner an amount to pay the debt in proportion to his ownership. In the end Sam Percy and Frank Small chose both courses. Each $1/64$ was assessed $300.00 (+/- $4,620 in 1998), bringing in $19,200. The balance, nearly $2,000, was paid out of the accrued freight receipts—mostly from that June voyage.

Percy & Small were on the hook for $3,000 (+/- $46,200 in 1998), thanks to their $10/64$ ownership. It is not known whether they had any insurance on these shares—share owners could, at their own option, purchase insurance—although insurance never paid the total loss. However, Percy & Small had one advantage: the firm, wearing its shipyard hat, benefited from the repairwork brought to it by its shipping arm. In fact, it benefited to the tune of $2,338.93 (+/- $36,000 in 1998) in the form of the commissions that it normally took on all repairwork—its profit margin. Annoying, embarrassing, and even costly, the collision between the PERCY and the WELLS was, however, not life threatening.

The collision assessment on the PERCY obviously affected the owners' return in the years that followed. She was not one of their best money earners during the fifteen years they owned her, which may explain why it took Percy & Small nine years before they built another six-master for their own account.[80] On the other hand, she did not experience any more expensive disasters while serving under the P&S house flag.

SHIPYARD FINE TUNING: 1901–1909

When the ELEANOR A. PERCY returned to her natal shipyard the first time—in disgrace—following her completion, a major change in the shipyard's layout was well under way. Percy & Small had successfully negotiated a deal with Frank Powers to purchase his mother's house and land that lay on the north boundary of the shipyard.[81] This purchase allowed the firm to consolidate its shipbuilding operations at one enlarged shipyard convenient to its shops and storage facilities rather than being spread out across Bath's south end. The Powers lot provided ample room for a second, longer set of building ways, and provided valuable new working and storage space.

There were a few things that needed to be done before the addition would be functional, however. The Powers lot included a public right-of-way along its north boundary with the W. T. Donnell property. As the Powers property was rather narrow, it would seriously subtract from the usable space. But Sam Percy simply ignored the right-of-way in the end with the connivance of city hall and had a portion of the new building ways plunked right down on it.[82] In fact, the north side of the ways was so close to the Donnell property line that when very large schooners were built on the north ways, the staging on that side had to be erected on the Donnell property.[83]

The other question revolved about the Powers house. Sam Percy and Frank Small were too much the good Maine Yankees to pay cash money for something and then just throw it away. The answer they came up with put them into the housing business for more years than the firm was in shipbuilding.

Remember the two houses sold to Fred Tobey, Sam's brother-in-law, in 1899 to make way for the new mill? Well, now the firm bought them back, along with the Marshall Street lot upon which they sat. And Sam Percy also bought additional abutting lots on Middle Street extension.[84] Then the two peripatetic residences were picked up and moved one more time to adjoining lots on the west side of Middle Street extension, where they have remained ever since.

The Powers house was then moved up the hill to the corner lot on Marshall Street just vacated by the two smaller houses. There it also found its final resting place, converted by Percy & Small into a double house. The three residences were subsequently rented to shipyard employees.

The purchase of the Powers property did not result in any major shipyard construction projects, a point that underlines the successful program to improve shipyard productivity in 1899–1900. Nonetheless, meaningful improvements that fine-tuned its operation were introduced throughout the rest of the decade.

As already mentioned, the first project the firm undertook was to clear and grade the site of what became the north building ways. In the process, P&S established what must have been the largest building slip in Bath, if not the state. Oak pilings driven to refusal and capped with hard pine bed logs made up the foundation to carry the construction supports and launching ways.[85] The slip appears to have been at least 350 feet long by approximately 50 feet wide.

Little else was done at the shipyard until 1902, when the firm added a brick pitch oven to its inventory of structures. Designed to heat pitch (crystalized resins derived from pine sap) that was payed into deck seams to waterproof the caulking, the oven was fueled with wood scraps from the shipyard. It also proved to be a popular attraction for neighborhood boys who delighted in dipping out an occasional bit for a tasty—and free—chewing gum substitute. Or at least they did until two of them saw a wiry old caulker with an impressive "chaw" of chewing tobacco—smoking was prohibited throughout the yard, except in the blacksmith shop—lean over the pitch pot and deposit said chaw and accumulated juice into the pot. Somehow, chewing pitch from Percy & Small palled after that.[86]

The next major project to improve the shipyard involved the small stub wharf built on the north side of the original building ways about 1898. It was widened in 1902 to take advantage of the land acquired from the Powers purchase, but not deepened. That project came in 1906, when the shipyard rebuilt the north wharf into a fitting-out pier, measuring a hundred feet square. The cost ultimately came to $2,303.60 (+/- $35,500 in 1998).[87] One interesting feature of the new fitting-out pier—aside from the fact that it now projected out to deeper water—was a timber ramp built into its southern side. This addition eased the problem of landing large timbers in the shipyard that had been floated down from the railroad yards and ferry slip after being dumped from the flat cars. It was particularly useful for handling the huge spar timbers that were shipped into Bath from the West Coast.

The final improvements during the first decade of the century waited until 1909. A two-story addition, measuring 75 feet by 17 feet, was added to the north side of the mill. The first floor addition provided a home for boat building which had hitherto been subjected to the laws of chance when it came to finding space about the shipyard. Percy & Small generally built the small boats that were part of a schooner's outfit—a large yawl boat (powered with a gasoline engine from 1902) about 26 feet in length and a Whitehall-type about 16 to 18 feet in length, propelled by oars. The second floor addition added ample storage for lumber used in the joiner shop, something that had been previously lacking.

The final addition to the shipyard facilities during the decade (in 1909) was a small transformer house placed near the northwest corner of the mill. No doubt it was an addition also welcomed by most of the shipyard's neighbors in the south end because it foretold the end of the dimming lights phenomenon that plagued the area every time the shipyard started its big motors. But now, at last, a source of electric power adequate to meet peak demand was at hand. Bath was to draw its electrical power from the new hydroelectric generating station at the falls in Brunswick. Two 11,000-volt high tension lines carried the power to Bath's generating station—to be used thereafter as a backup generating station—where it passed through a transformer substation and was then distributed to consumers throughout the city. Furthermore, industrial customers such as Percy & Small, Hyde Windlass, Bath Iron Works, etc., were to receive their power on

PERCY & SMALL
1901 - 1917

Tobey to P&S 1901
To P&S 1901
To P&S 1901
Middle Street
Middle Street Extension
Eliakim McCabe
Marshall St.
Stinson Lot
Timber Storage
P&S Office
Washington Street
1909 Addition to Mill
Paint & Treenail Shop
W. T. Donnell
Blacksmith Shop (burned and rebuilt 1913)
Transformer Building, 1909
C. E. Hyde
House
Shipbuilding Ways – South
P&S
Shipbuilding Ways – North
Pitch Oven 1902
Timber Storage
Oakum Shop
Outhouse
Fitting Out Pier (1906)
Timber Ramp
Kennebec River
0 50' 100'
R. L. Snow & D. K. Lee - 1997

Percy & Small Plan: 1901–17
D. K. Lee and R. L. Snow

distribution lines separated from those of residential customers and carrying higher voltage.[88] The higher voltage, in turn, required the installation of transformers for the industrial customers in order to "step down" the voltage to their motors' rated capacity. The two new transformers and the transformer house at Percy & Small were provided at the power company's expense.[89]

The investment Percy & Small put into their shipyard was made to facilitate the building of large wooden schooners. But it took more than just a modern plant to produce schooners.

When this photo was taken about 12 December 1909, Percy & Small had carved out its niche as the premier builder of very large schooners, a role epitomized by the schooner WYOMING enmeshed in staging on the north ways awaiting her copper bottom paint and a few finishing touches, and the S. P. BLACKBURN lying alongside. The shipyard's evolution is graphically documented: (from left to right) north building ways (1901), transformer building (1909), mill building (1899) with 1909 addition, office (1900), paint and treenail shop (1898); on the waterfront, (center) fitting out pier (1906), outhouse, south building ways. The blacksmith shop and caulker's shop are not visible.

N. E. Card/Rollins Photo, courtesy of Richard Card

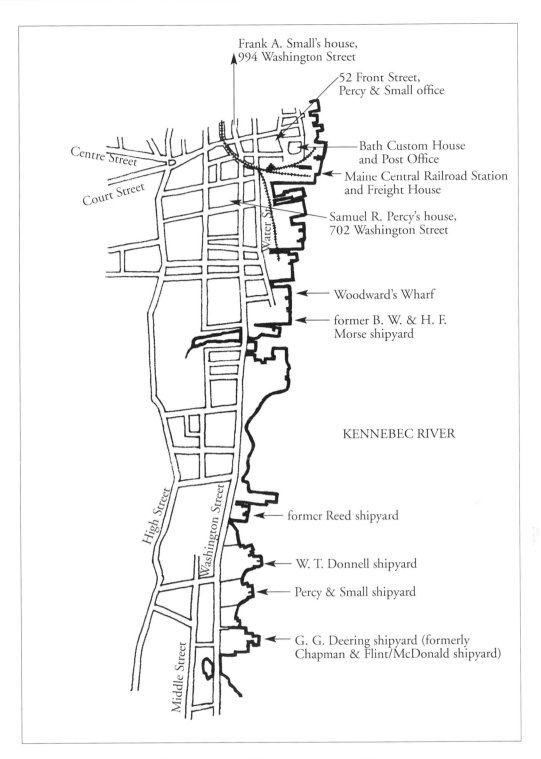

Frank A. Small's house,
994 Washington Street

52 Front Street,
Percy & Small office

Bath Custom House
and Post Office

Maine Central Railroad Station
and Freight House

Samuel R. Percy's house,
702 Washington Street

Woodward's Wharf

former B. W. & H. F.
Morse shipyard

Centre Street

Court Street

Water St.

KENNEBEC RIVER

former Reed shipyard

W. T. Donnell shipyard

Percy & Small shipyard

G. G. Deering shipyard (formerly
Chapman & Flint/McDonald shipyard)

High Street

Washington Street

Middle Street

The South End of Bath, Maine, circa 1900.

Courtesy: Maine Maritime Museum

[1] During 1899 Percy & Small committed to build one six-master and two five-masters, totaling 8,329 gross tons. This was nearly 3,000 more tons than delivered by all Bath shipyards in 1898.

[2] *PSJ*, p. 61, 8/10/1899; "For two story house/for 1 1/2 story house."

[3] *BT*, 9/8/1899.

[4] *BT*, 9/16/1899.

[5] When the building was located on the north side of the yard, its principal openings were oriented to the east and south into the shipyard. Once moved, these openings would face the Hyde property on the south and the west end of the blacksmith shop. By rotating the building, one set of openings still faced into the shipyard while the other set faced onto the street. When the building was documented in 1974, the architect found traces of two former exterior doors, one facing east onto the site of the long-gone blacksmith shop. The other opening faced south into the Hyde property which, during the last active years of the shipyard, was part of the shipyard. When that was no longer the case, there was no reason to keep the door; it was removed, boarded over, and the outside clapboarded. When the blacksmith shop was subsequently torn down in the 1930s, the same fate overcame that particular door. See: "Shipyard Restoration Plans," prepared by Bastille-Neiley Architects, 12/26/1973, Sheets 2, 3, MMM.

[6] *BT*, 9/30/1899.

[7] Information concerning the mill machinery is drawn from the following interviews: Samuel Barnes by Virginia Wood (9/25/1975, Summary Transcript 75-T-1, MMM); Charles A. Coombs, Jr., by Robert Schultz (11/27/1973, Tape #68-T-3, MMM); Raleigh Osier by Robert Schultz (Tapes #72-T-2,3, MMM); Homer Potter by Robert Schultz (Tape #72-T-4, MMM); William Donnell by Robert Schultz (Tape #72-T-1, MMM); Charles A. Coombs, Jr., by Maynard D. Lee (Tapes #68-T-1,2,3, MMM); Thomas Robson by R. Snow and J. Sturtevant (Tapes #72-T-5,6, MMM); and the author's examination of wear and mounting marks in the building and photographs.

[8] *I&E*, 5/16/1906.

[9] *I&E*, 12/9/1908; for example, P&S purchased 400 logs from the idle Shaw mill a short distance upstream from the shipyard and sawed most of the spruce into staging plank.

[10] Advertisement: Withby, Rugg & Richardson Co., *Scientific American*, Architects & Builder's Edition, August 1886, p. ii.

[11] Letter, Captain R. L. Arthur, USN, to Rear Admiral Mayo A. Hadden, USN, 12 January 1973. Author's P&S File. This planer was sold to the Boston Naval Shipyard in the late 1920s. *BI*, 2/17/1927.

[12] *BI*, 2/9/1901. The Hooker sawmill had what was claimed to be the largest Daniels planer in the world. Set up by Warren Carr, the machine was specifically designed to plane ship knees. Its arm was 4.5 feet long, and the table was 6 feet wide.

[13] Two of the former shipyard employees interviewed in the 1970s did not recall the lathe, but mounting holes on the floor by the east wall clearly indicate its presence. This observation was confirmed in the interview with Samuel Barnes who first worked at P&S in 1906. Notes of Barnes Interview conducted by Virginia Wood, 9/25/1975, Author's P&S File.

[14] Hutchins, pp. 394–95.

[15] *BE*, 4/24/1895; *BT*, 1/15/1896. Information on the early history of electricity in Bath comes from: *BI*, 8/29/1896, and *I&E*, 5/7/1904.

[16] When the joiner shop was moved to its current location in 1899, the motor was removed. However, the shaft, countershaft, and belt power transmission system—often called a jackshaft system—was extended from the blacksmith shop to the first floor of the building where it drove the treenail lathe.

[17] As told to the author circa 1975 by the daughter.

[18] Information was drawn from the 1903 Sanborn Insurance Map of Bath.

[19] Sanborn Insurance Map, 1909. By 1909 the mill contained two motors—100 HP and 75 HP. The 34 percent increase in power suggests that even the previous 90-HP motor was less than totally adequate.

[20] Sometimes two clutches were used, especially on larger pieces of machinery. In the case of the sawmill and Daniels planer, for example, one clutch controlled the blade mechanism and the other clutch drove the saw or planer table. The former needed much higher revolutions than the latter.

[21] Torque in foot-pounds force declines as revolutions per minute increase. A 90-HP motor delivers 274 foot-pounds of torque at 1,725 RPM; at 1,050 RPM, the same motor delivers 450 foot-pounds.

[22] SCRD, 81–250; Harry Stinson purchased the property from J. C. Ledyard, yet his father and mother supposedly had lived there since circa 1865, shortly after their marriage (See: James P. Stinson obituary, *BT*, 10/23/1917). Harry was married in 1909 to widow Winona Tilton Eaton and died during 1916, aged fifty.

[23] SCRD, 140–293. Percy & Small finally purchased the land outright in 1918 from widow Winona Tilton Stinson, Harry's wife and mother of young John F. Eaton who had spent no little time keeping a low profile during the events leading up to WYOMING's launching.

[24] *PSJ*, p. 92.

[25] *NYMR*, 3/16/1898.

[26] *BT*, 6/19/1899 and 3/3/1900; *BI*, 7/29/1899.

[27] *BT*, 6/12 and 11/22/1899.

[28] Interview with Charlotte Cahill, 8/24/1975, Notes,

Parker Collection; *BT*, 8/24, 25/1908.

29 Cahill entertained many of his New York clients and friends each summer at his Bay Point cottage (it had fourteen rooms!) at the mouth of the Kennebec.

30 *PSJ*, pp. 92, 231. Cahill received commissions totalling $543.30 (+/- $9,000 in 1998) for selling 21 percent of shares in the HELEN W. MARTIN, commissions of $796.28 (+/- $12,250 in 1998) for the sale of 23 percent of shares in the GRACE A. MARTIN, and $615 (+/- $9,500 in 1998) in commissions for shares he sold in the GOVERNOR BROOKS.

31 *BT*, 3/3/1900; guests at the launching from Gloversville were his daughters, his partner E. C. Naylor, E. W. Starr, Edward Parkhurst, and Charles W. Stewart.

32 *BT*, 8/25/1908.

33 *BT*, 3/3/1900. This hackneyed phrase appears so many times in the *Times* launching accounts that one can only be left with the belief that the newspaper used a "fill-in-the-blanks" launching story for the guidance of its reportorial staff.

34 Schooner HELEN W. MARTIN Dividends, Notes, Parker Collection. Captain Parker abstracted the data from *PSJ*.

35 *BT*, 6/2/1902.

36 *BT*, 3/13/1902.

37 *PSJ*, p. 308.

38 *BT*, 9/25–28/1911; *NYMR*, 9/27/1911.

39 *NYMR*, 7/14/1915.

40 *BT*, 7/14, 30 and 9/17/1915.

41 *NYMR*, 11/24/1915.

42 *Ibid.*; *BT*, 11/19, 20/1915; The stated destination of New York does not hold up in light of her location when she struck the mine. The MARTIN was in the North Sea less than a day's tow to the coast. This was an active war zone and a place a schooner sailing from Archangel to New York was not likely to pass through, especially a neutral vessel. It does appear that the schooner was, in fact, bound for an English port.

43 *NYMR*, 5/17/1916.

44 Personal Letter, Dr. Basil Greenhill to Author, 2/22/1996. Dr. Greenhill, formerly director of the National Maritime Museum at Greenwich and an internationally respected maritime historian, has a longtime interest in sailing vessels on the Baltic.

45 Instrument of Survey, Ship FENIX, at Gravesend, London, 5 November 1919. MS-54, MMM.

46 *Ibid.*; Greenhill Letter.

47 *NYMR*, 3/16/1898.

48 *NYMR*, 5/24/1899.

49 Construction Bill File, Schooner #7. Bill: McFadden (teamster) to P&S, 9/27/1899, Parker Collection. Fred Rideout, designer of #7, always dated and submitted his bills for design work about the time the vessel was launched, not when he did the actual modeling and lofting.

50 As the Winslow schooner was the next hull number after #7, she was obviously contracted for after the decision to go ahead with the six-master. Given the lead time needed to design the vessel, develop materials lists, estimate, and order and receive the shipbuilding timber for the vessel, it was likely that the contract was signed no later than September 1899.

51 *BT*, 7/20/1900. The exact terms of the lease are not known. Deering did not believe in tying up capital in his shipbuilding plant and completely eschewed the use of power machinery. P&S made needed repairs to the building slip, wharf, and other facilities, all of which accrued to his benefit when he began building there. By late July frames for two vessels were in the shipyard, suggesting that Deering was anxious to commence work.

52 *BT*, 12/6/1899.

53 *BI*, 4/21/1900.

54 *BT*, 4/27/1900. Percy & Small did not lease the closer Donnell shipyard, perhaps because Donnell was already committed to build the steam ferry HOCKOMOCK.

55 *BT*, 4/3/1900.

56 *BI*, 5/26/1900; *BT*, 5/16, 26/1900. Part of the problem appears to have been the lack of skilled shipbuilding labor. This was a boom shipbuilding year up and down the coast, which really taxed the labor supply. Percy & Small, suddenly expanding their production from one schooner to three, were unable to expand their workforce accordingly.

57 Captain W. J. Lewis Parker, "Percy & Small, Shipbuilders and Shipowners, 1894–1920." Paper presented at the Symposium in Maine Maritime History, Maine Maritime Museum, May 3, 1975.

58 *BT*, 8/13/1900. It is not clear from the published descriptions whether the strapping was on the outside *or* inside of the frame. William F. Palmer, in writing about the ELIZABETH PALMER in 1903, comments about the strapping on the inside of the frame "after the fashion of Percy and Small." Palmer to F. E. Corbin, 8/21/1903, Palmer Collection.

59 *BT*, 7/20/1900.

60 *BT*, 7/31/1900.

61 *BT*, 8/16/1900.

62 *BT*, 11/14/1900. The schooner was the JENNIE R. DUBOIS. Subsequently, he built vessels for the Portland Company and M. G. Shaw in Greenville. He never built another vessel in Bath. See: *BT*, 2/4/1931, obituary.

63 *BI*, 8/18/1900.

64 *BT*, 8/13/1900.

65 From 1900 through 1909, a total of ten oceangoing six-masted sailing vessels were built throughout the world. They were all built on the East Coast of the United States. Of the ten, one was built of steel by Fore River Shipbuilding Co. of Quincy, Massachusetts. The other nine were built of wood, all in Maine, and seven by Percy & Small.

66 *BT*, 7/18/1908. Voyage, Newport News to Boston; a

month earlier she came into Boston with 5,984 tons of coal, suggesting that P&S and Captain Jewett were striving to increase the PERCY's earnings.

[67] The author recognizes that technically 1900 was the *last* year of the nineteenth century, not the first of the twentieth century. However, the complete production history of the six-masters extended over exactly one decade, 1900–09. Therefore, I have arbitrarily placed all six-masters in the twentieth century. All detailed information concerning the ELEANOR A. PERCY is drawn from the following: *BT*, 10/10/1900, launching account; Construction Accounts, Schooner #7, Parker Collection.

[68] During World War I, many of the surviving five- and six-masters carried radio receivers and a few carried transmitters.

[69] *BT*, 11/15/1900.

[70] *BT*, 12/27/1900.

[71] *PSJ*: the first cash dividend was paid on 20 April 1901, $30.84 per $^1/_{64}$.

[72] *BI*, 7/6/1901; *BT*, 7/2, 3/1901; Denny M. Humphreys, Survey of Vessels (Repairs): 1905, MS-197, Frederick Drake Papers, MMM, hereafter cited as Humphreys, Survey of Vessels (Repairs).

[73] *BI*, 7/6/1901.

[74] *Ibid*.

[75] *BT*, 7/2/1901.

[76] Allen Irish File.

[77] W. F. Palmer to Captain J. E. Creighton, 8 July 1901, Palmer Collection.

[78] Humphreys, Survey of Vessels (Repairs).

[79] *PSJ*, pp. 110–11. Figures concerning the collision and subsequent costs all come from this source.

[80] The ELEANOR A. PERCY had an average gross return of 8 percent per year (1900–11); her return net of an annual 5 percent depreciation was 2.9 percent. Her best year was 1903 when she netted a 10 percent return after depreciation. As with most schooner investments during that period, however, it was World War I that converted marginal investments into big winners. ELEANOR A. PERCY Earnings, Notes, Parker Collection; and *PSJ*.

[81] Mrs. Powers died intestate in May 1900. SCRD, 97-184, 2/25/1901.

[82] Percy was not being a scofflaw; the general public had virtually unlimited access through the shipyard to the waterfront, and a number of the neighbors kept their small boats at the shipyard.

[83] This didn't appear to bother Mr. Donnell. At various times Percy & Small's sparmakers did their work in the unused Donnell yard and, in 1907, Percy & Small leased the shipyard itself for six years.

[84] SCRD, 97–218, 97–219, 102–310.

[85] During the mid-1970s, while setting up ways to haul out a vessel on the site, volunteers uncovered a number of the hard pine bed logs, buried since 1901. Aside from a shallow punky surface, they were still solid and, when cut, gave forth the pungent odor of fresh-cut hard pine.

[86] Charles A. Coombs Interview, Tape #68-T-1, MMM.

[87] *PSJ*, p. 324, 12/27/1906; *BT*, 5/19/1906.

[88] *BT*, 9/23 and 12/8/1909.

[89] *BI*, 9/25/1909.

Schooners by Design

A CAUTIONARY TALE

In 1899 the M. D. CRESSY broke new ground for Percy & Small with her five-masted rig and 2,000-plus gross tons. As with most trailblazing models, however, she soon revealed a variety of problems, many minor and some major. The major problems suggested that more thought had to go into building schooners if they were to continue to grow in size and be able to survive long in the marine environment.

Built from the popular CLIFFORD/BLACKBURN model but substantially larger than her predecessors, the CRESSY proved to be excessively limber. Although the ratio of length to depth-of-hold exceeded 10:1—the point at which the American Bureau of Shipping recommended installing so-called hogging straps—the designer (Rideout), the master builder (Willard Hodgkins), the owners (Percy & Small), and the American Bureau of Shipping through its surveyor in Bath (Denny M. Humphreys) did not make any efforts to reinforce the long hull against the increased stresses beyond using timbers of somewhat larger scantlings than called for in the tonnage tables. It was not enough.

Loren E. Haskell, son of Captain Ellis E. Haskell, recalled sailing with his father on the "old M. D. CRESSY" several times. Once, in 1902, when the three-year-old schooner was carrying phosphate rock from Tampa to Baltimore, she ran into trouble. But let Haskell tell the story:

> I would say that she was not a strongly built vessel, and seemed to leak plenty most of the time. Her pumps were going so much that it kept the engineer on the job twenty-four hours a day . . . . We were picked up by the Revenue Cutter ACUSHNET off Cape Hatteras in distress, with the loss of all our sails, and leaking badly. We were towed into Charleston, S.C., a sorry looking sight.[1]

Captain Haskell provided amplification of the report written many years later by his son:

> We left Port Tampa, Fla., Nov. 24, for Carteret, NJ, with phosphate rock. Sunday, Nov. 30, experienced hurricane from east, canting to southeast, with a dangerous cross sea running and breaking over the vessel from aft to forward. The schooner sprang a leak, but we kept the wrecking pump constantly going. We lost sails, spars, and everything movable from the decks. We used oil

The M. D. "Doctor" CRESSY appears to be in relatively good shape fifteen years after her launching from Percy & Small. Despite appearances, however, she had a long history of structural problems and within months of this interlude at Hoboken would be abandoned by captain and crew, salvaged, and repaired once again. Two years later, under new owners, she literally fell apart in a storm.

Courtesy: Captain W. J. Lewis Parker, USCG, Ret.

to advantage, and kept the vessel before the sea for safety during the storm, but the bad weather continued, and it wound up another hurricane from the northeast on Dec. 4. We lost our port anchor off Charleston, and our sails and rigging are damaged.[2]

The battered CRESSY was towed from Charleston to Newport News and then on to Baltimore. At each port she was reported to be "leaking badly" upon arrival.[3] A subsequent report in the *New York Maritime Register* claimed the CRESSY, drydocked after unloading her cargo, was completely recaulked from keel to deckhouses.[4] But Percy & Small, in an early twentieth-century effort at spin control, denied the report immediately, saying that all that needed recaulking was the schooner's topsides.[5] Any firm that realized that its prosperity was dependent upon the good opinion of investors and shipbuilding customers could do no less.

Denials of major structural problems notwithstanding (anyone familiar with wooden sailing vessels had no serious problem understanding the implications of a complete recaulking for a vessel barely three years old), Percy & Small brought the CRESSY back to their shipyard for "major repairs" in early December 1904.[6] Although it was never revealed publicly, the major repairs involved an effort to supplement the longitudinal strength members with the addition of a number of reinforcing strakes of ceiling through the entire length of the vessel.[7] The M. D. CRESSY's experience drove home the need to build large, strong hulls capable of resisting the stresses and strains to which such hulls were subject in their operating environment.

Throughout her long career with Percy & Small, the CRESSY continued to be prone to numerous problems ranging from gear failure and storm damage to the more worrisome—and dangerous—problems with structural integrity. Yet, for all of these problems, she was a surprisingly profitable investment for the managing owners and the other shareholders. In her first nine years, she generated a rate of return of 13.8 percent per year.[8] It was a decidedly better rate of return than many of her larger, later, fellow members

of the Percy & Small fleet experienced during the first decade of the century.[9]

But by the time the CRESSY was approaching the sixteenth anniversary of her launching, she was a pretty tired vessel, even though she had received her full-time survey, been overhauled, and reclassed at Percy & Small during November and December 1914. In March 1915 she cleared Gulfport, Mississippi, with a cargo of railroad ties destined for New York. Caught in a series of gales while working her way north past Cape Hatteras, the CRESSY became badly strained again and began to leak far faster than the pumps could handle. Captain Arey, Mrs. Arey, and the sailors were taken off the sodden schooner by the crew of the Diamond Shoals lightship. The next day the CRESSY was found floating on her cargo near the Wimble Shoal buoy and taken in tow by the SS D. N. LUCHENBACH to Norfolk. Captain Percy apparently paid the owners of the steamer for salvaging the battered schooner, and she received temporary repairs at Norfolk before being towed to New York to unload.[10] From there she went on to Percy & Small for "extensive repairs" just months after she had been overhauled in accordance with the surveyor's recommendations.

Aside from adding two full-length tiers of assistant keelsons on both sides of the keelson and nine strakes of 9- by 12-inch ceiling installed from the lower turn of the bilge to the hanging knee strake on both sides, the shipyard renewed virtually all the iron fastenings and re-treenailed the hull planking from the light waterline to the rail. The foremast was replaced (the CRESSY also appears to have been very hard on her masts), as were her wrecking pump (probably worn out by then), the boiler, and the forward deckhouse.[11]

With her class continued by the American Bureau of Shipping surveyor, the CRESSY returned to service, picking up a charter to carry coal to Bahia, Brazil. It was a long step from being abandoned to a cruise to South America, all in a matter of months, but the effect of World War I on the shipping business and charter rates was dramatic and underlay Percy & Small's decision to keep the old schooner in service.

However, she was finally sold in March 1917 to the American Union Line.[12] That firm, cashing in on the enormous, prepaid freight rates to Europe, was sweeping up whatever old hulks it could find at top-dollar prices, then chartering them for European ports at such high rates that a single passage reportedly would pay for the vessel and leave a very tidy profit as well. There was little concern on the part of the new owners, or the underwriters for that matter, whether a vessel such as the M. D. CRESSY, already eighteen years old (and hard years they had been), was up to crossing the North Atlantic in early spring.

The CRESSY sailed from New York on 7 April 1917 with a general cargo, bound for Havre. Two days later,

only 200 miles out of port, she encountered a gale and, in short order, sprang a leak and then literally began to disintegrate. The crew abandoned ship in two boats, one of which was lost along with the second mate and two seamen. The other boat, containing the captain, his wife, and ten members of the crew, one of whom died of exposure, was picked up by a British freighter after more than two days in the open boat.[13]

The CRESSY saga underscored an important lesson for Percy & Small and those who modeled and built their schooners: learn from experience. This they did.

DESIGNING THE GREAT SCHOONERS

Design of the great schooners, as of all vessels, encompassed such matters as size, hull form, scantlings, internal structure, specifics of individual rigs, and deck arrangements. The final result was, hopefully, a thoughtfully worked out design of a vessel that would be cost effective and operate successfully and profitably within its intended environment. In a few cases, these schooners were designed by academically trained naval architects, but most of the great schooners—including all built by Percy & Small—were the product of de facto collaborations between prospective owner, the shipbuilder(s), the modeler, and the classification society.

Long before the first published works on naval architecture saw the light of day in the sixteenth century, shipwrights had evolved an effective system of rules based on practical experience for proportions, hull shape, and size of structural timbers for new vessels—the basic elements of design.[14] By the time Percy & Small began building vessels in 1894, the rules on construction, scantlings, and materials were those of the various classification societies—American Shipmasters Association, Lloyd's Register, and Bureau Veritas—that established standards and ratings regarding the construction of a vessel for the guidance of marine insurers.

Hull size and form were established by the modeler and prospective owner based on considerations of the type of service the vessel would be in, the desired carrying capacity, and construction cost. In the coal

trade, for example, it was well known that, all things being equal, there were substantial economies of scale to be derived from building bigger schooners—i.e., larger schooners cost less per ton to build than smaller ones, and their operating cost did not increase in proportion to their increased cargo (earning) capacity. Therefore, the more the vessel carried, the greater the return on the investment.

However, there was another axiom in the coal schooner business: the bigger the schooner, the fewer markets it was able to serve. WYOMING, for example, with her 6,000-ton capacity and 27.5-foot draft, would find herself limited to four coal-loading ports and two delivery ports during the first eighty-eight months of her active service.[15] Lacking the ability of smaller schooners to move to other trades and other ports when there was a glut of tonnage in their own, the biggest schooners were sometimes forced to take charters at marginally profitable rates or to lay up until rates improved.

Percy & Small understood the limitations of the very large schooners, an understanding reflected in the ultimate composition of their own fleet—eight four-masters (697–1,756 gross tons), six five-masters (2,114–3,129 gross tons), and only two six-masters (3,401–3,730 gross tons). This wide distribution of size and carrying capacity played an important role over the years in the firm's ability to operate profitably.

Once size, carrying capacity, and cost were

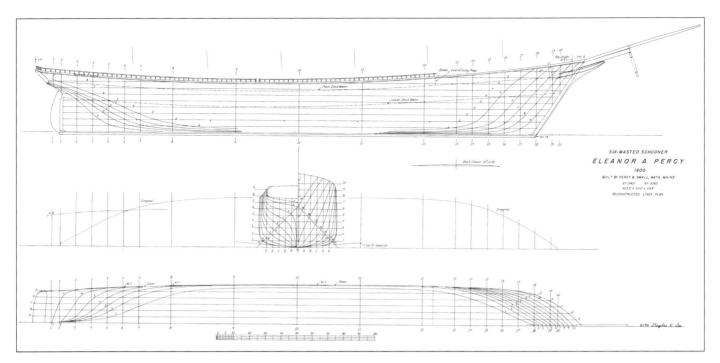

Reconstructed Lines Plan: ELEANOR A. PERCY
Douglas K. Lee

decided, the next step in the design process for a new schooner was the shape of the hull. By varying hull shape, a modeler could produce two vessels with the same registered dimensions but with dramatically different carrying capacities and sailing qualities.

The hull form favored by Percy & Small for their vessels—and for most of the great schooners—can be described in general as follows: a midship section characterized by a straight, gradual deadrise of the floors that ended with a rather sharp turn of the bilge and sides that were nearly vertical, or parallel, with little tumblehome; the shape of the midship section was carried well forward and aft with a proportionally short entrance and run; the strong sheer rose forward and met the high, raking stem; the stem rabbet developed a curve quite high, and the flare at the bow developed well up and forward on the stem; the entrance lines were hollow only at the lowest waterlines, if at all; the run started well aft of amidships and continued up to the high counter with a light, raking stern balancing the high raking bow.[16] It was a hull form that compromised between capacity and sailing qualities, with a small edge given to capacity.

It also produced good results in terms of minimiz-

ing draft per ton of burden, a desirable characteristic not only for the already noted problems with the controlling depth at various ports as well as at loading and discharging berths, but also when sailing through an area such as one encompassed by Vineyard Sound, Nantucket Sound, and the complex of shoals streaming south, forty-two miles, from Chatham to the Nantucket Lightship. One chart, for example, showed the controlling depth of the Pollock Rip Slue—a popular route for the big schooners around the southeast corner of Cape Cod—to be 29 feet at low water.[17] Given the frequent presence of large ocean swells on the shoals, it was not uncommon for these big schooners—loaded deep—to strike bottom a few times, even in the dredged channels.[18]

Aside from being burdensome, this general hull form, combined with its very heavy structure and lack of tophamper that characterized square-riggers, produced a relatively low center of gravity even when without cargo. This enabled the great schooners to sail light and arrive with clean-swept holds, ready to accept cargo upon arrival at their loading ports. Avoiding the handling of ballast saved significant time and money over the life of a vessel.

For all of their size and lack of the fine lines that distinguished the clipper ships of an earlier era, the great schooners were capable of a good turn of speed under the right conditions thanks to their long hulls. Sustained speeds of twelve knots were not uncommon. The six-master RUTH E. MERRILL, running light from Portland to Norfolk before a northwester in forty-five hours, averaged thirteen knots. And it was claimed the six-masted GEORGE W. WELLS could make fifteen knots and occasionally reached eighteen.[19] These speeds exceeded the capabilities of the steam collier and tug-towed barge competition of the day, but the schooners' average speeds were considerably lower than what they attained under ideal circumstances.

WORKING STRESSES

The internal structure of the wooden sailing vessel, dictated by a combination of custom and the rules of the above-mentioned classification societies, had one purpose: to maintain the integrity of the hull against the stresses of wind, wave, water, cargo, and its own structure that it could reasonably expect to encounter during the course of its working life. However, the growth of the wooden hull, especially amongst schooners, was pushing beyond the well-marked boundaries of the past and even challenging contemporary standards.

Before going on, a brief examination of those stresses is in order. Basically, they are four in number: (1) those that produce longitudinal bending; (2) those that tend to alter the transverse shape; (3) those that are local in nature, affecting some particular part of the hull; (4) and those that are due to the propulsion system.

Longitudinal bending manifested itself in two ways, hogging and sagging. Hogging—the bane of the great schooners—occurred when the ends of the vessel, less buoyant in proportion to their weight than the midsection, bent down as the midsection tended to rise.[20] This was a particular problem when the vessels sailed light which, as we know, was nearly half the time for the biggest of the great schooners. Sagging—the midsection becoming less buoyant than the ends—was more manifest when the vessel was heavily loaded. Both of these conditions were caused by the uneven distribution of weight and buoyancy along the longitudinal axis of the hull. What complicated matters in designing a hull to resist the hogging and sagging stresses when underway at sea was that these stresses were generally present at the same time, in varying intensities, while acting on different, and constantly changing, points of the hull. Almost the only time this was not true was when a hull was anchored in still water.[21]

The vessel's structure also had to contend with equally variable stresses that could alter the hull's transverse shape. As with the longitudinal component, transverse stresses were most apparent when the vessel was underway, rolling and pitching. The strains then were largely of the racking variety, distorting both the transverse and longitudinal hull forms, tending to force out the caulking between hull planking. The salty novelist's accounts of creaking and groaning timbers on board ship were grounded in fact.

Local stresses on the hull were set up by such things as the concentration of weight forward—anchors, chain, windlass, steam boiler and associated equipment, hoisting engine, bowsprit and jibboom—at a point where the hull had relatively little buoyancy. The heavy Oregon fir masts and their heavy steel wire standing rigging also set up strains around the mast partners and steps and at the chainplates. Strains set up from sailing were derived from the effects of the pressure of the wind on sails, masts, standing rigging, and the already mentioned rolling and pitching movement of the hull in a seaway.

Because a large, wooden hull was built of literally thousands of pieces of wood, its strength and ability to resist the stresses placed upon it were dependent not only on the sizes, quality, and placement of the shipbuilding timber, but also upon the care with which the pieces were fitted and fastened together. Although such considerations moved beyond the category of design to construction, the success of any design depended in

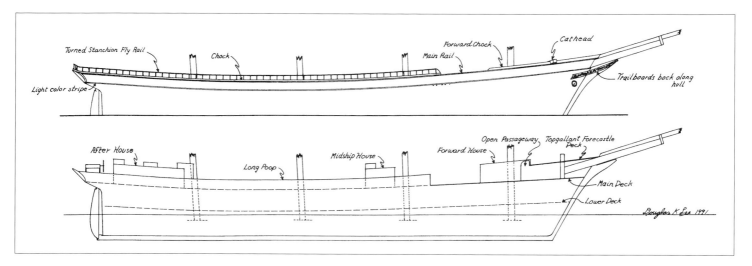

Deck Arrangement: Long Poop Schooners
Douglas K. Lee

substantial part upon the quality of construction.

The schooner rig's design was also the product of centuries of evolution, so little was to be added during the design phase of the vessel. The rake of the masts might vary according to the preferences of owner or captain, builder, or rigger, and each prospective captain had his own ideas where halyards should lead and snatch blocks should be located, but in the last analysis there was little difference in the rig arrangement between the great schooners.

DECK LAYOUTS

There was, however, a visible difference in deck configuration. Percy & Small built schooners with four basic deck layouts during their quarter century as active shipbuilders. The long poop model was particularly popular at P&S during their first ten years, where it was incorporated in no fewer than fourteen schooners—four-, five-, and six-masted. It was followed in 1902 by what we shall call the CORA F. CRESSY type, a configuration intended to address some of the problems of the long poop model. Three schooners were built to the original CRESSY layout; another—GRACE A. MARTIN—was a modified CRESSY, and then a group of four World War I schooners—the DUNHAM WHEELER type—were built to a further-modified CORA F. CRESSY deck layout. Many of the firm's largest schooners—nine in number—were built as true flush-deck vessels, and its smallest schooners—ten in number—were built to the more traditional short poop configuration.

The long poop model in its various manifestations was the most popular deck layout for the great schooners and latter-day wooden square-riggers through the 1890s and into the first years of the twentieth century. It appears to have evolved from the large cotton carriers built under the old measurement rules of the 1830s–1850s. Those rules, which assumed the depth of hold of a vessel equaled one-half its beam, also excluded from tonnage calculations sheltered spaces above the main deck. Shipowners soon figured out that extending the poop forward provided additional, tax-free space where perhaps another hundred or two hundred bales of cotton (a bulky but relatively light commodity) could be stuffed for the voyage to Europe. After the cotton was unloaded, the space could then be quickly converted into far from luxurious accommodations for the Irish immigrants who flocked to Liverpool and other Irish Sea ports seeking passage to America.[22] By the time of the great schooners, however, the long poop's perceived value had nothing to do with cotton, passengers, or untaxed cargo space.

The Percy & Small long poop model was charac-

Deeply loaded, the ELEANOR A. PERCY—the largest long poop schooner ever built—is drifting along
with all sail set to catch an illusive breeze while a "bay chaser" tug lies under her starboard quarter.
The tug's skipper is, no doubt, discussing towing terms with Captain "Linc" Jewett of the PERCY.
Courtesy: Maine Maritime Museum

terized by a full-length main deck, four to five feet below the main rail. It dropped away from the rail forward to provide more space for the upright boiler in the forward deckhouse and adequate clearance under the topgallant forecastle deck for the anchor windlass.[23] A long poop at the height of the rail extended forward to a break just ahead of the mainmast. Moving forward from the poop deck was the well deck, an open or weather deck (and part of the main deck), that lay between the poop and the topgallant forecastle deck and acquired its name from its solid bulwarks—also at the height of the rail—that gave the deck all the characteristics of a well, i.e., enclosed on five sides. The topgallant forecastle deck was also built at the height of the rail and extended aft from the stem to a point about four feet ahead of the forward house. The forward housetop extended over this space to the topgallant forecastle deck, forming a covered passageway—open on both sides—between the for-

ward house and the topgallant forecastle. A turned stanchion fly rail on the chock rail ran the length of the poop. The after and midship houses were sunk into the poop deck and sat on the main deck below. The forward house also sat on the main deck.

The long poop schooner presented a well-balanced, aesthetically pleasing profile. The long poop also provided a working space for handling sail and was significantly higher above the full-load waterline than the main deck (well deck) at the break. Although the poop deck was often awash when the schooner was fully loaded and thrashing through heavy seas, its height and the open nature of the turned stanchion fly rail meant that it shed boarding seas quite rapidly. This contrasted with the well deck, sided by solid bulwarks to the main rail, and closed off aft by the poop bulkhead and the forecastle forward. Only a few freeing ports and scuppers, however effective, were available to clear the well deck. When fully loaded, with heavy boarding seas, it was often converted into an enormous bathtub with many tons of seawater washing about, making sail handling difficult and often flooding the forward house. But the flooding of the well deck was more an inconvenience than a threat to the vessel's safety.

The long poop configuration did, however, possess a dangerous weakness that did not become fully evident until the length-to-depth ratio of the wooden hull began exceeding 10:1.[24] A dramatic illustration of this problem with large, long poop vessels involved one of Arthur Sewall's Big Four, SHENANDOAH. The largest wooden sailing vessel in the world when she was built in 1890, SHENANDOAH (3,407 GRT) was a four-masted bark destined for the Cape Horn trades. She was under the command of Captain James F. Murphy—sometimes known by such nicknames as "Shotgun" or "Shenandoah"—who was the deepwater equivalent of Captain "Linc" Jewett. Murphy loved SHENANDOAH—an appropriate stage upon which to practice his craft—and clearly regarded her as the finest vessel under sail anywhere in the world. But then she revealed her weakness—and the weakness of most of the large, long poop vessels. Murphy was devastated when he wrote to Arthur Sewall about the necessity of putting his crew to the pumps for thirty minutes every hour from Cape Horn to Liverpool:

> This ship from her poop forward works and bends both sideways and up and down and to my mind is getting worse every passage. Have seen her bow lift 3 ft then fall back. . . . Then in running in heavy rolling seas have seen her bow go sideways. When sighting the masts in line, the foremast head go[es] out of line and back from head of mainmast 4 feet.[25]

The movement of the forward section of the big bark ahead of the break in the poop resulted in the vessel "spitting-out" her caulking, causing the severe leaks. No doubt a contributing factor was her enormous and heavy tophamper, something that was less of a factor on the schooners, but many—if not most—vessels built to the long poop configuration suffered from problems of a similar nature.

The cause was easy to ascertain. The hull of a ship can be regarded as an enormous girder. The deeper the girder in relation to its length, the stiffer it is. But its overall strength is effectively determined at its weakest (read: shallowest) point. And the point where the effects of stress are most likely to appear is the interface with the shallowest point, i.e., that point where there is a discontinuity of the section modulus. On the long poop schooner, this point was just forward of the mainmast at the break of the poop. As we saw in the case of the M. D. CRESSY, Percy & Small soon became intimately aware of this problem and undertook various changes to address it. They built no more schooners with this deck layout for their own use after 1901 or for others after 1904.

The CORA F. CRESSY type (page 102) was Percy & Small's first radical response to the problems cropping up with the larger, long poop schooners. While unusual, her configuration was not altogether original. Next-door neighbor William T. Donnell built a version of this type in 1889, the CLARA A. DONNELL, and another schooner built at Mystic, Connecticut, the same year as the CRESSY, the JENNIE R. DUBOIS, shared the same deck layout.[26]

It was a simple, direct approach to the problems experienced by the great coal schooners and other, large, plank-on-frame vessels. As an answer to the limber nature of such hulls, the CORA F. CRESSY offered three mutually supporting solutions: an unusually deep hull for the length of keel, a flush deck, and the installation of hogging straps. The first solution strengthened the effective girder dramatically; the second did away with the trouble-prone zone around the break between the poop and the main deck by doing away with the break (eliminating the discontinuity in the section modulus) and carrying the weather deck all the way to the topgallant forecastle deck; and the third used two parallel, heavy, steel straps on each side of the vessel to reinforce the hull's structure against the bending forces imposed on the large, long hull.

What was truly striking about the CRESSY—making her the easiest schooner on the coast to identify—and to a lesser degree about her much smaller siblings, was her profile with its dramatic sheer forward and her truly imposing bow. During the long course of her

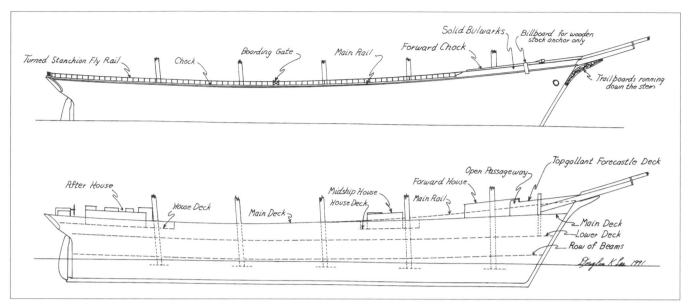

Deck Arrangement: CORA F. CRESSY-Type Schooners
Douglas K. Lee

career, the CRESSY's bow looming out of the fog jarred more than one daydreaming seaman on another vessel back to reality.[27]

This type had a full-length flush deck which dropped away from the rail forward. The turned stanchion fly rail and chock rail extended from the stern to a point abaft of the foremast standing rigging where it became full-height solid bulwarks. The proportionally greater sheer forward, defined by the fly rail and bulwarks, and the falling away of the main deck from that sheer line provided enough height forward under the topgallant forecastle deck to comfortably shelter the anchor windlass.

The after and midship houses were sunk into the main deck, resting on special house decks built 4 feet below the main deck. The forward house, however, was built on the main deck, its forward bulkhead 4 feet aft of the forecastle and its housetop extending over the space to the topgallant forecastle deck. The resulting passageway was open at the sides but provided a sheltered, full-height work space and access to the anchor windlass and heads.

This arrangement contributed to the CORA F. CRESSY's reputation for having the highest bow on the Atlantic seaboard. In fact, it was nearly 48 feet from the keel shoe to the underside of the topgallant fore-

castle deck. The 13-foot difference between that measurement amidships and at the bow dramatized the extent of the forward sheer.

The benefit of a deck arrangement, combining the advantages of the flush deck configuration with a flaring bow, topgallant forecastle deck, and full-height forward house, was relative dryness forward even when deeply loaded in heavy seas. Seamen preferred it to the "half-tide ledge" phenomenon of the long poop and flush deck configurations which were both notoriously wet.[28]

There was a downside, however. When light, the CRESSY's considerable freeboard, especially forward, was a problem that was quickly spotted by Percy & Small and competitors alike. William F. Palmer, forever willing to gossip about other schooner operators' problems, passed on the news to one of his captains: "Captain Harding tells me that he fell in with the CORA CRESSY and that he called her an exceedingly tender vessel. I think she takes as long an angle of heel as almost any vessel that sails."[29] This tendency to sail on her side, and her inability to point when light was so pronounced that Percy & Small eventually installed two hundred tons of sand ballast to provide more initial stability.[30]

In 1904 Percy & Small launched the 3,129-GRT

Although only a four-master, the FLORENCE M. PENLEY shared the unusual deck arrangement used on the
CORA F. CRESSY and the ill-fated MARGARET WARD.

Courtesy: Maine Maritime Museum

In an effort to reduce some of the windage problems experienced with the CORA F. CRESSY deck
arrangement, Percy & Small built the GRACE A. MARTIN with a reduced-height topgallant
forecastle deck, shown here to full advantage on launching day crowded with invited guests.

Courtesy: Maine Maritime Museum

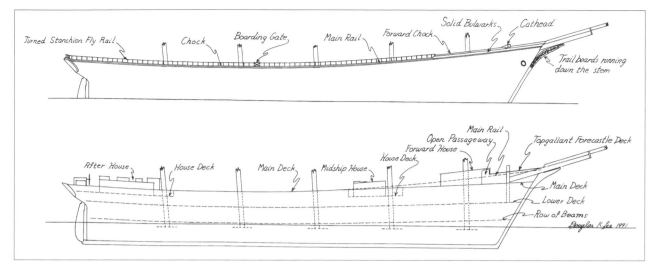

Deck Arrangement: GRACE A. MARTIN (modified CORA F. CRESSY) *Douglas K. Lee*

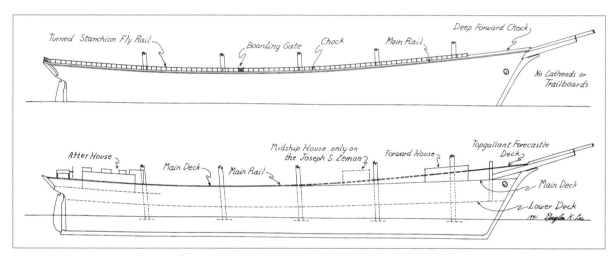

Deck Arrangement: DUNHAM WHEELER Type *Douglas K. Lee*

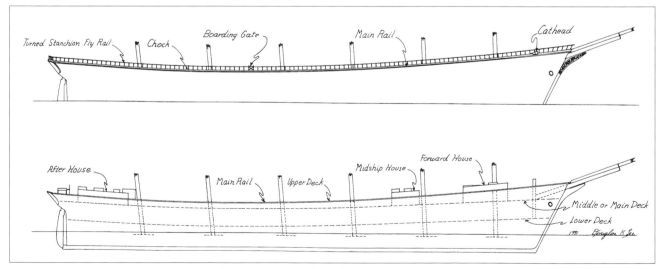

Deck Arrangement: Flush-Deck Type *Douglas K. Lee*

five-master, GRACE A. MARTIN. Her deck configuration represented an effort on the part of Percy & Small to preserve the advantages of the CORA F. CRESSY type without its major disadvantage—too much windage when light. The MARTIN closely resembled the CRESSY in general arrangement except that the solid bulwarks upon which the topgallant forecastle deck was built was constructed at half the height of the turned stanchion fly rail rather than at its full height. This required the main deck to fall away from the sheer more than on the CRESSY in order to achieve enough headroom under the topgallant forecastle deck for the windlass. The MARTIN's modified deck arrangement was not repeated in subsequent vessels, which leads to the conclusion that it did not altogether solve the problem noted on the CRESSY.

Yet, over a decade later, a further-modified version of the CRESSY deck configuration reappeared in four schooners, three five-masters and a four-master. Built during the wartime boom for other owners, the DUNHAM WHEELER type had two full decks with the flush main deck falling away from the rail forward. In an effort to further reduce the windage problem, this type had a topgallant forecastle deck built at the height of the main rail, which ran from the bow aft to the forward end of the forward house. The turned stanchion fly rail on top of the chock rail ran forward to the foremast. From there forward, the chock rail became deeper. The after house was sunk into the main deck and sat on a house deck below, and the forward house was built on the main deck. Only the JOSEPH S. ZEMAN had a midship house that was also built on the main deck.

Schooner DUNHAM WHEELER, unloading cargo at Gloucester, England, in 1919. She and her three near sisters are the final variant of the CORA F. CRESSY deck configuration.
Courtesy: Captain W. J. Lewis Parker, USCG, Ret.

Percy and Small used two other deck configurations in their schooners. The first was the flush deck layout (page 104) originally put in William F. Palmer's ELIZABETH PALMER. This was a true flush-decked vessel with no solid bulwarks or topgallant forecastle deck to interrupt the line of the uppermost deck. The weather deck—main or spar deck, depending on whether the vessel had two or three decks—extended from the taffrail aft to the very stem in one continuous sweep. A turned stanchion fly rail set on the chock rail ran the entire length of the hull. The after, midship, and forward houses were set into the spar deck, resting on the partially planked deck below which fell away from the sheer line of the spar deck forward to provide enough height for the upright donkey boiler in the forward house and the anchor windlass. The windlass, normally set on the uppermost continuous deck, was dropped down one deck to be out of the weather. It was placed in a compartment separated from the forward house by a bulkhead.

The largest schooners from Percy & Small were flush-deckers. With their continuous deck line, steel strapping, and very heavy scantlings, they were also some of the strongest wooden vessels ever built. Unfortun-

WYOMING, sailing light, demonstrates the continuous sweep of her weather deck, interrupted only by three deckhouses set into it and resting on the deck below. Blessed with the strongest deck configuration (all things being equal), the flush-deck schooners could be miserably wet, especially when deeply loaded.

Courtesy: Captain W. J. Lewis Parker, USCG, Ret.

ately, when deeply loaded and in the wrong sea conditions, they often fit the unpleasant description of "half-tide ledge," laboring heavily with deck awash.

The second most common schooner deck type at Percy & Small was the short poop schooner. No fewer than ten vessels—24 percent of P&S-built schooners—were built to this configuration, although the first two didn't appear until the firm had been in business for over a decade. This deck type was reserved for "small" four-masted schooners under a thousand gross tons, most of which were not built until the World War I years.

There was a single, full-length deck about 4 feet below the rail. A short poop deck—or quarter deck—built at the height of the rail extended forward to a break ahead of the spanker mast. A turned stanchion fly rail on top of the after chock ran the length of the poop deck. The rail and chock continued forward from the poop, resting on solid bulwarks, until it merged with the topgallant forecastle deck. The after house was sunk into the poop deck and rested on the main deck below. The forward house sat on the main deck.

These excellent, all-purpose carriers were capable of hauling more than 1,300 tons and could find work in a

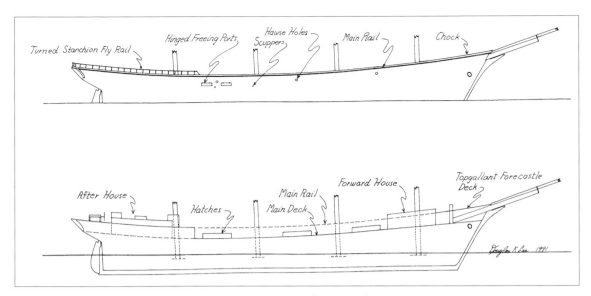

Deck Arrangement: Short Poop Type

Douglas K. Lee

The short poop deck arrangement was particularly effective for carrying large deckloads such as the dimension lumber being carefully stowed between the bulwarks in the waist of the ANNIE C. ROSS.

Courtesy: Captain W. J. Lewis Parker, USCG, Ret.

variety of trades. Their versatility was attested to by the ANNIE C. ROSS, the last working Percy & Small-built schooner, which earned her keep until 1941.

The solid bulwarks along the main deck between the poop and the topgallant forecastle deck created a large "well" that made for a wet vessel in heavy seas. However, the bulwarks were pierced by an assortment of freeing ports, scuppers, and hawseholes that all contributed to freeing the main deck of water.

This particular deck arrangement may have been wet on occasion, but it offered a big inducement not found in schooners with other deck layouts. It easily accommodated deck cargo. More often than not, the deck cargo was sawn timber or even logwood lashed down with heavy chains, but it could also be freight not easily gotten through the hatches, such as automobiles and, on occasions, even Mack trucks.[31]

THE MODELERS

In the course of a quarter century of shipbuilding, two men were unquestionably entitled to the primary credit for modeling Percy & Small-built schooners. The first, and most prolific, was Frederick Rideout, whom we met briefly in Chapter 1. He is also entitled to the credit for producing the first model for a six-master. The second was Bant Hanson who, with Rideout, learned his trade from the ground up in Bath shipyards without benefit of formal technical training. To Hanson goes the honor of modeling the largest wooden sailing vessel in the world—WYOMING—a feat that has gone virtually unremarked upon ever since.

William F. Palmer, ex-schoolmaster, managing owner of a remarkable fleet of coal schooners, and occasional Percy & Small customer, also has some claim to designer honors for Percy & Small-built vessels. A dozen of the fifteen schooners built for his fleet between 1900–09, including two of the four built by Percy & Small, have been credited to him. Unlike Rideout and Hanson, however, the Boston businessman had taken instruction in naval architecture as well as learned from the renowned Albert Winslow of Taunton, Massachusetts, the justly famous modeler of the largest two- and three-masted schooners, as well as the first four- and five-masters.[32] Exactly how much of the design work Palmer was actually responsible for is unknown, but he was a bona fide member of the Society of Naval Architects and Marine Engineers.

Frederick Rideout and Bant Hanson were "vernacular modelers," i.e., their talents were shaped principally by direct experience rather than academic training, a description that certainly fitted the majority of schooner designers in Maine.[33] Rideout was born into a Bath family that lived and breathed shipbuilding. His grandfather, the first Johnson Rideout, began building vessels in 1824, completing approximately seventy-two for his own account or for others by his death in 1866. It was in grandfather's shipyard that Fred first took up the shipwright's tools. His father, the second Johnson Rideout, also worked in the senior's shipyard before going to New York about 1840 to work briefly under the soon-to-be legendary Donald McKay. Upon his return to Bath, he became a master workman in his father's shipyard. After the first Johnson died in 1866, Johnson II went into the employ of Goss & Sawyer as designer and draftsman until he joined William Pattee—perhaps the greatest vernacular modeler of them all—in a partnership in 1874 known as Pattee & Rideout.

Fred turned his back temporarily on shipbuilding after his stint in the first Johnson's shipyard. In what may have been a case of youthful rebellion against the heavy hand of family tradition, he took to the water as crewman and then pilot of local tugboats before going on to skipper the first steam yachts on the Kennebec, George M. Patten's MIST and TWILIGHT. When that occupation palled, he returned to the shipyard, moulding timbers for Goss & Sawyer. He then moved on to the Pattee & Rideout mould loft, which he ultimately took over when his father retired in 1894.[34]

Bant Hanson, by way of contrast, was an immigrant, born in Arendal, Norway, in 1849. Two years after his birth, his family packed up and left that nursery of Norwegian seamen and shipbuilders for

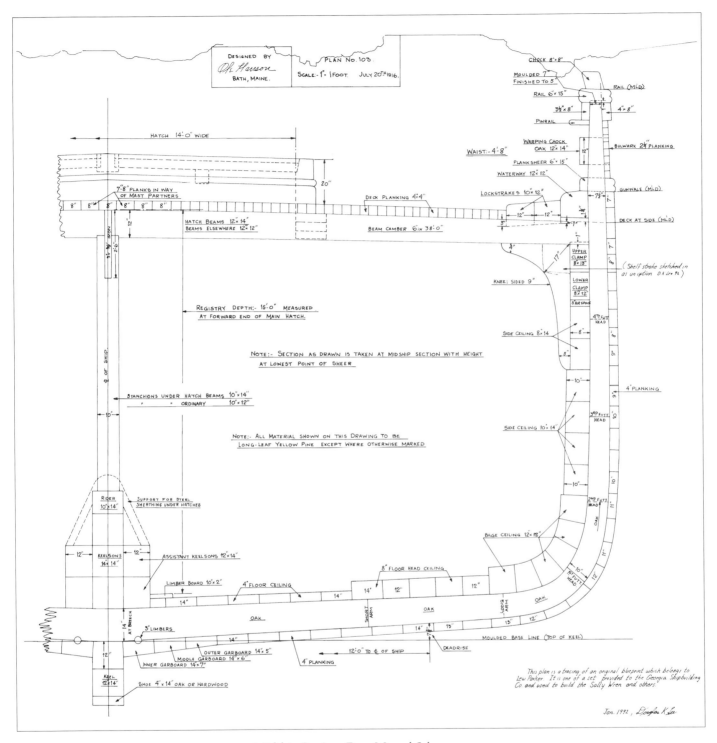

Midship Section: Four-Masted Schooner

Percy & Small did not build schooners from plans, but during the World War I shipbuilding boom, plans were prepared from schooners C. C. Mengel, Jr. and Sam C. Mengel built at the Bath shipyard for the use of the new Georgia Shipbuilding Company of Savannah, Georgia. By a strange quirk of fate, the plans were drawn by Ole Hanson, son of longtime Percy & Small modeler and timber surveyor Bant Hanson, who provided the model from which the schooners were built. Traced from the original by Douglas K. Lee.

Courtesy: Captain W. J. Lewis Parker, USCG, Ret.

Sherman, in Maine's Aroostook County. Young Bant lived in the remote village for the next twenty years, during the course of which his father marched off with the Maine Volunteers to fight in the American Civil War, leaving the teenager as the man of the house. When he turned twenty-two, Bant Hanson struck out on his own, moving to the city of opportunity on the banks of the Kennebec to be a ship carpenter. He found employment at the shipyard of Goss & Sawyer, Bath's famous "ship factory." Here he met Johnson Rideout the younger, and his son Fred.[35]

Hanson learned his trade well and became, in time, one of the Goss & Sawyer master builders. He so admired Captain Guy C. Goss, founder of the firm, that he named his third child and first son after the good captain and, subsequently, served as one of the honorary pallbearers for the captain's funeral cortege in Bath.

When Goss & Sawyer became the New England Company, Hanson became that firm's leading master builder and, eventually, moved over to Kelley, Spear Company. He briefly abandoned wooden shipbuilding in 1900 when he became the boss carpenter at Bath Iron Works, a position he filled for nearly three years. But even the challenge of supervising the installation of a pair of 12-inch breech-loading rifles weighing 236,000 pounds aboard the monitor NEVADA was not enough to keep him away from his beloved wooden shipbuilding.

He went out on his own in the fall of 1903, picking up a contract from Kelley, Spear Company to model a four-master. That firm built two schooners from the model.[36] But before Bant finished that commission, Fred Rideout was felled by a stroke and died three months later from a second stroke. Hanson was once again called upon to serve as pallbearer for a friend and fellow Mason. He also found himself to be the only still-active modeler of wooden vessels in Bath.

He acquired Fred Rideout's mould loft—formerly Pattee & Rideout—at 106 Commercial Street, probably with assorted half models, miscellaneous collections of papers and drawings, and moulds. He worked out of this loft until his death in 1915. In the course of this period, Hanson modeled vessels, served as a master builder and a timber surveyor, and even built a floating stage for the city.[37]

Rideout and Hanson, two men whose combined personal experience with the modeling and construction of wooden ships totaled approximately eighty years, were also the bearers of practical ship design and construction wisdom that was literally centuries old. Each had learned the practical techniques and their underlying principles from men of earlier generations. There was little they did not know about the form and structure of wooden sailing vessels or the materials with which they were built.

PLANS AND MODELS

By the late nineteenth century, a vessel's shape was defined on paper in two dimensions and in wood in three dimensions. Percy & Small, along with most schooner builders along the Maine coast, relied exclusively on the three-dimensional wooden half model when dealing with the shape of the vessel's hull.

Although this may seem to be a little too wedded to traditional techniques, two-dimensional plans as a design technique actually predate the use of models.[38] In fact the latter method was developed in response to the limitations of depicting accurately a three-dimensional object in two dimensions.[39] The models used were not the elaborate, detailed, and somewhat stylized Admiralty models of the seventeenth and eighteenth centuries, however. They were, instead, half models, i.e., a scaled-down representation of half of a hull divided on the longitudinal centerline. Solid and unadorned, rough or well finished, the working half model is one of our few direct connections with the ship modelers and builders of the past.

The medium in which Rideout and Hanson worked was far from being a primitive, unsophisticated approach to form. Howard I. Chapelle, an authority on nineteenth-century American ship design, once wrote:

Undoubtedly the half-model gives a more complete and precise impression of the hull form than does a lines drawing. The half-model produces the same three-dimensional effect as the finished vessel, something a lines drawing will not do. Hence a lines drawing may produce in the finished hull form an undesirable feature that would be discovered at once in a half-model. In general, the ability to design and judge hull form is more readily acquired by use of the half-model than by use of lines plans and other drawings. Many boatbuilders, ship carpenters, and even fishermen can quickly develop good judgment of hull form through use of the half-model, whereas some well educated naval architects, using only drawings, never acquire sound judgment of form.[40]

There were several stages of development. The early half models were carved from solid blocks of wood. Another version which enjoyed a little popularity early in the nineteenth century was the hawk's nest model. It had a plank backboard mounted with solid wood pieces—nailed from the back of the backboard—shaped to represent the shape of the frame at that point on the keel. Each was held rigid and vertical to the backboard by thin battens bent around and nailed to the frame pieces that also demonstrated the fairness of the form. Difficult to shape, it never achieved wide use. The lift half model was, by and far, the most commonly used then, and the best known type today. It started life as a laminated rectangular block composed of horizontal layers of boards cut to a thickness appropriate to the scale, called lifts, fastened together by toggles, tapered pegs, or iron screws. Various refinements evolved over the years, such as alternating pine lifts with walnut or mahogany.

Percy & Small's modelers, Rideout and Hanson, used a hybrid of the block and lift models. Their model blanks were put together like a lift model, but the lifts were glued together creating a permanently laminated block. This technique overcame problems concerning the drying out, warping, and splitting of large solid blocks of wood, and it also incorporated fixed waterlines as part of its structure, important ref-

erence points in the subsequent process of lofting.

With a model blank in hand, Rideout and Hanson attacked it with a variety of woodworking tools to create the practical work of sculpture that it would become. Draw knives and spokeshaves, chisels and hollow gouges, a variety of small planes including hollow- and round-sole types, scrapers and sandpaper made up the modeler's tool kit. When completed, the resulting model represented the shape of the hull at the outside of the frame (or inside of the plank) and to the underside of the rail, i.e., "the moulded dimensions."

The completed half model allowed the designer, builder, and prospective owner to see and criticize the scaled-down, three-dimensional form of the prospective vessel. Once all were satisfied that the form provided the requisite properties of capacity, acceptable sailing qualities, and seaworthiness, its lines were taken off and laid down full size on the mould loft floor. From the lofted lines, patterns (called moulds) were made for the frames and other structural members that gave the vessel its shape.

Percy & Small's surviving half models have since been embellished for display. Mounted on backboards, they now have such decorative elements as stems, keels, sternposts, rudders, bowsprit stubs, nameboards, and chock rails. The WYOMING model differs from the rest in that the horizontal lifts are mounted against a 3/8-inch vertical board which is integral to the model's structure, making it wider and slightly longer at the bow. At first considered an effort to enlarge an existing model, subsequent research suggests that it is an aesthetic element and a hallmark of modeler Bant Hanson.[41]

Unlike the half model, paper plans are far more vulnerable to the passing of time. Yet the few involving wooden shipbuilding in Bath that have survived underscore how little they were actually used in comparison, for example, to those used by steel shipbuilder Bath Iron Works, a contemporary of Percy & Small.[42] Wooden shipbuilders continued to work from the half model right up to the end of the industry in 1920–21.[43] In fact, the only known complete set of construction plans for a wooden schooner ever produced in Bath was drawn by Bant Hanson's son

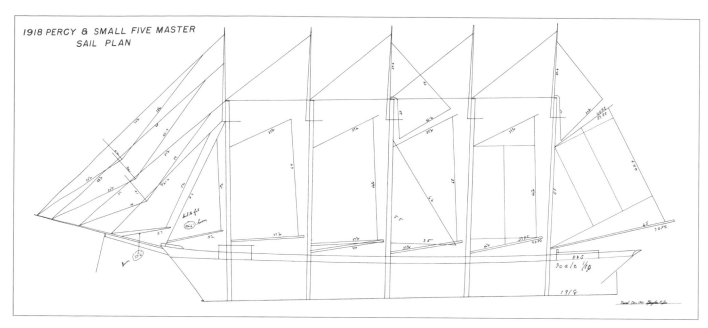

Sail Plan: Percy & Small 1918 Five-Master. Traced from original by Douglas K. Lee.
Courtesy: Captain W. J. Lewis Parker, USCG, Ret.

Midship Section: Hull #42 (Lieut. Sam Mengel). Traced from original by Douglas K. Lee.
Courtesy: Captain W. J. Lewis Parker, USCG, Ret.

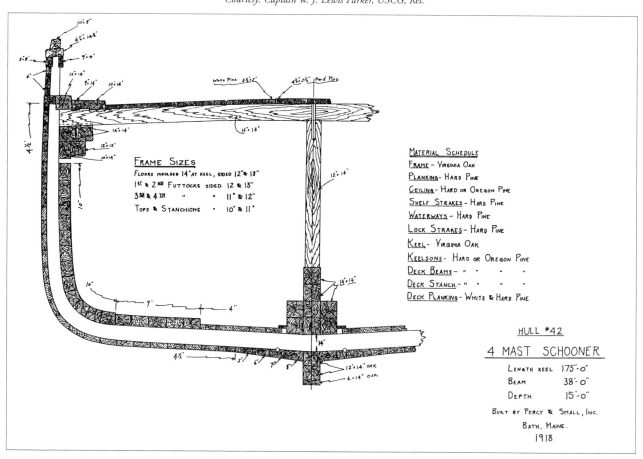

Ole—an academically trained naval architect—from schooners being built at Percy & Small at the time. Coincidentally, it is likely that the schooners from which Hanson the younger drew the plans were originally modeled by his father.[44]

Other scale drawings that have survived to the end of the century fall into three categories: (a) sail and rigging plans; (b) those drawings produced for the information of the surveyor or classification society at their request; and (c) working drawings, frequently on brown paper, of such things as deckhouse layouts and new or special features.

Sail plans were prepared for the use of the sailmaker. They focused on the sails and their dimensions, but everything else except the size and rake of spars were largely abstractions.

Five scale drawings in the second category concerning Percy & Small vessels still exist. Two are alternative formal midship sections of the schooners CORA F. CRESSY and GRACE A. MARTIN, signed "F. W. Rideout," and dated "1-'02" and "2-'02" respectively. Two others are unsigned midship sections of four-masted schooners built in 1918 and 1919. These may have been drawn by Allen Irish, Sam Percy's son-in-law, who was a trained marine draftsman and came into the firm about the time the shipyard's mould loft

was built. The local surveyor or the American Bureau of Shipping may have required these drawings as part of the information, including the construction surveys, that was submitted to the American Bureau of Shipping for evaluation and the classification of the subject vessel. The fifth drawing was probably prepared for the information of the American Bureau of Shipping concerning major efforts to stiffen the badly hogged six-master EDWARD J. LAWRENCE in 1920.[45]

Two plans of the brown-paper, working-drawing variety were discovered by the late Charles S. Morgan when he visited the long-idle Percy & Small Shipyard in 1938. He found the originals, rolled up under the eaves of the mill building in what had been the joiner shop. The plans were scale drawings of the after house layout of Percy & Small's largest schooners, the EDWARD B. WINSLOW and WYOMING. In addition, Maine Maritime Museum possesses deckhouse plans for the ELIZABETH PALMER and the FANNIE PALMER (II), along with a handsome outboard profile and sail plan for the former that are part of the Palmer Collection. They were apparently prepared for the guidance of the inboard joiners as they prefabricated the partition paneling, doors, drawers, and fixed furniture in the shop.[46]

FROM MODEL TO MOULD LOFT TO MOULDS

Translating the three-dimensional half model into the full-sized moulds needed to cut and assemble the frames of a new schooner was a critical step. And it was Fred Rideout and, subsequently, Bant Hanson, along with one or two trusted assistants, who carried out the job, called lofting, for Percy & Small schooners at the old Pattee & Rideout mould loft on Commercial and Commerce Streets just north of the city center. The second-floor loft, measuring approximately 150 feet by 50 feet, was located over a variety of businesses that over the years included junk shops, a produce store, and a bottling works.[47] Regardless of its less than impressive surroundings, the Pattee–Rideout–Hanson loft was of central importance to wooden shipbuilding in Bath and other shipbuilding communities along Maine's coast.[48]

Once the half model was approved by all concerned, the modeler, Rideout or Hanson, moved on to the next step. Placing the model flat side down on a smooth board, a line was carefully traced around it creating the sheer plan, and the intersections of the lifts (waterlines) were picked off on the board. After removing the half model from the board, the waterlines were drawn in as a series of evenly spaced, horizontal, parallel lines enclosed by the outlined profile of the model. Then, using a scale ruler, the modeler marked off selected frame stations from stern to bow along the base of the model before using a try square to draw in the perpendicular lines representing the frame stations on the model's centerline (flat) side. A corresponding set of lines was also drawn in on the simple sheer (profile) plan on the board.

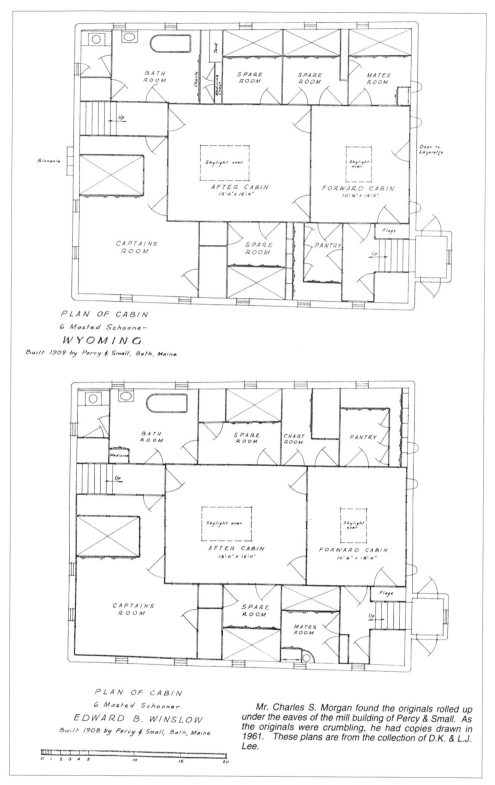

PLAN OF CABIN
6 Masted Schooner
WYOMING
Built 1909 by Percy & Small, Bath, Maine

PLAN OF CABIN
6 Masted Schooner
EDWARD B. WINSLOW
Built 1908 by Percy & Small, Bath, Maine

Mr. Charles S. Morgan found the originals rolled up under the eaves of the mill building of Percy & Small. As the originals were crumbling, he had copies drawn in 1961. These plans are from the collection of D.K. & L.J. Lee.

Plan of Cabin: Schooners WYOMING and EDWARD B. WINSLOW

Courtesy: Captains Douglas K. and Linda J. Lee

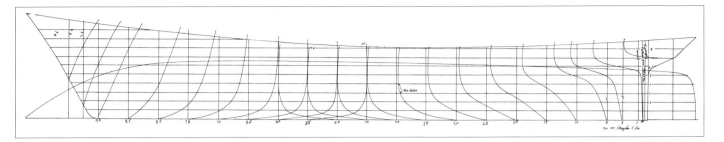

Bant Hanson Four-Masted Schooner Model
From a private collection.

The next step was to take off the shape of the hull at selected points and transfer these curves to the appropriate points in the sheer plan. This was done using either thin lead bars or calipers.

With the former, the bar was placed at the selected frame station marked on the model's back and then carefully bent around the shaped surface on the carved side until it intersected the other end of the frame station. The resulting curve was then traced onto the hull profile at the appropriate frame station. No buttock lines or diagonals were necessary since fairness had already been proved by the model.[49]

At this point, our modeler was ready to go on to the next step: lofting the vessel full size in order to make the necessary moulds. But there was a problem: lofting the entire sheer plan full size could not be done because the loft floor was too short. This necessitated foreshortening the vessel on the loft floor, but fortunately, the long midsection of these vessels with their parallel lines was not essential to the lofting process and was telescoped.[50] It was necessary, however, to loft the ends of the vessel full size where the greatest changes in shape occurred in the shortest distance.

To lay down the sheer plan, Rideout or Hanson first drew in chalk on the loft floor the line representing the top of the keel. Then the horizontal waterlines and vertical frame stations were drawn in full size (the half model and the simple sheer plan drawn on the backboard were done to a quarter-inch=one-foot scale—i.e., 1:48—so it was necessary to multiply all measurements taken from the scaled sheer plan by a factor of forty-eight).[51] What resulted was a grid com-posed of lines crossing at right angles. Now it was possible to plot and draw in the locations and angles of the vessel's stem and sternpost, the keelson, and keel. Once this was completed, the moulds for the stem, apron, stem knee, sternpost, inner post, and stern knee were made up.

The moulds for the frames were made from the body plan, a full-sized drawing of the vessel's hull as viewed end on, showing the curvature and height of the frames at a number of frame stations (one side of the centerline on the plan represented the forward half of the vessel, and the other side represented the after half of the vessel). This plan was created much the same way as the sheer plan with the line marking the keel and the horizontal waterlines.

In order to expand the frame shapes taken off the half model with the lead bars, the loftsman measured the distance from the centerline on each waterline to the point intersected by the outside of the frame. On the full-size body plan, he then ran the measurement out on the appropriate waterline times forty-eight. Once each waterline offset for a given frame station was run out and ticked off, the loftsman arranged a long flexible batten to pass through each of the ticked-off points and fixed it in place with pins or awls driven into the floor. He then traced the curve of the batten onto the floor with chalk.

It wasn't necessary to plot and draw in with chalk the outside line of all the frame stations even at the ends of the vessel, although the experienced loftsman delineated more stations where change was greatest. Once the selected frame stations were plotted and drawn in, that same loftsman then drew in, freehand, each of the remaining frame stations using its immediate neighbors as guides.

Once the frames were plotted and drawn on the body plan, the lofting crew turned its attention to making up all the necessary moulds—floors, futtocks, and top timbers—for each frame, or group of frames if they were identical or close in shape. The methods loftsmen used to transfer the lofted lines from the floor to the moulds varied. Larger mould lofts often used a device called a "banjo frame," but in Maine the loftsmen frequently resorted to a variety of simpler, homegrown methods. Elliott Gamage, for example, arranged copper tacks placed with points up along the outside of the moulded line of the frame. He then took the mould stock—comprised of thin pine boards—and pressed it carefully down over the tacks. Then by drawing a line along the inside of the tack heads, the bandsaw operator knew exactly where to saw out the mould.[52] Others used a homemade version of the banjo frame called a "spider batten." A long, green oak batten would be sawn out with a series of evenly spaced vertical cuts made on one side. The batten was then face-nailed to a series of two-foot-long pine wedges also spaced evenly. To lift the shape of a particular frame station, the batten was aligned, wedge side out, along the outline of the frame and then each wedge was fastened at the thin end with staging nails into the floor. Once aligned to the entire frame, the batten could be lifted enough to allow the mould stock to be slid under it; by tracing along the inside edge of the spider batten, the loftsman transferred the outside shape of that particular piece of the frame to the mould.[53]

Because the frames of the great schooners were "double-sawn" (two frames identical in shape fastened together but with joints well separated), two sets of moulds were needed for each frame station, one for the "short floored" frame called the "laying down frame" or "layer," and one for the long floored frame called the "cover." As many as twelve to sixteen moulds, depending on the size of the vessel, were required for each station with a full frame. Of course, the run of identical amidship frames required only one set of moulds.

Once the moulds for each frame were cut out with

a bandsaw, the next step was to make horning poles. These were long wooden poles square in section with carefully centered holes drilled through each side near the top of the pole. Then the sheer height for that frame was located on the centerline of the body plan and a nail driven in the floor at that point, over which was dropped the horning pole. The "layer" moulds were then set in place on the body plan—short floor, first futtock, third futtock, long top timber—for that frame.

The horning pole was swung in an arc starting at the centerline of the keel and moving on to the end of the short floor mould where it intersected the first futtock mould, end of first futtock mould where it intersected the third futtock mould, top of third futtock mould where it intersected the long top timber, and the top of the long top timber at the rail where it was also the half breadth (moulded). Marks were made on one side of the pole identifying the frame number and each of the intersecting points (see page 117). As we shall see, horning poles were routinely used during the actual framing of the vessel to ensure that all the frame components for each "layer" were properly aligned on both sides of the centerline. They could also be used to enlarge or shrink previously lofted vessels without relofting and making new moulds.

Each individual mould was marked with the appropriate frame number (numbers, if it was one of a sequence of similar frames), the number of frame pieces to be cut from this pattern, which piece it was (i.e., which futtock, floor timber, or top timber), and the degree of bevel to be cut into the frames (if any) at indicated points. One complete set of frame moulds was then bundled up and shipped to the firm that contracted to get out the frame. Because many of these moulds were apt to be damaged, lost, or destroyed while in the field, a second set of moulds was made from the first set and, along with the horning poles, was sent to the shipyard to await the assembly of the newly arrived frame. It is also possible that a third set of moulds may have been made and set aside as masters, in the event that some moulds in the "working" sets were lost or damaged.

The lofting for Percy & Small's schooners was a far less involved and detailed process—although no less

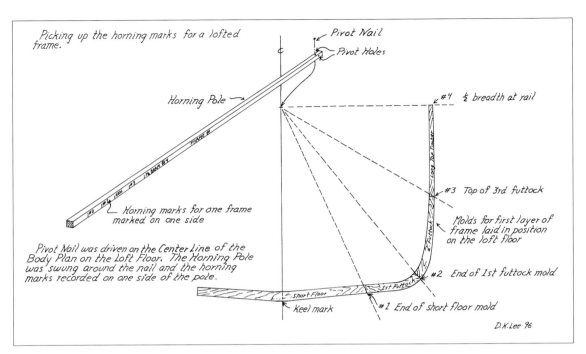

Picking Up Horning Marks for Lofted Frame

Douglas K. Lee

demanding of skill and knowledge—than the lofting of steel vessels, as can be seen by comparing the expenditures of Arthur Sewall & Company for the steel five-masted schooner KINEO and those of Percy & Small for the five-masted schooner OAKLEY C. CURTIS, two similarly-sized vessels. KINEO's bill came to $900 (+/- $13,800 in 1998) compared to $150 spent by Percy and Small on the CURTIS (+/- $2,300 in 1998), six times as much for steel as for wood.[54] True, the requirement for detail accuracy was much greater for steel than for wood, but this was more a reflection of the unforgiving and unmalleable nature of steel as compared to that of timber.

As Percy & Small moved from the design stage to the construction stage of a new schooner, there were no detailed plans of the vessel-to-be. The half model, it was true, represented the hull form but, as we know from experience, it did not necessarily represent size. The American Bureau of Shipping construction standards and scantling rules could convey a rough picture of the new vessel's structure, but only in the most generalized fashion. The prospective managing owner had his conception of the completed schooner, as did the builders. However, the only true and complete record of each vessel's specific design could be found in the schooner itself, as built.

1 Loren Haskell to Harold E. Jordan, 6/22/1963, Parker Collection.

2 Captain Haskell's report is quoted in *BT*, 12/8/1902.

3 *NYMR*, 12/10, 24, 31/1902.

4 *NYMR*, 1/28/1903.

5 *BT*, 1/22/1903.

6 W. F. Palmer to George Welt, 11/18/1902, LB 2/02–6/03, Palmer Collection.

7 Humphreys, Survey of Vessels (Repairs), 1/11/1905. "This certifies that the following work has been done on this vessel for the purpose of strengthening her. Three strakes of yellow pine 12 x 13" reinforcing ceiling in Poop, square fastened with 1 1/8" iron and edge bolted every frame with 1 1/4". Two Lock Strakes on Poop Deck 9 x 13". In between decks, strake of 9 x 12" on lock strake, and four strakes of 6 x 13" fastened to ceiling with 1 1/8" iron each timber and edge every frame, caulked outside from light water up. This work extends the whole length of the vessel."

8 Notes, Parker Collection.

9 Notes, Parker Collection. HELEN W. MARTIN: 9.9 percent; ELEANOR A. PERCY: 8 percent; CORA F. CRESSY: 13 percent.

10 The saga of crew and schooner can be followed in *BT*, 4/5, 6, 7, 24/1915 and *NYMR*, 4/7/1915.

11 Survey Report: M. D. CRESSY, 7/1/1915. Drake Papers, MS-8, MMM, hereafter cited as Drake Papers.

12 *NYMR*, 3/7/1917.

13 *BT*, 4/12/1917; *NYMR*, 4/18/1917. For all of her problems, the CRESSY had a longer than average life span for a five-masted schooner. Nonetheless, she was old and weary, and the new owners—who had full access to her previous surveys and repair records—were aware of her problems.

14 Diego Garcia de Palacio's *Instrucion Nauthica* of 1587, and the first work in English, Edmund Bushnell's *The Compleat Shipwright* of 1660.

15 Albert M. Barnes, "DOROTHY PALMER and WYOMING." Unpublished manuscript. Parker Collection. Her loading ports included Norfolk, Newport News, Baltimore, and Philadelphia. Her delivery ports were Boston and Portland, calling at Boston fifty-four times and twenty-eight times at Portland. She also stopped at New York once to be drydocked while going south light.

16 Captain Douglas K. Lee, "Reconstructed Plans of Schooners Built by Percy & Small." Unpublished manuscript, 1997. The bulk of the material on design is derived from this analysis unless otherwise credited.

17 U.S. Coast & Geodetic Survey, Chart 1209 (Corrected to 2/17/1925).

18 Frederick Sturgis Laurence, *Coasting Passage*. Concord, MA: C. S. Morgan, 2nd ed., 1968, p. 34.

19 *BT*, 1/4/1911: The CURTIS averages 12.37 knots for eight hours; Morgan, "Coasting Schooners," p. 17.

20 J. F. Coates, "Hogging or Breaking of Frame Built Wooden Ships: A Field for Investigation?" *Mariner's Mirror*, May 1980. Coates describes hogging in wooden vessels as "breaking" rather than bending, resulting from shear forces acting on caulking and planking rather than bending of heavy structural members. He also notes that the problem had existed since plank-on-frame vessels had been built.

21 Wooden vessels are not the only ones that have problems with stress. Early welded steel vessels were prone to many stress-related problems, not the least of which included breaking in two. The World War II Liberty Ship was a case in point. After a number broke in two, riveted crack arrestors and other modifications were soon added. One of the most famous cases involved a T-2 tanker built in an Oregon shipyard. SCHENECTADY returned from brief sea trials to her builder's dock. As the final items prior to delivery were being completed, she broke completely in two (1/16/1943) in calm water, tied up at a fitting-out pier! Modern steel vessels have not been totally cured of the problem.

22 Baker, I, p. 489.

23 Captain Douglas K. Lee, "Deck Configurations of Percy & Small Schooners." Unpublished manuscript, 1991. Deck terminology can be very confusing. In this book, the main deck is the so-called "tonnage deck," i.e., the second continuous deck above the keelson. The poop and topgallant forecastle decks are not continuous, but they are weather decks. The uppermost continuous deck of a three-deck, flush-deck vessel is the spar deck and is also the weather deck. Decks other than weather decks need not be completely covered by deck planking as long as the underlying structure—beams, carlings, etc.—is the same as that for a fully laid deck. On most of Percy & Small's schooners, the main deck was planked only in the way of the deckhouses, forecastle, and, of course, when it was the weather deck.

24 The ASA/American Bureau of Shipping "required" vessels exceeding this ratio to be fitted with hogging straps, a method dating back to the 1840s designed to stiffen long, wooden hulls. The underwriters apparently often waived the use of strapping if the builders used larger structural timbers than called for in the tonnage tables.

25 Captain James F. Murphy to Arthur Sewall & Co., 12/15/1892. Box 451, Folder 2, Sewall Family Papers, MS-22, Maine Maritime Museum. Hereafter cited as Sewall Papers. Murphy noted that she leaked five inches an hour at sea or in port. Yet for all her leaking, her cargo of bagged grain suffered no damage.

26 The DUBOIS's master builder was P&S's Willard Hodgkins, who left their employ after the botched launching of the WILLIAM C. CARNEGIE in August 1900. Was it more than simple coincidence that two shipyards, two hundred miles apart, were building vessels of similar size with

the same, unusual deck configuration at the same time?

[27] Conversation: John F. Leavitt with Author, May 1973.

[28] "Half-tide ledge," phrase used by Captain Henry W. Butler in letter to Captain Wiley R. Dickinson, 2/23/1905; Parker Collection. Captains Douglas and Linda Lee interviewed Captain Stinson Davis—the last living master of a great schooner—about 1987. He claimed sailors liked to go in her because she was dry forward when loaded.

[29] W. F. Palmer to Captain C. E. Risely, 10/4/1902; Box 3, Folder 2, Palmer Collection. The Harding mentioned was not the Harding then master of the CRESSY.

[30] Interview with Nancy Zahn by Captains Douglas and Linda Lee at Newcastle, Maine. Captain Percy visited the CRESSY in Bremen in 1938. Ms. Zahn quoted Captain Percy as saying the CRESSY "was an experimental model." Curiously, the only other P&S schooner that had permanent ballast installed was the HELEN W. MARTIN, a long poop model, which had six hundred tons of sand ballast installed at Percy & Small in 1906. *BT*, 7/12/1906.

[31] Charles S. Morgan, "Master in Sail & Steam: The Notable Career of One Maine Shipmaster." Paper presented at 1981 Annual Symposium of the Maine Maritime Museum at Bath, Maine, p. 53.

[32] Winslow was a stovelining patternmaker by trade. See: Parker, *Coal Schooners*, p. 31.

[33] W. H. Bunting, "Review: *Schooner Bertha L. Downs*." *WoodenBoat*, Sept/Oct 1996, p. 101. He also notes that while there were academically trained draftsmen and naval architects who indulged in schooner design—Edward and Starling Burgess, B. B. Crowninshield, and John Alden, to name a few—they added virtually nothing to the schooner world that their more rustic counterparts hadn't already established.

[34] Baker, II, pp. 787-88; *BI*, 10/26/1901; *I&E*, 2/27/1904; *BT*, 10/23/1903.

[35] Bant Hanson File, P&S Research Files: Snow Collection. There are twenty-nine newspaper references to Bant Hanson in this file, not to mention numerous references to his children. Hanson and his family were active and welcome participants in the community's political, religious, social, and business life. It is all the more surprising, therefore, that Mark W. Hennessy, the collector of enormous quantities of data on Bath's maritime industries, never mentions Bant Hanson. Baker, who relied heavily on Hennessy's research, also fails to mention Hanson, the last of Bath's vernacular ship designers.

[36] JOHN BOSSERT and LOUIS BOSSERT.

[37] Aside from the Bossert schooners, he designed some, if not all, of the following: CAMILLA MAY PAGE* (1904), ALICE MAY DAVENPORT (1905), ISABEL B. WILEY (1906), tug to be built in East Boston (1905), fishing schooner LOCHINVAR (1906), ESTHER ANN* (1909), MONTROSE W. HOUK* (1911), tug CHARLES B. GREENOUGH (1913 at

Cobb, Butler). He was master builder for those marked with *. His Percy & Small credits will be found in subsequent chapters.

[38] Baker, I, pp. 126–27.

[39] Baker, I, pp. 128–29. Baker suggests that their first use (about the beginning of the eighteenth century) may have been to precisely define the shape of the vessel's ends not otherwise delineated in contemporary drafting techniques.

[40] Howard I. Chapelle, *National Watercraft Collection.* United States National Museum (Smithsonian), GPO, Washington, 1960, p. 12.

[41] The WYOMING model was made by Bant Hanson. Another privately owned half model examined by the authors has the same unusual vertical board arrangement. That model's provenance and measurements point almost certainly to Bant Hanson.

[42] Maine Maritime Museum possesses a very large collection of BIW plans dating back to 1890 and through the period when P&S was active.

[43] Kelly, Spear did use detailed plans prepared by formally trained naval architects when that firm built the COLUMBINE, a so-called Ferris-hull wooden steamer, for the U.S. Shipping Board.

[44] SALLY WREN Plans, Parker Collection and Douglas K. and Linda J. Lee Collection.

[45] Midship Sections of Schooners CORA F. CRESSY, GRACE A. MARTIN, LIEUT. SAM MENGEL, MIRIAM LANDIS, and EDWARD J. LAWRENCE, Parker Collection.

[46] Morgan had tracings drawn from the crumbling originals in 1961. These plans are in the collection of Captains Douglas K. and Linda J. Lee.

[47] Sanborn Map Company, 1903 and 1909. Commerce Street has long since disappeared under a large parking lot, as has the site of the loft.

[48] It was also important to steel shipbuilders; Bath Iron Works had their first steel vessels, MACHIAS and CASTINE, lofted by Pattee, as were a number of their subsequent vessels. Arthur Sewall & Company had their steel sailing vessels lofted there as well.

[49] Captain Douglas K. Lee, "Reconstructed Plans of Schooners Built by Percy & Small." Unpublished manuscript, 1997. Master Builder Elliot Gamage of Rockland, Maine, recalled his father, John E. Gamage, also a master builder, telling him that his grandfather, John M. Gamage—master builder for I. L. Snow Co. at the turn of the century—did this. There are a number of extant half models with the sheer plan and frame stations drawn on the back of the backboard. The authors examined one such model that appears closely connected to Percy & Small. It is a practice that makes sense: the half model and sheer plan always stay together available for use—and there are no vulnerable paper plans to get lost or to deteriorate beyond use.

[50] In all the years Bath hosted one or more mould lofts,

only one was ever capable of lofting large, oceangoing vessels full size without foreshortening. The Bath Iron Works loft, completed in 1940–41 in East Brunswick, had a clear-span floor 750 feet by 90 feet. It was the largest clear-span mould loft in the country at the time.

[51] All known and presumed Percy & Small half models were done at the quarter-inch scale (1:48).

[52] The information on the "tack technique" of transferring lofted lines to the moulds comes via Jim Stevens, a longtime East Boothbay shipbuilder.

[53] Captain Douglas K. Lee learned this technique at Newbert & Wallace's shipyard at Thomaston, Maine. He later used it lofting the schooner HERITAGE.

[54] KINEO: Cost of Construction, pp. 384-87, Sewall Papers; OAKLEY C. CURTIS Construction Bill File, Parker Collection.

The Shipbuilders of Percy & Small

A DEMANDING WORLD

Charles A. Coombs, Jr., the son of Percy & Small's leading joiner, was a precocious young lad of three summers when he toured the gaily beflagged and about-to-be launched ELIZABETH PALMER with his aunt in hand. As he later recalled, "I expressed extreme satisfaction with the way the schooner was built and thought it would be a great thing to learn to build a thing like that."[1] Sixteen years later—by then a full-fledged joiner at the south end shipyard—Coombs was also aboard the JOSEPH ZEMAN, the last five-master built by Percy & Small, for its launching.

Coombs's history was, however, unusual. By the first decade of the twentieth century, it was becoming increasingly rare for Bath's sons to follow in the footsteps of their wooden-shipbuilding fathers.[2] Percy & Small and the other wooden shipbuilders along the Kennebec found the skilled labor pool shrinking and aging: Gard Deering commented in 1907 that he was running an "old man's home," a telling remark coming as it did from Bath's seventy-four-year-old senior active shipbuilder.[3]

Accustomed as we have become to retirement taking place at or before age sixty-five, not to mention our increasing familiarity with downsizing's phenom-

enon of "early retirement," the age to which many of Percy & Small's shipwrights worked until retirement or death overtook them is mind-boggling. One elderly gentleman, dubber James Tobey (also Sam Percy's father-in-law), took a tumble into the open hold of a schooner in 1897. Tobey—sixty-nine—died from his injuries.[4] Albert Sidelinger, a ship carpenter for his entire life, was injured when he fell into the hold of the EDWARD B. WINSLOW during the fall of 1908 as she sat on the north ways. Fortunately, the seventy-year-old Sidelinger suffered no broken bones and returned to work shortly thereafter.[5]

And then there was Percy & Small's veteran millwright, Henry W. Small, who filled that position for twenty years after a long career that included hitches in the Navy and 21st Maine Volunteer Infantry during the Civil War and as a seaman aboard the small coasting schooner ENIGMA. The latter experience was particularly harrowing: the schooner capsized in a gale, trapping the men below in the cabin. They cut their way with a small hatchet from the cabin to the hold and then from the hold to open air through the bottom of the vessel, a process that took three days. Their travail did not end there, however. For nine more days, they clung to life lashed to a wooden framework they had assembled and anchored in the centerboard opening next to the frequently awash keel before being rescued by the English brig PEERLESS. Throughout that time, they had had a few mouthfuls of fresh water, two small pieces of shark meat, and shared one flying fish. Not surprisingly, Small decided to find shore work after that adventure. He was still the boss at the Percy & Small mill when he died at seventy years, six months.[6]

But these men were mere youngsters compared to Charles Hamilton who was still working as a beveler at the shipyard when he died at age seventy-five, or Alexander McNeal who retired from shipbuilding at age seventy-six, and Patrick Charles McDonald, ship carpenter, who was still working at Percy & Small when he died at age eighty-three![7] Their ability to keep going is all the more remarkable considering that wooden shipbuilding was a physically demanding occupation that required not only skill but stamina to cope with

the fifty-five- to sixty-hour workweeks that were the norm in the Bath shipyards during this period.

Although there is no good statistical picture of the shipyard workers in Bath during the first decade of the century, Nathan Lipfert compiled a fascinating overview from the annual reports of the Maine Bureau of Industrial and Labor Statistics (1888–95) which is revealing:[8]

At this time the average wooden shipyard worker was forty-two years old and worked ten hours per day for $2.43, earning $541 (+/- $9,700 in 1998) per year from his trade. If anyone else in his 3.7-member family worked (there was a 17 percent chance of this), they brought in another $150 (+/- $2,700 in 1998), bringing the average gross family income up to $567. The annual cost of living averaged $474, including $200 for food, $100 for clothing, and $37 for

The soon-to-be launched ELIZABETH PALMER—"a great ark of a coal schooner"—inspired at least one young Bath lad to become a wooden shipbuilder.

Courtesy: Captain W. J. Lewis Parker, USCG, Ret.

fuel and lights (11 percent paid nothing for this item). For seventy-two working days out of every year the worker was unable to get work, primarily because of sickness and other causes. Forty-five percent rented living space, 11 percent lived in boardinghouses, and 44 percent owned homes (11 percent of the homes were mortgaged). The average shipyard worker's home was worth $1,508 (+/- $27,000 in 1998). Sixty-six percent of the workers belonged to labor organizations, 50 percent received weekly benefits when sick, and 23 percent had life insurance. Seventy-five percent had saved money during the past year, although only 36 percent actually had savings accounts.

One of the striking aspects of this analysis is the amount of time the average shipyard worker was out of work during the course of a year—24 percent of total working days each year.[9] The sources of this idleness were many and varied: gaps in shipbuilding contracts, weather and seasonal factors, delays in materials deliveries, illness, or personal choice (there were no paid vacations or holidays). Nonetheless, the loss of a day's pay for many of the shipbuilders in Bath had far less impact than we might normally expect. Many of these men and their families lived a semi-self-sufficient life with kitchen gardens, perhaps a family cow, and access to ample and often free quantities of fuel in the form of shipyard wood chips. As Lipfert also noted in his statistical analysis, 44 percent of these men owned their own homes, however humble they may have been compared to the mansions of Bath's maritime and commercial elite. It was a dramatic indicator of the average shipbuilder's ability to create a lot from a little.

The close relationship between shipbuilding and Bath's south end is captured in this photo by one of the Stinson brothers on 14 November 1900. Taken from High Street looking northeast, the picture includes four big schooners: (left) the OAKLEY C. CURTIS in frame being built by Percy & Small at the Reed shipyard; (center) the MARTHA P. SMALL in frame at Percy & Small's own yard with the completed ELEANOR A. PERCY lying alongside. The big six-master looming over the waterfront will depart for sea the next day. The schooner in frame on the right is Gard Deering's MALCOM B. SEAVEY, which followed the WILLIAM C. CARNEGIE on the ways at the former Chapman & Flint/ McDonald yard. Many of the male residents living in the houses visible here found work at these shipyards.

Stinson Brothers Photo, courtesy of Bath Historical Society

A large percentage of those who were employed on a regular basis at Percy & Small lived in Bath's south end, with the majority located in the area bounded by the Kennebec River on the east, South Street on the north, High Street on the west, and Lemont Street on the south. In fact, much of the residential development in Bath's south end can be traced to the relatively late shipyard development in the area commencing in the immediate post-Civil War era. Until then, Bath's shipyards had been found almost exclusively north of South Street. But after the Civil War, an area that had been largely wooded, interspersed by pastures, exposed ledge (a Bath specialty), gardens, open fields, and a few residences was transformed into a neighborhood of neat workingmen's homes with an occasionally more imposing residence marking the home of a more prosperous, middle class resident.[10] The entire neighborhood was within walking distance of the shipyard—and most of it within hearing distance, as well—but for those who were too tired or lived outside of the south end, there was the local trolley company, the L. A. & W. as it was known locally. It provided transport—sometimes problematical—along the north–south axis of Bath on Washington Street with daily "workingman specials" whose runs were coordinated with shipyard starting and closing times.

During average and good times, idleness was not a major problem. If a ship carpenter faced temporary unemployment at one shipyard, he could shop around among other local shipbuilders for work or even seek interim employment in the building trades. Or he could pack his tools and move temporarily to another location where shipbuilding or ship repair jobs were available. This was a common practice as attested to by a number of shipyard workers employed by Percy & Small. Young Charles Coombs's dad, for example, sometimes took temporary work in East Boston or Providence when things were slow at Percy & Small, returning to the joiner shop as soon as business picked up again.[11] Another Percy & Small employee, Francis Gallagher, a ship carpenter until the day he died, had quite a track record in following work during his career. He had also worked at the Sewall shipyard, Bath Iron Works, a shipyard in

Groton, Connecticut, and in New York, always maintaining his family in Bath.[12]

If times were bad nationally, as they were between 1893–98, it was a different story. There was little likelihood that work could be found anywhere with existing high rates of unemployment. When local ship carpenters did find jobs during these years in Bath shipyards, they often found that their wage rate was as depressed as the economy. This situation was underlined by a two-sentence news item in the *Bath Enterprise*: "'I have got $3 a day in the yard but now get $1.35,' said a Bath ship carpenter one day this week. Times are dull."[13] When plankers at Percy & Small struck in 1896 to increase their wage from $.175 to $.225 per hour, they were forced to return to work without the increase. "It is too bad for men to get no higher wages than they do," Captain Percy said, "but we builders can't help it. At the present state of shipping, we cannot afford to pay any more but would if we could. We think we are lucky to be building at all and surely half a loaf is better than none!"[14] Captain Percy did not mention that the partners had gone deeply into debt to finance the construction of their first three schooners during the 1893 depression.

If Bath shipbuilders responded to the siren song of work in other communities, so did many wooden shipbuilders come to Bath seeking work as the industry declined in their own areas, especially during the last two decades of the nineteenth century. A particularly large contingent from the Maritime Provinces (New Brunswick, Prince Edward Island, and Nova Scotia) were noticeable throughout the city. These migrants introduced new blood into the industry—although some of the new blood was pretty old—and to a degree made up for the declining number of replacements from local stock.[15] It is possible that as many as a fifth of the workers active in Bath's remaining wooden shipyards between 1900 and 1917 were from the Canadian Maritimes.

Willis Pinder was also a migrant to the shipbuilding city, seeking work at the shipyard on Bath's Long Reach (that broad three-mile stretch of the Kennebec running nearly north-south past the city), but he did not come from the Maritimes. For nine straight years Pinder arrived at Percy & Small early in May, ready to

The Lewiston, Auburn, & Waterville Street Railway Company ran "workingman specials" on their tracks in Bath timed to coincide with shipyard starting and knock-off times. Although long the butt of jokes, Bath's version of the "Toonerville Trolley" provided welcome relief to weary shipwrights coming off a ten-hour day, especially those facing long walks to their homes in Bath's north end.

Stinson Brothers Photo, courtesy of Maine Maritime Museum

work. Then in fall, as the trees shed their leaves, Pinder packed his gear and headed south once again to Dorchester in Virginia, where he resided in the winter when not out in the woods with a crew cutting and hewing white oak frames. Pinder became a summer fixture at Percy & Small, a man much admired for his skill with the broadaxe. The local press also demonstrated an uncharacteristic interest in Pinder not apparent with any other migrant worker seeking seasonal employment—except when they were suspected of crimes or became victims of accidents, fatal or otherwise. The truth of the matter was that Willis Pinder was black.

The *Bath Times,* which reported on his departure in 1901, noted that Pinder had once worked in Bath shipyards during the 1880s and had returned out of curiosity in 1901. Then the newspaper revealed that ". . . Pinder [was] one of the few colored men who has worked in Bath shipyards."[16] It was the only reference ever made by the paper to Pinder's race although subsequently, several items in the personal columns were printed over the decade mentioning his comings and goings.[17]

What Willis Pinder was returning to in Bath was employment largely governed by traditional practices concerning hours, organization, and compensation that were only partially impacted by the wave of industrialization sweeping the country.

WORKDAY, WORKWEEK, AND UNIONS

During the first half of the nineteenth century, Bath shipbuilders had worked according to the daylight rule, that is from dawn until dusk. This made for very long days in the summer, especially when the workweek was six days long. During the winter, with its minimum of eight hours of daylight, a man could actually become acquainted with his family, at least for a period of a few months.[18]

By 1850, however, the ten-hour day was rapidly becoming the established practice in Bath shipyards. The workers were expected to be ready to turn-to at 6:30 A.M., with an hour set aside for the noon meal ("dinner"), and knock-off coming at 5:30 P.M. During the four months of least daylight (November-

February), the hours were reduced to eight in those shipyards that worked through the winter (including Percy & Small), with the starting whistle or bell sounding at 7:00 A.M. and the closing whistle sounding at 4:00 P.M.

The workweek at Percy & Small was six days, except during the summer months when the men knocked off after a half-day on Saturdays.[19] Of course, the actual length of a man's workweek was determined by the amount of work available in the shipyard as well as the weather. But during the first decade of the century, Percy & Small had enough new construction and repairwork to keep a crew of men employed year-round almost continuously.

During this period there was a union active in Bath that claimed to represent the majority of Bath's ship carpenters. Its first effort on behalf of its membership was particularly successful, gaining a two-and-a-half cent per hour increase in 1899 without resorting to a strike, although this advance followed a period during the 1890s depression when hourly wages had actually declined.[20] But its next crusade, the nine-hour day—with nine-hours' pay—was stoutly resisted by Bath's shipbuilders, including Percy & Small, even though firms on and around Penobscot Bay were paying more for ship carpenters working a nine-hour day than Bath was paying for a ten-hour day.[21] Some of this resistance to "progress" may have been, in part, a backhanded recognition on the part of Percy & Small and a few of the shipbuilders in Bath that it would be difficult, if not impossible, to increase the skilled workforce pool enough to cover the shortfall of man-hours brought by a shorter workweek.

The first confrontation over the nine-hour-day demand occurred in March 1900 when workmen took advantage of the shift from the winter starting hour (7:00 A.M.) to the regular work starting hour (6:30 A.M.). Instead of reporting at the new starting time on Monday, the carpenters reported to their shipyards at the seven o'clock hour. Kelley, Spear and the New England Company immediately took a hard line, turning away all workmen who failed to report at the earlier starting time, effectively locking them out. Workers at the William Rogers shipyard and Percy & Small, however, commenced work at seven o'clock without a lockout, although Sam Percy allowed that the starting bell would be rung at 6:30 A.M. the next day.[22]

A storm intervened the next day and several of the shipyards didn't open for work because of the weather, but on Wednesday the confrontation continued. At the Rogers shipyard the men started at 7:00 A.M., but at Kelley, Spear and the New England Company work started at 6:30 A.M. with plenty of carpenters on hand for work. Captain Percy decreed work would start at his yard at 6:30, but only a few carpenters reported at that hour, a particular problem given Percy & Small's crowded production schedule involving the CARNEGIE in the Deering yard and the ELEANOR A. PERCY in their own shipyard.[23]

But the shipbuilders' resistance to the nine-hour day continued with only William Rogers conceding to the shorter day after receiving assurances from the carpenters' union that they would not ask for higher wages for at least a year. But with 500 ship carpenters locked out of their jobs and no sign that the other shipbuilders were ready or willing to shorten the workday, the union finally capitulated.[24]

The combination of limited opportunity to find employment in their chosen trades and economic necessity—a reduction of 10 percent in their weekly hours would have meant a reduction of 10 percent in their wages which was unsustainable—compelled the ship carpenters back into the ten-hour-day mold, but they never quite gave up on the goal.[25] In 1904 they reintroduced the issue but eschewed the strike as a means to support their request.[26] It went nowhere.

For some, those largely unencumbered by home and family, occasional help-wanted ads sometimes provided relief from the apparent obstinacy of Bath's dwindling roster of wooden shipbuilders. For example, the Stirling Shipyard & Machine Works of Greenport on Long Island once put an advertisement in the Bath Times for ship carpenters promising wages of $3 per day for a nine-hour day.[27] But there is little evidence that many Bath shipwrights packed their tools and caught the first train to New York in response to the ad's blandishments. Those who did were likely to find that any advantage in higher wages and shorter hours was largely canceled out by higher living costs and separation from family and friends.

Although there was occasional discontent on the part of the shipyard workers with their working conditions and/or employers, the relationship between the two generally appeared to range from non-confrontational to openly friendly. Those shipyard employees who lived long enough to be interviewed recalled the days of wooden shipbuilding not as nirvana but a combination of hard work relieved by the occasional fistfight, a rough sort of camaraderie interspersed with an equally tough competitive spirit, practical jokes, humor, friendships, and pride in work well done.

THE WORKPLACE

Today's workers would find the workplace amenities more than a little sparse, but Percy & Small's workmen had for the most part no complaint about their lot, although smoking was almost universally banned throughout the shipyard with the noticeable exception of inside the office and the blacksmith shop. So most of the workers addicted to nicotine resorted to chewing tobacco during the working day, a habit that once permanently discouraged young Charlie Coombs from dipping tar out of the pitch oven. The prevalence of the "chaw" at the shipyard is fully confirmed to this day by a collection of metal chewing tobacco seals carefully fastened over the years to a wall in the paint shop by anonymous shipyard workers.[28]

Those workmen who preferred to puff on their pipes, cigars, or the more recently developed cigarettes could find a smoking refuge in the blacksmith shop during their noon meal—they were not encouraged to hang out there otherwise—as long as they were acceptable to Len Gibson, the boss blacksmith. There was the added advantage, except during hot weather, of having one's dinner with its six or seven sandwiches, jug of soup, and jar of cold coffee in a warm area and, additionally, of being able to heat one's soup, coffee, or tea on red-hot iron clinch rings arranged on the hearths by the blacksmiths. There were also ongoing games of gin rummy and checkers carried forward from day to day during the noon hour, providing those assembled with ample opportunity to kibitz.[29]

For those not a part of the "blacksmith's set," there were three other places where heat was to be had and the men could find a place to eat, talk, and play cards or checkers while waiting for the bell to call them back to work: the aforementioned paint shop, the joiner shop on the second floor of the mill, and the little oakum shop perched near the river. In each, a stove fueled by wood chips from the yard provided a modicum of warmth during the cooler parts of the year.

During warmer weather, most of the men would take their meal out-of-doors, often seeking shade under the hull of one or another schooner perched on her keel blocks. It was also a time a worker could be assured of a large audience if he chose to demonstrate his physical prowess by performing acts of "derring-do." Young Coombs was once tempted to emulate one rigger who liked to show off by going hand-over-hand from masthead to masthead on the spring stay a hundred feet above the schooner's deck. Coombs rethought his plan as soon as he reached the crosstrees and looked down. Good sense prevailed over bravado, and he sheepishly descended to the deck.

And then there was Hans Mitchell, another rigger in Frank Palmer's gang of daring young men. Mitchell's basic feat was to make a running start on the forecastle deck and charge right up the bowsprit and jibboom before grabbing hold of the jib topsail stay and fore topgallant stay at the very end of the jibboom, sixty to seventy feet above the ground. There didn't appear to be many who challenged Hans Mitchell's sense of balance and lack of fear of heights—Coombs said many years later that Mitchell "was not afraid of anything." And Tom Robson summed up the riggers when he said, "the riggers were all men."

The workmen at Percy & Small, however hard their lives may seem to us, were also capable of exercising a little humor, even at the expense of the bosses. Miles M. Merry, the shipyard's universally respected master builder, was in the habit of carrying a measuring stick that he used to check the length of timbers before designating them for a particular place in keel, keelson, or framework of a new schooner. Some said his measuring stick was six feet in length, others said it was ten feet in length. It was agreed, however, that at one point, some brave soul found the stick where it had been laid by Merry when he was called over to render a decision on a particular construction problem. The finder, mercifully never identified by Merry, then proceeded to cut several inches off the official measuring stick of the master builder. Merry used his altered measuring stick for only a short time before he realized that there was a distinct conflict between ten feet—or six feet—as measured by his experienced eye and ten feet—or six feet—as delineated by his foreshortened measuring stick.

On another occasion in late spring, workmen uncovered a pile of snow buried under an insulating cover of sawdust and woodchips. A vigorous exchange of snowballs ensued until boss blacksmith Len Gibson sauntered by bound for the office. The snowballs disappeared as he passed by, then Percy & Small's longtime blacksmith received an icy reminder of winter past right in the back of the neck.[30] Gibson's response to the chilly surprise was not recorded.

As with any group that worked closely together for long hours, there were instances of personal friction. Some of these were spawned by perceived character faults in others, some resulted from the heat generated by competitive spirit. Louis B. Thebeau, a native of Nova Scotia, had come to Bath seeking work in the local shipyards as a young man, married and raised a large family, and worked the last nine years of his life at Percy & Small (1900–09) building the schooners' small boats with Harry Stinson. His constant companion on the job was a very large, furry, Newfoundland dog.

Thebeau, during the years he worked at the shipyard, acquired the reputation—rightly or wrongly—of being excessively neat; a neatness that primarily involved picking up unattended hand tools and adding them to his own tool chest. Sam Barnes recalled one occasion when the estimable Louis came across a solitary, unemployed broadaxe which promptly made its way into his tool chest. A short time later, the irate owner of said broadaxe, ship carpenter Lemuel Frye, confronted Thebeau and demanded to inspect the contents of the latter's tool chest. Sure enough, there was the missing broadaxe. But before the livid Frye could remonstrate further, Thebeau turned to his dog exclaiming, "that son-of-a-gun dog steals everything he sees."[31]

Fistfights were not a common occurrence at the shipyard, but they were known to happen. More often than not, they appear to have been ignited by a combination of the competitive spirit, an opponent's jeering, and an excess of testosterone. About the only sanctioned competition at Percy & Small involved the planking gangs assigned to the same vessel. Although never mentioned, it is more than a little likely that the competing plankers were not averse to a little betting action on which team would finish its side of the schooner first.

For the most part, however, the relations between the men who built the big schooners—shipwrights, leadingmen, foremen—remained solidly grounded on common interest. They were often neighbors, relatives, friends, co-religionists, and members of the same fraternal organizations that flourished during this period. Many were particularly active in Freemasonry, an association which brought together a diverse group of men associated with Percy & Small including Sam Percy, Frank Small, Miles M. Merry, Ocea Cahill, Fred Rideout, Bant Hanson, James Spinney, James Brewster, Fred Colby, Al Havener, and Henry Small. In fact, Sam Percy was so involved in the Masonic Order's top charitable organization, the Kora Temple, that he arranged for the colorfully uniformed Shriners with all their ceremonial regalia to grace a Percy & Small launching.

Life was a great deal simpler at the beginning of the twentieth century than it is today, and people did not expect the level of amenities that have since become the norm. Percy & Small, for example, provided one water faucet from which the workmen could draw water for drinking. It was located at the east end of the blacksmith and machine shop, next to the boiler room and the only place in the shipyard that was kept heated throughout the winter even when the shipyard was idle. It could be argued that this was not done for the convenience of the workmen but rather to keep the sole fire hydrant in the shipyard from freezing even during bitter weather. Nevertheless, the workmen did benefit and the shipyard even provided a tin cup, attached to the wall by a chain, for the convenience of its workforce.

Toilet facilities—"the necessary"—were, if anything, even more basic. There was a flush toilet in the office across the road from the shipyard, but this was reserved for office staff, Sam Percy, and the various "boss" workmen. The bulk of the shipyard workers had to rely on a flimsy privy overhanging the tidal basin, sandwiched between the fitting-out pier upon which it was built and the south pier.[32] It was the subject of considerable folklore on the part of those who worked at the shipyard; its lack of privacy and loca-tion did not encourage contemplative interludes, especially when the north wind howled down the Kennebec in the winter.

The shipyard crew had long agitated for a more hospitable arrangement according to Raleigh Osier, a planker during the war years, when someone came up with the perfect solution to the noisome, shabby, and uncomfortable privy. When the next launching took place, some of the launching crew placed the snubbing cable for the cradle around the structure. When the schooner launched, she took the offending privy with her, now reduced to kindling.[33] The next morning, Captain Percy had the carpenters build a new one in the place vacated the day before by its predecessor. The new one was, if anything, more primitive.[34]

SHIPYARD SAFETY

In a world of deadly sharp tools, dangerous machin-ery unprotected by anything more than the most rudimentary guards, and the lifting and moving of very heavy objects, on-the-job injuries—some fatal—were to be expected in a busy shipyard. These injuries were usually reported in the press, so it is possible today to gain some understanding of the on-the-job risks, the nature and frequency of the injuries, and the cause and frequency of fatalities at Percy & Small.

Unfortunately, no such data exists for disabilities such as bad backs, hernias, bad knees, and over-worked hearts that occurred over the long term. These were not usually reported in the press, so it is hard today to get a picture of the total price men paid to work in wooden shipyards in general and Percy & Small in particular.

During the twenty-three years Percy & Small actively engaged in shipbuilding and ship repair, fifty-three men were involved in accidents reported by the press. Six of these accidents resulted in death (11 per-cent), eight in broken bones (15 percent), and two resulted in the amputation of a finger or finger tips (4 percent). To place these figures in the broader industrial context, 146 workers died in a single fire at a New York shirtwaist factory in 1911.[35] In point of fact, employ-ment at Percy & Small almost represented the low end of risk for workplace injuries, although there were risks.

The most frequent accident at Percy & Small involved falls off staging, deck beams, or into a vessel's hold. Twenty such accidents were reported in the press—38 percent of total accidents reported. Three of the falls were fatal, including Sam Percy's father-in-law. Seven of the workmen who fell suffered broken bones but recovered, including Miles Merry who once fell fifteen feet from a deck beam, breaking his shoul-der.[36] Yet, given the fact that riggers routinely worked far above the ground, it is interesting to note that only one rigger at Percy & Small was ever reported to have fallen from aloft. Frank Duley fell 60 feet into the river—fortunately missing the vessel on the way down—while working aloft on the REBECCA PALMER at the shipyard for repairs. He emerged from the river wet and shaken but otherwise uninjured.[37]

The second largest group of accident victims (17 percent) were, ironically, the victims of a single, freak incident of a lightning strike. One man, Leander Miller, was killed and eight others suffered from vari-ous degrees of temporary disorientation and/or loss of hearing or sense of touch for weeks and even months after the incident.

Injuries involving squeezing or crushing were the third most common at Percy & Small, amounting to 13 percent of the total. None of the accidents resulted in fatalities although one involved broken bones and others were quite serious. Miles M. Merry was one of the victims of such an accident, one that could have cost him an arm if not his life as it turned out. A hands-on type of manager, Merry was supervising the setting of one of the hawse timbers in place in the bow of the ADDIE M. LAWRENCE with his hand on the timber when it pivoted and jammed his left hand against another timber. The force was so great that it nearly severed three of his fingers. After a visit to the doctor to have the injury dressed, Merry returned to work. Unfortunately, the wound became infected and the shipyard's stoical master builder was soon in bed. There he remained for months as he and the doctor fought the infection with the limited arsenal of weapons at hand. During Merry's extended absence, Eliakim McCabe served as acting master builder.[38]

Injuries resulting from sharp objects were next in the frequency sweepstakes with six instances reported, 11 percent of the total, and one resulting in death. The sixty-three-year-old Columbus P. Nash was at work under the ALICE M. LAWRENCE with his adze when he was tripped up by a line being used to haul a plank under the schooner. He fell on his adze and died the next day.[39] Most of these accidents, however, involved cutting the ankles or shins with an adze.

To caulker Ephraim Toothaker, who was killed when his coat caught in the messenger chain driving the gypsy head warping a schooner into the pier, goes the dubious honor of being the only person to be killed by machinery at the shipyard.[40] In fact, only five serious injuries were inflicted by machines, or careless behavior around them, including two involving lost fingers or finger tips. This is all the more remarkable considering the amount of machinery found in the mill and joiner shops, its constant use, and its almost total lack of protective equipment.

The smallest number of injuries resulted from blows and heat prostration. The former was usually the result of two or more persons wielding hammers or mauls to drive bolts or to bend and shape red-hot steel. Someone would get out of synchronization and two hammers or mauls would meet. The resulting injuries could be serious. Charles Varney and two helpers were hammering on a piece being fabricated in the blacksmith shop when their hammers hit in mid-swing. Varney's hammer flew back, striking him in the eye. For a time, Varney's sight in that eye was in doubt.[41] Blows came from other sources as well: Alexander Ferguson, a ship carpenter, was struck on the head by a falling staging plank. Dr. Fuller sutured the wound and announced that Ferguson's "skull was not fractured much."[42] Heat prostration was equally rare, but on one particularly hot day three men collapsed from the heat. After being revived, the firm hired hackney carriages to take them home.[43] Following this incident, Percy & Small adopted the policy of knocking off work on extremely hot days.

For the most part, Percy & Small's safety record appears to have been commendable in an era when concerns for a worker's health and safety were not high on the industrial agenda. This achievement perhaps had less to do with deliberate policy from the front office than it had to do with the experience level of its workforce. These were men who well knew the potential dangers lurking about them and consciously guarded against them.

SHIPYARD ORGANIZATION

It soon became evident after the formation of the Percy & Small partnership that the shipbuilding side of the business was Captain Sam Percy's bailiwick.[44] Once the south end shipyard became fully operational during the busy first decade of the new century, Percy spent more of his time at the shipyard than at the firm's Front Street headquarters.

The nerve center of the shipyard operation was at the office built across the street on the leased Stinson land. Although decidedly smaller and less luxurious than the firm's uptown quarters, the shipyard office was a busy, even frenetic place on occasion. It was here that Captain Sam hung his hat, conferred with Master Builder Merry and the assorted subcontractors, met with clients or talked with them by telephone, dickered with vendors over prices, dictated letters, and, no doubt, socialized with friends and fellow shipbuilders when the opportunity presented itself.

Nothing in the way of a description of the shipyard office has come down to us today, but from the few peripheral views in assorted shipyard photos, it was more than twice the size of the oakum shop, perhaps measuring 20 feet by 24 feet, but cramped compared to the uptown office. It did have a lavatory with a flush toilet situated in the southwest corner of the structure, and a chimney and stove in the northeast corner. Captain Percy had a desk here, as did Miles Merry. There was also space for at least a clerk/ typist who compiled the materials lists, typed up the orders, kept the time slips for all Percy & Small employees at the yard which were sent to the uptown office weekly, and generally kept track of orders and invoices, neatly organized in wooden boxes with hull number and/or initials of each new vessel.[45] That clerk remained anonymous until the last years of the shipyard when Ena F. Bucknam, the only woman so far identified as being in the employ of the firm, held the position of stenographer/typist at the shipyard.[46] The shipyard's accounting, including payroll, accounts payable, and billing were all handled in the uptown office where Frank Small, ably seconded by head bookkeeper J. Clifford Spinney, kept the firm's books, paid its bills, and collected its receivables.[47]

It is probable that another person also worked in the shipyard office as storekeeper. In order to ensure accurate cost accounting, it was essential that someone keep track of the materials ordered, delivered, and charged against each vessel. When materials were left over, the vessel's construction accounts needed to be credited for the leftovers that were then added to the shipyard's stock inventory or used in the construction of another vessel and so charged. On 1 January 1914, for example, an inventory of stock in the shipyard revealed $5,810 (about $77,000 in 1998) of stock charged to Schooner #32 and $26,130 (about $350,000 in 1998) of stock charged to the shipyard's general inventory.[48]

Nitpicking clerical and accounting details notwithstanding, Miles Melvin Merry was the man in charge of the day-to-day operations at the shipyard. Born in 1843, Merry had achieved the position of a master builder in 1865 at the age of twenty-two. By the time he came into the employ of Percy & Small in

1900, he had thirty-five years of cumulative experience as a master builder for William Rogers, Goss, Sawyer & Packard, and Arthur Sewall & Co., and over a hundred wooden vessels to his credit, including the ROANOKE, Sewall's last, and largest, wooden square-rigger. Before retiring in 1916, Merry oversaw the construction of more wooden sailing vessels exceeding 3,000 GRT than any other person in history.

Merry's entire life didn't revolve exclusively around shipbuilding, however. He was married twice—his first wife died in 1895—and had a son who died in 1901 at age thirty. Merry was also a well-known owner of some very fast trotting horses that he entered in races around the state. He was even known to take the reins himself on occasion. But with the turn of the century, he gradually wound down his stable and satisfied his thirst for speed with the new-fangled horseless carriage, starting with a product of Maine genius, the Stanley Steamer. Subsequently, he owned several automobiles. One, at least, put him in as embarrassing a situation as a ship refusing to launch when the automobile broke down in the country and required a tow by a farmer's team of horses back to town.[49]

Although he frequently insisted to wide-eyed little boys that the world was flat, Merry enjoyed enormous respect from his employers, their customers, and the men with whom he worked.[50] When the ALICE M. LAWRENCE was dragged over some of the ledges at the Graves as she was being towed into Boston Harbor, she suffered heavy damage to her hull that required immediate drydocking. At the request of managing owner Eleazer Clark, Merry was soon on his way to Boston to supervise the replacement of 130 feet of keel and eleven strakes of planking on one side and four on the other.[51] When William F. Palmer needed an expert witness to testify to the structural damage done to the big HARWOOD PALMER by the steamer JUNIATA, it was Merry who traveled to Boston to testify on behalf of the schooner's owners—he, after all, had supervised the schooner's repairs at Percy & Small.[52]

Merry and the sometimes-officious Palmer enjoyed an interesting relationship. On the one hand, the

Boston shipowner admired Merry's enormous reservoir of shipbuilding experience, so much so that he once tried indirectly to recruit Percy & Small's master builder to run the bankrupt George Welt shipyard in Waldoboro.[53] On the other hand, Palmer was not above asserting his authority as a customer and his ego as a "trained" naval architect. The Palmer Letterbooks contain numerous letters from Palmer to Percy & Small, admonishing Sam Percy—and Miles Merry— on this point or that. One can almost see the three men standing together discussing the rake of the masts, the vessel's sheer, or the number and placement of the hooks and pointers. All through Palmer's monologue, Miles Merry nods, as if in full agreement with the naval architect and managing owner's wishes. Yet from one such discussion came the following letter from Palmer to Captain Walter B. Wiley, soon to be skipper of the then-building FANNIE PALMER (II):

It makes me hopping mad to think that they [Percy & Small] have located those hooks and pointers so as not to have 6 forward and five aft. Myles (sic) Merry is a past master in buncoing us in this regard, but the deck itself forward and aft must be made into good hooks.[54]

It would appear that "Myles" was basically willing to listen to all the customer's theories on what made a good vessel and be agreeable. But he built the vessel his own way.

The size of the workforce that Merry directed varied considerably according to the shipyard's workload at any given time. As many as 250 men were working at the shipyard during the summer of 1908 and as few as a dozen worked there when contracts for new construction were lacking and ship repair business was slow as during the first three months of 1910.[55]

The workforce directed by Merry was composed of Percy & Small employees and a group of subcontractors and their workmen, some of whom were more or less permanently based at the shipyard. Of the latter, we have already met Len Gibson, boss blacksmith, who employed as many as six smiths and helpers in the shipyard's smithy.

Fred B. Scott, boss joiner, was associated with

Percy & Small for nearly a quarter century before a bad heart retired him and he was succeeded by Charles Coombs, Sr. As with Miles Merry, Scott's personal life was marred by tragedy. His only son, a brilliant student near the top of his class at the military academy at West Point, contracted malaria, dying at home not long after his twentieth birthday. Then, four years later, Scott's wife died suddenly from pneumonia. Yet he carried on, supervising the joiner work with up to ten men on nearly forty schooners before his ailments caught up with him in the fall of 1917.

Master joiner Scott and his men not only produced the elegant paneling and finish work found in the after house, but they also framed and finished all the deckhouses, and fabricated and installed all wooden deck furniture, including the turned stanchion fly rails. Sometimes this group was referred to as "inboard joiners" to distinguish them from their less-skilled "outboard joiner" counterparts. The latter, however, were regular shipyard carpenters assigned to such tasks as putting down the decks and scraping planking in preparation for painting.

Two other subcontractors also based much, if not all, of their operations at Percy & Small. Boss caulker Charles H. Oliver held forth at the oakum shop, the little frame building overlooking the waterfront, from the day it was built until the shipyard closed. He learned the caulker's trade at the New England Company and has been credited with supervising the caulking of one hundred new vessels during the course of his career.[56] Oliver, a man of imposing girth, struck quite a figure attired in his ever-present bowler hat, black suit (jacket tightly buttoned), white shirt with celluloid collar, and tie as he supervised his caulkers from the steps of the oakum shop.

With a crew that could number as many as thirty men when there were two vessels on Percy & Small's ways, Oliver was responsible for the caulking of up to twelve miles of seams—or more—on new vessels, not to mention the recaulking of older vessels in for repairs. When his men couldn't work on the schooners due to weather conditions, he put some of them to work in the shop spinning oakum into 25- to 30-foot hanks for future use.[57]

Another key subcontractor who also worked out of

Percy & Small for many years was James H. Cameron, sparmaker. A native of Mabou Bridge on Cape Breton, Cameron was actually trained as a ship carpenter and was once a master builder at the Bean shipyard in Camden. He returned to Bath to take over his younger brother Lewis's sparmaking business in 1906 after the latter was killed in a freak trolley car accident near his home.[58] James Cameron used the Donnell yard for many years to make spars, a definite convenience given that the bulk of his work was destined either for new Percy & Small vessels or vessels being repaired in their shipyard.[59]

Another subcontractor of long standing at Percy & Small was boss painter James R. Jewett, who worked out of the second floor of the paint and treenail shop with its wall decorated with plug tobacco seals. The walls were not only decorated by the seals, but with the archaeological remains of brush cleaning and experimental efforts with graining and other painting techniques. The painters, it should be noted, mixed virtually all of their own paint excepting varnish and the anti-fouling paint used below the light waterline on each schooner.

Subcontractors not based at Percy & Small, but who were consistently at work on P&S vessels, included Frank Palmer, who supervised the rigging of every vessel built or repaired by Percy & Small over a quarter century, and Charles S. and Fred Colby, whose crews fastened Percy & Small's schooners as well as those of G. G. Deering. William F. Palmer—no relation to Frank—rarely deferred to anyone's judgment but his own, but he specified that the final arbiter of the sizes and quality of standing and running rigging in his Bath-built schooners was to be Frank Palmer, the man who was in charge of installing it.[60] Sam Percy showed his confidence in Frank Palmer's talents by selecting him to do all Percy & Small rigging work for a quarter century. As Palmer maintained his own rigging loft in Bath, his crew did not appear at the shipyard until it was time to step the masts and install the already made-up standing rigging. Then his crew performed their assorted feats of derring-do, not the least of which was the actual stepping of the huge masts.

For many years the fasteners of choice at Percy & Small were led by Charles S. Colby, succeeded by son Fred N. Colby, who became foreman fastener at both Percy & Small and the Deering shipyards. Several years after the two shipyards had closed down, the younger Colby was senior assistant during the restoration of CONSTITUTION at the Boston Naval Shipyard.[61] The Colbys—father and son—were charged with the responsibility of making sure that the many thousands of pieces of timber that made up the great schooners were firmly attached to each other. Their crew included several men—including Sam Barnes, interviewed in the 1970s—who, among other things, must have possessed impressive shoulders considering the very deep holes the men drilled with the hand-cranked augers then in use through oak, hardwood, and yellow pine, not to mention the driving of many thousands of treenails, bolts, and ship spikes in every vessel they fastened. During the war years, Captain Sam Percy decided to install a fancy system of air-driven tools, including hammers and augers, to speed up production and reduce the need for manpower. The old-time fasteners, however, were not impressed, claiming that the air-driven augers left oblong holes that did not grasp fastenings as effectively as those holes drilled by the old hand-operated augers.[62]

Percy & Small also subcontracted one other specialized wooden shipbuilding trade, dubbing. This specialty involved only a few men who, with their razor sharp adzes, carefully trimmed the surface of the frames so that frame and planking fitted tightly together and each strake of planking remained fair.

Specialty firms also provided work crews at various stages of a schooner's construction for work not directly connected to wooden shipbuilding. There were masons, ship plumbers, a decorative wood carver, electricians, steelworkers, and steamfitters.

Bath Iron Works sent a team of machinists and ironworkers to fabricate and install bow and keelson irons; they also assisted in strapping some of the big schooners when required. Hyde Windlass Company, in turn, sent a crew of mechanics and steamfitters to install and hook up the extensive list of equipment provided by that firm, from boiler, hoisting engines, and wrecking pumps to windlass, steering gear, patent chain stoppers, and the steam heating system.[63]

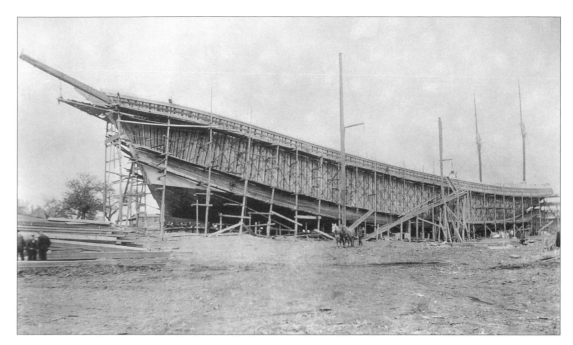

Above: The giant WYOMING provides shade for shipyard workers ranged along her keel from the bow as they eat their dinner, although the shipyard team appears to be doing without both. Note the heavy frame, diagonal strapping, and status of the planking. Probably most of the men tucking into their vittles make up the planking gangs, dubbers, and fasteners.

Perry Thompson Photo, courtesy of Maine Maritime Museum

Percy & Small's prime movers idling with their handlers. Stabled on Middle Street extension, a block from the shipyard, these teams were supplemented when necessary by hired teams.

Courtesy: Maine Maritime Museum

Opposite: Percy & Small Shipyard Workers: Date Unknown
About a third of these men are identified.
First row: (*left to right*) unk., Bert Preble, Willard Dodge, unk., Miles M. Merry, unk., Ed Hamilton, Alex Ferguson, Al Havener, unk., unk.
Second row: (*left to right*) Jim Gillis, Willard H. Sampson, John Sonia, unk., unk., unk., unk., unk., unk., Sam Soule, Franklin "Buck" Savage, Alex McCullough.
Third row: (*left to right*) unk., unk., Frank Sylvester, unk., unk., unk., Charles Burnham, unk., unk., Melville Williams.
Back row: (*left to right*) unk., unk., John Berry, unk., unk., unk., unk., unk., unk., Harding Zwicker, Charles Emero, unk., unk., unk., unk.

Courtesy: Maine Maritime Museum

J. A. Winslow & Son of Bath—no relation to J. S. Winslow & Company—was, for years, Percy & Small's ship plumber. Aside from installing the heads, the firm hooked up the internal water system that connected galley and after cabin with the vessel's water supply tanks, and installed the waste and deck drainage systems.

W. G. Bates of Bath usually did the masonry work on Percy & Small schooners. Such work involved the installation of masonry to protect the wooden decks in the way of the galley range and the schooner's donkey boiler. It also involved the cementing of all the caulked seams from the garboards to the light waterline (seams above the waterline were finished with white lead putty or seam paint).

Percy & Small's direct employees constituted the largest single block of workmen at the shipyard. Henry W. Small, of ENIGMA fame, was the boss millwright responsible for the maintenance and repair of all the machinery in the entire shipyard and the specific operation of the mill floor. Although the number of men working the mill has never been stated, during busy times it is likely that as many as six to eight persons operated the circular sawmill, Daniels planer, and jigsaw.

The biggest group of Percy & Small employees were the ship carpenters, a category that covered a number of specialized skills. For many years they came under the direct supervision of Miles M. Merry's number two in the shipyard, Eliakim McCabe. Numbering as many as 125–150 men at peak periods or as few as a dozen during dull times, this group was organized into highly skilled, temporary, task-oriented "gangs" who literally erected and clothed the vessel's skeleton. Once a gang completed its assigned task, it was dissolved and the men assigned to new jobs with other gangs. At Percy & Small they set up the keel, assembled and erected the frames, framed the stern, installed the deadwood and keelsons, installed deck beams and fore-and-aft stringers, and planked and ceiled the vessel. Others worked as outboard joiners, laying decks and scraping and planing the hull prior to painting, etc. The flexible gang system was an effective method of ensuring that the highly skilled and knowledgable ship carpenters were on hand for every phase of schooner construction, passing on their hard-won skills to dwindling numbers of apprentices.

Virtually all of the shipyard workers who used hand tools supplied their own. Joiners, ship carpenters, fasteners, dubbers, riggers, sparmakers, caulkers, and the smiths often had large, elaborately finished tool chests which they hauled from job to job during the course of their careers. These tools often represented a large investment on the part of the workman and were—literally—his stock in trade. It was no surprise that ship carpenters such as Lemuel Frye were more than a little protective of their tools. The shipyard furnished the powered machinery along with heavy planking and ceiling clamps and timber handling equipment such as peaveys and hooks.

The prime mover at the Percy & Small shipyard was the draft horse. The firm maintained two impressive teams stabled on Middle Street extension, opposite the two houses moved from Percy & Small in 1899. One team, purchased from Prince Edward Island, tipped the scales at 3,500 pounds. Another horse which had worked for the firm for fourteen years was so well trained according to teamster Totman, that he knew more than some men.[64]

The teams moved timber about the shipyard as needed, provided the principal pulling power for hoisting timber and equipment aboard the schooners, and were used to haul materials to and from the shipyard. During periods of heavy activity, the firm hired additional teams to do the grunt work while the shipyard's better-trained teams handled the jobs requiring precise control.

---

[1] Coombs Interview, Tape #68-T-3, MMM.

[2] Nathan Lipfert, "The Shipyard Worker and the Iron Shipyard," *The Log of Mystic Seaport* 35, no. 3, Fall 1983, pp. 75–87. Hereafter cited as Lipfert, "Shipyard Worker." Lipfert noted that few skilled wooden shipyard workers shifted over to iron/steel shipbuilding in Bath from the 1890s. The great majority of the younger generation that chose a shipbuilding career chose steel shipbuilding.

[3] Letter, C. V. Minott, Jr., to Captain Wiley R. Dickinson, Phippsburg, ME, Oct. 10, 1907. Notes, Parker Collection; *BA*, 10/26/1907, article stresses repairwork was being lost from Bath shipyards because of the shortage of ship carpenters.

[4] *BT*, 7/13, 14/1897.

[5] *BA*, 9/12/1908.

[6] *BT*, 11/28/1914. The story of the capsizing and subsequent rescue from the ENIGMA was recounted in the national magazine *Harper's Weekly*, and later appeared in a booklet by the Rev. L. J. Fletcher entitled *A Thrilling Account of the Loss at Sea of the Schooner "Enigma": October 1865*. A copy of the latter is in MS-53, Box 13/17, MMM.

[7] *BT*, 3/7/1907; *BT*, 5/6/1905; *BT*, 2/11/1909.

[8] Lipfert, "Shipyard Worker," pp. 76–77.

[9] There were approximately 307 working days in a year after subtracting Sundays and the almost-universally accepted holidays of New Year's, Memorial Day, Independence Day, Thanksgiving, and Christmas.

[10] *BE*, 5/4/1901. Robert Goddard, James W. Coombs, and William T. Donnell—all familiar names— were responsible for much of the development, particularly

between Marshall, Weeks, and Corliss Streets.

11 Coombs Interview.

12 *BT*, 1/31/1912.

13 *BE*, 1/16/1897.

14 *BE*, 4/22–26/1896.

15 One man, Patrick Charles McDonald, moved to Bath in order to find a shipyard job at age seventy-seven (*BT*, 2/11/1909). Another, Alexander McNeal, had moved to Bath from Cape Breton when eighteen. He retired from Percy & Small at seventy-six in 1901.

16 *BT*, 10/15/1901.

17 *BT*, 10/24/1904, 10/31/1905, 5/8/1908, 5/24/1909. Pinder was on good terms with Percy & Small management: he boarded summers at the old Powers house on Marshall Street and, when he was ready to return south in the fall, he sometimes went as a passenger on a Percy & Small schooner if one was leaving the shipyard at that time.

18 *BT*, 3/7/1900.

19 *BT*, 8/29/1908.

20 *BI*, 10/28/1899.

21 *BT*, 3/5/1900. The newspapers initially indicated that the workmen were asking for a nine-hour day with ten-hours' pay (*BI*, 2/17/1900). However, the original union demand stated that "as they [ship carpenters] are paid by the hour and are not asking for an increase in wages the loss falls upon them and not upon their employers." (Letter, Union to Shipbuilders, 2/8/1900, printed in *Bath Times*, 3/6/1900.)

22 *BT*, 3/5/1900.

23 *BT*, 3/7/1900.

24 *BI*, 3/17/1900. Ironically, it was William M. Rogers & Son (William Rogers) who had first agreed to the ten-hour day back in 1846, even though it was some time before the rest of the shipbuilders followed suit.

25 The fact of the matter was that the average ship carpenter was already putting in less than a nine-hour day on an annual basis, even when times were booming, and he could not afford to work less.

26 *I&E*, 4/16/1904.

27 *BT*, 8/26/1907.

28 Chewing tobacco came in "plugs" wrapped for protection. The wrapping was secured with a small metal seal painted red. When the plug was used up, the wrapping and seal were discarded.

29 The description of working conditions at Percy and Small are drawn from the following interviews done in 1973–74: Samuel Barnes, Charles A. Coombs, Jr., William Donnell, Sydney Eaton, Raleigh G. Osier, Homer Potter, and Thomas P. Robson.

30 *BT*, 6/6/1907.

31 Barnes Interview. Thebeau, who died in church, was the father of Eugene Thebeau who achieved some fame two decades later as one of the triumvirate who revived the moribund Bath Iron Works during the late twenties and thirties.

32 There was also a "relief tube," a precursor to the rather primitive sanitary devices found on many military aircraft around World War II, in the joiner shop. This may all sound rather crude, but Bath's system was no better. A series of outfalls along the river dumped raw, untreated sewage directly into the river.

33 Osier Interview; the schooner was probably the DUNHAM WHEELER.

34 Osier recalled some fifty-five years after the event that Captain Percy had a flush toilet installed for the crew under the mill. There was no evidence of this toilet when the building was restored in 1973–74.

35 Triangle Shirtwaist Company fire in New York City, 1911.

36 *BT*, 2/9/1906.

37 *BT*, 9/28/1911.

38 *BI*, 7/19 and 8/2/1902; *BT*, 7/31/1902; as a result of this accident, Merry received $500 (+/- $7,700 in 1998) in insurance payments; *BT*, 1/16/1903.

39 *BT*, 9/11/1906; *I&E*, 9/15/1906.

40 *BT*, 12/6/1910.

41 *BT*, 11/3/1903.

42 *BI*, 11/17/1900.

43 *BT*, 9/11/1897.

44 The principal source of information for shipyard organization comes from the interviews with Charles A. Coombs, Jr., Raleigh G. Osier, Samuel Barnes, and Thomas P. Robson.

45 Two of these boxes, with sliding tops and duly initialed, are in the Parker Collection.

46 *Bath City Directory*, 1919.

47 Spinney came to work for the firm in 1900 as a clerk/bookkeeper. He worked there for the rest of his life rising to the rank of treasurer following Frank Small's death. His pay in 1904 was $1,050 per year (+/- $16,200 in 1998). He died in 1924. *BT*, 9/16/1924.

48 See: *PSJ*, various entries; Summary Cost Accounts, Hull Numbers 16–18, 24, and Stock in Yard Jan. 1, 1914, Parker Collection.

49 *BI*, 12/4/1919; *BT*, 7/12/1900 and 5/31/1905.

50 Eaton Interview.

51 *BT*, 4/19/1907.

52 WFP to P&S, 10/26/1908, Palmer Collection. "On the seven o'clock train Saturday night I shipped you back one Myles [sic] Merry. Please acknowledge receipt of same. Mr. Merry made an excellent witness for us and undoubtedly did us good." Palmer won the suit against the JUNIATA owners who were compelled to pay for repair costs, loss of earnings, etc.

[53] W. F. Palmer to C. C. Dennett, 9/19/1903, Palmer Collection. "I wish to thank you once more for the prompt manner in which you took up the Miles Merry matter, and I am very sorry that Miles was not Merry (!) enough to go to Waldoboro."

[54] W. F. Palmer to Captain Walter B. Wiley, 1/9/1907, Palmer Collection.

[55] *BT*, 9/4/1908; Coombs Interview, Tape #68-T-3, MMM.

[56] *BT*, 1/13/1930.

[57] J. P. Stevens, *Reminiscences of a Boothbay Shipbuilder*, pp. 37–39.

[58] *BT*, 12/9/1927 and 7/16/1906. Lewis Cameron was Percy & Small's sparmaker until he was crushed between a trolley car and a power pole while shifting his seat on the trolley.

[59] "James Cameron in account with Percy & Small, 1913," James Cameron Papers. His account for 1913 included repairwork on spars for thirty-three schooners and new spars for but one scow. The work ranged from a low of $7.55 to a high of $223.70.

[60] Contract for Schooner No. Eleven of the Palmer Fleet, "Elizabeth Palmer," Parker Collection.

[61] *BT*, 12/24/1928. Several other former Percy & Small shipwrights also worked on "Old Ironsides," including Sam Barnes. Chief Naval Constructor John Lord was in charge of the project. He was a native of Bath.

[62] Robson Interview. Contemporary publications on shipbuilding reinforced Mr. Robson's observations. They recommended that when using air-driven augers, the bit should be as much as $1/4$ inch smaller than the fastening rather than the conventional $1/8$-inch difference used with hand-powered augers. See: Charles Desmond, *Wooden Shipbuilding*, p. 91.

[63] Percy & Small Construction Bill Files, various, Parker Collection. Hyde Windlass billed for 330 hours of labor for installation of their equipment on Schooner #27, Governor Brooks. The list of equipment and materials supplied runs for seven pages.

[64] *BT*, 6/12/1901, 10/30/1902, 11/15/1917.

Building the Great Schooners

TIME AND SHIPBUILDING

Miles M. Merry was more than a skilled artisan with wood. He was the organizer responsible directly to Sam Percy for the shipyard's day-to-day operations. Juggling production schedules, manpower, vendor delivery dates, the impact of weather, and customer expectations, his task was akin to playing three-dimensional tic-tac-toe while blindfolded.

The first consideration was the potential customer's preferred delivery date for the new vessel and the shipyard workload. Was it feasible? Merry knew that under average conditions it took approximately five to six months from keel-laying to launching to complete a four-master; a five-master would take from seven to eight months, and a six-master would take eight to nine months. But he also knew that there had to be a building ways available at the right time (the reason the firm built in three separate shipyards during 1900), and orders had to be placed with key vendors well before projected keel-laying dates.

Timing was particularly crucial when it came to ordering the frame and ship timber. These were normally gotten out during the deepest months of winter when the sap was down—reducing chances of rot—and when frozen ground and even snow assisted in

moving the timber from stump to the nearest shipping point. This meant that timber orders normally had to be placed by December or January at the latest if the vessel was to be delivered sometime during the next twelve months because the sawmills and frame cutters generally cut shipbuilding timber to order only.[1] Not only did Percy & Small find it advisable to move quickly to acquire the frame and ship timber, but they also found it advisable to place early orders for the masts, given the long lead time often needed to get the giant Oregon-fir sticks from the Pacific Northwest to Bath. Moreover, as with all other ship timber, the best spars came from winter-cut trees.

Hard as it may be to believe, railroads did lose mast shipments from time to time. Three flatcars (spars were blocked-up and secured to the outside flatcars, the middle car serving as a spacer or idler) and five 120-foot eight-sided spars shipped in October 1906 for the FANNIE PALMER II were lost several times before they finally arrived in Bath six months after being loaded on the rail cars at a mill in the state of Washington. At one point, they had traveled less than a hundred miles in three months. Yet the next year a shipment of spars arrived at Percy & Small after being in transit for just a month.[2]

With the signing of the contract to build a new schooner, or the decision to proceed with the construction of a schooner for their own account, Percy & Small also immediately placed orders for all the iron and steel bar, strap, and round stock, anchor chains and anchors unless these were already ordered through the managing owners, as was sometimes the case with Palmer and J. S. Winslow. In addition, they contracted for the so-called "steam outfit" from Hyde Windlass that included donkey boiler and condenser, steam pumps, steam whistle, steam hoisting engines, the steam heating system, all associated piping and valves, windlass, Adair pumps, power capstans, hawsepipes, chain stoppers, patent steerer, and assorted fittings.[3] By acting early, the shipyard was assured of having the materials and equipment on hand when needed.

The pattern revealed by Percy & Small's shipbuilding statistics underlines the importance of timing in shipbuilding: construction was started on vessels in every month of the year, but two-thirds of their schooners were started between March and July, the period when winter-cut timber and frames normally arrived from suppliers. October and December had the fewest monthly starts (one each), and the winter period (December through February) logged the

The crowd's attention is focused on the EDWARD B. WINSLOW's spectacular slide into the Kennebec (note the smoke rising from the ways lubricated with a mixture of tallow and cottonseed, and the schooner's stern wave) while ignoring the great piles of timber that more than a few have climbed seeking a vantage point. Yet it was from this raw timber shipped by water that Percy & Small's shipwrights fashioned great schooners. It is more than likely that this particular timber was ordered from the southern sawmills during the previous winter and was part of the 3,100 tons of yellow pine and white oak destined for WYOMING.

J. C. Higgins Photo, courtesy of Maine Maritime Museum

fewest seasonal vessel starts (five), although this was still fully one-eighth of their total schooner production. By way of contrast, delivery of new vessels was remarkably even across the four seasons with summer having a slight edge. Thus local seasonal weather conditions had little impact on the shipyard's building schedule even though as much as 90 percent of all work on a schooner was done out of doors, often during Maine's notorious winters.

CONSTRUCTION STAGES

Percy & Small developed their own approach to building schooners, both in terms of the specific sequence of events and of methods, but throughout the entire process the firm continued to be guided by centuries of tradition. The actual construction process as they practiced it can be divided into four distinct and frequently overlapping stages: framing—fabrication and assembly of the vessel's complete skeleton intended to resist the multitude of forces encountered in maritime service; planking and decking—enclosing the skeleton with the planking and decking and making the whole watertight; sparring and rigging—stepping and staying of the masts and other spars, setting up the running rigging, and bending on the sails; and, finally, outfitting—virtually everything else from painting the vessel to the installation of ship's plumbing and steam-hoisting machinery and boiler, finishing and furnishing cabins, and putting aboard stores.

Although the construction of a wooden vessel can be neatly grouped into carefully defined phases on paper, reality was more chaotic. In actual fact, two or more phases were often in progress at the same time, a point graphically made by a number of photographs of schooners under construction at Percy & Small.

PRELIMINARIES

Long before the ship timber arrived, men were hard at work on the new schooner. Len Gibson and his crew of blacksmiths were already fashioning the heavy steel mastbands and other fittings produced at the yard in order to keep ahead of the demand once the schooner was laid down. A couple of his men were also employed cutting and pointing the first of thousands of steel bolts in various lengths at the bolt cutter in the machine shop section of the blacksmith shop. The bolt cutter, powered by the same motor that turned the whetstones and the blowers for the forges, had been introduced to Bath shipyards in 1881. With it, one man could cut eighteen to twenty inch-and-a-quarter bolts per minute, three times as many as two men produced per minute before the process was mechanized.[4] In effect big nails, these bolts were intended to be driven, so were pointed at one end and were not threaded. The process of driving them created the bolt "head."

On the main floor of the paint and treenail shop, meanwhile, another workman was converting long, square billets of white oak and locust into treenails (pronounced "trunnels"), the wooden fastenings used extensively for framing, planking, and ceiling. A big schooner easily consumed 26,000–28,000 treenails in lengths ranging from 14 to 30 inches. Percy & Small usually subcontracted the work to someone to turn the treenails, supplying the work space, the treenail blanks, and the treenail lathe.[5]

The latter was a surprisingly simple device, reportedly developed by Bath ship fastener Francis Lightbody during the 1880s.[6] The treenail lathe had a rotating headstock—powered via the shaft, pulley, and belt system from the blacksmith shop motor—to which was attached the locust or oak treenail blanks. The cutter head, designed to shave the rectangular blanks into fixed-diameter treenails, much as a pencil sharpener but without a continuous taper in its blades, was pushed forward toward the rotating head, turning each wooden block to the desired diameter except for the end fastened to the headstock. The finished treenail was then stacked with its size mates

The keel blocks are in place, the keel has been laid, gin pole derricks and lifting sheers put in place, and the framing stage erected. In the foreground, it appears that someone on the framing crew has been organizing frame timbers.

Courtesy: Maine Maritime Museum

until the fasteners came in for armfuls of the wooden fastenings.

The serious work began as the timber began arriving in the shipyard. A crew cleaned up the debris around the building slip left from the previous schooner. Then new, red oak keel blocks—chosen for the ease with which they could be split out from under the keel for the launching—were spaced about four feet apart and set on cribbing to a height of about six feet above the slip to leave enough space under the vessel for the men to work. As the grade of Percy & Small's building slips was approximately five-eighths inch per foot, close to that desirable for launching medium- to large-sized vessels, little additional preparation was necessary. However, the master builder could modify that angle slightly for construction purposes by adjusting the height of the blocking and cribbing as one moved aft, and by adjusting the declivity of the launching ways when they were installed to adjust for the size of the vessel and anticipated temperatures at launching.[7]

If the keel being laid was for a larger schooner, the keel blocking was deliberately adjusted so that the keel would arc downward (called a "rocker" or sag) between the ends of the vessel. The rocker compensated to some degree for the tendency of the keel to bend under the brief but severe stresses encountered during the launching, and the hogging that took place over time.[8] Percy and Small, it has been said, built a 12-inch rocker into the keels of their big six-masters using this method, although it would hardly be noticeable in a schooner with a 300-foot keel.[9]

Most of the ship timber used by Percy & Small until late in its history was delivered by schooners from the Southern suppliers.[10] When the schooner arrived at the shipyard pier, the rough-sawn and/or hewn timbers underwent both measurement and critical inspection by a qualified timber surveyor as they were unloaded. The survey not only accurately nailed down the quantity delivered, but it also provided a checkpoint along the path to construction that helped weed out unsatisfactory materials before they ended up in the vessel or otherwise came to the attention of the American Bureau of Shipping surveyor—Captain Denny M. Humphreys—who periodically inspected a vessel under construction.[11] Unsatisfactory materials included pieces that were cross-grained, had too many knots, contained wanes and sapwood, displayed radial cracks (clefts) or separation along the grain (shakes), or were of the wrong species for the place and/or part for which they were designated.[12]

Miles Merry was particularly noted for his keen eye when it came to rooting out poor or unsatisfactory timber. Once a piece failed his eagle-eyed scrutiny, so the story goes, it was forever banned from use in Percy & Small vessels. A particular *bête noire* of his was tim-ber from the sweetgum tree that bore a resemblance to white oak but lacked its resistance to rot except when in a continuously wet environment. Nonetheless, from time to time some sweetgum frame timbers found their way into shipments of oak frames cut in the South.[13] One of the few cases where the contents of a Sam Percy letter has survived concerned the delivery of a white oak frame supplied by William Palmer's favorite frame contractor, E. A. Wentworth, that indeed contained a gum second or third futtock. The letter sounds as if the entire frame was riddled with the offending species, but in fact it turned out to be one or two pieces. There is no question, however, that the letter was inspired by an irate Merry.[14]

FRAMING

Framing the vessel principally involved the shipyard's own force of carpenters who were divided into specialized teams often called "gangs." One such gang, composed of Eliakim "Like" McCabe, Al Havener, and four sexagenarians—Pat Driscoll, Andy McAllister, Gran Miller, and Jack Sonia—was tasked to frame the aft end of the big six-master EDWARD B. WINSLOW from the inner sternpost to the counter.[15] Another gang, numbering as many as eighteen to twenty men depending on the size of the schooner, assembled and erected the half and full frames. The fabrication and installation of the keel, keelsons, fillers, deadwood, deck beams, carlings, lodging knees and the rest of the deck framework was the responsibility of yet another gang of Percy & Small-employed ship carpenters.

Joining the shipyard's various gangs of shipwrights in the framing of the schooner was subcontractor Fred Colby and his crew of broad-shouldered fasteners. Responsible for ensuring that the hundreds—even thousands—of pieces of timber that made up a schooner would hang together literally as one during the vessel's working career, the fasteners worked with handcrank augers, sledgehammers, mallets, and handsaws as their principal hand tools. No other subcontractor gang was so totally involved in the construction of the vessel as the fasteners.

With the arrival of the timber designated for the keel, stem, and sternpost, the work of turning it into these components of the frame began. The roughsawn timber had to be reduced to uniform dimensions with parallel opposing sides (squared), a job made all the more easy thanks to the Daniels planer. When the yard built WYOMING, for example, her keel was assembled from white oak timbers—sided 14 inches and moulded 13.5 inches— in two tiers with finished dimensions measuring 14 inches wide by 27 inches deep by 304.5 feet long.[16] Made up of seventeen pieces—eight in the top layer and nine in the bottom layer—the entire unit weighed (without fastenings) approximately 22 tons![17]

Of course it was not quite that easy. The relatively short pieces (approximately 40–44 feet) that made up each layer of the keel had to be made into a continuous longitudinal piece capable of resisting both bending forces and those that attempt to pull them apart. This was achieved by joining each section with nibbed scarf joints, long—4- to 6-foot—diagonal joints where the joining timbers overlap each other while maintaining the cross-sectional dimensions. Fashioned by experienced ship carpenters using adzes, slicks, and handsaws, the carefully fitted joints resisted separation with expertly fashioned nibs or hooks cut to mesh one face of the joining timber with the other.

With the keel stretched on keel blocks, cross spalls are temporarily secured to the keel stock
with cleats. The spalls, in turn, will support the planking upon which the frames are skidded
down the keel to their assigned station. The frames already in place appear to be half frames
fastened to deadwood at the narrowest point aft and, perhaps, a few full frames where the
hull becomes wide enough for the floors to cross the keel.

Courtesy: Maine Maritime Museum

Each joint was covered with a preservative compound—red lead, carbolineum, etc.—and then the
marriage was sealed by a series of galvanized iron bolts
driven vertically through the joint and clenched over
galvanized rings. The second layer of the keel was
assembled in the same fashion, with its scarf joints
spaced to fall halfway between the first layer's joints,
hence nine pieces to the latter's eight on WYOMING.
The two layers were also bolted together.

The ship carpenters making up the gang assigned
to fabricate the heavy structural units assembled the
keel on the keel blocks, piece by piece, moving

The framing gang is hard at work on the stage assembling the next frame. The top half of the frame—the cover—appears complete, but the bottom half—the layer—is missing one of the first futtocks. Perhaps one shipped from the frame supplier failed to pass inspection. In that case, Miles Merry will take the appropriate mould and search through a pile of "promiscuous" oak to find a piece that approximates the mould and passes muster. Note the frame timbers at the head of the staging; the rough surfaces from handhewing are clearly visible.

Courtesy: Maine Maritime Museum

forward from the after end of the vessel. If the keel was being fabricated of hardwood—birch, hard maple, rock elm—they also spiked on a 4-inch-thick oak shoe. But they didn't bother in the case of vessels with oak keels built for Percy & Small.[18]

Once the keel was laid and properly aligned in a straight line (it wouldn't do to have a keel snake its way up the keel blocks), it was secured in place against movement by diagonal braces, timber dogs, and treenails driven into holes in the keel blocks tight against each side of the keel timbers to prevent lateral movement. Then the ship carpenters turned to and erected the temporary staging needed for assembling and moving the schooner's frames.

It should be noted that far more wood went into building the great schooners than just that incorporated into their hulls. Staging plank and posts, rib-

bands, temporary battens, shores, braces, cribbing, keel blocks, cross spalls, boards used for spiling planking, and the moulds consumed prodigious quantities of lower grade timber and lumber throughout the construction process. Some was recycled for the next vessel, but much of it ended up as firewood.

For all but the largest schooners, the framing stage was erected at the forward end of the keel and took the form of a large platform several feet above the ground measuring approximately 60 feet wide by 35 feet in length, with its working surface of planks spiked down across the top of the keel.[19] Along the entire length of the keel, a series of evenly spaced spalls, fastened to cleats nailed temporarily to the keel's sides, extended outward at right angles, supported on temporary shores to the width of the framing floor or stage. This structure supported staging

In this photo of the Oakley C. Curtis being built at the Reed yard, the sternpost has been hoisted into position using sheer-legs, mortised into the keel, braced, and fastened. Shipwrights have also put in the fashion frame and are building up the transom and installing counter timbers. The schooner will obviously overhang the river by a considerable amount when completed.

Courtesy: Captains Douglas K. and Linda J. Lee

planks for the men and each completed frame as it was skidded, lying flat, to the point on the keel where it would be set upright.[20]

The largest schooners demanded a somewhat different approach due to the size and weight of their frames. The framing floor made up of loose planks was set up just forward of the first full frame space. Once that frame was slid and hoisted into position, the adjoining planks were moved to the upper side of the stage, making space for the next frame. With this technique, the framing floor literally marched up the keel just ahead of the frames.[21]

The men also set up two or more gin-pole derricks to assist in moving and lifting heavy timbers and equipment; one was usually placed at the head of the framing stage and a second derrick was located about halfway down the building slip, with a mate sometimes located on the opposite side of the ways. Placed in holes dug in the ground, the gin-poles were braced

by cables radiating from the top of the derrick out to anchors located around the shipyard.[22] At the lower end of the keel, sheer-legs were set in place to assist in raising the frames upright and to hoist the stern timbers into place.

Even as the framing stage was being assembled, Miles Merry was laying out the location of the sternpost, inner sternpost, deadwood (filler pieces), and the centers for the after half frames along the keel. Meanwhile, McCabe, Havener, and "the four old men" were busy getting out the sternpost, an operation that was facilitated by the machinery in the mill but still demanded the skilled use of adze, slick and gouge, especially to accommodate the rudder stock. But their biggest challenge lay in constructing the counter.

As there were no transverse frames aft of the sternpost on these vessels, the overhanging counter was framed with longitudinal counter timbers spaced

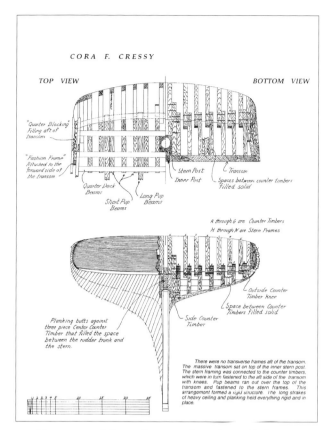

Transom and Stern Construction: Cora F. Cressy

Douglas K. Lee

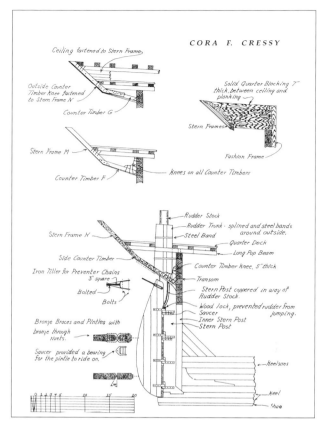

Details of Transom, Stern and Rudder Construction: Cora F. Cressy

Douglas K. Lee

across the lower aft side of the transom and held in place with knees, pup beams that were cantilevered out over the top of the transom, and stern frames attached to the counter timbers. The white oak sternpost and inner sternpost was hoisted into position using the sheers—its proper angle in relation to the keel established with one of the moulds taken off the lofting floor—mortised into the keel, shored up, and fastened. Then the transom timbers and fashion frame were installed, the rudder was hung, and the aft filler was fastened to the keel.

With the sternpost in place and secured, McCabe, Havener, and "the four old men" turned to and constructed the transom and counter, a complex structure dependent on a number of cantilevered, longitudinal pup beams and counter timbers locked together in a rigid triangle that supported the entire structure aft of the rudderpost.[23] When the counter structure was completed—i.e., everything but the

planking and ceiling—they turned their attention to the schooner's bow.

Meanwhile, the framing gang was also at work on the framing stage in an operation that often took twelve to fourteen weeks of unremitting and demanding toil. Sam Barnes, a fastener from New Brunswick who worked on several large Percy & Small schooners—including the Alice M. Lawrence and the Fannie Palmer II—during the mid-part of the decade, remarked in an interview nearly seven decades later that Percy & Small's shipbuilders built the huge schooners by ". . . skill, main strength, and awkwardness."[24] Nowhere was this more evident than with the framing gang.

A large five-master or six-master required the installation of 90 to 100 half and full frames—the largest measuring close to 50 feet across and over 30 feet high—whose shape was originally determined from the half model, then translated to full size on the loft floor in the form of patterns called moulds.[25] Often referred to as double-sawn frames, those used by Percy & Small were certainly double, but rarely sawn. Actually, each full frame was a pair of frames—layer and cover—each half of the pair composed of several pieces hewn from timber (oak, hardwood, or hackmatack) and roughly shaped in accordance with the appropriate mould. The bottom pieces of the frame that ran across the keel, the floor timbers, were anywhere from 14 inches to 16 inches deep at the keel (the moulded dimension), and 12 inches to 16 inches across (thickness or the sided dimension), the scantlings being determined by the size of the vessel. Each full frame had a long and a short floor timber, a number of futtocks (a corruption of foot-hook, meaning the curved timbers connecting the floor timbers to the top timbers), and top timbers and stanchions. A midship frame on a big schooner ordinarily contained fourteen to eighteen pieces of timber for the two halves of the frame, and such a vessel required eighty or more full frames.

The more than one thousand pieces of the vessel's frame arrived at the shipyard hewn roughly to shape, each with the outline of its mould and an identification code scribed with a race knife on the appropriate surface to indicate which frame it was to go into and where.[26] The floor timbers and first futtocks were often sufficiently generous in their hewn dimensions that consistent frame spacing required attention in the mill. The Daniels planer's ability to "slab" the large floor timbers and first futtocks (reduce them to a uniform sided thickness) quickly saved many hours of hand labor.[27] William F. Palmer, who constantly demanded extra-heavy frames, touched on that very same situation in a letter to E. A. Wentworth, his frame supplier: "You have gotten me in a scrape with

The framing gang working on the SAM C. MENGEL have assembled the half of the frame known as the "layer" on the framing stage. It appears that the next step will be horning the layer, a process described and illustrated in Appendix B. Some of the moulds for this frame have been laid on the floor timber and futtocks, and one shipwright (right) appears to be checking the horning pole for the number indicating which side of the pole has the horning marks for that particular frame. The center block from which the horning pole will be swung to ensure the accurate shape of the frame is on the left, aligned with the keel.

Ralph D. Paine Photo, courtesy of Captains Douglas K. and Linda J. Lee

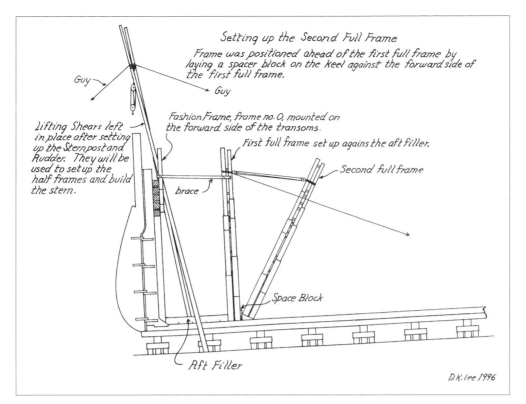

Setting Up the Second Full Frame

Douglas K. Lee

Percy & Small. My contract calls for a spacing of three feet on centers and your frame cannot be gotten into a spacing of three feet on centers. I shall probably have to pay for putting the frame through a Daniels planer."[28] It is also probable that the floor timbers were cut to their moulded dimensions and correct bevels, when required, using the mill's big jigsaw. Such a practice considerably reduced the amount of difficult overhead labor required when it came to dubbing the floor timbers in the cramped, ill-lit space under the vessel.

Assembling the frames on the framing platform and erecting and fastening the frames to the keel were operations conducted with even more than the usual care and attention to detail. The reasons were simple: frames that failed the mirror test—one side the image of the other—and frames fastened to the keel that were not perpendicular and/or at right angles to the keel would affect the form of the vessel, complicate all subsequent construction stages, and adversely affect the vessel's sailing qualities, as well. In short,

the frames gave the vessel her shape, a crucial aspect of her performance during her working life. The timbers fastened to her frames would give the vessel strength, an equally important consideration during her working life.

Once a frame was completely assembled on the framing stage (the actual assembly of a frame is described in the Appendices), the keel was greased and temporary runners were set in place on both sides of the keel. Snatch blocks were rigged, and the tackle was so arranged that the hauling parts came together, permitting the shipyard's team to exert an equal pull on both sides of the frame as it was skidded down the keel. A block was temporarily placed against the forward edge of the previous frame to ensure consistent frame spacing and the frame was carefully—for all its size and weight, it was a fairly flimsy structure—moved into proper alignment with the centerline of the keel. Once the floor timber was set against the space block, the tackles were reset to the widely spaced top timbers and either run through a block on

Cleats, long battens, and cross spalls temporarily hold the ADDIE M.
LAWRENCE's frames in place until the heavy internal structure of
keelsons, deck beams, stanchions, and ceiling can be installed.
Stinson Brothers Photo, courtesy of Captains Douglas K. and Linda J. Lee

the sheers to the team, or off a block secured to a well-braced full frame already in place.[29] Then the "frame up" call went out, and men converged on the platform to bear a hand wherever necessary. Hauled upright until perpendicular to the keel, the frame was joggled exactly into place and secured with temporary cleats to the adjoining frame. Then the fasteners went to work with their long crank augers, drilling down through the frame's floor timbers and into the keel for the first of several bolts that would secure and lock the frame in place.

The success of the framing job was far more dependent upon the experienced "eyes" of the master builder and the ship carpenters of the framing gang than upon technically advanced machinery or scientific instrumentation. One clear example of this was the final determination of the new schooner's sheer line. Chester McCabe, a pipefitter and machinist at Percy & Small during the war years and a longtime friend of Sam Percy, recalled that once the vessel was

framed, Miles Merry and Percy would team up to establish the sheer line. Merry would scramble around on staging with long battens that he affixed to the outside of the top timbers in accordance with shouted directions from Percy, who stood off far enough to get a full view of the hull. Once the battens reflected Percy and Merry's shipbuilding and aesthetic standards, carpenters sawed off the top timbers above the battens. McCabe claimed that the pair could tell if the sheer was out by as little as a quarter inch.[30]

The gang of ship carpenters that had stretched the keel were now at work fitting and fastening the stern knee and getting out and fitting the first of many keelson timbers that locked the frames in place and stiffened the great schooner longitudinally. The keelson—literally "son of the keel"—was a structure built-up of 14- by 14-inch yellow pine timbers with each tier joined by widely spaced scarf joints, much as the keel.[31] The difference lay in the final size of the structure. Where the finished keel might stand slightly over 2 feet high, the finished keelson stood as much as 7 feet high and was flanked by tiers of three or four sister or rider keelsons on either side, each timber also measuring 14 inches square. The entire assemblage was fastened vertically with long bolts, some driven through the floor timbers and into the keel. Horizontal bolts also fastened the keelsons and sister keelsons laterally.[32] This massive structure was the true backbone of the big wooden schooners.

The internal structure of a wooden sailing vessel went well beyond being a framed box. The keelsons, as already noted, provided the backbone of the vessel, but other key elements contributing to its longitudinal and transverse strength included the complex of ceiling, clamps, shelf logs, bow and stern hooks, waterways, lock strakes, hanging knees, lodging knees, deck beams, carlings, stringers, and stanchions that occupied more than a little space within the hull's massive, gloomy confines.

Once the schooner was framed up to approximately the amidships point with the after half frames erected, and the gang installing the keelsons having made a fair start, the planking gangs began fitting and installing the internal planking, called ceiling. Far

The internal structure of the hull, not the frames, provided most of its strength. In this rare photo of ship carpenters and fasteners hard at work, the crew standing on the keelson is driving long bolts through the five keelson tiers, the frame floor, and into the keel. The men on the left appear to be driving edge bolts through the latest strake of the ceiling into its predecessors. On the right, another group appears to be fitting a ceiling strake into place. The highest quality of construction demanded that all parts of the vessel fit tightly together, and there are a number of implements visible in the photo to assist the shipwrights in accomplishing that end.

The long poles resting on the keelson assisted in forcing each strake of ceiling hard against the dubbed-off frame; special ceiling and planking clamps—no doubt custom-made by boss blacksmith Len Gibson—to hold the ceiling in place until fastened are visible at the left foreground. Also note the chains that were probably used with opposing wooden wedges to force the top layer of the keelson tight against the previous layer.

Courtesy: Robert Colfer

heavier than the outside planking, ceiling was specifically designed to add additional longitudinal reinforcement to the vessel rather than keep out water. Although it was caulked in some shipyards in order to stiffen the vessel, the presence of openings for limbers along the keelsons and the frame ventilation openings called air strakes discounted any watertight claims for the ceiling.[33]

With its primary purpose of strengthening the vessel longitudinally, the heaviest ceiling strakes were located in the vicinity of the curve of the bilges, considered one of the weakest points in a vessel's hull. But from the limbers to the sheerline, ceiling timbers were frequently more than twice the thickness of the corresponding exterior planking.[34] It was not thickness alone that was relied upon for strength, however.

Ceiling planking was not only fastened through the frames—and in some cases through the exterior planking—but it was edge fastened as well. As each strake of ceiling was secured to the frames, fasteners with long crank augers drilled holes laterally through each strake at regular intervals into the adjoining ceiling strake. They then drove in long iron bolts, thereby increasing the ceiling's resistance to the longitudinal shear forces that caused wooden hulls to work and hog. Additional resistance to these forces could also be achieved by scarfing the joints between individual timbers in each strake, and spacing the joints of adjoining strakes.[35]

The ceiling was installed by the same gangs using

Two schooners are taking shape on the ways at Percy & Small, while a third appears to be delivering timber and receiving some minor repairs. The schooner on the left has completed the framing phase and work has begun upon the internal structure. Note the ramp that curves up into the hull at the turn of the bilge. Adjoining futtocks on two frames have been temporarily removed to allow the workmen to skid large timbers for keelsons, ceiling, and deck beams into the hull without resorting to high lifts. Many of those timbers are lying between the two schooners.
Martin Sandler Photo, courtesy of Maine Maritime Museum

essentially the same techniques used to plank the exterior of the vessel (see below), although some of the very heavy timbers presented something of a challenge to fit snugly into place, especially at the ends of the vessel. Very large "C" clamps, screw jacks, ringbolts, Spanish windlasses, and wedges were all devices of choice for the plankers when forcing each timber into position. Timbers that had to take on a permanent curve or twist were also thoroughly steamed in the steambox located along the north wall of the blacksmith shop before being sprung into place and clamped to await the attention of the fasteners.

STRAPPING

On the larger schooners built at Percy & Small, one last operation remained to be completed before a schooner was ready for the planking and decking phase: the fabrication and installation of the steel reinforcing strapping. Throughout the nineteenth century, shipbuilders had been busy seeking ways to stiffen the steadily growing hulls of wooden merchantmen. Keelsons grew to be enormous, and the scantlings of ceiling and other structural timber grew apace. Some shipbuilders in Great Britain, where the domestic supply of shipbuilding timber was approaching exhaustion, experimented with diagonal planking, diagonal iron trussing let into the frames, and iron framing planked with wood in an effort to find substitutes for the expensive and hard-to-find heavy timber used in more traditional wooden ship-

The DUNHAM WHEELER (circa February/March 1917) has had her ceiling and decks completed, the after house erected, strapping installed, and now the planking gangs are at work. The sheer strake has been hung and fastened as well as the garboards and a few bottom strakes. The crew now is at work on a strake that runs just below the steel belt strap to which the diagonal strapping is riveted.

Courtesy: Maine Maritime Museum

building.[36] The iron—later steel—strapping technique also gained early favor in the building of wooden steam vessels as their relatively long, narrow, and shallow hulls (to accommodate the side paddlewheels and maximize the effects of their thrust) required serious stiffening that often took the form of very prominent above-deck timber hogging frames (trusses) for those operating in American coastal and inland waters. A far less visible technique, and one far more suitable for oceangoing steamships, utilized diagonal iron strapping arranged in a crisscross, basket-weave pattern along the outside of the hull frames and under the planking. Although more expensive than hogging frames, strapping had been well tested and proven by the time the big five- and six-masted schooners began to take to the water.

Percy & Small's experience with their first two five-masters—the unstrapped M. D. CRESSY and HELEN W. MARTIN—not to mention the experience of other operators of great schooners, demonstrated the need to reinforce the long but relatively shallow hulls.[37] And the decision to build even larger six-masters and five-masters further underlined that need. In response, Percy & Small began to experiment with different patterns of strapping on their largest schooners, seeking the most cost-effective pattern, starting with Schooner #7, the ELEANOR A. PERCY. Before the firm closed up shop two decades later, fully 65 percent of its gross tonnage output had been strapped.[38]

Strapping a vessel was an expensive proposition. Our friend William Palmer, for example, stated categorically that it cost $6,000 (+/- $90,000 in 1998) to strap one of his "semi-composite" schooners.[39] Adding 5 percent to the capital cost of a vessel engaged in a constantly fluctuating trade, rife with economic and physical peril, was not an automatic decision.

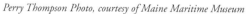

Approximately a month after the photograph on page 153 was taken, the planking gang has completed its work on the DUNHAM WHEELER, the forward deckhouse has been erected, and joiners are at work installing the turned stanchion fly rail. The men on the staging appear to include some outboard joiners (right) who are laboriously scraping and planing the planking smooth for the painters, who are putting on the first coat of paint.

Perry Thompson Photo, courtesy of Maine Maritime Museum

Two caulkers appear to be driving the final threads of oakum on the C. C. MENGEL, JR. as a third moves along the staging with his trusty mallet under his left arm and his caulker's tool chest-cum-rolling seat in tow. Note the temporary cleats spiked to the hull to support the staging cross pieces, the appearance of the planking where some of it has been scraped smooth by outboard joiners, and the vertical chalk lines which may have marked the frame spaces for the fasteners. In the lower left, a sparmaker in a broad-brimmed straw hat is at work on one of the schooner's masts with a broadaxe.

Ralph D. Paine Photo, courtesy of Captains Douglas K. and Linda J. Lee

Schooner operators had to carefully balance the additional cost against their projections of short- and long-term return. Palmer, however, was eventually able to convert the additional cost of his semi-composite strapping to a public relations advantage (as well, presumably, as a reduction in operating expense) when he prevailed upon the American Bureau of Shipping in 1904 to extend its rating on the so-called semi-composite schooners from fifteen years to sixteen years.

Percy & Small experimented with three less-expensive strapping patterns on their own large schooners, obviously attempting to balance effectiveness against cost. Even after they built the DAVIS PALMER, Percy & Small and principal customer J. S. Winslow & Company resisted the more expensive arrangement until the latter agreed to it in 1907 for the EDWARD J. LAWRENCE (and subsequently for the EDWARD B. WINSLOW). Percy & Small finally incorporated the semi-composite arrangement on the last very large schooner built for their own account, WYOMING.

When a schooner was to be strapped, the work sequence on the vessel was modified to permit the installation of the straps. The hull was fully framed (including decks) and ceiled, but the outside planking sequence beyond the garboards was delayed until the strapping was completely installed.[40] Additional production steps had to be taken including laying out the strap pattern on the frames, cutting the grooves with adzes so that the straps were let in flush with the moulded surface of the frames, and installing the straps.

The strapping was not lightweight material. On the schooners using the simpler arrangement of parallel hogging straps and trusses, the builders usually used $3/4$-inch by 12-inch steel. The ELEANOR A. PERCY had two parallel trusses on each side using 960 feet of strapping that weighed nearly fifteen tons. The more complex "semi-composite" strapping advocated by Palmer and ultimately adopted by J. S. Winslow and Percy & Small for their own schooners used lighter-weight materials—one linear foot of a $7/8$-inch by 9-inch belt strap weighed 26.78 pounds versus 30.6 pounds for the equivalent length of $3/4$-inch by 12-inch strap. But the combined weight of the belt strap along with the smaller diagonal straps needed to complete the diagonal criss-cross pattern that extended from the belt strap to the short floor timbers far exceeded the weight of other types of strapping.[41]

Shearing, drilling, and riveting the straps was a task done by Bath Iron Works employees or subcontracted to an independent steel worker. It is not entirely clear, however, whether the straps were installed by regular shipyard employees and subcontractors, or by a steel-working subcontractor. A surviving memo detailing the cost of strapping Schooner #39 (DUNHAM WHEELER), built in 1917, presents a mixed picture of the strapping operation. Riveting and shearing the straps was subcontracted to a steelworker (Moses Swett), but the shipyard blacksmith (already a subcontractor) was also paid to shear some of the straps and punch or drill them for riveting and fastening. However, the actual installation was done by shipyard labor, and the fastening of the strapping to the frame was done by the regular fastening subcontractor.[42]

PLANKING

One of the hallmarks of a well-built wooden ship was the care shipwrights exercised in fitting the many components together, and one of the most visible indications of that care was found by examining the exterior planking. The exterior planking served primarily as the vessel's watertight shell, although it played a secondary role in strengthening the hull.

Because the vessel's hull did not follow the parallel and right angle planes of a wooden box, all planking—exterior hull, deck, ceiling—was, of necessity, curved in one or two planes, a little, a lot, or somewhere in between depending on location. To ensure the best fit, the shipbuilders relied upon three processes: dubbing, lining, and spiling.

The dubber's job was to trim the faying surface (surface against which the planking set) of the frames so that the fairness of lines originally established on the half model and subsequently in the laying down of the lines was preserved in the real thing. As most of the frame stock used by Percy & Small was rough-hewn to only the approximate shape scribed on each timber when it arrived at the shipyard, the dubbers—a subcontracted specialty—often had considerable trimming to do with their adzes before the hull was faired and ready for planking.

Following the dubber came the liners who laid out the planking sequence from the keel rabbet to the sheer line. It doesn't sound like a difficult task in retrospect, but it required not only practical knowledge of the properties of the timber making up the planking, but also a real ability to conceptualize the entire hull three-dimensionally. At Percy & Small the liner worked under three strictures: (a) equal numbers of strakes on each side of the vessel; (b) the same number of strakes at the bow of the vessel as it took to plank the midship section; and (c) fore-and-aft hood ends (ends of each strake of planking where they butted into the stem or stern rabbet) that mirrored their opposites on the other side of the vessel.

Lining a schooner first required the liners to measure from the keel rabbet to the sheer line along the midship frame, the longest of all the frames measured. That length was then divided into the number of strakes of 14-, 12-, 10-, 8-, and 6-inch planking it would take to cover the distance. The widest strakes were on the underside of the vessel and became progressively narrower in stages at the bilge, at the wales, and then topside. The narrowest planking, exposed to the weather part or all of the time, was far better at resisting the effects of weathering than wide planking. As the measurements between the rabbet and sheerline forward and aft of the full midship section were less than those amidships, decreasing as one approached the bow and stern, the liners had to taper each planking strake as it approached the ends of the vessel.

The men who lined plank at Percy & Small appear, for the most part, to have also been employed as ship carpenters at the shipyard rather than working as sub-contractors, although there were exceptions. Henry Curtis, who lined the CORDELIA HAYES and the MILES M. MERRY, was paid as a subcontractor, but other identified liners—Daniel Higgins, James Brewster,

and one Pinson—appear to have been paid under the category of ship carpenters, Percy & Small's catch-all description for most of their direct employees. In all probability, they preferred to be employees rather than subcontractors, since they were paid for their time rather than at a piecework rate, i.e., for the job.

It is possible, perhaps probable, that some of the men who lined Percy & Small's schooners also spiled their planking. Spiling was the technique used to determine and lay out the exact shape of each plank so that it fit snugly in place against the previous strake on the one side and the liner's mark on the other. Once the plank was spiled, it went to a hewer, a ship carpenter skilled with broadaxe and adze, who then shaped the plank—a plank could be 6 inches by 14 inches by 45 feet long and weigh half a ton—in accordance with the spiling pattern. Once hewn, the plank was checked for fit and then had a $3/16$-inch bevel planed onto its outside edges by another ship carpenter—often referred to as a beveler—to form the caulking seams. Although the shipyard was equipped with machinery capable of mechanically getting out such planks, it appears that such equipment was used principally on the heavier ship timbers while manpower was used on the smaller, lighter (relatively speaking) planking.

The same process of lining and spiling the planking was used for both the ceiling and the outside planking. However, many ship carpenters felt that the ceiling was easier to do than the outside planking. There were fewer—though heavier—strakes. The necessary twists and bends were less acute (following inside curves as opposed to outside curves) and there were more available purchases for forcing the ceiling tightly into place. Finally, the ceiling simply did not demand the quality of finish that was applied to the outside planking.

Planking, more than any of the preceding operations, offered an element of excitement. Most of Percy & Small's schooners were planked by two gangs of men—usually numbering about eight to ten men each—working on opposite sides of the vessel. As their operations were virtually mirror images of each other, there was more than a little opportunity for the development of a lively competition and, perhaps, the placing of a few side bets. The late Charles Coombs recalled that, more than once, the competitive spirit between planking gangs sometimes boiled over into "a little skirmish" between the competing gangs.[43]

The plankers took each plank once it had been hewn to shape, and beveled and fitted it into place tight against the frames and neighboring planks, securing it temporarily with a variety of planking screws, clamps, and wedges. Fasteners, following directly behind the plankers, then proceeded to drill the necessary holes with their hand augers for the treenails and composition spikes (used to secure the plank's butts).

When the plank had to be bent or twisted to follow the lines of the hull and seat firmly against the frames and its neighbors, the plankers hauled it on their shoulders to the steam box alongside the blacksmith shop. The steambox, 50 to 60 feet long, was built of tongue-and-groove pine planks and open at the ends to allow the shipyard teams to draw the long, heavy planks into and out of the box. Once the planks were in position, heavy canvas flaps were dropped over the ends and the fireman in the boiler room opened a valve between the boiler and the steambox. The length of time the planks "cooked" was dependent on their size, but by the time they were ready to be removed, they were limber and hot.

Imagine, if you will, a planking gang led by Cole Frazier, his shirt seemingly always in tatters. Frazier— a hard driver if ever there was one—with Ralph Jewett, Harry Lounds, Howard Atwood, Charlie Pushard, Charles Burnham, Jack McDonald, and Tom Robson, carried the heavy, hot planks from the steambox using large two-handled tongs through the shipyard over and around piles of lumber, timber, sawdust, and woodchips and then up the none-too-steady ramps and along staging that was ". . . jumping up and down all the time."[44] If the gods of shipbuilding were in a beneficent mood, the gang soon had one end of the plank anchored with clamps; then, with every trick in the shipbuilder's arsenal, along with brute strength, the men forced the plank into its exact position, bends and twists included. Once clamped in place, the plank set itself permanently into position as it cooled and dried.

Sometimes, however, the gods of shipbuilding were less than cooperative. Occasional planks, even though they were carefully spiled, hewn, and steamed, simply would not accept the twists and turns. This meant getting out a replacement plank and repeating the entire operation.[45] But the ultimate planker's nightmare was to be planking the ends of a vessel (with all those twists and bends) during the coldest days of winter. Then Frazier and his cohorts (or anyone else, for that matter) really had to scramble to get the plank clamped into position before it froze solid. If it froze, they were compelled to beat an ignominious retreat back to the steambox to start all over again with, no doubt, the catcalls of their friendly opponents on the other side of the schooner ringing in their ears. Of course, the Frazier "gang" reserved the right to return the compliment when their opposites ran into their own problems.

The fasteners followed close on the heels of the planking gangs with the tools and apparatus of their trade. Percy & Small routinely "square-fastened" (sometimes called double-fastened) the planking on their schooners, a pattern that generally involved four fastenings at every frame (two in each futtock). One of every four fastenings was a composition bolt driven through plank, frame, and ceiling and riveted over clinch rings; one was a treenail also driven through the ceiling and wedged at both ends, and the final two were "short" treenails driven into, but not through, the ceiling and wedged only on the planking end. Normally, seasoned white oak treenails were used below the light-load waterline and locust treenails above. All planking butts fell on frame timbers and were "square fastened," i.e., with one composition planking spike a foot long and one bolt, both countersunk and plugged.[46]

Edge fastening, used extensively with the ceiling, had only limited use with the outside planking thanks to the latter's relative thinness. The first garboard strake (garboards were the extra-thick planking adjoining the keel) was edge-bolted to the keel. The second and third (and sometimes fourth) garboards were then edge-bolted into the first and second garboards.

There was considerable discussion in wooden shipbuilding circles in the early twentieth century over the efficacy of using wooden treenails for fastenings. One school of thought pointed to the superior strength and resistance to shear forces of metal bolts and their smaller impact (although not by much) when it came to drilling holes for them. Sam Percy lends some credence to the last point when, in an interview with Mark Hennessy, he noted that one of the reasons they used such thick ceiling, planking, and timbers was to compensate for the large number of holes drilled through them for fastenings.[47] The pro-treenail advocates, on the other hand, proudly pointed to the treenail's low cost, lighter weight (less weight in a ship's structure meant more capacity for cargo), and its immunity to corrosion resulting from oxidation and/or galvanic action.[48]

The actual holding power of properly sized and installed treenails was substantial, however. Sizing in terms of diameter was a critical factor in that holding power, with the rule-of-thumb practice requiring that treenails be one size larger (usually $1/32$ inch) than the holes into which they were driven. The treenail that passed completely through planking, frame timber, and ceiling with both ends wedged had the best holding power, but only a third or fewer of all treenails were in that category. The rest, wedged at one end only, depended upon a combination of the tight fit and length (the longer the treenail, the better the holding power).[49]

The actual fastening of the planking involved a veritable parade of Colby's men. One marked the location, depth, and type of fastening on the planking into the frame timber using a fastening pattern that would avoid the fastenings driven from the inside of the vessel. (It was important not to cut into or across those fastenings even if they were only treenails rather than iron bolts.) Then came the men with the big augers. Their task was easier in one way than when they made the holes for fastening together the huge keelsons: they didn't have as far to go—most through fastenings on a big five- or six-master involved cutting through perhaps 26 to 30 inches of solid wood. What made it harder were the angles at which they had to turn their augers: from straight overhead under the schooner to roughly the horizontal plane while working the sides of the vessel.

In the wake of the drillers came helpers with armfuls of treenails—a single 45-foot plank could take 42 treenails in two lengths—as well as the necessary bolts and butt spikes. The bolts and spikes were driven first, countersunk, and eventually plugged. Then the treenails were set into their holes and driven to refusal. It was a job requiring considerable physical effort (properly sized treenails drove hard) and care to drive the fastening straight along the path cut by the auger.

Once the treenails were driven in, another member of the fastening gang came along with a handsaw and cut the protruding square ends off flush with the plank. The sawn-off treenail ends were traditionally divided among the fasteners who used them for firewood. Then, with a heavy mallet and chisel, one of the fasteners split the end of each treenail and drove in an oak wedge. The wedge was shaved flush and the fastener moved on to the next treenail.

Even as the planking gangs and their cohorts were striving to hang a strake a day, another gang of ship carpenters were hard at work laying the schooner's decks. The weather decks were usually covered with clear white pine planks running fore and aft, while yellow pine was used on those portions of the interior decks that were planked.[50]

Caulking

As the planking gangs strove to reach the sheer line and the deck-laying gang the waterways, the caulkers were not very far behind. The practitioners of this arcane trade dating back more than two millennia accomplished their task in a manner reminiscent of a ritual dance. Charles Oliver divided his men into a number of teams, two to tackle the hull and one or two to address the deck's caulking needs. Each of the teams caulking the hull was composed of a man who caulked all plank butts and the stem and stern rabbets; another—usually an apprentice—who was responsible for reaming tight seams before the caulkers coming behind him began driving threads into the seams; and a driving gang normally composed of four to six men.[51]

The American Bureau of Shipping required that the first thread (or threads) driven be of spun cotton followed by oakum. The basic rule specified one thread of cotton per 4 inches of plank thickness or part thereof. Thus a 6-inch plank would have two threads of cotton and then the oakum.[52]

The butt man led the parade, caulking each plank butt. He left short tabs or ends of each thread protruding from the top and bottom of the seam that would be picked up in sequence by the caulkers driving the longitudinal seams when they reached the butt. They returned the favor when they reached the rabbets, and their tabs were picked up by the butt man who was also responsible for caulking the rabbets.

Although caulking the linear seams between each strake of planking was a fairly straightforward exercise, the desirability of having the planking tightly fitted together did require the frequent use of reaming irons so that the lead caulker could drive the first thread. It was also an excellent way to train the apprentice in the mysteries of the trade, as well as keep him hopping if he was to stay the minimum three reaming irons ahead of the caulker.

Once the first four threads were set into the seam, two men, one with a horsing iron (a moderately blunt iron with a two-foot handle) and the other swinging a large wooden maul called a beetle, set back the caulking, packing it more tightly into the seam. Then the balance of the threads were driven before the beetling process was repeated, using a somewhat blunter-edged iron called a making-in iron. This pass left the caulking tightly packed and set approximately $1/2$ inch into the seam. The seams were then "painted" with a special seam paint and sealed with Portland cement (below the waterline). Above the waterline the seams were painted with the seam paint and, in some cases, puttied.[53]

The decks were caulked with fewer threads of cotton and oakum, but the process was otherwise identical to that used on the planking. The seams, however, were sealed with hot pitch from the pitch oven rather than with putty or cement.

The well-equipped caulker at Percy & Small was outfitted with a toolbox on wheels to hold his assortment of standard and specialized irons and caulking mallets. It also served well as a seat while working on deck seams, allowing him to scoot along the seam in relative comfort. Such a minor comfort was probably much appreciated by the caulkers who had to endure endless hours hearing the ring of caulkers' mallets and irons—the background music of a wooden shipbuilding town—as they sometimes drove as much as seven tons of oakum and a ton of cotton to make a schooner watertight.[54]

SALTING AND JOINERY

Once the hull was caulked, it was ready to be salted. Rock salt acted as a preservative, providing some protection for frame timbers against rot in the poorly ventilated spaces between the outer and inner shell of the vessel. As the schooner was being planked, ship carpenters had installed a salt stop in each space between frames at about the light load waterline. The wooden stop, which was intended to keep the coarse rock salt from migrating into the bilges and blocking the limbers, had vertical holes drilled in it to allow the briny moisture to drain into the bilges. Each frame pocket was filled through ceiling air strakes just below the weather deck and was periodically topped off during the schooner's working life. The amount of salt used for the great schooners was prodigious: the ALICE M. LAWRENCE consumed no fewer than 252 hogsheads purchased for $529.20 (+/- $8,200 in 1998) from Houghton Brothers.[55]

Before, during, and after the decks were laid, Fred Scott and his inboard joiners moved aboard the schooner from their shop over the mill. They came to build the deckhouses and install the wooden deck furniture (wooden quarter and knighthead bitts, hatch coamings, turned stanchion flyrails, fife rails, etc.). Once the deckhouses were weathertight, the joiners focused on finishing their interiors. Most of the panel-

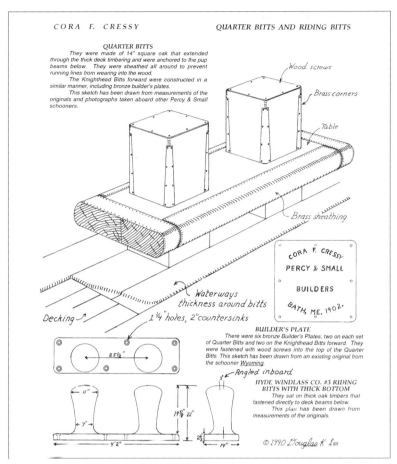

Quarter Bitts and Riding Bitts
Douglas K. Lee

ing for the after house had been gotten out in modular units by the joiners—along with much of the deck furniture—as the schooner was being framed. The much more austere interior finish found in the midship and forward houses was largely fabricated in place.

With the schooner completely planked, decked, and caulked and the houses in place, the second phase of the shipbuilding process drew to a close. With the exception of paint, she could be launched with every expectation that she would stay afloat. Yet only twice in their quarter century of shipbuilding did Percy & Small ever launch schooners so far from completion: the ELEANOR A. PERCY and GOVERNOR BROOKS. The rule of thumb then among shipbuilders, as it is today: achieve the highest level of completion possible before launching. It was easier, quicker, and more economical to finish a vessel on dry land than it was to do the same thing while the vessel was afloat.

SPARS, RIGGING AND SAILS

The entire process of rigging the vessel began even before the keel was laid. A spar and sail plan was prepared for the guidance of the sparmakers and sailmakers incorporating the particular attitudes and preferences of the owners-to-be regarding the rig, as well as the dimensions of all the specific elements. Although the big schooner rig was pretty straightforward and simple in comparison to the big three- and four-masted square-riggers of just a decade or two earlier, there was still room for differences.

It should come as no surprise that William F. Palmer and Percy & Small conducted a continuous

The inboard joiners held sway on the decks of the MARTHA P. SMALL (identified because she is the only long poop schooner built by P&S where the forward house top was faired directly into the topgallant forecastle deck) when this photo was taken. Aside from the normal clutter associated with shipbuilding, one can see the structures that were the responsibility of the joiners, including almost endless turned stanchion flyrails, quarter and knighthead bitts, and deckhouses. The partially concealed mechanical device in the left foreground is the part of the windlass machinery called the brake lever beam that theoretically permitted the manual, non-steam-assisted operation of the anchor windlass. The large boxes are personal tool chests of individual workmen. Note the large C-clamp in the center foreground.

Courtesy: Maine Maritime Museum

discussion during their relationship over various aspects of the schooner rig. During the years they did business together (1903–09), the debate touched on mast spacing (Palmer wanted his masts spaced exactly 52.5 feet on some schooners), the number and angle of the topmast stays (Palmer wanted to eliminate the topgallant stay and enlisted the opinion of boss rigger Frank Palmer), and the rake of the masts.[56]

The rake question elicited the following from the ever-vociferous Palmer:

It is now time to take up the rake of the masts on our schooners. You have a habit down there in Bath of raking the foremasts $^4/_8$ of an inch, the main mast a little more and so on until the

spanker sticks out over the stern. I have tried all kinds of rakes of masts, and I am satisfied that a vessel sails better with her masts absolutely plum [sic]. . . . I should like these masts raked exactly $^3/_8$ of an inch, every one. Then I shall ask Mr. Frank A. Palmer to string the masts forward until they are about plum [sic].[57]

He didn't leave it at that, however, for just over three months later he once again raised the rake question, just in case Sam Percy and Miles Merry may have forgotten his wishes:

I wish I could impress it upon the minds of some of you builders in Bath, that if you want to injure the steering of a vessel the nicest way I

A shipment of huge, roughed-out, Douglas-fir spars, destined for Percy & Small, arrives at the Bath freight yards from Washington State in the spring of 1908. Considerable care was needed mapping their passage east, with particular attention given to the sharpness of curves along the route. They will be rolled into the river and towed to Percy & Small.

Arthur H. Brown Photo, courtesy of Maine Maritime Museum

know of is to rake the masts in your Bath fashion. There is not a thing that fetches the center of effort of the sail further aft than by raking the masts. Just remember that we are not building a Baltimore bugeye. . . . I hear indirectly that you intend to rake the masts further aft than I gave you directions for, and if you do there is going to be a howl from, yours truly, Wm. F. Palmer.[58]

In the end, Palmer and Percy & Small struck a deal: all the masts would have the same rake (making Palmer happy), but the rake would be Percy & Small's preferred 1/2 inch.[59]

The sails were subcontracted out to a sailmaker—after the death of Bath's William Clifford, Percy & Small sent virtually all but Palmer's business to the sail loft in Portland operated by Captain Leslie B. Clark—who was provided the necessary sailcloth, roping, and sail hardware by the builder.[60] Palmer, as was his custom, insisted on being different by requiring that the principal sails on his schooners be made from "#0000 [4/0] Dorothy" cotton duck especially woven by Hall, Lincoln & Company. Whether this was really extra-heavy sailcloth or just 2/0 duck normally used for the heaviest sails of the great schooners can't be ascertained today, but it should be noted that the price for "#0000 Dorothy" duck was less than the more plebian 2/0 duck used by more common mortals.[61] The surviving invoices suggest that everyone else's 2/0 was Palmer's 4/0.[62]

The Cameron brothers, first Lewis and subsequently James, were the sparmakers of choice for Percy & Small. Lewis set up his spar yard in a portion of the old Deering–Donnell shipyard just behind his house at 305 Washington Street, close to his best customer, Percy & Small. Following his death from a freak accident, the business was taken over by brother James who continued to operate from the same location.

For all of the vaunted simplicity of the schooner rig, there was plenty of work for the Camerons and their workmen. The ALICE M. LAWRENCE, a typical six-master, required six finished masts of Oregon pine (Douglas fir) measuring 118 feet long each, with five having a maximum diameter of 30 inches, and one—

the foremast—with a maximum diameter of 32 inches. The six Oregon pine topmasts were each 56 feet long with the foretopmast measuring 20 inches in diameter. It didn't end there, however. A 21-inch piece of Oregon pine, 75 feet long, was made into the spanker boom, and another piece 21 inches in diameter and 80 feet long became the jibboom. Native Maine spruce was used to make the six gaffs, five booms, and the clubs for the forestaysail and jib.[63]

The Oregon pine spars arrived from the West Coast aboard flatcars. Strictly speaking, the big timbers were no longer raw material, having been hewn eight-sided before leaving the Pacific Northwest. Once they were rolled into the river at the Maine Central Railroad yard and towed to the spar yard, the sparmakers went to work finishing the task so roughly begun a continent away.

Their first job was to lay out the spar length, diameters, and taper from the spar and rigging plan. Then they proceeded to hew off the corners, making the stick sixteen-sided. The stick was then rounded, tapered, and made smooth using an assortment of planes. A mortise was cut in the mast heel to accommodate the maststep tenon, and the masthead was squared and tapered to accommodate the trestle and crosstrees and all the masthead hardware.

That hardware had occupied most of Leonard Gibson's and his gang of brawny blacksmiths' time since the decision to build the schooner had been confirmed. Virtually none of the many tons of specialized iron fittings designed for the standing and running rigging—as much as twenty tons worth for a six-master—came off the shelf but were custom-made of the heaviest feasible steel stock.[64] Most of the fittings were then sent on to Wilbur Oliver's Bath Galvanizing Shop on Vine Street where they were given acid baths and then hot-dipped galvanized.

The sparmakers finished their work on the vessel by fitting boom and gaff jaws, oiling all the spars (to reduce checking), and fitting and fastening in place all the bands and fittings. At this point the spars were turned over to the riggers, whose first job at the shipyard was to step and stay the masts.

The riggers had already been at work in Frank Palmer's loft, making up the shrouds and stays of wire

This spar obviously came into the shipyard as an unprocessed log with the bark still attached. Now the sparmakers are at work hewing the timber into an eight-sided stick with due allowance made for the spar's taper. The eight-sided stick is then made into a sixteen-sided stick by carefully removing the corners and, after this, into a properly round spar. A first-class sparmaker could produce a mast with broadaxe, adze, and spar planes that was as round in cross section and properly tapered as any produced by the modern spar lathes found in some shipyards today. Note the finished spar immediately to the left rear with the mortise cut into its base that will fit over the maststep tenon. It reappears in the photo to the right.

Ralph D. Paine Photo, courtesy of Captains Douglas K. and Linda J. Lee

This pleasant old gentleman with his white moustache and cap askew may well be boss sparmaker James H. Cameron. He is checking the portion of the mast from the hounds to the mast cap, often referred to as the doubling, where mast and topmast were joined. Note the plane resting on the doubling and the deep bed of woodchips on the ground. The small, crude, shed-like structure over the sparmaker's left shoulder is the shipyard outhouse. It appears to have been recently built, but no effort was exerted to place its quality of construction on a par with the schooners built here, or to protect privacy.

Ralph D. Paine Photo, courtesy of Captains Douglas K. and Linda J. Lee

This dramatic view of Percy & Small—and twenty-two masts on four vessels (*left to right*, WILLIAM C. CARNEGIE, EDWARD B. WINSLOW, FULLER PALMER, ELEANOR A. PERCY)—offers a rare glimpse of that most tricky of shipbuilding operations, sparring the great schooners. The two schooners on the ways have very recently had their masts stepped. So recently, in fact, that Frank Palmer's men have not yet set up any standing rigging on either. In fact, the EDWARD B. WINSLOW on the north building ways still has the sheer-legs in place that lifted and stepped the foremast. Even the lower main purchase block is still made fast to the sling that is lashed strategically just above the spar's center of balance, suggesting that the foremast was stepped on Saturday and the picture was taken the next day, Sunday. The hipped-roof house on the right was owned by Charles E. Hyde. Today that house is on a lot a short distance down Washington Street on the opposite side, and Maine Maritime Museum's Maritime History Building occupies this site.

Stinson Brothers Photo, courtesy of Maine Maritime Museum

rope supplied by Palmer. When the time came for them to perform their magic at the shipyard, the made-up standing rigging—coiled and labeled—along with many coils of rope destined for halyards and sheets, but first to be used to step the spars, was hauled by McFadden or Mason wagons and teams to the shipyard. Meanwhile, the mast hoops were slid over the boom saddles and temporarily tied off. Then, one-by-one, the lower masts were hauled from the spar yard to a point alongside the schooner using Percy & Small's version of gallamanders—pairs of wheels connected by axles—that were positioned over the spar, which was then snugged up against the axles clear of the ground and hauled by one of the teams to a position alongside the schooner. There they would lie until the schooner was ready to receive her masts.

With the possible exception of launching, the masting of the great schooners was about the most awe-inspiring aspect of the entire construction process. It is likely that all work not closely associated with the actual sparring came to a halt at the shipyard when one of the big lower masts was hoisted skyward preparatory to being stepped.

Frank A. Palmer never left a description of masting the great schooners, but fortunately his Penobscot Bay contemporary, Christian Henry Bohndell, detailed the riggers' work on the first six-master—GEORGE W. WELLS—in a notebook.[65] Although the two riggers may have differed in some of the specific steps, they were confronting the same challenges with essentially the same resources.

As there were no cranes or derricks at the shipyard

that were tall enough to do the job, the riggers assembled and erected sheer-legs on the deck of the schooner. The legs, approximately 100 feet in length and lashed together near the top, were set in a pair of large wooden shoes—sometimes referred to as "boats"—to protect the deck from damage from the compressive forces transmitted through the legs by the weight of the spar. The shoes, made up of three timbers bolted together with hollowed-out "bowls" in which to set the legs, could be skidded along the deck using shoe tackles so that the apparatus could be positioned at each mast hole in turn. Preventer lines were used to keep the legs from spreading apart and/or shifting along the deck while under a load. Secured at the crotch of the sheer-legs some ninety feet above the deck were a pair of quadruple-sheaved blocks (main and lower lifting blocks) of heroic proportions—each

block was 2 to 3 feet high—that would reduce the effort required to hoist the masts, some weighing twenty tons or more, to manageable proportions.[66]

Additional blocks were also lashed to the top of the sheer-legs. Two—the forward sheer tackle and the aft guy sheer tackle—controlled the adjustable fore-and-aft angle of the sheer-legs as well as guying the structure. A second pair of side blocks provided additional adjustable guying to contend with the different forces during a lift ranging from those trying to tip the sheers over the side to those attempting to pull the sheers aft.

Stepping each mast required three distinct operations. First, the sheer-legs were positioned ahead of the appropriate mast hole starting with the spanker and moving forward as each mast was stepped to the foremast, mast by mast. Once the sheer-legs were in

In this deck view, looking aft, on WYOMING, the sheer-legs (one of the sheer-legs is visible at the extreme right) have been positioned preparatory to lifting and stepping the foremast. One of the steam-driven warping heads used to provide the power to lift the enormous spars is visible on the forward house, and one of the shoe tackles that assisted in positioning and anchoring the sheer-legs is also visible with one end secured over a mooring bitt and tension maintained by using a crude Spanish windlass. The bulk of the rope used by the riggers to step the masts came from the stocks that would then be used to set up the vessel's running rigging.

Walter E. Snow Photo, courtesy of Captains Douglas K. and Linda J. Lee

position, blocking was built up slightly higher than the rail on both sides of the schooner to protect the rail from the crushing weight of the spar. On the ground alongside the schooner, riggers placed lashing for the lower main purchase block at the balance point on the mast so that it would come up in the horizontal plane. Once the block was secured to the lashing and control lines were attached, the riggers were ready for the first lift.

This lift involved raising the horizontal, +/- 120-foot "stick" approximately 40 feet vertically to clear the schooner's rail and turning it 90 degrees so that it could be set down athwartships on the blocking. The easiest part of this phase was providing sufficient power to lift the mast. The main purchase led through a large single block shackled to one of the heavy fair-lead staples, and from there to one of the warping heads driven by one of the schooner's own steam hoisting engines.

Getting the mast up onto the schooner was a more complex maneuver than the above description suggests. Remember, the sheer-legs had no ability to "boom out," that is, to place the center of its lifting effort over a load not located on the centerline of the vessel. Therefore, attempting to lift a spar lying alongside the schooner, perhaps 30 to 40 feet to one side of the main purchase block's lifting effort, could convert the mast into a huge battering ram capable of wiping out staging and even damaging the new vessel's hull once it was lifted clear of the ground. How the riggers avoided this outcome was not explained by Frank Palmer or Christian Henry Bohndell who both figured, no doubt, that if you had to ask, you did not need to know. It is possible that it took two lifts to get the mast on deck. The first lift would be near the top end of the mast, raising it above the level of the blocking while the mast butt remained firmly on the ground braking any tendency for the entire spar to swing into the staging and hull. Once the mast was nearly upright and leaning against the schooner, it would be temporarily secured. The lower main purchase block was then reset to a point closer to the mast's center of balance, and rope fenders, grease, sliding blocks, or some such method to facilitate drawing the mast over the block-

ing at the side of the deck was set in place.[67]

Once the mast was safely resting athwartship on the blocking, the riggers, their coils of rope and rope fenders strategically placed along the schooner's deck, reset the lashing around the mast, locating it a little above the center of balance. Ropes were tied around the mast heel and led to assorted bitts where a turn or two was taken. These served to dampen any tendency for the spar to swing once it was hoisted to the vertical, and also permitted the riggers to position the mast over the mast hole and align the mast's mortise fore and aft as it was slowly lowered until it mated with the maststep tenon. It was, in the words of the late Charles Coombs, "a ticklish job" and "work best not done on a windy day."[68]

With the lower masts in place, the big sheer-legs were removed and the riggers turned their efforts to lifting and setting up all the shrouds and lower stays, followed by stepping the topmasts. The topmasts lacked the sheer size of the lower masts—on the larger schooners they were approximately 60 feet long by 18 inches to 20 inches in diameter—but getting them setup required more than a little effort and skill. Once it was accomplished, the balance of the shrouds and stays were installed and adjusted.

The gaffs and booms were hoisted aboard to join the coils of manila rope (that could stretch more than seven miles on a six-master), and kegs and boxes of blocks of all descriptions.[69] The spanker boom was, in itself, an impressive spar, measuring 80-plus feet in length and 20 inches in diameter on the largest schooners.

Palmer, Anderson, Crowell, Duley, Mitchell, Spicer, Wright, and the other, anonymous members of the rigging gang installed blocks, rove off halyards, clewlines, lift and boom tackles, and sheets, and rigged the lazy jacks, arranging all the running gear to take maximum advantage of the hoisting engine or engines. It was work that necessitated a great amount of time spent aloft, yet in the twenty-five years Palmer's men rigged for Percy & Small, they had only one man fall from aloft, and he landed in the water and was only shaken up. The skill of Palmer's crew was evident, not only in its safety record, but in the track record its rigging enjoyed for durability.[70]

The four-master MIRIAM LANDIS was launched (25 September 1919) with just the masts
stepped and the shrouds in place. Eight working days later, the riggers had completed
their job right down to bending on the sails.

Courtesy: Captains Douglas K. and Linda J. Lee

The quality of their work notwithstanding, the riggers had one job left before moving on to the next schooner: bending on the sails. Whether they came from Stearn's loft in Bath or Clark's loft in Portland, the sails were guaranteed to be bulky, stiff, and very heavy. The fore, main, mizzen, jigger, driver, and spanker sails (on a six-master) were routinely made of the heaviest 2/0 duck. The rest of the sails were made from lighter sailcloth, the weight being determined by the use—lighter sails used only in lighter weather. The new suit of sails would last, on average, approximately three years in service with the most frequently used sails requiring repair and replacement first.

OUTFITTING AND COMPLETION

There were still myriad details to be completed before a new schooner was ready for sea. Take paint, for example. Every fleet operator had a basic paint scheme that was applied to most, if not all, of the schooners under that particular house flag. Most of the schooners Percy & Small built for J. S. Winslow & Company, for example, had bronze green hulls with white trim. The Palmer schooners were given white or dove gray hulls, and Percy & Small painted their schooner hulls a far more convenient and low maintenance black.[71]

Painting was far more than a decorative vanity, however. It protected the external fabric of the schooner against the elements and, when it came to copper bottom paint, it also discouraged marine growth that would slow the vessel down.[72] However, before the painters applied a gallon of bottom or hull paint, it was necessary for the outboard joiners to prepare the hull's surface for the paint. The planking had gone into place rough-sawn, and it had been subjected to considerable abuse throughout construction (clamping and forcing into position, as a nailing base for staging, etc.).

Preparation involved planing and scraping the hull smooth. For that, each of the outboard joiners carried a toolbox filled with eight to ten hand planes and an assortment of hand scrapers made from discarded handsaw blades. The nature of their work being what it was, they found it necessary to stop three or four times a day to adjourn to the blacksmith shop where they sharpened the plane and scraper blades.[73]

Behind the outboard joiners came the painters. Although some paints came ready-mixed—principally the copper bottom paint and small amounts used for decorative painting—most were mixed at the shipyard's paint shop. Using raw and boiled linseed oil that came in barrels, japan driers, whiting, white lead and bronze green pastes, and lampblack, the painters were able to create the colors favored by each schooner's managing owners: black/white/and shades of gray favored by P&S, bronze green and white favored by J. S. Winslow, and the white of the Palmer line. The painters mixed and applied three coats of paint for each schooner—the first with slow-drying raw linseed oil and the subsequent coats with quicker-drying boiled linseed oil.[74] Oak crosstrees and trestletrees were painted black, but the spars were oiled as was cabintop planking. Deckhouses, rails, and other structures were finished in white, or a combination white and varnished natural finish, depending on the managing owner's or captain's preferences.

The deckhouse interiors also received close attention with three or four coats of shellac (a sealer) and varnish (with sanding between coats) not being unusual, especially in the posh after house. The one example of surviving paneling from a Percy & Small-built schooner and surviving invoices for a number of Percy & Small-built schooners demonstrate that gilded capitals, decorative painting and gilding, and highly finished, exotic paneling were the standard in the after house of the period.[75] Tongue-and-groove North Carolina pine was the standard for the midship and forecastle houses, although they, too, glittered with several coats of shellac and varnish.

Between Hyde Windlass, the ship plumbers (J. A. Winslow & Son), and the technology of the day, Percy & Small's big schooners incorporated a level of amenities for officers and crew that would have been

The "Hyde" Improved Hoisting Engines

DESIGNED for use on shipboard for working the windlass, pumps, hoisting cargoes and hauling the vessel. These engines are of new design, and embody all the improvements that have suggested themselves to us in years of experience in building engines for this service. We have aimed at strength, simplicity and convenience in the construction of these engines, and feel confident that we have the best engines for all classes of hoisting duty ever placed on the market.

The cut shown on this page illustrates our single friction drum hoisting engine without gypsy heads. This engine is intended for installing inside a deckhouse, and couplings are fitted on extended shafts each side, carried out through the sides of the house and gypsies fitted. These engines are furnished in many different sizes. The ones most generally used are as follows:

```
6" diameter x  8" stroke
7"     "     x 10"    "
8"     "     x  8"    "
8"     "     x 10"    "
9"     "     x 10"    "
```

The "Hyde" Improved Hoisting Engines
From: 1915 Hyde Windlass Company Catalogue

unimaginable for someone aboard a wooden Down Easter on the Cape Horn route just a decade or two earlier. What made most of this possible and, in fact, made the great schooners themselves possible, was the steam auxiliary power plant.

Hyde Windlass Company, which had started as the Bath Iron Foundry then became the Bath Iron Works, was spun off from that firm in 1896 by its founder Thomas W. Hyde. The new firm concentrated on deck machinery and equipment, much of which had originally been developed under the BIF/BIW regime of the 1870s–1880s, while its progenitor concen-

trated on shipbuilding and marine propulsion systems.[76] During Percy & Small's active years, the Hyde Windlass firm possessed a reputation for superb engineering and quality manufacturing. It was also virtually next door, occupying the site of the Morse shipyard where Sam Percy and Frank Small cut their teeth as shipbuilders between 1893–96.

The deck machinery firm was, in fact, one of the major subcontractors to Percy & Small when it came to building schooners. It routinely provided materials, equipment, and services for each new vessel amounting to between six and eight thousand dollars

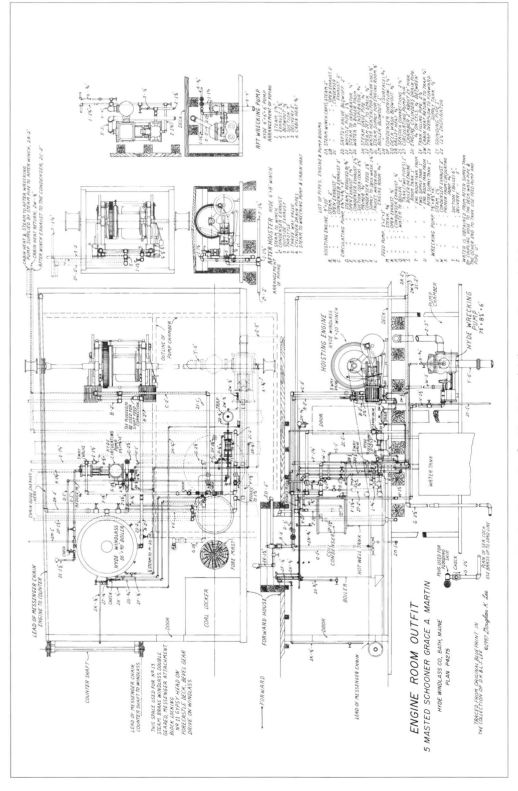

Engine Room Outfit: Five-Masted Schooner GRACE A. MARTIN

This plan, traced from the original, depicts the layout of the basic steam plant that, while not propelling the great schooners, made their very existence possible. Without the benefit of the steam hoisting engines and wrecking pumps, the small crews would have found it virtually impossible to set sail, hoist anchors, or keep the big hulls free of water.

Courtesy: Captains Douglas K. and Linda J. Lee

($92,000 to $123,000 in 1998), which were only exceeded by the outlays for ship carpenters, timber, and iron.[77] In the case of the ALICE M. LAWRENCE, fairly typical of the six-masters and large five-masters, Hyde provided the following equipment: a #13 Messenger attachment, Double-Geared Brake Windlass with steel gears and fitted for $2^3/4$-inch stud link chain; two Hyde horizontal hoisting engines, both 9 x 10; one 60-inch by 108-inch upright boiler with large coil condenser; two $7^1/2$ by $8^1/2$ by 6 Hyde Duplex Steam Pumps; two smaller steam pumps for salt water circulation (condenser) and fresh water boiler feed; two 6-inch Adair Pumps; one #4 Power Capstan; three large fresh water tanks; two #0 Patent Anchor Chain Riders; and one #11 Robinson Steerer with 72-inch wooden wheel. In addition, the firm provided all of the necessary piping, valves, gauges, and other fittings, along with 402.5 hours of labor by machinists and pipefitters to install the entire system.[78]

The work of installing and hooking up the Hyde Windlass-provided machinery and equipment began as soon as the schooner was in frame and before the decking was laid and the forward house was completely enclosed. On the ALICE M. LAWRENCE, a flush-decked schooner, the windlass was placed on the main deck, one deck below the spar deck and just forward of the recessed forward house. It was probably knocked down when it was lifted aboard the schooner via a gin-pole derrick and one of the shipyard teams, and was assembled in place. A close examination of the Hyde Windlass plan for the GRACE A. MARTIN's steam plant (opposite page) and auxiliaries illustrates the added, but essential, complexity steam brought to age-old wooden shipbuilding at the end.

When the LAWRENCE set sail from Bath, she had a system that hoisted her anchors and sails—something her crew could hardly do thanks to their limited numbers—and kept her hull pumped dry. But there was more. For the first time, a wooden schooner was fitted with a steam-driven dynamo, providing not only bright running lights, but electric light in the quarters as well. In later years, more and more of the big schooners were "electrified," and during World War I, many were also outfitted with radio receivers and some even with transmitters.[79]

Steam not only provided the means by which the great schooner's crew (captain, first and second mates, engineer, cook, and eight seamen) could handle the vessel's massive gear, but it also provided comfort. From the seamen's cramped forecastle to the captain's elegant quarters aft, all living quarters were steam heated. Hot water was also readily available to all for washing, shaving, and laundry, although the captain and his guests were the only ones with a bathtub and sink with hot and cold running water. The crew had to inject live steam into a bucket of water when they wanted hot water, or depend on the good humor of the cook.

J. A. Winslow and Son, ship and house plumbers, took care of the water supply and waste and drainage systems. They installed the marble-topped sink, claw-footed tub, and water closet—all with nickel-plated pipes and fixtures—in the captain's bathroom. Reserved for the use of the captain and his family, plus any guests of the captain or managing owners, the facility was more on the par with what one found at the most up-to-date hotels than in even the average middle class home of the period.

The rest of the crew had to make do with two hoppers, one on the port side forward for the common seamen and one on the starboard side for the mates, engineer, and cook. The facilities were a bit better than the seats of ease found aboard the old square-riggers (from which the term "head" is derived), but they certainly lacked the ambience enjoyed by captain and guests.[80]

It took more than timber, oakum, paint, steel and iron, canvas, and manila to complete a vessel. The schooner had to be furnished with the thousand-and-one items that made it livable and workable. Furniture: in addition to the custom built-ins, the ALICE M. LAWRENCE's after house was outfitted with one oak armchair, one box couch, oak desk and chair, several framed mirrors, three grass twine chairs, a rattan rocker, slipper chair, oak dining table and six matching chairs, and, after a big dinner, one could choose to stretch out on the Adams Adjustable Couch, or sit in comfort in one of the leather or mahogany armchairs in the main saloon.[81]

Although the builder paid the bill for these furnishings, it was customary for the managing owners to actually select the furnishings going into their vessel and the builder to pay a previously agreed-upon amount. If the owners exceeded that allowance, they made up the difference.

Some of the surviving contracts—probably drawn up by New York lawyers—included variants of the following wording:

> To have customary Bath outfit in cabin. To be furnished with side lights, anchor lights and signal lights. Liquid and brass compass, Taffrail log, mechanical foghorn, one set of flags, usual outfit of carpenter tools, leads, lead lines and cork fenders.[82]

This all appears rather vague, but Bath shipbuilders knew exactly what it entailed. The Bath outfit encompassed everything from pillows and pillow cases, mattresses and sheets, to linen, china and silver for the captain's table (glazed metal plates and cups for the crew), and all the pots, pans, and other utensils in the galley. Percy & Small paid $446.83 (+/- $6,800 in 1998) to two suppliers for these items, and an additional $445 for furniture, carpets, curtains, etc., for the GOVERNOR BROOKS.[83]

The shipbuilder was also responsible for providing a full set of tools for carpentry and maintenance of the auxiliary steam system. Of course, definitions of what constituted complete varied, especially between the managing owner and the builder, as this letter hints:

> Now the matter of chandlery, tools, etc; these Percy & Small may get in Bath. Be sure to get a very good outfit of engine tools, carpenter's tools and chandlery. Take this matter up with them and ask them whether they want us to buy them here in Boston. I judge some of them they will get down there and then we can give you a list of what we have been in the habit [of] furnishing up here. Then you can give them a list for as much more as you can make them stand for.[84]

The builder also provided an assortment of navigational instruments, including a pair of compasses, shallow and deep sea leads, a sounding machine, and a patent taffrail log with spare line and rotator. In addition, such items as a megaphone, hand-operated foghorn, illuminating torch, and flags—signal, national ensigns, jack, house, and burgee—made up part of the outfit. Captains were expected to supply their own navigation tools—charts, parallel rules, dividers, chronometer—but Percy & Small sometimes purchased chronometers outright for a vessel. The GOVERNOR BROOKS received a secondhand Dent chronometer (#2037) purchased from the Charles C. Hutchinson Company of Boston for $135, and the CORA F. CRESSY was the recipient of a London-made John Fletcher eight-day chronometer purchased secondhand from Bath's most famous living mariner, Captain James F. "Shenandoah" Murphy for $150 (+/- $2,300 in 1998).[85]

About the last thing that needed to be put aboard was the basic stock of groceries. As this was, for the most part, a cost charged directly to the owners and not the builders, few Percy & Small provision invoices have survived, but those that have are instructive. Captain Jewett stocked the ELEANOR A. PERCY for $218.40 (+/- $3,300 in 1998) before sailing from Bath in November 1900, but Captain Harding of the CORA F. CRESSY managed to run up a bill for groceries that came to $311 (+/- $4,800 in 1998). In fact, an examination of their respective purchases suggests that Captain Harding was fond of a varied and plentiful table, while Captain Jewett was a man of simpler tastes. One does wonder momentarily what use both vessels had for 500 pounds of tallow and flaxseed when it came to feeding the crew, but the materials were, in fact, intended to literally grease the way of each schooner into the river.[86]

With the shipyard work completed and with crew and stores aboard, each new Percy & Small-built schooner took a tow to the mouth of the Kennebec where, for the first time it harnessed the power of the wind in its sails. Some would have short lives, others long, but all would be hard.

[1] Percy & Small did build a few vessels from frames on hand—FANNIE PALMER (II) and GOVERNOR BROOKS—and frequently scouted extensively amongst other shipbuilders for available shipbuilding timber.

[2] *BT*, 3/25/1907; *I&E*, 4/22/1908.

[3] Schooner #11, Construction Invoices, Parker Collection.

[4] *American Sentinel*, 2/15/1883; 3/20/1890.

[5] Known Percy & Small treenail turners included Edison Jones, B. C. Jordan, and B. A. White. These men may also have worked at the shipyard as ship carpenters or fasteners when not turning the treenails.

[6] *BT*, 8/3/1916.

[7] Smaller vessels needed a steeper set for the ways to overcome inertia and accelerate enough to clear the end without damage or hanging up. Larger vessels needed less declivity because their mass was sufficient to overcome the effects of inertia and they developed enough speed to clear. If one were launching a vessel in winter, it was advisable to build launching ways with more declivity than one would do for a summer launching because of the effects of temperature on the launching grease. The differences, however, rarely exceeded 1/8 inch in a foot.

[8] William F. Palmer mentions this rocker in relation to the JANE PALMER which he bought unfinished on the stocks in East Boston. "In launching the craft slid the whole length on her keel, and took out all of the camber [rocker] built into her keel and possibly a couple inches more. The keelson scarphs show a great deal more than the rail." See: WFP to Captain Creighton, 8/19/1904, Palmer Collection. Palmer meant rocker; no one in his right mind ever built a great schooner with a cambered keel.

[9] Parker, *Coal Schooners*, p. 41.

[10] Oregon-fir spars were delivered to Bath on railroad cars, but were then dumped into the Kennebec and towed to Percy & Small. So they may not have come to the shipyard on a schooner, but they certainly arrived via water. Hardwood, hackmatack, and sawn white pine from Maine and other northern sources came via railroad. It was usually trucked to the shipyard in horse-drawn wagons or transhipped on scows or barges.

[11] Many of Percy & Small's surviving construction bill files contain the painstaking surveys of timber by ship designers Fred Rideout and Bant Hanson, and teamster George McFadden, broken down by rough-sawn dimensions (i.e., 14 x 15, 10 x 14, etc.), number of pieces, average length, board feet, cubic feet. See: Percy & Small Schooner #17, Construction Bill File, Parker Collection. Many of Captain Humphreys' surveys are at Maine Maritime Museum, in MS-8.

[12] Rock elm, hard maple, beech, and yellow birch were all used extensively by Maine shipyards for keels and floor timbers although sneered at by some including those who thought the last acceptable shipbuilding timber was English oak. Hardwoods were obtainable in the right sizes, available at a good price, nearly as strong as white oak and, as long as used in places that were always wet with salt water, were durable. White oak was stronger and could be used in dry, wet, or conditions of alternating wet and dry. Live oak, found along the southern coast of the U.S., was considered even better than English oak for frames, but it was very expensive and in short supply, a factor that ruled out its use on commercial vessels.

[13] Schooner #27, GOVERNOR BROOKS, Construction Bill File, Parker Collection. George McFadden surveyed the frame sold by Donnell to Percy & Small. He rejected about 5 percent of the frame timber, much of which was sweet gum rather than oak.

[14] Copy of letter from Percy to Palmer in WFP to EAW, 5/21/1908, Palmer Collection.

[15] Barnes Interview. McCabe may have been in charge of all framing. This gang also probably fabricated and hung the rudder and got out and installed the stem, knighthead, and hawse timbers.

[16] DMHSN #25. The newspaper accounts gave the dimensions for keel stock as 14 x 15; *BT*, 12/15/1909.

[17] The keel pieces totaled 828 cubic feet of oak weighing on average 55 pounds per cubic foot.

[18] Palmer insisted on shoes—a sacrificial structure designed to be easily torn off if the vessel ran aground, thus protecting the keel. Hardwood keels, along with yellow pine and Douglas-fir keels, also needed oak shoes.

[19] Barnes Interview.

[20] "Schooner Construction Notes," interview with Captain S. R. Percy, 9/19/1935, MWHRP. Hereafter cited as Percy Interview, MWHRP.

[21] McCabe Interview, Parker Collection.

[22] Some of the anchors were ringbolts set into ledge and are still visible. In other parts of the shipyard where no ledge was available, the anchors were probably heavy, buried timbers—called deadmen—with ringbolts.

[23] Captain Douglas K. Lee, "Transom, Stern, and Rudder Construction Sheets, CORA F. CRESSY Drawings."

[24] Barnes Interview, 9/25/1975. Unfortunately the tape of this interview has been misplaced. However, the author took extensive notes of the interview while preparing a symposium paper and, subsequently, an article for the National Trust on wooden shipbuilding published in 1976.

[25] Half frames did not cross the keel but butted against and were fastened to the keelsons and deadwood at the

narrow ends of the vessel. Full frames crossed and were fastened into the keel.

[26] A third futtock for frame station #46 would be marked: XLVI-3 and *p*(ort) or *s*(tarboard).

[27] Percy Interview, MWHRP.

[28] Palmer to E. A. Wentworth, 4/28/1905, LB 2/1905-6/1905, Palmer Collection.

[29] Percy Interview, MWHRP.

[30] McCabe Interview, Parker Collection.

[31] Some builders resorted to butt joints rather than scarf joints in the keelsons, but this was a practice rejected by most builders. Perhaps the best-known practitioner of the butt—rather than scarf—approach was Holly Bean of Camden.

[32] Bolts in the wooden ship era were not what we think of today with threads, heads, and nuts, but were long drifts up to 1.25 inches in diameter—basically big nails—that were driven with sledges. Depending on their use and location, they were either headed over clench rings at the driving end or at both ends.

[33] Caulking served to increase resistance to longitudinal shear forces—i.e., resisting the tendency of ceiling strakes to shift along their contact or faying surfaces. The limbers—longitudinal openings on each side of the keelsons—were normally covered by boards that could easily be removed when the hold was empty so that the limber holes and spaces between frames could be cleaned out, especially the ones that housed the bilge pumps' suction pipe strainers. These needed periodic maintenance so as not to become clogged with coal dust and other debris.

[34] WYOMING's ceiling ranged from 11 inches to 14 inches thick while her planking was 6 inches, except at the garboards where it was 8 inches thick.

[35] A limited number of butt-to-butt strakes of ceiling were permitted in the lower hold, but it required extra fastenings in the plank ends. All other ceiling joints were scarfed. See: "Ceiling and Lower Deck Beams," Contract for Schooner No. Eleven of the Palmer Fleet, ELIZABETH PALMER," Parker Collection.

[36] Robert Gardiner, ed., *Sail's Last Century: The Merchant Sailing Ship 1830–1930*. London: Conway Maritime Press, Ltd., 1993, p. 33. The iron-frame, wooden-planked type was known as composite construction. William F. Palmer referred to wooden-framed vessels with diagonal, basketweave strapping as the semi-composite type.

[37] Percy Interview, MWHRP.

[38] Of all the vessels measuring over 1,750 gross tons, only four were unstrapped, the last being completed in early 1901.

[39] WFP to F. H. Orr, 10/29/1904, Palmer Collection.

[40] In the two instances where strapping was on the inside of the frames (ADDIE M. LAWRENCE, ELIZABETH PALMER), the ceiling was obviously put on after the strapping.

[41] The diagonal straps measured $4^1/2$ inches by $^1/2$ inch.

[42] "Memorandum Cost of Strapping," Construction Bill File, Schooner #39, Parker Collection. Those subsequently interviewed did not recall or did not mention who actually installed the strapping.

[43] Coombs Interview.

[44] Robson Interview.

[45] Coombs, Osier, and Robson Interviews. The worst possible event was to have the plank in place and fastened and then have it crack or split as it dried. The treenails could be bored out, but getting the composition ship spikes out was a real challenge. For this reason, Percy & Small did not fasten planking with a lot of twist or bend until it had definitely taken the proper set.

[46] Contracts: ELIZABETH PALMER and FULLER PALMER, Parker Collection; Contract: JOSEPH S. ZEMAN, Douglas K. and Linda J. Lee Collection.

[47] Percy Interview, MWHRP.

[48] H. Cole Estep, *How Wooden Ships Are Built*. Cleveland, Ohio: The Penton Publishing Company, 1918, pp. 68-70.

[49] William F. Palmer to G. Welt, 6/5 and 6/6/1902 and WFP to Captain Leroy K. McKown, 10/24/1905, Palmer Collection. Palmer, forever persnickety, kept a close eye on the length of the treenails going into his schooners—he believed those not going all the way through to be wedged at both ends should be long enough to go halfway through the ceiling. He warned his builders to avoid "the Camden practice," and referred pointedly to the GEORGE W. WELLS and what she revealed while repairing at Percy & Small (presumably that Mr. Bean skimped on the length of his treenails).

[50] Lower decks were often planked only in the way of the deckhouses that rested on them or where pumps and other equipment were installed. The generally open nature of the hull's framework below the weather decks facilitated loading, trimming, and discharging bulk cargoes such as coal.

[51] Stevens, *Reminiscences of a Boothbay Shipbuilder*, pp. 36–46. The author, a shipbuilder with over a half century of experience and a devoted student of maritime history, describes the caulker's "progress" at the tail end of the wooden shipbuilding era.

[52] American Bureau of Shipping, *Rules for the Construction and Classification of Wooden Ships*. New York, 1921 edition, p. 212.

[53] Lee interview with Roy Wallace of Thomaston. Wallace had worked on the five-master EDNA HOYT when she was built.

[54] Construction Bills, Schooner #24 (ALICE M. LAWRENCE), Parker Collection. According to the invoices, 13,650 pounds of baled oakum and 2,100 pounds of cotton went into the seams of this six-master in addition to nearly 20 barrels of pitch.

[55] Houghton Bros. Invoice, Construction Bills, Schooner #24, Parker Collection.

[56] WFP to P&S, 4/12 and 5/12/1905, 9/27, 28, and 10/01/1906, 1/9/1907, 6/23/1908; WFP to Frank Palmer, 9/27 and 10/1/1906; WFP to Miles M. Merry, 9/28 and 10/1/1906, Palmer Collection.

[57] WFP to Miles M. Merry, 9/28/1906, Palmer Collection.

[58] WFP to P&S, 9/9/1907, Palmer Collection.

[59] WFP to Frank A. Palmer, 10/1/1906, Palmer Collection.

[60] Palmer required that Percy & Small have his sails sewn by C. C. Dennett and his successor W. F. Stearns in Bath. Percy & Small may have occasionally patronized the A. M. Cutler sail loft in Bath, as well.

[61] Contract, Schooner #16—FULLER PALMER, p. 17, Parker Collection.

[62] Construction Bills, Schooner #22, Parker Collection; Construction Bills, Schooner #24, Parker Collection. P&S purchased sailcloth from J. S. Winslow & Company for #24. Their 2/0 duck cost P&S $.34 per yard (discounted) versus $.26 per yard (discounted) for "Dorothy duck." The list price for "Dorothy duck" was also less than the Woodberry duck used on the Winslow schooner. It should also be noted that Hall, Lincoln & Company billed their "#0000 Dorothy duck" as 2/0 duck. The difference in the final price reflects Eleazer Clark's ability to never pass up an opportunity to make money, especially at the expense of investors in J. S. Winslow & Company schooners.

[63] Spruce was frequently used for all but the foretopmast, but not in this case.

[64] A typical four-master required approximately 240 individual steel fittings for its masts and spars alone.

[65] Christian Henry Bohndell Notebook, Private Collection; interviews with Henry Bohndell and James Stevens by Douglas K. and Linda J. Lee.

[66] Coombs Interview. Ignoring friction, the block arrangement provided an 8:1 mechanical advantage.

[67] It is possible that the riggers arranged large timbers much like loading ramps on one side of the vessel and as a strain was taken on the main purchase lead and the spar began to rise and swing under the center of effort, it began

to slide up the well-greased diagonal timbers that served to keep it clear from the shipyard staging and side of the vessel. When it was lifted high enough to clear the vessel's rails and the temporary blocking, the spar could be turned ninety degrees and set down on the blocking. The few photographs of P&S schooners being sparred indicate that the staging remained in place, but there was nothing present that resembled ramps or other structures that permitted the spars to be skidded up onto the athwartship blocking.

[68] Coombs Interview.

[69] Construction Bills, Schooner #24, Parker Collection. The ALICE M. LAWRENCE invoices included bills for 7,500 fathoms (45,000 feet) of manila ranging in size from $1^{1}/_{2}$ inches to 9 inches and 9,735 pounds of blocks purchased from the Boston & Lockport Block Company.

[70] Only one Percy & Small-built schooner's loss can be traced directly to rigging failure: the S. P. BLACKBURN rolled her spars out after being caught in the trough of the seas seventeen years after she was built.

[71] The Palmer schooners had their hulls painted black after the fleet was purchased by Winslow.

[72] For centuries, shipbuilders had "coppered" ship's bottoms using thin copper sheets and subsequently sheets composed of various copper alloys. Although effective, coppering was also expensive and needed to be renewed periodically. Enter bottom paints rich in copper oxides which tend to poison marine growth. Bottom paint was relatively cheap and could be applied quickly. P&S schooners normally were drydocked once a year to have their bottoms cleaned and repainted. However, when wooden vessels were likely to spend extended periods in the tropics they were still coppered. CORA F. CRESSY Owners Statements, 1902–22, Parker Collection.

[73] Samuel A. Barnes Interview by Virginia Wood, 9/25/1975. MMM Transcript and RLS Notes. Coombs Interview.

[74] Contracts, ELIZABETH PALMER & DAVIS PALMER, Parker Collection.

[75] Construction Bills, Schooners #7 and #11, Parker Collection; and MMM Collections, CORA F. CRESSY Panels.

[76] Snow, *Bath Iron Works: The First Hundred Years*, p. 24ff.

[77] Building Accounts, Schooners #18, 24, 26, 28 and 30, Parker Collection.

[78] Construction Bills, Schooner #24, Hyde Windlass Company Invoice, Parker Collection.

[79] Battery-powered telephones were standard equipment on these schooners because of their great size, connecting

quarterdeck, engine room, and forecastle.

[80] The smaller four-masters often relied on a bucket in the engineroom or under the forecastle deck.

[81] Construction Bills, Schooner #24, Walter Corey Company Invoice, Parker Collection. The furnishings from this vendor came to $437.23 (+/- $6,750 in 1998).

[82] Contract, P&S Hull #43, Douglas K. and Linda J. Lee Collection.

[83] Summary Cost Account, Schooner #27; Construction Bills, Schooner #27, D. T. Percy and J. A. Winslow Invoices, Parker Collection.

[84] WFP to Captain Leroy McKown, 11/10/1905, Palmer Collection.

[85] Charles C. Hutchinson Invoice, Schooner #27; Construction Statements and J. F. Murphy Invoice, Schooner #11, Construction Statements, Parker Collection.

[86] T. G. Campbell Invoices, Schooners #7 and #11, Construction Statements, Parker Collection.

To the Top of the Class

A NEW CENTURY

On 1 January 1901, the first day of the new century, Percy and Small were hard at work. At the Reed yard north of their main yard, the OAKLEY C. CURTIS was virtually complete and was scheduled to go overboard about midmonth for delivery to J. S. Winslow & Company. The five-master, built to the same model as the CARNEGIE but somewhat smaller, was well ahead of the other five-master the firm was building at its own yard that was not scheduled for launching until spring. That schooner, named the MARTHA P. SMALL for the wife of Percy & Small's junior partner, was being built from the model of the WILLIAM H. CLIFFORD, a much smaller vessel.[1]

Aside from the two schooners on the ways, J. S. Winslow & Company had placed an order for a four-master that would follow the CURTIS at the Reed yard, and Percy & Small already planned to build a four-master as a replacement for the NOTMAN, sunk the previous June in a collision, and an additional five-master for their own account.

BUILDING SCHOONERS BIG TIME

After the frenetic shipbuilding activity of 1900, Percy & Small settled into a more stately pace through the end of 1909. At least it seemed more stately as the firm moved to consolidate its shipbuilding operations into one enlarged shipyard by the late summer of 1901, following the launching of the CORDELIA E. HAYES from the Reed yard.

The truth of the matter, however, was that the surge in demand for new schooners that emerged in 1898 had peaked and never again would Bath's wooden shipbuilders match the 35,276 gross tons of shipping launched in 1900.[2] Although the decline was uneven, reversing itself some years, the general trend was down. This became strikingly apparent during the last half of the decade as output from Bath shipyards dropped precipitously from the 1900–04 average of 24,575 gross tons per year to an average of 9,964 gross tons per year between 1905–09.

Nonetheless, during that same ten-year (1900–09) span, Percy & Small delivered twenty-five vessels, all but one of which were schooners, and eighteen of the twenty-five vessels measured greater than 2,000 gross tons.[3] Altogether, Percy & Small's share of the wooden hull market increased during the decade from approximately a quarter of those built at Bath to over half (1900–04: 26 percent; 1905–09: 52 percent), but its actual tonnage output declined during the second half of the decade (1900–04: 32,550 GRT; 1905–09: 25,917 GRT). Even so, the firm's record tonnage year was not achieved until 1908 when its shipbuilders delivered 9,834 GRT.

It could be argued that if Percy & Small was becoming the biggest frog in the schooner-building pond, it was more a case of the pond shrinking rather than Percy & Small growing. In one respect this was true, since their total new tonnage output declined during the second half of the decade. Nonetheless, they had secured for themselves unchallenged domination of the production of five- and six-masted schooners.[4] It was a classic case of servicing a niche market, with Percy & Small's particular niche occupied by J. S. Winslow & Company of Portland, William F. Palmer of Boston, and—of course—Percy & Small of Bath.

CUSTOMER: J. S. WINSLOW & COMPANY

J. S. Winslow & Company became Percy & Small's first—and best—outside customer in 1897. By the time the Portland firm accepted delivery of its last new schooner from the Bath firm in 1908, they had acquired 27,016 gross tons built to order, purchased while under construction, or purchased directly from Percy & Small's fleet. In fact, in the period between 1900–09, J. S. Winslow took delivery of more new tonnage than even Percy & Small's own fleet.[5]

Two of the schooners launched under the Winslow flag were under construction for Percy & Small's own account when purchased: MARGARET WARD and EVELYN W. HINKLY. A third schooner, the MILES M. MERRY, was purchased by Winslow after it was already in Percy & Small service. Obviously, Sam Percy and Frank Small operated on the principle that the first rule of business was to keep the customer happy. And happy J. S. Winslow & Company was, in the person of Eleazer Clark, if his orders for five six-masters were any indication.[6]

Clark was no "barefoot Captain" in the image of his firm's founder and namesake. He was, however, amazingly adept in the forging of alliances that assured J. S. Winslow & Company a major share of the business carrying coal into Portland. While this did not come close to the tonnage of coal carried to Boston, Maine's largest city was the principal coal discharge port and distribution center for much of Maine's textile and paper industry, as well as the gas and electric generating industries and Maine Central Railroad, all big consumers of coal. Clark, through his alliances, was able to assure a steady flow of business to the Winslow fleet even in the face of competition from steam colliers and tug-barge fleets.[7]

The secret to Clark's success was to persuade as many as possible of those engaged in the distribution of coal, or major consumers of it, to make substantial investments in Winslow schooners. The roll call of the namesakes of the big Winslow schooners testified to his success: Oakley C. Curtis, Addie M. Lawrence, Ruth E. Merrill, Alice M. Lawrence, Edward J. Lawrence, and Edward B. Winslow.

Curtis was a nephew of J. F. Randall, principal partner of Portland's largest wholesale coal dealers, Randall & McAllister, former manager of that firm, and a prominent member of the Democratic Party. Ruth E. Merrill's father was also a manager of Randall & McAllister for many years, son-in-law to Mr. Randall, and a big investor in coal schooners. Edward J. Lawrence (and daughters) controlled the cotton mills in Waterville on the Kennebec, big consumers of coal. Finally, but by no means least, there was Edward B. Winslow (no relation to J. S. Winslow), a major producer of vitreous pipe and consumer of coal, and an acknowledged leader of Portland's business community. These were people of considerable influence who, in modern parlance, networked. They not only operated prosperous firms and were members of the same fraternal lodges, but they frequently had

Launchings attracted investors—actual and potential—so it behooved the captain-
designate (also an investor) to make himself sociable with especially deep-pocketed
individuals for the good of the firm. Captain William "Billy" Kreger commanded three
J. S. Winslow & Company six-masters, all named for members of the Lawrence family
whose textile mills dominated the economy around Waterville on the Kennebec.
Gathered here for the launching of the first—and smallest—Winslow six-master, the
ADDIE M. LAWRENCE, Captain Kreger (left) is joined by three prosperous, upright-
looking gentlemen who probably include Edward J. Lawrence, a good friend and
Fairfield neighbor of Captain Kreger, and Eleazer Clark, the good captain's boss.
Courtesy: Captain W. J. Lewis Parker, USCG, Ret.

adjoining seats on the boards of important local corporations and banks.

It was certainly enough assurance to Clark that,
despite the inroads that modern technology might
make on the coal trade at Portland and other East
Coast ports, J. S. Winslow & Company and their big
coal schooners would receive their share. It was
enough of an encouragement, in fact, to have Percy &
Small build them a new six-master every other year,
starting in 1902. By the end of the decade, the
Portland firm had added five six-masters to their fleet,
fully half of the class ever built.[8]

On the one hand, Clark was adventuresome
enough to stake much of the firm's future on six-

masted schooners at a time when coal schooners were
coming under increasing competitive pressure. On
the other hand, he was sufficiently conservative to
stay with the long-poop schooner layout even after
others, including Percy & Small, had concluded its
strength was inadequate for very large schooners.
Winslow's first flush-decked six-master did not go
into service until 1906, when the ALICE M.
LAWRENCE took to the Kennebec River.

Another example of Clark's conservatism was evident in a far less functional matter. Most of the great
schooners still retained a few of the traditional decorative elements passed down through generations of
vessels, among them carved and gilded trailboards at

the bowsprit. The trailboards—really planks on either side of the cutwater that originally served as braces or stiffeners for the traditional carved, wooden figure-head—were carried aft a short distance along the flare of the bows. They were, however, purely vestigial elements with no structural role to play after the figure-head was replaced by the simple billethead. Percy & Small recognized this in 1902 when they equipped their CORA F. CRESSY with a set of carved trailboards that were mounted on and followed the curve of the upper cutwater. All but one of their subsequent schooners had this feature, as did those built for William F. Palmer, who substituted a carved eagle

head for the simpler billethead.[9] Trailboards and billetheads disappeared finally during World War I when functionality—and cost savings—became the principal criteria. Nonetheless, Clark's resistance to change has long eased the task of schooner "watchers" attempting to identify six-masters, first in real-life and then in photos: if she had a flush deck and the traditional trailboard placement, the schooner had to be one of three Winslow schooners.[10]

Unlike Percy & Small, who lost but one schooner—and that in 1900—during the decade, the Winslow fleet suffered an unusually high casualty rate. Among the twelve schooners built for, or sold to,

The MARGARET WARD, seen here drying sails, shared the CORA F. CRESSY deck layout but not her durability or good fortune. Sold on the stocks to J. S. Winslow & Company shortly before her launching—she has the "modern" trailboard configuration rather than the Winslow-preferred version—the schooner had already claimed one life in a freak accident before she was launched. Eight months after her launching, she was sunk by a steamer with three lives lost, including the captain's two small children and one seaman.

Courtesy: Maine Maritime Museum

the Portland firm by Percy & Small between 1897 and 1908, no fewer than five had been lost by the end of 1909.[11] We have already heard the fate of the CLARK and the CARNEGIE, the first schooners built for Winslow by Sam Percy and Frank Small. What of the others?

The MARGARET WARD was an elegant four-master of only 1,074 GRT that duplicated the deck configuration of the much larger CORA F. CRESSY, launched from the same ways just months earlier. Originally started for Percy & Small's own account, she was sold to the Portland firm on the stocks as she neared completion in July 1902 and was launched 9 August 1902. Her captain was Jason C. McKown, a member of one of Boothbay Harbor's more famous seagoing clans.

For those with a superstitious turn of mind, the WARD could already be considered a jinxed ship when she was sold to the Portland firm. On 15 July an approaching thunderstorm and driving rain led a number of Percy & Small workers to seek temporary shelter under her bow. Suddenly a bolt of lightning struck the pile of chain and anchors piled on the ground by the bow, waiting to be hoisted aboard. One man, Leander Miller, was killed instantly, and several others were knocked to the ground.[12]

The WARD sailed from the Kennebec with several hundred tons of ice destined for Washington at the end of August. Those aboard included Captain McKown's young wife and their two young children, a son and daughter. For the next eight months, the family sailed on the new schooner from various ports on the eastern seaboard to ports in the Caribbean. Then, early in the spring, before the hurricane season descended, the WARD was chartered to carry a cargo of steel rails from Baltimore to Galveston.

Early on the 13th of April (not a Friday), the WARD was anchored twenty-eight miles east of the Galveston bar in seven fathoms, anchor lights brightly burning and anchor watch on deck. At about 3:00 A.M., the watch spotted a steamer bearing down upon them and the mate roused the crew and called the captain. All hands turned to, ringing bells, blowing the steam whistle, and shouting for all they were

worth as the Southern Pacific steamer EL RIO inexorably approached: she struck the schooner aft about thirty feet forward of the taffrail, carried away the wheel box and steering gear, and ripped a massive hole extending well below the waterline.

There was no time to launch a boat, so everyone aboard was ordered into the rigging. Captain McKown, son in his arms, was scrambling to safety when gear falling from aloft knocked him momentarily unconscious and knocked his son from his arms. As Mrs. McKown struggled to get aloft with her daughter in her arms, a sailor attempting to assist her took her daughter, but he and the little girl were swept overboard as the schooner plunged to the bottom just thirty seconds after the collision.[13]

If there was some sort of hex on the WARD, there was certainly none on the 1,281-GRT CORDELIA E. HAYES which Percy & Small built for the Winslow fleet in 1901. Launched from the Reed yard, the HAYES was commanded by Captain Elmer Ellsworth Ross—often called "praying Ross" thanks to his propensity to preach the gospel in public places while in port (he was no relation to Captain Alex Ross). Ross not only succeeded in finding a bride who was happy to make the schooner her home, but he also performed a daring rescue of crew and passengers from the foundered British steamer KELVIN in the fall of 1904.[14] For the latter feat, Captain Ross received a silver urn from the British government. Unfortunately for Captain and Mrs. Ross, the HAYES was wrecked on Diamond Shoals six weeks before the presentation of the award; she had been temporarily under the command of a relief captain as they enjoyed a vacation ashore. All that was salvaged was a miscellaneous collection of gear, the naphtha launch, and Mrs. Ross's piano, which formerly graced the schooner's main saloon.[15]

The MILES M. MERRY (1,589 GRT), built from the ubiquitous model of the WILLIAM H. CLIFFORD, was the designated replacement for Percy & Small's first schooner, the CHARLES P. NOTMAN, lost in a collision. The MERRY, whose name suggested the esteem in which the shipyard's master builder was already held by the firm's partners, also had the honor of being the first schooner built on the shipyard's new north building ways. Captain Sydney G. Hupper, a resident of Rockland, owned the master's interest in the new schooner.

Captain Hupper didn't have much time to enjoy his new command, however. Barely five months after she was launched, the MERRY was sold to J. S. Winslow & Co. for an unspecified price. The good captain found himself on the beach when the Portland firm selected Captain Fickett for its newly acquired vessel.

It appears that the schooner and Captain Fickett managed a fairly uncomplicated existence for the next sixty-five months or so with few, if any, untoward events. Then things began to unravel. First, the MERRY managed to get ashore on the south shore of Long Island near Moriches—forty miles east of Fire Island—in a heavy fog. Loaded with 2,500 tons of coal consigned to Bangor, the schooner grounded at high tide, which put her far up on the beach, virtually

Launching day at the Reed shipyard, 17 August 1901, and the CORDELIA E. HAYES is almost ready to join the J. S. Winslow fleet. Located a block north of Percy & Small's own shipyard, this rather spartan facility was refurbished by the firm in 1900 during the rush of contracts. Percy & Small built two schooners here, the OAKLEY C. CURTIS and the HAYES, for the Portland firm. For the six weeks prior to this launching, they also repaired the grievously wounded GEORGE W. WELLS here.

Courtesy: Captain W. J. Lewis Parker, USCG, Ret.

The MILES M. MERRY underlines one of the perils that constantly engaged the attention of coasting captains, the danger of getting ashore. Built for their own account, the Percy & Small schooner was later sold to best-customer J. S. Winslow & Company. This particular misadventure at Moriches, Long Island, however, avoided disaster when a powerful salvage tug managed to pull her off before storm and heavy surf did her in. She was not so lucky the next time she hit the beach, almost in the same spot, seventeen months later.

Courtesy: Captains Douglas K. and Linda J. Lee

in the front yard of the Moriches Life Saving Station. Although there was some initial concern, she was quickly pulled off the beach and on her way again.[16] Damage was slight.

Then in November 1908, while enroute to Portland with a load of coal, the MERRY encountered a gale. This time she lost sails and a topmast. After discharging cargo, she was towed to Percy & Small for repairs just in time to be present for the launching of the giant EDWARD B. WINSLOW, the Portland firm's last Percy & Small-built schooner.[17]

Captain Fickett chose to take a winter vacation during February 1909, just a few months after the schooner returned to service from repairs at her builder's yard. His relief, Captain Farrow, then took the MERRY south to load coal but he only got as far as—you guessed it—Moriches, Long Island. Once again she got ashore—in heavy surf—within a half-mile of the lifesaving station. This time she stayed. The crew and relief captain were taken off the schooner by the breeches buoy rescue apparatus, and

Merritt and Chapman—the well-known marine salvage firm—was called in to get her off. After two weeks of futile efforts, the vessel was stripped of movable gear and she was abandoned. The next day the stranded hulk burned.[18] At the time of her loss, the MERRY was valued at fifty thousand dollars (+/- $750,000 in 1998). She was reportedly uninsured.[19]

The irony of the MILES M. MERRY's attraction to the beach at Moriches, however, was compounded six weeks after the schooner burned. It was then that her fellow Percy & Small-built fleetmate—WILLIAM C. CARNEGIE—slammed ashore on that very same beach. All in all, 1909 was not a good year for J. S. Winslow & Company, having lost to stranding no fewer than three Percy & Small-built schooners.

Some of the schooners built for—or sold to—J. S. Winslow had short, if interesting, lives during the first decade. Others survived a little longer. The first Winslow six-master—and Percy & Small-built six master—to be lost was the big ALICE M. LAWRENCE (3,132 GRT).[20] Launched in 1906, she was the first flush-decked schooner built for the Winslow firm and the first of the great schooners to be outfitted with a steam-powered generating plant and electric lights.[21] Eight years later, sailing light for a coal port, she went aground in Nantucket Sound on Tuckernuck Shoal during a gale on 5–6 December 1914. Unfortunately, she was also hung up on the hulk of an earlier wreck that had a cargo of stone. It broke her back. However, captain and crew stayed aboard the schooner salvaging virtually all her standing and running rigging, blocks, and anything else removable before abandoning the hulk to the elements on 17 December.[22]

As with Percy & Small, World War I brought dramatic change and exceptional opportunity to the offices of J. S. Winslow & Co. First, freight rates shot up to unbelievable levels and then continued to climb.

Then, shippers offered to prepay all freight charges (whether or not the cargo arrived). And finally, people began offering to purchase great schooners that just months before were regarded as a glut on the market, at prices that boggled imaginations and even encouraged a little larceny. Eleazer Clark joined Percy & Small in the big sell-off during 1917, placing much of the Winslow fleet with the deep-pocketed France & Canada Steamship Company. Among the vessels Clark sold to France & Canada were the four surviving Winslow six-masters.

The ADDIE M. LAWRENCE (2,807 GRT), the first of J. S. Winslow's P&S-built six-masters, survived for a full fifteen years before going ashore on the coast of France near St. Nazaire in 1917. The coast of France was also the site of the EDWARD B. WINSLOW's (3,424

Many an authority on schooner aesthetics placed the WILLIAM C. CARNEGIE at the top of the five-master list. When she went ashore for the first and final time at Moriches on Long Island—within eyesight of the MERRY's final resting place—on 1 May 1909, she still retained that quality, although now battered by surf.

Courtesy: Captains Douglas K. and Linda J. Lee

GRT) funeral pyre at the same time, although the WINSLOW was still a relative youngster of nine years.[23] At a time when rumors of Hun perfidy and sabotage abounded, it was said that the WINSLOW succumbed to a fire set by a German agent disguised as a sailor.[24]

Two of the former Winslow six-masters survived into the third decade of the century. The RUTH E. MERRILL (3,003 GRT), delivered by Percy & Small in late 1904, was to be the last of the long poop schooners built by that firm. Nonetheless, she set some significant records under her first skipper, Captain George H. Wallace. During 1906, she made no fewer than fourteen round trips between the coal ports—principally Baltimore—and Portland. One of the longest runs possible in the trade, the MERRILL averaged 6.2 days northbound from Baltimore and 5.5 days southbound during the period.[25] On one trip, she made the run from Portland to Philadelphia in thirty-eight hours, averaging 13.5 knots.[26] She proved to be a leaker, however, a point brought home when she hove to and anchored off Montauk Point during a fierce winter gale. Heavily loaded with bituminous coal, she was boarded continuously by huge seas and became badly strained as she pitched and rolled. Although her pumps succeeded in keeping up with the inflow, Clark decided to have her towed into Boston from the Vineyard, where she could be dry-docked and repaired after unloading.[27]

The late March light (26 March 1906) shows off the ALICE M. LAWRENCE to great advantage as she is warped into the pier at Percy & Small, her hundreds of guests having tasted the delights of the launching buffet and those in the know having sampled the lethal punch. The first flush-decked six-master built by Percy & Small, she has a sweeping sheer and elegance of line that puts to rest the old notion that to be big was to be ugly.

Holmes Photo, courtesy of Captains Douglas K. and Linda J. Lee

Some claim that the best looking—and, perhaps, best built—six-master was the EDWARD B. WINSLOW. After being purchased by the France & Canada Steamship Company in 1917, she was dispatched to France with a mixed cargo of steel, wire, leather, and rice totaling nearly 5,000 tons. She caught on fire—set by a secret German agent shipped as a crewman, according to many stories—off the coast of France and sank.
Courtesy: Captain W. J. Lewis Parker, USCG, Ret.

The slow years—1909–15—resulted in periodic lay-ups, but the war and shipping shortage took care of that. Charters to Spain, South America, and France made up for the slack years. During this period she was sold to the France & Canada Steamship Company. Then peace again and a charter with coal to Hango, Finland. It became the charter from hell, with a failing rudder and failing boiler, lost anchors, worn-out hoisting gear, and a leaky hull. The protest submitted by the captain was a litany of day-to-day crises that saw them towed into Hamburg for repairs that took almost five weeks. Finally, after passing through the Kiel Canal and, subsequently, suffering from such a leaky boiler that it was impossible to raise the anchors, the schooner got as far as Oskarshamn in Sweden at the end of a towline where her cargo of 4,391 tons of Pocahontas coal was transferred to barges for the balance of the journey to Hango.[28] The voyage had taken three months, and now she had to return.

She didn't leave Oskarshamn until the following March, loaded with pit props destined for the British port of Hull. Apparently her boiler was repaired along with the anchor windlass, but the rudder remained a major problem all the way to England. After a long tow from Oskarshamn to the Skaw, the MERRILL cast off and proceeded under sail, passing within ten miles of the remains of her fellow Percy & Small-built schooner FENIX, ex-HELEN W. MARTIN.

The MERRILL moved across the North Sea in fits and starts as rudder problems and adverse winds compelled the captain to anchor so that the array of cables and chains rigged to control the rudder could be re-rigged and tightened. In all, it took twenty-five days to reach Hull—not exactly the "steamer time" the MERRILL was used to posting in her youth.

The longest-lived of the six-masters, the RUTH E. MERRILL slides gracefully into the Kennebec, 23 November 1904. Note that the boiler stack on the shipyard's blacksmith/machine shop is smoking furiously, a sure sign that for all of the pomp and circumstance connected with the launching, shipyard workers were hard at work steaming planking for the four-master EVELYN W. HINKLY on the south ways. If one looks closely at the HINKLY's sunlit port forward quarter, you can see she is planked to a point above her timber ports and that the dubbers have been at work just above the topmost staging planks fairing the frames to receive the planking.

Courtesy: Captains Douglas K. and Linda J. Lee

The RUTH E. MERRILL being unloaded at the Maine Central Railroad dock in Portland. The railroad was a good customer of J. S. Winslow and Percy & Small, consuming 168,903 tons of coal in 1900 alone. The MERRILL had a reputation for fast passages. She once completed two round trips between Portland and the coal ports in a single month and fourteen round trips in 1906 under her hard-driving captain, George H. Wallace.

Courtesy: Maine Historic Preservation Commission

Repaired in Hull, she returned across the Atlantic and went back into the coastwise trade. But the glory days of well-paying charters were over, and any charter was hard to come by. Nonetheless, she managed to find cargoes sufficient to keep going. One of three surviving six-masters at this point (EDWARD J. LAWRENCE and WYOMING), the MERRILL and her sisters were sold by France & Canada to A. W. Frost & Co., a Portland-based shipping firm.

The end came 12 January 1924 when, strained during heavy weather and leaking copiously, the schooner and her 4,500 tons of coal settled to the bottom at the west end of L'Hommedieu Shoal between Woods Hole and Vineyard Haven. She was not insured.

The last of J. S. Winslow's fleet of six-masters, the EDWARD J. LAWRENCE was still afloat when the MERRILL sank, but just barely. Ordered in 1907, the LAWRENCE was supposed to challenge the ELEANOR A. PERCY's title as largest six-master. In this she failed by fifty-one gross tons. But through the use of a heavy frame, diagonal steel strapping long advocated by William F. Palmer (see below), and the flush-deck configuration, J. S. Winslow & Company expected they had the strongest of the six-masters. But within a few years, the LAWRENCE was to dash their hopes as she proved to be both trouble-prone and strangely attracted to sand bars and ledges.

Her beginning, however, was auspicious. Just two weeks after she left her builder's yard, the dark green-hulled schooner pulled into Portland with a hefty 5,708 tons of coal.[29] But by June she was in trouble for the first time. While being docked at East Deering, her jibboom and bowsprit were broken off, necessitating a return to Bath for repairs. Later, in early fall, she ran aground in Hampton Roads without any apparent damage.[30] She was reported aground twice more in the next two years, both in Nantucket Sound. The first time it was Cross Rip Shoal, but the

Bright as a newly minted coin, the EDWARD J. LAWRENCE shows off her graceful sheer and massive hull before departing from her builder's yard. The authors believe she was the first of three schooners built from the Bant Hanson model labeled as WYOMING. Note the numbered frame timbers in the left foreground that are probably destined for the LAWRENCE's sister, the EDWARD B. WINSLOW.

Courtesy: Dr. Charles E. Burden

LAWRENCE floated free on the rising tide. Fifteen months later, near the same location, she ran onto a shoal and required assistance from the revenue cutter ACUSHNET in getting off.[31] Although no damage was ever reported in these instances, the fact of the matter was that the long, heavily loaded, wooden hull was subjected to a great deal of stress on these occasions, perhaps starting some of her caulking or fastenings.

However, it was an October gale in 1913 that really hurt her. Loaded deep with coal consigned to Portland, the LAWRENCE sailed from Norfolk on 29 September. After a lackadaisical passage, the schooner cleared the Nantucket shoals and turned north around Cape Cod on 13 October, only to run into a savage northeaster by nightfall. Laboring heavily with decks constantly awash, the LAWRENCE's captain confronted four critical problems simultaneously. The wind was threatening to blow her down on the infamous Peaked Hill Bars off the northeast end of Cape Cod. Then her cargo shifted, giving the deeply laden vessel a dangerous list; sails blew out and the fore and driver gaffs were smashed. Then she began to leak. Even with her wrecking pumps and bilge pumps in operation, there was soon seven feet of water in her hold.

Captain William R. Kreger, a resident of Edward Lawrence's hometown of Fairfield and captain of each of the Lawrence schooners successively, later claimed it was the worst time he ever spent at sea, and he had spent a lot of time at sea.[32] First he anchored the big schooner to keep her off the bars—demonstrating just why the coal schooners carried such heavy ground tackle. Later, when the wind moderated slightly, Kreger raised the anchors and the LAWRENCE was able to stagger into Provincetown Harbor. From there, the battered schooner was towed to Portland to unload. It was clearly evident that the EDWARD J. LAWRENCE was badly strained during this episode, opening a number of seams and starting scarf joints and fastenings. It is also possible that the big hull was wracked so badly during her experience that the basketwork of steel straps designed to reinforce the longitudinal strength of the hull parted at a crucial point.[33]

After a two-week repair (and recaulking) interlude at Percy & Small, the LAWRENCE went back into the coal trade. Two months later, she survived another violent gale without damage, whose near-hurricane force winds and freezing spray claimed two of her Percy & Small-built sisters, the GRACE A. MARTIN and FULLER PALMER.[34]

World War I had a way of converting struggling investments in schooner property to gold mines, and the LAWRENCE turned into one of the gold mines. In the fall of 1915, J. S. Winslow & Company chartered her to carry 5,000 tons of coal to Barcelona, Spain, at $10.50 (+/- $131.00 in 1998) per ton, prepaid. She made the passage under Captain Kreger's command—he stood to make $2,625 (+/- $32,800 in 1998) in primage for that leg of the passage alone—in a very creditable thirty days. It took her five months to get back to the States, carrying 5,400 tons of salt delivered at the fishing port of Gloucester. Unfortunately, while being towed to her anchorage, the big schooner hit a ledge which did extensive damage to the keel and bottom and necessitated drydocking for repairs. Nonetheless, it had been a profitable voyage for all concerned.[35]

The LAWRENCE made at least one additional passage to Barcelona under the Winslow house flag with Billy Kreger in command, although she was forced into an intermediate port for repairs. Upon her return to the United States, the LAWRENCE was sold to the France & Canada Steamship Company and Kreger left her to retire to his home in Fairfield, albeit only briefly.[36]

Captain Frank Hewitt Peterson took over the LAWRENCE from Captain Kreger in New York and prepared the big six-master for another transatlantic crossing, the destination being La Pallice on France's Bay of Biscay coast near La Rochelle. This time she carried a more warlike cargo than coal—4,990 tons of six-inch steel artillery shells (unloaded). The passage across was uneventful, taking just twenty days from New York to the Bay of Biscay. After being discharged by heavily guarded German POWs, the LAWRENCE cleared port under tow in company with another Percy & Small-built schooner, the CARL F. CRESSY. They were taken two hundred miles due west before

The EDWARD J. LAWRENCE was one of the first of the great schooners to take advantage of the impact of World War I on trade and shipping. The gross freight for her first passage to Barcelona, Spain, in 1915 was over $52,500. Here she lies at Barcelona after a thirty-day passage, unloading using her own hoisting engines. Contrast this arrangement with those enjoyed by the RUTH E. MERRILL at Portland (page 189, bottom photo).

Courtesy: Dr. Charles E. Burden

casting off the towing hawsers and filling away on starboard tacks for the southward. During the night, Captain Peterson received a radio message—by now most of the largest schooners were outfitted with radio receivers, and some carried transmitters—warning that a German U-boat was operating about sixty miles ahead on the course they were sailing. Unable to contact the radio-less CARL F. CRESSY, Peterson tacked ship and headed northwest. The next morning, the CRESSY—the last schooner Percy & Small built for their own account—was stopped by the rampaging U-boat, the crew ordered into the boats, and the schooner sunk.

Peterson and the LAWRENCE stuck with a northerly route back to North America, making landfall at Cape Race, Newfoundland. One day while enroute, the second mate—in a state of agitation—interrupted Captain Peterson who was hard at work at his desk. The ship, he reported, was in danger of breaking up. When asked what caused this concern, the mate took

Peterson on deck to the rail amidships. There he pointed at a flyrail scarf joint that was opening and closing four inches as the schooner worked in the seaway.[37] Limber she was, but the schooner kept on sailing all the way to Norfolk.

Over the next two years, the LAWRENCE's perambulations are more than a little obscure. But she probably made at least one passage to South America, as well as one to the Gulf of Mexico. In March 1919 she was in a Mobile, Alabama, drydock for extensive repairs, and in November came into Charleston, South Carolina, in distress after a passage from Amsterdam.[38] She was eventually towed to Percy & Small and surveyed, the results of which were pretty sobering, especially for anyone who had recently crossed the Atlantic on her. The shipyard installed three tiers of sister keelsons, 14 inches by 14 inches, on each side to stiffen her failing and badly hogged hull.

She made an additional trip to South America and

Few photographs were taken aboard the great schooners while under sail, and even fewer were taken on transatlantic passages. Sold to the France & Canada Steamship Company in 1917, the LAWRENCE lost her skipper of nine years, Captain Kreger, who retired to his home in Fairfield, Maine, after making two round-trip crossings of the Western Ocean. His replacement was Captain Frank H. Peterson who sailed the big schooner to France loaded with 4,990 tons of steel shell casings. Such a voyage took the schooner into the war zone and an area frequented by German U-boats. Peterson successfully evaded the latter, although the big schooner's flexible hull alarmed the second mate. The midship deckhouse is at the left. Note the lifeboat and spare gaffs—both sensible precautions on such a passage—lashed down abaft the house.

Courtesy: Captain W. J. Lewis Parker, USCG, Ret.

back, "showing no sign of strain."[39] Then, as with the other France & Canada schooners, the LAWRENCE was sold to A. W. Frost & Co. of Portland for less than a tenth of what she had brought five years earlier. For the next two years, under the command of Captain Joe York, she scraped together a dozen or so coal charters, but not enough to make a living. And her condition continued to deteriorate as even basic maintenance, never mind major repairs, was deferred. Her severe hog had grown more pronounced with the passage of time and she sported a 43-inch crown in her keelson by early 1922. Because of her hog, her maximum summer draft had now reached 31 feet 6 inches, making her too deep for

most ports.[40] After the owners refused to pay assessments on their shares to meet past operating expenses, the schooner was seized by the U.S. Marshall and posted for sale at auction. The day after Christmas 1925, while anchored in Portland Harbor, she burned to the waterline and sank.[41] She was the last six-master.

Percy & Small's Hull #21 must have appeared to be a mouse among pachyderms when her keel was laid in August 1904. With one exception, and that by just one ton, she was the smallest schooner built by the firm, measuring 698 GRT. Modeled by Fred Rideout, she was built explicitly for the hard pine trade, with an eye, no doubt, to carrying much of the timber

The last six-master, EDWARD J. LAWRENCE, burns on the day after Christmas, 1925,
allegedly the victim of an illegal still (operated by her shipkeeper) that got out of
control. The big schooner had been laid up for long periods of time since the early
1920s: too big, too old, and in too poor condition.

Courtesy: Dr. Charles E. Burden

brought to Percy & Small every year by water. As a timber carrier, she was outfitted with bow ports and no main hatch, a not-uncommon arrangement for schooners intended for the yellow pine trade, especially for those that would carry deck loads.

Her construction was well advanced when, once again, J. S. Winslow & Company decided that the little four-master was just what they needed. Negotiations were initiated and in early November it was announced that the new schooner had been sold on the stocks to the Portland shipping firm.[42] In the deal, Percy & Small agreed to sell her for $47,000 (+/- $723,000 in 1998) and purchase one quarter of her shares.[43] Her new managing owners selected

Captain J. F. Hinkly as captain, and named the schooner for his wife Evelyn. She was launched 19 January 1905.

At that point, the HINKLY's career became routine. She had no dramatic passages, no collisions, no serious groundings. She did haul timber, but she also hauled virtually everything else—even coal—although loading and trimming a coal cargo with her hatch layout must have been something of a challenge. In October 1917 the HINKLY sailed from New London and disappeared from the face of the earth. She had finally achieved a record: the first, and only, Percy & Small-built schooner to be lost without a trace.

William F. Palmer was not one of the boys. Where they had grown up around shipbuilding, ship handling, and the shipping business, he had grown up on the farm, attended Williams College, and taught school.[44] It was only when he moved to Taunton, Massachusetts, a prosperous manufacturing city with strong economic ties to coastal shipping, that he was exposed to the mechanics of the coastwise shipping trades, coal schooners, and sailing vessel design. He also met and married his second wife, Marie Elizabeth Convers—his first wife died nine years earlier—who shared his drive and ambition and was no shrinking, know-your-place housewife of the late Victorian era.[45]

Palmer was a self-assured individual, confident of his own views on a wide range of subjects. He even claimed, with some justification, to be the designer of most of the schooners in his fleet.

The first white schooner of the new Palmer fleet was laid down in June 1899 at the William Rogers shipyard in Bath. Named the MARIE PALMER, the 1,594-GRT four-masted schooner was soon followed by a near sister, the MAUDE PALMER. Also built by Rogers, and probably designed by Palmer, the MAUDE had a white oak frame actually cut locally, in Woolwich. However, Stinson Davis, one of her captains, felt she was a very poor sailer—dragging a lot of water behind her. According to the voluble Davis, if

Ghosting along off Vinalhaven Island, the EVELYN W. HINKLY, along with her twin ROBERT P. MURPHY, were the smallest schooners ever built by Percy & Small at 698 and 697 GRT respectively.
Leroy Coombs Photo, courtesy of Captain W. J. Lewis Parker, USCG, Ret.

you dropped a cord of wood over her stern off Cape Cod, it would still be under her stern when she reached Bangor.

But Palmer, aided by an uncanny ability to convince investors that coal schooners represented the cutting edge of twentieth-century investment, expanded his operation at a prodigious rate. By 1903 he was managing a fleet of seven schooners totaling 13,633 GRT. Percy & Small, by way of contrast, also operated a fleet of seven schooners totaling 15,806 GRT, but they had been in business six years longer.

Because Palmer was attempting to expand his fleet quickly, he contracted with four different shipbuilders for schooners between 1899–1902 before settling briefly on the George Welt shipyard in Waldoboro.[46] That shipyard ultimately built six of the fifteen Palmer schooners, but worsening relations between Palmer and Welt, along with the shortcomings of the shipyard and location, finally convinced the former to shift his business elsewhere.[47]

Palmer and Percy & Small came to do business in the spring of 1903. Palmer, disgusted with Welt's lack of progress on various contracts, began shopping around for another shipyard but had not been pleased with the responses he received from William Rogers, the New England Company, and even W. T. Donnell, Percy & Small's next door neighbor.[48] Then he discovered that Sam Percy and Miles M. Merry were hard at work on a new schooner for Percy & Small's account. Built on

William F. Palmer (1859–1909): schoolmaster, naval architect, schooner manager and promoter, letter writer, gadfly, Percy & Small customer.

Courtesy: William F. Palmer Collection, Maine Maritime Museum

the same model as the ADDIE M. LAWRENCE, Hull #17 was to be 18 inches deeper than her J. S. Winslow predecessor, but otherwise the same.[49]

Her keel was laid down during the first week of March, and #17 was moving right ahead when Palmer betook himself to the shipyard. He liked what he saw but there would need to be some important changes made if he were to purchase her. First, he wanted her rigged as a five-master. Palmer regarded six-masters as products more of vanity than practicality. Five years after #17 was built, he rejected a sixth mast on the schooner to be the FULLER PALMER because it would add an additional $3,000 to the total cost of the vessel and not effectively improve her performance.[50] The other change was Palmer's insistence that the schooner be built with a flush deck rather than use the long poop or CORA F. CRESSY arrangements that the shipyard had used up until then. His persistence in demanding the stronger flush-deck configuration starting with his first schooner ultimately influenced other schooner operators, including Percy & Small and J. S. Winslow & Company, to follow in his footsteps. However, he did not get the Palmer-preferred semi-composite construction utilizing diagonal steel strapping on the exterior of the frame. Percy & Small had already installed "hogging straps" arranged as steel trusses on the inside of the frame.[51]

Palmer's requirements were set forth in a contract, dated 8 May 1903.[52] The document itself—all fifteen pages including annexes—reflects Palmer's detail-oriented business management style, and contrasted dramatically with Percy & Small's contracts with J. S. Winslow & Company, which rarely exceeded one page.[53] Particularly striking were Palmer's "teacher's corrections" done in red pencil.

For delivering the ELIZABETH PALMER to the new owner, Percy & Small received $134,000 (+/- $2,060,000 in 1998). For that sum, Palmer received what he would later describe as "a veritable coal ark to carry 4,800 tons."[54] In addition, he also held title to the largest wooden five-masted schooner—although a year later she dropped into third place behind the

JANE PALMER and GRACE A. MARTIN. But at 3,065 GRT, the ELIZABETH was larger than even six-masters GEORGE W. WELLS and ADDIE M. LAWRENCE. Palmer, a nitpicker who tried the patience of ship-builders up and down the Maine coast beyond endurance—driving at least one into bankruptcy and possibly to drink—found in Sam Percy and Miles M. Merry the type of people who were comfortable with their own capabilities and not easily buffaloed by his assertive and self-assured manner. He also got a non-confrontational relationship with his shipbuilders for the first time in his career. In a letter to one of his shareholders, he wrote: "It is also refreshing to state

ELIZABETH PALMER, "the veritable coal ark," curtsies to the shipyard and spectators as her cradle drops off the end of the launching ways. The stiff south wind blowing upriver has also caused the third-largest five-master ever built to heel to starboard. Note the enormous crowd of guests on board for the launching.

Courtesy: Captains Douglas K. and Linda J. Lee

that we built our ELIZABETH, from the first to last, without a single syllable of dispute. The builders tried to do everything they could for us, and we went away satisfied."[55] He also got a schooner capable of doing her job well.

Eighteen months after the ELIZABETH went overboard, Palmer and Sam Percy were discussing the building of another schooner for the Boston firm. The only things that Palmer felt needed to be changed were raising the sheer at the stern by six inches and using what he liked to call semi-composite construction.[56] The former issue was, for the most part, a matter of aesthetics. The latter issue represented Palmer's most significant contribution to the design and construction of the great schooners (see Chapter 6).

The ELIZABETH PALMER turned out to be a profitable and lucky vessel for the Palmer fleet. During her career under the Palmer flag she paid good dividends, returning 62 percent of her cost in less than six years, and avoided serious accidents.[57] Then, in 1910, she and her surviving fleetmates were transferred to the management of J. S. Winslow & Company which had purchased the first Palmer fleet a decade earlier.

Her luck began to change then, perhaps a reflection on the law of averages. As she was being towed from the Mystic docks through the Chelsea drawbridge in October 1913, the bridge began to close. Considerable damage was done along her port side, including ripped-off chainplates and turnbuckles and scarred planking.

The final event of her career occurred on 26 January 1915 at 3:30 A.M. Bound south from Boston, the ELIZABETH was under full sail and making eight knots. At that point the American–Hawaiian freight steamer WASHINGTONIAN entered the picture: apparently not seeing the big schooner's lights until it was too late, she steamed right across the PALMER's course. The PALMER slammed into her head-on, opening up a huge hole in the steamer amidships and smashing in her own bow. The WASHINGTONIAN sank within ten minutes, all but one of her forty-man crew escaping to the lifeboats. The PALMER, having bounced off the fatally wounded steamship, staggered along for another mile or so before captain and crew got her

into the wind and dropped the anchors. With the schooner leaking heavily and down by the bow, they abandoned ship and were picked up by another passing steamer and carried to New York.[58]

The ELIZABETH PALMER remained afloat for three days after the collision. A tug and the revenue cutter MOHAWK tried to tow her to shallow water in order to beach her, but with her anchors down she refused to move. Then she rolled over on her beam ends and sank in eleven fathoms.[59]

Before the end of the decade, Percy & Small completed three more schooners for the Palmer interests: the DAVIS PALMER (2,965 GRT) in 1905, the FANNIE PALMER (2,233 GRT) in 1907, and the FULLER PALMER (3,060 GRT) in 1908. Each was accompanied by a deluge of correspondence (and not a few telephone calls as well) from Boston touching on the smallest details and all the other trappings of doing business with William F. Palmer, who regarded himself as an authority on ship design and construction, an authority on the shipping business, and a horse-trader capable of driving very hard bargains.[60]

One of Palmer's more interesting business habits, once he was ready to let a contract for a new vessel, was to make a series of contracts with various suppliers and then, once a shipbuilder was signed up for the vessel, to assign those contracts to the chosen shipbuilder. For example, in the FULLER PALMER contract, Palmer assigned the contracts for yellow pine, the oak frame, anchor chain, and sail canvas. This practice had certain advantages for Palmer: timely delivery of crucial materials was facilitated by early orders; the managing owner could negotiate the terms of sale, including ownership shares in lieu of cash; additionally, the managing owner was able to direct some of the business generated by building the vessel to suppliers favored by his firm.[61]

Palmer's horse-trading talent probably contributed to the demise of the Welt shipyard and probably contributed to bad feelings between Palmer and two other shipbuilders. In letters to investors in his schooners, he boasted of his ability to keep the cost of Palmer schooners around the $40 per gross ton level. Of course, the firms that built these schooners didn't do too well. In one letter, Palmer estimated that

William Rogers lost $10,000–$20,000 on the two schooners he built, Cobb-Butler lost $10,000–$20,000 for one schooner, and Welt had lost from $15,000–$20,000 dollars on the first three schooners he built. He did grant that Percy & Small may have cleared a small profit on the ELIZABETH. As a matter of fact, it appears that Percy & Small did far better than that. A close examination of the ELIZABETH PALMER's Building Account shows that Percy & Small included a charge of $13,208.32 labeled "Balance to P&S." However, the other expense categories are well covered, including the use of the mill, materials, etc. It appears that P&S made a great deal more on the PALMER than William F. gave them credit for.[62]

Percy & Small made a profit on each of the succeeding Palmer vessels, as well. The DAVIS PALMER brought a profit of about $6,000 (+/- $92,000 in 1998) on a $132,000 contract; with FANNIE PALMER (II), the profit was a nominal $773.24 (+/- $12,000 in 1998) in 1907, but this was taken as a make-work project in bad times so little was expected; but the last Palmer schooner, the FULLER PALMER, netted $9,630.68 (+/- $148,000 in 1998) in 1908 on a $141,000 contract.[63]

Captain Leroy K. McKown was the master-designate of the DAVIS PALMER, Percy & Small #22. A Boothbay Harbor native and son and

brother in a seagoing family, McKown had the reputation of a driver which he had earned on the three-masters LUCY DAVIS and GEORGE W. JEWETT, and the four-master JACOB M. HASKELL.[64] As with any seagoing family, McKown was no stranger to tragedy: it was his brother Jason's two children who drowned the night the schooner MARGARET WARD was sunk. There would be more losses.

The captain maintained his home with his wife and two small children in Boothbay Harbor during the construction of #22, commuting back and forth to Bath on the local steamer. This led to a little friction between the captain and Palmer as McKown agitated for the completion of the yawl boat—being built at Percy & Small by Harry Stinson—in Palmer's words, " . . . so that he [McKown] can play with it."[65]

For all of his irritation with Captain McKown, Palmer was delighted with the new schooner. The launching went off without a hitch, with a big crowd aboard representing the Boston investors, as well as a large flock of McKown family and friends from Boothbay Harbor. Palmer was also delighted to observe that the launching was so smooth that nowhere could he find a seam where the pitch or paint had even cracked. He passed his compliments on to Percy & Small—with just a touch of skepticism: "I renew my

The DAVIS PALMER's career spanned just forty-nine months, but she was the Palmer fleet's "highliner" thanks to her hard-driving skipper, Leroy McKown. Anchored off Newport News awaiting a turn alongside to load on 1 August 1909, the schooner's white hull shows the results of hard service with stains and scrapes marring her paintwork. Less than five months later she was lost with all hands. Note the barge on the right, which appears to have begun life as a square-rigger.

Courtesy: Maine Maritime Museum

congratulations on the launching. I could not find a place on either of the rails or the waterways where even the paint had been broken. I note that you skillfully bolted rail boards at places most likely to show. Inasmuch as there was never known a launching without some sign of it, I should be pleased to hear from you just where you found any evidence."[66]

During her first two full years of operation, the DAVIS PALMER looked to be a winner under young McKown and was the "highliner" of the Palmer fleet. She paid twenty-five dividends and returned to the investors 42 percent of her original cost.[67] The next year, 1908, was not so good. Charters were slow in coming and freights were low. The big coal schooners often swung on their anchor chains for weeks on end before a cargo could be found, and the DAVIS PALMER proved to be no exception to the rule as her dividends dropped 80 percent in one year.

Business began to show some signs of life in 1909, but the worst gale to strike the northeast Atlantic Coast since the infamous "PORTLAND Gale" of 1898 wrote *finis* for the DAVIS PALMER and Captain McKown.[68] Coming north from Newport News with 4,822 tons of coal, McKown had vowed to have the big schooner in Boston by the Christmas holidays so that he could join his wife and two small children living at 150 Salem Street in nearby Malden. When Christmas day dawned, the PALMER was working her way through the Nantucket Shoals with a southerly wind. If the weather held for a while longer, they had a good chance of being snug and safe in Boston Harbor before the sun rose on Boxing Day. Unfortunately, other weather indicators suggested that an easterly storm was brewing—it was already spreading havoc along the seaboard south of Long Island with high winds and heavy snow. McKown could play it safe and seek shelter in Nantucket Sound in the lee of Monomoy. But it might take three or four days for the winds to become fair again and allow him to resume the trip to Boston. Or, he could run for it, gambling that the PALMER had enough time to work around the Cape and reach the safety of a protected Boston anchorage before the storm struck. Even if the storm struck before the schooner reached the safety of

Boston Harbor, McKown may have reasoned, the DAVIS PALMER's massive anchors—8,500 pounds each—could hold her safe until the storm passed, just as they had done many times before. The captain decided to go for it.

William P. Coughlin, a crewman aboard the Boston tug NEPONSET docked at the end of Lewis Wharf, was also thinking of getting home before Christmas passed. A "bay-chaser," the tug was standing by awaiting reports—via telegraph from marine reporters stationed at various key points along the coast—of sailing vessels approaching Boston.[69] "Bay-chaser" tugs then steamed out to intercept the incoming vessels, at which point the tug captains attempted to negotiate towing fees with the sailing vessel's captain. If the weather was good or the opportunity to go immediately into an unloading berth was not dependent upon beating others into port, the schooner captain enjoyed considerable negotiating latitude with the tug. If, however, it was a question of reporting in first to get an immediate unloading berth or the weather was deteriorating, the tugboat skipper gained the upper hand.

Around noon on Christmas Day, as Coughlin recalled years later, a report was delivered to Captain Sears of the NEPONSET that the big five-master DAVIS PALMER had moved off the shoals south of Cape Cod and was making a run for Boston, a hundred miles away as the schooner sailed. So much for a Christmas at home for the tugboat crewman.

The NEPONSET's crew cast her off from her berth at Lewis Wharf and headed out into Boston Harbor and Massachusetts Bay where they hoped to intercept the big white schooner somewhere between the Boston Lightship and Stellwagen Bank. By the time they passed the lightship, the weather was definitely turning sour. The wind was backing around into the east and then into the northeast. Clouds thickened and lowered and by late afternoon, as darkness came, snow began to fall.

Captain Sears, Coughlin, and their fellow crewmen now found themselves in "wild seas, gale winds, blinding snow and zero visibility." Realizing that it was unlikely that they could spot the big schooner in the roaring darkness, Captain Sears turned back towards the lightship, where the tug jogged about for a time in hopes that the schooner might loom up out of the storm and they could get the towing hawser aboard. Finally, they gave up their storm-tossed vigil and headed back into the shelter of the harbor, finally taking cover in the lee of Georges Island where they tied up at the government wharf.

Four other vessels caught sight of the DAVIS PALMER that day. The five-master HENRY O. BARRETT—built by G. G. Deering—spotted her after crossing the Nantucket Shoals.[70] The captain of the tug ONTARIO then saw her off Pamet River, Cape Cod, late in the afternoon before the storm closed in, and the skipper of the barge he was towing added a poignant note when he reported that the PALMER's crew ". . . was on deck, singing and celebrating in true sea fashion."[71] Then there was the sighting by Captain Barlow aboard the rudderless GOVERNOR BROOKS before his assisting tugs towed him around into the lee offered by Cape Cod's sandy fist. The final act, however, can only be conjured up from a few known facts.

The gale, with driving snow, descended about dark before the Palmer schooner had a chance to raise the Boston Lightship. It is even possible that tug NEPONSET and schooner DAVIS PALMER may have unknowingly passed within hundreds of yards of each other as the storm clamped down. For some reason—desire to get to his family?—Captain McKown did not veer off into Cape Cod Bay as the wind shifted into the northeast to seek shelter in the Cape's lee. Instead he drove on across Massachusetts Bay, probably passing north of the Boston Lightship, invisible in the snow. Continuing on the same course, he came to The Graves, whose light and foghorn may have alerted him to the fact that he was further west and north than he had thought—he had missed Boston Light by nearly three miles—and he was entering a dangerous, shoal cul-de-sac called Broad Sound. There was only one thing to do: round up into the wind, let the anchors go, douse whatever sails she was still carrying, and pray there were no ledges or shallows nearby.

Some believed that the big white schooner's anchors failed her—or the chain on the starboard anchor parted—and she dragged across the bottom until she fetched up on a ledge where, bilged, she sank in seven fathoms. Others believed that the big vessel's plunging at the end of her anchor chains caused her to hit bottom in the relatively shallow sound.[72] Either way, she went down quickly. No one aboard had a chance of surviving in the gale-driven seas long enough to reach safety.

Wreckage from the big schooner was discovered early on the morning of the 27th, washing up on the beaches near Hull and Nantasket. Found in the debris were her signal flags and burgee, a quarterboard, bits and pieces of cabin furniture and paneling, and even soggy bills made out to the Schooner DAVIS PALMER. Beachcombers also discovered the large, white, power yawl boat—the same that McKown had pestered Palmer about during the summer of 1905—washed up on Lovell's Island in Boston Harbor. It was split open from bow to stern after pounding on the rocks. However, the remains of Captain McKown and her thirteen crewmen were never recovered. Fortunately for William F. Palmer, he never had to face the tragic loss of life and his big schooner. He had died three months earlier.

Percy & Small's #25 became, in time, William F. Palmer's FANNIE PALMER (II). A replacement for one of the Welt-built five-masters that had the misfortune of going aground, the third schooner Percy & Small built for the Palmer fleet had unusual origins as well as an unusual construction feature.

During 1905 the law of supply and demand was once again asserting its authority upon the shipbuilding community. The output of Bath's wooden shipyards dropped to half that of the previous year, reflecting a major slowdown in the demand for wooden hulls along the entire coast. The schooner-building boom experienced over the previous five years had now created surplus tonnage on the coastwise shipping market, and shipping rates fell precipitously.

The falling rates did encourage many of the big schooner operators, banded together as the Atlantic Carriers' Association, to lay up their vessels in hopes of driving the rates back up. The Atlantic Carriers' Association also did something else that could have gotten them into serious legal problems with the federal government if the courts and the government ever seriously enforced the Sherman Antitrust Act: the Association, through its members, agreed to limit the letting of contracts for the largest of the great schooners—five- and six-masters—for at least the year 1905.[73] Subsequently, the Association members extended the agreement on a yearly basis through 1907.[74]

This placed Percy & Small in a bind. The firm had purchased a frame during 1904, probably using the moulds from the Martha P. Small–William H. Clifford model, with the intention of building another schooner of approximately 2,100 GRT for its fleet.[75] The limitations on building additional large tonnage left Percy & Small with money tied up in an expensive frame. It was not a good situation to be in, especially as many of the firm's big schooners were swinging idly at their chains awaiting a rise in the freight rates.

With the plan to restrict large tonnage came the decision that only William F. Palmer and Captain John G. Crowley's Coastwise Transportation Company would be allowed to contract for large schooners during 1905. Although Palmer turned to Percy & Small to build his allotted schooner, it was to be a vessel considerably larger than could be gotten

The Fannie Palmer II makes an impressive picture as she awaits the launching ceremony later that day. Just visible under her bow is the shipyard's pitch oven.
Courtesy: William F. Palmer Collection, Maine Maritime Museum

out of the existing frame. Thus Percy & Small were stuck with a frame they could not use.[76] Then the only firm that got the go-ahead from the Association to build a very large schooner in 1906 was J. S. Winslow & Company, which negotiated a contract with Percy & Small for the six-masted ALICE M. LAWRENCE, a schooner also much too large for the existing frame. But then William F. Palmer managed to get approval for another five-master for 1906 by pleading the effective loss of the FANNIE PALMER (I) from his fleet after she stranded, was salvaged, and sold at auction.

First, Palmer thought the Percy & Small frame was too small for his needs, but he soon changed his mind as an advantageous situation blossomed, seemingly for his sole benefit.[77] Bath's Kelley, Spear Company, which had received an order from New York parties to build a huge car float designed to carry seventeen loaded railroad cars, had the order canceled just as timber ordered for the project began to arrive in Bath. The timber, approximately half a million board feet of Douglas fir, much of which was in 90-foot lengths, had been shipped by rail from the Pacific Northwest.[78] The use of the fir—often called Oregon pine—for structural purposes represented a distinct departure from the normal practice of Bath ship-builders, even though it had been introduced to Bath in the 1870s by Captain Guy C. Goss at his famous "ship factory." Since then, however, it had principally been used for masts and spars. The readily available yellow pine, although limited to lengths averaging 40–45 feet, was the preferred timber for structural purposes because of its reputation for being rot-resistant, its accessibility, and its cost.

Kelley, Spear's resort to Douglas fir reflected two hard realities: the commercial "strip mining" of the yellow pine resource was seriously reducing the ready availability of suitably sized ship timbers; and the reduced availability of the timbers inevitably led to an increase in their price.[79] As the shipping via rail of large spars from the Pacific Northwest to Maine had become fairly routine by mid-decade—virtually all of the spars used by Percy & Small came this way—it was not a major step to arrange the shipping of long lengths of ship timber in the same manner. The

450,000 board feet of fir ordered by Kelley, Spear required thirty-five railroad cars to carry it east.[80]

The third leg of the stool was put in place when a local dealer in iron and steel stock fell upon hard times and was compelled to sell some of his stock to raise cash.[81] Palmer, who bragged that he watched this situation—along with the aging frame at Percy & Small, and the influx of Douglas fir destined for a car float that wasn't to be built—evolve over six months until it exactly fitted his needs, closed with Percy & Small on their hull #25 during the spring of 1906. What he got, however, was not quite the marvelous bargain that he regaled his investors about—actual and potential—during the course of the FANNIE II's construction. His contract with Percy & Small called for a price of $115,000 delivered (+/- $1,770,000 in 1998), or $51.50 per gross ton.[82] The actual cost to Percy & Small (materials and labor and some over-head) was $114,226.76. Yet in 1907 the firm built a slightly larger schooner for their own account, the GOVERNOR BROOKS, that cost (labor, materials) only $47.06 per ton.[83] Even if Percy & Small had used the more expensive diagonal strapping on the BROOKS, she would still have cost less per gross ton than the FANNIE PALMER (II).

Of course, Percy & Small's profit on the Palmer project was virtually nil and, if you took into account uncharged overhead, it was, in fact, illusory. But the firm more than made up for the lost profit on its next and final schooner contract for Palmer—Schooner #29, the FULLER PALMER.

The construction of the FANNIE was slow, largely because of the learning curve involved with using the Douglas fir. The ship carpenters as a group were not familiar with the techniques needed to handle keelson and ceiling timbers that ran up to 90 feet in length. To facilitate this part of the contract, Percy & Small turned to Bant Hanson who, since the death of Fred Rideout, had done most of the firm's lofting and tim-ber surveying. Being an alumnus of the Goss shipyard operations, Hanson was one of the few active ship-wrights in Bath familiar with the peculiarities and requirements of Douglas fir in shipbuilding.[84]

Of course, no project involving Mr. Palmer of Boston was complete without a blizzard of correspondence on whatever topics had won the former school administrator's particular attention. This year he stumped for the replacement of the standard Adair bilge pumps with a manual diaphragm pump and an additional steam wrecking pump.[85] But the future of the Adair pump was not the only thing on Palmer's mind. He engaged in a three-way correspondence with Percy & Small and rigger Frank A. Palmer (no relation, although addressed as "Sir and Brother") concerning the number and placement of topmast stays, the rake of the masts, the bowsprit angle, and hoods and pointers in the bow and stern.

When the FANNIE II at last took to the water on 25 May 1907—much to Sam Percy and Miles Merry's relief—she was sponsored by her seven-year-old namesake (assisted by five-year-old brother Paul) who scattered a large bouquet of flowers over the bow. A large list of invited guests aboard for the launching enjoyed the buffet luncheon served by caterer Malo of the Dewey (Restaurant) and some, no doubt, found the "knock-out drops" available in the forward house.[86]

The FANNIE enjoyed what was essentially an unremarkable career following her launching. After her first passage, Palmer wrote to his sailmaker, "I am in receipt of the first letter from Captain Wiley. He writes that his vessel is tight as a bottle and that she steers well, and that he thinks she will go well in a breeze."[87] Four months before he died, Palmer wrote to Percy & Small:

> I have been meaning for some months to tell you of a curious thing that happened on the "Fannie Palmer." She has already been a remarkably tight vessel, not only remarkably tight, but almost bottle tight. She went for nearly six months without being pumped, and she has not been pumped for over four months.
>
> Before she was hauled out for painting down at Newport News she made just a little water. After she was hauled out at Newport News we discovered one butt in which there had never been any oakum, only a little cement, and another with only one thread of oakum half way across the butt, and the third with but one little

thread. These butts were all close together and the queer thing is that the vessel should have been tight under these conditions.[88]

The FANNIE PALMER (II) joined the other survivors of the Palmer fleet in transferring to J. S. Winslow management in 1910. The change, initiated in part as a captain's revolt against the management of Mrs. Marie Palmer and Dr. A. L. Fuller, Palmer's assistant, saw not only a change in management, but also a change in color. Eminently practical, Eleazer Clark saw no point in painting vessels white so that every rust stain, coal dust streak, and scrape on the hull stood out like a sore thumb. He ordered them all to be painted black. It saved on maintenance and upkeep.

The most exciting thing that happened to the FANNIE (II) during these years occurred during a long bout of gale-force winds while enroute from the coal-loading ports. The saga actually began during the last week of November 1909, when Captain Walter Wiley, the FANNIE's only captain, set sail from Newport News for Portland with 3,600 tons of coal. Passing out past Cape Henry that same evening, the schooner encountered freshening southwest winds as Captain Wiley shaped his course to the northward. By the next evening, the wind had increased to gale force and backed around to the north and northeast. Wiley, fixing their position to be off the Five Fathom Banks off the Delaware capes, dropped the anchor and payed out 125 fathoms of chain and prepared to ride out the gale. The wind increased to seventy miles per hour during the next day and soon the entire crew, including the captain, found themselves trapped forward in the midship and forward houses as the giant combers repeatedly swept across her decks. Captain Wiley made do with a bench in the engine room for his bed for the next two days before the seas moderated enough so he could return aft to his own quarters. They were able to get underway again on 28 November but were forced to anchor and ride out another gale for two days near Abescom Inlet. They finally made Portland on 8 December after a stormy passage of over two weeks, much of it spent at anchor riding out winter gales.[89] Several months later, the

FANNIE (II) fetched up on the Salt Cay Banks in the Bahamas and was described as being in a precarious condition, but she was gotten off—although the actual extent of damage is unknown.[90]

In 1915 J. S. Winslow & Company, taking advantage of the war-induced shipping shortage, began putting their schooners into the offshore market. The FANNIE (II), one of the first schooners to take a coal charter to South America, went to Rio in a round-trip passage that consumed four months.[91] She made additional passages to South America, one of which got her on the notorious British "Black List" of neutral merchantmen suspected of trading with the enemy or their agents. Nonetheless, she was chartered to Cartagena, Spain, with 3,100 tons of coal as 1916 began to wind down. But approximately 500 miles west of Gibraltar, she lost her rudder during a hurricane and, unsteerable, fell off into the trough and began to labor heavily. Her seams opened as the hull continued to work, and the pumps became hard pressed to keep ahead of the leaks. Eventually, a British steamer (SS LADY PLYMOUTH) spotted the wallowing schooner and her anxious crew of thirteen and came to their aid. After an abortive attempt to tow her into port, the crew—including Captain Wiley—was removed and the towline cast off.[92] The foundering schooner was never seen again.

The building of the FULLER PALMER in 1908 brought no letup in William F. Palmer's correspondence, although he was suffering from health problems. But this time Percy & Small got a contract that promised a reasonable return on their efforts to please an exceedingly demanding customer. Signed on 10 December 1907, the contract provided for the delivery of a five-masted schooner slightly larger than the DAVIS PALMER.[93] Palmer inserted his usual clauses regarding frame timbers, hard pine, sail canvas, and sailmaker, assigning contracts he had already made to Percy & Small.

Although Palmer again received queries from other shipbuilders, including Robert Bean, son of Camden's famous Holly Bean, there is no evidence that he seriously entertained proposals or bids from other than Sam Percy. For example, Palmer wrote to Bean: "As I

have previously explained to you my relations have been very friendly with Percy & Small whereas I have had controversies with all the other builders of my ships; and that I naturally incline to Percy & Small, price and other things being equal."[94] Three days later, Palmer wrote to the Singleton brothers—two of his principal investors—that the new vessel ". . . will be built in the yard of Percy & Small . . . ."[95]

The ill Palmer—he was plagued by what he described as rheumatism, which necessitated sojourns at various health spas—still managed to keep the postman busy, but the correspondence was muted, with little in the way of admonitions to the builders or prospective captain—Otis Clark. His major concern was to maximize the gross tonnage of the vessel enough so the cost to investors fell at or below his projected level. To achieve this end, he kept reminding Sam Percy and Miles Merry to remember to "horn-out" the frame, one of the techniques wooden shipbuilders used to enlarge the vessel, and increase the depth of hold.[96]

The major complaints emanated from Captain Percy. He was not happy with the frame provided by E. A. Wentworth of Rockport, Maine, Palmer's preferred frame contractor. He was also not happy with the hard pine delivered by another pre-selected Palmer contractor, George A. McQuesten & Company, headquartered in Boston.

As Sam Percy saw it, the frame delivered to the shipyard had several drawbacks, not the least of which was the use of gum wood in place of white oak in places where the former would quickly fall victim to dry rot. In addition, Captain Percy complained that a number of the timbers were beveled on the wrong side, a problem that could not be corrected by simply turning the timbers upside-down. The worst problem, with which even Palmer concurred, was Wentworth's division of the floor timbers into two pieces (i.e., two pieces for the short floor and two pieces for the long floor) and his failure to provide a second rudderstock.[97]

Captain Percy, who was unusually crotchety at this point, was also upset with the delivery of the hard pine. The contract, placed with the George A. McQuesten & Company of Boston for 900,000 board feet at $36 per thousand, was substantially over-run, creating a glut of timber in Percy's shipyard and another spate of letters attempting to sort out the problem. Palmer found himself in the unusual role of peacemaker, attempting to smooth over incipient hard feelings between the Bath shipbuilders and the Boston wholesale timber dealer.[98]

The irritation evinced by Sam Percy with the various Palmer-assigned contracts carried over to the launching of the FULLER PALMER on 10 November. The usual profuse launching stories in the local newspapers rattled on about the distinguished out-of-town guests, the schooner's construction details, and the elegant decor and finish of the after quarters. Nowhere can one find even the slightest hint of a problem marring the launching celebration.[99] Yet something did happen, according to William F. Palmer.

In a letter to Captain Otis "Ott" Clark, skipper of the new schooner, Palmer wrote in connection with the schooner's cost account, "Had it not been in consequence of getting on the ledge and that Sam Percy abused some of our owners and told them where to go to, there would have been another bill for about $600 extra and the vessel would have been in the hole."[100] It was an intriguing, if incomplete, description of events that launching day.[101] However, it is possible to work out the broad outline of the events of that afternoon, events that the local newspapers diplomatically cloaked in a veil of silence.

The FULLER PALMER was built and launched from Percy & Small's south building ways. East and a little south of the river end of the ways, about fifty to seventy-five yards from shore, lay a ledge that was submerged about eight to ten feet at low water. At high water the ledge was theoretically covered by enough water to permit safe launchings, but local

A flotilla of small boats, ranging from a dory to skiffs and whitehalls, joins the
launching of the FULLER PALMER.
Courtesy: William F. Palmer Collection, Maine Maritime Museum

CHARLES P. NOTMAN
Artist: S. F. M. Badger
Courtesy: Kenneth Kramer

HELEN W. MARTIN
Artist: S. F. M. Badger
Courtesy: Captains Douglas K. and Linda J. Lee

MARTHA P. SMALL

Ship portraits are often formulaic and formalized, with each artist developing his own standardized settings. This view of the
MARTHA P. SMALL places the schooner off Cape Cod Light (a k a Highland Light), southbound, light, with all sail set
and flags flying. The date can also be approximated because the SMALL did not have a captain whose name began
with an "H" until Captain Hodgkins took her from Portland to New York to Rio starting in late
February 1915, so this painting was commissioned by Captain Frank M. Hodgkins. Compare
this painting with those of the CORA F. CRESSY and the GOVERNOR BROOKS.
Artist: S. F. M. Badger

Courtesy: Maine Maritime Museum

CORA F. CRESSY

Artist Andrew Nesdall has also used Cape Cod Light and the Highlands as the setting for his recent painting of the CRESSY. The schooner is showing a good turn of speed but not all sails are set. The flags are flying, however; the Union Jack flies from the foretopmast; P&S's house flag from the maintopmast; ship's burgee from mizzentopmast; captain's personal flag (in this case William Harding) from the jiggertopmast; and the national ensign and a signal hoist from the spanker topmast. The signal hoist is for the benefit of the marine reporter, in this case Isaac M. Small, based at Highland near the lighthouse. No doubt Harding is requesting that Small telegraph the ship's agent in Boston to report his imminent arrival.

Artist: Andrew J. Nesdall

Courtesy: Captains Douglas K. and Linda J. Lee

EVELYN W. HINKLY
Artist: Antonio Jacobsen
Courtesy: Maine Maritime Museum

GOVERNOR BROOKS
This painting by Badger has almost the exact setting as that of the MARTHA P. SMALL. However, this painting predates that of the
SMALL even though she was built six years earlier. The GOVERNOR BROOKS is flying Captain McLeod's personal signal,
but he commanded this schooner only between November 1907 and October 1909.
Artist: S. F. M. Badger

Courtesy: Maine Maritime Museum

wind and weather conditions could change this.[102] This ledge was one of the reasons Percy & Small had the largest schooners built on the north ways, where there was no danger from grounding on an offshore ledge. Sam Percy, in fact, admitted years later that when the firm put the big ELEANOR A. PERCY overboard from the south ways (then the only ways) in October 1900, he was more than a little concerned, but nothing happened. Nor did anything happen when the 3,129-GRT GRACE A. MARTIN was launched in the summer of 1904.[103] But Percy & Small were pushing their luck if you believed in the three time rule—third time never fails—as it applied to launching 3,000-tonners from the south ways.

It is not clear whether the PALMER hit the ledge after leaving the ways, or after the launching when the tugs were maneuvering the schooner into her berth at the shipyard's fitting-out pier. But the latter circumstance appears more probable, since photographs of the launching all appear normal. One can well imagine the guests who were aboard for the launching, partaking of caterer O'Brien's luncheon of salads, rolls, cold meats, sandwiches, coffee, cake, and fruit—and a few of the "elect" partaking of the "launching fluid"—as the tugs worked the big schooner around to get her alongside the pier: then, crunch! Captain Percy, who reportedly was never aboard Percy & Small-built vessels for their launchings, would have observed this developing situation from shore. Whether it was caused by inattention on the part of one or more tug skippers, or caused by local current and wind conditions, can't be determined today in the absence of testimony from those who were present, but to Sam Percy it was a blot on the firm's reputation. Whatever the cause, it appears that the FULLER PALMER remained hung up on the ledge for some time before the tugs—perhaps aided by shifting the two hundred or so guests back and forth—succeeded in getting the schooner off the ledge and docked.

At this point, the guests began leaving the schooner, no doubt passing a very embarrassed, humiliated Captain Percy whose patience had been strained to the breaking point. During the disembarkation, someone must have made an unwise remark to Percy or within his hearing, a remark that may have been intended as humorous rather than critical and may have been fueled by too many visits to the punch bowl. But to Sam Percy, Cape Horner and schooner captain who had the voice and vocabulary to get someone's immediate and full attention, even in a full gale, it was the last straw.

Exactly why Sam Percy's outburst saved the FULLER PALMER six hundred dollars remains a mystery. It appears to be far too much for additional charges to get the schooner off the ledge. Despite these events, the relationship between Percy & Small and Palmer remained cordial right up to the latter's death. Although Palmer never ordered the frame for the schooner to follow the FULLER PALMER, he continued to send various members of the Palmer fleet to Percy & Small for routine and not-so-routine repairs.

Perhaps the governing reason for Palmer not ordering a new frame was the state of the coastwise shipping business that greeted the FULLER PALMER. After making one passage loaded with coal to Boston, the PALMER tugged at her anchor chain in Boston Harbor from 28 December until 11 March 1909, when she sailed for Hampton Roads. Operating on the theory that if things are bad, they can get worse, the PALMER then got into a collision with the Italian steamer TAORMINA off Five Fathom Bank. Loss of her headgear and a damaged stem forced the schooner to anchor until she could be towed into port to be repaired.[104]

Once repaired, the FULLER PALMER was again back in the coal trade for which she was intended—but not for long. On 2 December the big schooner left Baltimore with 5,000 tons of coal consigned to the Maine Central Railroad docks at Portland. As usual, winter gales intervened. While anchored off Absecom Inlet during one such storm, a rogue sea smashed into her rudder, twisting the rudderhead.[105] The to-do over the lack of an extra rudderpost two years previously now took on new meaning. Captain Clark managed to get the schooner to Martha's Vineyard before the steering gave out completely. From there the FULLER PALMER was towed to Portland where, once the coal was unloaded, a team of shipwrights from Percy & Small went to work replacing the rudder.

When barely five years old, the FULLER PALMER became another victim of winter gales along the Atlantic seaboard. This particular storm claimed another Percy & Small-built schooner—the GRACE A. MARTIN—as well as another alumna of the Palmer fleet, the SINGLETON PALMER. Yet, even under the extreme conditions leading to the loss of the three schooners, only one person was lost. The rest of this story appears in Chapter 8.

The shipbuilding side of Percy & Small's activities benefited enormously from the contracts received from J. S. Winslow & Company and William F. Palmer. Without them, Percy & Small could never have afforded the investment in shipyard and equipment that made the greatest of the Great Schooners economically feasible. The contract business also allowed the shipyard to provide a more consistent level of employment for its own people, as well as the subcontractors, than if Percy & Small relied solely on building its own schooners. Consistent employment ensured the ongoing availability of a reliable, highly skilled labor pool at a time when wooden shipbuilding skills in Maine and elsewhere were in rapid decline.

---

[1] BT, 4/20/1901. The story says it was built from a model of the S. P. BLACKBURN, but the half model carrying the MARTHA P. SMALL name (in a private collection) is marked on the back "PS #2," the WILLIAM H. CLIFFORD. For a detailed discussion of schooner family trees, see Appendix B.

[2] Between 1900–04, Bath shipbuilders delivered 122,887 gross tons of wooden hulls: 1900—35,276; 1901—22,703; 1902—23,826; 1903—19,397; 1904—21,685. Only 68 percent of that tonnage was in schooners, however. Almost all of the rest of the tonnage was made up of the schooner's arch enemy, the coastwise coal barge.

[3] The non-schooner was the scow sloop UMBAJEJUS, 68 GRT. Under 100 GRT: 1; 100–1,000 GRT: 2; 1,001–2,000 GRT: 4; 2,001–3,000 GRT: 9; 3,001+ GRT: 9.

[4] Percy & Small built seven of ten six-masters (70 percent) and fifteen of the fifty-six (27 percent) East Coast-built five-masters.

[5] Delivered to Winslow: 23,806 gross tons; delivered to Percy & Small: 23,270 gross tons.

[6] Captain Jacob S. Winslow died in 1902.

[7] The first cargoes of bituminous coal delivered via barges to Portland were received soon after 1900. Henry F. Merrill Interview, ca. 1950, Notes, Parker Collection.

[8] J. S. Winslow & Company also had purchased the managing owner's interest in the "other" Palmer (Nathaniel T.) fleet in 1901–02, purchased the barely year-old four-master MILES M. MERRY from Percy & Small, and had that firm build three new four-masters, as well as the five-master OAKLEY C. CURTIS, delivered in January 1901.

[9] It is not known who actually initiated this practice with the trailboards, but photographs of vessels built prior to 1900 definitely rule out Percy & Small.

[10] ALICE M. LAWRENCE, EDWARD J. LAWRENCE, EDWARD B. WINSLOW.

[11] The losses were more a product of increased exposure to risk due to the large size of the Winslow fleet, rather than incompetence or poorly maintained vessels.

[12] BT, 7/16/1902.

[13] BT, 4/14, 18/1903; NYMR, 4/15/1903. Captain and Mrs. McKown returned to Boothbay Harbor where the captain went into the coal business. He eventually went back to sea.

[14] BT, 9/27/1902.

[15] BT, 1/18 and 1/25/1905. Captain Ross died at sea six years later while in command of the ADDIE M. LAWRENCE. Mrs. Ross was still sailing with her husband, as were their two children. BT, 7/31/1911.

[16] BT, 9/11/1907.

[17] NYMR, 11/25/1908.

[18] NYMR, 2/24, 3/10, and 3/17/1909.

[19] I&E, 3/10/1909.

[20] The first six-master lost was the MERTIE B. CROWLEY, built by Cobb, Butler in Rockland in 1907. She stranded on Wasque Shoal in January 1910. The GEORGE W. WELLS was lost in 1913.

[21] BT, 12/1/1906. Baker says that a Rockland-built schooner may have been the first to carry a generator plant. Baker, II, p. 763.

[22] BT, 12/17/1914. Most of the salvaged gear was used on other Winslow schooners in the course of time.

[23] BT, 7/17/1917; NYMR, 7/18/1918.

[24] Loren E. Haskell, "The Glorious Six-Masters," Down East, April 1965, p. 24. She was beached after the fire.

[25] Parker, Coal Schooners, p. 57.

[26] BT, 9/18/1906.

[27] BT, 1/28/1908.

[28] The details of this voyage are found in "Schooner RUTH E. MERRILL, Adjustment of General and Particular Average." Frank B. Hall & Co., Inc., Average Adjusters, 67 Wall Street, New York, NY, Parker Collection.

[29] I&E, 4/25/1908; NYMR, 4/29/1908, says 5,106 tons, but this is an obvious error.

[30] NYMR, 6/24 and 9/30/1908.

[31] NYMR, 6/23/1909 and 9/7/1910.

[32] BT, 10/20/1913.

[33] Drake Papers contain an interesting but undated draft document on Percy & Small stationery. It reads:

"At the request of Messrs. J. S. Winslow & Co., we, the undersigned were called on to examine the Sch. 'Edward J. Lawrence' and found the following repairs were necessary to make her sea-worthy.

"All the lower deck beams from the forward hatch to the after hatch were broken in three places and would have to be renewed, there being thirty in all. 40 new stanchions under same and 60 new straps. 26 new 12" hanging knees too.

"The bet. decks to be renewed, 190' in length by 35' in width.

"One horse [hawse] pipe renewed and five new scuppers."

This survey was probably done in 1915 when she returned to P&S for a month during the summer, just before she sailed for Barcelona. Much of the damage is consistent with the continued operation of a vessel with broken strapping.

[34] BT, 1/17/1914.

[35] BT, 4/10 and 5/8/1916; NYMR, 5/17/1916.

[36] Captain William R. Kreger (1852 1924) was born in Germany and came to the U.S. as a young sailor. His first command was the Bath three-master NORMAN, built and managed by Adams & Hitchcock. He commanded more six-masted schooners than any other captain. In 1918 he helped finance and supervised the construction of the five-master JENNIE FLOOD KREGER at Matthews Brothers shipyard in Belfast, Maine.

[37] Morgan, Master in Sail & Steam, pp. 34–37. Captain Parker recalls from a conversation with Captain Peterson that the mate called the captain to look down into the hold through an open hatch. There, before their eyes, several feet of water was sloshing back and forth as the schooner worked her flexible and leaking way through the swells. For fear of panicking the crew, Captain Peterson then ordered the hatch cover replaced. The pumps were started and with more moderate weather, the leak was kept under control.

[38] NYMR, 3/19 and 11/5/1919. American authorities banned American-flag sailing vessels from the war zone in the summer of 1917 due to losses to submarines. The ban was lifted after the signing of the armistice in November 1918.

[39] Boston Marine Insurance Company Notes, Parker Collection. This particular report originated with Captain James E. Creighton, who was France & Canada's marine superintendent at the time.

[40] Boston Marine Insurance Company Notes, Parker Collection. Comments by surveyors included: "I respectfully recommend that after next Fall you keep off her (insurance) both hull and cargoes." (C. E. Littlefield) "The LAWRENCE has her iron strapping broken and is badly hogged, causing her to work all kinds of ways at sea." (C. L. Pascal)

[41] One story has it that her shipkeeper, Captain Joe York, whiling away the idle hours around the Christmas holidays, attempted to operate a still—Prohibition was at its height. The still got out of control and the whole works went up in flames.

[42] BT, 11/11/1904.

[43] Schooner Notes, Parker Collection. P&S apparently lost $741.05 when the final costs were added up. See: Building Account Schooner #21, Parker Collection.

[44] Palmer was born in Webster, Massachusetts, in 1859. His father was killed in action during the Battle of the Wilderness in 1864. He received his BA from Williams College in 1880 and his MA in 1883. For the next sixteen years he taught and administered at a series of high schools. On the way, he had taken correspondence courses in naval architecture and met and learned from Albert Winslow of Taunton, Massachusetts, a man who had a legitimate claim to being one of the progenitors of the great schooners. Although Palmer's obituaries subsequently magnified his contributions to naval architecture in general, and the great schooners in particular, William F. Palmer was a major player in the first decade of the twentieth century when it came to the coal schooners.

[45] Morrison Bump, "Notes on the Palmer Fleet." Unpublished manuscript, January 1992. Marie Palmer ran the business when her husband was out of town or ill. After his death in September 1909, she attempted to carry on the business, but there was simply too much opposition from shareholders in Palmer vessels to having her permanently manage the operation.

[46] William Rogers and the New England Company in Bath; George I. Welt in Waldoboro; Cobb & Butler in Rockland.

[47] Welt was in deep financial trouble which, coupled with a serious drinking problem, effectively led to Palmer taking over the operation of the Welt shipyard until his contracts were completed. At one point, Palmer tried to lure Miles Merry to Waldoboro. See: Palmer Letter Books, 1901–04, Palmer Collection.

48 Palmer to W. T. Donnell, 3/27/1903; Palmer to William Rogers, 4/11/1903; Palmer to New England Company, 4/29/1903, Palmer Collection.

49 *BT*, 3/3/1903.

50 Palmer to Captain O. W. Clark, 5/25/1908, Palmer Collection.

51 Palmer to Captain Denny Humphreys, 11/8/1905, Palmer Collection.

52 Contract, Schooner #11, Parker Collection. The hull number is Palmer's, not Percy & Small's.

53 Contract, Schooner #29, October 14, 1907, Parker Collection.

54 Palmer to Captain James E. Creighton, 5/14/1903, Palmer Collection. As it turned out, she was a bigger ark than even Palmer suspected, with a deadweight capacity closer to 5,100 tons.

55 Palmer to Fred T. Clayton, 9/1/1903, Palmer Collection.

56 Palmer to P&S, 3/1/1905, Palmer Collection.

57 Parker, *Coal Schooners*, Appendix No. VI, pp. 125-27.

58 *BT*, 1/26, 28/1915. Captain George Carlisle, who was relief skipper of the ELIZABETH on this trip, had been experiencing an extraordinary run of bad luck. About a year earlier, he had lost his wife to illness and the schooner PRESCOTT PALMER in a gale. Then in December 1914 he took command of the DOROTHY PALMER which, within days, was badly damaged by the British steamer LIMON and towed to Percy & Small for repairs.

59 *NYMR*, 2/3/1915.

60 The Letterbooks in the Palmer Collection include a deluge of letters from Palmer to the shipbuilder(s) of the moment. The construction of the DAVIS PALMER called forth over forty letters on various details.

61 The tradition of demanding rebates on substantial orders does not appear to have been a business practice of either Palmer or Percy & Small.

62 Palmer to Prentiss Howard, 5/4/1904, Palmer Collection.

63 The profits on the schooner contracts are found in Percy & Small Financial Statements: 1906, 1907, 1908, Parker Collection.

64 His father was M. D. McKown, and siblings included Captain Eugene McKown (HENRY W. CRAMP and MOUNT HOPE), Captain Jason McKown (MARGARET WARD), and Captain John McKown (H. E. THOMPSON).

65 Palmer to Percy & Small, 6/23/1905, Palmer Collection.

66 Palmer to P&S, 11/29/1905, Palmer Collection.

67 Parker, *Coal Schooners*, Appendix VI, pp. 126–27.

68 The events leading up to the loss of the DAVIS PALMER have been drawn from the following: *BT*, 12/27/1909 and 12/29/1909; Captain William P. Coughlin, "The Christmas Gale," *Northshore*, 12/21/1968; Unidentified and undated clippings, Douglas K. and Linda J. Lee Collection.

69 Three key marine reporters were based at Highland on Cape Cod (Isaac Small), at Chatham on Cape Cod, and at Vineyard Haven on Martha's Vineyard.

70 The HENRY O. BARRETT rode out the gale anchored off Minott's Ledge Light. She suffered some damage including a stove-in yawl boat and flooded after house after being "pooped" by an enormous sea.

71 *BT*, 12/29/1909.

72 A diver subsequently went down to examine the wreck. She was lying on her starboard side pointing northeast with her port anchor chain stretched taut. Part of her deck aft and her after house were torn up, and the starboard standing rigging was slack on the spanker, jigger, and mizzen masts, all of which was suggestive of major hull damage on the starboard side.

73 Palmer to Dr. John M. Hills, 3/11/1905, Palmer Collection.

74 WFP to Dr. Hills, 8/28/1906, Palmer Collection. Palmer noted that only one five- or six-masted schooner was to be launched in 1906 and his own new schooner would not be launched until 1907. "There may be more. The matter will be settled in January."

75 *PSJ*, p. 296. Entries read: "Carpenters #25" and were dated 7/9, 16, 30, and 8/6/1904.

76 Palmer had the DAVIS PALMER built at Percy & Small; Coastwise Transportation Company had Holly Bean build the HELEN J. SEITZ. Aside from the Palmer schooner, Percy & Small cranked out two small four-masted schooners, the EVELYN W. HINKLY and the ROBERT P. MURPHY.

77 Palmer to E. A. Wentworth, 3/9/1906, Palmer Collection.

78 *Zion's Advocate* (Portland), 10/11/1905. It was the largest single shipment of timber to the Northeast up to that time.

79 Notes, Parker Collection. Yellow pine cost +/- $22.375 per M in 1900. By 1905 P&S were paying $24.50, and a year later the price had risen to $26.30. By the time WYOMING was built, yellow pine had gone up to $31.25 per M—an increase of 39 percent in the course of the decade.

80 *Zion's Advocate* (Portland), 12/13/1905.

81 Palmer to Dr. Hills, 8/28/1906, Palmer Collection.

82 *Ibid.*

83 Building Accounts Schooner #25 and #27, Parker Collection.

84 *PSJ*, p. 328. Hanson received $1,850 for this job. Of course, the shipyard could cut the fir timbers into more manageable lengths, but this step would completely negate the advantages gained—i.e., long lengths without joints—

from such long pieces. See: Palmer to Prentiss Howard, 9/7/1906, Palmer Collection.

[85] Palmer to P&S, 6/?/1906, Palmer Collection. The law required a manual pump, although most big schooners relied on their steam wrecking pumps for routine pumping. The Adair pump could also be driven by a messenger chain from the steam hoisting engine. The later FULLER PALMER had an Adair pump.

[86] Palmer to Dr. H. E. Johnson, 5/16/1907, Palmer Collection.

[87] Palmer to W. F. Stearns, 6/3/1907, Palmer Collection.

[88] Palmer to P&S, 5/7/1909, Palmer Collection.

[89] *BT,* 12/9/1909.

[90] *BT,* 7/9/1910.

[91] *BT,* 6/23/1915.

[92] *BT,* 12/29/1916 and 1/24/1917.

[93] Contract for Schooner "Number Sixteen" of the Palmer Fleet, Parker Collection. All handwritten contract additions and deletions were done in red ink by Palmer who, it would seem, never quite shed the habits of the schoolmaster. Sam Percy must have loved it. Palmer considered the DAVIS PALMER "the best performing schooner on the coast without any single exception." See: Palmer to E. A. Wentworth, 11/18/1907, Palmer Collection.

[94] Palmer to II. M. & R. L. Bean, 11/15/1907, Palmer Collection.

[95] Palmer to James & Ernest Singleton, 11/18/1907, Palmer Collection.

[96] Palmer to P&S, 5/5, 6/23, and 6/29/1908, Palmer Collection.

[97] Palmer to E. A. Wentworth, 4/18, 5/21, 6/29, 7/8, and 7/11/1908; Palmer to P&S, 7/11/1908, Palmer Collection. Good rudderstock material was getting more difficult to find, so it was a normal precaution to order an additional piece in the event the first proved unsatisfactory once the ship carpenters began to shape it. If the second rudderpost proved unnecessary, it could usually be quickly placed on another vessel. It should also be noted that Palmer was practicing a little deception on Percy & Small by telling them that the contract for the frame was for $18 per ton when he had negotiated a price with Wentworth for $17 per ton. Given that the total frame measured out at over six hundred tons, this constituted a not-insubstantial piece of change. See: Palmer to E. A. Wentworth, 7/11/1908, Palmer Collection.

[98] Palmer to P&S, 5/22, 6/4, and 7/8/1908; Palmer to George McQuesten Company, 4/18 and 6/9/1908, Palmer Collection. One continuing source of irritation was a bill of $122.71 for some second grade yellow pine that Palmer, through a misunderstanding, paid too much for. He wanted Percy to split the additional cost, but Sam apparently refused. In Palmer's pocket notebook, where he figured the total cost for the new schooner, is a notation assigning that cost to the vessel above and beyond Percy & Small's contract price. See: Box 12, Fleet Records, FULLER PALMER, Palmer Collection.

[99] *I&E,* 11/11/1908.

[100] Palmer to Captain Otis Clark, 11/24/1908, Palmer Collection.

[101] There had been a grounding involved with the launching of the ELIZABETH PALMER, as well. That time, however, it involved managing owner Palmer. He had taken a party of friends and associates in his gas engine-powered yacht, PALM, on a morning cruise to Merry-meeting Bay. They got aground for a spell, forcing a delay in the scheduled launching. *BT,* 8/27/1903.

[102] The combination of an extended drought and strong north winds, for example, could reduce the margin considerably.

[103] Percy Interview, MWHRP.

[104] *NYMR,* 3/24/1909.

[105] *BT,* 11/11/1908. Her white oak rudderpost was 22 inches in diameter and 45 feet long. One of the most vulnerable points of a big schooner was its rudder. Massive of necessity, rudderposts were increasingly difficult to find in oak timber clear of rot and other problems and of sufficient size. One critical point was where the patent steering gear clamped to the rudderhead. Too loose and the rudder could slip, too tight and the clamps crushed the wood fibers. When the large surface area was struck by a big wave, considerable torque was applied to the rudderpost, but there was very little give in the worm gear steering mechanism to absorb the sudden shock.

Schooners for the Firm

A DECADE OF GROWTH

Although the tonnage built by Percy & Small for J. S. Winslow & Company and William F. Palmer during the first decade of the century was almost half again as great as that built for their own use, the shipyard still serviced the firm's needs for new construction as well as repairs and maintenance to those vessels already in the fleet. During the course of the decade (1900–09), the ship-building side of the business completed 23,270 GRT for Percy & Small composed of two six-, five five-, and three four-masted schooners. Even taking into account the loss of the CHARLES P. NOTMAN and the sale of the MILES M. MERRY a few months after her completion, Percy & Small managed to quadruple their fleet's gross tonnage between 1900–09.[1]

Percy & Small definitely preferred the five-master for their own use, rather than the more spectacular six-master that they had helped pioneer and whose production they dominated throughout the period. After opening the decade with the ELEANOR A. PERCY, it took nine years before the firm took delivery of its second—and last—six-master, WYOMING. On the other hand, six five-masters, starting with the M. D. "Doctor" CRESSY of 1899, constituted the bulk of the tonnage built for their own account through 1909.

As a group, the Percy & Small five-masters built for their own use during the decade were about as varied as they could be in size and external appearance, even though three were built from the ubiquitous model of the WILLIAM H. CLIFFORD. The MARTHA P. SMALL, launched in 1901, measured 2,178 GRT and though she sported the popular long poop deck configuration, she was easily identifiable because her forward housetop was at the same height as the topgallant forecastle deck and blended smoothly, one into the other, without a break. She was also one of the smallest five-masters built at the shipyard during the decade, being slightly smaller than the peripatetic HELEN W. MARTIN, whom we met in Chapter 5.

THE CORA F. CRESSY, the next five-master off the shipyard ways in 1902, was probably the most recognizable wooden schooner ever built and measured a healthy 2,499 GRT.[2] Modified while under construction with an eye to eliminating or ameliorating the problems associated with the long poop and flush-decked schooners, she proved to be one of the longest-lived five-masters, although her design was never exactly duplicated.

Two years after the CRESSY went into service, Percy & Small built their next five-master, the GRACE A.

MARTIN, a 3,129-GRT giantess. The MARTIN incorporated a modified CRESSY configuration, retaining the same flush-deck arrangement to the forward house, but without the prominent bulwarks carried at the full height of the rail forward to the bow. In an effort to reduce the windage that proved such a problem with the CRESSY, Percy & Small carried the bulwark forward at only half the height of the rail.

The last five-master built for their own account, the GOVERNOR BROOKS (2,628 GRT) of 1907, was different from all her Percy & Small predecessors, possessing a true flush deck that ran from the after rail to the bow, broken only by hatches and low-slung deck houses. In profile, she bore a distinct resemblance to the three flush-decked Winslow six-masters and, finally, to WYOMING herself.

MARTHA P. SMALL: HULL #10

When Percy & Small began planning for Schooner #10 in 1900, their shipbuilding business was going full out to deliver three schooners for J. S. Winslow & Company under construction at the new Deering (McDonald) yard and Reed yards and to complete the queen of their own fleet, ELEANOR A. PERCY, in their yard. They were so well organized that

when the PERCY went overboard in October 1900, they were able to lay the keel for Schooner #10 on the same building ways only nine days later.

Number 10, named for Frank Small's wife Martha, shared the same model as at least nine other schooners built by the firm over two decades, that of the WILLIAM H. CLIFFORD.[3] Although the CLIFFORD

Under shortened sail, the new MARTHA P. SMALL clears the Kennebec on her maiden voyage. The lack of sail suggests that Captain Barlow may be getting a feel for the schooner's handling under various sail combinations. Perhaps that is the captain standing on the starboard side just forward of the jiggermast shrouds.

Courtesy: Maine Maritime Museum

was a vessel of a third less tonnage than the SMALL, in the hands of a skilled master builder such as Miles M. Merry, the considerable size difference was not an obstacle to using a proven hull form, thus saving on the cost of a new model, lofting, and making new sets of moulds (a detailed explanation of the techniques of widening the vessel by horning out the frame and the use of rising rods to deepen the vessel, all without relofting the vessel, can be found in Appendix B). It remained to be seen whether the structural weaknesses just being revealed in Percy & Small's first two five-masters would be addressed in the new schooner.

The MARTHA P. SMALL experienced few, if any, problems while under construction. Laid down nine days after the PERCY was launched from the same ways, the SMALL was already partially framed by the time the big six-master was rigged and left the shipyard in mid-November. Work continued on throughout the coldest, darkest months of the year—contrary to the oft-stated belief that Maine shipyards closed down in winter—with the schooner completely framed and six strakes of planking on by early February.[4]

Almost the only crisis appeared to be a replay of the question of whether the schooner would have four or five masts.[5] It seems likely that the confusion existed largely in the minds of the press, who may have interpreted references that the SMALL was being built from the CLIFFORD/BLACKBURN model to mean that she, like they, would have four masts.

Although she was built from the model that had also produced the M. D. CRESSY and HELEN W. MARTIN (the firm's first five-masters, noted for their snake-like qualities in a seaway), the SMALL incorporated some nonvisible modifications designed to stiffen her hull.[6] They were not dramatic departures from past practice, underlining the normal and conservative gradualist approach to change in wooden shipbuilding, but they were an indication that Percy & Small were responding to the difficulties with long and relatively shallow hulls. Her beam was increased significantly, and two parallel "hog straps" running most of the length of the hull were let into the frames.[7] While by no means a perfect solution to the longitudinal weakness demonstrated by her two near sisters, the measures appear to have eliminated the

necessity of reinforcing the hull longitudinally during most, if not all, of her subsequent career, although she had hogged considerably by the end of her working life.[8]

The SMALL also introduced a new captain to the Percy & Small fleet, George F. Barlow. A native of New Brunswick, Barlow had long skippered the Bath-built BENJAMIN F. POOLE, a Providence-based four-master, before he was selected for command of the SMALL. Barlow brought some investors with him from the Providence area, as he and they took a 7/64 ownership position in the schooner.[9] Along with a new command came a new residence. Because the POOLE was owned principally in Providence and called there regularly, Barlow had maintained his shore residence there. But now he shifted to Portland, which was his new schooner's primary port-of-call.

Barlow avoided the publicity actively sought by some of the more colorful characters on the coast and proved to be a steady and reliable shipmaster. He stayed with the SMALL for eight years, leaving her in 1909 to take command of the GOVERNOR BROOKS for Percy & Small. Then in 1911, retirement beckoned to the good captain, and he sold the captain's interest to Captain Willard Wade. With that money he purchased a farm at Grand River, New Brunswick, "on which to live in a quiet and comfortable manner away from the dangers of the sea."[10]

Captain Barlow and his new command sallied forth to face the unpredictability of the coasting trade in early May 1901. They had to contend with the usual mix of weather, navigation, and business hazards. Of the three, the latter proved the most expensive. Shipping charters were sometimes hard to get at prices the managing owners regarded as being remotely profitable. Sometimes the big schooner spent weeks—at one point eighty-one days—unchartered, swinging idly at her anchor in Boston Harbor during the anthracite coal strike of 1902.[11] Another time it was three months in Portland Harbor before a charter to carry railroad ties from Brunswick, Georgia, to New York freed the schooner from the thrall of idleness.[12]

Surprisingly, given the nature of the trade she was engaged in, the SMALL suffered little from the usual traps lying in wait for a coasting schooner. Aside from one grounding on the usually deadly Peaked Hill Bars in 1910, the schooner appears to have avoided most of the pitfalls that ensnared her sisters. Even the Peaked Hill Bars adventure was substantially less than life threatening. Bound light from Portsmouth for Norfolk, she grounded on the shoals in a moderate wind as the tide was going out. A few hours later, on the rising tide, she floated free without any apparent damage.[13]

World War I opened new vistas and opportunities to the SMALL, as it did for most of the surviving great schooners, and those opportunities often lay in the South American trade. For six years the five-master principally carried case oil south. Return cargoes included quebracho wood and linseed cake.[14] Although the cargoes were pretty mundane, the dividends to the owners were not, especially after years of sparse earnings: for example, $297 per $1/64$ (+/- $3,700 in 1998) in December 1915.[15]

In August of the following year, the SMALL underwent her full-time survey, having reached the ripe old age—for five-masted schooners—of fifteen years. The surveyor reported:

> This vessel opened very fine, finding just one poor timber aft, but the top of which was all right. Tried all the knees and beams, also transom, stem, apron, all of which were sound. Rudder unhung and repaired where necessary, new bowsprit, new spanker topmast, new spanker boom, rigging all gone over and renewed where necessary. This vessel has been re-treenailed from light water up, and will have some turnbuckles put into her to help strengthen. . . . This vessel is in good sea-worthy condition and fit to carry dry and perishable cargoes.[16]

If this were a report card on surviving the effects of aging, the MARTHA P. SMALL would have been entitled to a B or B+. Some wear and tear was inevitable on a vessel her age, but there was nothing in the report that suggested the excessive working of the hull that had been experienced by both the M. D. CRESSY and HELEN W. MARTIN. Although the surveyor mentioned turnbuckles to help strengthen the vessel, he was referring to the installation of lateral steel tie rods that could be tightened or loosened by the turnbuckles. This was not an uncommon installation on wooden vessels even when new, but it does suggest that the SMALL was not immune to racking stresses.[17]

After completing repairs and with a clean bill of health, the schooner left the Percy & Small shipyard for the last time. Back to hauling case oil to South America, the SMALL was sold by Percy & Small in the spring of 1917 to the France & Canada Steamship Company for a reported $180,000 (+/- $1.8 million in 1998), substantially more than she cost new sixteen years earlier.[18]

The subsequent career of the SMALL is not well documented, in part because the government clamped down on the publishing of shipping arrivals and departures after Congress declared war on the Central Powers in April 1917. However, she probably continued in the lucrative South American trade as sailing vessels were soon banned from the war zone around Europe. We do know that her last charter in 1920 took her from Norfolk with coal consigned to Buenos Aires, but she didn't quite make it. About 350 miles short of her destination, off Cape Polonio, Uruguay, she lost her rudder and suffered other damage in a storm and was forced to anchor until a salvage tug arrived to tow her to Montevideo.

Once in port, her cargo was discharged and then she was drydocked for repairs. As the dock was being de-watered, however, she rolled off the keel blocks and suffered additional damage. After being redocked, the necessary repairs were made but at this point the owners—France & Canada Steamship Company—failed to pay their bills and the vessel was seized by the local authorities.[19] She lay at anchor for two years until April 1923 when she was sold to pay her debts for $2,300 (+/- $16,800 in 1998)— a far cry from the $180,000 she brought six years earlier. The new owner then broke her up for her fittings and timber.[20]

The MARTHA P. SMALL and Percy & Small's Schooner #11 had two things in common: they were built by the same firm for their own use, and they ranked among the longest-serving five-masters ever built. Beyond that, they were as different as day and night.

Where the SMALL was a standard long poop schooner, the CRESSY was almost unique in her layout (see Chapter 5). Where the SMALL received little attention over the years while plying her trade, the CRESSY was a frequent subject of stories even long after her sailing days had ended. Where the SMALL avoided most of the hazards of the coastwise trade, the CRESSY appeared to welcome them with gusto, whether it be collision, grounding, lost anchors, blown-out sails, or failed rudders. And, finally, where the SMALL left little in the way of a documentary trail, the CRESSY left a stack of paper and, as importantly, she left herself.[21]

If the MARTHA P. SMALL represented a restrained effort at improving the physical shortcomings of the great schooners, the CORA F. CRESSY represented the firm's head-on attack. Yet, the most visible feature of change—the raised, flaring bow—appeared only after she had already been framed up. Two photographs taken approximately four months apart reveal that the CRESSY was virtually framed by early July 1901, although the deck beams do not appear to have been installed. From this first photo, it appears that the new schooner was to have the standard, long poop deck configuration.[22]

The second photo was taken in November, probably on Sunday the 10th; it shows the MILES M. MERRY almost ready to be launched from the new north building ways, and the five-master HELEN W. MARTIN alongside for repairs. The CRESSY was still in frame, but with the after house in place, deck beams installed, and with a partial row of new top timbers being added forward as part of the solid, full-height bulwarks and raised topgallant forecastle deck that ultimately marked the CRESSY's forward profile.[23]

Captain Percy and Miles Merry decided early in

This photo can be dated to early July 1901 thanks to the presence of the ELEANOR A. PERCY without her headgear and the absence of the Powers house, removed to the corner of Marshall and Middle Streets about a month before to make way for Percy & Small's new north shipbuilding ways. The schooner in frame behind the mill is the CORA F. CRESSY. Compare this photo with the one on page 217, taken four months later.

Stinson Brothers Photo, courtesy of Bath Historical Society

The MILES M. MERRY, first to be built on the north ways, is almost ready for
launching, but work on the CORA F. CRESSY has made only glacial progress. She is still
in frame although deckbeams and after house have been installed. However, note the
forward end of the schooner: a new row of top timbers is being installed, giving her the
solid, full-height bulwarks forward and the raised topgallant forecastle deck that were
her trademarks. In the time span between the two photos, the authors believe Percy &
Small chose to convert the big schooner from a conventional long poop schooner into a
deck arrangement that was far less conventional in an effort to overcome structural
problems that had cropped up with earlier five-masters.

Stinson Brothers Photo, courtesy of Bath Historical Society

the construction to change the original deck configuration, no doubt in response to problems that
were becoming all too evident with the M. D. CRESSY
and the HELEN W. MARTIN. So construction was suspended before it advanced so far that changes would
be too expensive. Fred Rideout was brought into the
redesign effort as well, possibly making a second half
model and supplying additional moulds and some
drawings.[24]

What they created was a schooner with a deep hull
whose ratio of length to depth of 9.78:1 was the lowest of any schooner built by Percy & Small and one of
the lowest in the business, giving her a very high
effective girder rating. Moreover, with this design
they did not simply extend the poop deck forward to
the bow—many flush-deck schooners were described

as having a "full poop"—with the conventional
+/- 4.5-foot spacing between the poop and the main
deck with all deckhouses resting on the main deck.
Instead, the main deck on the CRESSY served also as
her spar or weather deck. The second deck, approximately 9 feet below this deck, was too deep to serve as
a foundation for deckhouses, so special "house decks"
were constructed in the way of the deckhouses to support the after and midship houses. A row of beams supplemented the two full-length decks and the platform
decks. The combination of a flush deck and deeper hull
(and, perhaps, the unconventional spacing of her
decks), along with hogging straps, gave the CRESSY one
of the strongest wooden hulls in the business.

The new schooner was flush decked, but with a
difference. Instead of recessing the forward house into

the deck along with the midship and after houses that were set on special house decks 4 feet below the main deck, it sat full height on the main deck, sheltered from head and quartering seas by the raised solid bulwarks that underpinned the topgallant forecastle deck and carried aft along both sides of the forward house. This created a semi-enclosed space ahead of the forward house that contained the anchor windlass, crew heads, and storage.

The CRESSY appeared to have proportionally more sheer forward than other types of schooners, an impression enhanced by the solid bulwarks forward. In addition, since the topgallant forecastle deck was built at the fly rail height, the bowsprit, which protruded from the hull right under this deck, was raised an amount equal to the height of the solid bulwarks. All in all, her reputation for having the highest bow on the coast was well deserved.[25]

Ironically, this was Percy & Small's most effective design in some respects, even though they chose to apply it subsequently to only two four-masters and, in modified form, to four five-masters. The CORA F. CRESSY was still working in the commercial charter business as late as 1928—and probably would have been at it a few years longer if there still had been business for big schooners. And this was taking into account that for nearly a decade her owners had been less than diligent in matters of maintenance and repair.

Prophets are rarely announced, and the CRESSY was no exception. In fact her construction was delayed twice: first, as the firm worked out a new deck configuration; and second, as they sought to replace her complement of blocks after a fire destroyed the supply being fabricated by J. S. Jackson & Son, blockmakers, of Bath. The basic suite of blocks that the Jackson firm was contracted to supply ultimately came from the Boston & Lockport Block Co. of Boston.[26] Then there was one more delay—the weather.

Scheduled to launch on Thursday afternoon, 10 April 1902, the CORA F. CRESSY attracted quite a crowd of visitors to Bath, even on a stormy, raw spring day. One group aboard the sleeping car "Helicon" arrived on the morning train from Boston. Headed by Mr. and Mrs. Cressy—the latter with an elegant bou-

quet of roses and pinks for the launching—the party of twenty registered at Bath's Shannon House. Among the friends of the Cressys were several in the group who had purchased shares for the first time in a new schooner and were looking forward to the pomp and circumstance associated with launchings.[27] But the weather refused to cooperate.

The visiting Bostonians had to be satisfied with a tour of the schooner led by Captain and Mrs. Harding. Then a special trolley car took them to the New Meadows Inn where the launching banquet—without benefit of the launching—was enjoyed by all. Late in the evening, the train to Boston, with "Helicon" attached, picked up the Boston-bound, leaving Mrs. Cressy and her friend Mrs. Jopp to await the actual launching rescheduled for Saturday.

The ceremony went off without a hitch. Those who were invited to ride the schooner into the river enjoyed the usual lunch after the ceremony, and the *Bath Times* reporter, pressed to meet his deadline because the launching was in mid-afternoon, completely overlooked the rather unique nature of the new schooner, noting that her after cabin furnishings were "very tasty." The only innovation in her design and construction noted by him was the equipping of one of her small boats with a Palmer gasoline engine—the first such installation on any schooner—which initiated a yawl boat war among schooner captains.[28]

The CORA F. CRESSY may have enjoyed a very long career, but it was one that was not exactly trouble free. On the one hand, the CRESSY and her compatriots had to deal with the unsettled nature of the coal business, which included coal strikes, boycotts, and growing competition. On the other hand, the always present hazards of navigation lay in wait.

Business conditions led to the CRESSY lying idle in Boston Harbor in 1902 for four months after only two trips to the coal ports. Her next charter took her to Brunswick, Georgia, to load railroad ties for New York before returning to the coal business just as the year was ending. So in her first eight months of service, the schooner was able to make only four trips under charter with net earnings of $108 (+/- $1,660 in 1998) per $1/64$, a return of 6 percent on original

Myron D., Cora F., and Dustin G. Cressy admire the latest vessel to bear the Cressy surname on her visit to Boston. Before Percy & Small went out of the shipping business, four vessels carried the Cressy name. The two young women are unidentified.

Courtesy: Maine Maritime Museum

investment.[29] But 1903 temporarily made up for the slow start, with the schooner returning $299 (+/- $4,600 in 1998) per 1/64, a return of 17 percent on investment.[30]

The next year, however, was a complete dud. The CRESSY was involved in what appears to have been a "no-fault" collision with the SS PARTHIAN off the Delaware Capes in late March, inflicting considerable damage to the steamer, as well as upon herself.[31] By the time repairs were completed, an entire month was lost and the schooner had disbursed $2,580.44 (+/- $39,860 in 1998) for legal fees, towage, surveys, dry-docking, and repairs.[32]

It does appear that Percy & Small took advantage of the visit to the Newport News Shipbuilding & Drydock Company to also address the CRESSY's tenderness problem (see Chapter 4) when sailing light. Prior to this repair period, she carried an average of

3,979 tons of coal per voyage for fifteen voyages. After the repairs, the next fifteen cargos averaged 3,841 tons per voyage, suggesting that 150 tons of ballast had been installed.[33]

After her brush with the steamer, the CRESSY enjoyed a brief return to the coal trade before she laid up in the James River, above Norfolk and Newport News, as many schooner owners protested against low freight rates. It would take another year for the vessel's earnings to even remotely approach profitability once again.[34]

Despite a not always favorable business climate, the usual wear and tear on the vessel, and an annoying series of lost anchors (seven in ten years), the CRESSY moved on into her second decade. An extended time charter provided steady employment between Norfolk and Portland starting in 1912 and carrying through into 1915 with rates that were at

The CORA F. CRESSY aged well, considering the hard service she saw. Here she is at age ten, being pushed away from the coal docks in Portland before setting sail once again for the coal ports.

Courtesy: Captains Douglas K. and Linda J. Lee

least marginally profitable. Then came the war boom and a series of charters to Brazil (coal and case oil) with return cargoes of ore and quebracho wood to the U.S.[35] The case oil charter was particularly lucrative: three trips with 85,000 cases each at $.35 per case or a gross freight for three trips of $90,000 for the southward leg alone. Unfortunately, on her third trip south she went aground at Bahia, causing considerable damage to her hull, as well as to 7,000 cases of oil. She received extensive repairs at Rio, a notoriously expensive port for shipwork, and didn't arrive back in the States until the following April, just as the country declared war on Germany.[36] Then she was involved in a collision with some barges while she was under tow in New York Harbor, an accident which took over five years to adjudicate in New York courts and delayed the final distribution among Percy & Small's Cora F. Cressy owners until 13 December 1922, as her net earnings from that voyage had been held in escrow pending a final judgment.[37]

In August 1917 Percy & Small sold the Cressy along with the Small to the France & Canada Steamship Company. The Cressy brought $202,500 to her owners. Captain Wiley R. Dickinson, a retired deepwater and coasting shipmaster, as well as a Cressy shareholder, noted on the letter from Percy & Small conveying his share of the sale price: "This was a satisfactory investment."[38] It certainly was: Cora F. Cressy returned over 313 percent of the original investment, and that figure does not include approximately thirty dividends for which there are no surviving records.[39]

Little is known of the Cressy's movements after she moved under the house flag of the France & Canada Steamship Company, especially after the U.S. government clamped down on reporting ship movements. It is likely, however, that the Cressy continued to sail to South America until the ban on sailing vessels going to Europe was lifted after the Armistice. Then she crossed the Atlantic to France.

Aside from a photograph or two, the only record of that voyage can be found in the diary of a seventeen-year-old Australian girl, Mary Barker. Captain James Platt Barker, her father, had been prevailed upon to take the steel British square-rigger

TAMAR from Sydney to Bristol after her regular captain suffered a serious accident. Captain Barker posed two conditions that proved acceptable to the ship's owners: the government would give him a leave of absence from his post in Australia, and he could take his wife and five children. Young Mary, whose birthday fell just one month into the voyage, had fortunately decided to keep a diary "as a record of an experience that few girls—if any—would ever enjoy," a Cape Horn passage aboard a square-rigger. Under the date, Sunday, 7 September 1919, she recorded:

> Temp. 79°. Nice day, going about 6 knots. There is a five-masted schooner and a square-rigged ship in sight. After dinner, the schooner came to windward of us and gained on us fast. I snapped her. Her name was the Cora F. Cressy. She did look nice bowling along with all sail set. She had a wireless and a patent log astern, she wouldn't be American if she hadn't, still it's annoying to be beaten by a Yankee.[40]

Fifty-four years later, Mary Barker Leeming pondered the changes that had taken place in her century, from rounding Cape Horn in a sailing ship and being overhauled by a Yankee great schooner, to jet planes and men landing on the moon. "My father was a graduate of Trinity House in Hull," she wrote. "Their motto was 'Spes Super Sidera'—Hope Beyond the Stars. Surely the achievements of this century bestow a prophetic quality on those words."

The France & Canada Steamship Company prospered for a time with its fleet of great schooners, many purchased from Percy & Small and J. S. Winslow & Company. But the Armistice and a seemingly unstoppable flow of shipping from the emergency shipyards in the United States rapidly deflated the shipping boom during 1921. With new tonnage—mostly modern steel steam vessels—flooding into the market, freight rates plummeted. The value of the big schooners that only a year or two earlier had commanded top dollar evaporated like a morning dew in the desert. And the schooners, more than a little tired after having been worked hard and undermaintained to maximize the return on investment, saw their value decline even more quickly.

This is a photograph we believe was taken by Mary Barker from her father's full-rigged ship TAMAR in the Western Approaches on 7 September 1919. The CRESSY is pushing right along—she overhauled and passed the TAMAR—even though her sheer has straightened out a little. Note that she has a clothesline radio antenna strung between her mizzen topmast and spanker topmast. At this time she was owned by the France & Canada Steamship Company.

Courtesy: Captain W. J. Lewis Parker, USCG, Ret.

France & Canada also got itself into financial difficulties involving a post-war scheme to transport oil to Europe (as it also involved Percy & Small, we shall examine it more fully in a subsequent chapter). So by 1920, France & Canada was trying to unload its fleet of obsolete schooners, all suffering from varying degrees of decrepitude, at the same time values were plunging. By the end of 1921, a buyer for several of the big schooners was found—Captain Alfred W. Frost of Portland, a former skipper of Sam Percy's last command, the HENRY P. MASON, and the CORA F. CRESSY.

Frost, the head of a Portland syndicate of thirty-six investors, purchased the CRESSY along with the WYOMING, EDWARD J. LAWRENCE, and OAKLEY C. CURTIS for the fire sale price of $125,000 (+/- $850,000 in 1998). France & Canada had paid over $502,500 (+/- $5 million in 1998) for just the CRESSY and WYOMING four years earlier and had recently spent $116,000 (+/- $750,000 in 1998) on repairs for the CURTIS and WYOMING.[41]

The CRESSY's return to Maine ownership did not reduce the hazards of the coasting trade. In fact, they placed the CRESSY into the limelight once more in 1924, albeit briefly. The press bestowed the title "Queen of the Atlantic" on her after she managed to claw her way off the Nantucket shoals in the gale that claimed WYOMING and made her way safely into Portland. But in the end, it was not the perils of weather and navigation, or even age, that did her in.

The move back to Maine had not solved the problems of dwindling charters and marginal charter rates. Just a year after being proclaimed the "Queen of the Atlantic," the CRESSY and her surviving compatriots in the Frost fleet—EDWARD J. LAWRENCE and OAKLEY C. CURTIS—were seized by U.S. Marshals after the owners refused to pay assessments to clear them from a heavy debt.

Yet there was still someone who had an appetite for sailing ship property. In December 1925 the CRESSY was in Portland Harbor completing a general overhaul, before being towed to Boston to be drydocked, presumably financed by her new owner, Clinton T. Swett.[42] Shipowner Swett did not make his fortune with her, however. Enroute to Norfolk, she was blown offshore in a storm and didn't straggle into port (Mayport, Florida) until nearly four weeks later. She did manage a few coal charters through 1926 and on into the next year when she was towed into New York leaking and with sails blown away while enroute to Searsport with coal.[43]

She eventually arrived at Searsport, unloaded her coal, and then was anchored with a watchman near the entrance of Searsport's harbor. But Mr. Swett, his patience and pocketbook apparently exhausted by the demands of a superannuated schooner, had enough

and effectively abandoned her in place. The watchman departed. Local "salvagers" ransacked the vessel, hatches were left open, and she partially filled with water, developing a pronounced list.[44] Although the Coast Guard took some measures to secure her, she remained anchored at Searsport until she broke free from her moorings and went ashore on the rocks. But all was not lost. Floated by the Coast Guard, she found a new owner—J. S. Harrower—and an old captain, Alfred W. Frost.[45]

Frost, who was apparently a glutton for punishment, had been the CRESSY's skipper for several years before she was sold to France & Canada and later was her managing owner for another two years. Both soon

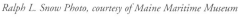

CORA F. CRESSY's towering bow and sheer size loom up out of the fog in 1972 as she lay in a cove in Bremen, Maine, an impressive reminder of the great schooners. The authors, assisted by Maynard D. Lee (in the skiff, left center), Terrance Geaghan, and others, were removing the schooner's rails for Maine Maritime Museum. Over a half century since Mary Barker "snapped" her, the CRESSY—the largest surviving wooden sailing vessel hulk—has been a crucial source of data on turn-of-the-century wooden shipbuilding practices at Percy & Small.
Ralph L. Snow Photo, courtesy of Maine Maritime Museum

demonstrated that infirmities of age notwithstanding, they still had some of the "right stuff." In what must have seemed to be a scenario from *Twilight of the Gods*, they made a roundtrip passage from Boston to Newport News for coal in a far from shabby thirteen days.[46] But it would not last: Captain Frost was not a young man, and the CRESSY was worn out—sails, gear, steam donkey plant—from over a quarter century of hard use. She was sold once again, this time to become "Levaggi's Showboat," a glamorous caricature of her former self. But even show business could not reverse the downward spiral of unpaid bills and U.S. Marshal sales. After nightclub stints in Boston, Providence, and New Haven, she returned to Boston, owned by a bank who found it necessary to keep a watchman aboard to keep a portable steam pump running. There she sat until 1938.

Bernard T. Zahn operated a Maine lobster business on the Medomak River in Bremen. On a business trip to Boston, he happened on the CRESSY in all her bedraggled glory. A visit on board with the watchman elicited the information that the bank was anxious to sell what must have become a discouraging burden. That visit also made it clear that the pumps were recycling Boston Harbor water through her hull on an all too frequent basis.

Zahn had the germ of an idea, so he went to the bank and made contact with the appropriate vice president. The first price quoted was a little steep in the lobster dealer's opinion, especially as the bank had to pay a full-time watchman and for the operation of the pumps. Besides, who wanted to buy at almost any price a big old hulk of a schooner that leaked like a sieve? With that question firmly planted in the banker's mind, Zahn went on to complete his business before returning to Maine.

On his way back to Bremen, Zahn stopped in Bath to look up Captain Sam Percy, still very much alive. He spoke with the captain about the schooner and mentioned the leak. Percy suggested that the source of the leak might be a rusted-out seacock and drew a sketch indicating where the valve could be found.

On his next visit to Boston, Zahn again visited the schooner and hired a diver to inspect the seacock. It was indeed letting water into the hull in a steady stream.[47] So back to the bank with a definite offer for the vessel that was far lower than the bank's asking price. Reminded that the CRESSY was a constant drain on cash, the bankers capitulated and accepted Zahn's offer of $200 (+/- $2,000 in 1998) for the schooner.[48] Zahn immediately rehired the diver, who again donned his hard-hat diving suit, went over the side, and drove a wooden plug into the seacock. A few minutes later the pumps sucked dry.

Ever mindful of economy, Zahn then had the vessel stripped of her rigging, spars, windlass, boiler, hoisting engines, and pumps. The money derived from the sale of the gear more than covered the new owner's payment to the bank and the cost of then towing the hulk to Bremen, where Zahn hoped to adapt her to his lobster buying and shipping business as a combination breakwater/office (in the main cabin), with lobster tanks on the lower deck. She has been there ever since.[49]

Schooner #18: Grace A. Martin

After Percy & Small sold Hull #17 while still on the stocks in the spring of 1903 to William F. Palmer, they immediately restarted the process of building another big five-master for their own account. As it turned out, this not only entailed re-ordering the materials now going into the ELIZABETH PALMER, but also rethinking the design of the schooner-to-be. This step was particularly important in light of the early operating experience of the CORA F. CRESSY, whose first skipper, William F. Harding (who previously commanded the CLIFFORD and the M. D. CRESSY), had planned to take #17 until she was sold to Palmer and he became the captain-designate of #18. His report on the new schooner's performance, strong points and weak points, and such matters as the effectiveness of the unusual CRESSY deck configuration was of utmost importance to Captain Percy and Miles M. Merry.[50]

Schooner #18 became, in reality, something of a hodgepodge in terms of design elements. The deck configuration was a version of that used on the CORA F. CRESSY, but scaled down to reduce windage, especially forward. But the deck spacing pattern was the same for both schooners, necessitating the use of house decks for the after and midship houses. Yet, curiously, the builders chose to use the moulds from the model of the ADDIE M. LAWRENCE rather than the CRESSY, as they had also done with #17.[51] Apparently Captain Sam Percy concluded that his experiment embodied in the CRESSY had gone, if not too far, far enough. But there was one small exception where she led all Percy & Small vessels. She was the first schooner in the fleet to be delivered with two stockless anchors—two very big stockless anchors that weighed 8,600 pounds each![52]

Design hybrid she may have been, but large she definitely was. With a registered length of 302 feet and a gross tonnage of 3,129 tons, the GRACE A. MARTIN was for a very brief time the largest five-masted schooner in the world until surpassed by the JANE PALMER of 3,139 GRT. Her bigness was attested to when a crowd estimated at one thousand boarded the five-master for the launching. Another four thousand observed the events from vantage points in and around the shipyard and from the fleet of boats in the river.

Among those aboard the new schooner were large contingents of investors from upstate New York, led by John Martin of Gloversville, and from Boston, led by M. D. Cressy. And circulating through the crowd was the ever-agreeable drygoods salesman and schooner investment promoter, Ocea Cahill.

Martin, assisted by daughter Grace, then hosted a banquet for seventy-five at the popular New Meadows Inn. There, host Cahill put on one of his famous shore dinners that even impressed hotel men from such urban areas as Albany and Washington, D.C. Toasts were offered to Miss Martin, the host, Percy & Small, Captain Harding, Miles M. Merry, and Landlord Cahill. Then the speeches began.

Captain Percy, of course, spoke for the firm; Captain Harding, no doubt, spoke of his heartfelt thanks for the opportunity to command such a fine and capacious vessel. Another called to the podium was E. C. Plummer, attorney and authority on coastwise shipping who, it so happened, was secretary of the Atlantic Carriers' Association, the trade and lobbying organization for the great schooner operators. Robert P. Murphy, a noted hotelier from Albany, spoke enthusiastically of his first trip to Maine and vowed to bring a large party of his own to the next launching of a Percy & Small schooner. Some at the affair may have quietly dozed off following the big dinner and the hours of speeches, but Ocea Cahill carefully noted Mr. Murphy's promise. The next schooner to join Percy & Small's fleet of coasters was the ROBERT P. MURPHY.[53]

The banquet broke up at 10:30 P.M., but the celebration was not quite over. Captain Percy, who knew the value of good press and good feelings, laid on a steamboat excursion for the next day for all the guests at the banquet. The Sunday excursion aboard the SS M & M gave the party an opportunity to view the activities along Bath's waterfront before proceeding down the Sasanoa River to Boothbay Harbor. After a big dinner at the Menawarmet Hotel, the party reboarded the steamer and was given the chance to really go to sea, passing out of the harbor, past Squirrel Island and out past Cape Newagen between the Cuckolds and Damariscove Island—encountering a sizeable swell that may not have set too well with the landlubbers in the party after a big dinner—before turning into the more sheltered waters of the Sheepscot. After an exciting race with the steamer WIWURNA, the party returned to the dock at Bath at 5:00 P.M.[54] It had been a memorable weekend for the Bostonians and New Yorkers, and they would remain loyal Percy & Small investors.

The launching, dinner, and steamer trip occurred on 16–17 July 1904, but the GRACE A. MARTIN did not leave her builder's yard for her first charter until the third week of October, three months later. The delay had nothing to do with the shipyard and un-completed work. It was, instead, a reflection of the coal charter market and the boycott of the coal shippers by the Atlantic Carriers' Association members that dragged on through the summer and into the fall. Most of the largest schooners had remained laid up since late spring, as the owners insisted upon higher freight rates and better lay days. In the absence of the big schooners, the coal shippers relied upon small schooners, the barge operators, and the steam colliers to close the tonnage gap.[55]

Captain Harding who, you will recall, had a penchant for moving from schooner to schooner in quest of bigger carrying capacity (hence bigger primage payments), was temporarily sidetracked as a result of the boycott, but in October the Atlantic Carriers' caved in and accepted prevailing charter rates. Percy & Small immediately negotiated a charter for the MARTIN to carry coal from Philadelphia to Portland. So, four months after her launching, the GRACE A. MARTIN completed her maiden voyage, carrying 5,004 tons of coal and a promise from Harding that she would carry 5,400 tons in summer ". . . when the cargo could be trimmed to better advantage than in winter."[56]

Harding and the MARTIN slipped along quietly for five years except for one incident dealing with the perils of shoreside navigation that proved embarrassing for the good captain. He was relieved of $615 (+/- $9,500 in 1998) by an adept pickpocket as the captain examined some curios in a shop window. To make matters worse, it was not Harding's money, but the balance of the MARTIN's freight money. It is not known whether he was required to make up the loss out of his own resources, but it can be assumed that Captain Harding no longer casually stuffed large rolls of bills in his most convenient pocket.[57]

The partners must have held Captain Harding in high regard, since he continued in the service of Percy & Small virtually to the end of his life. In the spring of 1910, the fifty-one-year-old captain was forced by heart trouble to relinquish command of the MARTIN as she lay off Vineyard Haven. Leaving the first mate in command, Harding went ashore for the last time. He died four months later at his home in Massachusetts.[58]

Captain Lincoln Jewett, officially retired a year earlier, temporarily took command of the schooner after she arrived at Boston. Throughout the balance of the spring, summer, and into early fall "Linc" Jewett sailed up and down the coast in the MARTIN until relieved by Captain Simeon J. Smith, formerly of J. S. Winslow &

Company's four-masted JACOB S. WINSLOW. Smith died in service in the spring of 1913.

His replacement, Herbert H. Wallace of South Portland, was a Harpswell native who had previously commanded Percy & Small's S. P. BLACKBURN.[59] It was Wallace's particular destiny to be the last skipper of the GRACE A. MARTIN.

They were coming north having sailed from Norfolk on 4 January 1914 with 5,000 tons of coal consigned to Portland parties. After a long passage marked by unusually bad weather, the GRACE A. MARTIN was anchored in Nantucket Sound waiting a chance to get around the Cape for Portland. In company were three other schooners, the FULLER PALMER, REBECCA PALMER, and PRESCOTT PALMER. Only one of the four would reach her destination.

When the winds shifted to the west, the four captains decided to break out their anchors, hoist sail, and make their respective ways north around Cape Cod. But it was not the typical weather pattern that follows a winter northeaster, at least not in degree. As the storm low moved off into the Maritimes, the winds backed around into the westerly quadrant but instead of slowly decreasing as the low pulled away, the winds increased. And to compound the situation, the bottom fell out of the thermometer as temperatures plunged to near record lows. The skipper of the REBECCA PALMER, the only schooner of the four to make port, later recalled, "I was never so cold in my life."[60] In the end, the combination of cold and wind destroyed three great schooners in the most devastating loss to the class in a single storm.[61]

As the westerlies increased in ferocity, Captain Wallace had a decision to make: anchor in the lee of Cape Cod's "backside"—the eastern shore—until the wind diminished to a safe level or make a run for Portland. The first option was not a popular one with any experienced coaster captain; Cape Cod was a notorious graveyard for the unwary and unfortunate vessels that passed that way. The second option carried the danger of being blown far offshore thanks to the schooner's inability to heave-to safely in adverse wind and sea conditions.[62] Wallace, a captain with a reputation for taking chances, took the second option.[63]

The combination of ferocious winds, bitter cold, and confused seas finished the GRACE A. MARTIN thirty miles south of Matinicus Rock. Driven by the winds, her entire forward end encased in ice, the MARTIN's seams opened as the great, laboring hull was wracked and strained by the combination of the heavy load of ice and the enormous seas. Pumps clogged with coal dust and then with slush ice in the bitter cold. Finally at 8:00 A.M. on the 14th, as her bow sank deeper and deeper under the load of ice and water, Captain Wallace ordered all hands to gather extra clothing and food and abandon ship. It was a slim chance as the fourteen-member crew crowded into the open yawl boat, especially after it was discovered that the extreme cold had frozen the gasoline line from tank to engine.

Nevertheless, they managed to get clear of the wallowing schooner and, in Captain Wallace's words:

> . . . we watched our vessel sink her head slowly, dreadfully, and then with a slipping, sliding motion, she suddenly shot down out of sight. We stared at each other with blanched faces to see not a sign of the big five-masted schooner which had brought us 1,000 miles from Norfolk.[64]

There they were, in the Gulf of Maine in an open boat, drifting powerless toward the open ocean before the bitter wind: Captain Herbert Wallace, First Mate Joseph McPhee, Second Mate John Remby, Engineer O. D. Henderson, Steward John Phillips, Stewardess Loraine Phillips, and Seamen Joseph Marshall, George Griffin, Peter Tevaris, William James, Alexander Josephs, Joseph Goodwin, Edward Jones, and N. Watson. With the exception of the officers and engineer, all were black.[65]

They drifted for twenty-one hours. Then as dawn approached, someone remembered they had a signaling torch aboard the boat that might provide enough heat—it used an open flame—to thaw the fuel line. The torch was located and someone went to work on the fuel line. As dawn broke, a steamer was spotted, and the torch was waved with a certain desperate enthusiasm. "We were answered from the bridge of the approaching steamer," Captain Wallace recalled, "and at five o'clock we were hoisted up out of our boat with a hand line. I never felt so glad of anything in my life as I did of the prospects of the bunk aboard the A. W. PERRY while I was being lifted over her rail."[66]

All hands arrived safely in Boston that afternoon and four of the crew were taken immediately to the Marine Hospital for treatment of severe frostbite. Captain Wallace met with the press and heaped particular praise on Loraine Phillips: "She proved herself to be the best man of us all and bore the frightful cold and hardship with an ever ready smile and cheer."[67]

It was a remarkable story, all the more so as the FULLER PALMER and PRESCOTT PALMER were also blown far offshore, heavily iced, severly strained, and sinking. Yet only one person aboard the three schooners died, for rescuers arrived, seemingly out of nowhere, just as all appeared lost.

SCHOONER #27: THE WESTERN CONNECTION

Percy & Small suspended building five-masters for their own fleet for nearly three years after the MARTIN took to the water, although they had ordered and taken delivery on a frame for an additional five-master in 1904. The unsuccessful boycott by the Atlantic Carriers' Association of the coal shippers in an effort to force higher freight rates was followed by another measure. This time the members of the Atlantic Carriers' Association sought to drive up charter rates by reducing competition, in this case by putting severe restrictions on the number of new large schooners members could build. Percy & Small, heavily invested in a frame, were not cleared to build an addition to their fleet, so the frame lay around the shipyard for two years before Palmer, with Atlantic Carriers' Association permission in hand, struck a deal with Sam Percy to build the FANNIE PALMER II (Chapter 7).

Curiously, Schooner #27 appears to have originated in somewhat the same manner. This time, however, the purchaser of the frame was William T. Donnell, Percy & Small's next-door neighbor and former owner of the Blaisdell shipyard that became the foundation of their shipbuilding plant. Donnell's shipyard, literally in his backyard, had last produced a schooner in 1896, the ALICE M. COLBURN. Since that time only one new vessel had been built there, the small steam ferry HOCKOMOCK (known locally as "Hinky-Dink") which was launched in 1901.

It appeared obvious that Mr. Donnell, getting along in years and apparently comfortably situated, had retired from the shipbuilding business. Yet, in late 1904, Donnell purchased a large oak frame from J. S. Hoskins, the Maryland-based firm that frequently supplied Percy & Small. The timber began arriving at Donnell's shipyard in late December aboard the schooner ANNIE F. KIMBALL.[68]

It does not appear that Donnell was planning to build a large schooner at his own shipyard, but that he acquired the frame at a good price with the intent of reselling it at a better price. It is also possible that the frame was actually intended for Percy & Small and hewn from their moulds.[69]

Before Percy & Small proceeded further into the construction of a new schooner, the financial backing had to be nailed down. It was a little more difficult now that the rate of return on the coal schooners had declined from the peak at the turn of the century. Nonetheless, a number of Percy & Small's loyal corps of investors from the Boston area, as well as upstate New York, had signed up for shares in the new schooner. But more were needed if Schooner #27 was to become a reality.

John Brooks, one of Ocea Cahill's recruits from the Hudson Valley, turned out to be the key to opening new sources of capital. Aside from his partnership in Tower, Brooks, an Albany dry goods firm, Brooks—a native of Bernardston, Massachusetts, in the Connecticut River Valley north of Greenfield—was also a partner in a western ranching venture. It appears that the men in the Brooks family followed the advice of Horace Greeley, although some with more enthusiasm than others. John went east to Boston before moving on to Albany; his father went to Chicago; and younger brother Bryant Butler

Brooks, at age nineteen, went to the Wyoming Territory where he worked as cowboy, trapper, and finally as a rancher.[70]

John Brooks was part of Ocea Cahill's circle of acquaintances. In fact, he and Mrs. Brooks were among those who attended the launching of the GRACE A. MARTIN and the subsequent festivities. In 1905 Brooks purchased 1/64 of the ROBERT P. MURPHY for himself, and another 1/64 for his niece Lena Brooks.[71] Somewhere along the line, John Brooks must have mentioned to Ocea Cahill or Percy & Small that his younger brother, an ex-cowboy and trapper, was now the managing owner of B. B. Brooks & Company, a livestock and real estate firm centered upon a 100,000-acre ranch in Natrona County, Wyoming. The younger Brooks also happened to be governor of Wyoming, dividing his family's time between the governor's mansion in Cheyenne and the ranch near Casper.[72]

Brother John was involved in other things besides the dry-goods business and ranching. He organized expeditions of like-minded capitalists designed to explore investment opportunities in various underdeveloped regions such as Mexico. These trips also appear to have had a strong social and recreational component as well.[73] But the expedition to Wyoming organized by Brooks was aimed at raising capital for a new schooner from a yet untapped source.

Accompanied by Captain Sam, Brooks met his brother in Cheyenne, as well as a number of leading Wyoming businessmen, before moving on to the ranch where they stayed for a few days. It turned out to be a profitable few days for Percy & Small and John Brooks if the local newspaper is to be believed:

Percy & Small, shipbuilders of Bath, Maine, will launch a new schooner, "Governor Brooks," the latter part of September. The schooner will cost about $130,000; it has five masts and carries 4,000 tons. Fully one-third of the stock [ca. $44,000] has been taken by Wyoming men, and about $10,000 of the stock has been taken by Casper men.

The schooner will carry freight along the coast and will return to its owners dividends on the

Sisters Lena (left) and Abby (right) Brooks accompany their uncle John Brooks for a ride around the Natrona County, Wyoming, ranch of B. B. Brooks. In 1905 Albany-based John Brooks purchased shares in Percy & Small's ROBERT P. MURPHY for himself and niece Lena and subsequently introduced Percy & Small to his brother, then governor of Wyoming.

Courtesy: Shelley McCleary Trumbull (granddaughter of Lena Brooks McCleary)

Governor and Mrs. Bryant B. Brooks stand on the porch of the V-V Ranch with their children: (left-right) Jean, Silas, Melissa, Abby, Lena. It was to Cheyenne and to this ranch that John Brooks brought Sam Percy on a successful mission to line up new investors in Percy & Small schooners. Captain Sam returned home to Maine with substantial investment pledges, some Wyoming oil stock, and a collie puppy.

Courtesy: Wyoming State Museum

average of about 15 per cent, the dividends being made every time the ship makes a trip, and about ten trips each year are generally made.[74]

Francois Dickman, in his recent article about WYOMING, could only positively identify five persons from the state as shareholders in the GOVERNOR BROOKS aside from the Brooks family.[75] Were John, Sam Percy, and the governor indulging in more than a little hyperbole in hopes of attracting additional investors? Or was the article generally accurate—aside from its assessment of a return on investment—and the list of original investors actually included a number of unidentified Wyomingites?

There is a bill of sale for $^1/_{64}$ share of the GOVERNOR BROOKS that appears to indicate that as late as November 1907, Percy & Small still owned $^{50}/_{64}$ of the vessel with no owners listed from Wyoming.[76] However, an examination of Bath's ship property tax assessment for 1908, the first year the GOVERNOR BROOKS appeared, shows the partners retaining only a $^{21}/_{128}$ interest in the vessel, and the firm's monthly trial balances list at least twenty-eight persons during 1907 making payments on their shares in the vessel.[77] It is likely that some of the $^{50}/_{64}$ shares ascribed to Percy & Small in the Bill of Sale were held in trust by the firm, while others pledged by the Wyoming investors had not yet been paid in full and transferred to the new owners. But the key indicator of a successful mission to Wyoming was the fact that the schooner was named, not just the GOVERNOR BROOKS, but named months before it was completed. Percy & Small rarely publicly revealed the names of their vessels until just weeks before their scheduled launchings.

Captain Sam Percy brought more than investment commitments home from Wyoming. He brought a number of shares in a Wyoming oil firm managed by the Richardson Brothers who, it so happened, had also invested in the GOVERNOR BROOKS.[78] He also acquired a four-month-old collie puppy. The Maine shipbuilder had long owned a handsome English collie named Dick who was much admired by the local newspapers. Often called "King Dick," his undeniable talents as a rider on the local trolley line often appeared in the press.[79] But Dick, alas, was stricken

down with the ailments of age, dying in April 1907, just before the captain's trip west. Not surprisingly, the new dog was named Dick also, and he, too, became something of an item in the local papers.[80]

The GOVERNOR BROOKS was the last vessel built by Percy & Small that was constructed outside of their own shipyard. This time, however, the schooner was built in the old Donnell shipyard adjoining their own north building ways. The FANNIE PALMER II was being finished up on the south building ways and the north ways were reserved for a big six-master for J. S. Winslow & Company that was scheduled to be laid down during June. So an arrangement was reached with owner William T. Donnell, and Percy & Small overhauled and expanded the Donnell building ways before laying the keel for the GOVERNOR BROOKS.[81]

This schooner represented something of a departure for vessels built for their own account: she was their first true flush-decked vessel. After the builders had abandoned the longpoop model for their own use, they had experimented with the CORA F. CRESSY type, completing four schooners (two five-masters, two four-masters) to the type or variants thereof. Percy & Small, however, had already built four flush-deckers since 1903: three for William F. Palmer and one for J. S. Winslow & Company, who had been reluctant to give up on the long poop model until 1906 with the construction of the flush-decked six-master, ALICE M. LAWRENCE.

We have no direct evidence of the specific model from which the BROOKS was built. The bill files for the schooner make no reference to a model, but they do specify that Bant Hanson billed for thirty-three hours' drafting and forty-five hours' making moulds.[82] This is not enough time to completely loft a new model and make the moulds, but it is enough time to reloft and modify an existing set of lines. Given Percy & Small's propensity to build schooners from the WILLIAM H. CLIFFORD/MARTHA P. SMALL "universal" model, it is more than a little likely that the BROOKS, modified to accommodate the flush deck, owed much to those schooners.

The central problem with building this schooner was coordinating her launching with the expected arrival of Governor Brooks and his party. The original projected launching in late September slipped into late October before a firm date was fixed: Tuesday, 22 October. For a while, there was some concern that the BROOKS would be launched without any masts stepped, since the long-ordered spars had failed to arrive from the Pacific Northwest. Then, on 14 October, the shipment of five 118-foot Douglas-fir "sticks" arrived at Bath's railroad yard. They were quickly dumped into the river and towed to Percy & Small. Four days later boss rigger Frank Palmer had all the lower masts stepped, although the standing rigging would have to wait until after the launching. It was fast work, especially when you consider how quickly sparmaker Colby and his crew shaped and finished the big spars.

On Monday, 21 October, the investors from the Boston area, upstate New York, and Wyoming crowded into town for the big event. Governor and Mrs. Brooks and daughter Abby were the guests of Captain and Mrs. Percy and daughter Eleanor; the rest checked in at the Phoenix Hotel.

Abby Brooks, nineteen, the designated sponsor for the new schooner named for her father, was attending Dana Hall in Wellesley, Massachusetts, preparatory to going on to Wellesley College.[83] Daughters of a wealthy rancher and leading politician and born in the first state to recognize the right of women to vote, Abby and her sisters enjoyed a combination of education and freedom unusual for women of the time.

Coming to Bath, however briefly, brought Abby Brooks and her family into a world essentially maritime and foreign to their experience. But they made

Abby Brooks was sponsor for the schooner named for her father. Then a student at Dana Hall, she went on to graduate from Wellesley College in 1911.
Courtesy: Shelley McCleary Trumbull, granddaughter of Lena Brooks McCleary

up for that lack during their forty-eight-hour stay in the Shipbuilding City and environs. A shore dinner at the famous Cahill establishment on the shore of the New Meadows was the first order of business upon arrival. The following morning, bright and early, Miss Abby and her parents were taken to the Percy & Small shipyard to be introduced to the governor's namesake and to get the grand tour of shipyard and schooner. Captain Angus McLeod did the honors on the new vessel, while Captain Percy did the shipyard tour.[84]

Perhaps the Wyoming party was a little disappointed not to find the GOVERNOR BROOKS in her crowning glory, fully rigged. But she was bedecked with colorful flags including one that puzzled most of the spectators: a white flag with "V-V" in red. One captain, when queried by a newspaper reporter, replied: "I never saw it in my code [book] and suppose it is some Masonic sign."[85] It was, in fact, the registered brand of B. B. Brooks & Company. And for those who wanted to admire towering spars, two Percy & Small four-masters, the WILLIAM H. CLIFFORD and FLORENCE M. PENLEY — dressed with all their flags— were docked at the shipyard.

The launching went without a hitch with Abby repeating the appropriate verbal formula and scattering the bouquet of roses and pinks over the bow as the schooner "smoked" into the Kennebec. There followed the usual light lunch aboard the schooner served by caterer Malo as the invited guests continued their examination of the schooner, now anchored in mid-stream. No doubt many exclaimed over the elegant finish found in the after house: quartered oak and mahogany with white spruce and cypress ceilings, hardwood floors, and decorated with gold trimmings. About a decade later, however, T. Clarke Conwell—a future captain in the merchant marine—found the cabin ". . . large, dark, and somewhat foreboding."[86]

After the tug docked the new schooner, the invited guests disembarked, crossed the shipyard, and boarded three special cars on the L. A. & W. Street Railway for the trip to—you guessed it—the New Meadows Inn. Here, a group including local bigwigs, captains retired and active, investors in the newly launched schooner, and shipbuilders assembled as guests of Percy & Small. Every guest found a souvenir menu at his or her place featuring a photo of Governor Brooks on the front page. Inside were listed gastronomic delights that had probably never graced a menu in Wyoming:[87]

Lobster Stew
Crackers Celery Pickles
Steamed Clams
Drawn Butter Clam Broth
Tomato Ketchup (Heinz)
Worcestershire Sauce (L & P)
Lobster Salad
Fried Clams Plain Lobster
Potato Chips
Cookies Rolls Doughnuts
Coffee Tea Milk

Payne's Second Regiment Orchestra, from Lewiston, provided the musical background as Charles Cahill once again proved that more than brother Ocea in the family could turn a dollar out of shipbuilding

The GOVERNOR BROOKS—no abbreviations here to save money—was built in the adjoining Donnell shipyard and launched before she was completed. The fact that she even had her lower masts finished and stepped was a testimony to the determination of sparmakers and riggers. The unfinished spars arrived at Bath only a week before the launching, yet were finished and in place on launching day. Note the flag flying just below her burgee. "V-V" was the governor's registered cattle brand.

Courtesy: Maine Maritime Museum

without being a shipbuilder.[88] Meanwhile the invited guests—from the governor and Abby to "Post Hole Pete from the Big Muddy"—pitched in with determination, if not enthusiasm.

Once the meal was cleared, the speeches began. How many of the 141 diners nodded off is not recorded, but the names of those who spoke are here forever recorded: Frank A. Small (chairman of the Bath Common Council and P&S junior partner); Bath Mayor George E. Hughes; Toastmaster E. C. Plummer; Governor B. B. Brooks of Wyoming; former diplomat Harold M. Sewall; former governor, college president, Civil War hero, and Medal of Honor winner Major General Joshua Chamberlain; and Captain Angus McLeod. When Captain McLeod finished his (mercifully) brief remarks, E. C. Plummer stood once more and raised his glass to Abby Brooks, expressing the hope that she might linger in Bath long enough to make it necessary for Governor Brooks to come to Maine each year to visit his daughter and son-in-law. Then brother Plummer called for three cheers for the young lady, which was given by the assembled guests with a will.

The next morning, sixty of the party assembled at the steamboat wharf in Bath to board the steamer ELDORADO for a boat trip that combined a foliage tour and a passage to Boothbay and return with lunch, all courtesy of Percy & Small. On arriving back at the

Captain Angus McLeod (circa 1856–1928) was the first skipper of the GOVERNOR BROOKS and WYOMING. The Cape Breton-born seaman had a well-earned reputation for steadiness under stress and careful management of vessels under his command.
Cadet John Brooks Photo, courtesy of Captain W. J. Lewis Parker, USCG, Ret.

wharf in Bath, the Brooks family and Boston and New York members of the party boarded the late afternoon train for Boston. As he turned to go, Governor Brooks summed up his impression of the visit:

Since arriving in Bath I have had the best time imaginable, every detail offered for our pleasure was new and interesting and we will never forget the entertainment given us by Percy & Small and the citizens of the Shipping City. I hope to have the pleasure of coming to see you again.[89]

With the departure of the invited guests, Percy & Small turned their attention back to completing the schooner, now docked alongside at the shipyard. Much remained to be done, however. Frank Palmer had to finish the rigging of the vessel and bend on the sails. Hyde Windlass Company had to complete the installation of the windlass, hoisting engines, wrecking pumps, steam heat for each of the deckhouses, and the steam donkey boiler and associated equipment. Ship carpenters, joiners of both varieties, and the painters finished up innumerable half-completed jobs. And, finally, the numerous items from towels and sheets to galley pots and pans, from tools to navigation equipment that made up the schooner's "Bath Outfit" had to be ordered, received, inventoried, and put aboard in the appropriate locations.[90]

Captain McLeod and his wife moved aboard the BROOKS in mid-November, once the steam heating system was operative. Mrs. McLeod, who would stay aboard until such time as the vessel departed, was living in Bath when she married her Cape Breton-born husband in the shipbuilding city in 1893. He was then skipper of the four-masted GEORGE P. DAVENPORT, built and managed by William T. Donnell.

McLeod, whose name leaves no doubt about his ancestry, took command of his first Bath schooner—Adam & Hitchcock's ELLEN M. GOLDER—in 1881 at the age of twenty-five. In 1887 he was offered command of the new four-master KATIE J. BARRETT by

builder and managing owner Donnell. In January 1890 the BARRETT went ashore near Nauset Inlet on Cape Cod. Donnell abandoned her to the insurers and elements after several attempts to get her off failed (she was later salvaged, rebuilt, and renamed). This hiccup in the captain's career was not held against him by Mr. Donnell, however.

In 1891 he took command of the brand-new four-master GEORGE P. DAVENPORT, again built and managed by Donnell. He remained with her for five years before he moved on to the ALICE M. COLBURN, named for his bride and, once again, built and managed by William T. Donnell. But by 1907, with the COLBURN the last schooner built by Donnell,

A month after the launching, the GOVERNOR BROOKS was ready for sea. The Sunday before she sailed, Captain McLeod dressed ship for the benefit of the neighborhood and passersby. She was the first of two flush-decked vessels built for Percy & Small's own account.

Courtesy: Captains Douglas K. and Linda J. Lee

it was evident that if McLeod wanted to go to a larger vessel, he would have to move on to another managing owner.

After the McLeods married, they made their "land" home in Bath until 1904 when they moved to Somerville outside of Boston. And it was while they lived in Bath that it just so happened that they became very close friends with Frank and Martha Small. Before the GOVERNOR BROOKS reached a point where she was habitable, for example, the McLeods were the guests of the Smalls rather than staying at a local hostelry or renting rooms. It is probable that this friendship played a significant role in bringing Captain McLeod under the blue and white flag of Percy & Small, where he rounded out his thirty-five-year career of command at sea, culminating with the largest wooden sailing vessel in the world.

The BROOKS cleared Bath for Newport News in late November and arrived back in Boston with 4,000 tons of coal on 12 December. As with virtually all voyages under Captain McLeod, it was without incident—in part, because the good captain was not a man to take risks or drive a vessel too hard. He was methodical, precise, and cautious, as his record of a decade of service with Percy & Small proved.

When McLeod left the BROOKS in 1909, he was succeeded by Captain George Barlow, formerly of the MARTHA P. SMALL. Barlow did not enjoy the trouble-free operation of the schooner that had been her plank-owning skipper's lot. In fact, "Murphy's Law" appears to have been operative on this trip.

Barlow relieved Captain McLeod in November while the BROOKS was unloading coal in Portland. On the morning of 24 November, he took his new command to sea for the first time, bound for Norfolk.[91] He didn't get very far when the wind increased to gale force, carrying away the sails one by one. After running under bare poles for several hours, Barlow managed to get both anchors out, and although the schooner was swept by several heavy seas, she finally came up into the wind and rode out the rest of the storm. The next day, under jibs and spanker, the only sails not blown out, the BROOKS staggered into Boston Harbor and anchored. New sails were ordered from the Portland Sailmaking Company and so they lay there for a week before the new sails were delivered and bent on. Once again they put to sea, making Norfolk in just three days and four hours.

The BROOKS, carrying 4,000 tons of coal, departed Norfolk on 10 December, her cargo consigned to Portland. After two days of moderate weather, another gale set in. The captain decided to play it safe and anchored about six miles southwest of the Fire Island lightship to ride out the storm. Sometime during the night in the 65-MPH wind, the schooner's rudder carried away. The full extent of the damage was not evident until daylight, when the captain discovered his rudder was completely gone.

Fortunately, the wind had moderated considerably, so Barlow decided to make for Martha's Vineyard, creeping along under his jibs and literally steering by using his anchors. Every time the schooner began to swing off course, out of control, her anchors were let go. Once she was under control again and the sails properly trimmed, up came the anchors and off they went—a testament to the value of the steam donkey engine on the great schooners. For six days the BROOKS made her painfully slow and halting way along the south shore of Long Island, past Block Island, and into Vineyard Sound. There she found a revenue service cutter and a tug that got her into harbor.

On 24 December—this is the same time Captain McKown was trying to get home for Christmas in the DAVIS PALMER, you will recall—two large tugs arrived to take the crippled schooner to Boston. One towed and the other served as rudder. After spending the night anchored off the Handkerchief Lightship, they rounded Cape Cod heading north. The wind kicked around into the southeast during the day (as the trio made its way north) and began to increase, reaching hurricane force by 1:00 A.M. The tugs hauled the BROOKS around under the lee of Provincetown, where Barlow put both anchors out with 112 fathoms of chain. The tugs then took shelter in Provincetown Harbor. Before anchoring, Barlow reported seeing the DAVIS PALMER as she jibed off into Massachusetts Bay. He was probably the last person to see her afloat.

The run of bad luck that had challenged Barlow and the BROOKS had fortunately run its course. Both rode out the hurricane force winds with no further damage, and after the storm passed, the tugs ventured forth and continued the tow to Boston where, once the cargo was discharged, the schooner was drydocked and the rudderpost and rudder were replaced. Captain Barlow, who retired to a farm two years later, summed up the events with a masterful understatement: "The trip just completed was my first one in the GOVERNOR BROOKS and I shall probably never forget it as it was surely one of many misfortunes." Unlike Captain McKown of the DAVIS PALMER, however, he had lived to tell about it.

Ironically, just a year later, Captain Ellis Haskell—substituting for Barlow who was spending some time ashore—drove the BROOKS from Boston to Norfolk in three days, spent three days loading, and then made it back to Boston in three additional days: nine days for a roundtrip. During part of this nine-day span, a severe gale had savaged the Atlantic Seaboard. Captain Haskell's explanation for this brilliant performance: "It's an ill wind that blows nobody good."[92]

In the spring of 1915, Percy & Small were able to charter the BROOKS for case oil to Santos, Brazil. It was a profitable charter with the schooner earning $125 per $1/64$ for the southbound freight alone. Unfortunately, on her return passage, loaded with linseed cake from Buenos Aires, she ran into another hurricane off Cape Hatteras, became badly strained, and began leaking heavily. She put into Southport, South Carolina, and was eventually towed to New York to discharge and for repairs. A month later she was on her way to Montevideo with 88,000 cases of oil and had a return charter for dyewood from Buenos Aires.

After several years of marginally profitable coal freights, the investors from Wyoming were beginning to reap those 15-percent returns bragged about in 1907. Former Governor Brooks recovered his entire original investment by July 1916. A year later the schooner was sold to the France & Canada Steamship Company. It is probable that the price was in excess of her original cost, giving the original shareholders more than a 200 percent return on their investment.[93] Not too shabby!

But the inflated freight receipts and sales price exacted their own heavy charges on the GOVERNOR BROOKS in hard driving and postponed maintenance as the new owners sought to recover and then capitalize on their investment. Captain T. Clarke Conwell, who commented on the schooner's gloomy after house, also remembered Captain George A. Goodwin remarking "that the schooner was so hogged that a man standing on the ceiling in the forward part of the hold could not see another man standing likewise in the after end."[94]

The end came in March 1921. After departing Norfolk on 7 May 1920, the schooner sprung her rudderhead and opened seams in a gale on 25 July; she was forced to put into Rio for repairs. While in port, to add insult to injury, she was hit by another vessel.[95] This was not a port, however, in which one wanted to make extensive repairs. It was very expensive, very slow, and the quality of the work left something to be desired. The BROOKS, which had to discharge her cargo before being repaired, reloaded it and finally cleared Rio for Montevideo on 8 February 1921, six months after she put in in distress. Encountering more foul weather, her seams opened again off Cape Castillo and her crew abandoned ship and made it safely ashore.[96] But the GOVERNOR BROOKS was not yet ready to call it quits. The British steamer HIGHLAND LOCH spotted a five-master floating abandoned several days after the crew had left her. A boarding party inspected her, found her indeed deserted, and removed several flags, including the burgee marked "GOVERNOR BROOKS." Because she was a menace to navigation, they set her afire before returning to the steamer.[97] A week later, her barely awash hulk with four masts projecting 50 feet above the water was sighted by another vessel. She was never seen again.

Although Percy & Small started their fleet and shipbuilding operations with four-masters, that class of schooners fell into a definite minority status during the first decade of the new century. The firm had built five schooners through 1899, four of which (80 percent) were four-masters. During the next ten years (1900–09), Percy & Small built twenty-five schooners, only six of which (24 percent) were four-masters.

What is more striking is that aside from their per-

centage in the total mix, their size began to shrink just as the size of the five-masters and six-masters began to grow. The Percy & Small four-masters built in the 1890s averaged 1,622 GRT as opposed to the 1,082 GRT of those they built between 1900 and 1909. This apparent anomaly was a recognition of the complex nature of the shipping market, especially the role of the smaller of the great schooners in working very profitably around the edges.

In 1901 Percy & Small completed two four-

Built as a replacement for the Margaret Ward, which had been sold to J. S. Winslow just before launching, the Florence M. Penley shared the same deck configuration, clearly visible here, as her predecessor and the Cora F. Cressy. Note the view of the shipyard under her bowsprit and jibboom. On the left is the blacksmith shop, paint and treenail shop, and one corner of the office. The launching ways upon which she was recently perched are also visible, along with a tantalizing view of the interior of the mill. The Penley was launched on 2 April 1903, just eleven days before her sister ship was tragically lost to collision.

Courtesy: Maine Maritime Museum

masters; one on order from J. S. Winslow & Company (CORDELIA E. HAYES) and the other to replace the sunken CHARLES P. NOTMAN (MILES M. MERRY). But within months of her completion, the MERRY also ended up—having been sold on the hoof, as it were—with J. S. Winslow's rapidly expanding fleet of great schooners (see Chapter 7).

However, Percy & Small had not given up on the four-masted schooner. Fred Rideout modeled and lofted one of approximately 1,100 GRT that incorporated the CORA F. CRESSY deck configuration. As we have already learned, the first schooner built to this model, the MARGARET WARD, was sold on the stocks to J. S. Winslow & Company just weeks before she was scheduled to be launched. Percy & Small immediately ordered another frame and prepared to lay down a duplicate, which became Schooner #16-2. This break in their hull-numbering sequence served principally one purpose: it made up for the skipping of number thirteen in the sequence of hull numbers, a widespread practice among shipbuilders.

Completed as the FLORENCE M. PENLEY, #16-2 was named for the daughter of Ferdinand Penley of Auburn, Maine, a childhood friend of Frank Small.[98]

The ROBERT P. MURPHY, at 697 GRT the smallest schooner built by Percy and Small, is being moved into her dock at Galveston, Texas. Although configured for the timber trade with just two hatches and a pair of bow ports, it is likely she is carrying steel rails on this voyage, for she does not appear to have a deck cargo. She was commanded for many years by Bath native Fred L. Dunton.

Courtesy: Captain W. J. Lewis Parker, USCG, Ret.

The schooner's name and her captain—M. L. Jameson—had originally been destined for #16-1, but the prospect of a quick sale saw their respective moments of glory postponed for eight months. However, the PENLEY survived the perils of the sea long after her twin was tragically cut down and sunk just eleven days after the PENLEY was launched.

It took thirteen years before she succumbed to a tropical hurricane 450 miles south of Hatteras in September 1915 while enroute from Rio de Janeiro to Baltimore with a cargo of manganese ore. It had already been a difficult passage with severe leaks forcing her into port twice for repairs. After departing Rio, she returned on 20 May leaking at the rate of fourteen inches per hour.[99] After expensive repairs, she sailed once again on 12 June, only to put into Barbados on 14 August and sailing again the next day. A day short of a month later, the schooner sank after Captain Jameson and the crew were taken off by the steamer SIXAOLA. Thus ended a career that underlined the adaptability of the smaller schooners. In her relatively short life of a dozen years, the PENLEY had frequently carried cargoes of coal, lumber, steel rails, and railroad ties to such ports as Bath, Portland, Boston, Havana, Rio, and Galveston.

Robert P. Murphy, Albany hotelier and friend of Ocea Cahill, had promised at one Percy & Small launching to someday host a launching banquet of his own. He finally got his wish on 16 December 1905. In a remarkable parallel with the events of three years earlier, however, he discovered that the schooner he thought was "his" was sold on the stocks to J. S. Winslow & Company when over 50 percent complete to become the EVELYN W. HINKLY. Yet two months after the HINKLY was launched, Schooner #23 was laid down, ending the longest period of no work (new construction or repair) in the shipyard since 1899.[100]

Both schooners were built from the same model and established a record for the shipyard: they were the smallest schooner-rigged vessels ever built by the firm, their gross tonnage being measured at 698 and 697 tons respectively. Both were built principally for the lumber trade with bow ports and only two hatches instead of the usual three found in schooners of this size. In terms of their deck configuration, they were the first built by Percy & Small to use the traditional short poop, short topgallant forecastle deck, and long main well deck configuration suited to carrying large deckloads.

Although she was a relatively small schooner, the MURPHY took big schooner time to complete. Most of the delay appears to have been caused by the slow arrival of yellow pine. The summer of 1905 turned out to be very dry in the South making it difficult to float saw logs from the areas the loggers were cutting to the mills. Then one of the largest sawmills burned down, compounding the problem.[101]

Finally, on 16 December 1905, the MURPHY was launched. No boat tours and no big banquets at the New Meadows Inn appeared on Bath's social calendar. Bath's newspapers, usually gossipy to a fault, even failed to mention who was aboard the new schooner for the launching except for the sponsor, a Miss Alice Rullman.[102] It was, in a few words, a low-key launching.

Albion B. Hipson, a thirty-three-year-old mariner from South Edgecomb, Maine, was selected to command the new schooner. In the fifteen years since he had gone to sea, Hipson had worked his way from the forecastle to the quarter deck and showed great promise, having previously commanded the LEORA M. THURLOW and ADDIE P. MCFADDEN. Unfortunately, in four months he would be dead from one of the perils of the trade, typhoid fever.[103] On her maiden voyage, the MURPHY was chartered to carry ice and spars from Rockport to Nassau. Sailing light, she proceeded to Carrabelle on the Florida panhandle to load lumber for Philadelphia. While at Carrabelle, young Hipson ingested a fatal dose of the bacterium *Salmonella typhosa*. He died at a hospital in Philadelphia.

The partners then picked Captain Fred L. Dunton, formerly of the DAISY FARLIN. A local boy, Dunton was married to the former Jennie Harnden, also from Bath. He retained command of the MURPHY until she was sold in 1917. By then she had carried him on voyages to ports far and near: Georgetown in British Guyana, Rio de Janeiro, Buenos Aires, Rochefort in France, Jacksonville, Galveston, Port

Arthur, Sabine Pass, Apalachicola, Brunswick, New York, Boston, Portland, and Bath.

One voyage was particularly long. The MURPHY sailed from New York with a cargo of anthracite coal destined for Rio in early April 1916. Percy & Small had arranged a return charter from Buenos Aires with linseed cakes, but the demand in Europe for grain—the war being in full swing—had driven up freight rates to the point that it was worthwhile for the firm to cancel the linseed charter with the resultant penalties and take a cargo of grain to France. Dunton reported his arrival at Rochefort on 2 November 1916 after a rough crossing of the Bay of Biscay. "The MURPHY behaved herself very nicely," he wrote, "although at times it was hard to tell whether she was supposed to sit up straight[,] on either end[,] or on her side. After the storm she concluded it was better to sit up straight and keep her keel under her."[104]

Captain Dunton got to know the port well before he finally sailed for Nova Scotia. German prisoners of war, heavily guarded, acted as stevedores but didn't work very fast. However, the French were fascinated by Dunton's "big" schooner, which was the first American coaster to call at this port. They were amazed at the smallness of the crew and the fact that Captain Dunton planned to sail light, without cargo or ballast, to Nova Scotia.[105] The captain, on the other hand, was suitably impressed by the menu and—one assumes—the cuisine at the Hotel de France which was far removed from that dished up by the MURPHY's cook. He had plenty of time to enjoy it, as the schooner did not arrive back in a U.S. port (via Nova Scotia) until July 1917, after being out of American waters for fifteen months. The MURPHY was sold shortly after her return.

She outlived her sister, the HINKLY, by several years, finally perishing by fire in 1924 at Puerto Plata, Dominican Republic. The MURPHY's nineteen years of hard service without serious damage speaks well for her builders and her captains.

Percy & Small's Hull #20 was unique in their shipbuilding annals. It was the smallest sailing vessel built by a firm noted for its very large schooners. And, it wasn't a schooner. But let Marston Hamlin tell the story of his encounter with UMBAJEJUS, a Kennebec River scow sloop:

> One fine summer's day around 1906 or 1907 my brother Talbot and I were bound Down East in our sloop VALKYR. Somewhere off Old Orchard Beach we sighted a craft to the eastward heading towards us, apparently just coming out of Casco Bay. We couldn't make her out. She fitted into no category we knew. At first we saw only a lofty mast and topmast with a great gray mainsail and a couple of gray jibs. Then a dingy gray hull became visible, surmounted by a dingy gray deckload, the bow throwing a tremendous welter of white foam. Finally, as we came abreast of each other, her full glory appeared. Her hull, as gray and innocent of paint as the barn of a long abandoned farm, was straight sided and looked about 60 or 70 feet long. Her bow and stern were square with some rake. Her single mast was lofty and surmounted by a topmast reaching to the clouds, and it supported a great gaff mainsail, a fore staysail and a jib, the latter reaching down to the tip of a mighty balk that formed her bowsprit. On her deck was a load of tons of hay eight or ten feet high covered by gray tarpaulins. . . . there . . . neatly lettered on her name board in black paint (the only paint visible on her by the way)—UMBAJEJUS.[106]

Hull #20 appears more a job to satisfy an important supplier than an effort to make big money or reputation. The UMBAJEJUS was built for the M. G. Shaw Company, a major producer of sawn lumber that based its cutting operations around Moosehead Lake in north-central Maine and its timber-sawing operations in Bath. The cost of the big scow as set by the contract was $3,300 (+/- $50,000 in 1998). However, it was not a big moneymaker for Percy & Small. They had to charge off $84.99 worth of hard pine to stock in order to break even on the contract.[107]

Although intended for hauling lumber, the UMBAJEJUS—named for a lake near Millinocket—carried virtually every cargo available along the coast, from hay to lime. Her perambulations in the interest of a paying cargo took her from Penobscot Bay to

Portsmouth, New Hampshire.[108] Under the command of Captain J. M. Pottle, the scow sloop was famous along Maine's "up west" coast as she slogged her way along loaded with boxboards or hay or lime.

M. G. Shaw eventually sold its operations in Bath and the scow sloop acquired new owners and another name (Pottle as owner and McCormick as name). For several years her principal venue was hauling boxboards from the New Meadows River to Portland to be loaded on the railroad cars. But on one trip, she brought white oak frames cut by former Percy &

Small subcontractor Alonzo Parks to the shipyard. Perhaps the last white oak frames cut in the area, they were destined for a small Moosehead Lake steamer that was to be erected at the lake.[109]

Captain Pottle turned command over to his son, Captain J. H. Pottle. Six years later, on 20 November 1921, the McCormick, ex-Umbejejus, burned and sank off Parker Flats on the lower Kennebec. She had not been the object of romance and adventure, but she got the job done.

The Ultimate Schooner: Wyoming

After completing the Eleanor A. Percy, Percy & Small focused on building five-masters for their own account over most of the decade. Nevertheless, the firm built no fewer than five six-masters for J. S. Winslow & Company, all but the last, the Edward B. Winslow, smaller than the pioneering Percy.

The Bath firm's reluctance to invest in further six-masters probably stemmed from two factors: (a) the higher level of investment required for construction, and (b) the desire to evaluate the efficacy of various improvements designed to address the problems of very large wooden hulls.

The Rideout-designed Percy model was used only for that schooner, with a new model and moulds being prepared for the first of the Winslow six-masters, the Addie M. Lawrence. That model, in turn, was used for the next two Winslow six-masters—the Ruth E. Merrill and the Alice M. Lawrence—as well as two five-masters. But then someone decided—J. S. Winslow & Company? Percy & Small?—that the design needed further improvement. The design assignment was turned over to Bant Hanson, as Rideout had died two years earlier.

Hanson produced a half model representing a very burdensome schooner with a 275-foot keel, 47.6-foot beam measured to outside of planking, and a 28.6-foot depth of hold.[110] Although no vessel was ever built to those exact dimensions, it does appear that the last three six-masters built in the world came from that model: the Edward J. Lawrence, Edward B. Winslow, and Wyoming. Unfortunately for his-

torical certitude, there is no surviving letter, invoice, or journal entry that ties the "Wyoming" model to the other two schooners. And only one published statement ties the design of the Wyoming to Bant Hanson, the brief article published in *International Marine Engineering* in 1910. However, the writer of the article apparently drew his information directly from Percy & Small, and possibly from Bant Hanson, himself.[111]

Tying the "Wyoming" model to the Lawrence and the Winslow is a little more problematical. Unfortunately, none of the bill files for these three vessels have survived, although the summary cost accounts have. None of the latter, however, list the expense category "Model & Moulds" found in the accounts of earlier schooners using original models. But the person (or persons) who compiled the summary cost accounts was not a shipbuilder and tended to categorize costs by the name of the vendor rather than by the type of service or material provided. For example, designers Fred Rideout and Bant Hanson also provided extensive services surveying ship timber delivered to the shipyard. Percy & Small's bookkeeper had the habit of lumping *all* of their services under the surveying category rather than breaking them out into type of service rendered.[112]

It is instructive to look at the "Surveyor" charges on the last three six-masters as set forth in the individual summary cost accounts: Edward J. Lawrence—$584.19; Edward B. Winslow—$326.64; Wyoming—$238.36. The charges for the

LAWRENCE are way out of line when compared to her two near sisters, even when Bant Hanson's charge of $129.89 for "repairing moulds etc." is subtracted.[113] However, they would not be out of line if a part of the total was for half or a third of the cost of model and moulds, the rest being charged to the other two schooners.

Although Hanson's charge for repairing moulds appears to suggest that the LAWRENCE was being built from a pre-existing model, the actual timing is wrong. The billing was dated after the moulds had been shipped back from Virginia with the frame timber. It is apparent that Hanson needed to replace missing or damaged moulds before the ship carpenters could begin assembling the frames. It is also likely that a portion of the "Surveyor" costs for the WINSLOW and WYOMING were actually charges to repair and/or replace damaged or missing moulds.[114]

There is one more factor that points to three vessels built from the same model. These three schooners, with the exception of some minor cosmetic differences, were so close in appearance as to suggest common parentage. So it was that the last six-master and her two sisters were the most advanced wooden sailing vessels built with traditional techniques in the world. They also represented the most successful traditional response to the stresses placed upon large wooden hulls.

It took courage to go forth and raise the funds for a giant schooner in 1908, a schooner that required an investment of $2,575 per $1/64$ (+/- $95,000 in 1998).[115] Although this was a substantial cost, the two big Winslow sisters went for considerably more, reflecting Eleazer Clark's tendency to charge heavily for the firm's services and the generous contract terms worked out with Percy & Small.[116] Less expensive notwithstanding, Percy & Small still had to raise the money, an exercise made difficult by the sudden death of super-salesman Ocea Cahill. But there were those willing to fill Mr. Cahill's capacious shoes: John Brooks—brother of Governor Brooks—and S. L. Dodd (otherwise unidentified). Between them, they raised 21 percent of the total cost.[117]

Following her launching (see Chapter 1), WYOMING went into service. After her dramatic three-week trip to Newport News—dramatic, at least, in the eyes of the press and shareholders whose expensive investment apparently disappeared—she put into port no less the worse for wear. That was the most excitement the big schooner generated for the next seven-and-a-half years. The rest of it was the endless sailing back and forth from the coal ports to Boston and Portland. Throughout the period she sailed under the Percy & Small colors (December 1909–April 1917), she made eighty-three trips north with coal, thirty to Portland, and the balance to Boston.

Under the meticulous and experienced command of Captain McLeod, WYOMING avoided all the perils that appeared to lie in wait for her fellow coal schooners. Groundings were unheard of, as were lost anchors, and limping into port with sails blown out, gear adrift, rudder disabled, or hull badly strained was an unknown phenomenon as far as the biggest schooner was concerned. She was apparently not only lucky, but for all of her great size, WYOMING was considered to be a good sailer, easily handled and responsive to her helm. McLeod, who had spent forty years at sea before taking the Bath giant claimed, "She is as handy as a yacht and the best working vessel I ever put my foot into."[118]

McLeod never commented on what he thought of the series of time charters Percy & Small arranged for the big schooner starting in 1914. A good arrangement when business was slow and layups were likely, the time charter could turn into a huge burden on a rising charter market. But it did provide a fixed charter rate for the "time" of the charter, a sort of guaranteed wage which, with careful management of the vessel, would assure a steady, if unspectacular, return on investment.

When freight rates began to skyrocket in 1915 and into 1916, some shipping firms canceled their time charters, preferring to pay the penalties and/or substituting another vessel—obviously less capable—to carry out the terms. But Percy & Small appear to have carried out all their charter terms at considerable cost to themselves and the owners by late 1916 and early 1917.[119]

When WYOMING came out from under her $.70 per ton charter with International Paper Company in

April 1917, she was immediately sold to the France & Canada Steamship Company for a price variously reported to be $300,000, $350,000, or $500,000.[120] The former figure, although widely accepted, appears low under the circumstances. The only two schooners at all comparable to WYOMING were the LAWRENCE and WINSLOW, her smaller sisters. The WINSLOW officially sold for $325,000 and the LAWRENCE for $315,000 within weeks of WYOMING. But we now know that the real sale price for the LAWRENCE—the

oldest and more hardworked of the trio—as well as the WINSLOW, was approximately $400,000 (+/- $4 million in 1998) each in an apparent scheme engineered by Eleazer Clark that was designed to line his pockets at the expense of the owners. It was detected by one captain (Orville S. Pinkham, formerly of the MAJOR PICKANDS) who passed his suspicions along to a large owner in Winslow vessels, James W. Parker. The latter threatened Clark with exposure and jail and Clark eventually disgorged most, if not all, of the

WYOMING at Santos, Brazil, during the late fall or early winter of 1917, unloading coal using her own gear and hoisting engines. Percy & Small was never able to take advantage of the foreign charter market for WYOMING thanks to a lengthy time charter with International Paper Company. As soon as she was free of that charter, she was sold to the France & Canada Steamship Company, who sent her first to France and then to Brazil. Note the clothesline radio antenna strung between the jigger topmast and spanker topmast.

Courtesy: Penobscot Marine Museum

funds collected from France & Canada above the reported sale price.[121]

Even if Captain Percy was totally unaware of the fiduciary lapse of his best customer (and connived in by France-Canada)—and there is absolutely no reason to believe that he even had an inkling—the public sale prices for the two big Winslow six-masters suggests that the $300,000 figure for WYOMING is too low. It does not seem possible under the circumstances that Percy & Small would have settled for less than $350,000 for their flagship, a newer and larger schooner in better shape than the two Winslow six-masters.

How well did WYOMING shareholders come out on their investment in the big schooner? The short answer is that we do not know. The financial records for the big schooner are virtually non-existent. Only one dividend statement survives, dated February 17, 1911. Additional information can also be found in Percy & Small's Annual Statement for 1915, but it is limited specifically to that year and the net receipts from dividends accruing to Percy & Small's shares in the vessel.[122] It's a shocker, however. Percy & Small's dividends from WYOMING for that one year appear to total $8,341.50!

Percy & Small either owned more shares in the schooner than it was telling the Bath tax collector, or it was acting as trustee for a number of non-local owners. According to the *Bath Ship Book*, Percy & Small were paying taxes on $3/128$ of WYOMING, but the 1915 dividends were definitely not generated by so little an ownership position. Given the number of trips made

that year (thirteen), the amount of coal carried (estimated at 76,000 tons), the average rate ($.70 per ton), and the estimated annual operating cost of $29,000, her net earnings for the year would be approximately $24,200 or $378 per $1/64$.[123] In order to generate $8,341.50 in dividends, Percy & Small would have to control $22/64$ of the vessel shares, about a third of the total ownership, far too much even if the firm was concealing a portion of its holdings from the Bath tax collector. It is more likely that Percy & Small held a number of shares in trust agreements, a situation reflected in the high level of earnings.

WYOMING's net income can be estimated using the EDWARD B. WINSLOW as a guide and adjusting for the increased cargo capacity and operating cost of the larger schooner. On the basis of that estimate, it appears that the Percy & Small schooner had already paid her owners approximately 80 percent of her original cost when sold to the France & Canada Steamship Company. If the $350,000 sale price was, indeed, the benchmark, WYOMING owners received nearly three dollars for every dollar plunked down on the world's largest wooden sailing vessel. It was a substantial return, amounting to 40 percent per year over the life of Percy & Small's managing ownership.

The success of an investment is more often than not a matter of timing. Those who supported the construction did very well by their commitment of financial resources to the big schooner. Those who built her, however, had to be satisfied with hard work, skills applied, a living wage, and the knowledge of a job well done.

---

[1] At the beginning of 1900, 6,981 GRT of shipping sailed under the P&S house flag. When 1909 drew to a close, the fleet had grown to 27,144 GRT.

[2] See Chapter 4.

[3] A detailed discussion of the CLIFFORD/SMALL model can be found in the appendices.

[4] *BT*, 2/7/1901.

[5] *BT*, 2/7 and 2/27/1901.

[6] WFP to Captain D. H. Sumner, 5/6/1901, Palmer Collection. Palmer wrote: "With regard to the HELEN W. MARTIN, we all admitted in a spirit of great friendliness,

that the vessel had started in her scarfs and butts in a great many places, and that in general she did not seem to be wearing well." The MARTIN had then been in service just over a year.

[7] *BT*, 4/20/1901; "There are two steel 'hog straps' on each side twelve inches wide and six eighths thick, running well forward and pretty well aft."

[8] "Memorias del Capitan Daniel," Museo Maritima, Montevideo, Uruguay. Copy from Douglas K. and Linda J. Lee Collection. Captain Henry Daniel surveyed the SMALL in 1921 at Montevideo after she had been drydocked and

fell off her blocks. At the time he found her "badly hogged."

[9] Reprinted in *BT*, 3/23/1901. Barlow then lived in Providence and it was reported that [7]/64 of the SMALL was owned in that city.

[10] *BT*, 6/20/1911. An earlier story (1/31/1911) had Captain Ellis Haskell buying the captain's interest but this appears to have fallen through.

[11] *BT*, 9/6/1902; Parker, *Coal Schooners*, pp. 87–89.

[12] *BT*, 3/10/1909.

[13] *NYMR*, 10/12/1910.

[14] MARTHA P. SMALL & Owners in account with Miller & Houghton, Inc., etc; materials found in the Frank M. Hodgkins Account Book, SM 43/7, MMM.

[15] *BT*, 12/18/1915. The SMALL made basically two trips per year to South America, more than doubling her earnings per year over that which she earned in the coal trade prior to the war.

[16] Schooner "Martha P. Small," Report of Survey, Record of Foreign and American Shipping, 8/21/1916, Drake Papers, MS-197, MMM.

[17] Charles Desmond, *Wooden Shipbuilding*. New York: Rudder Publishing Co., 1919. See Figures 42a and 50, pp. 55, 63.

[18] *BT*, 8/9/1917.

[19] It was the SMALL's misfortune to fall off the blocks in 1920 and not a year earlier. Then, it would probably have been worth the owner's effort to pay her bills. But by mid-1920 the shipping business was saturated with tonnage, and sailing vessels had become a glut on the market.

[20] Captain Henry Daniel Account, Douglas K. and Linda J. Lee Collection; *NYMR*, 7/28/1920 and 6/13/1923.

[21] Aside from the numerous stories and items in the press, occasional entries in *PSJ* and Percy & Small Trial Balances, the CRESSY's construction bill files and approximately three-quarters of her earnings statements while under the P&S house flag have survived. The latter are particularly useful in tracking her itinerary, charter rates, earning history, and repair record.

[22] The CORA F. CRESSY was being built from a different model than the SMALL, but configuration of decks was a design decision separate from hull form. The CRESSY's half model, in the collection of Maine Maritime Museum, depicts a schooner with the long poop configuration. The photograph was taken by Ernest or Frank Stinson from their home on the west side of Washington Street in mid-July 1901. The photo date is confirmed by the presence of the ELEANOR A. PERCY, sans her headgear, in the background, following her collision with the GEORGE W. WELLS. The PERCY arrived in Bath for repairs sometime between 7 and 14 July.

[23] This photo was also taken by one of the Stinson brothers from the family's front yard. The MERRY appears to be ready for launching (11/14), and the MARTIN left the shipyard on the 11th or 12th. Lack of any activity or workmen means the photo was taken on a Sunday, hence 10 November.

[24] Schooner #11 Construction Bill File, Parker Collection; *PSJ*, p. 135. Unfortunately, Rideout's bill is not in the file, but McFadden Bros. delivered two models to the shipyard from Rideout's loft on 25 October 1901, the cost of which was charged to schooner #11. Fred Rideout charged P&S a total of $560.04 for his services on the CRESSY. Although he did some timber surveying, it is unlikely that his bill for this would have exceeded $150. This leaves the balance of his bill, +/- $410, for making models, lofting, moulds, etc., about twice what that work would normally cost. Certainly, from conception to completion there were some serious design changes.

[25] Captain Douglas K. Lee, "Deck Configurations of Percy & Small Schooners." Unpublished memo, 12/15/1991.

[26] Construction Bill File, Schooner #11, Parker Collection.

[27] *PSJ*, pp. 136–37; *BT*, 4/10/1902. Sixty-eight owners had purchased shares in the CRESSY ranging from [16]/64 to [1]/256. Fully 55 percent of the ownership was local, many being the usual subcontractors or suppliers. Aside from the group of Cressy friends and associates, other owners included several of Ocea Cahill's upstate New Yorkers.

[28] Adding power to the yawl boat enabled schooner captains to report quickly to the coal docks for order in loading or unloading. Yawl boats soon became another focal point in the competitive arena of the coal business. Captain Harding sold the CRESSY's small power boat within a year and had Harry Stinson build her a full-sized, powered yawl boat.

[29] CFC Statements of Earnings, #1–3, Parker Collection. If one took into account straightline depreciation of 5 percent per year, her return, net of depreciation, was 1 percent.

[30] CFC Statements of Earnings, #4–13, Parker Collection. This was her best year until ca. 1916–17, but her earnings statements are not complete for that period.

[31] CFC Statements of Earnings, Parker Collection. Nowhere in the statements are credits for payments from the owners of PARTHIAN, nor are there any charges against owners of the CRESSY for payment to the owners of the PARTHIAN.

[32] CFC Statements of Earnings, #14, Parker Collection.

[33] Interview with Bernard T. Zahn by Douglas K. and Linda J. Lee, 1985–86. Zahn removed 67 tons of sand ballast after bringing the schooner to Bremen. CFC Statements of Earnings, #1–24, Parker Collection. After

1909, as rates declined and charters were harder to come by, the CRESSY began carrying tonnages close to what she had averaged before ballast was added. Her largest recorded cargo was 4,034.5 tons, carried in 1914—not bad for a schooner that was rated at 3,850 tons when new.

[34] CFC Statements of Earnings, #15–23, Parker Collection. Net earnings in 1905 totalled $9,600 vs. $1,152 the previous year.

[35] CFC Statements of Earnings, #101, #104, Parker Collection; BT, 4/5, 6/17, and 10/27/1915, and 2/4/1916.

[36] NYMR, 10/25, 11/1, 11/29, and 12/6/1916. For all the expense, the schooner had a net balance in favor of its owners of $29,186.83 when she returned from Brazil. This was held in escrow until a legal case was subsequently decided in the courts.

[37] CFC Statements of Earnings, #106, Parker Collection.

[38] P&S to Captain W. R. Dickinson, 8/29/1917, in CFC Statements of Earnings, Parker Collection.

[39] CFC Statements of Earnings, Parker Collection. Total dividends including sale price for which there are surviving records come to $352,702 against her original cost of $112,652.80.

[40] Letter: (Mrs.) Mary B. Leeming to Samuel L. Lowe, 7/16/1973, Curatorial Files, Maine Maritime Museum. Captain James Platt Barker later joined the "Yankees" when he commanded the last square-rigger under the U.S. flag in commercial service, TUSITALA (ex-SIERRA LUCENA, ex-SOPHIE), owned by James A. Farrell.

[41] NYMR, 4/18/1917; BI, 1/26/1922.

[42] NYMR, 12/2/1925.

[43] NYMR, 1/19/1927.

[44] NYMR, 4/13/1927.

[45] NYMR, 10/19 and 12/28/1927, 3/21 and 4/25/1928.

[46] NYMR, 6/20/1928.

[47] Interview, Bernard T. Zahn with Douglas K. and Linda J. Lee, 1985–86. Zahn said that the bronze seacock valve had been smashed by the watchman to insure his pumping job.

[48] Copy of Bill of Sale, Douglas K. and Linda J. Lee Collection.

[49] Conversations between author and Bernard T. Zahn, August 1972, at Bremen, ME.; Interviews of Bernard T. Zahn and Nancy Zahn by Douglas K. and Linda J. Lee in 1985–86.

[50] Hulls #17 and #18 were built from the same model as the ADDIE M. LAWRENCE (#15), although they were longer and, thanks to different deck configurations, considerably deeper than the orginal.

[51] BT, 7/16/1904. As far as the authors can determine, Percy & Small never used the model of the CORA F. CRESSY again.

[52] Ibid.

[53] BT, 7/18/1904.

[54] Ibid.

[55] See Chapter 9 for a more detailed discussion of the shipping business.

[56] BT, 11/14/1904.

[57] I&E, 8/30/1905.

[58] BT, 8/20/1910.

[59] BT, 1/16/1914.

[60] Parker, Coal Schooners, p. 68.

[61] The storm was known thereafter as the PALMER Gale.

[62] A square-rigger could set just enough sail to hold her on the wind without driving ahead. The great schooners had to be driven hard to prevent falling off into the trough which, in turn, frequently caused them to labor heavily. See William H. Hill, "At Sea in the Blizzard of '98," Rudder, June 1951, p. 19.

[63] BT, 10/9/1913.

[64] BT, 1/16/1914.

[65] Black crews were quite common on the great schooners. See Chapter 9.

[66] BT, 1/16/1914.

[67] Ibid.

[68] "Memorandum of Southern Oak Timber Measured from Schnr. Annie F. Kimball To Wm. T. Donnell," Geo. A. McFadden, Surveyor. 12/23/1904 to 1/6/1905. Schooner #27 Bill File, Parker Collection.

[69] Percy & Small, good customers of Hoskins, may have been offered a very good price on an additional frame but did not want to tie up their cash. Mr. Donnell then agreed to put up the cash and hold the frame until the firm was in a position to buy it with a reasonable profit accruing to Mr. Donnell. Just as with the FANNIE PALMER II frame, it took longer than originally anticipated to make use of it.

[70] Information on the Brooks family was drawn from: Francois M. Dickman, "America's Largest Wooden Vessel: The Six Masted Schooner Wyoming," Wyoming Annals, Spring/Summer 1994, volume 66, nos. 1 & 2, p. 42; Bryant Butler Brooks, Memoirs of Bryant Butler Brooks, Glendale, CA: Arthur H. Clark Company, 1939.

[71] PSJ, p. 285.

[72] "Wyoming: Historic Governor's Mansion," Brochure, Information & Education Services Office, Division of Parks & Cultural Resources, Wyoming Department of Commerce, 5/93. Natrona County Tribune (WY), 6/12/1907, "Mrs. B. B. Brooks and the children came up from Cheyenne last week and will spend the summer on the ranch."

[73] WFP to SRP, 4/22/1907; WFP to John Brooks, 4/18/1908, Palmer Collection.

[74] Natrona County Tribune, 6/12/1907.

[75] Dickman, footnote #14, p. 43. He identified the

Richardson Brothers (they founded and ran for many years the Consolidated Royalty Oil Co.) and J. A. Fullerton of Cheyenne; Harold Banner, a large rancher at Glenrock, near Casper; Patrick Sullivan from Casper; and J. D. Woodruff, a business associate of the governor. It should be noted that Lena Brooks McCleary (sponsor of WYOMING) and her husband later purchased the Banner Ranch.

[76] Bill of Sale of Enrolled Vessel, Sam'l R. Percy & Frank A. Small Copts. To B. B. Brooks Co., Casper, Wyo. Entered: 12/13/1907, Parker Collection.

[77] *BSB*, 1908; also see entries May–December 1907 in Percy & Small: Trial Balances (December 1901–December 1916), Parker Collection.

[78] Notes of Parker interview with Eleanor Percy Irish, 10/24/1954, Parker Collection. The Percys collected dividends far longer on their Wyoming oil investment than the Wyomingites collected on schooners. Mrs. Irish still had the stock in 1954.

[79] *BT*, 4/24, 26/1907; *BE*, 5/14/1902; *BI*, 6/9/1900.

[80] *I&E*, 6/26 and 10/5/1907; *BT*, 2/4/1908 and 7/6/1915.

[81] *PSJ*, p. 350; Percy & Small paid Donnell for the use of his shipyard for new construction, docking and repairing vessels, and for storage over a period of several years. See Schooners #28, #30 Summary Construction Statements, Parker Collection.

[82] Bant Hanson to P&S, 6/6/1907, Schooner #27 Construction Bill File, Parker Collection.

[83] The three oldest Brooks daughters graduated from Dana Hall and the youngest graduated from Chevy Chase. Abby received a BA from Wellesley College, and returned to Wyoming to teach.

[84] *BT*, 10/22, 23/1907; *BI*, 10/26/1907.

[85] *BT*, 10/22/1907.

[86] Captain T. Clarke Conwell to James Stevens, 2/1/1977, courtesy James Stevens.

[87] *BT*, 10/23/1907. A copy of the menu can be found in the collections of Maine Maritime Museum in SM 25/19.

[88] Payne's Second Regiment Orchestra to P&S, 10/22/1907, Schooner #27 Construction Bills, Parker Collection; New Meadows Inn to P&S, 10/28/1907, Schooner #27 Construction Bills, Parker Collection. The orchestra—seven men—cost $24.70 (+/- $380 in 1998), and the inn charged $103.75 (+/- $1,600 in 1998) for 141 dinners, extra lobster salad and celery, 75 cigars, and an extra tip of $8.00 to the waitresses—ah, the good old days!

[89] *BT*, 10/24/1907.

[90] Schooner #27 Construction Bill File, Parker Collection. Dated entries on accounts from Johnson Brothers (ship chandlers), Hyde Windlass, and W. W. Mason and McFadden Bros. (teamsters), J. A. Winslow Co. (ship plumbers), and David T. Percy & Sons (department store) illustrate the quantity and type of work being completed.

[91] *Portland Express*, 12/31/1909, interview with Captain Barlow.

[92] *BT*, 12/21/1910.

[93] Brooks, *Memoirs of B. B. Brooks*, p. 264.

[94] T. C. Conwell to J. P. Stevens, 2/1/1977.

[95] *NYMR*, 7/28/1920.

[96] *BI*, 3/31/1921; *NYMR*, 3/30/1921.

[97] *NYMR*, 5/4/1921. Where did that burgee go?

[98] *BT*, 9/14/1915.

[99] *NYMR*, 5/26, 9/19, and 9/22/1915.

[100] *BT*, 3/29/1905.

[101] *BT*, 1/6/1906.

[102] *BT*, 12/16/1905.

[103] *BT*, 4/16, 20/1906.

[104] *BT*, 11/25/1916.

[105] *Ibid.*; *BT*, 11/27, 12/5, and 12/7/1916.

[106] Marston L. Hamlin, "The Old and Not-So-Old," *Rudder*, March 1948, p. 64.

[107] Summary Construction Statement for Hull #20, Parker Collection.

[108] *BT*, 4/17/1912.

[109] *BT*, 9/17/1915.

[110] The half model is in the collections of the Patten Free Library in Bath. Captain Douglas K. Lee scaled off the model's dimensions.

[111] "Six Master Schooner Wyoming," *International Marine Engineering*, v. 15, January 1910. The drawing for this article was done by Jacob A. Stevens, then working as a draftsman at Bath Iron Works. The "Stevens brothers" were credited for the text. The detailed information in the drawing and the text appear to have been drawn from Percy & Small and Bant Hanson.

[112] Construction Bill File, Schooner #18, Parker Collection. The Rideout bill totals $193.73 for surveying timber and repairing moulds, both costs being broken out. But the Summary Cost Statement, Schooner #18, Parker Collection, lumps it all together under the category "Surveyor, F. W. Rideout."

[113] *PSJ*, p. 337; entry is dated April 25, 1907.

[114] *PSJ*, p. 378; there are two entries charging schooner #30 for unspecified services of Bant Hanson dated 1/20/1908 (16 months before construction started) for $21.73 and $120.00. At that point in the process, these are more apt to represent work on the moulds.

[115] Percy & Small: Monthly Trial Balance Ledger (1902–16), entries for November and December 1909, Parker Collection.

[116] EDWARD J. LAWRENCE: $2,800 per 1/64; EDWARD B.

WINSLOW: $2,730 per ¹/₆₄. Percy & Small's contract with the Winslow firm set the shipyard's price for each schooner at $172,800. The price to the shipyard for WYOMING appears to have been $164,800.

¹¹⁷ Summary Cost Statement, Schooner #30, Parker Collection. The two gentlemen collected a total of $869.06 in commissions which, at a 2.5 percent commission, represents ²⁷/₁₂₈, or 21 percent of the total ownership.

¹¹⁸ *BT*, 1/31/1910.

¹¹⁹ *BT*, 4/7/1916 and 3/27/1917.

¹²⁰ *NYMR*, 4/18/1917; *BT*, 4/12/1917; *BI*, 8/11/1921.

¹²¹ Information on this curious scheme which saw Clark and Maynard Bird form a corporation to "buy" the EDWARD J. LAWRENCE at the published price of $315,000 and immediately resell to France & Canada for +/- $395,000, thus gaining an instant profit of $80,000 (+/- $800,000 in 1998) can be found in the following sources: Parker, Notes of Conversation with Mr. Willis Hay, Cape Elizabeth, 23 September 1962, Parker Collection; this is supported by a small file of letters from J. S. Winslow & Co. to Mrs. Mildred Hay involving the sale of her ¹/₁₂₈ of the LAWRENCE and a memo simply entitled Sale of Schr. "Edward J. Lawrence" which has three entries re: the sale of the vessel as follows: "June 1917 Sale of Schr. Per 64th . . . 4,675.78"; "Nov. [1917] 2d sale so called . . . 1,280.65"; "Mar. 1918 Settlement through Lawyer . . . 449.49." Another paper in the collection gives in tabular form the amount received for each of five Winslow schooners. The figures strongly suggest that Clark attempted to work his scheme on at least four other schooners besides the LAWRENCE if one compares the price received by the tabulator and the published price of the sale. Schooner EDWARD J. LAWRENCE File, Edmund Blunt Library of Mystic Seaport Museum.

¹²² Schooner WYOMING & Owners, Statement #12, Cameron Papers; Statement, Year 1915, ending Dec. 31, Parker Collection.

¹²³ This is an average based on the figures for the EDWARD B. WINSLOW, adjusted for the larger WYOMING. The WINSLOW figures are from: Schr. Edward B. Winslow Statements, 1908–17, Parker Collection.

Coal for the Hearths of New England

Lest we forget, the original—and for many years co-equal—business of Percy & Small was the coastwise charter trade, principally carrying coal. But the boom that marked the end of the nineteenth century and had encouraged our partners to greater heights began to show signs of uncertainty as Percy & Small eased into the twentieth century. The situation, in fact, took on all the characteristics of a dormant volcano that once again began to rumble, shake the earth, and emit clouds of steam and ash. Was this a sign of a return to another period of predictable activity to be followed by another spell of dormancy, or did it presage a fundamental change in the historical pattern?

SHIPPING BUSINESS BASICS

The basic agreement in the shipping business was the charter party, a contract between the shipper and the vessel's managing owners. The charter could be for one voyage, for a specified tonnage of cargo delivered, or for a stated period of time. Also included in the agreement were clauses dealing with cost of service (priced by the ton for coal, by the board foot for lumber and timber, and by the actual count for railroad ties, for example), and the number of so-called lay days permitted for loading and unloading once the vessel reported ready to take on or discharge cargo.

The shippers, the charterers of the coal schooners, fell into three categories. There were the wholesale coal dealers, for example Boston's C. H. Sprague and the Warren & Monks Company, or Portland's Randall & McAllister. There were also major industrial customers such as S. D. Warren Co., the Maine Central Railroad, gas companies, and other major consumers of bituminous coal. Some of the large coal mining firms also maintained sales offices, especially in Boston, and were active in the shipping market.[1]

The managing owners maintained constant contact with all the shippers, attempting to place their available tonnage at the best possible terms. The shippers, of course, were attempting to move their coal to the Northeast at *their* best advantage, meaning as cheaply as possible. As we shall see, the resulting tension between the operators and the shippers led to some bitter struggles during the first decade of the century over freight rates and such arcane issues as demurrage and turn in loading.

Percy & Small relied principally on the single-voyage charter during their early years, especially when the freight rates were generally on an upward trend. In later years, when business became more unsettled and competition for coastwise charters intensified and rates were declining, the firm put increasing emphasis on time charters that provided guaranteed work for one or more vessels, albeit at reduced or relatively low rates.[2] Although time charters provided guaranteed work when times were slow, there was always the danger that new business at higher rates could be lost, witness Percy & Small's experience with WYOMING and the CORA F. CRESSY when freight rates shot up during the early years of World War I and the two schooners were tethered to time charters. (See Chapter 10.) On the other hand, if the daily charter rate declined during a time charter, the owners could find their schooner receiving more per ton than vessels currently in the market.[3]

The inclusion of lay days in the charter contract, known as a charter party, was intended to protect the vessel owners from excessive delays when loading or unloading, since some shippers were not above using a chartered vessel as a floating warehouse rather than invest sufficient capital and energy to ensure prompt dispatch. Others played the game of locking as many schooners into charters at favorable rates as possible, thus keeping the carriers away from their competition, but without the facilities and/or coal to ensure

The basic business contract in the shipping business was the charter party that defined the terms between the shipper and the shipowner. The Percy & Small-built DUNHAM WHEELER is seen here loading railroad ties at Pensacola using her own steam hoisting gear. Among other things, her charter party set the freight charge per tie, number of days to load and discharge, destination of cargo, and who was to pay for loading, discharging, and insuring the cargo. Note the pier has lost its outboard end, no doubt from a Gulf hurricane, one of the calculated risks for schooners delivering or loading cargo there.

Courtesy: Captains Douglas K. and Linda J. Lee

prompt dispatch. These delays were expensive for the owners but, thanks to demurrage clauses in the charters that defined when compensation for unreasonable delay kicked in, they became even more expensive for the shippers and, by extension, the consumers.[4] It should come as no surprise to learn that William F. Palmer was the uncrowned king of demurrage and his insistence upon every penny did little to endear him, or his fellow schooner operators for that matter, to the coal shippers.[5] In fact, heavy demurrage charges may have contributed to accelerating the development of port facilities, thereby accelerating the decline of the great schooners.

A key part of the demurrage issue was the debate over "absolute turn in loading," a phrase that became the battle cry of coal schooner operators. The master of a schooner arriving at the loading port made haste (underscoring the importance of the engine-powered yawl boat) to report his vessel's presence and readiness for loading to the shipper. This put his vessel at the bottom of the loading list behind all the vessels that had previously reported and were yet to load. It also started the clock on the lay days. All subsequent arrivals would, in turn, take their respective places *after* him on the list. The same routine was followed when the schooner arrived at the delivery port.

Some schooner operators—with justice—believed that this custom was being eroded by the shippers who not only gave steamships priority to bunker at the coal docks, but applied that same priority to steam colliers and barges to load their cargo. Percy & Small's own S. P. BLACKBURN experienced this kind

Heavy consumers often had their own coal docks, sometimes equipped with the latest in unloading equipment. But even that could be overtaxed; witness this view of the Portland waterfront in 1911 as three six-masters (*left to right*, ELEANOR A. PERCY, ADDIE M. LAWRENCE, RUTH E. MERRILL) overwhelm the port facilities at the gas company and Maine Central Railroad coal pockets.
Courtesy: Captains Douglas K. and Linda J. Lee

When port facilities were pushed over the limit, schooner masters were compelled to anchor to await their turn to come alongside to load or unload. Such is the fate of the deeply loaded EDWARD B. WINSLOW on a breezy fall day in 1910 as she lies at anchor off Portland's Promenade. However, demurrage clauses usually specified loading and unloading in turn and assessed penalties against shipper or consignee for undue delays.

Courtesy: Captains Douglas K. and Linda J. Lee

of treatment when chartered to the Garfield & Proctor Coal Company to carry a cargo of bituminous from Baltimore to Boston at $2 per ton. Percy & Small reported that it took *thirty-seven* days to load 2,737 tons from the time the BLACKBURN was reported ready to take on cargo, as opposed to the seven or eight days one might normally expect; the shipper refused to load the schooner in turn, allowing later reporting barges and steamers to haul into the loading berth ahead of her, and to provide her with a full and complete cargo in accordance with the charter.[6]

This and a number of similar incidents ultimately brought forth an unequivocal statement from the schooner operators who, through their industry coalition, called the Atlantic Carriers'

Association (ACA), declared:

We, the undersigned, hereby covenant, promise and agree, to and with each other, not to close any charter for any vessel in any way controlled by us, to load coal in any port, unless it be specially agreed therein that such vessel shall be loaded in her turn and that no priority for loading shall be given to any steamer, barge or other vessel, except only steamers calling to fill their bunkers for their consumption, and vessels loading coal for the United States Government.[7]

As a practical matter, they also modified the standard charter party, inserting a clause that each vessel would be loaded in turn.[8]

It should be noted, however, that the ACA was not the first organization to raise this issue; the Vessel Owner's and Captain's National Association, headquartered in Philadelphia, was founded during the 1880s to promote the causes of the shipowners. Although it was supplanted by the Atlantic Carriers' Association after the turn of the century, many of the ACA's causes—absolute turn in loading, rate of discharge, and limiting the length of barge tows to two barges—had been high on the agenda of the Vessel Owner's & Captain's National Association.[9]

Of course, not all coal shippers felt obliged to honor the written contract, therefore, William F. Palmer felt obliged to sue. His suit, *Harding v. Cargo of 4,698 Tons of New Rivers Steam Coal*, generated a landmark decision from the Federal District Court that confirmed the principle of absolute turn in loading.[10] It was one of the few significant victories won by the coal schooner operators in the twentieth century.

Ironically, Percy & Small subsequently lost a case against Union Sulphur Company for demurrage that revolved about absolute turn in loading and the question of when the lay day clock was started.[11] The Federal District Court had sustained Percy & Small's contention that lay days for the CORA F. CRESSY, Captain E. E. Haskell, began as soon as Captain Haskell reported his schooner ready to load cargo at the shipper's pier at Sabine Pass, Texas. But, when the Union Sulphur Company appealed the decision to the Circuit Court, the latter overturned the District Court in an example of legal hairsplitting that must have left Federal District Court Judge Hale, the man who had decided the *Harding v. 4,698 Tons of New Rivers Steam Coal* case four years earlier, spinning in his judicial chair.[12]

The Circuit Court of Appeals decision was based on the clause typed into the charter following the usual statement that lay days commenced after the vessel arrived and reported ready to receive cargo. The typed clause, "vessel to take turn in loading," was in the minds of the justices enough to delay the start of lay days until such time as the CRESSY took her turn to come alongside the loading dock at Sabine Pass. This decision effectively required that the schooner operators have a clause written into every charter specifying that lay days started upon reporting even when turn in loading was observed if they were going to avoid lengthy delays or collect demurrage.

ATLANTIC CARRIERS' ASSOCIATION

When the Vessel Owner's & Captain's National Association failed to pursue an aggressive campaign, a number of coal carriers came together in 1900 to form the Atlantic Carriers' Association (ACA). The new organization's membership list grew to include schooner operators (Percy & Small, J. S. Winslow & Co., Gardiner G. Deering, William T. Donnell, William F. Palmer, Crowell & Thurlow, J. S. Emery & Co., John G. Crowley, etc.) and barge operators (Luckenbach, Scully, Thames Towboat, Staples Coal Co., etc.). Palmer would later claim that Atlantic Carriers' included 90 percent of all schooners, 85 percent of all schooners and barges combined, and 72 percent of all schooners, barges, and steamers.[13] It was, however, an organization whose dominant thrust reflected the interests of the schooner operators, particularly those from Maine.[14]

The longtime president of the association, Fields Pendleton, was a native of Islesboro although his fleet headquarters was at New York City. Vice president was our own Frank A. Small and treasurer was none other than Eleazer Clark. The only paid staff member was Edward C. Plummer, the Yarmouth (Maine)-born Bath Admiralty lawyer, who not only provided legal advice and services to the membership, but also served as the group's principal lobbyist in the halls of Congress.

Although the Atlantic Carriers' Association remained in existence for nearly a quarter century, no known records of its meetings, official correspondence, or finances have survived to this day. Even Plummer's autobiography dismissed in a few words his many years' service as the organization's linchpin.[15] However, hints of the association's activities can be gleaned from news stories and from the letters of William F. Palmer.

Purportedly organized to challenge the Virginia compulsory pilotage law and to throttle the Atlantic Coast Seamen's Union (the first successful seamen's union on the East Coast) before it grew too powerful, the ACA soon found itself embroiled in a variety of other issues as well. These included the previously discussed turn in loading, as well as higher freight rates, limitation of new coal schooner tonnage and competition in general, and eagle-eyed oversight of the laws protecting coastwise trade and American-built vessels.

Virginia's compulsory pilotage law was an anachronistic holdover from the early republic when the regulation of pilotage was reserved to the states. In 1871 Congress enacted legislation that placed authority for licensing pilots of coastwise steamers with the federal government, but left coastwise sailing vessels at the tender mercies of the several states. The seaboard states north of the Mason-Dixon line soon abolished compulsory pilotage—after all, most of the coastwise sailing fleet was owned in the North—and Maryland, seeking to strengthen its role as a coal shipping center, eliminated compulsory pilotage for vessels entering state waters to load coal. Virginia, however, was a different story.[16]

Home of the leading coal ports in North America, if not the world, the state was a stickler for the observance of compulsory pilotage. This, it should be noted, was not a position dictated by the desire for greater marine safety even though it was often couched in those terms. The real impetus behind the state's diligent support of the law was money—for the pilots and for the state.

Most of the skippers of the big coal schooners knew their way around Virginia's Hampton Roads and the coal ports at Norfolk and Newport News better than their own backyards. But they were required by law to have a licensed (in Virginia) pilot aboard when moving in these waters. Instead of hiring a pilot every time one was needed, the various schooner operators solved the problem by having Virginia license each of their captains as a pilot. The license was good for a year and cost ten cents per net register ton of the specific vessel. Thus the Virginia compulsory pilotage laws cost the owners of the CORA F. CRESSY $208.90 per year (+/- $3,200 in 1998).[17]

The ACA attempted to get a bill through Congress in 1902 to abolish state control of pilotage but it foundered, it would appear, on the rocks of political maneuvering. Nonetheless, the association continued to kick and scream—William F. Palmer even tried to enlist the assistance of the Atlantic Carriers' Association's arch enemy, the Atlantic Coast Seamen's Union![18] Virginia finally abolished compulsory pilotage in 1908. At that late date, it could only be described as a Pyrrhic victory for the ACA.

Another unsuccessful legislative effort on the part of the association focused upon legal ways and means of hamstringing the union by threatening seamen with immediate imprisonment if the person "… refuse[s] or neglects to join, or deserts from or refuses to proceed to sea in any vessel in which he is duly engaged to serve …."[19] It would effectively preclude any job action on the part of union seamen once they had shipped on a vessel. The "Seamen's Imprisonment Bill," as it was labeled by the union, also failed to make its way into law, thanks to the more aggressive, and successful, lobbying efforts of the union.

But the war was far from over. The Atlantic Carriers' Association collectively—with one notable exception—and individually pursued a number of anti-union measures.[20] They harassed the union by every means possible—legal and extralegal—and even went so far as to establish their own seamen's "union," the American Seamen's Federation.

SEAMEN AND THE UNION

Following the Civil War, service before the mast in the American merchant marine acquired a certain notoriety. Tales abounded of bully mates with hair-trigger tempers, belaying pins, marlinspikes, and brass knuckles, blood running in the scuppers, and food so bad that even the rats and cockroaches deserted at the first opportunity. Some of these tales were all too true; others were more imaginative than factual. But for the most part the tales applied to the deepwater merchant service, not to coasting. The latter service was subject to the same laws and abuses as the former but a major safety valve in the form of short voyages took much of the heat out of potentially explosive situations.

Historically, common seamen were regarded as being somewhat childlike, hapless, unreliable, and incapable of doing anything except under the direction of their superiors.[21] This attitude was even reflected to a degree in laws passed in the 1890s that were designed to improve the seaman's lot by abolishing the more notorious practices of shoreside crimps and providing regulations governing the sailors' rations and berthing spaces.

Childlike or not, seamen were shipped by the act of signing the shipping articles in the presence of representatives of the U.S. Shipping Commissioner. These same officials were also charged with adjudicating disputes between seamen and the captains. The articles served as a contract, binding the seamen to a period of service for a specified rate of pay and the rations and accommodations crewmen were entitled to by law.

Coal schooner crewmen were ordinarily shipped in northern ports for the passage to the coal port and return, or for a term of thirty days. If a long delay developed at the loading port, most of the crew was discharged after the thirty-day period, although the captain usually retained the chief mate, cook, engineer, and sometimes a seaman or two who, in exchange for a bunk and meals, were willing to stay aboard, stand anchor watches, and do necessary ship's work. When the vessel was finally loaded, the captain shipped the balance of his crew for the passage north.

Wages for seamen were not very high, although one study by the U. S. Shipping Commissioner noted that those engaged in the coasting trades in schooners received an average of $33.66 (+/- $520 in 1998) per month during 1901–02, a higher sum than averaged by men shipping on square-riggers and schooners engaged in foreign trade, but less than crewmen received on all categories of steam vessels.[22] The surge in schooner construction that followed the end of the 1893 depression created an additional demand for

men to man these vessels, enabling the Atlantic Coast Seamen's Union to get the acquiescence of the schooner operators in 1902 to a pay scale based on vessel tonnage.[23] However, the decline in freight rates in the following year made the reduction of the wage scale and the elimination of the Atlantic Coast Seamen's Union one of the foremost objectives of the Atlantic Carriers' Association after 1903.

The union members, in turn, resorted to a boycott against shipping aboard schooners whose management refused to pay scale. The union's "walking delegates" (business agents) intercepted gangs of seamen on their way to ship aboard schooners in port and attempted to persuade them not to sign the shipping papers. They appeared aboard the vessels that had already shipped some or all of their crews and sought to convince the non-union crews to leave the vessels—an act viewed as desertion by the owners and the law—in an effort to force the schooner operators to accept the union scale.[24] And sometimes the union delegates resorted to threats and other forms of coercion.

The Atlantic Carriers' Association countered these tactics by appealing to the law and by recruiting principally African-American seamen (as well as West Indians and Bravas) willing to work for $5 less per month than their largely white counterparts in the Atlantic Coast Seamen's Union. For encouraging desertion, union delegates were arrested by local authorities for enticement, and crewmen who walked or were talking of deserting were jailed by local authorities and even restrained by some of the schooner captains and mates. Although lawyers for the union argued that no laws existed on the books that entitled authorities to take such steps, the courts supported the owners.[25]

In due time the black seamen became members in the American Seamen's Federation, the puppet of the Atlantic Carriers' Association, that was funded by members of the association through a "yellow-dog" (anti-union) fund started by Fields Pendleton in New York, but also mirrored in Boston and Norfolk. By establishing sailors' boardinghouses in the principal coal ports, the association attempted to de-claw the seamen's union by recruiting blacks to whom $30 per month was good pay, especially when that included

The crews of many of the great schooners were composed of white officers and engineers, with the bulk of
the deckhands being made up of African Americans. This was more a reflection of the owners' struggles
with the Atlantic Coast Seamen's Union than any effort on their part to promote the cause of blacks in
America. That, however, made little difference to the helmsman on the DAVIS PALMER, who probably
regarded $30 per month and the relatively good food on the big schooners to be a pretty good deal.

Courtesy: Palmer Collection, Maine Maritime Museum

food and lodging.[26] Although it was said that the blacks recruited to sail the big schooners lacked experience, necessitating the shipping of additional men, they soon came to dominate the crews shipped by Palmer, Percy & Small, and other Atlantic Carriers' Association operators.[27] Only one fleet—the Coastwise Transportation Company run by John G. Crowley—acceded to the Atlantic Coast Seamen's Union's demands, a position that assured Crowley of fairly quick dispatch for his schooners, but earned him the utter contempt of William F. Palmer, one of the movers of the counter-union movement.[28]

Palmer, who wore his prejudices on his sleeve, was indefatigable in the anti-union efforts at Boston. In one letter to Percy & Small, he wrote of a secret arrangement he had made with Boston's Police Commissioner to have a police boat put non-union crews aboard schooners (despite public statements to the contrary) to head off the walking delegates, and of how he made a three dollar donation to the union (he got a letter back thanking him and asking for more) in an effort to trace the union's bank account so that the Atlantic Carriers' Association could find a legal way to tie it up. "Let us then hang up our crews in Boston," he concluded, "until we get this Union broken. If we do not it will be our Waterloo and if we do the question will probably be settled for a long time."[29]

Percy & Small schooners were prominently involved in the strife between the Atlantic Carriers' Association and the Atlantic Coast Seamen's Union. After assembling six non-union Norwegian seamen for the ELEANOR A. PERCY, Captain Leroy McKown (acting for the ACA at the direction of Palmer) was escorting them to the ferry when John Lind, a union walking delegate came along and talked the men out of boarding the schooner. McKown then had the Boston police arrest Lind for enticing members of the crew to desert.[30] This case and a similar one involving the ADDIE M. LAWRENCE were tried in Boston and the union delegates were found guilty. The Massachusetts Supreme Court also got in on the act when it granted a permanent injunction prohibiting the union from interfering with non-union crewmen employed aboard coasters.[31]

In a more extreme case, the S. P. BLACKBURN, the first schooner to pay the Atlantic Coast Seamen's Union scale, became a battleground that ended with one man dead after a confrontation between non-union and union men as the schooner lay alongside a pier in Providence. Manned by a non-union crew of six black seamen from the Norfolk area, the schooner was boarded by five union representatives. A heated argument followed and shots were fired. One of the union men, Ernest Frohnhoffer, was mortally wounded. The local police arrested everyone present (where were the schooner's officers?) and launched a search for the Atlantic Coast Seamen's Union walking delegate who had disappeared following the shooting and was, ironically, an African American.[32]

In the end the Atlantic Carriers' Association prevailed over the Atlantic Coast Seamen's Union, although it did not have long to savor its victory. The union's wage scale was discarded and seamen could expect no more than $30 per month, even on the largest schooners.[33] The American Seamen's Federation came into being and served to funnel a considerable number of blacks, Bravas from the Cape Verde Islands who had settled around New Bedford, and more than a few Norwegians into the schooner fleet at the lower rate. By 1905 many of the longtime, white American seamen were abandoning their calling, complaining bitterly of the encroachment of the blacks upon what they regarded as their territory. One former seaman, reflecting some of the racist attitudes that have plagued American society in general and the labor movement in particular, offered the following appraisal of the situation:

The trouble is that captains will hire the negro sailors and leave the white man out of employment. They can get them for five and ten dollars a month less than they can get white men and they fill their vessels with them, for white men and negroes cannot work side by side in the same vessel before the mast.[34]

The ultimate purpose of the Atlantic Carriers' Association was to ensure that the membership's vessels maintained a competitive advantage over any and all possible rivals. Breaking the Atlantic Coast Seaman's Union, compelling adherence to the absolute turn in loading, and repealing Virginia's compulsory pilotage laws were all objectives that contributed to that end. These, and a few other successful battles, however, did not add up to final victory. By the end of the twentieth century's first decade, the schooner operators had been decisively defeated—even if some did not yet realize it.

The first of two principal rivals to the great coal schooners were the tugs and barges that began to appear in serious numbers during the 1890s.[35] The barges, either built-to-purpose schooner barges ranging up to 2,000 GRT or superannuated square-riggers that had been barged (converted to barges), were towed along the coast by powerful seagoing steam tugs that dropped them at their destinations. Picking up waiting "empties," the tug then hauled that string of barges back to one of the coal ports where they were assigned turns in loading. If this were a well-organized firm, the tug could then ideally pick up a string of already loaded barges anchored nearby and haul them north, returning later with the barges, now emptied, it had hauled north previously.

The oceangoing barges were not the typical harbor lighters, but large—often with two decks—wooden vessels resembling the sailing vessels from which they were derived. Many of these barges were built by Kelley, Spear, upriver from Percy & Small. Generally they carried a crew of four to five men aft in a prominent deckhouse topped by an enclosed wheelhouse. A small donkey boiler provided steam for the anchor and towing windlass and pumps, as well as for heating the crew's quarters. Most of the barges carried a baldheaded gaff rig with three or four masts and a single headsail that provided some assistance to the tug or even a modicum of self-propulsion capability.

Some barge companies, Luckenbach and Scully being two of the most prominent, took the less-expensive route of purchasing older wooden sailing vessels and barging them. Shorn of their soaring rigs, often with ugly wheelhouses plunked down on their after deckhouses and the name of their current owner billboarded prominently on their sides, some of America's most famous wooden square-riggers ended their days ignominiously at the end of a towline.[36]

By the first few years of the new century, barge operators were making serious inroads into bituminous coal traffic. They had pretty well eliminated the coal schooners from ports along Long Island Sound to New Bedford, although the perils of rounding Cape Cod still served to restrain the barge trade to the more eastern ports.[37] Part of the success of the barges west of Cape Cod was, in Mr. Palmer's view, attributable to the fact that the biggest, therefore the most competitive, schooners were too deep for those ports while the smaller, shallower barges were more economical than their schooner equivalents.[38] Smaller crews, no primage, more or less predictable times enroute, and a tug that didn't have to wait for its barges (waiting was always expensive for any steam vessel) as they navigated the delays and frustrations of the loading and unloading docks, all pointed to a competitor that could haul coal nearly as cheaply as the big schooners, but without the unpredictability of being strictly dependent upon wind and weather.

The tug/barge operators represented a small but significant block of the Atlantic Carriers' Association in its early years. Although some were in direct competition with the schooner operators (some, like Staples, had formerly operated fleets of coal schooners[39]), they shared enough common interests to make common cause, at least for a while. It was in both their interests to force the issue on turn in loading; it was in their common interests to break the union; it was in their common interests to prevent an opening up of America's coastwise coal trade to foreign flag vessels. The latter issue raised its ugly head during the 1902 anthracite coal strike.

Across the Northeast, users of anthracite adapted their boilers and furnaces to bituminous by replacing grates configured for burning anthracite to those designed for bituminous, and the demand for the latter fuel skyrocketed. Unfortunately, the infrastructure supporting the mining and transport of soft coal from the mines in West Virginia and western Maryland and Pennsylvania was totally incapable of handling the additional demand. Matters were further complicated by the Atlantic Carriers' insistence that they would not take charters that did not recognize the principle of absolute turn in loading.[40] Schooners awaiting cargoes clogged the southern ports as other schooners swung on their chains in Boston and Portland Harbors as the receiving ports also became jammed with more traffic than the coal docks were capable of handling.

Angry politicians, having received more than a few earfuls from constituents—private and corporate—who feared a winter fuel shortage, came up with the usual simple solutions to complex problems. Congressman McCall (Connecticut) introduced a resolution in the House of Representatives to lift, at least temporarily, the prohibition of foreign flag vessels partaking in the coastwise coal trade. It is more than a little likely that McCall's political friends included those who did not want to see the turn-in-loading proviso put into effect, and saw the standstill in coal shipments as a convenient way to place all the blame on the schooner operators

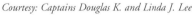

One key factor in the ability of the great schooners to remain economically viable as long as they did was the failure of the coal industry to keep up with the enormous increase in demand. Steam vessels could not afford long stays in port due to slow-moving or limited port facilities, but schooners could. The Helen W. Martin is shown here unloading coal at Galveston, Texas. There are no gantry cranes here with grab buckets capable of unloading 4,000 tons of coal in less than four days into strings of hopper cars. Instead, two grab buckets are suspended between the main and mizzen masts and the jigger and spanker masts and operated by portable boiler/donkey engine units on the pier. The grab buckets were hoisted full out of the hatches, then hauled sideways and emptied into large hoppers set up on legs on the pier. Horsedrawn coal carts were positioned under the hoppers, a lever was thrown, and coal poured into the carts. One trusts that Captain Harding and his crew were not expecting a quick turnaround at this port.

Courtesy: Captains Douglas K. and Linda J. Lee

and the Atlantic Carriers' Association.

But the schooner operators fought back. The normally reticent Frank Small, Sam Percy's junior partner, spoke out firmly on the issue in Bath a few days before Christmas:

> If it was our fault that the people are not getting coal more readily the [McCall] bill would be all right; but that is not the case. Why, we are unable to get either loaded or discharged in any reasonable time. Our vessels are tied up for weeks and months in the coal ports waiting to be loaded, and are again tied up for long periods in the ports of delivery waiting to be discharged.
>
> There is more tonnage than is needed to transport the coal already. The trouble is with the delivery of coal at tidewater, and with the facilities for discharging it at Boston and other northern ports.
>
> There is the ELEANOR A. PERCY. She arrived in Baltimore Nov. 11. She has taken on 2,600 tons of coal and we received word last night that there was enough coal on the cars to bring the amount to 4,300. She will then lack 1,300 tons of a full cargo and will have been in the loading

The ELEANOR A. PERCY shares Norfolk & Western Railway Coal Pier 3 with a small steam collier. Hopper cars of coal were pulled up by steam engine-driven endless chains, positioned over the appropriate bins, and then the hopper doors were opened, pouring the coal down into the bins and on through chutes into the recipient's hold or bunkers accompanied by a cloud of coal dust that often enveloped the entire ship in a gritty, black cloud.

Courtesy: Library of Congress

port more than six weeks, almost an eighth of a year. In that time, if she had been loaded and discharged promptly, she could have made 2 1/2 trips.

One of the big Palmer schooners has been in Boston more than three weeks with 4,200 tons of coal.

The MARTHA P. SMALL has been in the same port with a big cargo since Dec. 2 and not a pound had been taken out of her last night.[41]

The problem, as Frank Small saw it, was the shore-side infrastructure. The mines did not produce enough coal; the railroads did not possess enough rolling stock to move with dispatch that which the mines did produce; the coal loading facilities lacked sufficient berths and storage capacity to handle the demand at peak periods; the discharging docks also lacked adequate berths and equipment to deal with peak traffic. Of course, we don't know whether Frank Small realized that once the inadequacies in that infrastructure were on the way to being addressed, the great coal schooners might well find themselves becoming supernumeraries in the coal trade.

In the meantime, the Atlantic Carriers' Association mustered its political friends in Congress and the McCall Bill went into the trashcan. One more victory for the Association.

The relationship between the schooner and barge operators began to unravel, however, as the first decade of the century advanced. The sources of this decay were, no doubt, the downward effect on the shipping rates the barges were beginning to have, and the continuing inroads being made by the barge operators into areas formerly largely controlled by the schooners (north of Cape Cod) as more and more barge operators dared the perils inherent in rounding Cape Cod, especially in winter.[42]

The effect on rates became the most immediate problem, with its impact already noticeable by 1902 when some barge operators reduced their rates between Hampton Roads and Boston from $1.75 to $.90 per ton.[43] The impact of this decrease would have been far more noticeable at the time if the coal-shipping business had not then become beset by the anthracite strike and its various consequences. But once the strike ended and the pent-up demand for coal was satisfied, freights again descended with an alacrity that alarmed the schooner operators who, it would seem, regarded a dollar per ton to be theirs almost by natural right. The CORA F. CRESSY's freights during 1903 and the first half of 1904 charted that decline:[44] starting at $1.25 per ton (Norfolk-Boston) the rates dropped steadily to $.70 per ton (Norfolk-Portland) by June 1904, a decline of 44 percent. This state of affairs had schooner operators claiming their vessels could barely make expenses at the lower rate and searching diligently for some way to run the rates back up to those halcyon levels enjoyed back in the golden age, i.e., early 1903.[45]

The solution that many, and perhaps the most influential, members of the Atlantic Carriers' Association arrived at was to insist on a specific freight rate floor and a redefined schedule of lay days. Using the Virginia ports of Newport News and Norfolk as the base, the schooner operators insisted that $.90 per ton to Boston was the floor rate and lay days were to be calculated on the basis of sixteen days for a cargo of 4,000 to 5,000 tons, fourteen days for 3,000 to 4,000 tons, and twelve days for 2,000 to 3,000 tons, the same given the steam colliers.[46] Although the schooner operators, including William F. Palmer, avoided the phrase, they had effectively declared a strike against the coal shippers in order to enforce their demands.

The obvious hope was that the abrupt removal of two or three hundred thousand tons of carrying capacity from the market would soon force the rates up to their desired minimum levels. It was a monumental miscalculation akin to accidentally shooting one's self in the foot.

First, there were a number of small schooner fleet operators (not members of the ACA) who were not averse to putting it to the big operators. Second, there were some large fleet operators, even ACA members, such as the Crowley interests, that marched to their own drummer. There were also barge operators who were not members of the ACA, and even those who were, who regarded $.90 per ton as the nirvana of freight money even if it meant rounding Cape Cod

The consignees who handled large quantities of coal—such as electric, gas, and railroad companies—soon found that investment in cargo-handling facilities was far wiser a financial investment than paying demurrage charges. WYOMING is unloading at the Boston Edison dock in South Boston, which boasts of two gantry cranes.

Hildebrand Photo, courtesy of Captains Douglas K. and Linda J. Lee

(after all, it was the summer season with its generally moderate weather). Finally, it *was* summer, historically the season of lowest demand for coal. The ACA had proved themselves to be the masters not only of bad strategy, but also of bad timing.

The schooner operators let it be known in the press that the rates they were being offered to carry coal were below the break-even points for their schooners and they stood firmly for the $.90 rate.[47] But they were engaged in a struggle with the coal shippers who, it would appear, were considerably smarter than they. The Newport News *Daily Express* ran stories, frequently quoted in the *Bath Daily Times*, on the strategy of the shippers. By utilizing divide and conquer tactics, the shippers kept the amount of coal moving through the Chesapeake & Ohio docks at an unusually high rate, and most of it was carried in small schooners at a dollar per ton. Meanwhile, the shippers were offering less than $.90

per ton to the big schooners laid up by the strike.[48] Certainly, it demonstrated that the coal shippers were as determined to fix rates favorable from their point of view as the schooner operators were from theirs, and were not above taking advantage of the lack of solidarity between the "big" schooner operators and the "little" schooner operators by playing the two off against one another.

The resulting impasse did not hurt the shippers, who found many takers from the small schooner fleet operators and the barge operators. However, the striking big schooner operators had to lay up many, if not all, of their schooners in a veritable replay of the disastrous season of the anthracite coal strike just two years earlier.[49] Percy & Small, who had three of their big five-masters—the CORA F. CRESSY, HELEN W. MARTIN, and MARTHA P. SMALL—anchored in Hampton Roads, finally had them towed up the James River to Claremont to join a congregation of big schooners that were literally "taking the waters," fresh water that is.[50] The schooners congregated here, just above the site of historic Jamestown and Williamsburg, to rid themselves of the marine worms and other growth that had attached themselves to the schooners' hulls with the surrounding fresh water.

Despite predictions in the press that the ACA was about to fold its strike for $.90 freights by early September, the hard-liners held out until the first week of October. In the meantime, the "James River fleet" swung on its rusty chains in the largest collection of vessels—and largest, individually—to ever be seen on that river. Captain E. E. Haskell of the CORA F. CRESSY has left us some glimpses of life on the James during the late summer and early fall of 1904.

The good captain found his big schooner overrun with visiting Virginia farmers who acted as though they had never seen a big sailing vessel before, never

mind ever being aboard one. Nonetheless, making the best of a bad situation, Haskell acquired a veritable barnyard of livestock and fowl who took up residence on the deck of his idle schooner. At one point, Haskell boasted of having two hogs, forty-two chickens, two dogs, fourteen pigeons, ten white mice (!), and miscellaneous other stock on board. One of those hogs, no doubt suspecting the worst, broke the sleepy monotony of the life on the James when said porker decided to desert. But let Haskell tell the tale:

> I was seated on the forward deck, reading a [Newport News] *Daily Press* and enjoying the bracing breeze, when I heard a noise and before I could port my headgear, I was upset by one of my porkers. The pig placed his snout under my chair and hurled me into space, then darted towards the stern of the vessel. The next thing I

Even small Maine ports began to boast of sophisticated equipment to efficiently handle coal. At the Bangor and Aroostook Railroad dock at Searsport, the DAVIS PALMER could be worked by three gantry cranes at once.
Courtesy: Captains Douglas K. and Linda J. Lee

Sailing close-hauled in light airs, the deeply loaded WYOMING is barely making steerageway. The entire watch is visible on deck: helmsman and mate aft by the wheel, three seamen abaft the forward house, and even the cook is catching a breath of fresh air by the coach house for the midship house. For some reason, Captain McLeod has chosen not to set the topmast staysails to give her an added push along.

Courtesy: Captain W. J. Lewis Parker, USCG, Ret.

The GRACE A. MARTIN rides high out of the water as she heads for a loading port. Her sailing qualities will be entirely different when she returns, loaded. That may be Captain William F. Harding at her rail exchanging pleasantries with the tugboat skipper.

Courtesy: Captain W. J. Lewis Parker, USCG, Ret.

saw of him he was swimming like a porpoise for shore. The distance was half a mile, and I thought surely he would be drowned but later a farmer announced that a stray pig had landed on his farm and I got my porker back.[51]

What fate awaited the above pig following his unauthorized shore leave was not revealed. Captain Haskell wrapped up his enforced vacation on the James with a brief essay praising Virginia. Part reminiscence, part geography, part history, part folklore, and part poetry (his own, apparently), he shared the pleasures of a peaceful "blockade" on the James River with the folks in Bath.[52] Then, one by one, the big schooners passed their towing hawsers over to eager tugs, hoisted anchors, and moved back to Newport News or Norfolk to load coal. The strike, a total failure, was over.

Palmer tried to put the best possible face on the ACA's caving in by explaining to one investor (who hadn't seen much in the way of dividends lately) that the schooner operators decided to lower rates "for a few days" to move some coal and, "incidentally, [to] kill off a lot of little vessels." Arch nemesis Crowley also entered into the equation: as with the seamen's union, Crowley failed to support the ACA line and accepted a number of term charters at low rates that were due to expire in early October. The other members believed that if they kept their tonnage off the market it would only serve to improve the rates for Crowley's benefit, something they very definitely did not want to do. Finally, Palmer also mentioned another fear that must have lurked at the back of the mind of each and every schooner operator: the proposed conversion of several Great Lakes tank steamers to colliers to replace the striking great schooners.[53]

Those members of the ACA, including Percy & Small, who participated in the boycott achieved very little at great cost. Many of their captains were unhappy to have lost three to four months of work during the season of the year with the best sailing conditions. Although they continued to receive their pay—$40 per month—the bulk of their income came from primage and dividends and that was based on freight carried. One schooner captain observed that, "The general impression among the Captains in the fleet is that the Association [ACA] have bungled[,] in so much that they did not take into account the amount of tonnage on the coast outside the Association."[54] This rather astute observation came from Frank W. Patten, skipper of the steel five-master Kineo, and the only man to ever take one of the great schooners on a circumnavigation of the globe.

The impact on earnings was dramatic. The Cora F. Cressy paid $230 (+/- $3,540 in 1998) per 1/64 between May 1903 and June 1904 even with the extraordinary expenses involving the collision with Parthian; between July 1904 and June 1905 (including the boycott) she managed to pay only $17 (+/- $262 in 1998) per 1/64![55] The impact on Percy & Small's earnings, exclusive of shipyard operations, is particularly telling: in the five-month period July–November 1903, the fleet paid the firm $6,326 (+/- $97,420 in 1998) in dividends; during the same months in 1904 the dividends from the schooners totaled only $2,490 (+/- $38,340 in 1998) and the firm suffered a net loss in the period of $5,286 (+/- $81,400 in 1998) as it advanced funds from the partnership's pocket to meet each schooner's current expenses, insurance on their shares, and interest on loans.[56] It is unlikely that Sam Percy and Frank Small shared brother Palmer's optimism when he wrote to Myron Wick after the boycott ended: "Our waterfront in Boston is lined with little vessels [schooners that carried much of the coal during the strike] that cannot get a living at 60 cents and we are now engaged in a survival of the fittest. We are the fittest."[57]

Once the schooner operators accepted the lower rates, they did indeed drive many of the smaller schooners out of their trade with the larger New England ports east of Cape Cod. But the small schooners were not the critical competition.

Before long, the big schooner operators realized this and became more vociferous in complaining about their erstwhile allies, the barge operators. They even enlisted support in Congress with Senator William P. Frye (R-ME) offering a bill to regulate coastwise tows. The *New York Maritime Register* editorialized: "The present unnecessarily long tows of these barges when in crowded harbors, causing much obstruction to shipping and increasing the liability to accident, is a nuisance that should be abated. The owners of the seagoing barges are at present a law unto themselves . . . ."[58]

Long tows involving three or more seagoing barges and one tug were especially unwieldy in the confines of busy harbors. Incidents involving collisions, crew injuries, and death were all too numerous as through inattention, poor visibility, or crowded harbor conditions, vessels unwittingly attempted to cross between barges making up a tow in a maritime version of "clotheslining."[59] Schooner masters also complained that even outside of the harbors, the not very maneuverable barge strings often interfered with critical maneuvers of their own vessels, often placing them in some danger.

The good Senator Frye, always prepared to support Maine's shipping interests, also noted that the poor safety record of the barge operators required attention. In speaking for his bill, subsequently passed by the Senate, Frye reported that 15 percent of

four hundred seagoing barges in American waters had been lost in the previous year (1907) along with a quarter of their crewmen.[60] Fortunately for the senator, he did not have to explain the loss statistics run up by the schooner fleet for the year 1909 and through the winter season ending in March 1910.

The *Bath Times* reported that the Maine-owned fleet of vessels, including steamers, had suffered a net decrease of 8,000 tons in 1909 from casualty losses alone. It was in this year, you will recall, that J. S. Winslow & Co. lost no fewer than four schooners, three of which were built by Percy & Small. In a report covering a broader geographical area but during a shorter period, the *New York Maritime Register* noted that 225 persons had lost their lives during the winter of 1909–10 by shipwreck in New England and the Canadian Maritimes. Shipwreck casualties included sixty-two schooners, many of which were small fishing vessels, but among them were one six-master, two five-masters, and four four-masters.[61]

For nearly thirteen years, Percy & Small—unlike many of their competitors—lost nary a vessel to grounding, collision, fire, or foundering. This all changed in January 1913 when the aging S. P. BLACKBURN, Baltimore to Galveston with coal, reverted to an early fault of the great schooners and rolled out her spars. Eight of her ten-man crew were rescued by the S. S. TIVERTON, but the engineer and cook refused to jump into the raging sea. Four days later, the S. S. ESPERANZA saw the derelict, but upon sending a boat to investigate found a cabin light burning, no one aboard, and the battered derelict slowly foundering.

Courtesy: Maine Maritime Museum

The barge operators managed one more victory over the schooner operators in 1914 with the opening of the Cape Cod Canal. Too shoal for most of the great schooners, the canal offered a safe and relatively quick, if rather pricey, route between the coal ports to the southwest and the coal discharge ports around Massachusetts Bay, avoiding the Cape's deadly "backside," especially during the winter season. Although the canal's initial depth at low water was only 18 feet, by mid-May 1916 the controlling depth had been dredged to 25 feet.[62]

There was a far bigger competitive threat to the great coal schooners than a motley collection of barges, however. Steel steam colliers were superior to the wooden great schooners in reliability, overall performance, and profitability as long as there was a supporting infrastructure—facilities and organization—capable of maximizing their potential. Where such facilities existed, as in parts of the anthracite trade, the steam colliers had flourished since the 1870s.[63]

One of the principal reasons the coal schooners survived, and even flourished on occasion, in the bituminous trade was the inadequate infrastructure. It had not kept pace with the growth in demand for the product, and its organization could best be described as chaotic in contrast with the more mature anthracite industry.[64] The mines produced the coal, the railroads transported it to the tidewater and loaded it aboard colliers. The colliers then carried the coal to seaport destinations where it was unloaded, stored, and eventually distributed to the ultimate consumer. There was little or no coordination or planning throughout the process with the result that coal was frequently in short supply at the coal ports at the same time that colliers—sail and steam—waiting to receive cargo accumulated at an alarming rate. Of course, the opposite scenario was often the case at the discharging ports when, after a sustained period of bad weather and empty unloading berths, a large flock of schooners and barges arrived on the doorstep overwhelming the port's facilities and running out the demurrage clocks on those forced to wait their turn. It was this situation that kept the schooners in the running and discouraged the use of the steam colliers.[65]

The steam colliers simply could not operate profitably in this type of environment. They needed a fast turnaround time in the loading and unloading ports to justify their initial capital outlay and their high operating costs. In time, and with the development of suitable facilities, these vessels were able to reduce their time in the coal ports to a matter of hours.[66] Obviously, the high demurrage costs and turn-in-loading issue flogged by the schooner operators encouraged the bituminous coal shippers to improve both their loading and discharge facilities.

The knell of the great schooners was sounded in 1909. The Virginian Railway from the as yet untouched coal fields in the Kanawha River basin of West Virginia to Norfolk signed the death warrant. Stretching 446 miles from its western terminus at Deepwater to the new coal piers with their 36,000-tons-per-day dumping capacity at Sewall's Point, the railroad followed a downhill and direct route to the tidewater, bypassing potential freight-producing cities. This was a railroad whose primary function was to haul coal in one direction and empty coal cars in the other. Other business would serve only to detract from carrying the coal from Deepwater to Norfolk.[67]

The New England Coal & Coke Company, in anticipation of the increased efficiency in the movement of coal represented by the Virginian Railway, had ordered three steel steam colliers to be delivered in 1907 by the New York Shipbuilding Company at Camden (New Jersey): the EVERETT, MALDEN, and MELROSE. Their delivery was intended to approximate the opening of the new railway, but the railway was completed two years later than originally planned.[68] So the new colliers entered into a bituminous trade beset by much the same difficulties involving delays in loading and discharging that plagued all those involved since the beginning. It was not an auspicious start for the steam colliers, but it encouraged the schooner operators, including Percy & Small, to invest in additional very large schooners as they indulged in one more burst of shipbuilding as the decade drew to a close.

The start was so inauspicious, in fact, that the New England Coal & Coke Company was soon rumored to be attempting to unload their three "white elephant" colliers onto the U.S. Navy. When the Navy refused to purchase the hapless trio, they began to be referred to in the shipping press as "misfits all around."[69]

New England Coal & Coke, however, had the last laugh. Company President Richards, speaking at a luncheon honoring the launching of the new collier NEWTON (sister of the EVERETT, MALDEN, and MELROSE) in October 1911, permitted himself the pleasure of saying "I told you so." After admitting he had not been particularly confident that the half-million dollar EVERETT would repay her investment when she took to the water in 1907, he went on:

I am pleased to say to you today that our most sanguine expectations have been realized. That others as well as ourselves have found that the type of boat carrying coal like the EVERETT, of which the NEWTON is practically a duplicate, is a success, is demonstrated by the fact that since the EVERETT was launched, six other ships of like design have been built, three of which have been constructed by others than ourselves.

In order to utilize a ship of this character and make it pay, one must have satisfactory terminals for the loading and discharging of coal. We have a very large amount of money invested in our terminal in Everett, where we have large [coal] pockets and ground storage, a traveling bridge, more than 20 miles of railroad track connecting with steam railroads and 27 feet of water at low tide.... I said we expected to be able to unload one of these ships [EVERETT-class collier], carrying over 7,000 tons, in not more than ten hours. At our Everett terminal we now discharge two of these boats at one time, and our record for unloading one of them is seven hours and 40 minutes .... This type of ship would be unsuccessful unless it could be both loaded and unloaded quickly, for the expense, involving interest and depreciation, is more than $400 per day per boat.

You railroad men know the great value of these boats to railroad transportation, because of the regularity of the service, and all the consumers of coal in this section must realize their value, for they have not only been the means of settling the demurrage questions to a large extent, but have equalized and lowered water freights materially, and we do not now see water freights $1 and over during the winter months as we did just preceding the advent of these boats.[70]

It was a message that the much-maligned Captain Crowley had already read. In 1909, with the promise inherent in the opening of the Virginian Railway and the Sewall's Point docks, Crowley ordered two steam colliers for his firm, the Coastwise Transportation Company. Named, conveniently, COASTWISE and TRANSPORTATION, and costing a half million dollars each, these colliers were expected to haul between them 400,000 tons of coal annually, and the Boston & Maine Railroad agreed to invest $100,000 in coal-handling machinery to discharge the new colliers.[71] Between 1912 and 1915, Crowley was selling off the last of Coastwise's schooners, including the only steel six-master, the WILLIAM L. DOUGLAS, and the wooden five-masters VAN ALLENS BOUGHTON, MARGARET HASKELL, and MARCUS L. URANN.[72] Even Crowell & Thurlow, another schooner-based—and unlike Crowley—loyal member of the ACA, began to turn to steam colliers in 1914 when it took delivery of the EDWARD PEIRCE, capable of hauling 8,500 tons of coal.[73]

A number of Great Lakes-built whaleback steamers designed for the ore trade also migrated to the East Coast to meet the demand for steam colliers. The F. J. LISMAN, built at Detroit in 1911, joined the Shawmut Steamship Company to carry 4,000 tons of coal between Baltimore and Hampton Roads ports to Maine's eastern ports.[74] There were also reports of more Great Lakes steamers making the long transit via the St. Lawrence to the Atlantic Coast. One, the GEORGE E. WARREN, a Lake-built whaleback, went to work for Harper Transportation Company in the Fall of 1912, carrying coal from Newport News to the International Paper Company in Portland on her first voyage.[75]

The impact of the Virginian Railway and the first major successful deployment of steam colliers in the bituminous trade was immediately evident.

No further six-masters were built following WYOMING in 1909. The construction of smaller great schooners also ground to a virtual halt with only two five-masters and seven four-masters delivered by Maine shipyards between 1910 and 1916, all of them built in Bath.[76] The attrition rate of the great schooners, in fact, began to exceed their rate of replacement.

For all of their efforts, the schooner operators had, at best, only slightly delayed the advance of technology in their realm. Stringent rules concerning turn in loading, bitter battles with the seamen's union, boycotts against the coal shippers, and even efforts to limit the amount of new schooner tonnage entering the market had all come to naught during the decade. But there was one hope glittering like the proverbial beacon in the storm: empire.

THE BENEFITS OF EMPIRE?

When "Imperial America" emerged with the twentieth century, there was hope among some ship operators that the new age would particularly benefit America's merchant marine. Cuba, Puerto Rico, the Hawaiian Islands, Guam, and the Philippines had all come rather suddenly and dramatically under the protection of the United States, thanks to a bungling Spanish government, a rabid "yellow press," a president described by his vice president as possessing "the backbone of a chocolate eclair," a "splendid little war," and the political machinations of a group of wealthy American sugar growers in one of the true natural paradises on earth.

Empire opened new opportunities for American shipowners, potentially expanding the boundaries for protected coastwise trade from the North American continent to the South China Sea. The issue was, simply put, whether the Constitution followed the flag, i.e., whether the Constitution applied in the new territories along with all other pertinent laws of the United States—including the laws prohibiting foreign flag vessels from America's "coastal" trade. The anti-imperialists insisted that wherever the flag went the Constitution was close behind, a position that was, for the most part, abhorrent to the imperialists who shuddered at the prospect of hundreds of thousands—if not millions—of non-white, non-Europeans being regarded as equal under the law with themselves—this, in a society which had already carefully and thoroughly subjected the black population to legal inferiority.

In the end, the Supreme Court, in a series of decisions known as the Insular Cases, decided that the Constitution did not automatically follow the flag, but was dependent upon the will of Congress. Thus Hawaii and Puerto Rico became territories of the U.S. and were included under the navigation laws that governed American coastwise shipping. The Philippines, on the other hand, did not enjoy the same treatment, much to the dismay of some American shipowners—Arthur Sewall & Company, William F. Palmer, and John G. Crowley—who had seen the island group's annexation as opening up a huge and protected "coasting" market literally on the Asian continent's doorstep.[77]

William F. Palmer was one of the first coal schooner operators who realized the opportunity an annexed Philippines presented. As an American naval base to protect the islands from rapacious imperialist European states and protect American interests throughout the Far East, large quantities of coal would be needed to bunker warships at Cavite or Subic Bay. Of course, stores of bunker coal for merchant vessels were also necessary as steamships continued to supplant the sailing vessel in world commerce. The coal, it was hoped, would be mined by American miners at American coal mines, carried in American bottoms, and profit American business, a virtual certainty if the islands were granted territorial status.[78] The only problem was a doozy: finding return cargoes to continental ports. It was, after all, one thing to deadhead a schooner for 750 miles and another thing to sail light for thousands of miles.[79]

The indefatigable and almost always optimistic Palmer described his schooners as being: "General-cargo vessel[s] designed for both foreign and coastwise trade . . . ."[80] Actually, Palmer had already sent the REBECCA PALMER to France and England on a

The critical role hoisting engines played in the operation of the great schooners is
no more graphically illustrated than in this photo of the crew hoisting and setting
sail on the DAVIS PALMER. Halyards litter the deck as six crewmen carry out
various assignments. A seventh man is in the fore shrouds making his way aloft,
no doubt to clear some fouled gear (the foresail has only been partially hoisted).
These men, along with the mates, constituted the manpower that handled the
DAVIS PALMER's oversized gear.

Courtesy: Maine Maritime Museum

voyage in 1901 that created quite a stir, the big white schooner being only the second five-master seen in European waters.[81] However, it was probably not very profitable in spite of all the publicity, and Palmer did not repeat it. It took more than a dozen years before the war-induced shipping shortage encouraged the managers of the five- and six-masters to risk their big charges in the transatlantic trade.

Meanwhile, Arthur Sewall & Company did test the viability of the Manila coal trade with their nearly new steel five-master, KINEO. Under command of the last seagoing member of the web-footed Patten clan (Frank W.), the KINEO departed Norfolk with a load of coal destined for the navy's coal pocket in Manila. Accompanied by his wife and young daughter, both of whom had previously been tested by adversity on the high seas, Patten sailed for the Philippines via the Cape of Good Hope. They were not too far behind another Sewall vessel also bound for Manila, the big four-masted steel bark EDWARD SEWALL, which was serving as an informal trial horse.[82]

The KINEO arrived in Manila in July after a trying voyage. Patten reported that the big schooner could show her stern to square-riggers while in the trade-wind belt, but had nothing but problems the rest of the time. The long swells often encountered while running down her easting caused the sails to slat badly, especially in light winds, tearing sails, breaking boom and gaff jaws, and forcing the crew to lower sails. When gales threatened, the harried captain was forced to shorten sail long before he would aboard a square-rigger to avoid having to handle the huge sails with his decks awash (schooner sails were almost all handled from deck rather than aloft).

From Manila the Sewall schooner filled its water ballast tank and sailed for Newcastle in Australia to load coal for Hawaii. Its course was marked by misfortune including a devastating typhoon, baffling calms, torn sails, broken gear, and virtually an entire crew down with beriberi. Patten put into Brisbane after efforts to obtain fresh food came to naught in Guam and the Solomons, with one man dying and

First Mate Norman McLeod takes his ease perched on WYOMING's rather substantial power yawl boat as he keeps a watchful eye on the youthful helmsman. By the looks of things, however, the big schooner is barely making steerage way so the helmsman's job can't be too demanding at the moment.

Photo by John B. Brooks, courtesy of Captain W. J. Lewis Parker, USCG, Ret.

virtually everyone else aboard seriously ill and barely able to work the schooner.[83]

With health restored and the marine forest that had taken root on the schooner's bottom removed, KINEO moved on to Newcastle and then to Kahului on the island of Maui in the Hawaiian chain. The voyage from Australia's east coast to the fabled islands was remarkably uneventful, taking only two months and avoiding all forms of catastrophe.

Lying offshore in the roads, KINEO's cargo of Australian coal was slowly discharged into lighters. Then with an equally measured pace, the same lighters began to deliver the 3,081 tons of bagged sugar consigned to the Spreckles sugar refinery in Philadelphia. Finally, in May 1906, schooner, Patten, family, crew, and sugar cleared for home. Two hundred five days later they arrived, safe but exhausted.

Once again, all the problems with the schooner rig noted outbound to Manila reappeared as KINEO and company ran down her easting past Cape Horn. But it became even worse than that. As the schooner slogged past the fabled cape her boiler failed: no steam, no heat, no steam hoisting engines, no steam pumps. The KINEO had become the largest hand-puller schooner in the world, underscoring the great schooner's vulnerability with its small crew when the steam auxiliaries failed. Nonetheless, Patten refused to panic and pushed on all the way to Philadelphia even as stories in the press began to speculate on the overdue schooner's fate. In closing his arrival report to the Sewalls, Captain Frank Patten throttled any ambitions that the Sewalls, Crowley, Palmer, or Percy & Small had of creating a new trade for their big schooners outside of the Atlantic basin: ". . . my experience in the KINEO off Cape Horn is a repetition of what the GOV. AMES went through and what every other big schooner will go through."[84] Prophetic words; not a single great schooner followed the trail blazed by KINEO or the GOV. AMES.[85]

What experience didn't squelch, the federal government eventually did when the navy opened the coal charters to Manila to foreign flag vessels.[86]

UNDER SAIL IN THE GREAT SCHOONERS

However complex, unpredictable, frustrating, or blatantly political the business milieu in which the great schooners operated, they still had to be sailed to their destinations to load or unload cargo. That in itself was often a challenge of near Olympian proportions.

Captains and crews had to move some of the largest sailing vessels in the world—the VLCCs (Very Large Cargo Carriers) of their day—whose handling qualities were not always as yacht-like as those Captain McLeod claimed for the giant WYOMING, especially in light airs. For the most part, they also sailed vessels with split personalities given the nature of the coal trade: northbound, their schooners were deeply loaded, wet in any sort of sea, stiff in strong winds, sluggish in light airs, and subject to severe laboring in a beam or confused sea; southbound they were usually light, crank or tender to the point that some were prone to sailing on their sides, making almost as much leeway as headway.[87] These qualities challenged the ingenuity of the great schooner skipper.

Captain Stinson "Stin" Davis, formerly in the four-master MAUDE PALMER, once described to one of the authors a tactic many of the big schooner skippers used to sail south to the coal ports in light summer winds. With a prevailing southwest wind, they would set a course to take them well offshore on a starboard tack. Then they would wear ship, timed usually in the middle of the night so they would come onto land in the middle or late afternoon. Instead of wearing ship again—not enough room—they would sail right up to the beach, luff up into the wind, come to a stop, and anchor. Headsails and foresail were backed to starboard and the spanker backed to port. Then, with the steam hoisting engine puffing and windlass and anchor chain clanking, the schooner hauled up and over the anchor, picking it up on the run. With the sails backed as they were, and the forward momentum of the vessel coming up on the anchor, the schooner would then head off on the offshore starboard tack.[88] Nothing to it!

The fact of the matter was that the principal

source of energy that drove these vessels was the fickle, ever-changing wind, and its partner in crime when they operated along the coast, local tidal currents. Of the two, the tidal currents were far more predictable than the winds, a fact that all captains of the great schooners certainly took into account as they slogged their way north or south along the coast.

The great schooners were built principally to carry coal to New England. This they accomplished by sailing from Hampton Roads or the mouth of Chesapeake Bay between Cape Charles and Cape Henry after loading at Newport News, Norfolk, Baltimore, or Curtis Bay. Other schooners loaded at Philadelphia and sailed from the mouth of the Delaware River. In either case, their basic route to their destinations north of Cape Cod was virtually the same.

The choice of that route to the ports north of Cape Cod appears obvious at first: when leaving Chesapeake Bay, for example, steer northeast. That course, providing open-water sailing all the way, brings the schooner to the east of Nantucket and Cape Cod, at which point a new course can then be laid for the destination port. Simple and direct, it was an option not frequently used by the captains of the great schooners, and for good reason, as a quick glance at a chart of the region reveals.[89]

Clusters of shoals radiate seaward from the island of Nantucket, with Nantucket Shoals extending up to seventy miles to the south and southeastward, and Georges Shoal (part of Georges Bank) marking the eastern boundary of this maze of ever-shifting shallows over a hundred miles out to sea from Nantucket! Between Georges Bank and the Nantucket Shoals, however, there is a north-south passage called the South Channel which has sufficient depth to allow safe transit of deeper draft vessels.

There are serious drawbacks in using the South Channel, especially for sailing vessels. It is well out to sea, totally open to the effects of the wind from all points of the compass. Moreover, it is a channel that threads through shallows and shoals, often with breaking seas on both sides, and is devoid of aids to navigation or visible landmarks from which to fix a schooner's position. It certainly was not a good place for a big schooner loaded deep to be caught in an easterly gale, with limited visibility, a beam sea, and shoals ahead and astern, to leeward and windward.

For these reasons, the great schooners' captains often preferred a course that passed east of Montauk Point, Long Island, and east of Block Island into Vineyard Sound and on into Nantucket Sound. Although this alternative had numerous drawbacks, such as relatively narrow and shallow channels and heavy traffic, it enjoyed some crucial advantages: it was, in effect, a covered way offering shores to shelter under in adverse winds. At Vineyard Haven on Martha's Vineyard, a number of services were available including tugs for those anxious to get to their destinations, a marine reporter with a telegraph link with the mainland, ship chandleries, and a marine hospital in the event of a medical emergency. But most importantly, this fifty-mile passage was liberally dotted with navigational aids in the form of lighthouses and light vessels, as well as the usual channel buoys. From the Vineyard light vessel marking the northwest corner of Vineyard Sound and Gay Head Light anchoring its southwest corner to the Pollock Rip Light Vessel at its eastern end, fourteen lighthouses and light vessels lined the passage through and around the shoals.

The narrowness of the channels, the vagaries of the wind, and the constant traffic of sailing vessels, steam vessels, and tugs with barges led, however, to a steady litany of collision reports. The saga of the WILLIAM H. CLIFFORD and the five-master MARGARET HASKELL on one passage offers a case in point.

Northbound from Norfolk to Bangor with coal, the CLIFFORD was involved in two collisions on Vineyard Sound within twenty-four hours. After anchoring off Gay Head Light following a shift in the wind, the schooner was struck by the schooner HATTIE H. BARBOUR bound from St. John to New York with lumber. The BARBOUR lost her headgear and had to be towed to New Bedford for repairs, but the damage to the WILLIAM H. CLIFFORD was limited to a portion of her rail and the mizzen rigging. After assessing the damage, the captain sailed the schooner to Vineyard Haven, arriving late in the afternoon. But as she passed West Chop, lo and behold, the CLIFFORD fouled the schooner MARGARET HASKELL, at anchor, carrying away the HASKELL's jibboom and headgear in

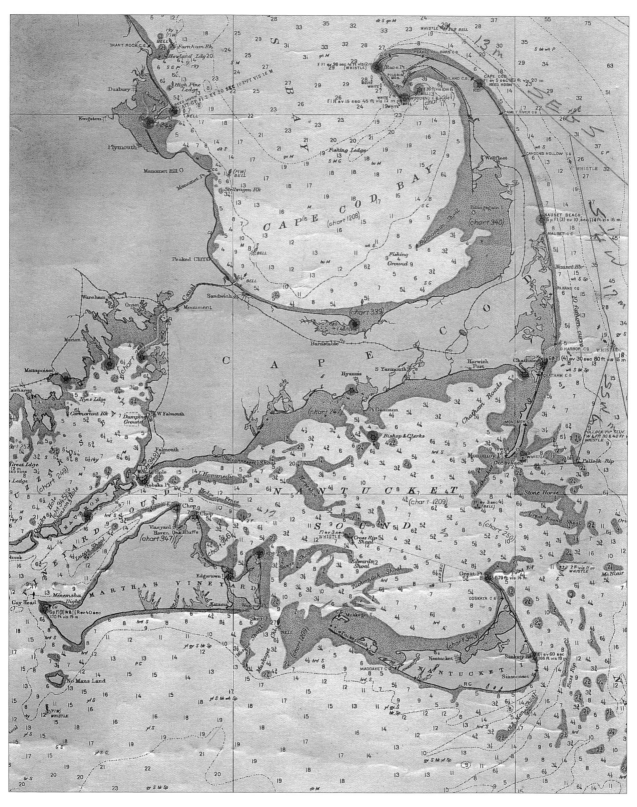

Detail from U. S. Coast & Geodetic Survey chart, *Georges Bank and Nantucket Shoals*,
2 February 1924, soundings in fathoms.

Courtesy: Captains Douglas K. and Linda J. Lee

exchange for her own spanker boom, spanker sail, and spanker rigging.[90]

The CLIFFORD repaired her damage at Vineyard Haven before proceeding on her belated way to Bangor. The MARGARET HASKELL was not so fortunate, however. Still at anchor a few hours after her brush with the CLIFFORD and now awaiting a tow to her destination, the damaged HASKELL was struck again, this time by the five-master GEORGE P. HUDSON (ex-FANNIE PALMER [I]) when the latter missed stays while passing across her bow.[91] It had been an eventful twenty-four hours on Vineyard Sound.

The reluctance of many coasting captains to take the South Channel route may also have been motivated by a notable unwillingness to place heavy reliance on the preciseness of their celestial navigation and dead-reckoning calculations in a stretch of water crowded with perils on every hand. By way of contrast, the "inside" route through the Vineyard and Nantucket Sounds offered a multitude of known landmarks and seamarks upon which any competent coasting captain could get bearings that accurately fixed his position.

But we are apt to forget in this modern age of electronic navigational systems just how the traditional art of navigation was impacted by local weather and other conditions: limited visibility due to fog or storm concealed landmarks; overcast skies prohibited making sun and star sights; a patch of floating seaweed could foul and carry away the spinning rotor on the patent taffrail log. These interruptions to the flow of information into navigational computations sometimes proved to be costly and even fatal, as the sad fate of the DAVIS PALMER demonstrated in Chapter 7.

When Frederick Laurence took passages north and south in coal schooners, he was exposed to the rough and ready, and sometimes extemporaneous, navigational techniques of Captain Billy Kreger on the one hand, and the cool, technical, deep-water precision of Captain Bunker on the other.[92] Sailing north in the four-masted schooner SARAH C. ROPES commanded by Kreger, Laurence detailed navigation by land and seamarks when visible, by dead reckoning (using compass and patent log) when they were not, and twice—after losing the patent log rotor—by inquir-

ing of nearby vessels the bearings to prominent but not visible marks.[93] Later that summer, Laurence went south in the four-master ALICIA B. CROSBY commanded by Captain G. W. Bunker, a man who was proud and confident of his ability to navigate by celestial observation. It was a good thing, as on this voyage they took the South Channel and didn't sight land from the time they left Portland until they arrived off the Virginia capes.[94]

Captains of the great schooners needed to know more than where they were at any given time. They had to know the handling qualities of their vessels in a variety of different situations. These were determined by schooner size, individual design, how deeply they were loaded, wind direction and velocity, sea condition, and the sail combinations being used at any given time.

Great schooners loaded with coal did not float like ducks on the water. Some observers claimed that just to get them underway required a fresh breeze (17–21 knots) to overcome the inertia of their deep-laden, long hulls. And in a seaway, the heavily laden hulls barely rose to meet the wave crests but plowed on through, decks awash and timbers creaking.

When the great schooners were light, an almost entirely different situation was operative. Decks remained dry in fair weather, but many a captain discovered his almost cork-like vessel would not tack, requiring the time- and space-consuming practice of wearing ship—or its seemingly suicidal variant described previously by Captain Stin Davis. Another discovery that was made while sailing light was described by F. L. Eno when he was in the five-master JENNIE FRENCH POTTER as she ran light before the wind, bound for Brunswick, Georgia:

Toward the latter part of the afternoon it blew harder than ever, and the sea became steep and angry; the schooner was wallowing along, rolling and pitching and sending the foam in broad sheets on either bow; a good eleven knots by the log and still breezing.

. . . Running before it as we were, she slid over the seas in a regular rise and fall that gave no indication [of their size]; but as I stood in the

Cabin boy Bailey makes the long trek from WYOMING's after house, carrying the remains of a meal back to the galley located in the midship house. The only other person visible on deck is the man at the wheel back aft, although mate Norman McLeod is apt to be prowling around on deck out of sight.

Photo by John B. Brooks, courtesy of Captain W. J. Lewis Parker, USCG, Ret.

Foul weather and limited visibility increased the level of danger confronting any ship crew as they traversed the heavily trafficked, peril-strewn waters along the East Coast. With the wind rising and visibility decreasing, the duty watch on the ELEANOR A. PERCY is reducing sail. The huge gaff-headed spanker has already been lowered and furled, and part of the crew is out on the end of the jibboom getting ready to lower and furl the jib topsail. The shadowy figure in the right foreground is probably Captain Jewett scanning the lowering horizon off the port bow with binoculars. Perhaps he is tracking a dimly perceived landmark or another vessel crossing the PERCY's track.

Courtesy: Maine Maritime Museum

When loaded, the big schooners were notoriously wet even in fair weather and moderate seas. With her spar deck awash, the FULLER PALMER thrashes her way into Vineyard Sound off Gay Head in August 1913. The peculiar arrangement of yacht skylights superimposed on the more common flat-top skylights (right) found on great schooners was the product of one of William F. Palmer's personal idiosyncrasies.

Courtesy of Captains Douglas K. and Linda J. Lee

waist my eye was on the level with the long poop-deck, and when the stern settled in the hollow and the next sea getting under [the counter], rose around the quarter, I could see that deck curl up; and then as the sea passed under her and she hung on it amidships, the ends of her dropped, and along in the wake of the mizzen mast the deck humped up and hogged; and as the stern settled she straightened out, curled up, straightened out, curled up, and straightened out.[95]

Captains who had learned their trade in square-rigged sail discovered another big schooner trait that could be very dangerous in heavy weather. Unlike square-riggers that with a few staysails set and a reefed and backed lower topsail could be held bow to the wind during a bad storm, big schooners had to be driven to keep from falling off into the trough. But driving big schooners into head seas caused a vessel to labor heavily, and falling off into the trough could well end with the masts being rolled out of her. If the schooner could not anchor in this situation, the captain's best course was to slack sheets and run before wind and wave.[96]

The men who shipped as seamen on the great schooners were a mixed lot. As already noted in this chapter, Percy & Small and William F. Palmer favored African-American crews through most of the first decade of the century, crews that were liberally sprinkled, however, with Norwegians. The deck officers, mates and captain, were white and, for the most part, native of the coastal New England states or the Maritimes.

Those who went in the coal schooners and subsequently retailed their adventures in print had varying opinions, generally, of the class of men—whatever their color or national origin—who lived in the forecastle. Laurence described the four seamen who were shipped to sail the SARAH C. ROPES north as ". . . a pasty faced anemic looking lot, indescribably filthy in person and clothing and dressed commonly in old derby hats and frayed out store clothes, the mark of a deep sea sailor usually . . . . Only when the real merchant sailor got into oilskins did he look like anything one could recognize as a sailor. Later on, when dressed that way, I saw the men on the ROPES do things which nobody but a real sailor could do, the captain's

Harnessing the energy of wind and current, the EDWARD B. WINSLOW, Captain Henry Butler, parades her stuff in this classic photo as she drives across the Gulf of Maine for Portland Harbor with 5,800 tons of coal aboard, leaving two other schooners far astern.

Courtesy: Captain W. J. Lewis Parker, USCG, Ret.

observations (generally disparaging) to the contrary notwithstanding."[97]

Mr. Eno was in no way so complimentary in describing the first mate and seamen shipped for the trip on the JENNIE FRENCH POTTER to Georgia. The second crew of seamen shipped for the trip—the first group had run—was described by Eno as ". . . a group of six reeling, drunken beasts, cursing heaven and hell and all between, who were helped up the ladder and over the rail, and who immediately disappeared below, where fight and revelry held sway, judging from the sounds that made their way aft."[98] Eno's harsh views concerning the crew moderated only slightly during the passage.

On the other hand, there were men such as Charles Barth, a young Norwegian who came to America in the small steamer ALADDIN as a crewman about 1919. The sixteen-year-old recalled being washed from the ship's deck during the crossing but then being returned by the next wave. Upon arrival in the United States, he went to Norfolk to join his father and older brother employed at that city as pipe fitters.

After recovering from injuries he received aboard the ALADDIN, Barth began to visit a sailor's hangout run by two Norwegians near the coal docks. It was here he learned that the big schooner WYOMING was shipping crewmen for a trip to Boston. He signed on, receiving $30 per month (+/- $205 in 1998) and one of eight bunks in the forecastle. The eight sailors, two mates, captain, cook, and engineer made up the entire crew of the largest wooden sailing vessel in the world.

Once the schooner was underway, Barth found himself standing watches, six hours on and six hours off. As little work was done on maintenance while underway, the watch—four seamen and a mate—devoted most of its time to steering the vessel, look-outs, and handling sail. Barth recalled that WYOMING was hard to steer with her wooden wheel standing high above his head.

Meals were eaten in the midship house adjoining the galley. The young Norwegian, who had an enormous appetite, recalled that the cook was an African American. He also recalled that he was perpetually hungry while aboard the schooner, although he did not recall whether the food was good or bad, plentiful or stingy.

After several trips in the big schooner, Barth fell ill while enroute to Boston. The captain—probably Glaesel—sent him to the Chelsea Marine Hospital where he was placed in the care of Dr. Paul Dudley White who, many years later, as a renowned heart doctor, cared for President Eisenhower. The seaman, however, was suffering from typhoid fever. After he recovered, he stayed on at the hospital for a time serving as an orderly, thus missing the final voyage of WYOMING.[99]

Whatever the problems the great schooners may have presented to their officers and crew on occasion, they turned out to be a remarkably efficient form of transportation in the service for which they were intended.

PROFITABILITY

The fragmentary nature of the Percy & Small financial records makes it difficult to reconstruct the firm's financial performance throughout its quarter century of operations. However, enough records from the first decade of the century have survived to offer some substantial clues.[100]

The first decade of the twentieth century was, if anything, volatile, in the coastwise collier business. As noted above, 1904 was probably one of Percy & Small's weakest financial years during the decade, with many of their vessels deeply in debt or "running astern," to quote one of William Palmer's more colorful phrases.[101] Dividends from their schooners dropped to almost half the level of 1903 which, as we already know, had been a so-so year thanks to the anthracite strike and overtaxed coal-handling facilities. A slow recovery followed, so slow in fact that Percy & Small may have seriously considered selling out the management of their vessels at one point.[102] But by 1906 net profits, including those from shipyard operations, climbed to $27,709 (+/- $426,000 in 1998). The next year, 1907, was another banner year, with net profits from schooner operations and shipbuilding rising to $31,500 (+/- $485,000 in 1998).

Percy & Small achieved their best peacetime earnings in 1908. But the big source of income for that year came not from schooner dividends, but from the shipbuilding business. In fact, schooner dividends nose-dived 43 percent from their 1907 level to only $16,399 in 1908 (+/- $250,000 in 1998). Yet the firm posted an overall profit of $63,216 (+/- $975,000 in 1998), with most of it coming from shipyard operations and the booking of profits from the construction of Hulls #26–29.

Although complete accounts do not exist for the entire decade, it is likely that Percy & Small managed to eke out a profit from its operations in excess of $200,000 (+/- $3.1 million in 1998) for the period.[103] They also ended the decade with property (vessel, real estate, shipyard), cash, and accounts receivable with a book value of $260,000 (+/- $4 million in 1998), a gain of 50 percent in eight years.[104] All things considered, Sam Percy and Frank Small had done well given the nature of the business they were engaged in and the turmoil that marked the period. But between 1910 and 1914, they probably wished for the return of those halcyon days of the previous decade.

1 Parker, *Coal Schooners*, p. 85.

2 Statements of Earnings for the CORA F. CRESSY: 1902–17, Parker Collection. Time charters are usually identifiable as a string of voyages between the same two ports, often at the same rate. For example, the CORA F. CRESSY made at least five voyages between Newport News and Searsport (ME) in the summer and fall of 1906 at $.725 per ton.

3 *Ibid.* The CORA F. CRESSY had a six-month time charter in 1908 (Norfolk-Searsport) with the rate set at $.80 per ton. Her next charter, a shorter voyage to Boston, paid only $.60 per ton, the spot rates having declined throughout the summer and fall with many of the great schooners laid up for lack of business.

4 *Ibid.* Statement #36. The penalty was $.05 per cargo ton per 24 hours.

5 Parker, *Coal Schooners*, pp. 89–90. Parker quotes an article in the *Nautical Gazette* that notes that the MAUDE PALMER, on a six voyage charter from Baltimore to Boston, had used up all her laydays, already collected forty-one days of demurrage at $240 per day, and had only completed two trips!

6 *BT*, 12/26/1899. P&S subsequently libeled the cargo as did two other schooners—the ALICE M. COLBURN and the GEO. E. WALCOTT—who ran into the same problem at the same time.

7 *BT*, 7/18/1902.

8 *BT*, 8/12/1902.

9 *BT*, 6/3/1899.

10 *Harding v. Cargo of 4,698 Tons of New Rivers Steam Coal,* 147 Federal Reporter 971 (1906). The schooner was the DOROTHY PALMER.

11 *Percy, et al. v. Union Sulphur Co.,* 173 Federal Reporter 71 (1909).

12 *Union Sulphur Co. v. Percy, et al.,* 180 Federal Reporter 862 (1910).

13 W. F. Palmer to J. G. Hannah, 9/9/1904, Palmer Collection.

14 Parker, *Coal Schooners*, p. 96.

15 "For twenty-one years I served as attorney and Washington representative of this organization [ACA], resigning from that position in 1921 to become a Commissioner of the United States Shipping Board." Edward Clarence Plummer, *Reminiscences of a Yarmouth Schoolboy,* p. 248.

16 Parker, *Coal Schooners*, pp. 98–99.

17 Statements of Earnings for the CORA F. CRESSY: Statements #1, #9, #15, etc., Parker Collection.

18 W. F. Palmer to W. H. Frasier, Atlantic Coast Seamen's Union, Palmer Collection. The effort was apparently unsuccessful.

19 *Philadelphia Press,* 2/25/1902.

20 Atlantic Coast Transportation Company, operated by John G. Crowley.

21 *NYMR*, 1/15/1890. A shipmaster described seamen as "childlike" and easily led.

22 *NYMR*, 7/30/1902.

23 *NYMR*, 12/17/1902; *Boston Globe*, 1/30/1901. The S. P. BLACKBURN paid the highest wages on the coast when it shipped a crew at Providence in December 1901 for $35 per month. The union scale was: to 799 GRT, $25 per month; 800–1,500 GRT, $30 per month; above 1,500 GRT, $35 per month.

24 *BT*, 1/14 and 2/25/1904.

25 *BT*, 3/23, 4/2, and 8/30/1904. The cases reported involved enticing duly articled seamen away from the schooners ADDIE M. LAWRENCE and ELEANOR A. PERCY. The walking delegates, so-called, received a month each in the slammer and a $100 fine. Subsequently, the Massachusetts Supreme Court issued an injunction against the union, prohibiting it from interfering with non-union seamen.

26 W. F. Palmer to P&S, 2/13/1904; W. F. Palmer to Eleazer Clark, 3/2/1904 and 6/13/1907, Palmer Collection.

27 Parker, *Coal Schooners*, p. 60.

28 *BT*, 1/29/1904; W. F. Palmer to P&S, 2/13, 15/1904, Palmer Collection.

29 W. F. Palmer to P&S, 2/13/1904, Palmer Collection.

30 *BT*, 2/25/1904. It is not clear whether Captain McKown was relief skipper of the PERCY at the time, or acting on behalf of the ACA.

31 *BT*, 8/30/1904.

32 *BT*, 3/15, 16/1904.

33 In 1914 seamen on the big six-masters were paid only $25 per month. *BT*, 12/24/1914.

34 *BT*, 10/23/1905.

35 One of the pioneering firms in the seagoing barge system was the Kennebec Steam Towage Company of Bath, part of the extensive Morse interests, that had two huge barges (2,254 and 2,383 GRT) built in 1889 and 1893, INDEPENDENT and KNICKERBOCKER.

36 Among the barged square-riggers were the GEORGE R. SKOLFIELD, the WILLIAM F. BABCOCK, SHENANDOAH, the A. G. ROPES, GLORY OF THE SEAS, and the DAVID CROCKETT.

37 Parker, *Coal Schooners*, pp. 90–91. But it still continued to grow at the expense of the schooners.

38 W. F. Palmer to Wm. H. Thayer, 4/3/1908, Palmer Collection.

39 Parker, *Coal Schooners*, p. 23.

40 *BT*, 8/12/1902.

41 *BT*, 12/20/1902.

42 Chapter 7; recall the last voyage of the DAVIS

PALMER—one of the last reports of her progress came from the captain of the coal barge HOPATCONG, part of a string of barges being towed by tug ONTARIO, off the Cape's backside.

43 *NYMR*, 8/20/1902.

44 Statements of Earnings for the CORA F. CRESSY: Statements #4–15, Parker Collection.

45 The CORA F. CRESSY's average break-even point during her first seven years in service was $.59 per ton of cargo delivered.

46 *BT*, 6/15/1904.

47 *BT*, 8/5/1904. This was patent balderdash; see fn #45. A few years later many of these same schooners were returning at least an anemic profit on freights considerably below those being quoted in 1904. See: Statements of Earnings for the CORA F. CRESSY, Parker Collection.

48 *BT*, 6/25/1904. This approach was logical from an economic point of view. All else being equal, a 1,500-ton schooner cost more per ton of cargo to operate than a 2,000-ton schooner; and a 2,000-ton schooner cost more to operate per ton carried than a 3,000-ton schooner.

49 The ELEANOR A. PERCY was at Newport News for two months awaiting a charter; J. S. Winslow & Co. had nine of its largest schooners in Portland with shipkeepers aboard; *BT*, 8/6/1904; W. F. Palmer to A. E. Hemphill, 8/9/1904, Palmer Collection.

50 *BT*, 9/27/1904; the other schooners in the James River fleet included the JACOB M. HASKELL, EDWARD H. COLE, ELIZABETH PALMER, and the SINGLETON PALMER.

51 *BT*, 9/7/1904.

52 *BT*, 9/27/1904.

53 W. F. Palmer to Prentiss Howard, 10/1/1904, Palmer Collection.

54 Captain F. W. Patten to Arthur Sewall & Co., 8/22/1904, Sewall Papers.

55 Statements of Earnings for the CORA F. CRESSY: #6–17, Parker Collection. The dividends represented the net profit from the vessel's operation, but were gross profit to Percy & Small which had to pay their insurance and interest charges.

56 Percy & Small, Monthly Statements, July–November 1903 and 1904, Parker Collection.

57 W. F. Palmer to Myron D. Wick, 10/21/1904, Palmer Collection.

58 *NYMR*, 4/15/1908.

59 Statements of Earnings for the CORA F. CRESSY: Statement #106, Parker Collection. The CRESSY, under tow herself, was pulled across a string of Consolidated Coal Company barges being towed by the tug CUMBERLAND. One of the barges was heavily damaged and a barge crewman killed. It took five years to settle the case.

60 *NYMR*, 5/6/1908.

61 *BT*, 12/14/1909; *NYMR*, 3/30/1910.

62 William P. Quinn, *Shipwrecks Around Cape Cod*, p. 101. An early and enthusiastic canal user was Captain J. H. Curtis of the three-masted schooner WINNEGANCE. The captain was impressed by the ease of the transcanal passage, the time and anxiety saved, and the fact that the canal was electrically lighted throughout its entire length. *NYMR*, 2/17/1915.

63 Parker, *Coal Schooners*, pp. 93–94. The Reading Railroad operated a fleet of small iron coal steamers built in 1874 between Philadelphia and New England ports with thirteen of the original fourteen still in active service in 1902. In addition, they controlled the mines, the railroad between the mines, and the Philadelphia loading docks.

64 Parker, *Coal Schooners*, pp. 93–95.

65 It cost approximately four to five times as much per day to keep a fully manned steam collier waiting as it did a schooner of the same capacity.

66 *NYMR*, 11/29/1911. The collier NEWTON loaded and trimmed 7,000 tons of coal and 600 tons of general cargo in four hours and 55 minutes at Baltimore.

67 Parker, *Coal Schooners*, p. 101.

68 *NYMR*, 1/27/1909.

69 *Ibid.*

70 *NYMR*, 10/18/1911.

71 *NYMR*, 6/16/1909.

72 *BT*, 6/1/1912 and 12/7/1915.

73 *BT*, 10/19/1914. Crowell & Thurlow subsequently had two colliers built at the Bath Iron Works.

74 *BT*, 4/24/1914. The LISMAN later joined the World War I offshore trade rush.

75 *BT*, 11/6/1912.

76 Bath's G. G. Deering delivered the two five-masters in this period (COURTNEY C. HOUCK and JEROME JONES). The seven four-masters were also delivered by Bath shipbuilders including two by Deering (MONTROSE W. HOUCK and LYDIA MCLELLAN BAXTER), one by Kelley, Spear (WILLIAM C. MAY), and four by Percy & Small (DUSTIN G. CRESSY, CARL F. CRESSY, CHARLES D. LOVELAND, and C. C. MENGEL, JR).

77 Arthur Sewall & Co. built the five-masted steel KINEO (1903), Crowley built the giant steel seven-master THOMAS W. LAWSON (1902), and six-master WILLIAM L. DOUGLAS (1903) in anticipation of this trade. Palmer was convinced that wooden schooners could do the job and they were considerably cheaper to build.

78 The only coal mined at that time on the West Coast was in British Columbia, so the presumed source was the Appalachian bituminous mines. Coal was also mined in large quantities in eastern Australia, a lot of which was shipped to the west coast of Canada and the U.S. and to Hawaii, but the route from Sydney to Luzon was essentially uphill for sailing vessels.

[79] The two principal exports from the Philippines at the time were manila fiber and sugar.

[80] Contract For Schooner "Number Sixteen" of the Palmer Fleet, 10 December 1907, Parker Collection.

[81] The GOV. AMES arrived in Liverpool in the spring of 1894.

[82] The SEWALL and KINEO both followed the same rough itinerary all the way round the world. It is not known whether this was deliberate planning or sheer happenstance.

[83] Patten's eight-year-old daughter, the cabin boy, and one crewman apparently were not affected.

[84] As quoted in Mark W. Hennessy, *The Sewall Ships of Steel*. Augusta, ME: *Kennebec Journal* Press,1937, p. 372.

[85] Patten noted that he had used up fourteen sails on the circumnavigation, an observation that generated some discussion of pairing big schooners with large oceangoing tugs for the difficult Cape Horn passage, but this never went beyond the talking stage.

[86] W. F. Palmer to Captain James E. Creighton, 2/11/1905; W. F. Palmer to D. B. Dearborn, 3/3/1905, Palmer Collection. These letters expressed great interest on behalf of Palmer and Percy & Small regarding the "Pacific" trade. The latter also expressed considerable doubt over obtaining return cargoes and the ability of the great schooners to stand up to the rigors of the Cape Horn passage.

[87] There are comparatively few first person accounts of sailing the great schooners that have come down to us today. Frederick Sturgis Laurence's account of his passage north in the SARAH C. ROPES is a classic (*Coasting Passage*). Less well known, but very informative, is F. L. Eno's article, "A Few Days Off Shore," published in the 20 November 1903 issue of *Forest and Stream*. He went in the JENNIE FRENCH POTTER, a moderate-sized five-master, from Portland to Brunswick, Georgia. Finally, William A. Hill published an article in the June 1951 issue of *Rudder* entitled "At Sea in the Blizzard of '98" which apparently was derived from an interview with Lester Harriman of Prospect, Maine, who had been first mate in the four-master WESLEY M. OLER on a passage in late 1898 that saw the schooner and her crew fighting for survival in the infamous PORTLAND Gale. A recent book by Sebastian Junger, *The Perfect Storm*, New York: W. W. Norton & Company, 1997, describes in considerable detail just how bad wind and wave, individually and in combination, can be.

[88] Stinson Davis Interview by Captains Douglas K. and Linda J. Lee, 1989, Lee Collection.

[89] U.S. Coast & Geodetic Survey, Chart 1107, Georges Bank and Nantucket Shoals, 1913.

[90] *NYMR*, 10/29/1913; *BT*, 10/25/1913.

[91] *BT*, 10/25/1913.

[92] Frederick Sturgis Laurence, *Coasting Passage*. Second Edition. Concord, MA: Charles S. Morgan, 1968.

[93] Kreger crossed the Atlantic four times in the big EDWARD J. LAWRENCE during World War I, confident in his ability to navigate by celestial observation.

[94] Laurence, *Coasting Passage*, p. 41.

[95] F. L. Eno, "A Few Days Off Shore," *Forest and Stream*, November 20, 1903.

[96] William H. Hill, "At Sea in the Blizzard of '98," *Rudder*, June 1951, pp. 18–19, 63. Hill credits this account to first mate Lester Harriman of the WESLEY M. OLA [*sic*] which should be spelled OLER.

[97] Laurence, *Coasting Passage*, p. 15.

[98] Eno, "A Few Days Off Shore."

[99] Conversation with Mr. Charles Barth, September 1995; Notes of Conversations with Charles Barth by Evelyn Hannaren (his daughter), January 1996. Barth is undoubtedly the last surviving crewman of the largest wooden sailing vessel.

[100] *PSJ*; P&S Trial Balances, 12/1901–12/1916, Parker Collection; Miscellaneous Monthly and Annual Balance Sheets, Parker Collection.

[101] W. F. Palmer to Prentiss Howard, 11/14/1904, Palmer Collection. P&S did not build a five-master for their own account for three years, between the launching of the GRACE A. MARTIN in 1904 and the start of the GOVERNOR BROOKS in 1907, after building four between 1899–1902.

[102] W. F. Palmer to J. S. Winslow & Co., 3/16/1905, Palmer Collection. "Now, confidentially, do you think it is true that P&S have approached various parties in Boston to sell out the management of all their vessels?"

[103] P&S Annual Statements, 1906–08, Parker Collection. Net profit from all operations in this three-year period alone came to $122,425 (+/- $1.9 million in 1998).

[104] P&S Trial Balances, entries for December 1901 and December 1909, Parker Collection.

TEN

The Final Years: 1910–1921

Captain Sam Percy and partner Frank Small couldn't help but feel twinges of concern as dawn of the first day of the new year of 1910 rolled westward through Bath. Their newest and biggest schooner, WYOMING, was overdue at her loading port after sailing from the Kennebec two weeks earlier on her maiden voyage. To compound their concerns, among those aboard the big new vessel was a young military school cadet, John B. Brooks, son of one Percy & Small investor and nephew of the governor of the state of Wyoming.

As matters turned out, WYOMING and all aboard had been blown far offshore by a bitter winter gale, but the staunch vessel and her skilled master (Captain Angus McLeod) weathered the danger and a week later, she was safe in port with young Cadet Brooks on his way back to military school. A few years after his adventures aboard the world's largest wooden sailing vessel, he became one of the earliest recipients of pilot's wings from the U.S. Army and many years later, retired as a major general in the U.S. Air Force.

Reassured by the safe arrival in port of WYOMING,

Sam Percy and Frank Small turned their attention to larger concerns. Although they had just added an additional 6,000 tons of carrying capacity to their fleet of schooners, raising their total capacity by 16 percent, charter rates for coal continued to decline as more of the market went to the steam colliers. And to make matters worse, the demand for additional schooner tonnage that had looked so bright in 1907 and encouraged a wooden shipbuilding boomlet during 1907–08 rapidly dried up, so much so, that one frame ordered by Percy & Small in 1908 for a small four-master lay unused in the shipyard throughout 1909.[1]

It had become patently obvious during the waning of 1909 that the great coal schooners were losing the competition for market to the steam colliers. Even as Percy & Small strove to complete the world's last six-master and largest wooden sailing vessel in the world, the market for new large schooners, a niche filled principally by Percy & Small for the previous decade, had all but disappeared. The future was not looking too bright.

France & Canada Steamship Company purchased a huge quantity of schooner tonnage in 1917, principally from Percy & Small and J. S. Winslow & Company, at unbelievably high prices. Three of those schooners lie at the France & Canada pier in New York, probably about 1919–20: the MARTHA P. SMALL (left, front), an unknown five-master, possibly the CORA F. CRESSY (left, rear), and the EDWARD J. LAWRENCE (right).

Photo by Captain James E. Creighton, courtesy of Captains Douglas K. and Linda J. Lee and Captain W. J. Lewis Parker, USCG, Ret.

A SATISFACTORY INVESTMENT

It is altogether possible that Percy & Small would have lived out their days as financial flops if it were not for one of the most murderous interludes in human history: World War I. But in the interim, they lost two schooners—largely uninsured—within the span of five years. And, along with everyone else in the coal schooner business, they saw charter rates decline to levels below those of the very dull year of 1908. The Great War figuratively tossed life rings (many of solid gold, it would appear) to a small coterie of owners in Maine-built, Maine-operated schooners who had been contemplating the rapid

devaluation of their schooner investments, but had not worked up the courage to sell or find buyers at a price they were willing to accept.

As noted in the previous chapter, 1907 had been a very profitable year for shareholders in Percy & Small schooners. Charter rates reached levels last seen at the beginning of the decade, even in the face of a financial panic on Wall Street that ultimately led to the passage of the Federal Reserve Act of 1913. But the effects of the panic were soon reflected in a concomitant decline in freight rates and dividends paid to shareholders. Unfortunately, the earnings records of Percy & Small schooners become very fragmentary after 1907, but fortunately, we can track the state of the business through the collective records of a few J. S. Winslow schooners whose experience approximated that of their Bath sisters during this period.[2]

The rates then began to recover slowly during 1909 and J. S. Winslow & Company posted slight gains in the returns from their big six-masters—1909 at 10 percent, 1910 at 12 percent, 1911 at 11 percent, 1912 at 15 percent. However, if one assumed a depreciation rate of 5 percent per year—rather low given the lack of investor interest in the big schooners after 1909—the return, net of depreciation, averaged 7 percent over those four years. This was not an insignificant return, but one far below returns the big schooners racked up in 1906–07, when the big Winslow six-masters earned on average 14 percent after deducting depreciation.[3]

Following a moderate but brief recession during 1910–11, an anemic "recovery" marked the succeeding three years as commodity prices stagnated, stock market prices went into a slow, irregular decline, and the coal schooners found themselves increasingly pitted against a wave of steam colliers coming into the shipping market. Schooner earnings, which rebounded somewhat in 1912, once again sagged downward during 1913–14. J. S. Winslow's big six-masters, for example, saw earnings of 10 percent after depreciation in 1912 nose dive to approximately 3 percent in 1914, the year the Great War got underway.

The onset of the war did not immediately drive coastwise rates up, but a number of idle or under-employed schooners were soon under charter again as shippers began to anticipate the dislocation of normal peacetime trade. It did not take long before the nature of the war's impact began to take shape. By early 1915, Argentina was receiving only 50 percent of its normal coal supply from the Welsh mines.[4] In June 1915, Spanish coal stocks, imported largely from the same Welsh mines, were approaching exhaustion. And in Brazil and Greece, the need to create new links to new suppliers was more than self-evident as their own coal piles dwindled.[5]

The government of Greece took immediate steps,

ordering 100,000 tons of coal from American mines even as the battle lines across France stabilized.[6] Additional orders for coal began pouring into the U.S. from Brazil and Argentina, who had also previously relied upon Welsh coal shipped in British-flag vessels. Soon, the best opportunities in the shipping business were to be found going offshore as the coastwise charter rates increased at a more sedate rate, held down by the steam colliers, barge traffic taking advantage of the new Cape Cod Canal, and a series of big schooner time charters taken earlier at low rates.[7]

Nonetheless, the surplus tonnage—largely in the form of underemployed or idle great schooners—began to melt away and freight rates moved upward. The CORA F. CRESSY's experience was typical. After a long series of coal cargoes to Portland at $.70 per ton, the rate jumped to $.75 per ton during the fall of 1914 for a time charter that was fulfilled by March 1915.[8] As soon as Percy & Small had the CRESSY out from under that time charter, they had her signed up for the lucrative South American trade where she remained until sold to the France & Canada Steamship Company in August 1917.

On her first trip south of the equator, the CRESSY carried a load of coal to Rio with a prepaid freight of $7.25 per ton. Her return cargo, 3,013 tons of manganese ore, brought an additional $10,328.81 in freight monies, bringing her total gross revenue for the round trip voyage to approximately $32,000 (+/- $401,000 in 1998).[9] This was considerably more than the veteran five-master could earn during the same period of time trudging back and forth between the coal ports and Portland with freights at $.75 per ton.

Subsequently, the CRESSY was joined by other Percy & Small schooners, including the MARTHA P. SMALL and the GOVERNOR BROOKS hauling case oil to the River Plate and returning with cargoes of quebracho wood and linseed cake.[10] When the SMALL returned to the United States following her first voyage, Percy & Small declared a dividend to her owners of $297 per 1/64![11] Throughout 1915, freights to South America mounted at a satisfying pace; the EDWARD B. WINSLOW's charter in December 1915 to Rio had advanced 10 percent over that paid the CRESSY and the WINSLOW for the same destination several months earlier.[12] By mid-1916 coal freights to Rio had risen to $16.50.[13]

But Sam Percy and Frank Small had something else besides the latest and future charter rates on their minds. By the first of July 1915, their fleet was composed of a dozen schooners ranging in size from the "little" four-master ROBERT P. MURPHY of 697 gross tons to WYOMING, the 3,730-gross-ton giant. More important, however, was the age of their schooners: with an average age of eleven years they were approaching great schooner old age. Four of their vessels were fifteen years or older, four more ranged between ten and fourteen years, and four fell into the under-ten category. The first group were, in fact, getting close to wearing out, a condition that Percy & Small were all too familiar with when it came to keeping their first two five-masters in service throughout the last decade.

There was a larger concern than the aging of the fleet, however. That problem could, after all, be addressed by building additional schooners (the most recent addition, the CARL F. CRESSY, was launched on 6 January 1915) to replace some of the tonnage that had been lost or was becoming superannuated. Did Percy & Small wish to continue in the shipping business, especially since the war had started to drive up freight rates and open new opportunities for increased vessel earnings? Or was this the time with its strong and growing market for tonnage—any tonnage—to phase out the shipping

Dustin G. and Carl F. Cressy joined their parents as namesakes of Percy & Small schooners launched in 1912 and 1915. These were the last schooners the firm built for their own account.

Courtesy: Maine Maritime Museum

operation gracefully but completely? In the end, Percy & Small chose to phase out the shipping end of the business, although the final decision was deferred until late 1916 or early 1917.

On the surface at least, this choice appears to be obvious. It was becoming clearly evident as early as 1908 that the days of the schooners were numbered and the intervening years with their limited returns and the growing involvement of steam colliers in the coal shipping market had underscored this point. William F. Palmer, writing to one of the investors in his schooners in 1908 acknowledged that the great schooners were obsolete and ultimately doomed, but optimistically predicted that they wouldn't see this in their lifetime.[14] In Palmer's own case he was absolutely correct: he died eleven months later.

There were other, more substantial, straws in the wind. Captain John G. Crowley disposed of the Coastwise Transportation Company's schooners and replaced them with steam colliers by 1916. Although Crowley had actually reorganized his shipping business into a full-blown stock corporation more than a decade earlier, the growing movement to steam colliers required so much capital that the long practiced methods of ownership in individual vessels was effectively doomed.[15]

There was also no question that between 1910–14 there was little or no interest in buying great schooners except at greatly discounted prices. The owners faced the prospect, therefore, of selling at considerable loss to themselves or of sticking it out, earning dividends on the newer schooners that, while not promising to recover their original investment would, at least, ameliorate their potential loss. Ocea Cahill's widow, an example of the former, sold all her shares in Percy & Small schooners in June 1914 to none other than Gard Deering, "for less than the cost of a share in one vessel."[16] The wily Deering turned a very tidy profit within three years, but the poor widow lost what, in a few years, would have been a small fortune. It was too bad in her case that the very human tendency to hope that, in time, the coal shipping business would improve was not strong enough to overcome her lack of faith and need for cash.

The war and the demand for additional tonnage began to raise the hopes of the typical Percy & Small investor. And the offshore voyages to South America with their generous dividends, along with the growing demand for tonnage to carry supplies to a Europe wracked by war, rekindled interest in schooner property. Percy & Small began to sell off their oldest vessels. The rather limber HELEN W. MARTIN—extensively rebuilt once—was the first to go in July 1915 at age fifteen for $60,000 (+/- $750,000 in 1998) to A. H. Bull & Co. of New York. We followed her subsequent career in Chapter 8.

Five months later, the firm sold off its longtime fleet flagship and, for many years, largest schooner, the six-master ELEANOR A. PERCY, also fifteen years of age. Her sale price of $125,000 (+/- $1.56 million in 1998) probably mirrored more demand for hulls, her substantially greater cargo capacity than the MARTIN, and possibly her marginally better structural condition. The new owners, a New York firm named Harby Steamship Company, Inc., operated the big six-master for eight months before selling her to the Norwegian firm of Theo B. Heisten & Sonnen of Kristiansand, which renamed the proud schooner DUSIE and placed her under the Norwegian flag.[17] She lasted three more years and changed hands one more time, getting back her original name and flag.[18] But her long hull, already severely strained a number of times, gave out one last time on a voyage to Denmark with a cargo of grain on Christmas morn-

ing 1919. Of her eighteen-man crew, five were rescued by the Swansea trawler WELWYN CASTLE after four days in an open boat. The rest of the crew also got away from the vessel but were never seen again. Nearly two years later, the PERCY's logbook, tightly wrapped in canvas, washed ashore at St. Mary's in the Scilly Isles.[19]

In February 1916, Percy & Small sold their oldest and the last surviving schooner not built in their south end shipyard, the WILLIAM H. CLIFFORD. The CLIFFORD, six months shy of twenty-one years of service, brought $70,000 (+/- $780,000 in 1998), a remarkable figure considering her original cost of $72,000 in 1895 (+/- $1.29 million in 1998), advanced age, and relatively small size.

Curiously, the M. D. CRESSY remained unsold for another year, although she was older than the HELEN W. MARTIN and the PERCY. The only reasonable explanation for the long delay in selling Percy & Small's first, and most problem-laden five-master, was her reputation. It was in 1915, you will recall, that, badly strained and leaking with a cargo of hard pine, she was abandoned by officers and crew. Subsequently salvaged, towed to port, and given an extensive overhaul at Percy & Small, all well publicized in maritime circles, she resumed work. It is highly likely that her reputation for straining and leaking—going back to early in her career—was pretty common knowledge along the waterfront, thus complicating her sale. Following her overhaul and one voyage to Bahia (Brazil), she once again reappeared at Percy & Small for extensive repairs that took three weeks, one more indication that she was a basket case.[20] Nonetheless, Percy & Small found a buyer in the form of the American-Union Line. As you recall, on her first voyage bound for Europe for that firm, the CRESSY literally disintegrated in a storm after she had barely cleared New York.

With Percy & Small's first five-master finally sold, the firm still controlled a fleet of seven vessels totaling 13,492 gross tons that included one six-master, three five-masters, and three four-masters. It was a good mix of vessels whose ages ran from sixteen to two years and whose physical condition was good to excellent. With the freight rates for South America,

The WILLIAM H. CLIFFORD, sold out of the Percy & Small fleet in early 1916, was sailing light for the United States six hundred miles west of Nantes, France, on 8 September 1917. Captain Lewis Blackwood, who had brought a cargo of case oil safely to France through the German *unterseebooten*, was probably congratulating himself on avoiding the submarine menace when a distinctly unfriendly shell went whistling through the rigging. Kapitan-Leutnant Franz Schuster, skipper of the submarine UB-50, backed by the authority of an 8.8 cm deck gun, ordered the American crew to abandon ship. A German detachment then boarded the schooner and removed a few stores, valuables, and the ship's papers before setting fire to her. When this didn't appear to accelerate the old schooner's trip to the bottom, an impatient Schuster ordered his gun crew to open fire, an event recorded in this picture. The first shell was short, but subsequent rounds struck and fatally wounded the old schooner. Captain Lewis and crew, who observed all this from the lifeboat, were then given bread, water, and a compass course to steer for the Irish coast. They landed in France. Schuster and the UB-50, along with the pictures, returned safely to Imperial Germany.

Courtesy: Dr. Jürgen Meyer

Europe, and the Mediterranean climbing into the stratosphere, Percy & Small and the other owners in their schooner property were poised to rake in enormous dividends. Yet, within a span of four months, the firm sold off the balance of its fleet.

There appear to be three factors that influenced the decision to sell rather than going on for a while longer, although exactly what weight each was assigned in the final decision is speculative. First, there was Frank Small, the firm's junior partner and business manager. It was Small who knew most about the intricacies of the shipping business and had estab-

lished a network of contacts with shipping agents and shippers. He developed a particularly close relationship with Eleazer Clark, the longtime boss of J. S. Winslow & Company, who frequently arranged for charters of Percy & Small vessels and long served as the Bath firm's best customer for new construction and repair work. Although Clark's reputation for personal probity was soon called into question by some, their joint working relationship appears to have been strictly aboveboard. But the fifty-four-year-old Frank Small was in rapidly failing health by the spring of 1917. He died suddenly on

21 June at the Somerville (MA) home of his old friends, Captain and Mrs. Angus McLeod.[21]

Second, the J. S. Winslow & Company had also been engaged in selling off some of its fleet, disposing of the surviving four Palmer vessels (Clark had purchased the managing owner's interest in the Palmer fleet in 1910) in March for a price reported to exceed a half million dollars.[22] Within a month after Percy & Small sold WYOMING to the France & Canada Steamship Company, J. S. Winslow & Company followed suit with the sale of most of its remaining fleet, including the four six-masters and the five-master OAKLEY C. CURTIS to the same firm.[23] It appears from all of this that the two firms had certainly discussed what steps to take and possibly even coordinated the sale of their vessels, although each negotiated separately with the buyers.[24]

Finally, there was the deteriorating situation vis-à-vis Imperial Germany. That nation demonstrated a particularly heavy-handed approach to the United States, whose neutrality toward the Kaiser and his government was sorely tried by a series of incidents and activities including the sinking of the LUSITANIA and SUSSEX, attempts to draw Mexico into a war with America, and the reversion to unrestricted submarine warfare. It was clear by early 1917 that the United States was moving toward a declaration of war against Germany and her allies. Such a move would effectively create a whole new ball game in the shipping business, offsetting the potential for extravagant freight rates with the additional risk of destruction by enemy action even when trading with neutral nations outside of the war zone. This was not the shipping business Frank Small, Sam Percy, and their friends and associates knew and were comfortable with.

So Percy & Small chose to take advantage of the situation existing in the spring and summer of 1917, selling the remainder of their fleet for a healthy profit.

WYOMING was reportedly sold for about $350,000 (+/- $3.5 million in 1998) and the five-masters CORA F. CRESSY and MARTHA P. SMALL brought $382,500 a few months later.[25] The prices for the GOVERNOR BROOKS and the three four-masters were not published, but Winslow's HENRY F. KREGER, a thirteen-year-old four-master of 991 gross tons, was sold that summer for $140,000. It is more than likely that each of the CRESSY twins brought more than the KREGER, being roughly of the same size and several years younger. The BROOKS must have brought at least as much, if not more, than the smaller and older CORA F. CRESSY, which sold for $202,500. Therefore it is probable that the final sell-off of the Percy & Small fleet grossed approximately $1.5 million (+/- $15 million in 1998), less the 5 percent seller's commission that went to Percy & Small, divided among the various shareholders. To this must be added the earlier sale of the older schooners that brought an estimated $350,000 (+/- $4.1 million in 1998).[26] It was a substantial return for any of the original investors in Percy & Small schooners who, through thick and thin, had stayed the course, unlike Mrs. Cahill.

Of course, it could be argued that by sticking it out another year, Percy & Small and the other vessel shareholders would have done even better both from substantial dividends and an even more inflated vessel market. However, with a future obscured by the rapid unrolling and unpredictability of events, and the loss of Frank Small, a key member of the Percy & Small team, the decision was reasonable and prudent. Thus, the firm left what had been its primary business when it was organized nearly a quarter century before.

Captain Wiley Dickinson summed up the results best in a note he wrote on the letter transmitting the check for his $1/128$ share of the sale proceeds for the CORA F. CRESSY: "This was a satisfactory investment."[27]

SHIPBUILDING LANGUISHES

The shipping business went into a long decline in 1908, interrupted by the war. The wooden shipbuilding business followed suit two years later. After arguably the most profitable year in the history of the shipbuilding arm of the firm in 1908, Percy & Small produced their *magnum opus*, WYOMING, and then the shipbuilding business all but collapsed. In fact, if it were not for their ship repair business—see below—the south end shipyard would have been largely idle over the next six years. In the period 1910–15, Percy & Small delivered exactly two schooners to themselves (both four-masters) totaling only 1,760 gross tons. In addition, the shipyard built three lowly coal lighters whose combined tonnage equalled that of just one of the four-masters. The 2,617-gross-ton output between 1910–15 stood in stark contrast to the twelve schooners totalling 32,095 gross tons delivered during the previous six-year period.

The wooden shipbuilding crisis did not affect Percy & Small alone. Not one great schooner was launched from Maine shipyards in 1910 and only two in 1911. Those were built for Gard Deering's fleet, one at the shipyard south of Percy & Small, and the

This photo of the DUSTIN G. CRESSY taken sometime during the winter of 1911–12, underlines the lack of urgency to complete the schooner. Although she only requires her sails to be bent on and is already in her launching cradle, the CRESSY did not go overboard until 12 July.

Courtesy: Captains Douglas K. and Linda J. Lee

other at the old New England Company yard at Bath's north end. The latter schooner, the MONTROSE W. HOUCK, was designed by Bant Hanson for Captain James Hawley but construction was suspended by Hawley, and Deering subsequently purchased her on the stocks. Hanson not only designed the HOUCK, but he served as her master builder for Hawley and, subsequently, for Deering. Her model, scaled down slightly, was recycled by Percy & Small for their last nine four-masters (see Appendix B).

In the 1910–15 time period, Maine shipbuilders delivered only six great schooners: five four-masters and one five-master. All were built in Bath with Deering getting credit for three, Percy & Small two, and Kelley, Spear one. It was not until 1917 that the first great schooners built outside of Bath since 1909 were launched from other Maine shipyards.

The two schooners built by Percy & Small were for their own account and were named for early investor Myron D. Cressy's two sons, Dustin G. and Carl F., thus giving the family the distinction of having a vessel named after each of its members.[28] Planned during 1908, the moderate-sized four-masters shared an elegance of line that was sometimes lost in the translation to the larger five- and six-masters. The schooners' moderate size also made them well fitted for carrying timber and general cargo, as well as coal, particularly to and from the smaller outports along the eastern seaboard. In this role they had some success before the war intervened.

Their construction, however, was deliberately drawn out by Percy & Small. The first expenditures

A respectable crowd of spectators joined by the tug SEGUIN was on hand on a cold, windy 6 January 1915 when CARL F. CRESSY took to the Kennebec. Although all went well with the launching of the last schooner built for Percy & Small's account, Captain Sam and Miles Merry must have been mortified to learn that the ship's name had been misspelled on her hull—Carle rather than Carl.

Courtesy: Andrew J. Nesdall

involving the DUSTIN G. CRESSY (Schooner #31) were posted in the trial balances as early as October 1908, probably representing the purchase of moulds from Bant Hanson.[29] The frame, timbers, and planking for #31 were ordered before the end of 1908 and were in the shipyard by the spring of 1909, although actual construction did not begin for another twelve months. Even then progress on the vessel only moved ahead in fits and starts, with the hull sitting on the building slip for months at a time with no visible advance toward completion.[30] From keel laying to launching, the DUSTIN G. CRESSY took twenty-six months to complete, and her stablemate the CARL F. CRESSY later consumed twenty months. Percy & Small, who routinely built two schooners simultaneously and normally completed vessels of this size in four to six months, spread their construction over fifty-two months.

It appears that Sam Percy and Frank Small's decision to go forward with the construction of schooners #31 and #32—they were numbered sequentially even though one of the coal lighters (#33) was built before construction actually started on #32—was motivated principally by a desire to keep the shipyard in operation and a core group of highly skilled shipbuilders on the payroll lest they disappear to greener pastures. In effect, both schooners served as "fillers" for the shipyard's reduced workforce, bridging gaps in the flow of repairwork (see below) that flooded the yard between 1910–15 and the construction of the three coal lighters (Hulls #33–35). Although Percy & Small's workforce fell well below the level it achieved in 1907–08, a reliable cadre of workmen was assured a reasonable amount of continuing work at a time when virtually all wooden shipyards in Bath, in Maine, and along the East Coast of North America were idle.

The two schooners were virtually identical in size, as well as appearance, but they experienced two vastly different careers. The elder of the two started off by being the only Percy & Small vessel ever christened by a member of the male gender, namesake Dustin G. Cressy.[31] She then went on to a career marked by several brushes with disaster, yet she managed to remain in service until 1929. The disasters included a brush

with the shoals on Cape Cod's notorious "back side" when the CRESSY became badly iced up and unmanageable while bound to Portland with lumber. After fetching up on a sand bar off the Pamet River Life Saving Station and being subjected to a severe pounding, she was literally snatched from the breakers by the revenue cutter ACUSHNET just as a northeast snowstorm struck.[32] She had experienced a similar adventure the previous winter in the vicinity of Nantucket and was rescued by the tug NEPONSET.[33]

A few years later, in 1917, she almost met her end after being hit broadside by the Cunard steamer VALERIA while entering the Narrows into New York Harbor. Cut open clear to the turn of her bilge, the CRESSY filled rapidly, rolling over onto her beam ends as the crew made its way to safety. However, she didn't quite sink, thanks to her cargo of logwood, and eventually grounded out near Governor's Island. Salvagers placed a temporary patch on the jagged hole in her side and then righted and pumped out her soggy hull. She was then towed to her destination to discharge the wood before coming to Percy & Small for the necessary major repairs, all at Cunard's expense.[34] Percy & Small sold her just as repairs were being completed. After a few years of profitable service, she was sold again when the war boom began to collapse. She went through two or more owners during the 1920s, the last of whom was Charles E. Gremmels of New York, who purchased her for $1,250 (+/- $9,900 in 1998) in a marshal's sale.[35] She was eventually laid up until sometime after 1933, when she was towed as far up the Hackensack River (New Jersey) as possible and abandoned to the tender mercies of firewood gatherers.

Her "sister" schooner enjoyed a relatively trouble-free and prosperous career—for thirty-two months. Coming into service just as the demand for tonnage to South America began to accelerate, the CARL F. CRESSY turned a number of profitable case oil charters to Brazil under the Percy & Small house flag. Following her sale to the France & Canada Steamship Company, she received a very lucrative charter to carry case oil to France. The EDWARD J. LAWRENCE and the CARL F. CRESSY sailed from New York in company. After unloading their respective cargoes, they departed together under tow by a pair of French gunboats to get them safely through the submarine-infested Bay of Biscay. Two hundred miles offshore, the gunboats cast off the schooners who filled away on starboard tacks to the south. That night Captain Frank Peterson, skipper of the LAWRENCE, received a radio message warning of U-boats ahead and tacked ship and headed northwest, but the radio-less CRESSY continued south, where she was intercepted by a German submarine and sunk by gunfire. All hands were subsequently rescued.[36]

The coal lighters built by Percy & Small do not appear to have experienced much drama in their careers. The first, RANDALL & McALLISTER #2, was built in a month then towed to Portland, where she transported coal around the harbor for a firm very familiar with Percy & Small thanks to its connection with J. S. Winslow & Company.

The other two lighters, PEQUOSETTE and POCA-HONTAS NO. 1, were larger and outfitted with more sophisticated steam hoisting equipment for service in and around Boston Harbor. Their new owner, the Charles W. York Company, had contracts for bunkering a number of steamships calling regularly at Boston, including those of the United Fruit Company. To that end, the POCAHONTAS—however ugly in appearance—represented the cutting edge of bunkering technology in 1914 with her ability to transfer 1,250 or more tons of coal daily to hungry steamships.[37]

The war and demand for additional vessels soon changed the rather lackadaisical production schedule that Percy & Small had followed for six years. Although production would not achieve levels equal to the best years during the previous decade, it was substantial and profitable.

Struck broadside on 19 February 1917 by the SS VALERIA in New York's lower harbor, the DUSTIN G. CRESSY filled and rolled over on her beam ends—but floated on her cargo of log wood. Merritt, Chapman, & Scott succeeded in righting the schooner, getting a temporary patch over a hole running from the rail to the turn of the bilge, and pumping her out. She then was towed to her destination port, discharged, and towed on to Percy & Small, who completed her repairs.

Courtesy: Captains Douglas K. and Linda J. Lee

The aesthetic qualities of the three coal lighters built at Percy & Small between 1911–14 apparently did not appeal to photographers. The POCAHONTAS NO. 1 seems to have been the only one photographed.

Courtesy: Maine Maritime Museum

THE REPAIR BUSINESS

Far less glamorous than building great schooners —or even coal lighters for that matter—was the firm's repair business. It had grown since 1894 from basically minor repairs rendered to schooners delivering lumber to the shipyard to a substantial component of the shipyard's business, especially—but not exclusively—after 1909.

While many of the vessels undergoing repairs at Percy & Small over the years were naturally from their own fleet, J. S. Winslow & Company and William F. Palmer, as well as other owners, also sent their schooners to the Bath shipyard for routine maintenance and repairs. Although Percy & Small lacked drydocking facilities, the shipyard was capable of carrying out extensive repairwork of damage caused by collision, fire, and other mischance. The GEORGE W. WELLS

and ELEANOR A. PERCY, you will recall, caused a major stir in Bath when they were brought to the shipyard to repair their collision damage in 1901. Others followed over the years, among them the fire-damaged JANE PALMER, and the victims of collision— the HARWOOD PALMER, PRESCOTT PALMER, ALICIA B. CROSBY, DUSTIN G. CRESSY, and EDWARD B. WINSLOW.

Much of the work that Percy & Small craftsmen performed on visiting schooners fell into the category of the more routine maintenance that once had been carried out by a sailing vessel's relatively large crew during the course of long voyages. A square-rigger bound for San Francisco usually arrived at her destination with everything inboard of her bulwarks freshly painted, masts and spars gleaming with slush, decks recaulked, sails neatly repaired, and all exposed metal-work chipped and painted. This was not the usual case with the great schooners. Their short passages and small crews mitigated against more than the most limited maintenance being done at sea, confined mostly to time spent "soogeeing" coal-stained deckhouses and paint. And when a schooner arrived in port, the short turnaround times (during the better times) limited in-port work to the most essential repairs.

Percy & Small, J. S. Winslow, and Palmer generally sent their largest five- and six-masters to the Newport News Shipbuilding Company for an annual drydocking that included cleaning the bottom, inspection, and an application of a coat of antifouling paint. But it also became standard operating procedure after unloading to have their big schooners towed from Boston or Portland to the shipyard on the Kennebec where some of the schooners had first taken to the water. Palmer summed up the feeling of many of the schooner operators when he wrote, "Boston is no place to repair JANE PALMER [damaged in a bad dock fire] and I shall tow her to Bath where we get good labor of 10 hours a day, and where people know something about ships."[38]

The key was "knowing something about ships," especially wooden ships. Even when vessels suffered

Ship repair became an important, albeit secondary, source of revenue for the Percy & Small shipyard. The work encompassed not only schooners from their own fleet, but also included J. S. Winslow, Palmer, and other vessels as well. Here, the big HARWOOD PALMER is having damage repaired from her collision with the steamer JUNIATA in October 1905. The ROBERT P. MURPHY is nearing completion on the south ways (center), and the DAVIS PALMER on the north ways (right) appears to be closed in.

Stinson Brothers Photo, courtesy of Captains Douglas K. and Linda J. Lee

Charles Oliver (1855–1930), boss caulker, stands out in his bowler and paunch as a gang of his men interrupt their work recaulking the deck of either the EDWARD B. WINSLOW or EDWARD J. LAWRENCE to pose for the photographer during the World War I era. Recaulking the deck of a big six-master was no small job: count the number of strakes of deck planking visible in this picture, multiply that number by two to get the total number of strakes and then multiply it again by 340 to get the approximate number of feet of seams these caulkers had to fill. It's no small wonder a caulker's tool box was also a mobile stool.

Courtesy: Captain W. J. Lewis Parker, USCG, Ret.

damage requiring drydocking, the owners frequently retained Percy & Small—in the character of Miles M. Merry—to go to whichever port the stricken vessel lay to superintend repairs.[39] In some cases, Merry and Sam Percy were also called as expert witnesses testifying to the extent of the damage in admiralty court when it came to extracting compensation from the guilty parties.

Much of the repairwork was pretty basic: caulking decks and the hull above the light waterline, over-hauling machinery and rigging, replacing broken or damaged spars, and painting. A newer vessel might come in once every one or two years for a week or two of yard time, but as the schooners aged, their need for attention increased. In addition, seven to eight years after they were launched, each schooner was sub-jected to a half-time survey by the American Bureau of Shipping. The surveyor directed the removal of

selected planks and ceiling in order to inspect the condition of the frame timbers, and some fastenings were bored out in search of signs of rot. Upon com-pletion of the inspection, the surveyor specified the work necessary for the schooner to continue her class. Much of this work was carried out at Percy & Small, even on schooners they did not build.[40]

Then, as you already have learned, a number of the schooners were brought back to the shipyard in efforts to strengthen their sagging hulls. The M. D. CRESSY, HELEN W. MARTIN, and EDWARD J. LAWRENCE were each "stiffened" by Percy & Small one or more times during their careers.

The heaviest concentration of repairwork at the shipyard occurred between 1910–15, a bit of seren-dipity for Percy & Small, for it coincided with the period of minimal shipbuilding. This was not al-together sheer coincidence. The schooner fleet was

The great schooners were normally drydocked once a year to have their bottoms scrubbed, inspected, and covered with another coat of copper bottom paint. Prior to World War I, the big five- and six-masters normally had this done at Norfolk or Newport News in the large commercial graving docks available in those cities. This all changed during World War I, when the demand for shipping justified having vessels hauled wherever facilities were available. Thus WYOMING, sporting her new home port on her counter, is drydocked at the Winnisimmet Shipyard at Chelsea, Massachusetts, shortly after her purchase by the France & Canada Steamship Company.

Courtesy: Captain W. J. Lewis Parker, USCG, Ret.

aging and required more work. A number of firms that formerly built and repaired schooners shut down for lack of business. And it appears that Sam Percy pushed all the buttons and pulled all the levers developed from his lifetime in the business to bring repair work to his shipyard. It worked. At least twenty-two schooners came to the yard in 1910, twenty-eight during the next year, nineteen during 1912, and twenty-two again in 1913.[41] At times it appeared as if there was a schooner traffic jam at the south end shipyard, as Percy & Small frequently docked vessels at their yard, at Donnell's next door, and at the nearby Reed yard just upriver. Gard Deering also contributed to the congestion on occasion with one or two of his schooners adding to the forest of masts.

By 1914 the amount of repairwork began to fall off as freights improved and ship owners concluded that time was more important than money, thus sending their schooners to more expensive but also more convenient repair yards or deferring yard periods altogether in the interest of making money. Yet throughout the war period many a tired, worn out, and weary schooner made its way to Bath to be rejuvenated one more time.

A Contract Shipyard

Seven months after the CARL F. CRESSY was launched from Percy & Small, the firm proceeded to lay down its next schooner, which became in time the CHARLES D. LOVELAND. Another four-master that was a smaller version of the CRESSY twins, the LOVELAND was apparently a speculative venture on the part of the firm, and her construction marked the beginning of the final phase of shipbuilding that focused on meeting wartime demand.

In the course of the next five years (1916–20), the shipyard completed ten more schooners—seven four-masters and three five-masters—totaling 12,167 gross tons. It was a record that was surprisingly lackluster when compared to the shipyard's performance throughout the previous decade and in light of the growing demand for new schooners that sparked a rapid but short-lived revival of wooden shipbuilding in Maine.[42]

A number of factors contributed to the drop in tonnage production to less than one-third that of the century's first decade. The labor supply presented Percy & Small with its single greatest challenge, one that it never overcame during its last few years. During the first decade of the century, the shipyard relied on a locally based but aging workforce, supplemented by itinerant ship carpenters from other parts of the state and the Maritime Provinces. But a number of workers had since moved on following the stagnation of wooden shipbuilding in Bath. Fastener Sam

Barnes, you will recall, packed his bags and joined the 1915–16 exodus of Bath shipwrights to the shipyards of the Pacific Northwest. Other skilled shipbuilders were attracted to new shipyards being set up in Georgia and other southern coastal areas to take advantage of their proximity to the hard pine supply by promises of work, high pay, and a salubrious climate.[43] In some cases, Percy & Small lost workmen to a shipyard in Savannah which they played a minor role in founding (see below). And finally, the longtime pool of skilled labor from the Maritime Provinces dried up as younger men were recruited for military service and older men found work closer to home.

Percy & Small also found itself competing more and more for manpower with shipyards that were being reactivated or started from scratch along the coast including the huge Shattuck shipyard in Newington, New Hampshire, which was created to build wooden steamers for the government.[44] Then, the heirs of William T. Donnell—Percy & Small's next-door neighbor—sold his shipyard to Fields S. Pendleton of New York and Islesboro during 1917. After cleaning up the facility and putting it in shape for shipbuilding, the Pendleton Bros., Inc. proceeded to start work on their first new schooner—the BRINA P. PENDLETON. Although the Pendleton yard rarely employed more than twenty-five men, one of them was a longtime Percy & Small shipwright and Miles M. Merry understudy, Eliakim McCabe. At long last, he was able to claim the formal title of master builder. How many other regular Percy & Small workmen were pulled into the Pendleton operation is not known, but the loss of McCabe did not go unnoticed at Percy & Small.[45] This was especially true because Miles M. Merry retired after the launching of the C. C. MENGEL, JR. in August 1916, ending a career in wooden shipbuilding at the age of seventy-two that had begun fifty-six years earlier. But with Merry's departure, McCabe—who often was acting master builder in Merry's absence—did not succeed to the all-important position. Instead, Sam Percy brought in W. Judson Baker.[46]

Matters were further complicated locally by a labor market dominated by two steel shipbuilders, the Bath Iron Works and the recently organized Texas Company, a subsidiary of current-day Texaco, with both expanding their operations during 1916.[47] As a result, the workforce at Percy & Small doesn't appear to have exceeded a hundred men during the last five years and generally wavered between fifty and seventy-five men, well below the levels achieved between 1900 and 1909.

If availability of ship carpenters put a crimp in Percy & Small's productivity, the supply of suitable ship timber further complicated their building of more schooners. The fact of the matter was that high quality ship timber (yellow pine and white oak) was already overharvested in the South during the heyday of the great schooner. The most accessible, sizeable, best-quality timber had been figuratively strip mined. The result was steadily increasing prices for both oak and yellow pine—the latter also popular in the construction of homes and industrial buildings. Back in 1894, Percy & Small had purchased yellow pine for $18 per thousand board feet but the price had climbed to $31.25 during the next fifteen years, a 74 percent increase. The price for good quality yellow pine ship planking would nearly double once again between 1909 and 1918.[48]

The price jump was attributable to both the increasing rarity of good yellow pine ship timber and a sudden, even overwhelming, demand for the commodity to build more vessels, a program that, by 1917, was being avidly pursued by both private enter-

prise and by government. We have already seen that by 1916, Maine shipyards—new and recycled—were coming on line to build more schooners.

The federal government also got into the act starting during 1916 with the passage of the law establishing the U.S. Shipping Board (precursor to the Maritime Commission) and its wartime production arm, the Emergency Fleet Corporation. The latter, charged with the construction and—if necessary—operation of sufficient tonnage to meet America's shipping needs as a neutral or belligerent nation eventually put together an ambitious shipbuilding program assisted by a $50 million appropriation (+/- $560 million in 1998).

The Emergency Fleet Corporation, formally—if belatedly—organized just days after the U.S. declared war on Germany, immediately began requisitioning merchant vessels (steel) under construction in existing shipyards and letting contracts for additional vessels. Because America's steel shipbuilding capacity was limited, and much of that was dedicated to naval construction, a program was also instituted to build emergency shipyards, the largest of which was the enormous fifty-slip Hog Island plant at Philadelphia.[49]

The Emergency Fleet Corporation did not limit its efforts to steel shipbuilding, however. A smaller but still significant portion of the shipbuilding program was dedicated to the production of a proposed fleet of approximately 400 middle-sized (3,500 DWT) wooden freight steamers designed by Theodore E. Ferris, a naval architect employed by the Shipping Board.[50] The half-baked assumptions underlying this program presumed that enough steel could not be produced to meet the shipbuilding needs of the nation in the short term; that a wooden shipbuilding infrastructure, including an ample supply of skilled labor, was already in place and would pick up much, if not most, of the program; and that sufficient reserves of suitable shipbuilding timber were readily and conveniently available. They were basically wrong on all three counts.[51]

Sam Percy certainly considered contracting for some of the Ferris hulls (machinery and boilers were installed by a government subcontractor in Portland)

The CHARLES D. LOVELAND was apparently started for Percy & Small's own account, but sold on the stocks in January 1916 to S. C. Loveland. A smaller version of the CRESSY twins, the LOVELAND sports an American flag painted on her hull, asserting her neutrality (obviously before the U.S. entered the war), as she lies at a pier in Philadelphia.

Courtesy: Captains Douglas K. and Linda J. Lee

with their $300,000 price tag (+/- $3 million in 1998). But in the end, for reasons unstated, he chose to remain exclusively in the schooner building business. Ironically, Percy & Small's last significant work involved some of these much-maligned Ferris steamers.[52]

The emergency shipbuilding program seriously impacted upon Percy & Small's—and everyone else's—traditional sources of timber, starting with an initial order for 140 million board feet of yellow pine for delivery as fast as the mills could saw the timber![53] After 1916 Percy & Small increasingly resorted to Douglas-fir timber (for ceiling, shelves and clamps, keelsons, and deck beams) as a substitute for yellow pine, even though the former had to be transported over three times the distance and

contend with numerous rail bottlenecks.

For the most part during this period, Percy & Small built for "one-ship" corporations. Three of the one-ship corporations involved David Cohen of New York whose firm owned the Stanley Navigation Company (JOSEPH S. ZEMAN), the Landis Navigation Company (MIRIAM LANDIS), and the Cecilia Cohen Navigation Company (CECILIA COHEN), or at least had a controlling interest in each. David Cohen also purchased Percy & Small's ROBERT P. MURPHY during the 1917 sell-off.[54]

The exceptions were the three schooners built for the C. C. Mengel & Brothers Company of Louisville, Kentucky. That firm had long traded with the west coast of Africa, principally at Axim in modern-day Ghana, for some of the more exotic varieties of timber such as mahogany. Formerly reliant upon British shipping that had since been diverted to the Allies' war effort, the Mengels found it necessary to build up a small fleet to maintain their link to West Africa. The Mengel "navy" grew to include three steam schooners, the Bath-built steel, four-masted bark DIRIGO, and the three Percy & Small-built sisters: C. C. MENGEL, JR., SAM C. MENGEL, AND LIEUT. SAM MENGEL.[55]

Built from the same model as the CRESSY twins and the CHARLES D. LOVELAND, these schooners were delivered to the owners in successive years between 1916–18. They each possessed one characteristic that set them aside from their predecessors: their bottoms were fully coppered as a defense against marine borers. These were the first vessels built in Bath to be coppered on the stocks since 1892, when the Sewalls coppered the giant four-masted bark ROANOKE. And then there was another difference involving the SAM C. MENGEL. She was the only engine-powered vessel ever built by Percy & Small.

The Mengels preferred schooners with auxiliary steam engines. Such equipment theoretically permitted the captain to power out of areas of calms and

Percy & Small built three schooners between 1916–18 for the Mengel Box Company, which imported mahogany from West Africa into the United States. The first of these schooners, the C. C. MENGEL, JR., is unloading timber from Axim at a pier in Pensacola. Her first master, Frank Peterson, may be the gentleman standing on the chock rail just forward of the main shrouds. This was the first schooner coppered on the stocks in a Bath shipyard since 1892. She also served as Ole Hanson's model of a four-masted schooner when he drew up construction plans for a Georgia shipyard.
Courtesy: Captains Douglas K. and Linda J. Lee

contrary winds, saving considerable passage time. So Percy & Small contracted to deliver the vessel ready for installation of her machinery. The Mengels, in turn, contracted with an engine builder for building and installing the machinery. Unfortunately for the owners, the machinery deliveries fell well behind schedule.

The MENGEL was outfitted with twin screws, twin triple expansion engines rated at 150 IHP each, twin oil-fired Talbot water tube flash boilers, and a pair of steam-driven generator sets.[56] The sophisticated power plant—flash boilers were very compact, fast, generators of steam—along with the necessary oil tanks, occupied one-sixth of the schooner's hull, making serious inroads into payload. The twin propellers (four-bladed and 7.5 feet in diameter) also proved to be literally a big drag on her performance under sail.[57] When the power plant was finally installed, it also proved to be unreliable. On her departure from Bath in June 1917—she was launched in January to clear the building ways—her boilers failed before she reached the mouth of the river. She was towed by tug to Boston.[58] Subsequently, the machinery, propellers and shafts, and oil tanks were removed. Almost a year to the day after she left the Kennebec in tow, the SAM C. MENGEL was stopped and sunk by a U-boat approx-

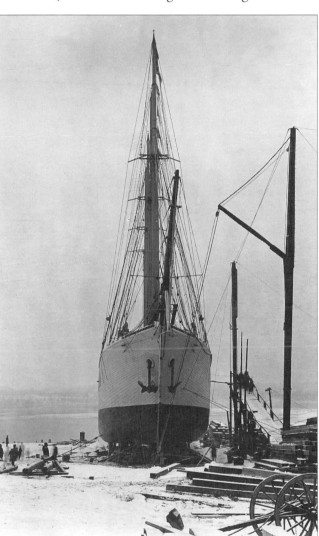

Launching day for the SAM C. MENGEL was as bitterly cold as the picture suggests (the ghost figures were the result of the cold slowing down the camera shutter). A near sister of the C.C. MENGEL, JR., the new schooner shows off her Bant Hanson-designed form and the amount of bending and twisting of plank that was necessary at the ends of a vessel.
Courtesy: Maine Maritime Museum

imately 175 miles southeast of Sandy Hook.[59]

The first two Mengel schooners also served as a model for naval architect Ole Hanson, son of WYOMING designer Bant Hanson, as construction progressed. Young Hanson had been retained by Captain John C. Darrah, a retired sea captain and resident of Richmond, upriver from Bath. Darrah was retained by the newly organized Savannah-based firm named the Georgia Shipbuilding Company, whose principal investors were more knowledgeable regarding finance than shipbuilding. Darrah, son of a shipmaster and master of at least four schooners himself before his own retirement, came from a shipbuilding community on the most prolific shipbuilding river in America and was, therefore, something of an authority on the subject.[60] He was also familiar with some of the leading businessmen of Savannah, thanks to a number of calls at that port to pick up lumber.

When asked if he could obtain plans for a suitably sized four-master, Darrah may have developed a coughing fit, knowing how most Maine shipbuilders ignored such unnecessary luxuries. But he did know that Percy & Small was active and building four-masters that were within the size and cost parameters of the Savannah enthusiasts. All he needed was to sit down with Sam

Percy and hammer out the details on transferring technology.

We don't know the exact arrangement Captain Darrah and Captain Percy formulated, but what has come down to us eight decades later is a unique set of plans drawn from life of a small, but representative, great schooner at the end of the age of wooden sail, drafted by Ole Hanson, son of the original modeler/designer.[61]

Bant Hanson had died in the fall of 1915 while his son Ole was employed as a naval architect for the Erie Canal Commission. Unlike his father, young Hanson was an academically trained naval architect, having completed the three-year course at America's foremost naval architectural school (ask any Webb graduate) after a year at Bowdoin College. He returned to Bath and apparently sought to continue his father's business operating the last active mould loft in Bath as well as holding down a paying day job in the Bath Iron Works' drafting department.

The SAM C. MENGEL, stern view. Propeller shafts and propellers for the auxiliary propulsion plant are in place, but the boiler and steam engines have yet to arrive and be installed by the engineering works. Nonetheless, Percy & Small is preparing to launch the schooner to clear the ways for the next hull. Note her coppered bottom: the alloy sheets and the steel propellers, struts, and shafts must have created an electrolytic nightmare—and no "zincs" in sight. Note also how the liner neatly matched the hood ends of the planking on both sides of the hull.

Courtesy: Maine Maritime Museum

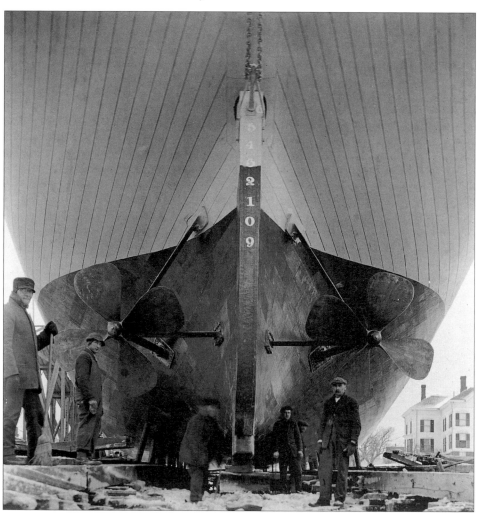

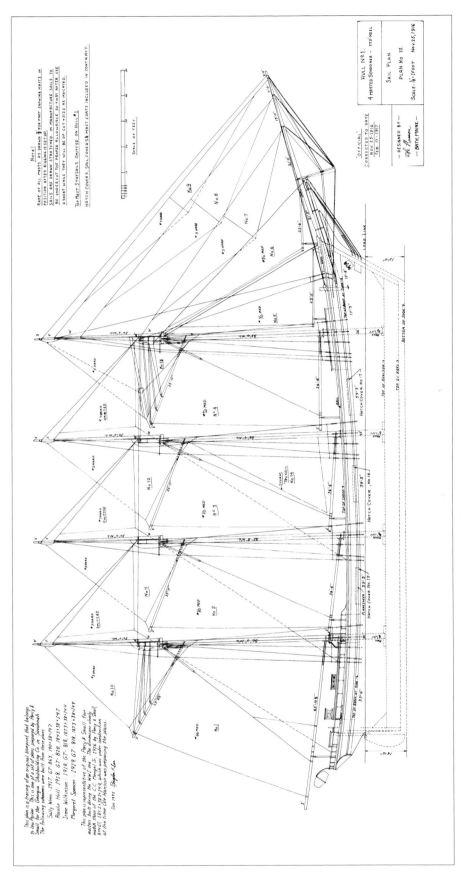

Sail Plan: Hull No. 1
Georgia Shipbuilding Co.
Traced from original by Douglas K. Lee.
Courtesy: Captain W. J. Lewis Parker, USCG, Ret.

The last of the trio of Mengel schooners, LIEUT. SAM MENGEL, sports a yard on her foremast
that carries a square foresail and raffee. It was a far better solution for schooners making
long ocean passages than the expensive, steam auxiliary engines fitted to her middle sister.
Courtesy: Captain W. J. Lewis Parker, USCG, Ret.

Darrah's commission required that young Hanson visit Percy & Small frequently—probably on weekends—to note the numerous construction details of the C. C. MENGEL, JR., as well as review his father's notes and develop a lines plan and table of offsets from the well-used half model. With this data, he developed a full set of detailed construction plans and specifications. His completed plans were sent south, probably in the company of several former P&S employees, including longtime liner James Brewster, who was hired to be master builder at the southern shipyard, and Willard Dodge, a longtime ship carpenter.[62]

The LIEUT. SAM MENGEL, the last of the trio, was vested with something that distinguished her from her sisters: she was fitted with a yard on her foremast. A rig variant that made sense for any schooner making long ocean passages and far more successful than auxiliary steam engines, it proved so successful that the Mengels reportedly retrofitted the C. C. MENGEL, JR. with the same rig.[63]

Because the three schooners were as nearly alike as peas in a pod, their construction costs provide an interesting commentary on war-driven inflation and its impact on shipbuilding, especially when comparing costs associated with the C. C. MENGEL, JR. and the LIEUT. SAM MENGEL and their peacetime-built sister, the DUSTIN G. CRESSY. The latter cost $64.08 per GRT (+/- $850 in 1998), with construction starting in 1910. The C. C. MENGEL, JR., started six years later, cost $76.93 per GRT (+/- $860 in 1998), and the LIEUT. SAM MENGEL in 1918 cost $137 per GRT (+/- $1,205 in 1998).[64]

Unlike most of the Percy & Small war-built schooners, the career of the two surviving Mengel schooners has been better documented than many of their contemporaries. Sold by the Mengel Company in the years after 1918, they were purchased by a corporation made up of some wartime naval officers who had served together in destroyers. Banking on a continuation of the shipping shortage for a few more years as the victors—especially France and Belgium—sought to overcome the war's devastation, the stockholders reasoned that they could get a few good years of returns on their investment and, if nothing else, would also own pretty sizable four-masted "yachts." Most of the investors returned to their employment in banking, securities, and insurance even as they invested a small amount of capital as a down payment to purchase the C. C. MENGEL, JR. for $105,000. The one paid "hand" in the corporation was John T. Rowland, who served as president and general dogsbody for a salary of $200 per month (+/- $1,800 in 1998). The other stockholders apparently received no dividends, being largely content to walk in the ghostly footsteps of some of America's great maritime entrepreneurs.[65]

After roughly two years operating a single-ship corporation, Rowland's stockholders decided he was doing so well with one schooner that it would be a good idea to purchase her sister, the LIEUT. SAM MENGEL. Doing well meant meeting the carrying costs of a sizable mortgage on the vessel (+/- $30,000 per year) and her operating costs. By purchasing the second schooner on considerably better terms than the first—schooner prices were descending rapidly from their wartime highs at this point— they could double their receipts without doubling their costs. So the two schooners were once again in harness together.

During his tenure as shipping company executive, Rowland found charters for his schooners carrying deals, barrel staves, asphalt, piling, and gypsum along the East Coast from Nova Scotia to the Caribbean,

The LIEUT. SAM MENGEL idling along in the Bay of Fundy and showing off her raffee and square foresail in action.
John T. Rowland Photo, courtesy of Captains Douglas K. and Linda J. Lee

and even across the Atlantic. He also managed a voyage or two on his charges replete with a few photographs. But time was running out for the great schooners, especially those that carried a heavy load of debt.

THE C. C. MENGEL, JR., with a case oil charter to the West Indies, had been entrusted to a new skipper who came to Rowland with excellent references. But then Rowland began to hear reports that the new captain was hitting the bottle pretty hard. He attempted to intercept the schooner at Port-au-Prince, its next scheduled port of call, but the MENGEL came to grief before she reached that port 150 miles to the southwest on Morant Cay. As it turned out, the captain had become despondent after learning that his wife had left him.

The firm managed to struggle along for a while longer with just the LIEUT. SAM MENGEL. A number of charters carrying construction materials during the fall of 1925 and winter of 1926 for the big Miami real estate boom barely managed to pay the bills. But freights were falling and it was getting harder to find charters. Then Rowland received an offer for the schooner from William Beebe, a noted marine biologist famous for his deep ocean dives in a bathysphere to observe marine life. So one of Percy & Small's finest started a brief career as a scientific expedition mother ship. By 1933, however, she had been converted to a

The ANNIE C. ROSS footing along in West Penobscot Bay in June 1941. At age twenty-four, she was the last Percy & Small-built schooner in active service.

Betty Fox Photo, courtesy of Captains Douglas K. and Linda J. Lee

barge. Two years later, while under tow by the tug WELLFLEET inbound to Boston from Norfolk, she foundered off the Boston Lightship.[66]

Percy & Small's Hull #40 proved to be a particularly durable schooner, staying afloat until the mid-1950s. Laid down in May 1917, she was built for a syndicate that included longtime Percy & Small captain (S. P. BLACKBURN, HELEN W. MARTIN, and ELEANOR A. PERCY) Alex Ross, who owned the largest single share in the vessel. Among the other shareholders were such familiar names as Cora F. Cressy, Dustin G. Cressy, and E. T. Nalor of Gloversville, New York.[67] The E. P. Boggs shipping firm of Boston was the managing owner, retaining 15 percent of the shares spread among five members of the Boggs family, including the schooner's sponsor, five-year-old Elizabeth T. Boggs.[68]

The ANNIE C. ROSS, named in honor of the captain's wife, was the sixth in the series of four-masters built from the model created by Bant Hanson.[69] There was, however, one significant difference between her and all but one other Percy & Small schooner: the ROSS did not carry steam-powered pumps and hoister. In their place was a Fairbanks-Morse gasoline donkey engine that ran the hoister, anchor winch, and pumps. This outfit took less space, weighed less, cost less, and required one less crewman; the first mate or a mechanically inclined crewman was assigned responsibility for the engine room. Dispensing with the engineer effectively eliminated one of the highest paid crew members without the necessity of replacing him, an important consideration especially as the shipping business became increasingly competitive in the post-World War I era and owners sought to further reduce costs.[70] Other than that, the ROSS was a typical Percy & Small four-master of the period with a registered length of 175.5 feet, beam of 38.2 feet, and depth of hold of 14 feet.

As with the CORA F. CRESSY, the ROSS enjoyed a long operating life. She sailed for twenty-four years and actually remained afloat until 1955, thirty-eight years after she left the Kennebec River for the first, and last, time.

Captain and Mrs. Ross sailed in her for seven years, carrying cargoes of hard pine north and occasional cargoes of fish scrap or coal south. Being both an investment *and* the family home, she was well and carefully maintained. Then in 1924 Captain Ross retired, being replaced by Captain Bennett D. Coleman, who only stayed in her for several months before buying the master's interest in the ANNA R. HEIDRITTER. Captain Frank J. Peterson then took her for just over a year, completing several passages from southern hard pine ports to New York and New England. On one of these passages, the ROSS hit the beach on Santa Rosa Island (Florida) when Captain Peterson confused lights on the grounded schooner ROBERT L. BEAN with those of a lighted buoy. The schooner was soon pulled off, and it was the only time that she would find herself in serious trouble throughout her long working career.[71] Captain Peterson sold his master's share in the schooner to Captain Joseph Zuljevic late in 1926. The new captain eventually acquired the managing owner's shares in the schooner, although several of the original shareholders still retained their interest in the vessel.

Amazingly, the Yugoslav-born captain kept the aging schooner going in the hard pine trade for another fifteen years. It helped that he had learned much of his trade at the hands of tightfisted Yankee and "Blue Nose" skippers, who could make every dime do the work of a dollar. From the historic— and artistic—point of view, Zuljevic also benefited from some of those who chose to ship aboard his aging schooner, regardless of his penurious ways: John Noble, a struggling marine artist who occasionally shipped aboard her in order to pick up some ready cash and who used her as a model for many of his most famous drawings; Fred Kaiser, a Brooklyn

schoolboy whose love affair with the schooner has been recalled in words and photographs;[72] and Captain Francis "Biff" Bowker, author and one of the last of the schoonermen, whose sojourn as "acting mate" on the ROSS in early 1940 he recounted in a letter to the editor of the *National Fisherman* in 1981 and is worth quoting at length here.

For some reason Captain Zuljevic attracted a certain amount of loyalty from Kaiser, John Noble and Jordan, the cook. I have often thought that Captain Zuljevic probably heated his home from the chips squeezed out of the buffalo on nickels hoarded in his cellar. He once told me that a Turk could always get the best of a Greek and a Greek could get the best of a Jew but a Yugoslav could give them all a headstart and wind up ahead every time . . . . I don't know if he ever matched wits with some of the Downeast skippers, or shippers, but it could have been a battle of experts.

Unlike Mr. Kaiser, I came aboard the ROSS as a professional schoonerman. I'd sailed in three-, four- and five-masted schooners and, in my own mind, considered myself a capable seaman. I came aboard on the last day of February 1940, as an able seaman. That day the mate had a row with the skipper, who came forward and asked if anyone wanted the job. John Noble wasn't interested and the old squareheads [Scandinavians] weren't interested. I was full of ambition and thought it great when he offered me an extra ten dollars. I didn't know at the time, but I found out when we paid off that he meant exactly what he said . . . .

I joined the ship at Bossert's Lumber Company wharf at Newtown Creek, a foul stretch of water on the Brooklyn side of the East River, and soon took up my duties. Beside the captain and myself, the crew consisted of a black cook named Fred Melvin, who was filling in for Jordan, the regular cook, John Noble, John Lindquist and two other squareheads named Hugo and Pete. Except for the rather inexperienced mate, it was as good a crew as one could wish and even the mate wasn't too bad . . . .

The mate of a schooner was in charge of deck work, in charge of the port watch, in charge of the engine room, pumps, and lights. In addition, I found that I had also taken on Fred Kaiser's chores as "go fer." John [Noble] was appointed to teach me the workings of the old Fairbanks & Morse horizontal engine. I hadn't the least interest in engines before that trip but had to learn fast. Eventually I managed to break an eccentric on the pumps and John came to the rescue on that. I was learning that mate of a schooner was a trade that demanded one to be a jack-of-all-trades . . . .

We left New York on March 5th and arrived off Jacksonville Bar on March 14. It was a fair weather passage for that time of the year but we had a snow storm while loading. Our cargo consisted of heavy construction timbers, some for the Bangor and Aroostook Railroad and the balance for Portland people. By the time the hold was filled we were nearly to our marks but took a few 12" x 16" on deck . . . .

While in Jacksonville, Captain Zuljevic's thrifty nature again showed up. He had discovered that the cook was a vegetarian but thought the crew should have a treat. There were seven of us aboard so he went ashore and bought six pork chops, the cook didn't need one. On another occasion he asked the cook to give him a list of stores for the trip north. Poor Fred told him he needed a few pounds of coffee and a case of canned milk. Captain Zuljevic flew into a rage. "Milk," he screamed, "What did you do with the twelve cans I bought in New York . . . ?"

Eventually things quieted down but Fred was informed that from then on it would be one can of milk for two days for the sailors. The cook was almost in tears and the list of stores grew considerably shorter . . . .

[The cook's personal road to Gethsemane at the hands of the captain continued after the Ross anchored off Nobska Point, Martha's Vineyard, to ride out a southeaster. Bowker continues, quoting from his diary:] Cook caught hell last night for leaving a fire in the galley to raise bread. SOME SHIP. The skipper even makes him lock the place up at night so the sailors can't get in. It was general practice in American schooners to leave the galley open and a pot of coffee going for the watch.

All was not happy aboard the ANNIE C. ROSS and some of the crew were talking about leaving at Searsport, without even discharging our part cargo at Searsport and finishing at Portland. The sailors were growling that they had only three cans of milk since leaving Jacksonville and I couldn't seem to please the captain, no matter how I tried. The captain watched me every time I reached out for butter at the table and I took good care to take plenty. This was not the last such experience I had but I learned to lather it on under hostile scrutiny.

We rounded Cape Cod in good order and arrived at Searsport, where all hands stayed by. It was a relief to have a tug tow us to Portland and there we paid off. On Sunday, April 21, we lay at anchor in Portland while a violent snow storm made us drop a second anchor as we dragged down on a Danish steamer. Captain Zuljevic offered us each ten dollars extra to stay by the vessel and go to Promised Land, Long Island, for a load of fish scrap. I'd heard about the stuff and wanted no part of it. The crowning blow was when the captain gave me ten dollars extra for going mate when I had expected to be paid at the rate of ten dollars a month extra. The four-master, HELEN BARNET GRING, was fitting out for a trip to the West Indies and I headed to Boston to join her.[73]

By the time Captain Bowker sailed on the ROSS, her glory days were over. Despite Captain Zuljevic's gallant efforts at keeping her going—which, in fact, required more than a little tightfistedness in matters of expense—the four-master was definitely beginning to show her age. In the summer of 1941, the ROSS made her last trip to Maine waters. That December she was bound for New York from one of the hard pine ports when the Japanese attacked Pearl Harbor.

Laid up in early 1942 at Bossert's Lumber Yard on Brooklyn's noisome Newtown Creek, long her winter berth, the ANNIE C. ROSS waited for the call to return to sea once more. When photographed shortly after World War II, however, the combination of long neglect and age—she is clearly hogged—had taken their toll.

Andrew J. Nesdall Photo, courtesy of Captains Douglas K. and Linda J. Lee

After discharging her cargo, Zuljevic had her towed to Newtown Creek in early 1942 to be laid up. She never sailed again.

The captain and principal owner took a shore job and put the ROSS on the market. In October 1942, a report was circulated that she had been sold for $45,000 for the offshore trade—half what she had cost new a quarter century before—but the prospective owner never picked up his option and she languished with minimum care, sails stowed in the hold. Then, in 1947, Captain John Rosario purchased Zuljevic's shares and proceeded to outfit the thirty-year-old schooner as a Cape Verde Island packet. He died before the work progressed very far and the schooner essentially became abandoned. A fire set by vandals burned out her after deckhouse while others pillaged gear. The state of New York then got in the picture, offering her at auction. Bid on by a TV personality and actor named Scott Moore, she then became the focal point of a lawsuit brought by several of the surviving owners whose shares had never been purchased. Moore finally made a small cash settlement, thus effectively ending the last shareholding shipping venture involving an American vessel. But Moore found himself saddled with a vandalized ghost, severely hogged and raddled with age and neglect. He, in turn, finally sold her for $2,000 in 1954 to the Catholic Sea Cadets of America, who had plans to convert her into a training ship. It was a harebrained scheme, as time would quickly prove. After a cursory cleanup and some paint therapy, she was towed from Newtown Creek to a more appropriate setting at Glen Cove, Long Island. There, in 1955, her weary timbers succumbed to age and she sank, almost thirty-eight years after she had been launched.

One of the Percy & Small-built four-masters, the MIRIAM LANDIS, came back from the dead, in a manner of speaking. She was owned by one of David Cohen's single-ship corporations and named for the niece of Judge Kennesaw Mountain Landis, the Moses-like commissioner of baseball. Neither her namesake nor her managing owner were present when, only partially rigged, she went into the Kennebec on 25 September 1919, christened by Percy & Small's only female employee, Ena Bucknam.

Proctor Hagan was selected to command the new schooner. This was the same Proctor Hagan about whom a news item headlined "An Expensive Kiss" was published in his hometown paper, much to the delight of his friends and his own embarrassment. In 1892, young Hagan was a carefree bachelor in command of the schooner CORA, then in Baltimore. The good captain, on his way back to his ship after an evening out with the boys, ran across " . . . a pretty young woman who was not so bashful as to stand upon the order of introduction, but who entered merrily into conversation with the seaman." One thing led to another and they were soon engaged in some affectionate necking. But then the young lady recalled that she needed to be elsewhere and they bid a fond farewell. Shortly thereafter Captain Hagan had need for something in his wallet only to discover—you guessed it—no wallet. And no $205 (+/- $3,100 in 1998) in cash that had very recently dwelt there. To make a long story short, Hagan complained to the law, and one Josephine Neal was soon identified, arrested, and arraigned, pleading not guilty in the Jefferson Market Court. But when Hagan learned he would have to stick around to testify, he balked. CORA was loaded and ready to sail, so he declined to place a formal charge. He later commented that $205 for a few kisses was a much higher tariff than prevailed down in Maine.[74]

Since his brief but expensive encounter on the streets of Baltimore, Hagan had risen further in the world. He took command of the big new Minott-built FRANCIS M in 1896 and acquired a wife who presumably took care of his osculatory needs. He stayed with the FRANCIS M for twenty-one years before a change in ownership put him on the beach for a well-earned rest. He later learned that he and his wife's longtime home (she frequently accompanied

him on his voyages) was lost to a German U-boat off the coast of Spain. But now that the war was well over, Captain Hagan had only to concern himself with the shipping business, shiphandling, navigation, and the routine perils of the sea. In the fifteen or so months he commanded the LANDIS, he had plenty to concern himself with.

Percy & Small completed the schooner and sent her on her way during the second week of October 1919. Captain Hagan first went to Norfolk to load a cargo of coal for Lisbon, Portugal. From there, they sailed light to Gulfport, Mississippi, to load hard pine timber for delivery to France where it would be used in the massive rebuilding effort along the trace of the Western Front. Once discharged, they cleared for Haiti to load a cargo of log wood that was exchanged in a U.S. port for more coal destined for the French port of Marseilles. Mrs. Hagan joined her husband in Haiti and planned to stay aboard until they returned from France.

Slightly over a year after departing from Bath, the LANDIS sailed from Marseilles bound once again for the United States. For the first few days the weather appeared to have been ordered by a press agent— balmy temperatures, fair winds, and the fabulous blue Mediterranean. Then came the problem: strong westerlies that gradually drove the unballasted schooner closer and closer to the North African coast while exhausting captain and crew in a seemingly endless tacking contest.

When it appeared that they had almost made the fabled Pillars of Hercules, disaster in the form of a sudden vicious storm and an outdated chart took a hand. In the limited visibility afforded by the weather, Captain Hagan mistakenly identified a key navigation beacon for another thanks to changes in their flash sequences and, believing he was well clear of the Moroccan shore and in the straits, he changed course—too soon! At 3:00 A.M., the LANDIS hit the beach, pounding hard as the surf washed over the stricken schooner. But through some miracle—Mrs. Hagan credited their salvation to the sermon on "Dawn" preached by Reverend Mr. Hardin at Bath's Winter Street Church just before they sailed from Bath on the LANDIS's maiden voyage—the schooner

The MIRIAM LANDIS, named for the niece of Judge Kennesaw Mountain Landis, went overboard from Percy & Small only partially rigged on 25 September 1919. The schooner alongside is the ANNA G. LORD, recently launched from the old Donnell shipyard by the Pendleton family from Islesboro. They had lured Eliakim McCabe away from Percy & Small with the promise he would be their master builder.

Courtesy: Captains Douglas K. and Linda J. Lee

had gone ashore on a sandy stretch of beach surrounded by rocky cliffs and partially shielded from the worst of the storm-driven surf; "the nicest little beach in Morocco," as Mrs. Hagan put it.[75]

Cast up broadside onto the beach, the LANDIS and her bedraggled but relieved humanity soon had other worries. A crowd, seemingly from nowhere, gathered on the beach to observe the distressed vessel and, no doubt, contemplate the potential for a little marine salvage. Two of the Moors, well mounted on Arabian horseflesh, were dispatched with a message to be wired to the American consul in Gibraltar, and the Hagans settled down in what was now a beachfront home to await rescue.

It took nearly ten days to get the battered schooner free; Captain and Mrs. Hagan and the crew stayed aboard to discourage the locals from helping themselves. A second storm, arriving inconveniently just as a salvage tug was hauling the battered schooner free, caused the vessel to pound heavily, opening seams, and then drove her back up on the beach after the tug had to let go the towing hawser. When she was finally hauled off by the salvage tug—a job that also required considerable dredging between the ship and open water—the LANDIS was towed to Gibraltar with her wrecking pumps hard at work keeping her afloat. Subsequently drydocked and examined by marine surveyors, the LANDIS had suffered enough damage to justify selling her "as is, where is." David Cohen apparently agreed, and a year after she hit the beach she was sold for £900.[76] But the barely three-year-old schooner was far from done. Renamed KENTON, she remained in service for thirteen more years before foundering on 30 January 1935 off Brava in the Cape Verde Islands.

The last schooner delivered by Percy & Small, the CECILIA COHEN, was also part of David Cohen's

The last four-master launched by Percy & Small (9 February 1920) was the CECILIA COHEN, complete with the same deck configuration as the five-master DUNHAM WHEELER. The COHEN, it turned out, was to have a short life.
Courtesy: Captain W. J. Lewis Parker, USCG, Ret.

stable of vessels. Slightly larger than her four-masted predecessors—measuring 1,102 gross tons—she was built with another version of the CORA F. CRESSY's deck configuration which Percy & Small had used on the three five-masters they built between 1917–19. The COHEN, as with the ANNIE C. ROSS, was also outfitted with a big gasoline donkey engine (Mianus) in place of the heavier, more complex steam auxilliary systems.

Captain Molear Christianson, a grizzled old Norwegian seadog with fifty years of sea time under his belt (thirty-four years as a shipmaster), was selected for command by David Cohen. With his Norwegian, British, and American master's licenses in hand, the good captain and his wife sailed away in the COHEN in February 1920, the last schooner to depart from the shipyard on her maiden voyage.

Seventeen months later, Captain Frank Peterson—apparently attempting to set the record for the number of Percy & Small schooners commanded by one person—was ordered by the owners of his current command to take over the CECILIA COHEN in Tampa and bring her to Philadelphia.[77] Peterson failed to mention what had happened to Captain Christianson, but he reported aboard the COHEN early in July 1921, finding the schooner loading phosphate rock and nearly ready to sail.

As the schooner and her crew passed through the Florida Straits, their problems began, as Peterson was later to relate:

We were beating up through the Straits. After we made Alligator Reef Light, I went below leaving the Mate in charge. The wind headed her and the Mate let her go onto Pickel's Reef. I tried to wear her off, but we swung wide onto Conch Reef and stayed. A tug pulled us off and towed us into Key West leaking four inches per hour. There were no facilities to haul out, and a diver reported only that he found the false keel split through. Informed of the problem, the owners insisted that we proceed. When I remonstrated with them, they said if I wouldn't bring her east, they'd find somebody who would. So we took aboard all the gasoline we could get, to run the engine which she had to

power the winch and the pumps, and started out. I soon found it was impossible to tack her, probably because the keel had been twisted in the stranding. The leak increased in heavy weather encountered on August 6, and the pumps had to be kept running continuously. Sixty miles east of Hatteras we ran out of gas, and on August 7, 1921, we abandoned her with twelve feet of water in the hold. Just before being taken off by the freighter WEST KEENE, we set her afire so she would not be a menace to navigation. She must have sunk very shortly.[78]

The CECILIA COHEN had been launched just eighteen months earlier.

David Cohen proved to be a good Percy & Small customer during their last few years in the shipbuilding business. Not only had he purchased the ROBERT P. MURPHY in 1917, but he also had the shipyard build the two four-masters whose contrasting fortunes are outlined above. But the first new vessel he ordered from Percy & Small was the five-master JOSEPH S. ZEMAN, the final sister in the trio of five-masters built between 1916–19. Thus, by some quirk of fate, Mr. Cohen was responsible for the final three vessels delivered by the Bath firm.[79]

The five-masters—call them the DUNHAM WHEELER Class—were virtually identical in appearance and in size. They also shared the latest and final manifestation of the CORA F. CRESSY deck configuration (see Chapter 4). That configuration, you will recall, combined the strength benefits of a true flush-decked vessel with the advantages derived from a raised forecastle. Carrying the natural sheer of the main rail forward from the mizzenmast while limiting the forward rise of the main deck permitted the installation of a full-height forward house with ample room for donkey boiler and associated equipment and a topgallant forecastle with adequate height to install the windlass. The topgallant forecastle, forward deckhouse, and the solid bulwarks extending aft almost to the mizzenmast all contributed to reducing the impact of being swept by head seas, a problem with pure flush-deckers.

Deck configuration was one thing, but who

Captain Frank Peterson was compelled to abandon the CECILIA COHEN sixty miles east of Cape Hatteras eighteen months after she was launched. Despite damage received in a grounding in the Florida Straits, the COHEN's managing owner insisted the vessel proceed. When the fuel for the gasoline donkey engine operating the pumps was exhausted, the schooner rapidly filled. Taken off by the SS WEST KEENE, the captain and crew set fire to their ship to prevent her from becoming a menace to navigation.

Courtesy: Captains Douglas K. and Linda J. Lee

actually modeled these schooners? One clue appeared in the launching account of the WHEELER, referring to the class progenitor as ". . . one of the new modeled craft, the first of her model constructed by Percy & Small."[80] This appears to be substantiated by an invoice in her construction bill file from none other than E. S. Crosby (he who had divided the Adams & Hitchcock fleet with Sam Percy back in 1893) charging Percy & Small $185.00 for a set of schooner moulds.[81]

However, the two successor schooners, identical in virtually all respects, were clearly credited to Fred Rideout and his model of the WILLIAM H. CLIFFORD.[82] So how to explain the disparity? First, the newspaper description "one of the new modeled craft" referred *not* to the hull form, but to the new deck

configuration. And E. S. Crosby's role in all of this was, in the absence of Bant Hanson (recently deceased—November 1915) and Ole Hanson (yet to move back to Bath—April 1916), to reloft the vessel and make new moulds: an important and necessary step given that the moulds from the CLIFFORD had not been used for more than a decade, if they had survived at all.[83]

The three members of the DUNHAM WHEELER Class were the smallest five-masters built by Percy & Small. The three schooners ranged from 1,926 GRT to 2,046 GRT, not an excessive variation for vessels built to the same model when wood was the material of choice. Perhaps the only deliberate variations involved some of the scantlings for some structural timbers (reduced slightly due to shortages) and a

The first of Percy & Small's three war-built five-masters, the DUNHAM WHEELER outlived her two sisters before foundering off Cape Canaveral, Florida, in late 1930.
Courtesy: Captains Douglas K. and Linda J. Lee

slight increase in depth of hold (thus increasing the effective strength of the "girder") of the follow-on schooners, although the differences in the registered dimensions could also have been derived from normal variations in hewn keel and frame stock.[84]

Of the three, the WHEELER was the longest lived. Probably started on a speculative basis by Percy & Small, she ultimately cost the firm $143,782.55 (+/- $1.5 million in 1998). There is no indication of how much her new owners paid.[85] As with all of the war-built schooners at Percy & Small, she had no carved trailboards or billethead, these final remnants of traditional decoration falling victim to the no-frills attitude of wartime investors.

The thirty-ninth Percy & Small vessel was named for the general manager of R. Lawrence Smith, Inc., the New York owners, and her first master was Captain Millard G. Dow of Bucksport. Dow's previous experience included command of the Deering-built three-masted schooner FAIRFIELD and the steamer NAVAHOE, a Pacific Coast-built passenger-freight steamer that operated for a time out of Portland, Maine.

The WHEELER managed to find employment through the war and immediate postwar years, making passages to South America and Europe. Throughout the 1920s, she appears to have been largely engaged in the hard pine trade, bringing ties and sawn lumber principally from Jacksonville to New York, Boston, and Portland, as well as coal Downeast. Her owners, Pendleton Brothers, Inc., were approached by Ocean Tours Corporation of New York in early 1930, who came up with the idea of converting her to a training vessel for two hundred boys under the command of her captain, John A. McIver.[86] The project didn't fly—fortunately, it would appear—with either the Pendletons asking too much for their nearly 2,000-ton schooner or Ocean Tours realizing it was treading on very thin ice. Eight months later the WHEELER, now owned by Harold G. Foss, foundered off Cape Canaveral, Florida, during a gale. All hands, including Captain McIver, were rescued.

The next contract for a Percy & Small five-master was signed by W. S. Job, president of the W. S. Job Company in New York. For a price that must have been considerably in excess of $200,000 the investors—another single-ship corporation—became the owners of a five-masted schooner with a registered length of 254.1 feet, beam of 43.3 feet, and a 23.9-foot depth of hold.[87] When the admeasurer finished his job and toted up his calculations, the gross tonnage came to 2,046 tons. Although the new schooner fell into the category of a small Percy & Small five-master, she was capable of carrying 3,250 tons, fully loaded.[88] This made her one of the largest schooners built along the East Coast in the post-1909 period.

Mr. Job, a native of St. John's, Newfoundland, determined to name his new schooner in honor of his birthplace; hence she became—temporarily—ST. JOHNS, N.F. upon her launching on 9 May 1918. That event did without the traditional banquet following the "dip" as a part of wartime austerity, but the flowers cast over the bow were still very much a part of the ceremony. The event was unique for Percy & Small in that it was recorded by movie news cameraman Daniel Maher for Universal Weekly, a newsreel firm.[89]

Captain Frank Peterson assumed command of the schooner, but as matters turned out, he didn't have her long. He sailed the white-hulled schooner with her newly varnished brightwork into New York to load general cargo for Rio, accompanied by his wife and sons. Shortly after arriving, however, he had some sort of falling out with Job's port captain and Captain Peterson packed his bags and went ashore.[90]

ST. JOHNS, N.F. survived the vicissitudes of war without serious problems, but after shipping rates collapsed during 1920, W. S. Job & Company found it difficult to keep her going. It is possible that she had been built with largely borrowed money in the first place, with the plan being to meet the high carrying

ST. JOHNS, N.F. might appear a peculiar name for a ship, but she was in fact named for the capital city of Newfoundland. The second, and largest, of the Percy & Small war-built five-masters was sold to Portland owners in 1922 and renamed.

Courtesy: Captains Douglas K. and Linda J. Lee

costs of such loans out of the very generous freight rates being paid to all types of vessels. It is problematical whether two years was long enough for the vessel to have paid off the loans, especially if the shareholders in her corporation were unwilling to surrender big dividends in the interest of a fast pay-down on loans. In 1922 she was sold for $60,000—somewhere between one-third and one-quarter of her price just four years earlier—to the Portland syndicate headed by Captain A. W. Frost, and joined its fleet of tired great schooners (WYOMING, EDWARD J. LAWRENCE, RUTH MERRILL, CORA F. CRESSY, OAKLEY C. CURTIS).[91] The first thing the new owners did was to rename ST. JOHNS, adopting the name EDWARD B.

WINSLOW in honor of a Portland native son and the schooner lost to fire in 1917 that had carried his name.

The Frost syndicate kept her going for six more years, finding charters to carry coal and lumber. She even survived a vicious hurricane in the Gulf of Mexico that drove her from the Dry Tortugas to within 150 miles of the Mexican coast.[92] She also acquired some "firsts," including the first five-master and the largest sailing vessel to enter Miami Harbor. She also, it turned out, became the first five-master and largest sailing vessel to go aground in that harbor's turning basin.[93]

Although the other schooners in the Frost fleet fell

EDWARD B. WINSLOW (II), ex-ST. JOHNS, N.F., was purchased by Portland's Frost syndicate for $60,000 in 1922. She joined the fleet that included WYOMING, EDWARD J. LAWRENCE, RUTH E. MERRILL, CORA F. CRESSY, and OAKLEY C. CURTIS. It appears that inadequate maintenance was the primary cause of her loss in 1928.

Wilson Photo, courtesy of Captain W. J. Lewis Parker, USCG, Ret.

on varying degrees of unemployment and/or misfortune, the EDWARD B. WINSLOW, ex-ST. JOHNS, N.F., plugged along for a few more years. She achieved some notoriety after one arrival in Portland with a load of lumber from the south when the ship's cook was murdered by two members of the crew—an often threatened but rarely performed deed. Shortly thereafter, Captain Charles Publicover was hired to take her on a coal charter to Bermuda but fell ill before he could get underway. Captain John O. Hall, who lived in Portland's Stroudwater district, was then engaged for the voyage.

After arriving in Norfolk to pick up the coal, Captain Hall put the schooner into a drydock to clean and paint the bottom. At that time, the marginal nature of her operation became apparent when it was determined her caulking needed to be renewed from the light load waterline to the main deck. The work was deferred, ostensibly because of time rather than the expense, although the latter surely played a major role in the decision (the prepaid freights of the World War I era were history).

After the loading and trimming of 2,800 tons of coal (big schooners normally carried smaller cargoes offshore than they carried coastwise), the WINSLOW was towed through Hampton Roads and past Old Point Comfort. She anchored near Thimble Shoal to await a favorable wind, but there were already signs of a serious problem. As the coal had poured into her holds and she settled deeper into the water, the schooner began taking on water through those very seams that needed recaulking. Captain Hall later said, ". . . the schooner was found to be leaking quite badly [at Norfolk] but not enough to cause uneasiness to the crew or myself."[94] But once into the Gulf Stream and in the grip of a winter gale, the situation became decidedly worse.

The crew of the WINSLOW hove up her anchor on the morning of 5 December 1928 as they got underway for Bermuda. At first things went well, the wind gave them a good slant for Bermuda and one pump was able to keep ahead of the leaks. But then a heavy and confused sea caused the vessel to labor heavily and the leak to increase to the point that it was necessary to run one pump continuously. Then they were struck

by a full gale and Captain Hall was forced to shorten sail and bear off to reduce the schooner's laboring in the heavy seas. By now the single pump could not keep up with the leaks, and the water in the hold had increased to over 6 feet and was gaining.

By the morning of the ninth, the situation was looking a bit bleak. The Robinson Steerer had failed when a casting broke, forcing all hands to jury-rig the steering gear with relieving tackles. Then, during a particularly heavy roll and slat, the main and jigger sheets and boom tackles carried away, causing no little excitement and a lot more work before everything was secure once again. The leak got worse: two pumps were now running continuously but the water level in the hold continued to rise, reaching ten feet. The engineer, exhausted by endless hours of keeping up steam and tending the pumps, had to be relieved by the mates in turn, who themselves were far from well rested. Captain Hall decided it was time to seek help, so he had the national ensign hoisted with the union down (an international distress signal), and all hands now focused their efforts on keeping the struggling schooner afloat until they could be rescued.

Unable to keep up with the inflow of water with the ship's two big steam pumps (by noon on the tenth there was 13 feet in the hold), the engineer jury-rigged a third pump. The circulating pump suction pipe was disconnected from the seacock and connected to a pipe run into the hold, taking advantage of the more than ample supply of water in the hold to condense the exhaust steam from three hardworking pumps. For a while this appeared to do the trick, along with a moderation in the weather. By 11 December the seas had gone down slightly and the pumps had actually gained two feet. But Captain Hall took no chances and had the yawl boat provisioned and lowered, to be towed astern in the event a quick exit was in order—a prudent precaution given that the freshwater supply for the boiler had been exhausted and they were now forced to use salt water for making steam, a sure way to bring about boiler failure.[95]

As 11 December became history, it was apparent that time was running out. Salt was oozing out of every valve and fitting in the steam supply system, boiler pressure was dropping, and the pumps were gradually slowing down. To make matters worse, burdened not only with a cargo of coal but with many tons of water as well, the laboring hull was beginning to fail. Perhaps the working of the big wooden hull forced more and more caulking out of the seams, perhaps a planking butt opened under the strain. Whatever happened, it was soon evident that the water was again gaining in the hold and the WINSLOW was settling by the head.

By noon on the twelfth, the water had reached the 14-foot mark in the hold. Hall kept an anxious watch for a passing vessel from the masthead as the crew struggled to get more coal out of the hold for the failing boiler. Then, about mid-afternoon, a steamer on a parallel course was spotted. She—it turned out to be the American tanker CERRO EBANO—had an alert

lookout who spotted the schooner in distress. An hour later the captain and crew of Portland's last working five-master were safely aboard the tanker. When they left their schooner, the water in her hold was up to 20 feet. She foundered sometime during the night.

The JOSEPH S. ZEMAN, Schooner #43, was delivered to David Cohen and his associates at the end of March 1919, just nine months after signing the contract with the Stanley Navigation Company, a corporation owned by David Cohen & Company.[96] This represented unusual dispatch—the only mention of delivery date in the contract was ". . . to be completed as quickly as possible, or about January 1919"— for Percy & Small during this wartime period considering the difficulties in obtaining timber and the fact

The last of the war-built five-masters was the JOSEPH S. ZEMAN launched 28 March 1919. She differed from her sisters in that she was the only one with a midship deckhouse, although it was not recessed into the main deck but built full height on it. The yard's recently built mould loft is visible under her bowsprit. Also visible is the five-masted CARROLL A. DEERING on the ways at G. G. Deering's shipyard.

Courtesy: Andrew J. Nesdall

The JOSEPH S. ZEMAN struck the Metinic Island Ledge in thick weather while bound for Searsport on 3 February 1922. Determined efforts to salvage the big schooner and her cargo of coal by John I. Snow of Rockland came to little when it became apparent her hull was too badly damaged. The salvage tug SOMMERS N. SMITH (left) and steam lighter SOPHIA (right) were part of the salvage effort.

John I. Snow Photo, courtesy of Dr. Richard Snow

that the shipyard was operating with a reduced work force. The keel of the new schooner, a duplicate of the preceding pair of five-masters, was stretched only in mid-September so much of the work was pushed through the difficult winter season, a situation further compounded by the influenza pandemic that swept much of the western world and claimed as many as a half million Americans. All in all it was a creditable performance, given the difficult conditions existing at the time.

The ZEMAN was not quite an exact copy of her sisters. They had been built with two deckhouses, the one forward containing the forecastle, engine room, engineer's stateroom, and galley. Percy & Small's final five-master reverted to the original pattern found on the large four-, five- and six-masters built previously: a midship house containing the galley and messroom. It was built, however, right on the main deck—reminiscent of the old-time "caboose"—rather than being recessed into the deck.

The skipper-designate of the new craft was none other than the local Bath boy, Captain Fred L. Dunton, formerly of the ROBERT P. MURPHY. It was Dunton who made an extended tour in the MURPHY, even getting to try out his high school French in France. His wife, Jennie Harnden Dunton (also a Bath native), did the honors when the schooner was launched on 28 March 1919.

Dunton continued his roving ways in the ZEMAN. Her first charter involved carrying 12,000 barrels of oil—a good reason *not* to recess the galley deckhouse, with its always burning stove, into the hold—300 tons of steel, and a deck load of lumber to Genoa, Italy. According to one estimate, the gross freight for the voyage would reach $200,000 (+/- $1.4 million in 1998)! This did not pay off her contract price of $310,000 (+/- $2.1 million in 1998) in one fell swoop, but one or two more charters of that nature would see her free and clear of debt.[97] Fifteen months later, a letter to friends in Bath from the captain of the

ZEMAN reported that he was at Punta Delgada, Argentina, loading barley for Antwerp. Since sailing from Bath, the peripatetic skipper had logged over 28,000 nautical miles on the ZEMAN.[98] That was probably one of the last really profitable charters the schooner was to receive.

Then on 3 February 1922, while under the command of another Maine skipper, Captain Jim Fales of Thomaston, the ZEMAN fetched up hard on Metinic Island Ledge in the early morning hours as she was making her way in a thick southeaster to Searsport at the north end of Penobscot Bay with 3,000 tons of coal. After two weeks of concerted efforts by the John I. Snow Marine Salvage Company of Rockland, the attempts to haul her off were abandoned. An attempt was then made to salvage as much of the cargo and gear as possible from the three-year-old, fully insured schooner. It is a really ill wind that doesn't bring someone some good.

Then there was Percy & Small's Schooner #46,

The LAURA ANNIE BARNES, seen here waiting for the tide in Nantucket Sound, was the last great schooner built on the Kennebec River and one of the last built in the world. One story has it that her frame and timbers were intended for Percy & Small's Hull #46, whose construction was suspended in the late spring of 1920. They were instead sold to Frank S. Bowker, who disassembled the completed frame and shipped the timbers to his own shipyard downriver in Phippsburg, where she was completed and eventually sold to Captain C. H. Barnes.

Henry Bunting Photo, courtesy of William H. Bunting

whose fate—and name—remains something of a mystery, even to this day. Not long after the CECILIA COHEN was launched, workmen at Percy and Small began to prepare the ways for another schooner. By early February 1920, timber was being delivered to the shipyard and by March the keel was stretched and the framing gang began making up and erecting the frames.[99] But work was soon suspended on what must have been a speculative venture on Sam Percy's part. The shipping rates crashed during 1920, and the market for new vessels dried up. Some claim the frame, partially erected, stayed in the yard for a considerable time before Sam Percy sold it for firewood to some enterprising entrepreneur.[100] But others say that shortly after Sam Percy suspended construction, he sold the frame and timber to Frank S. Bowker of Phippsburg, the last major active shipbuilder in that community just downriver from Bath.[101] Bowker, the story goes, then built one more schooner on speculation, launching her unnamed and unsold at the end of November 1920. Ten months later she was sold to Captain Charles H. Barnes, who named the schooner for his wife, Laura.[102] True or not, it is a great story, especially since the LAURA ANNIE BARNES brought an end to an industry devoted to building wooden sailing vessels that had flourished for 312 years on the Kennebec River, North America's cradle of ships.

THE SHIPYARD'S FINAL CONFIGURATION

When the CECILIA COHEN cast off her mooring lines from the Percy & Small fitting-out pier on a chilly February day in 1920, she left a shipyard that had changed enormously over the previous ten years—never mind the last twenty years. An expanded land base, additional buildings and facilities, and a new blacksmith shop rounded out the changes of a decade that began on a deceptively low key, but appeared to be heading for an upbeat ending.

Fire had long been a major concern at Percy & Small, as at all wooden shipyards. For this reason, smoking in all but the blacksmith shop, as well as in the open-air areas around the shipyard, was banned. However stringent the precautions, fire occasionally raised its ugly head, often coming from the most unexpected sources. For example, in 1898 next-door neighbor Charles E. Hyde was burning grass early in the spring. Apparently some of the embers managed to cross the fence between residence and shipyard and lodge in a stack of timber. Late that night, a passing pedestrian saw the flames and pulled the lever at the nearest fire alarm box (#17). The firemen soon had the flames extinguished and then proceeded to thoroughly wet down the stacks of timber.[103]

During subsequent years, the threat remained although measures were taken to address it. The shipyard retained a full-time night watchman—Elwell Pinkham—to keep a close eye on things. Captain Percy had also endowed the local fire substation—on Marshall Street above Middle Street extension—with a flagstaff. Although this station housed only a man-pulled hose cart, it was staffed by a collection of young men from the neighborhood who, in many cases, had a vested interest in the shipyard because it provided much of their employment.

Over the years there were remarkably few incidents that actually threatened Percy & Small. A forest fire in 1903, driven east by strong winds, crested on the high ridge west of High Street just a few blocks from the shipyard. A number of householders were forced to temporarily abandon their homes and Sam Percy dispatched a number of his workmen into Bath to purchase all the usable buckets that could be found in the event they were needed to fight the fire. They were not.[104] A more sinister danger appeared a few years later in the form of a child's toy. Some bright entrepreneur had conceived of a toy hot air balloon comprised of a colorful paper balloon open at the base with an attached carrier for a candle that provided the heated air to lift and illuminate the contraption. The only problem with the toy—innocent in purpose—was the reality that it was an incendiary device of potentially great effectiveness. One such toy descended into a nearly deserted Percy & Small on 5 July 1909, the day being celebrated as a holiday by the firm. It landed in a pile of woodchips and soon had them fully ablaze. Fortunately, watchman Elwell Pinkham spotted the conflagration and soon had it under control.[105]

The worst fire incident at the shipyard began unobtrusively with a minor incident reported on 5 June 1913. A small fire broke out in a pile of sawdust and chips beside the mill. Whether it was caused by the careless disposal of banned smoking materials, spontaneous combustion, or some other factor was never determined, but the quick use of carbon tetrachloride "grenades" had the situation under control with only a minor scorching of paint on the side of the mill.[106] Less than forty-eight hours later, the fire dragon struck once again, this time with serious effect.

The ever-present Elwell Pinkham was making his midnight rounds through the shipyard, checking building security, tending the boiler for the steambox, and keeping a sharp eye and nose out for fire. At 12:25 A.M. he spotted flames in the blacksmith/machine shop. After ringing in the alarm at Box #17, he returned to the building, but the flames made it impossible for him to reach the hose and hydrant located at the east end of the structure. The local fire laddies responded vigorously, however, and soon had their hose hooked to the nearest hydrant and were playing it on the fire when the first horse-drawn steam pumper arrived from the central station. Assistant Fire Engineer Babb, one of the first on the scene, saw that the entire shipyard and neighboring residences were in danger as a strong south wind whipped up the flames and sent sparks and burning embers streaming across the yard and onto the adjoining Donnell property. He immediately rang in a second alarm, calling out the rest of the department and its equipment.

It was a near thing. The blacksmith/machine shop and boiler room/steambox went up in flames. The attached paint and treenail shop's wall—barrels of highly flammable turpentine and oils used to mix paint were stored on the second floor—actually burst into flames at one point but a heavy concentration of high pressure streams of water inside and out saved the building. The mill also was endangered, the flying embers and sparks landing on its roof where a crew of men equipped with buckets and hoses kept damage to a minimum. Another group of firefighters and volunteers equipped with buckets, brooms, wet blankets, and whatever else came to hand patrolled the Donnell property, beating out embers and sparks before they started new fires, as well as keeping the carpet of woodchips and sawdust and stacks of timber at Percy & Small thoroughly soaked down. Fortunately for all, there was no schooner rising on the ways adjoining the burning blacksmith shop that could be turned into an enormous windblown torch.

By dawn the damage was done but the fire was out. Percy & Small lost the first building it had built in the new shipyard, along with all its machinery and tools. Len Gibson, the boss blacksmith, was also a big loser in tools. But Frank Small assured all and sundry that a new, bigger, and better blacksmith/machine shop would soon spring from the ashes of the old. In the meantime, the shipyard rented the old blacksmith shop at the long-idle Donnell shipyard.[107] Once the site was cleaned up, Fred Scott, boss joiner, was put in charge of building the new, larger shop and repairing the damaged paint and treenail shop. The new blacksmith/machine shop, measuring 96 feet by 26 feet, also contained a new boiler and an attached steambox. It was in service by the end of July.[108]

Three years passed before more changes were instituted at the shipyard. Each reflected the need to address the increase in new shipbuilding work and changes in traditional supply patterns. In 1916 Sam Percy, who was always fascinated by the latest developments in machinery, had the shipyard equipped with compressed air-driven hand tools; these replaced the handcranked (and slow) augers with air-driven drills and the big sledge hammers used to drive long bolts with air hammers. The air drills were fast—one man could do the work of three or four using hand augers—but as previously noted, many old-timers believed that fastenings driven into the air-drilled holes did not hold as well as those drilled by hand. The air hammers speeded up construction and reduced manpower needs. They could also be dangerous.

Raleigh Osier was part of a team fastening the hawse timbers and knightheads on one schooner. The driller had finished his job and Osier and company were driving the bolts when the man who placed the heavy galvanized washers over the end of each of the bolts dropped the washer just as the pneumatic hammer man pulled the trigger. Without the washer, the bolt shot through the timber, out the other side, striking one of a two-horse team at work in the yard right between the eyes. The horse dropped in its tracks, dead.[109]

The air tools relied upon a compressor driven by a large electric motor and a large air storage tank. Powerlines were extended between the ways down to the fitting-out pier. One circuit provided night lighting for the shipyard and the other fed the compressor motor. The latter, along with the air storage tank that measured ten feet by twenty feet in diameter, was housed in a crude, flat-roofed shed situated just inboard of the fitting-out pier between the ways.[110] Hoses to the various tools being operated on a vessel were connected to a large manifold in the compressor shed.

A shortage of workmen was one problem Percy & Small confronted during the World War I shipbuilding revival. The combination of labor-saving machinery and a reduced production schedule allowed the firm to navigate that particular set of rapids. But the shipyard also had to contend with a new problem: the breakdown of the traditional shipping links that brought shipbuilding timber directly to the shipyard via water.

High wartime freight rates to South America, as well as European ports, drew off the very vessels that

Percy & Small Plan: 1917–21
D. K. Lee and R. L. Snow

long carried the cargoes of oak and yellow pine north to Percy & Small, including vessels in their own fleet. The next logical link was the railroad that had hauled materials to Bath for Percy & Small, ranging from 130-foot spars to four-ton anchors. Even ship timber had been delivered by rail when it came from Maine's North Woods. But this approach was slow and unwieldy when it came to moving the materials from the Maine Central freight yards to the shipyard nearly two miles away. With the exception of the big Oregon pine spars, virtually all of the materials had to be painstakingly transferred from freight cars to horse-drawn freight wagons, then hauled to the shipyard to be off-loaded once again.

Yet Bath had a standard gauge street railway that went right past Percy & Small and was already connected to the Maine Central tracks. The L. A. & W. undertook a program during 1916 to develop freight as well as passenger traffic on the north-south line. Although the primary impetus for the additional investment came from the newly established Texas Company shipyard—dedicated to building large, steel steam vessels—being developed in Bath's north end, Percy & Small and G. G. Deering also became beneficiaries of the move.[111] The street railway company acquired powerful electric freight engines and began replacing the original light 48-pound steel rails on its tracks with 60-pound rails. Sidings were also installed at Percy

& Small—at the head of the north building ways—and at Deering's.

Henceforth, flatcars loaded with timber and other supplies destined for Percy & Small were disconnected from the Maine Central trains, hooked up to an electric freight engine, shifted onto the street railway track, and hauled to the shipyard siding to be unloaded. Of course, in the real world things don't always work out as planned. Washington Street south of the railroad yards had a couple of low hills with rather steep grades that had long been a challenge for Bath's streetcars—often requiring the disembarkation of passengers and even an occasional hearty push. Even with the new, more powerful freight engines, it was sometimes found wise to lighten the load on the Percy & Small- and Deering-bound flatcars at the freight yards.[112]

The next development at the south end shipyard caught the city by surprise. On the first day of August 1917, Percy & Small purchased the large adjoining property that formerly belonged to Charles E. Hyde. Hyde had moved to New York about 1912 and in 1914 sold his house and three acres to a Thomas M. Waller who, two years later, resold the property to Chester McCabe. McCabe, a machinist at Percy & Small, was, in addition, a good friend of Sam Percy and would remain so throughout his lifetime.

In 1917 he also had something that Sam Percy felt was necessary for the future operation of the shipyard: a large piece of property with 300 feet of frontage on Washington Street and the L. A. & W. tracks. It provided additional space for a first-class railroad siding and adjoining timber storage in what was then Chester McCabe's front yard. Percy offered to buy the entire property, rent McCabe the house at a very fair rate, and allow the former owner to keep his sizable vegetable garden between the house and the river.[113]

Part of the newly acquired property was exposed ledge that overlooked the shipyard. Unusable for storage—or gardens—a purpose was very quickly found for it—so quickly, in fact, that one can only assume that the purpose had been divined before the deal with McCabe was consummated. The shipyard needed a mould loft and here was the place to put it. So it was that construction began within the month on the 75 by 40-foot building perched on the uneven ledge.

Why did the firm now need a mould loft after being in business for nearly twenty-four years? The short answer is that there simply wasn't one available elsewhere in Bath or the general vicinity short of the Bath Iron Works or the Texas Company, and those facilities were totally taken up with their own work. Bant Hanson, as we know, died in 1915 and, although his son returned to the city in 1916 and attempted to keep the business going even on a part-time basis, that proved to be impossible and the loft started by William Pattee on Commercial Street silently disappeared.

But Percy & Small continued to have need for such a facility. Although they were relying upon old and proven models during this last surge of shipbuilding, the moulds developed from the lofting had a finite—and hard—life, especially when they were used time and again. It so happened that Sam Percy's son-in-law, Allen Irish, was a trained loftsman and draftsman and had for a number of years been in charge of the Iron Works' drafting room. When Frank Small died, Irish left BIW and joined his father-in-law at the shipyard as superintendent. He was also directly involved in the lofting at the shipyard.

From time to time additional changes in the shipyard reflected developments elsewhere. For example, in late 1918 the firm finally purchased that portion of the Stinson property that had been leased since 1899. Work began immediately on the shipyard office which was doubled in size to accommodate the move of the firm's business office from Front Street in downtown Bath to the shipyard now that the latter had become the almost exclusive focus of activity.[114]

Finally, in the spring of 1920, another building appeared on the shipyard's waterfront. Serving as the pipe shop for a major conversion the firm was about to undertake (see below), the building was moved to a point adjoining the south building ways from the Hyde-McCabe house next door. Formerly, the structure had been part of an ell containing a shed with two small rooms above, perhaps former servant quarters. With the pipe shop in place, the final working layout of the shipyard was finally achieved.

The mould loft, completed in 1917, was a sizable, if lightly built, structure that was perched rather precariously on exposed ledge. The schooner is the MIRIAM LANDIS.

Perry Thompson Photo, courtesy of Maine Maritime Museum

WITH A WHIMPER, NOT A BANG

The wooden shipbuilding business was definitely slowing down by early 1920. The CECILIA COHEN was delivered by mid-February, and work was soon suspended on Hull #46 as the market for new schooners became nonexistent. But there was little in the way of gloom at Percy & Small. Two major overhaul jobs on the schooners OAKLEY C. CURTIS and EDWARD J. LAWRENCE extended into the new year. The CURTIS arrived in November 1919, for example, and was extensively rerigged, received a new boiler and freshwater tanks, had her hoisting machinery overhauled, and a new keelson installed. The bill for

this work reportedly came to $80,000 (+/- $540,000 in 1998) before she sailed away for the last time in January.[115]

The ever so weary EDWARD J. LAWRENCE also made another appearance at Percy & Small—this was the last six-master to put in at the shipyard, as well as the last to come up the Kennebec—after one more voyage to Europe. Arriving at the yard in late November 1919, the LAWRENCE's extensive repairs took until April to complete. She was also filthy and overrun with rats and huge cockroaches, as one man who worked on her recalled. The pests were so bad that the workmen had to clean out their tool chests every time they removed them from the vessel.[116] While at Percy & Small, the LAWRENCE underwent yet another attempt to stiffen her sagging hull by reinforcing her ceiling and keelson with, it would appear, as much success as previous attempts.

Both the CURTIS and the LAWRENCE were then owned by the France & Canada Steamship Company which had purchased a good portion of the Percy & Small and Winslow fleets during 1917. That firm had spent an enormous sum in 1917—most of it probably borrowed—to finance the purchase of those vessels, expecting that skyrocketing charter rates would be more than ample to meet the carrying costs of the loans while returning generous dividends to the stockholders. Now someone in the France & Canada front office had a bright idea: purchase at knock-down prices some of the completed but engine-less Shipping Board Ferris and schooner barge hulls that were creating an embarrassing and visible surplus of useless vessels. They then would convert these ships to oil tank barges that would work in tandem with engine-powered tankers, similar to the arrangement pioneered by Anglo-American Oil's successful IROQUOIS-NAVAHOE horsecart combination.[117]

France & Canada Steamship Company purchased three hulls from the Shipping Board, two built at the Shattuck shipyard at Newington, New Hampshire, and the third built at South Freeport.[118] Two were Ferris steamers without their propulsion machinery—HARRASEEKET built at South Freeport and WINAPIE built at the Shattuck yard.[119] The third hull was ULAK, also built by Shattuck, but intended as a schooner barge rather than a merchant steamship. As large as mid-sized five-masters, the Ferris hulls lacked the elegant lines that even the largest of the great schooners shared. They were, in a word, ugly. But the France & Canada Steamship Company was more impressed by their potential utility than by any aesthetic standard.

The first to arrive at Percy & Small was the Shattuck-built WINAPIE which was docked there on 13 May, two weeks later than expected. It was just as well she was on hand as far as the workmen at the shipyard were concerned; the three schooners that

had been repaired at the yard over the winter—CURTIS, EDWARD J. LAWRENCE, and CAMILLA MAY PAGE—were long gone, and work on schooner #46 had ground to a halt in April.

There was enough work to be done on WINAPIE and her cohorts to keep the men employed for as much as a year. Both of the Ferris hulls came complete with their midship superstructures in place. These had to be removed and the donkey boilers and associated equipment necessary for operating auxiliary machinery, oil tank heating coils, and cargo and bilge pumps had to be installed under their bridgedecks.[120] Miles of piping for pumps servicing the cargo tanks and providing steam heating for the cargo—crude oil could be very viscous when cold—also needed to be installed. It was the piping requirements that led Sam Percy to detach an ell from the old Hyde/McCabe house and move it down to the waterfront, there to fill the role of shipyard pipe shop. But the hardest work involved dividing the big open hull into a series of oil-tight cargo compartments. These were created by building wooden transverse bulkheads and a single longitudinal bulkhead. The inner skin of the hull—the ceiling—also had to be made absolutely oil-tight. This work took approximately four months before WINAPIE was delivered back to her owners and towed away.

In the midst of the work on WINAPIE, another customer arrived on the Percy & Small waterfront. She, too, was a bit odd as far as the neighborhood was concerned. A four-masted, baldheaded schooner with an auxiliary gasoline engine, built in Seattle, Washington, in 1919, SNETIND represented a version of schooner architecture that was a little foreign to most Percy & Small shipbuilders. Purchased by J. W. Gorman, she was to be thoroughly rebuilt—she was less than two years old!—the engine removed, and rerigged East Coast style with proper topmasts. That job took two months, with the schooner leaving the yard in early October. She was, parenthetically, the last big wooden schooner to depart from the shipyard for the open ocean.[121]

The ULAK and HARRASEEKET project dragged on into late fall when Percy & Small abruptly announced that it was suspending all work on the hulls

The last significant ship work at Percy & Small involved the conversion of a West Coast baldheaded schooner to the East Coast rig, and conversion of two war-built Ferris steamer hulls and a barge hull into tank barges for the France & Canada Steamship Company. The engineless steamer WINAPIE lies alongside at Percy & Small shortly after her arrival from Newington, New Hampshire, where she was built. Note the building on the left: it was formerly attached to the Hyde house before being moved to the shipyard waterfront where it served as the pipe shop. The rectangular radio shack just forward of WINAPIE's mainmast was salvaged when the deckhouse was removed and converted to a shed for a Bath residence. It is now preserved at Maine Maritime Museum.

Courtesy: Maine Maritime Museum

WINAPIE (right) has completed her conversion to a tank barge and is anchored in midstream awaiting a tow. The schooner SNETIND (left) and barge ULAK are tied up at Percy & Small. Percy & Small's mast sheers are in place by the schooner's foremast, which has apparently just been stepped.

Courtesy: Maine Maritime Museum

The view from WINAPIE's poop deck following her conversion reveals the second, and as yet unconverted, Ferris steamer HARRASEEKET moored at the Deering shipyard. These two vessels, along with SNETIND and ULAK, faintly visible (upper right) at the shipyard, were the last vessels worked on by Percy & Small.

Courtesy Maine Maritime Museum

until further notice.[122] The problem: France & Canada had failed to pay some rather substantial bills owed Percy & Small, and the latter immediately libeled the vessels. The threatened marshal's sale was postponed after the owners posted a bond totaling $114,000 (+/- $775,000 in 1998) on the two hulls. In time—February 1921—France & Canada paid the bill, the libel was lifted, and the two hulls were removed from the shipyard.[123] Of the three, only

ULAK, reportedly the largest towing schooner barge ever built, ever operated as originally planned.[124] Her compatriots did see some service over the years as conventional tank barges.

With their departure, no more serious work remained. After a quarter century, the shipyard fell silent for the last time. The age of the wooden sailing vessel had come to an end.

---

[1] P&S Trial Balances, entry dated October 1908 for Schooner #31, Parker Collection. The frame, intended for Hull #31, was not erected until the summer of 1910, and the schooner DUSTIN G. CRESSY was not launched until two years later.

[2] Entries for the J. S. Winslow six-masters, Schooner Investment Account Book, SM 43/1, MMM. The Percy & Small schooners roughly tracked the earnings of their Winslow counterparts, and in the absence of specific data on the former, the latter data accurately reflects trends, if not specific earnings. The average gross return on invest-ment for the three existing Winslow six-masters in 1907 was 24 percent, declining to 9 percent in 1908; it moved up to 10 percent in 1909 largely due to the addition of the EDWARD B. WINSLOW, and it rose during the next year. This book, a record of one individual's investments in schooner property and the dividends paid (or not paid), may have been kept by Captain William (Billy) Kreger who was master in each of the LAWRENCE six-masters.

[3] *Ibid.*

[4] *NYMR,* 3/24/1915.

[5] *NYMR,* 10/7/1914, 6/16 and 8/4/1915.

[6] *NYMR*, 10/7/1914. The Western Front cut off France from most of her domestic coal supply, which the British made up from production that formerly went to South America, Spain, and Mediterranean countries.

[7] *BT*, 12/22/1915 and 3/6/1917. WYOMING, ELEANOR A. PERCY, CORA F. CRESSY, and EDWARD B. WINSLOW all appear to have been locked into time charters to Boston or Portland early in 1915 at $.70–.75 per ton. The spot charter rates to Portland reached the $3.00–3.50 range by end of 1915 and appear to have stabilized there through most of the war.

[8] Statements of Earnings for the CORA F. CRESSY: #94–99, Parker Collection.

[9] *NYMR*, 3/24/1915; Statements of Earnings for the CORA F. CRESSY: #101, Parker Collection.

[10] *NYMR*, 11/3/1915; Schooner "Martha P. Small" in account with Miller & Houghton, Inc., 12/8/1915, SM 43/7, MMM. The SMALL received $.30 per case to haul 75,000 cases of oil to the River Plate and $24,881.52 in freight for carrying 2,644 tons of linseed cake back to the U.S.

[11] *BT*, 12/18/1915.

[12] *NYMR*, 12/1/1915. J. S. Winslow & Co. cancelled a time charter locking the EDWARD B. WINSLOW into $.75 freights, paying a cash penalty of $4,200 (+/- $52,500 in 1998).

[13] Statements of Earnings for the Schooner EDWARD B. WINSLOW: #79, Parker Collection.

[14] W. F. Palmer to Prentiss Howard, 10/27/1908, Palmer Collection.

[15] Percy & Small incorporated their business but not the schooners in late 1916. G. G. Deering had done the same in 1905. Both firms retained the traditional ownership arrangement through shares in individual vessels.

[16] Interview with Charlotte Cahill, 8/24/1975. Notes, Parker Collection.

[17] Certificate of Registry No. 53 of the Schooner ELEANOR A. PERCY (136844), Port of New York, 2/21/1916, National Archives, Record Group 41. *BT*, 11/7/1916. Her second sale involved three other, smaller schooners as part of an $800,000 package (!) according to the news reports. This figure seems rather high, considering she had just put into Funchal, Madeira Islands, leaking 15 inches per hour. Forced to discharge her cargo, she sailed to New York for "extensive repairs."

[18] *Merchant Vessels of the United States*, 1919. Under her original name, the owners were listed as Kinn, Ltd., of New York City.

[19] *South Wales Echo*, 1/1/1920; American Consul (Plymouth, England) to Percy & Small, 12/30/1921, photostat in Parker Collection. The log book ended up in the collection of the Mariners' Museum at Newport News, but it is in an advanced state of deterioration.

[20] *BT*, 11/28 and 12/20/1916.

[21] *BT*, 6/21/1917.

[22] *BT*, 3/21/1917.

[23] *BT*, 5/10/1917.

[24] The sale of the balance of the Percy & Small fleet was delayed until they returned to the United States, as it was customary to effect the transfer of vessel property subject to safe arrival in a U.S. port and a satisfactory inspection report.

[25] *BT*, 4/12 and 8/9/1917. One report set the price paid for WYOMING at $500,000.

[26] MARTIN—$60,000; PERCY—$125,000; CLIFFORD—$70,000; CRESSY—est. $60,000.

[27] P&S, Inc. to W. R. Dickinson, 8/29/1917. Statements of Earnings for the CORA F. CRESSY, Parker Collection.

[28] The schooner's name has often been misspelled as CARLE, even on the schooner's first set of nameboards.

[29] Trial Balances, October 1908, Parker Collection. $146 posted to Schooner #31.

[30] *BT*, 11/13/1911; vessel was being painted and rigged, but was not launched for another eight months.

[31] *BT*, 7/12/1912. Male sponsors were unusual but not unheard of. The Bath Iron Works built several trawlers for F. J. O'Hara named for Catholic colleges during the 1920s and 1930s, all but one of which were christened by men.

[32] *BT*, 2/12/1914.

[33] Captain William B. Coughlin, "The Languid Lady and the Stout-Hearted Tug," *North Shore*, April 26, 1969.

[34] *BT*, 2/20, 2/23, 3/12, 4/2, and 5/9/1917.

[35] *NYMR*, 10/17/1928.

[36] Charles S. Morgan, "Master in Sail & Steam: The Notable Career of One Maine Shipmaster." Paper presented to Ninth Annual Symposium on Maritime History at Maine Maritime Museum, pp. 35–36.

[37] *BT*, 3/13/1914.

[38] W. F. Palmer to S. W. K. Brooks, 8/28/1907, Palmer Collection.

[39] *I&E*, 4/3, 20/1907; W. F. Palmer to P&S, 10/26 and 11/2/1908, Palmer Collection.

[40] W. F. Palmer to Captain Campbell, 7/1/1907, Palmer Collection. The MARIE PALMER, built by William Rogers in 1900, underwent her half-time survey at P&S. She apparently required about four carloads of new frame timber and a heavy salting to have her class continued.

[41] Data on ship repair business at Percy & Small is drawn from references in the local newspapers, but it is likely that more vessels came there than were reported.

[42] Percy & Small schooner output 1900–09: 58,399 gross tons and twenty-four vessels; schooner output 1916–20: 12,167 gross tons and twelve vessels. Average

annual output 1900–09: 2.4 schooners measuring 5,840 gross tons versus 2.4 schooners grossing only 2,433 gross tons in the 1916–20 period.

[43] *BT*, 7/10, 13/1916 contain a brief story and advertisement concerning a recruiter for a Florida shipyard. But the southern experience was not enjoyed by all: Fred Nickerson of Waldoboro returned to Maine after discovering promises of high pay at a Savannah shipyard were in fact equaled by what he could get at Bath. Food was very expensive, lodging scarce, crowded, and overpriced, immorality rampant, and the southern lifestyle less than agreeable to this true son of Maine. *BT*, 2/26/1919.

[44] *BT*, 8/9/1917. The largest builder of Ferris steamers in New England, the Shattuck yard pulled in thousands of workers including Percy & Small's former master builder, Horatio N. Douglas.

[45] *BT*, 2/16, 8/11, 9/19, and 12/17/1918. McCabe may have been open to the change because he was passed over as Merry's successor.

[46] Baker, in contrast to his predecessors, maintained a very low profile in the local press.

[47] The Texas Company shipyard, made up of the former New England Company and Sewall shipyards, was organized in 1916 to take advantage of the demand for steel steamships for the merchant service. The yard produced the largest merchant ships built on the Kennebec until 1940.

[48] Memos on Costs of Ship Timber, Notes, Parker Collection.

[49] Considered the largest, most efficiently laid out, and modern shipbuilding plant in the world in 1918, Hog Island shut down at the end of the emergency program and was subsequently dismantled. It is now the site of Philadelphia's International Airport.

[50] *BT*, 8/28/1917. Ferris relied on input from experienced wooden shipbuilders, including Sam Percy and Gard Deering. The final Ferris design included Deering's continuous shelf and clamp system in lieu of hanging knees and the system of diagonal strapping ultimately adopted by Percy & Small.

[51] Steel production was never a serious problem, in part because it took so long to get the newly created shipyards up and running. In Maine, most existing wooden shipyards preferred to build schooners for private customers. Of the twenty-five Ferris hulls built in Maine, only two appear to have been built by previously active shipyards (Kelley, Spear in Bath and G. A. Gilchrest in Thomaston). The balance were built by newly formed corporations with no previous shipbuilding history. The Ferris design had three versions tailored to the timber supply in the region where they were to be built. Those built in the South and along the Gulf Coast were to be built exclusively of yellow (longleaf) pine—frames, timbers, planking. Those built in New England would have hardwood and hackmatack frames with yellow pine timbers and planking. Those built in the Pacific Northwest were to utilize Douglas fir exclusively. The latter supply was more than adequate to meet the demand, but the supply of yellow pine proved to be inadequate, a point the Shipping Board could easily have ascertained *before* they launched the program rather than a year after they started.

[52] *BT*, 6/30/1917.

[53] *BT*, 6/5/1917.

[54] *BT*, 3/29/1919.

[55] *BT*, 5/24/1916. The Sewall-built DIRIGO was the first steel square-rigger built in the U.S. The steam schooners were the BELMONT, the O. E. SALLMOASH, and the WILLIAM J. MURPHY.

[56] *BT*, 12/23/1916.

[57] *BT*, 1/13/1917.

[58] *BT*, 6/6/1917.

[59] *BT*, 6/5/1918. She was sunk on 2 June 1918. The Mengels had previously lost DIRIGO to submarines.

[60] Darrah's commands included the HENRY F. KREGER, EDWARD T. STOTESBURY, EDITH L. ALLEN, and HORATIO G. FOSS. Born in Richmond on the Kennebec, he retired from active seafaring in 1907.

[61] Greenhill and Manning, *Schooner*. This useful publication with many fine detail drawings of the subject vessel is heavily grounded upon the SALLY WREN/C. C. MENGEL, JR. plans in the collection of Captain W. J. L. Parker.

[62] Hanson File, Author's P&S Research Files. Young Hanson, on his return to Bath, lived within a few houses of Sam Percy's residence on Washington Street. The Georgia Shipbuilding Company of Savannah built four schooners from the plans: the SALLY WREN (1917), ROSALIE HULL and IRENE S. WILKINSON (1918), and MARGARET SPENCER (1919).

[63] John T. Rowland, *Wind and Salt Spray: The Autobiography of a Sailor*. New York: W. W. Norton, 1965, photo caption between 128 and 129. Rowland noted that the two Mengel schooners crossed a yard. The authors have not seen a photo of the C. C. MENGEL with the foreyard. She was lost in 1922.

[64] Summary Construction Accounts, Hulls #30, #37, #42, Parker Collection. The per ton cost of the Mengel schooners does not include the coppering.

[65] Rowland, pp. 115–50.

[66] *NY Journal of Commerce and Industry*, 10/16/1935. The schooner sank on 10/15/1935.

[67] Frederick J. Kaiser, *Built on Honor, Sailed with Skill: The American Coasting Schooner*. Ann Arbor, MI: Sarah Jennings Press, 1989, p. 139; Frederick J. Kaiser Collection, PC-80, Maine Maritime Museum; *BT*, 10/3/1917.

[68] *BT*, 10/3/1917. Miss Boggs also had the distinction of being the youngest sponsor in the shipyard's history.

[69] Kaiser, p. 138. "She was designed by B. Hanson of Portland [sic], associated with her builder, Percy & Small." Kaiser served aboard the ROSS as unpaid volunteer and paid seaman during his summer vacations from school late in the schooner's career and became well acquainted with her last captain-owner. He ultimately researched and wrote a series of articles for *National Fisherman* on the schooner's long career, as well as his own experiences aboard her. These were eventually compiled and published in book form.

[70] Specifications for ROSS Schooner, Parker Collection. Calls for steam outfit, but vessel was actually built with gasoline "one-lunger"; see Building Account, Schooner #40, Parker Collection. Category for machinery divided with $3,324.53 going to Hyde Windlass and $1,349.95 to Gray-Aldrich. If the vessel had a steam donkey engine, Hyde Windlass would have been the only vendor. Gray-Aldrich supplied internal combustion engines.

[71] Morgan, "Master in Sail and Steam, pp. 53–55. This was Peterson's sixth Percy & Small-built command and his last sailing vessel. He subsequently commanded steam tankers, was trials captain for the Bethlehem Fore River Shipyard, and a member of the board of Pilot Commissioners for Boston.

[72] See fn #65.

[73] Francis E. Bowker to David R. Getchell, 8/8/1981, courtesy of Captain Francis E. Bowker.

[74] *Bath Sentinel*, 10/27/1892.

[75] This account is drawn from Mrs. Hagan's account in a letter published in *BT*, 12/15/1920. They apparently went ashore near the Spanish-controlled city of Ceuta on Point Almina, almost directly across the strait from Gibraltar.

[76] *NYMR*, 11/30/1921. Open market prices for vessels were dropping fast by the end of 1920. Cohen may have figured that he would never collect more on his investment than from the insurers.

[77] At that time he was in command of the JAMES R. FOX, another Cohen-owned schooner. Peterson commanded for varying lengths of time the following Percy & Small-built schooners: C. C. MENGEL, JR., EDWARD J. LAWRENCE, ST. JOHNS, N.F., CORA F. CRESSY, CECILIA COHEN, and ANNIE C. ROSS. See: Morgan, "Master in Sail & Steam."

[78] As quoted by Morgan, "Master in Sail & Steam," pp. 47–49.

[79] Cohen also had another schooner built in Dennysville named the DAVID COHEN. Captain W. J. L. Parker once visited Mr. Cohen at his New York shipping office a number of years later, but found him unwilling to reminisce about his association with Percy & Small or his shipping business experiences. Personal communication with authors.

[80] *BT*, 7/2/1917.

[81] E. S. Crosby to P&S, 2/26/1914, Construction Bill File, Schooner #39, Parker Collection.

[82] *BT*, 5/9/1918 and 3/29/1919.

[83] See Appendix B.

[84] The WHEELER had a northern "hardwood and hack" frame. The ST. JOHNS, N.F. had an oak frame with hard-pine tops, while the ZEMAN came with an all white oak frame. Specifications, Schooners #39, #41, #43, Parker Collection.

[85] Building Account, Schooner #39, Parker Collection. An attached memorandum noted that the hull strapping (materials and labor) represented 2.6 percent of the vessel's total cost.

[86] *Portland Press Herald*, 3/3/1930.

[87] Building Account Schooner #41, Parker Collection. The shipbuilder's cost was $192,526.16 (+/- $1.7 million in 1998).

[88] A. W. Frost & Co. to Boston Insurance Co., 10/25/1922, Notes, Parker Collection.

[89] Maher worked the Maine scene for over two decades. Prints of some of his footage, his camera, and other gear are preserved at the Northeast Historic Film archive at Bucksport, Maine, but not footage of this launching unfortunately.

[90] Morgan, "Master in Sail & Steam," p. 41.

[91] *NYMR*, 6/28/1922.

[92] *NYMR*, 12/5/1923.

[93] *NYMR*, 12/2/1925.

[94] "Captain Tells of Last Journey of Old Five-Master, WINSLOW," *Portland Press Herald*, 8/17/1935.

[95] The steam auxiliary plants on these schooners were closed loop systems, with steam being made from fresh water stored aboard ship. Some of that steam was recycled back to water after driving the machinery by passing it through tubes in the condenser which were cooled by seawater pumped through it by the circulating pump. But the system did not operate at 100-percent efficiency, and some steam was lost. The plant did not include evaporators that permitted conversion of seawater to fresh water.

[96] Contract between Percy & Small, Inc. and Stanley Navigation Co. for Hull #43, Bath, Maine, June 25th, 1918, Douglas K. and Linda J. Lee Collection. The contract was signed by Sam Percy and David Cohen. One of the witnesses was Joseph S. Zeman, an official in Cohen's firm.

[97] *Ibid.*; *BT*, 3/29/1919.

[98] *BT*, 6/14/1920.

[99] *BT*, 2/10, 3/18, and 3/19/1920.

[100] Osier Interview.

[101] Coombs Interview.

[102] *Ibid.*; Baker, II, pp. 758-59.

[103] *BT*, 4/11/1898.

[104] *BT*, 6/3/1903.

[105] *BT*, 7/6/1909.

[106] *BT*, 6/5/1913.

[107] *BT*, 6/7/1913; Coombs Interview.

[108] *BT*, 6/26/1913.

[109] Osier Interview.

[110] William Donnell Interview.

[111] The Texas Company shipyard occupied the former New England Company and Sewall shipyards. Track was laid from the new shipyard, up Bowery Street to Washington Street where it intersected the existing street railway line.

[112] *BT*, 7/8/1916, 10/23 and 11/14/1917.

[113] SCRD, 135–490. The large front yard sloped gently away from Washington Street to a low ridge upon which the house was built. The ridge, in turn, sloped gradually towards the water. Today Maine Maritime Museum's Maritime History Building occupies the approximate site of the old Hyde-McCabe House and museum parking the old front yard/rail siding/storage yard. The house was moved to a lot a short distance down Washington Street.

[114] *BT*, 12/10/1918.

[115] *BT*, 1/26/1922.

[116] Robson Interview. John F. Eaton, who grew up in the Stinson house across the street from the shipyard, also recalled that every time a schooner came in for repairs, the neighborhood was suddenly overrun with rats. Eaton Interview.

[117] Built by Harland & Wolff in 1907–08, the pair operated successfully together until 1930.

[118] *BT*, 4/16/1920.

[119] The Ferris design was not only tailored to a variety of different materials combinations, but also offered steam propulsion or semi-diesel engine options.

[120] While the men were stripping the deckhouse off the vessel, someone saw some likely salvage in the radio shack perched on the aft end of the boat deck. It was removed intact and transported to a Bath backyard where it took on a new life as a shed. More recently, it has been acquired by Maine Maritime Museum. It may be the largest surviving piece of the unloved and unlovely class of Ferris steamers.

[121] "Supplement Vessel Reconstruction at Percy & Small," William A. Baker Collection, MS-57, MMM. The SNETIND ended her sailing days in 1928 when she was laid up at a wharf in Boston. She was subsequently sold to self-described poetess Ann Winsor Sherwin and her mentally challenged son who had visions of sailing her away, but in the meantime took up residence aboard. For the further misadventures of schooner and owners, see: William P. Quinn, *Shipwrecks Around Boston*. Hyannis, MA: Parnassus Imprints, 1996, pp. 151–53.

[122] *BT*, 12/4/1920.

[123] *BI*, 1/27/1921; *BT* 2/10/1921.

[124] Baker, fn #119. One story has it that the ULAK was loaded with oil and towed to Europe behind a conventional tanker. Upon arrival, it was discovered that a substantial portion of her cargo had soaked into the wood. Coombs Interview.

Epilogue

The last vessel worked on by Percy & Small, the ULAK, was towed to Portland for drydocking in early February 1921.[1] With her departure, a quarter century of sometimes intense wooden shipbuilding and ship repair activity at the shipyard spluttered to a halt. The neighborhood no longer rang with the sound of caulking mallets on driving irons, the scream of a saw through hard pine, or the distinct sound of the Daniels planer blissfully slabbing a massive floor timber. An unnatural silence descended upon the shipyard and the neighborhood.

Oh, there was still some activity in the shipyard. Stacks of hard pine once destined for a schooner that would now never be built were manhandled into the river by a gang of day laborers, made up into rafts, and towed upriver to Kelley, Spear to be fabricated into a pair of barges. Occasionally smoke could be seen issuing from the blacksmith shop, or the rumble of the drive shafts in the mill could be heard as some craftsman or another made use of the well-equipped shops. And across the street in the firm's office, one could sometimes see Sam Percy and certainly run into Allen Irish or J. Clifford Spinney looking after the firm's ever-diminishing pile of paperwork. For a brief time during the twenties, one might even imagine a return to the glory days when a five-master was tied up at the shipyard's fitting-out pier. But the MARY F. BARRETT, a Deering-built schooner, was just one of a number of

great schooners collected at various harbors and backwaters along Maine's coast to await the inevitable. The BARRETT was eventually towed to Robinhood Cove, where she was beached and eventually broken up. Most of the time, however, the buildings sat silent as if brooding over a past irretrievably lost.

After 1920 the passage of time brought with it the inevitable wastage amongst Percy & Small-built vessels. Three were lost during 1921, including the scow sloop McCORMICK, ex-UMBAJEJUS, the GOVERNOR BROOKS, and the eighteen-month-old CECILIA COHEN. Two more became history during the first part of the next year when both the C. C. MENGEL, JR. and the JOSEPH S. ZEMAN became victims of strandings within a month of each other. But it was during the first quarter of 1924 that the often transitory nature of man's best works was really driven home.

Six-master RUTH E. MERRILL was first to go, followed a month later by fire-victim ROBERT P. MURPHY. But the crowning blow was the loss of WYOMING—the creation of Bant Hanson, Sam Percy, Miles M. Merry, *et al.*, the pride of Percy & Small, the world's largest wooden sailing vessel—still looking remarkably good despite nearly fifteen years of hard work and, in recent years, some neglect. But now her long and largely untroubled career came to an abrupt and tragic end.

Owned by the Frost syndicate in Portland and

managed by Chase, Leavitt & Co., the big schooner was chartered to carry 5,000 tons of coal from Norfolk to St. John, New Brunswick. When she sailed from Hampton Roads on Leap Day (February 29, 1924), the late winter passage offered no more risk to the schooner than any of the many others she had successfully carried out during the course of her career. Her progress north was slow thanks to a combination of weather and the caution of Captain Charles Glaesel who, it appears, was reluctant to resort to hard driving; she didn't pass Vineyard Haven until 8 March and anchored near the Pollock Rip Lightship the next morning to await a fair wind. Here she was soon joined by the CORA F. CRESSY, Captain C. N. Publicover, as a northeast storm began to rake the area. The two schooners remained side-by-side for two days on the shoals as the storm grew in strength. Then, fearing the worst in such an exposed position, Captain Publicover got some sail on the CRESSY, hoisted her anchors, and made a run for open water to the eastward. WYOMING was last sighted from the lightship at 3:00 A.M. on the twelfth when the visibility improved briefly. Her anchor lights were bright and she appeared to be riding out

the seas without difficulty. But during the next day, wreckage began coming ashore on the island of Nantucket, including pieces labeled "Wyoming." Captain Glaesel and his twelve man crew were never seen again.[2]

At the yard, the passage of time also brought the inevitable peeling paint, roof leaks, weeds and brush pushing through a couple of feet of slowly rotting woodchips. It also brought about the inevitable dissolution of Sam Percy's painstakingly assembled shipbuilding plant. The first land to go was half of the lot originally leased from the Stinson family and subsequently purchased. The land where once there had been the stacks of timber that young Johnny Eaton saw as forts was sold as a house lot even before the body was cold.[3] But a few more years would pass before the changes became irreversible.

The great Daniels planer attracted the attention of John A. Lord, a Bath lad who made a career in the Navy. He was now charged with the responsibility of restoring the nation's oldest naval vessel, the USS CONSTITUTION at the Boston Naval Shipyard, and he was looking for machinery and skilled workmen around Bath to further the job. He got both at Percy

By the mid-1920s many of the big schooners that had been eagerly sought at virtually any price by investors in 1916–18 were anchored in sheltered coves and harbors awaiting the next boom that never came. Portland Harbor was no exception. Part of Alfred W. Frost's fleet of castoff schooners, the CORA F. CRESSY (left), OAKLEY C. CURTIS (center), and EDWARD J. LAWRENCE, idly swing on their chains awaiting their next charters.

Courtesy: Maine Maritime Museum

An unknown photographer caught WYOMING on silver nitrate as she was being towed out to her offing through Hampton Roads, Virginia. The date is 29 February 1924—Leap Day—and her destination is St. John, New Brunswick, with a cargo of 5,000 tons of coal. This is the last known recorded image of the greatest of the great schooners.

Courtesy: Captains Douglas K. and Linda J. Lee

& Small. Sam Percy agreed to sell the big planer in 1927 for $1,400 (+/- $11,000 in 1998) delivered to Boston.[4] Charles Colby and Sam Barnes were among the several shipwrights recruited locally by Lieutenant Lord, no doubt with glowing recommendations from Captain Sam.

The departure of the Daniels planer opened the floodgates. Much of the remaining woodworking machinery, along with the jackshafts and motors, was sold to a dealer in used mill equipment. The balance, including the wood-turning lathe in the joiner shop and the big bevel jigsaw in the mill, along with the air compressor, contents of the blacksmith shop, and a miscellaneous collection of odds and ends were sold to R. G. Bailey in March 1930.[5]

The breakup of the Percy & Small landholdings proceeded apace. In August 1929 the firm sold the former Hyde/McCabe property along with its former mould loft to Mrs. Helen Hardy for a residence.[6] Four months later, the office and its lot went to the Maine Conference of Seventh Day Adventists.[7] It appeared that the balance of the shipyard property, the core shipyard and its buildings, would soon follow the rest.

The General Utilities Company, a Bangor firm, announced it was going to set up a manufacturing plant in Bath to assemble refrigerators, washers, and other household appliances. Working with the Bath Board of Trade, President H. C. Buzzell announced the plant would be located at the former Percy & Small shipyard and the Board of Trade agreed to sell the company's securities to local investors.[8] The projections for the appliance manufacturer were encouraging: an initial plant investment of $60,000 (+/- $475,000 in 1998), fifty employees by mid-summer 1930 increasing to 200 employees by the summer of 1931, and orders for 2,000 refrigerators and 3,000 washing machines.[9] But there was a problem called the Stock Market Crash of 1929, then the Great Depression that followed.

The project never went beyond the talking stage and the shipyard remained unsold for another eight years. At the end of 1931, Captain Percy and Allen Irish dissolved Percy & Small, Inc., dividing the remaining assets between them.[10] In the interim, the buildings slowly deteriorated and the grounds of the once busy shipyard became overgrown with weeds, brush, and young trees.

During the summer of 1938, one young man who had learned about the great schooners at the feet of Captain Frank Peterson at the Boston Marine Society watched the CORA F. CRESSY being stripped of her spars, rigging, and machinery at Boston before being towed to Bremen, Maine. Charles S. Morgan came close to suffering serious bodily injury, if not death, when the riggers placed the hoisting sling below the center of gravity on one mast which, once freed from the constraints of the mast partners, immediately flipped butt end up as the unbalanced topmast end crashed down into the barge lying alongside—the same barge that Morgan was standing on observing the operation. The topmast portion broke off with a resounding crash when the spar hit the barge, shortening the mast and shifting the center of gravity to a point above the sling, causing the spar to flip once more with the mast butt slamming down onto the barge as the upper end flipped upward. It was a Charlie Chaplin moment.

Fortunately, this near miss did not discourage Morgan from pursuing his interest in schooners or the men who sailed them. Perhaps about the time of this incident, he learned that the shipyard that built the CORA F. CRESSY was itself facing the breakers. Whatever the cause, he made a journey to Bath that summer and spent a day prowling through the silent, long-idle shipyard with camera in hand. Someone, perhaps Chester McCabe, took him through the empty mill where he found two brown paper sheets of after house floor plans for the EDWARD B. WINSLOW and WYOMING, rolled up and tucked under the eaves in the joiner shop where they had lain for nearly thirty years. His photographs are the last known of the shipyard with the blacksmith shop in place.[11]

In November 1938 Captain Percy signed the deeds transferring the shipyard property to Richard C. Morse "for one dollar and other valuable considerations."[12] "Within a short time," the local press reported, "the last vestige of what was one of Bath's greatest industrial plants, with the exception of the land upon which the buildings stand, will have disappeared. Richard C. Morse of Phippsburg has purchased the land and buildings comprising what was

When this picture was taken in August 1938, the Percy & Small shipyard had been idle for over seventeen years and time was taking its toll. Some of the mill's awning doors have been roughly patched, peeling paint is commonplace, and brush and weeds are taking over. A small "For Sale" sign announces the owner's willingness to part with the property—at a price negotiable—to a willing buyer.

Charles S. Morgan Photo, courtesy of Captains Douglas K. and Linda J. Lee

This is one of the last known pictures of the more or less intact shipyard. The edge of the
last outhouse is just visible at the left, and the blacksmith shop (#2) can just be made
through the verdant growth of saplings flourishing on a couple of feet of rotting woodchips. The mould loft, paint and treenail shop, and mill are clearly visible. A few months
later the shipyard was sold, and the new owner announced his intention to develop the
property as a residential subdivision. The first building to go was the blacksmith shop.

Charles S. Morgan Photo, courtesy of Captains Douglas K. and Linda J. Lee

formerly the Percy & Small shipyard and will at
once commence razing the buildings, salvaging the
lumber, windows and other material used in their
construction, and once the land has been cleared pro-
poses opening it for the sale of house lots."[13]

Morse made a start in his project, tearing down the
1913 blacksmith/machine shop and its attached steam
box. All the salvageable materials were stored in the
other buildings for the time being. But thanks to the
curious juxtaposition of a continuing depression that
was almost instantly transposed into a boom, Morse
found that no market existed for his proposed shipyard houselots. A few years later, in 1941, he found a
tenant for the remaining buildings. Sears, Roebuck &
Company had just built a large retail store in downtown Bath, but it lacked warehouse space for such
bulky items as tires and appliances. Morse overhauled
the buildings, using some of the salvaged materials

from the blacksmith shop to convert the mill into a
proper and secure warehouse. Thus it was that
America's favorite catalog and department store
retailer ensured the survival of the remaining shipyard
buildings for another quarter century until the siren
call of the shopping center lured it away to nearby
Cook's Corner.[14]

Captain Sam Percy remained active throughout the
thirties, although age and infirmity slowly began to
overtake the former sea captain and shipbuilder. He
still enjoyed an occasional trip to his camp on
Moosehead Lake with Chester McCabe and a few
special cronies. He and Mrs. Percy also enjoyed their
summer cottage at Sabino, where they were often
joined by daughter Eleanor and son-in-law Allen
Irish. Then every winter they traveled west by rail to
San Diego to spend a few months in the sun, away
from the snow and ice of Maine.

The Final Muster, 1 July 1937: *(left to right)* John J. Wardwell; Captain Sam Percy; Oliver Matthews; Chester Pascal; and Captain Jim Creighton..

Courtesy: Maine Maritime Museum

But Sam Percy was an increasingly lonely man. Most of his closest associates—many of them part of his inner circle of friends—had passed away: partner Frank Small in 1917; boss joiner Fred B. Scott, who had been with the firm from the beginning, died in 1918, aged sixty-four; that giant amongst wooden shipbuilders, Miles M. Merry, retired in 1916 at age seventy-three and died three years later; J. Clifford Spinney, who joined the firm as an office clerk in 1900 and rose to be the corporation's vice president and the shipyard's assistant superintendent, was only forty-five when he passed away in 1924. Then in 1930 two of Percy & Small's stalwarts, boss caulker Charles H. Oliver and the incomparable Frank A. Palmer, one of Maine's greatest riggers, were laid to rest in Bath's Oak Grove Cemetery.

An extraordinary gathering took place in Bath on a bright and sunny first of July in 1937. Five old men—none of them under eighty—who were Maine's most senior shipbuilders met in Bath for a chance to swap sea stories and well-entrenched opinions on ships and shipbuilding: Oliver Matthews of Thomaston, still a shipyard blacksmith at age ninety; John J. Wardwell of Rockland, designer of the first six-master and a longtime master builder, aged eighty-five; Chester Pascal of Rockport who was a foreman at the Carleton & Norwood shipyard in 1885 when that firm built America's third four-masted bark, the FREDERICK BILLINGS; Captain Jim Creighton, long-time confidant and senior captain of William F. Palmer, as well as a shipbuilder; and, of course, Sam Percy. They enjoyed their get-together and the trip to Bath's city hall to look over the half models and pictures displayed by the Kennebec Marine Museum.[15] Then it was time to have a group picture taken.

Captain Sam Percy crossed the bar on 7 October 1940. By that time, only one Percy & Small schooner was still sailing, the ANNIE C. ROSS, and she would lower her sails for the last time within fourteen months. According to the probate records in the Sagadahoc County Courthouse, Percy's estate was valued at $226,745 (+/- $2.2 million in 1998), a level that suggests that the captain was certainly comfortably well off. Of course this represented the value of holdings that had very recently weathered the Great Depression.

Sears, Roebuck & Company concluded their unintentional and unconscious role as preservers of an industrial past in 1967 when they closed their Bath retail store and moved to the new shopping plaza several miles away at Cook's Corner. Once again the fate of the surviving buildings at the old shipyard was up for grabs.

This time, however, Bath was far more conscious of its maritime heritage and sheltered a small, but growing group of preservation activists. In 1962 a group of local citizens formed the Marine Research Society of Bath with the goal to publish a maritime history of Bath to be written by Mark Hennessy. Provision was also made for the future creation of a museum devoted to Bath's maritime heritage.

Hennessy was stricken with cancer shortly after he resigned his reporter's job on the *Portland Press Herald* to devote full time to the history, and he died just a year later. The Marine Research Society then turned to naval architect and maritime historian William Avery Baker to carry out the task, which was accomplished in 1973 with the publication of the two-volume *A Maritime History of Bath, Maine and the Kennebec River Region.*

The museum side of the equation appeared in 1964 with the opening of the storefront Bath Marine Museum in downtown Bath. It soon moved to the former home of Harold M. Sewall, thanks to the generosity of his daughter, Mrs. Walter E. Edge. There the museum grew and flourished, expanding its collections and attracting attention from maritime history enthusiasts and historians worldwide.

Some of those involved with the new museum soon discovered the Percy & Small shipyard, thanks to William Donnell, a descendant of shipbuilder William T. Donnell. The younger Donnell had undertaken the restoration of the small schooner MARY E at the old shipyard, a project that received considerable publicity. That publicity caught the attention of Dr. Charles E. Burden, a very active—and considered by some to be a very radical—member of the museum's Board of Trustees.

When word circulated that the Percy & Small shipyard was soon to be abandoned by Sears, Roebuck and the Morse family was seeking to sell it, Burden and other members of the museum community advanced the idea of acquiring the property, but this idea was quickly quashed on the grounds that the organization's plate was already too full with its obligations toward publishing the maritime history and the costs of operating the Sewall House headquarters.

The activists were not to be denied, however. Mr. and Mrs. Lawrence M. C. Smith of Philadelphia and Wolf Neck in Freeport, who had a record of providing generous amounts of seed money to get selected projects off the ground, were entertained at an elaborate dinner at the Burden home.[16] In time, they agreed to purchase the property and hold it until such time that the museum was ready and able to take it over. The Smiths took title to the property on 9 January 1968.[17]

The museum's board, however, was reluctant to get involved with the old shipyard, which some members frankly regarded as a falling-down dump. The Smiths took their role seriously, nonetheless, and invested money in essential repairs. It wasn't until 1971 that the pro-shipyard forces on the board finally prevailed, much like water dripping on a rock, getting approval to open the shipyard to public visitation. In subsequent years, the Percy & Small shipyard achieved the status of a National Historic Site, received grants for architectural surveys and restoration plans, and in early 1974 was the beneficiary of a major acquisition and restoration grant from the Maine Historic Preservation Commission. The value of the property donated to the museum was used to match the state and federal grant for completing the first stage of a long-term restoration process at the shipyard. In the fall of 1974 title passed to the museum. The following summer the refurbished buildings, appearing much as they did when new three-quarters of a century earlier, were dedicated and a plaque was unveiled honoring Mr. and Mrs. Smith for their role in making it all possible.

Shipbuilding activity also returned to the overgrown shipyard. William Donnell, as noted above, acquired and restored the small schooner MARY E during the mid-1960s. Then in 1971 Douglas and

Linda Lee brought a former New Jersey oyster dredge—the ISAAC H. EVANS—to the shipyard, where they spent two years rebuilding the old schooner for the Penobscot Bay cruising trade, where she remains active to this day.

Another schooner was built from scratch at this time as well, but its construction bore little resemblance to what had gone on before at the shipyard. Built of ferro-cement, the RACHEL & EBENEZER did, in her own way, succeed in duplicating the launching fiasco that marred the debut of the WILLIAM C. CARNEGIE over seventy years earlier.

The adjoining property that had formerly been the William T. Donnell shipyard and residence came on the market in 1977. Once again, Mrs. Smith—now a widow—agreed to purchase the property for the benefit of the museum. She conveyed title to the museum in 1981.[18]

Then in 1978 there was an opportunity to reincorporate the former Hyde/McCabe property back into the shipyard; the only problem was a lack of money to consummate the purchase. However, a group believing it was absolutely essential to acquire this property for the future interpretation of the shipyard and the future development of the museum organized a private company, called the South End Holding Company, put in enough money to make the down payment on the property, and mortgaged the rest. The loan-carrying charges, taxes, and maintenance for the residence were covered by rental of the property to a private family. The museum was able to purchase the property from the South End Holding Company in 1981, following receipt of a major grant from the Maritime Preservation Program of the National Trust for Historic Preservation.

The acquisition of these properties has not only brought almost all of the original components of the shipyard together, but it has allowed the museum to consolidate its operations in one place. Additional land purchases have included the G. G. Deering shipyard, made possible through the generosity of the late Elizabeth Noyce, and other small parcels linking the holdings together into one block.

Today, the Percy & Small shipyard still exists to interpret a key phase of our industrial past: wooden shipbuilding.

---

[1] *BI*, 2/10/1921.

[2] *Portland Press Herald*, 3/14, 15, 16, 18, 21/1924. Much was made of the fact that the MERRILL (lost two months earlier) and WYOMING each carried thirteen persons when lost. A more remarkable coincidence was the presence of former Governor Bryant B. Brooks and Mrs. Brooks in nearby waters while aboard a passenger ship bound from Europe via Halifax to New York in Cape Cod waters. They learned of the loss upon arrival in New York. B. B. Brooks, *Memoirs*, p. 265.

[3] SCRD, 147–263.

[4] Letters: Captain R. L. Arthur, USN, to Rear Admiral Mayo Hadden, USN, 1/12/1973; and Virginia Wood to Raymond A. Small, 11/3/1974. Letters in author's files. Efforts to locate the planer in the early seventies just prior to the closing of the Navy Yard came to naught. Once stored in Building 36, it was probably broken up for scrap during World War II.

[5] Agreement between R. G. Bailey and C. H. McCabe, 3/19/1930. SM 2/6, MMM.

[6] SCRD, 173–104.

[7] SCRD, 173–249.

[8] *BI*, 3/13/1930.

[9] *Ibid.*

[10] SCRD, 209–113.

[11] The late Charles S. Morgan related these events to the authors at various times.

[12] SCRD, 209–128.

[13] *BI*, 11/10/1938.

[14] Martin and Snow, *Good Times and Hard Times in Bath*, 46, pp. 181–82.

[15] Mark W. Hennessy, "Ghosts of Old Time Shipbuilders Conjured by Five of the Breed," *Portland Press Herald*, 7/2/1937.

[16] Among other things, they purchased beach front property at Popham Beach and turned it over to the state to be made into a public beach and recreation area and donated the land that became Wolf Neck State Park in Freeport.

[17] SCRD, 358–552.

[18] SCRD, 401–654.

Appendix A

HULL LIST

Commercial shipbuilders often assign sequential numbers to vessels they build to simplify accounting for material purchases, labor allocation, and use of capital equipment. Data in the Percy & Small hull list is arranged from left to right as follows: first line—P&S hull number, vessel name (number of masts), Blt (shipyard where built), MO (managing owner); second line—registered dimensions (in feet and tenths), gross register tonnage (measurement tonnage), MB (master builder); third line—LD (approximate date keel laid), LND (date vessel launched), First Master (name of first Master). Data for dimensions and tonnage is drawn from the *List of Merchant Vessels of The United States* published annually by the Bureau of Navigation, an office of the Treasury Department until 1903, when the Bureau was transferred to the newly created Department of Commerce and Labor. Additional information is drawn from Captain Denny Humphreys' American Bureau of Shipping (ABS) Survey Notebooks.

There is probably nothing more arcane in history than the system for measuring vessels. Below you will find each vessel's gross register tonnage (GRT) which is a measurement of volume (one ton = 100 cubic feet) rather than weight. This figure is derived from a series of carefully defined measurements of the vessel by the admeasurer.

The admeasurer is also responsible for determining the vessel's official registered dimensions (length/beam/depth of hold). Registered length is defined as the "inside clear measurement along the center fore-and-aft line of upper surface of the tonnage deck." And the registered depth measurement is taken from the underside of the second deck from below (also the tonnage deck) on vessels with two or more continuous decks. Thus the registered depth figure, especially on flush-deck vessels can be very misleading. Take the schooners EDWARD B. WINSLOW and WYOMING, for example. Very near sisters, the former has a registered depth of 23.7 feet and the latter's is 30.4 feet. In fact, the WINSLOW's actual depth to the underside of her highest continuous deck is 29 feet, but that deck is the third deck from below, while WYOMING has only two continuous decks.

To further compound the confusion, there are additional measurements that can describe the length of a vessel: length over all (LOA), i.e., measured length of the uppermost continuous deck; length over rig (LOR), i.e., length measured from tip of jibboom to aft end of spanker boom. Thus WYOMING's registered length is 329.5 feet, her LOA is 350 feet, and her LOR is 450 feet. The latter figure was the one the captain was most concerned about, especially when docking or undocking his schooner.

Now that you are thoroughly confused, let's take it one more step. Vessel size is also described in terms of weight. A vessel's light displacement tonnage (weight of water displaced by vessel) gives you the basic weight in long tons of 2,240 pounds of the vessel hull and all fixed equipment. Full load displacement includes the former plus the crew, fuel, supplies, and cargo. The difference is called deadweight tonnage (DWT) when describing the carrying capacity of a merchant vessel. Thus WYOMING, which measured 3,730 GRT, had a light displacement of approximately 4,800 tons, a full-load displacement of approximately 10,800 tons, and a deadweight capacity of 6,000 tons. Simple!

1	CHARLES P. NOTMAN (4)	Blt @ Morse SY	MO: Percy & Small
	219.3 x 42.5 x 20.5	1,518 GRT	MB: H. N. Douglas
	LD: 4/94	LND: 8/29/94	First Master: Lincoln W. Jewett

Remarks: Percy & Small's first vessel, the NOTMAN was considered a fast vessel and a good earner. She had paid a reported $80,556 in dividends against her original cost of $71,600 when lost.
Disposition: She was sunk by the SS COLORADO June 1900 in a collision; Captain Jewett (on his last trip before taking command of the-then building ELEANOR A. PERCY), wife, and crew managed to escape only with the clothes on their backs, Captain Jewett's chronometers, and the yawl boat. Mallory Lines, owner of COLORADO, paid $55,000, of which about $700 went to each $1/64$.

2	WILLIAM H. CLIFFORD (4)	Blt @ Morse SY	MO: Percy & Small
	221.6 x 43.5 x 19.6	1,593 GRT	MB: H. N. Douglas
	LD: 12/8/94	LND: 8/6/95	First Master: Wm. F. Harding

Remarks: Built on a new model, the CLIFFORD was uncommonly accident prone throughout her long career but held the record for longevity under the P&S house flag. She also was a frequent carrier of ice cargoes from the Kennebec. She was sold in February 1916 for $70,000.
Disposition: A war casualty, the CLIFFORD was sunk by a U-boat 600 miles off the coast of France on 8 September 1917 at 48–30N, 17–46W.

3	S. P. BLACKBURN (4)	Blt @ Morse SY	MO: Percy & Small
	233.7 x 43.9 x 20.1	1,756 GRT	MB: H. N. Douglas
	LD: 1/20/96	LND: 6/24/96	First Master: Alexander Ross

Remarks: Built on the CLIFFORD model, this schooner spent her entire life under the P&S flag. Reportedly the first schooner (1907) to engage in the sulphur trade from Sabine Pass. In 1909 she was outfitted with a radio and operator.
Disposition: She was abandoned at 30–45N, 70–38W after being dismasted in a severe winter gale 26 January 1913. The engineer and steward refused to leave the vessel when the other nine crewmen were picked up by a British steamship. On 1 February another steamer spotted the hulk and sent a boat to investigate. They found no one aboard, the ship's boat gone, but lamps still burning in the cabin.

4	ALICE E. CLARK (4)	Blt @ Percy & Small	MO: J. S. Winslow
	227.4 x 43 x 20.7	1,621 GRT	MB: H. N. Douglas
	LD: 6/16/97	LND: 1/24/98	First Master: Leslie B. Clark

Remarks: Built on the successful model of the NOTMAN, the CLARK was holder of two Percy and Small "firsts"— the first vessel built in P&S's new shipyard and the first built under contract for other owners. She returned to the shipyard in 1906 for repairs following a collision with the MARY F. BARRETT.
Disposition: The CLARK grounded on Coombs Ledge at Islesboro on 1 July 1909; after unsuccessful salvage efforts, she was declared a total loss.

5   M. D. CRESSY (5)   Blt @ Percy & Small   MO: Percy & Small
      264.4 x 43.9 x 21.6   2,114 GRT   MB: W. A. Hodgkins
      LD: 7/19/98   LND: 5/11/99   First Master: Wm. F. Harding

Remarks: The first P&S-built five-master and first sailing vessel to be outfitted with a stockless anchor, the "Doctor" CRESSY was prone to problems related to structural weakness throughout her career. Once abandoned off Diamond Shoals, she was salvaged and repaired.

Disposition: Sold to the American-Union Line in 1916, she foundered at 31–31N, 60–40W, enroute to Havre, France, 9 April 1917; four lost.

6   HELEN W. MARTIN (5)   Blt @ Percy & Small   MO: Percy & Small
      281.6 x 44.8 x 20.9   2,265 GRT   MB: W. A. Hodgkins
      LD: 6/19/99   LND: 3/3/00   First Master: Alexander Ross

Remarks: A slightly enlarged CRESSY, the MARTIN suffered from many of the same problems. She was sold on 7/6/1915 for $60,000 to A. H. Bull & Co.

Disposition: She made a forty-eight-day passage to Archangel (Russia) with cotton; on the return voyage with timber for England, she struck a mine in the North Sea. Badly damaged and floating on her cargo, she was beached, salvaged, and eventually sold to Swedish interests and renamed, appropriately, FENIX. As such, she was the largest schooner-rigged vessel ever registered in Sweden. She went ashore 14 January 1920 on the Danish coast.

7   ELEANOR A. PERCY (6)   Blt @ Percy & Small   MO: Percy & Small
      323.5 x 50 x 24.8   3,401 GRT   MB: M. M. Merry
      LD: 3/20/00   LND: 10/10/00   First Master: Lincoln W. Jewett

Remarks: The third-largest wooden sailing vessel (the Sewall-built square-riggers ROANOKE and SHENANDOAH were larger) when built, the PERCY was the second six-masted schooner. She was one of only three vessels P&S ever launched that was not completely rigged. Eight months later, the only two six-masted giants on salt water (PERCY and WELLS) tried to cross the same point of ocean at the same time. They were repaired at Percy & Small, giving Bath an enormous boost in that summer's tourist business.

Disposition: Sold in late 1915 for $125,000, the PERCY was lost on a voyage from Rio de Janeiro to Copenhagen 26 December 1919 at 48–30N, 17–45W. Five crewmen were rescued.

8   WILLIAM C. CARNEGIE (5) Blt @ Deering SY   MO: J. S. Winslow
      289.2 x 46.3 x 22.4   2,663 GRT   MB: W. A. Hodgkins
      LD: 1/20/00   LND: 8/13/00   First Master: Mitchell Reed

Remarks: The largest five-master when built, she stuck on the ways on her scheduled launching day, greatly embarrassing Captain Percy and resulting in the replacement of Hodgkins by Miles Merry as P&S's master builder. She was considered by many to be one of the most handsome five-masters.

Disposition: She was a total loss after going ashore, coal laden, Norfolk to Portland, near Moriches, Long Island (NY), 1 May 1909, not far from the site where the MILES M. MERRY was lost.

9   OAKLEY C. CURTIS (5)   Blt @ Reed SY   MO: J. S. Winslow
      265 x 46.2 x 22.9   2,374 GRT   MB: M. M. Merry
      LD: 6/22/00   LND: 1/19/01   First Master: M. E. Hodgdon

Remarks: The CURTIS served sixteen years hauling coal under the J. S. Winslow flag before being sold to the France & Canada Steamship Co. in 1917.

Disposition: After lying idle at Portland in the late 1920s, she was converted to a pontoon barge for raising the naval ram KATAHDIN. She was scuttled with the ram off Cape Henry in July 1930.

10   MARTHA P. SMALL (5)   Blt @ P&S   MO: Percy & Small
264.6 x 45.7 x 21.5   2,178 GRT   MB: M. M. Merry
LD: 10/19/00   LND: 4/20/01   First Master: G. F. Barlow

Remarks: Named for Frank Small's wife, this schooner had a long and successful career under the P&S house flag. She was sold in 1917 for $180,000.

Disposition: She fell off her keel blocks in drydock in Montevideo, Uruguay. She was repaired, but her owners failed to pay the bills, so she was broken up there in 1923.

---

11   CORA F. CRESSY (5)   Blt @ P&S   MO: Percy & Small
273 x 45.4 x 27.9   2,499 GRT   MB: M. M. Merry
LD: 5/1/01   LND: 4/12/02   First Master: Wm. F. Harding

Remarks: It took over eleven months to complete the CRESSY thanks to a design change while on the stocks and then a fire that destroyed her blocks. A profitable, if not always lucky, earner for P&S, she was sold to the France & Canada Steamship Co. in 1917 for $202,500.

Disposition: She soldiered on for two or three different owners until 1928 when she was sold to become a "showboat." Eventually she ended up in Bremen, Maine, where she served as a lobster pound breakwater and a first-class source of artifacts and data on wooden shipbuilding practices at the end of the sailing vessel era. Her hulk could still be seen in 1998.

---

12   CORDELIA E. HAYES (4)   Blt @ Reed SY   MO: J. S. Winslow
202.5 x 40.3 x 18.7   1,281 GRT   MB: M. M. Merry
LD: 3/01   LND: 8/17/01   First Master: E. E. Ross

Remarks: She had a three-and-one-half-year career under the J. S. Winslow flag. She once rescued forty-one passengers and crew of the British steamer KELVIN.

Disposition: The HAYES was wrecked off Diamond Shoals, Cape Hatteras, 16 December 1905.

---

14   MILES M. MERRY (4)   Blt @ P&S   MO: Percy & Small
215.2 x 43.2 x 20.1   1,589 GRT   MB: M. M. Merry
LD: 7/2/01   LND: 11/14/01   First Master: S. G. Hupper

Remarks: Built as a replacement for the NOTMAN and named in honor of Percy & Small's master builder, she was the first vessel to be built on the newly expanded shipyard's north building ways. She was built to the same model as the successful W. H. CLIFFORD and was sold to J. S. Winslow & Co. in 1902.

Disposition: She was wrecked at Moriches, Long Island, 17 February 1909, near the location where she had gone ashore previously.

---

15   ADDIE M. LAWRENCE (6)   Blt @ P&S   MO: J. S. Winslow
292.4 x 48.3 x 22.2   2,807 GRT   MB: M. M. Merry
LD: 5/02   LND: 12/17/02   First Master: Wm. R. Kreger

Remarks: The smallest of the P&S-built six-masters, she was sold to the France & Canada Steamship Co. in 1917.

Disposition: The LAWRENCE met her end 9 July 1917 when she was wrecked at Les Boeufs, near St. Nazaire, France.

16-1   MARGARET WARD (4)   Blt @ P&S   MO: J. S. Winslow
191.5 x 38.7 x 20.7   1,074 GRT   MB: M. M. Merry
LD: 5/21/02   LND: 8/9/02   First Master: Jason McKown

Remarks: Originally intended for their own fleet, she was sold on the stocks by Percy & Small (circa 15 July 1902) to J. S. Winslow & Co.

Disposition: Her subsequent career was brief. She was sunk by the steamer EL RIO on 13 April 1903, drowning Captain McKown's two small children and a seaman off Galveston, Texas.

16-2   FLORENCE M. PENLEY (4)   Blt @ P&S   MO: Percy & Small
         195.5 x 40.9 x 20.6   1,154 GRT   MB: M. M. Merry
         LD: 11/?/02   LND: 4/2/03   First Master: M. L. Jameson

Remarks: Built as a replacement for the WARD, the PENLEY took hull number 16-2, even though she was actually #16. Percy & Small had previously skipped unlucky #13.

Disposition: She was lost on a voyage from Rio after springing a leak off Barbados during a vicious Caribbean hurricane in September 1915.

17   ELIZABETH PALMER (5)   Blt @ P&S   MO: W. F. Palmer
         300.4 x 48.3 x 28.3   3,065 GRT   MB: M. M. Merry
         LD: 3/3/03   LND: 8/26/03   First Master: D. B. Smith

Remarks: Modeled on the ADDIE M. LAWRENCE, she was purchased on the stocks (8 May 1903) by William F. Palmer and modified while under construction into P&S's first flush-decker. Management interest sold to J. S. Winslow & Co. in 1910.

Disposition: She rolled onto her beam ends after sinking the freight steamer WASHINGTONIAN in a collision in 1915.

18   GRACE A. MARTIN (5)   Blt @ P&S   MO: Percy & Small
         302 x 48.1 x 28.6   3,129 GRT   MB: M. M. Merry
         LD: 9/29/03   LND: 7/16/04   First Master: Wm. F. Harding

Remarks: Built as a replacement to the P&S fleet following the sale of #17, she had a modified CORA F. CRESSY deck arrangement.

Disposition: She was lost in a bitter winter gale off Matinicus Rock, Maine, after becoming badly iced up with her pumps frozen, 14 January 1914.

19   RUTH E. MERRILL (6)   Blt @ P&S   MO: J. S. Winslow
         301 x 48.2 x 23.7   3,003 GRT   MB: M. M. Merry
         LD: 4/25/04   LND: 11/23/04   First Master: G. H. Wallace

Remarks: She was sold to the France & Canada Steamship Co. for a reported $300,000 ($377,000 by another account) during 1917 when the price for shipping was sky high.

Disposition: The MERRILL stayed in service until she pounded to pieces on L'Hommedieu Shoal off Woods Hole, Massachusetts, after her seams opened during a gale on 12 January 1924.

20   UMBAJEJUS (scow sloop)   Blt @ P&S   MO: M. G. Shaw
         70.5 x 22.2 x 5.6   68 GRT   MB: M. M. Merry
         LD: 12/2/03   LND: 1/21/04   First Master: J. M. Pottle

Remarks: Named originally for a lake in northern Maine and eventually renamed the MCCORMICK, this unlikely product of Percy & Small spread 400 square yards of sail. She was in service on the Kennebec, Sheepscot, and New Meadows Rivers, as well as along the coast carrying lumber and hay.

Disposition: She burned and sank off Parker Flats 20 November 1921.

21   EVELYN W. HINKLY (4)   Blt @ P&S   MO: J. S. Winslow
         179.4 x 37.1 x 12.5   698 GRT   MB: M. M. Merry
         LD: 8/8/04   LND: 1/19/05   First Master: J. F. Hinkly

Remarks: Originally destined for P&S's fleet, this schooner was sold to J. S. Winslow two months before she was launched. Her layout suggests she was primarily intended to carry timber rather than coal.

Disposition: After a long career with J. S. Winslow & Company, the HINKLY sailed from New London in October 1917 and was never seen again. She is the only P&S-built vessel lost without a trace.

22	DAVIS PALMER (5)	Blt @ P&S	MO: W. F. Palmer
	305.4 x 48.4 x 27.2	2,965 GRT	MB: M. M. Merry
	LD: 5/1/05	LND: 11/28/05	First Master: Leroy K. McKown

Remarks: The first fully strapped vessel built at P&S, the DAVIS PALMER was intended for foreign, as well as domestic, trade.

Disposition: She succumbed during a wild winter gale when, dragging her anchors, she struck a ledge and went to pieces in Broad Sound, Boston Harbor, the day after Christmas in 1909. All hands were lost.

23	ROBERT P. MURPHY (4)	Blt @ P&S	MO: Percy & Small
	175.3 x 37.1 x 13.5	697 GRT	MB: M. M. Merry
	LD: 3/20/05	LND: 12/16/05	First Master: Albion B. Hipson

Remarks: Built as a replacement for the HINKLY when the latter was sold to J. S. Winslow, the MURPHY was a profitable vessel. She made one passage from New York–Rio de Janeiro–Buenos Aires–Rochefort (France)–Nova Scotia during 1916. She was sold in 1916/1917 during the war boom.

Disposition: She was destroyed by fire on 20 February 1924 at Puerto Plata, Dominican Republic.

24	ALICE M. LAWRENCE (6)	Blt @ P&S	MO: J. S. Winslow
	305.1 x 48.2 x 22.6	3,132 GRT	MB: M. M. Merry
	LD: 3/26/06	LND: 12/1/06	First Master: Wm. R. Kreger

Remarks: Under the command of one of the more colorful "big schooner" skippers, the LAWRENCE proved to be a fast sailer. She was the second schooner (the first was the THOMAS W. LAWSON) to be completely lighted by electricity.

Disposition: She stranded on Tuckernuck Shoal, breaking her back, 6 December 1914. Much of her gear was salvaged and later used to repair other big schooners. Her hulk burned about eighteen months later.

25	FANNIE PALMER II (5)	Blt @ P&S	MO: W. F. Palmer
	263.7 x 45 x 21.3	2,233 GRT	MB: M. M. Merry
	LD: 5/26/06	LND: 5/25/07	First Master: W. B. Willey

Remarks: She was originally intended for their own fleet and to be a duplicate of the MARTHA P. SMALL, but P&S sold the frame to Palmer following the stranding and sale of the original FANNIE PALMER. Oregon fir was used extensively in her keelsons and ceiling.

Disposition: Management interest sold to J. S. Winslow & Co. in 1910; this vessel foundered on Christmas Eve 1916, 500 miles west of Gibraltar.

26	EDWARD J. LAWRENCE (6)	Blt @ P&S	MO: J. S. Winslow
	320.2 x 50 x 23.9	3,350 GRT	MB: M. M. Merry
	LD: 6/13/07	LND: 4/2/08	First Master: Wm. R. Kreger

Remarks: Probably built from a model by Bant Hanson, the LAWRENCE combined all of the positive attributes of this class with many of the negative traits. Part of the big sell-off of the Winslow fleet in 1917, she went to the ubiquitous France & Canada Steamship Co.

Disposition: When she burned at her mooring in Portland Harbor on 27 December 1925, the era of the giant, six-masted schooners came to an end.

27   GOVERNOR BROOKS (5)   Blt @ Donnell SY   MO: Percy & Small
      280.7 x 45.8 x 26.5   2,628 GRT   MB: M. M. Merry
      LD: 4/27/07   LND: 10/22/07   First Master: Angus McLeod

Remarks: Built in the adjoining Donnell shipyard due to the other building ways being bespoken, the GOVERNOR BROOKS was P&S's last five-master built for their own account. She was sold 1917/1918.

Disposition: She was abandoned in sinking condition off Montevideo, Uruguay, 23 March 1921.

28   EDWARD B. WINSLOW (6)   Blt @ P&S   MO: J. S. Winslow
      318.4 x 50 x 23.7   3,424 GRT   MB: M. M. Merry
      LD: 4/6/08   LND: 11/24/08   First Master: Henry Butler

Remarks: Probably designed by Bant Hanson and a near sister to the EDWARD J. LAWRENCE and WYOMING, this schooner was believed by many to be the most handsome of the class. She was, indeed, one of the most profitable. She was part of the 1917 sale to the France & Canada Steamship Co.

Disposition: She burned within sight of the French coast on 10 July 1917.

29   FULLER PALMER (5)   Blt @ P&S   MO: W. F. Palmer
      309.4 x 48.9 x 27.4   3,060 GRT   MB: M. M. Merry
      LD: 5/12/08   LND: 11/10/08   First Master: Otis W. Clark

Remarks: A slightly enlarged DAVIS PALMER, the FULLER PALMER was the last vessel built for William Palmer, whose health was failing. He died ten months later. The management interest in the surviving Palmer vessels was eventually purchased by J. S. Winslow & Co.

Disposition: She was abandoned during a gale after becoming badly iced up with pumps frozen 154 miles SE of Cape Cod, 12 January 1914. It was the same storm that claimed the GRACE A. MARTIN.

30   WYOMING (6)   Blt @ P&S   MO: Percy & Small
      329.5 x 50.1 x 30.4   3,730 GRT   MB: M. M. Merry
      LD: 4/5/09   LND: 12/15/09   First Master: Angus McLeod

Remarks: Designed by Bant Hanson, she was the last six-master and the largest commercial wooden sailing vessel ever built (doubters are referred to Dr. John Lyman's article in *Log Chips*, v. I, no. 3, November 1948, p. 28). She was sold in 1917 to the France & Canada Steamship Co. for a reported $350,000.

Disposition: Sold to A. W. Frost & Company of Portland, she was lost on the Nantucket Shoals with all hands 11–12 March 1924.

31   DUSTIN G. CRESSY (4)   Blt @ P&S   MO: Percy & Small
      182.3 x 38.2 x 15   862 GRT   MB: M. M. Merry
      LD: 5/18/10   LND: 7/12/12   First Master: Harry B. Dobbin

Remarks: Built from a model by Bant Hanson, she was long in building. A collision victim in New York Harbor in 1917, the CRESSY was raised and then repaired at P&S. Sold in 1917 as part of the deal with the France & Canada Steamship Co., she continued to soldier on until laid up in 1929.

Disposition: She was broken up after 1933.

32   CARL F. CRESSY (4)   Blt @ P&S   MO: Percy & Small
      189.1 x 38.3 x 15.5   898 GRT   MB: M. M. Merry
      LD: 7/7/13   LND: 1/6/15   First Master: Norman Merry

Remarks: The same model as #31 and the last schooner built for Percy & Small's own account, she was sold in 1917 to the France & Canada Steamship Co.

Disposition: She was the victim of a U-boat in the Bay of Biscay, 23 August 1917, at 45–52N, 11–13W.

33   RANDALL & MCALLISTER #2   Blt @ P&S   MO: Randall & McAllister
    95.5 x 28.6 x 7.2   164.68 GRT   MB: M. M. Merry
    LD: 10/26/11   LND: 11/25/11

Remarks: A coal lighter with a capacity of 400 tons, she served in Portland Harbor.

34   PEQUOSETTE   Blt @ P&S   MO: C. W. York
    113.7 x 30 x 3.4   248 GRT   MB: M. M. Merry
    LD: 8/14/13   LDN: 10/15/13

Remarks: Equipped with Hyde machinery, this coal lighter was built for service in Boston Harbor.

35   POCAHONTAS NO. 1   Blt @ P&S   MO: C. W. York
    118.9 x 32.2 x 13.4   444 GRT   MB: M. M. Merry
    LD: 1/18/14   LND: 3/13/14

Remarks: This lighter was equipped with elaborate coal-handling equipment to allow her to bunker United Fruit ships in Boston Harbor. She could carry 1,250 tons.

36   CHARLES D. LOVELAND (4)   Blt @ P&S   MO: S. C. Loveland
    179.6 x 37 x 15   776 GRT   MB: M. M. Merry
    LD: 8/24/15   LND: 4/6/16   First Master: C. H. Saunders

Remarks: Started for their own account, this schooner was sold on the stocks by Percy & Small in January 1916. Later in her career she was renamed the ESTHER MELBOURNE.
Disposition: She was wrecked at Miragoane Bay, Haiti, 10 August 1928.

37   C. C. MENGEL, JR. (4)   Blt @ P&S   MO: Axim Trans. Co.
    184.2 x 38.2 x 14.9   844 GRT   MB: M. M. Merry
    LD: 3/30/16   LND: 8/3/16   First Master: F. H. Peterson

Remarks: This was the last vessel to be supervised by Miles M. Merry. This schooner and #38 are believed to be the source for the detailed construction plans and specifications that were drafted by Ole Hanson in 1916–17 for the Savannah shipyard's SALLY WREN and her three sisters. She was also the first vessel to be fully coppered on the ways at Bath in twenty years, and was intended for the West African mahogany trade.
Disposition: She was wrecked on Morant Cay, British West Indies, 7 January 1922.

38   SAM C. MENGEL (aux. 4)   Blt @ P&S   MO: Axim Trans. Co.
    186.9 x 38 x 15.7   915 GRT   MB: W. J. Baker
    LD: 6/14/16   LND: 1/13/17   First Master: J. E. Bradford

Remarks: Outfitted with a pair of triple expansion engines producing a total of 300 IHP, this was the only powered vessel built by P&S. The highly sophisticated power plant was a failure. First, it took nearly five months to deliver her following the launching due to delays in delivery of her machinery. Second, on departing Bath under her own power, she suffered a boiler failure and had to be towed to Boston. Finally, the machinery and fuel tanks eliminated one-sixth of her cargo capacity. The MENGEL beached her engines/boilers within a year. She was also the first vessel built by P&S since 1900 not supervised by Miles Merry.
Disposition: She was sunk by a U-boat, 2 June 1918, 38–07N, 73–46W.

39   DUNHAM WHEELER (5)   Blt @ P&S   MO: East Coast T. C.
    254.5 x 44.2 x 23   1,926 GRT   MB: W. J. Baker
    LD: 11/?/16   LND: 7/2/17   First Master: Millard G. Dow

Remarks: She was the first five-master built by P&S since 1908. She was laid down in late November but the severe winter delayed construction.
Disposition: She foundered off Cape Canaveral, Florida, 15 November 1930.

40   ANNIE C. ROSS (4)   Blt @ P&S   MO: F. G. Boggs
     175.5 x 38.2 x 14   791 GRT   MB: W. J. Baker
     LD: 5/17/17   LND: 10/3/17   First Master: Alexander Ross

Remarks: She was the last P&S-built schooner in operation and afloat. Laid up after the attack on Pearl Harbor, she was later acquired by Sea Scouts in the early 1950s.
Disposition: She foundered at her mooring in Glen Cove, Long Island, on 4 September 1955.

41   ST. JOHNS, N.F. (5)   Blt @ P&S   MO: St. Johns, NF Trans. Co.
     254.1 x 43.3 x 23.9   2,046 GRT   MB: W. J. Baker
     LD: 9/10/17   LND: 5/9/18   First Master: F. H. Peterson

Remarks: Later renamed EDWARD B. WINSLOW, she was purchased by Capt. A. W. Frost in 1922 for $60,000.
Disposition: She foundered on a voyage from Norfolk to Bermuda, 12 December 1928.

42   LIEUT. SAM MENGEL (4)   Blt @ P&S   MO: Mengel Box Co.
     187.7 x 38.4 x 15.2   907 GRT   MB: W. J. Baker
     LD: 4/16/18   LND: 9/5/18   First Master: Hans T. Hansen

Remarks: She crossed a yard on her foremast and was designed for the West African mahogany trade. She was barged in 1933.
Disposition: She foundered off Boston Lightship, 16 October 1935.

43   JOSEPH S. ZEMAN (5)   Blt @ P&S   MO: Stanley Nav. Co.
     253.2 x 43.2 x 23.7   1,956 GRT   MB: W. J. Baker
     LD: 9/13/18   LND: 3/28/19   First Master: Fred L. Dunton

Remarks: She was the last of fifteen five-masters built by Percy & Small.
Disposition: The ZEMAN was wrecked on Metinic Island Ledge, Penobscot Bay, Maine, 3 February 1922.

44   MIRIAM LANDIS (4)   Blt @ P&S   MO: Landis Nav. Co.
     187.4 x 38.4 x 15.3   904 GRT   MB: W. J. Baker
     LD: ca. 5/19   LND: 9/25/19   First Master: Proctor Hagan

Remarks: Christened by P&S's stenographer, Ena Bucknam, the LANDIS survived a particularly exciting adventure on the coast of Morocco which led to her eventual transformation into a Brava packet.
Disposition: She was abandoned in sinking condition off Brava, Cape Verde Islands, 30 January 1935.

45   CECILIA COHEN (4)   Blt @ P&S   MO: Cecilia Cohen Nav. Co.
     199 x 38.4 x 19.2   1,102 GRT   MB: W. J. Baker
     LD: 9/?/19   LND: 2/9/20   First Master: Molear Christianson

Remarks: The owner's insistence that the vessel proceed without an inspection after grounding with a cargo of phosphate rock sealed her doom.
Disposition: Abandoned sinking off Cape Hatteras, she was set on fire to remove any menace to navigation, 7 August 1921.

46   Unnamed   P&S   Built on speculation
     ?   ?
     LD: 2/?/20

Remarks: Probably same model as the COHEN, construction was suspended by early spring as the frame was being erected.
Disposition: Later disassembled on the ways, the frame timber was reportedly sold to Bowker, who used the timbers to build the LAURA ANNIE BARNES.

Appendix B

Models, Moulds, Layers and Covers, Horning Out, and Rising Rods:
A Primer on the Arcane World of Traditional Wooden Ship Design as
Practiced by Percy & Small[1]

In the days of wooden vessels, schooners—even the largest—were almost always "modeled" rather than "designed." Modeling involved the process of making a three-dimensional scale model—normally a half model—out of wood to represent the shape of the proposed vessel's hull, rather than attempting to represent a three-dimensional object on paper in two dimensions. The experienced modeler—a Fred Rideout or Bant Hanson—much in the manner of a sculptor, transformed the basic dimensions specified by the prospective owner into a finished, graceful representation of form. "If it looks right, it is right," was the watchword of modeler and shipbuilder. The shape of the hull was then translated full-size to the lofting floor where it was used to make patterns—called moulds—of stem and sternpost, as well as of the frames that gave shape to the vessel.

During the great schooner era, the models were usually made of glued-up pine board lifts with contrasting dark—usually mahogany—thin lifts laid in at points approximating the light and load waterlines. The waist of the model was also frequently represented by a number of layers of alternating, thin, light and dark lifts sprung to the run of the sheer. Shaped by experienced hands guided by the well-trained eye, the models were often completed with the finish of fine pieces of furniture, to be admired, examined, and criticized.

Not surprisingly, many shipbuilders and shipowners came to treat these functional objects as works of art.[2] Whether mounted on a simple backboard and displayed on an office wall, or affixed to a framed backboard and elaborately detailed with keel, stem, sternpost, rudder, chock rails fore and aft, painted and gilded trailboards, and an engraved brass plaque detailing pertinent information, these models often remain the sole documentation of a vessel's shape. But determining which vessel (or vessels) they represent can be a challenging endeavor.

Half models have proved to be unreliable when attempting to equate their dimensions with the dimensions of built vessels. In short, identifying a half model by means of measurements alone can be an almost hopeless task. This point is underscored by the history of a Percy & Small half model made by Fred Rideout that is identified both as the William H. Clifford *and* the Martha P. Small, two schooners of considerably different dimensions.[3]

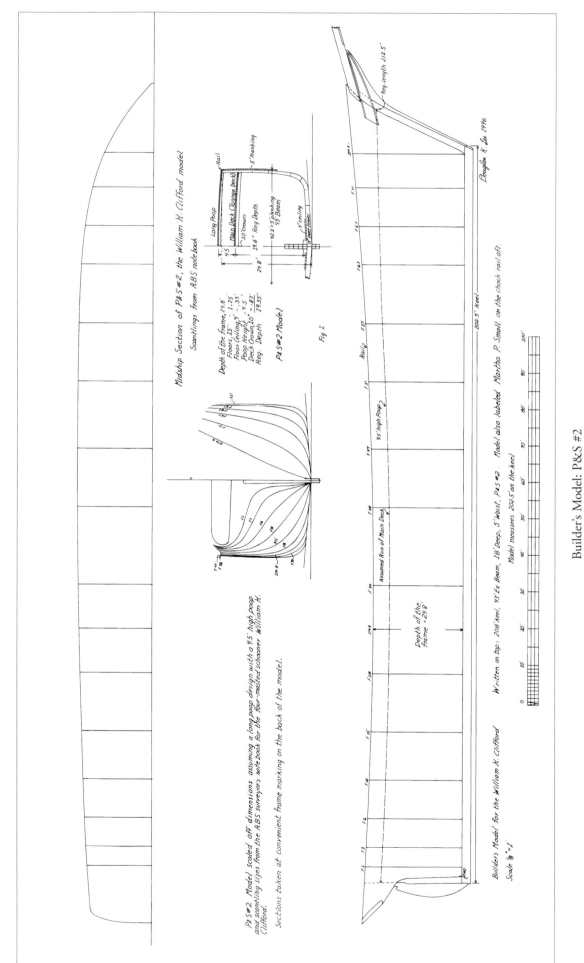

Midship Section of P&S #2, the William K. Clifford model

Scantlings from ABS notebook

Long Poop
Rail
Main Deck (Steerage Deck)
5" Planking
~10" Crown
19.6' Reg Depth
14.2'2" Planking
4'5"
43 Beam
4" Ceiling
24' 8"

Depth of the frame, 24.8'
Floors, 15" – 1.25
Floor Ceiling, 4" – .33
Poop Height, – 4.5'
Deck Crown, 10 – .83'
Reg. Depth   19.55'

P&S #2 Model

Fig 1

P&S #2 Model scaled off dimensions assuming a long poop design with a 4.5' high poop and scantling sizes from the ABS surveyor's note book for the four-masted schooner William K. Clifford.

Sections taken at convenient frame marking on the back of the model.

Reg. length 212.5'

Douglas K. Lee 1996

202.5' keel

45° high Poop

Assumed Run of Main Deck

Depth of the frame = 24' 8"

Written on top: 208' keel, 43' Ex Beam, 18' Deep, 5' Waist, P&S #2. Model also labeled Martha P. Small on the chock rail aft.

Model measures 202.5' on the keel

Builder's Model for the William K. Clifford

Scale ⅛" = 1'

Builder's Model: P&S #2

Douglas K. Lee

The Clifford/Small Model

This half model, which remains in the possession of members of the Small family, scales out for a vessel with a registered length of 212.5 feet, registered breadth of 43 feet, a registered depth of 19.6 feet, and a 202.5-foot keel. The Clifford, the first schooner built from this model, had a registered length that was 9.1 feet longer and a keel length that was approximately 7.5 feet longer. Although the breadth of the new vessel was greater by a half foot than that represented by the model, the depth was the same. These differences between model and schooner are not significant, particularly when you take into account the flexibility shipwrights enjoyed working with wood that often came into the shipyard oversized.

For example, it is likely that when the keel stock was finished and laid down, it measured several feet longer than the specified length. Percy & Small, building for their own account, were not averse to taking advantage of some of that additional length—the longer the vessel, the more tons of cargo that could be carried. And the added length could easily be accommodated in this case simply by increasing the frame spaces by one inch, from thirty-two inches to thirty-three inches, a perfectly acceptable adjustment that fell well within the rules of the American Bureau of Shipping or its predecessor. The increase in frame spacing, when combined with floor timbers hewn slightly thicker than specified, easily provided the necessary stretch without adding additional frames.[4]

Before the half model of the William H. Clifford/Martha P. Small was retired from active service, it provided the moulds for as many as ten schooners built by Percy & Small between 1895–1919. Only two other Clifford descendants were four-masters (S. P. Blackburn and Miles M. Merry, the latter coming the closest to the model's full-sized dimensions), with the rest built as five-masters. The five-masters fell, in turn, into three distinct groupings by size. The range of their dimensions is particularly startling considering that all of the schooners listed in the table were built from the same half model.

Clifford Model Schooners

		Reg. Dimensions		
	Length	Beam	Depth	GRT
Model	212.5	43	19.6	1,500
Group I: Four-Masted Schooners				
*Clifford	221.6	43.5	19.6	1,593
+Blackburn	233.7	43.9	20.1	1,756
*Merry	215.2	43.2	20.1	1,589
Group II: Large Five-Masted Schooner				
+H. W. Martin	281.6	44.8	20.9	2,265
Group III: Medium Five-Masted Schooners				
+M. D. Cressy	264.4	43.9	21.6	2,114
*M. P. Small	264.6	45.7	21.5	2,178
#Fannie Palmer	263.7	45	25.5	2,233
Group IV: World War I Five-Masters				
+D. Wheeler	254.5	44.2	23	1,926
+St. Johns, N.F.	254.1	43.3	23.9	2,046
*Joseph Zeman	253.2	43.2	23.7	1,956

Key To Symbols
* Direct attribution as built from Clifford model.
+ Strong probability of being built from the model based on direct and circumstantial evidence.
# Probably built from model based on circumstantial evidence.

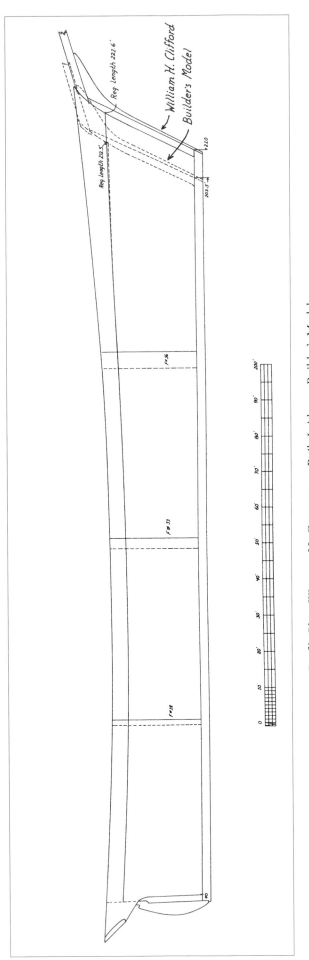

Profile Plan: WILLIAM H. CLIFFORD as Built Laid over Builder's Model

Douglas K. Lee

Profile Plan: MARTHA P. SMALL Laid over Profile Plan of P&S #2 as Modeled

Douglas K. Lee

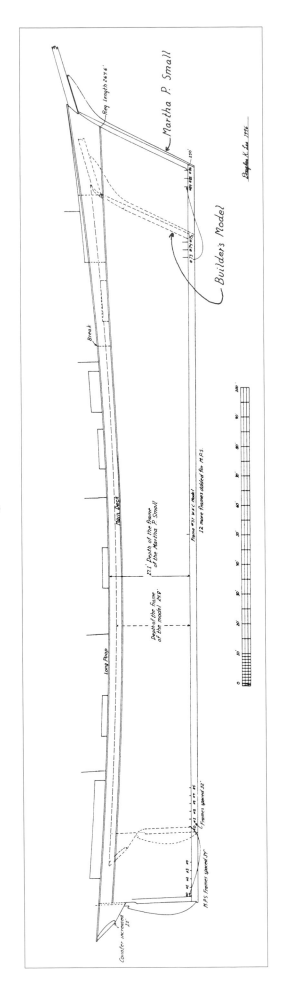

The second name on the half model, MARTHA P. SMALL, logically presupposes that the schooner so named was built from that model. However, the newspaper account of the launching of the SMALL specifies that she was in fact built to the model of the four-master S. P. BLACKBURN.[5] So how do we square the half model of the CLIFFORD/SMALL with the newspaper statement that it really was BLACKBURN/SMALL?

The answer is pretty simple. No model was made for the BLACKBURN *per se* because she was built from an existing Percy & Small model.[6] And there were only two such models extant in 1895, that of the NOTMAN and that of the CLIFFORD. The SMALL was built from the BLACKBURN model according to the local press, but the fact that her name is literally attached to the CLIFFORD model leads to the conclusion that the BLACKBURN also came from that model. In fact, only one other schooner—the ALICE E. CLARK—has ever been credited to the NOTMAN model.[7] Obviously, Sam Percy much preferred the CLIFFORD model over the NOTMAN model, although we have no way today of knowing why.

Having established the connection between the CLIFFORD and the SMALL, we must then ask why would a shipbuilder choose to use a half model that scaled out significantly smaller, or larger for that matter, than the vessel to be built? Why not make a new model that scaled close to the size vessel desired? The answers to these questions are threefold: save time; save expense; continue a proven model in service.

A significant increase in size over that represented by a half model required something more than the minor adjustments in frame spaces that enabled the builders of the CLIFFORD to stretch her registered length by approximately nine feet. On the surface, at least, it would appear that the best course would be to make a new model of the appropriate size, loft it, and make new moulds. But this took both time and added expense, the latter being a particular anathema to frugal Yankee shipbuilders. Also there was no guarantee that a larger or smaller model would possess the successful characteristics that marked those of the original.

But the traditional modeler and wooden ship-builder possessed a collection of "tricks of the trade," shortcuts passed down from generation to generation of master shipwrights, that allowed him to expand or contract a particular hull form without going back to the beginning, at the same time preserving the integrity of the form and the fairness of the lines. With the MARTHA P. SMALL, it is evident that Fred Rideout and Miles M. Merry had plenty of opportunity to exercise their talents as they created a new vessel half again as large as that represented by the model.[8] This growth in size was achieved by using a variety of techniques including increasing frame spacing, adding additional frames amidships, horning out the frame to increase the beam, and probably by using something called the rising curve and rising rods.

Frame space changes, as we have seen with the CLIFFORD as built, were effective in adding as much as 4 or 5 percent to the registered length of a vessel without requiring major changes in breadth and depth. It was, however, risky to make major additions in a vessel's length without adjustments in the breadth and/or depth in order to strengthen the effective girder (Chapter 4), a point underlined by the experiences of two of the CLIFFORD model offspring, the "Doctor" CRESSY and the HELEN W. MARTIN, who proved to be structurally challenged.

Major increases in length required the insertion of additional frames amidships in addition to a small increase in frame spacing. For example, analysis of the MARTHA P. SMALL documents, including the ABS surveyor's notebook, shows that Percy & Small achieved her 52.1-foot increase in registered length over the CLIFFORD model (+24.5 percent) by increasing frame spacing from 32 inches to 34 inches on center and adding a dozen frames amidships.[9] In addition to the hefty increase in length, Percy & Small prudently increased her beam (2.7 feet or 6.3 percent) and depth (1.9 feet or 9.7 percent) in an effort to enhance the effective girder.

MAKING FRAMES
Before going on to examine the esoteric methods used by Percy & Small and the other shipbuilders at the tail end of the wooden shipbuilding age to enlarge vessels, it is important to understand just how a ves-

sel's frames were assembled. (If you wish to review the process of lofting and making up the moulds and horning poles, please refer to Chapter 4.)

A framing floor where the frames were to be assembled was built across the forward end of the keel. As each frame was completed, it was slid along the top of the keel and temporary runners which were set up on each side of the keel to support the frame. When Percy & Small built some of their largest schooners, the framing floor—made up of thick planks—was laid just ahead of the location for the next full frame. Then the crew only had to slide the heavy frame a short distance before it was stood up in place. After the frame was erected in place, several of the planks at the lower end of the platform were moved to the upper end to make room for the next frame. In this manner, the floor moved up the keel rather than having the much heavier and limber frames moving down the keel.[10]

The frames were made of two overlapping layers that were treenailed together. The two layers were chocked (blocked) apart for ventilation and salting. The bottom pieces of the frame that ran across the keel were the long and short floor timbers. Anywhere from 14 to 16 inches deep at the keel and 12 to 16 inches thick depending on the size of the vessel, these timbers were backbreakingly heavy. Several of the frames near the forward and aft ends, where the deadrise became too steep to get out long and short floors, were made with mirror-image, overlapping floor timbers. They had one long arm and one short arm on each floor timber.

However, most of the frames were made with long and short floor timbers, a number of futtocks, and finally, top timbers (often the last top timber was called the stanchion). All of these pieces decreased in the moulded dimension (measured inside to outside), as well as decreased in thickness (siding) as they approached the top of the frame. Each piece was roughly hewn or sawn to shape with the outline of its mould scribed thereon. At Percy & Small the floors and first futtocks were probably milled to the finished moulded dimension using the large bevel jigsaw and thickness (the latter called slabbing) with their Daniels planer, which saved a considerable amount of

hand labor, especially dubbing underneath the schooner.

When assembling a frame on the framing floor, the bottom layer of the frame was called the "layer" and the top layer was called the "cover."[11] The layer was started by setting the short floor timber into position with its center aligned with the centerline drawn on the framing floor. It was set on supporting blocks that held it off the floor so that holes for the treenails that held the two layers together could be bored and the wooden fastenings driven. Then the other futtocks and top timbers that made up the layer were moved into approximate position. Those pieces were usually blocked up or chocked higher than the floor timber as the thickness of the stock decreased so that the centerlines of the floor timber, futtocks, and top timbers of the layer remained in a straight line as shown in the drawing on page 359.

A centerline had been marked previously on the framing floor and on a long block of wood (called the center block) which was also blocked up to the same height as the floor timber and dogged to the framing floor. The horning pole for that frame was laid along the centerline of the frame with the keel mark on the horning pole at the bottom center of the floor timber just as it had been on the lofting floor. A nail was driven through the hole in the upper end of the horning pole into the center line on the center block. That positioned the nail at the sheer height of the frame and became the pivot point for horning the frame. The horning pole was then swung to each end of the floor timber to line it up with the horning marks. Then the other futtocks and the top timbers were horned in the same manner. The butts of the frame pieces were sawn in if necessary to ensure exact alignment. After horning the layer portion of the frame, it was temporarily held in place by timber dogs that fastened it to the framing floor as shown in the drawing on page 359.

Next, the long floor timber was laid in position on top of the short floor timber, along with all the futtocks and top timbers making up the cover. The floors were usually chocked apart 2 inches and the other futtocks and top timbers chocked apart by a greater amount to account for their decreasing thickness.

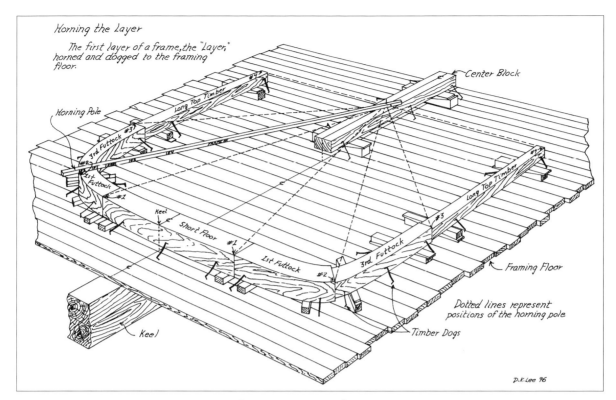

Diagram: Horning the Layer
Douglas K. Lee

This was done so that the centerlines of the cover and the layer remained parallel (see drawing on page 360).

Once completed, the frame was skidded down the keel to the spacer block. It was then hoisted to the vertical, joggled into position, and secured in place by temporary ribbands and long bolts driven through the floor timbers into the keel.

Increasing Breadth

The widening of the vessel involved the process of horning *out* the frame.[12] Literally an extension of horning the frame described elsewhere—i.e., the process using a horning pole and reference marks to ensure the frame is assembled in the lofted shape and remains symmetrical—horning out preserved the fairness of the hull while effectively adjusting the moulds to achieve more beam.

The widening process began by drawing a horning curve on a deck plan or waterline plan of the vessel that had all the frame stations ticked off on the centerline. The horning curve was drawn parallel to and offset from the centerline one-half the desired increase in breadth. The curve then tapered inward as it approached and blended into the stem and, if desired, the sternpost. The distance the horning curve was offset from the center line was then recorded at every frame. When a frame was being horned, the centerline horning pole nail on the framing floor was offset the same amount on each side of the center line as shown in the top drawing on page 361. The horned frame remained fair while ending up being the increased breadth.

William F. Palmer once wrote Percy & Small regarding the horning curve for the DAVIS PALMER, "I am very anxious to get the [increase in] beam, however, and when the horning curve is thrown in I will arrange to be down there to see that it is thrown in so as to get as much capacity as possible from forward to aft."[13] In effect, he was saying increase her beam (and carrying capacity) and carry that increase as far forward and aft as possible before tapering the horning curve into the stem and sternpost.

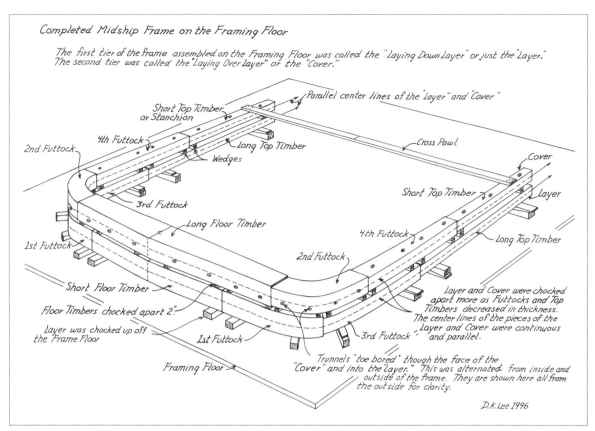

Diagram: Completed Midship Frame
Douglas K. Lee

If the increase in the beam was to be relatively small, a foot or less (as was the case with the DAVIS PALMER), instructions to the supplier of the frame to leave an additional 6 inches on the ends of the floor timbers and lower futtocks was sufficient. If the increase was to be more than that, it was probably a good idea to make new floor timber and lower futtock moulds by tracing around the existing moulds and adding an amount to the ends that covered the increased breadth. At the ends of the vessel, a little more imagination was required due to the shape of the frames in determining which futtocks were to be lengthened. None of this required time-consuming and expensive relofting.

INCREASING DEPTH

The depth of a wooden vessel could be changed a small amount just by moving the sheer batten up a little, the technique by which small adjustments in the sheer fore and aft were normally handled. This was possible if enough extra length had been left on the top timbers, which was usually the case, and the changes were limited to several inches or less.

Extending the height of the top timbers more than a small amount had the effect of increasing or decreasing deck width depending on whether there was tumblehome or flare to the topsides. Therefore, if the increase in depth or sheer was more than a minor adjustment, a more involved procedure was undertaken in order to maintain fairness of the deck outline by utilizing a rising curve and rising rods.[14]

To increase the depth of a vessel and maintain fairness, one first needed an original profile plan of the schooner with all of the frame stations drawn in. Then a new sheer was drawn in representing the increased depth of the hull. At this point, a "rising curve" was drawn from bow to stern delineating the transitional point between the vessel's bottom and topsides. Amidships, the curve also followed the point of maximum beam, but at the ends the curve dipped

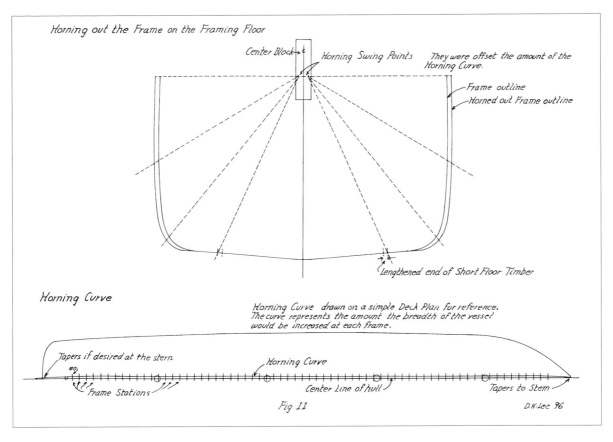

Diagram: Horning out the Frame
Douglas K. Lee

Diagram: Horning the Layer with Rising Rods
Douglas K. Lee

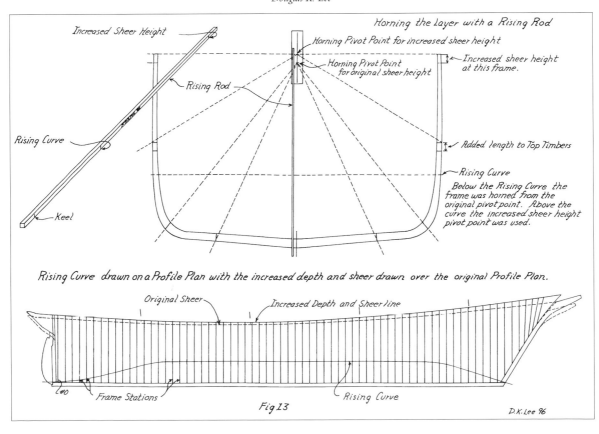

down to intersect the keel at or before the stem and sternpost. Since the rising curve represented the point at which the frame was divided between that portion horned from the original sheer pivot point (underside of the rising curve) and the portion horned from the increased sheer pivot point, it was preferable to have the curve run through each frame at a point where the futtocks were reasonably straight. It had to be a fair curve, however, in order to maintain the fairness of the hull. The moulds for the futtocks intersected by the rising curve had the extra length added to make up the additional rise and were sent on to the ship timber supplier.

A number of rising rods were also made from the measurements taken off this plan, even as the appropriate moulds were adjusted. Similar to horning poles, the sides of each rising rod had the appropriate frame number, the keel mark, rising curve mark, and the new sheer height duly inscribed. And, as with the horning poles, the rising rods were made to provide the basic information on the framing floor needed when horning the frame. The rising rod was laid along the centerline with the keel mark lined up with the bottom of the center of the floor timber. That section of the frame below the rising curve mark on the rising rod was horned in the usual manner using the original sheer height. In this way the underbody of the vessel was not changed when horning the frame above the rising curve, which lifted the upper part of the hull to the height of the new sheer. As long as the position of the rising curve was chosen carefully, fairness of the hull was maintained.[15]

When all was said and done, there always remained ample material in the frame stock for skilled liners and dubbers—not one of them a graduate of an engineering school—to transform the frames into a shining monument to naval architectural fairness.

PERCY & SMALL HALF MODELS[16]
During the course of its quarter century of shipbuilding, Percy & Small probably used no more than a dozen half models to build forty-one schooners.[17] The number of surviving, documented half models of their schooners currently hovers at five in number. Of these, Maine Maritime Museum possesses three, only

one of which apparently was used for more than one schooner.[18] Then there is the CLIFFORD/SMALL model that has remained continuously in the hands of Frank A. Small's descendants. If we accept that ten schooners were built from this model, that brings the total number of schooners built from known models to fourteen, just over a third of the total.

One other identified half model of a Percy & Small schooner exists. Patten Free Library owns the very handsome model identified by the attached brass plaque as WYOMING. There are some anomalies associated with the model, however. The plaque identifies the modeler as Frederick Rideout, who had died nearly six years before the schooner was built. It also represents a substantially smaller schooner than its namesake, although it is a difference by no means as great as we find with the CLIFFORD model and some of its siblings.[19] There is one other thing about the model, however, that goes a long way in ruling out Rideout as its maker. It is simply not done in his style.

All identified Rideout models are made of a series of glued-up horizontal lifts. The WYOMING model, however, has a striking difference. Part of her breadth is represented by a $^3/_8$-inch vertical mahogany board applied to the back of the horizontal lifts that is skillfully faired into the center line extremities of the vessel and is part of the modeled form. The authors have only seen one other model done in this style, and it too has strong connections to Percy & Small. Finally, the only contemporary account that named a designer—read: modeler—was in *International Marine Engineering*, and that journal named Bant Hanson.[20]

This leads us to the conclusion that the WYOMING model has had a career that parallels that of the MARTHA P. SMALL model: it started as some other schooner but received the name of its most prominent offspring. It also leads to the inevitable questions, "Which schooner was the model originally made for and which schooners were built from it?"

It is the authors' considered opinion that the six-masters EDWARD J. LAWRENCE, EDWARD B. WINSLOW, and WYOMING were derived from this model. As built, their dimensions are close, suggesting that they used the same "adjusted" moulds. And, aside from some minor differences in decorative elements, these three schooners could well be identical triplets.

It is also possible that the five-master GOVERNOR BROOKS could claim kinship to this model as well, even though she was a bit smaller. The processes for growing a vessel described above could also be applied to "shrinking" another vessel while retaining form and fairness. However, there is at least one major criticism of such an attribution. The BROOKS's oak keel, floor, and futtock timbers were largely purchased from William T. Donnell, who had acquired them two years earlier.[21] There must have been a set of moulds involved in getting out the frame timbers, but it does not appear probable that said moulds were from the WYOMING model, so-called, although they may have come from another Percy & Small model.[22]

Where are the rest of the models? It is probable that at least two—CARNEGIE and HAYES—eventually found their way to J. S. Winslow & Company or one of its designees. The third model that had its origins with the Winslow operation was that of the ADDIE M. LAWRENCE which went on to be the model for a number of other big schooners as well.[23] It, too, probably went to the Portland firm.

Then there were the Percy & Small-built Palmer schooners. Of the four they built, Palmer provided the moulds for two—DAVIS PALMER and FULLER PALMER—the other two being built from pre-existing Percy & Small frames. Palmer had developed two basic hull forms for the five-masted schooners built to his design—one for the smaller schooners and one for the larger ones. It is also likely that he developed these initially from formal lines plans rather than from the half models preferred by most traditional Maine shipbuilders. However, Maine Maritime Museum does possess four schooner half models purchased along with Palmer's papers, photographs, and other materials in 1993 from his descendants. One of the half models undoubtedly represents the DAVIS PALMER and FULLER PALMER, two of the largest Palmer schooners built to his design. The model, however, was probably made after the lines plan and may, in fact, have been a decorative model rather than a working half model.

During the 1930s, Sam Percy gave two half models to a close friend and employee. It is reasonable to assume that these models were associated with either Adams & Hitchcock or Percy & Small as Percy was not in the habit of collecting models not related to his own operation. These models have remained in the same family for over a half century. One is executed in the same style as the aforementioned WYOMING half model that is credited to Bant Hanson. The authors, who have never seen any other models executed with the 3/8-inch mahogany vertical board inserted behind the lifts as part of the model, have concluded that this unusual, if not unique, style is a Bant Hanson trademark.

The Hanson model translates to a schooner of the following registered dimensions: length = 200 feet; depth = 19 feet; beam = 40.4 feet; and keel length = 186 feet. Unfortunately, there are no obvious candidates in Percy & Small's hull list to fill that slot except the last schooner Percy & Small built, the CECILIA COHEN. But as we know, model dimensions and vessel-as-built dimensions are not necessarily even close, and the builders could, with relative ease, adjust moulds and manipulate the number of frames and spacing to get the size vessel they wanted.

Bant Hanson was retained by James Hawley in late 1908 or early 1909 to model, loft, and supervise the building of a schooner of approximately 1,000 gross tons. It was the type of assignment that Hanson had already successfully carried out twice for Hawley.[24]

About this time, Sam Percy was also in the market for a new model for a four-master or two he planned to build once WYOMING was out of the way. Hanson would be too busy to model a new schooner, but he did have the model and moulds for the schooner he was starting for Hawley. Why not adjust the moulds to accommodate Percy & Small's size needs—slightly smaller—and go with that? Hawley wouldn't object because the charge for using his model and moulds would reduce his costs.

In 1910 Hawley suspended construction of his schooner in the face of a depressed shipping market. It was subsequently sold on the stocks to Gardiner G. Deering and completed as the MONTROSE W. HOUCK. Deering, who normally built his schooners from two or three sets of his own moulds, was probably not interested in the model/moulds, so those eventually reverted to Percy & Small. It is, therefore, likely that all of the post-1910 four-masters built by Percy & Small were variants of this model.

During the early 1970s, another half model that had links to Percy & Small surfaced briefly in the Damariscotta area. Examined by the late William A. Baker who, as usual, methodically recorded his observations, the model had the legend "P&S #19" penciled on its deck. Hull #19, however, was the big six-master RUTH E. MERRILL, far too large a vessel to be built from a half model with scaled dimensions of 176.2 feet by 35.5 feet by 15 feet. The model comes very close, however, to the two small four-masters Percy & Small built in 1904–05, the EVELYN HINKLY and the ROBERT P. MURPHY—Hulls #21 and #23. This half model was later sold by an antiques dealer to an out-of-state owner.

---

[1] Captain Douglas K. Lee, "The WILLIAM H. CLIFFORD Model," and "Reconstructed Plans of Schooners Built by Percy & Small." Unpublished manuscript, 1997. Most of the material for this section is drawn from these papers.

[2] Some half models were made as works of art rather than as one of the tools used in the construction of a vessel. These so-called decorative half models were sometimes presented to major shareholders in a vessel by the builder or managing owner.

[3] Applied to the model's quarter is the label MARTHA P. SMALL, apparently added after it served its primary purpose. Then there is the inscription written on the top of the model in pencil: "P&S #2, 208' KEEL, 43' Ex BEAM, 18' DEEP, 5' WAIST, SCALE $1/4$"= 1'." In addition, written in pencil on the reverse side of the backboard, is the legend: "William H. Clifford."

[4] Lee, "CLIFFORD Model." As modeled, the CLIFFORD had 74 frames with floors 2.5 feet thick (cover plus layer plus space chocked apart—14 + 14 + 2) arranged along her keel with 2-inch "rooms" (frame space) between frames. By just adding 1 inch to each frame space, the schooner could be "stretched" by just over 6 feet from the 202-foot modeled length of keel to 208 feet.

[5] BT, 4/20/1901.

[6] Summary Construction Account, S. P. BLACKBURN, Parker Collection. The $100 spent on moulds was too little for model and moulds for a schooner this size, but perhaps covered the cost for making a new set of moulds. The NOTMAN'S model, moulds, deck plan and amidships section, for example, came to $147.65. See: F. W. Rideout Bill, Construction Statements: P&S Schooner #1, Parker Collection. The "set of moulds" for the NOTMAN came to $107.65.

[7] BI, 6/12/1897.

[8] The MARTHA P. SMALL has the closest connection to the CLIFFORD model by virtue of her name being applied to the model. The larger HELEN W. MARTIN also shares the same basic provenance—built from the model of the BLACKBURN, hence from the CLIFFORD. But the process of enlarging her was the same as used for the SMALL and other larger offspring of the original.

[9] Lee, "Clifford Model," pp. 8–9.

[10] Chester McCabe Interview, Notes, Parker Collection.

[11] Maine wooden shipbuilder Elliot Gamage called the two tiers of frame the "layer" and the "cover," but James P. Stevens—long associated with Goudy & Stevens of East Boothbay—called them the "laying down layer" and the "laying over layer."

[12] W. F. Palmer to P&S, 4/12/1905, Palmer Collection. Palmer states in connection with the construction of the DAVIS PALMER that the moulds will come for a moulded beam of 46.5 feet, but he wants the vessel horned out to 47.5 feet. He expects to be able to get the additional beam from the extra length in the floor timbers normally supplied by frame supplier Wentworth.

[13] Ibid., 4/12/1905, Palmer Collection.

[14] Master builder Elliot Gamage once told Captain Lee that his father and grandfather spoke of using a "rising rod up on the framing floor." Elliot, however, had no personal knowledge of its use. We have not been able to find any other reference to a rising rod or rising curve. The use of the former is straight forward, but the run of the rising curve is somewhat in doubt. Although there is probably no one alive today who has ever done this procedure, Captain Lee has applied his own experience from the lofting floor and framing stage to reconstruct the technique.

[15] Photographs of schooners built from the moulds of smaller vessels indicate that many were deepened by just adding height along the sheer. Those vessels show that the added depth was built on top of the stern without lifting the stern and counter up. It was a rather crude solution

when compared to the excellent results achieved by Percy & Small when they "horned-out" and, with rising rods in hand, deepened the new vessel.

[16] Douglas K. Lee, "The WILLIAM H. CLIFFORD Model" (1997), "The Builder's Half Model for the WYOMING" (1997), and "The Bant Hanson Four-Masted Schooner Model" (1998). Unpublished manuscripts. The aforementioned have been heavily relied upon for the preparation of this section.

[17] The half-modeled schooners included: NOTMAN, CLIFFORD, PERCY, CARNEGIE, C. F. CRESSY, HAYES, ADDIE M. LAWRENCE, WARD, HINKLY, WYOMING, DAVIS PALMER, DUSTIN G. CRESSY.

[18] The museum's collection includes three Rideout-modeled schooners: CHARLES P. NOTMAN, ELEANOR A. PERCY, and CORA F. CRESSY. Only the NOTMAN ever produced a second vessel (ALICE E. CLARK).

[19] The model represents a two-deck vessel with the following registered dimensions: length = 298 feet, breadth = 47.6 feet; depth = 28.6 feet.

[20] "Six-Masted Schooner Wyoming," *International Marine Engineering,* pp. 1–2.

[21] Construction Bill File, Schooner #27, Parker Collection. The timber to Donnell was surveyed between 12/23/1904 and 1/6/1905, over two years before the BROOKS or the EDWARD J. LAWRENCE were laid down.

[22] The GOVERNOR BROOKS is the Percy & Small orphan, with no specific attributions of its lineage. Dimensionally, however, it comes close to the HELEN W. MARTIN, but with a flush deck. If so, this would make her the eleventh schooner built from the CLIFFORD, Percy & Small's favorite model.

[23] At least five big schooners were built from this model: ADDIE M. LAWRENCE, ELIZABETH PALMER, GRACE A. MARTIN, RUTH E. MERRILL, and ALICE M. LAWRENCE.

[24] CAMILLA MAY PAGE in 1904–05 and ESTHER ANN in 1908–09.

$\mathcal{A}$ppendix C

PERCY & SMALL EMPLOYEES, SUBCONTRACTORS, AND SUBCONTRACTOR EMPLOYEES

Compiling a list of persons who worked at the Percy & Small shipyard anytime during that firm's quarter century of activity is no small challenge, especially as only one shipyard time book has come down to us and only a few pages of timekeeping notes from shipyard subcontractors survive.

But we are fortunate in having the recorded reminiscences of former employees and neighbors of the shipyard, city directories (1901, 1905–06, 1919) that sometimes listed places of employment, and the almost always gossipy local press. From these sources the authors have compiled a list of approximately 320 names. Some may be duplications due to spelling variations in the sources.

Technically, many of the persons listed below were not direct employees of Percy & Small. They worked for various subcontractors, moving from shipyard to shipyard as work offered. But as wooden shipbuilding concentrated more and more in fewer and fewer yards, many itinerent workers spent most, if not all, of their time at Percy & Small.

Nonetheless, this firm did have a number of regular employees at their shipyard at the south end. These included the shipyard's master builder, ship carpenters, millwright and assistants, teamsters, and watchman. Their numbers varied considerably in proportion to the work load, ranging from as few as a half-dozen to as many as seventy-five.

New construction and repair work sometimes combined to bring the total work force—in-house and subcontractors—up to 250 men, as in the summer of 1908.

Data is organized as follows: last name, first name/initial, [source(s)]: dates, if any; trade; other information/source; residence, if known.

ABBREVIATIONS
BA—Bath Anvil
BE—Bath Enterprise
BI—Bath Independent
BT—Bath Daily Times
I&E—Independent & Enterprise
SB—Samuel Barnes interview
JHC/TB—J. H. Cameron Time Book
C/S—Construction statement
CAC—Charles A. Coombs interviews
WD—William Donnell interview
RL—Roger Luke
JM—Jim McGuiggan
RO—Raleigh Osier interview
PS/TB—Percy & Small Time Book (7/1898–12/1899)
HP—Homer Potter interview
TR—Thomas Robson interview
#1 *Bath City Directory*, 1901
#2 *Bath City Directory*, 1905–06

#3 *Bath City Directory*, 1919
* Persons identified in group photo
? Persons who may have worked at P&S
obt.—obituary

PERCY & SMALL MASTER BUILDERS

Baker, W. Judson [#3, CAC]: 1916–20; resided Hyde house per CAC.

Douglas, Horatio N. [*BT*]: 1894–98.

Hodgkins, Willard A. [PS/TB, *BT*]: 1898–1900; 22 Goddard St.

Merry, Miles M. [*, *BT*]: 1900–16; 69 Dummer St.

Watson, Ebenezer [*BT*]: in 1896 described as "superintendent of Percy and Small Shipyard."

SHIPYARD FOREMEN, SUBCONTRACTORS, WORKERS

Adams, F. [PS/TB]

Adams, L. [PS/TB]

Adams, W. [PS/TB]

Allen, Peter [#3]: laborer.

Anderson, John O. [*BE*]: rigger.

Arnold, Fred: cut ankle with adze at P&S—*BI*, 9/15/1900.

Arsenault, Joseph [SB]: ship carpenter; 34 Floral St.

Atwood, Clarence [CAC]: one of "the Atwood boys."

Atwood, Harold [#3, CAC]: planker; one of "the Atwood boys"; 29 Pine Street.

Atwood, Howard [CAC]: another of "the Atwood boys."

Ayer, Arthur [#3]: ship carpenter.

Baker, George [#3]

Barnes, Leonard [SB]: uncle of Sam Barnes; worked on WYOMING.

Barnes, Lincoln [#3]: saw filing and listed in 1919 directory as millwright; CAC identified as possible wood lathe operator.

Barnes, Sam [SB]:1906–08; fastener; worked in several shipyards in Bath, New York City, and went to Aberdeen, Washington, to work in shipyard there—*BT* 5/5/1916.

Bates, Charles [#2]: joiner; listed as engineer in 1905 directory.

Bates, W. G. [C/S]: subcontractor, "cementing schooner."

Berry, John [PS/TB, *]: ship carpenter; 360 Washington St.

Bishop, A. [PS/TB]

Black, William H.: master builder of the AUGUSTUS BABCOCK— "formerly worked at Percy and Small"— *BT* 9/13/1904.

Blackman, Clarence L. [#3]: ship carpenter.

Blackman, Warren L. [#3]: ship carpenter.

Blake, Frank R. [#3]: ship carpenter; lived in houseboat community to rear of 345 Washington St.

Brewster, James [PS/TB, #2]: liner; Miller's pallbearer—*BT* 8/4/1916; went to Savannah, GA, shipyard to be master builder there—*BT* 8/9/1916.

Brewster, Thomas [#2, 3]: ship carpenter.

Bruce, A. [PS/TB]

Buckman, E. R. [C/S]: painter.

Bucknam, Ena F. [#3]: stenographer/typist at shipyard office.

Burnham, Charles [PS/TB, *, #3, CAC]: planker, caulker; 17 Corliss St.

Butler, George W. [#1]: joiner; 468 High Street.

?Butler, James C. [*BT*]: ship carpenter; died at eighty, born Nova Scotia, father of Nelson, obt.—*BT* 11/23/1910.

Butler, Nelson [#2]: ship carpenter; in charge of ceiling new six-master; employed by firm for several years—*BE* 7/2/1902; injured by lightning—*BT* 7/15/1902; died of TB, aged forty-two, born Nova Scotia, obt.—*BT* 7/22/1908.

Cameron, James H. [*BT*]: subcontractor, foreman sparmaker; succeeded late brother at Percy & Small; with brother was one of five major P&S subcontractors.

Cameron, Lewis [*BT*]: subcontractor, foreman sparmaker; died from injuries received in trolley accident near shipyard—*I&E* 7/18/1906.

Campbell, Merton [CAC]: blacksmith.

Cantalo (or Cantelo), Howard [#1]: 456 Washington St.

Clark, C. [PS/TB]

Colby, Charles S.: subcontractor, foreman fastener; injured in fall into hold—*BT* 10/27/1897; worked P&S and G. G. Deering, obt.—*BI* 11/9/1907.

Colby, Fred [PS/TB, #3]: subcontractor, fastener, foreman fastener; son of Charles S., took over father's job.

Comeau, A. [PS/TB]

Coombs, Charles A., Jr. [CAC]: 1917–20; joiner.

Coombs, Charles A., Sr. [#3]: subcontractor; joiner, foreman joiner; BT 5/7/1909—completing a 22-foot motorboat for own use; succeeded Fred Scott as boss joiner in 1917–18—BT 3/14/1918; lower Washington Street.

Coombs, Frederick [PS/TB, CAC]: joiner; lower Middle St.

Coombs, F. W. [C/S]: foreman sparmaker on the NOTMAN.

Coombs, James [C/S]: hostler; 75 1/2 Court St.

Craigh, James A. [#3]: ship carpenter.

Crooker, Harry: ship carpenter; injured in fall from deckbeam—I&E 10/18/1905.

Crouse, H. C.: P&S employee returned to Waldoboro for two-week vacation—BT 7/24/1902.

Crowell, A. [C/S]: a rigger on the PERCY.

Curtis, Henry [C/S]: subcontractor; liner on HAYES and MERRY.

Dalton, William: injured by adze at P&S—BT 6/27/1904.

Danforth, M. [PS/TB]

Davis, John [PS/TB, #1]: Robinson St.

Deering, J. [PS/TB]

Dern, Harry [JHC/TB]

Deveaux, A. [PS/TB]

Deveaux, G. [PS/TB]

Deveaux, L. [PS/TB]

Deveaux, M. [PS/TB]

Dickinson, William [PS/TB]: ship carpenter; nearly loses two toes in accident—BI 9/28/1901.

Dodge, Willard [*]: ship carpenter; broke leg from fall from schooner—I&E 9/8/1906; Robinson St.

Donnell, J. [PS/TB]

Donnell, Scott: injured foot at P&S—BE 7/13/1901.

Doucette, P. [PS/TB]

Dougherty, Angus [#1]: Robinson St.

Dow, W. [PS/TB]

Dowling, Thomas B.: sawyer; employed previously at M. G. Shaw, obt.—BT 5/23/1910.

Doyle, Martin [PS/TB]: injured at P&S—BT 12/10/1907.

Driscoll, Patrick [#2, SB]: ship carpenter; one of four old men who framed the WINSLOW's stern in 1908—SB.

Duley, Frank [#3]: rigger; injured while working on chain—BT 5/23/1907; fell 60 feet from rigging of the REBECCA PALMER and landed in river uninjured—BT 9/28/1911.

Durant, T. [PS/TB]

Durgin, I. H. [PS/TB, C/S]: identified as having worked on the NOTMAN.

Eaton, Frank E.: subcontractor; foreman painter at P&S for past twelve years, obt.—BT 4/23/1907, age seventy-one.

Edgett, W. A.: sparmaker; worked on spars for P&S—I&E 4/17/1907.

Emero, [or Emro], Charles [*]: noted in obt. for Robinson as pallbearer, BT 9/3/1913.

Fahey, Patrick: lumper and ship carpenter; died from heart attack at friend's home—I&E 7/13/1904.

Fancy, Frank [SB]: planker.

Ferguson, Alex [PS/TB, #2]: ship carpenter; born Nova Scotia, master builder at McDonald yard and built one schooner for Gilbert Transportation, obt.—BT 4/12/1909; lived eighteen years at 233 Washington St.

Flagg, Albert E. [C/S]: subcontractor; foreman dubber.

Flannigan, Mark [#1]: Robinson St.

Flannigan, Michael [#1]: Robinson St.

Foster, Henry L. [#1, #2]: 23 Corliss St.

Frazier [Frasier], Cole [CAC, JHC/TB]: planker; in 1900 employed at New England Co. shipyard; "shirt in tatters"—CAC; 41 Milan St.

Frederickson, J. [PS/TB]

French, Ephraim F. [PS/TB, #1]: 13 Pine Street.

French, W. [PS/TB]

Frye, Lemuel C. [PS/TB, SB, CAC]: carpenter; East Lane.

Fuller, A. [C/S]: subcontractor; decorative painter on the ELIZABETH PALMER.

Furbish, Charles E. [PS/TB, #3]: ship carpenter.

Gallagher, Francis: ship carpenter; died aged sixty-five, had worked at Sewall's, Groton, BIW, and P&S, obt.—BT 1/31/1912.

Gallant, D. [PS/TB]

Gallant, Maxime [#2]

Gibson, Leonard H. [CAC]: foreman blacksmith; one of the five major subcontractors working with P&S.

Gillis, Jim [PS/TB, *]: ship carpenter; off 454 High St.

Goodwin, James: joiner; lost finger in buzz planer— *BT* 8/9/1911.

Griffin, William A. [#3, JM]: laborer; 175 Middle St.

Hall, G. W. [C/S]: subcontractor; decorative painter on the NOTMAN.

Hamilton, Charles [PS/TB, #2]: beveler; died aged seventy-five, obt.—*BT* 3/7/1907; 525 High St.

Hamilton, Ed [PS/TB, *]: laborer; 31 Vine St.

Hamilton, John: injured in fall— *BT* 11/14/1901.

Hanscom, Samuel [#1]: boarded with John Davis, Robinson St.

Hanson, Bant [C/S]: subcontractor; lofting, designer, surveyor; circa 1904–13; succeeded Rideout as P&S designer and even operated out of Rideout's former loft at 100 Commercial St.; residence on Drummond St.; Ole's father.

Hanson, Ole [see text]: drafting; probably moonlit the plans for the SALLY WREN while working at BIW; rented apartment at 708 Washington St., near Captain Percy's home; Bant's son.

Harris, J. [PS/TB]

Harrison, Thomas [#3]: ship carpenter.

Harrison, William [#3]: ship carpenter.

Hart, C. [PS/TB]

Havener, Alpheus [#2, *]: ship carpenter; mentioned by Sam Barnes as one of the old men who framed the stern of the EDWARD WINSLOW; coincidently, he is buried in Oak Grove Cemetery in same section as Frank Small and Ole Hanson.

Helmes, George H. [#1]: 847 High St.

Heskitt, William [SB]: adzeman.

Heywood, E. W. [PS/TB]

Hicks, J. [PS/TB]

Higgins, Daniel: liner—*BT* 7/28/1905.

Higgins, Herbert D. [#3]: ship carpenter.

Hill, James [JHC/TB]: sparmaker, 1919.

Hill, Robert [JHC/TB]: sparmaker, 1919.

Hill, William [JM]: ship carpenter; injured self with

adze at P&S—*BT* 8/13/1907; also listed in JHC/TB, 1919; 69 Middle St.

Humphreys, Alex [C/S]: teamster during construction of the CORA F. CRESSY.

?Humphreys, George H. [*BT*]: teamster; team runs away at P&S—*BT* 11/25/1904.

Hunt, Oakman [#1]: 50 Beacon St.

Hunt, Zina [PS/TB]

Huse, J. [PS/TB]

Hussey, A. [PS/TB]

Hutchins, Chesley [#1; JM]: caulker; photo with Hose Company—*I&E* 6/26/1909; 175 Middle St./Goddard St.

Ingraham, F. [PS/TB]

Irish, Allan [*BT* 8/2/1917]: drafting and lofting; shipyard superintendent, 1917–20; Captain Percy's son-in-law.

Jardine, E. [PS/TB]

Jewett, James [CAC]: subcontractor; foreman painter.

Jewett, Ralph [CAC]: planker.

Johnson, A. [PS/TB]

Johnson, J. W. [C/S]: subcontractor; teamster.

Jones, Alden C. [#3]: fastener.

Jones, Edison [CAC]: subcontractor; turned treenails.

Jordan, B. C. [C/S]: subcontractor; foreman dubber on the PERCY.

Kennedy, John B.: subcontractor; foreman dubber; injured by lightning—*BT* 7/15/1902.

Kenney, J. [PS/TB]

King, David: split finger with maul—*BT* 9/15/1908.

Lang, J. [PS/TB]

Lebel, John [TR]: ship carpenter.

Lemont, G. T. [C/S]: subcontractor; "turning and sawing ventilators."

Lermond, T. [PS/TB]

Lincoln, George [C/S]: subcontractor; teaming.

Long, J. [PS/TB]

Lord, Frank P. [C/S]: subcontractor; electrician for the PERCY and other P&S-built schooners.

Lord, James S. [#3, JM]: teamster, ship carpenter; 177 Middle St.

Lounds, Harry [CAC]: planker.

Luke, Joseph [PS/TB, RL]: ship carpenter, 1890s.

McAllister, Anthony [#2]: ship carpenter; one of four

old men who framed stern of EDWARD WINSLOW in 1908—SB; mentioned as pallbearer in Miller's funeral.

McAllister, J. [PS/TB]

McCabe, Chester [#3]: pipefitter, machinist; longtime friend and employee of Captain Percy.

McCabe, Eliakim [#3]: ship carpenter; framed sterns—SB; in 1919 listed as assistant superintendent; later was master builder at the Pendleton shipyard; 11 Marshall St.

McCabe, Henry R. [PS/TB, #3]: ship carpenter.

McCabe, James R. [#1]: teamster; High St. at Getchell.

McCabe, Ray B. [BT 9/11/13]: ship carpenter.

McCullough, Alex [*]: fastener; off 102 Academy Pl.

McDonald, Charles [JHC/TB]: sparmaker.

McDonald, Jack [PS/TB, TR]: planker; overcome by heat—BT 9/11/1897; probably the John McDonald listed in JHC/TB; 5 Federal St.

?McDonald, Patrick Charles [BT]: ship carpenter; moved to Bath from Prince Edward Island six years earlier to work, died aged eighty-two years, eleven months, obt.—BT 2/11/1909.

McDonnell, D. [PS/TB]

McDonnell, Howard [#1]: boarded with Davis.

McDougall, John [C/S]; subcontractor; foreman dubber.

McFadden, N. [PS/TB]

McGregor, William [BT]: liner; 1243 Washington St.

McGuiggan, Charlie [JM]: ship carpenter; son of Edward; Washington St.

McGuiggan, Edward [JM]: ship carpenter specializing in installing cant and other half frames; formerly master builder at the Courtney Bay shipyard, St. John, New Brunswick; father of Edward and John.

McGuiggan, John H. [#3, TR, JM]: ship carpenter; 223 Middle St.; son of Edward.

McInnis, Daniel A.: injured by adze—BT 7/24/1908; fractured two ribs in fall at P&S—BT 3/19/1917.

McIntyre, H. [PS/TB]

McIver, George [PS/TB]: ship carpenter; had worked at his trade up to a few years ago, obt.—BT 10/6/1913.

McKeever, G. [PS/TB]

McKenzie, Angus: ship carpenter; injured when a shore collapsed—BT 11/14/01; 1229 Washington St.

McKinnon, J. [PS/TB]

McNeal, Alexander [PS/TB]: ship carpenter; father-in-law of Al Havener; son Alexander master builder at Deering—I&E 5/6/1905.

McNeal, Charles [JHC/TB]: sparmaker.

McNeil, J. [PS/TB]

McPhee, Angus [PS/TB]: ship carpenter; came from Prince Edward Island in 1890, worked most of his career at P&S, obt.—BT 12/26/1917.

McPhee, John: fell from vessel, dislocating collar bone and hip, seventy years old—BI 1/1/1910; brother to Angus.

McPherson, J. [PS/TB]

McQuarrie, Daniel: ship carpenter; injured while driving bolt to fasten ceiling of the CORA F. CRESSY—BE 1/25/1902.

Madden, Aden [#1]: 3 Farrin Place.

?Madden, Isaac: 2 Farrin Place.

Mains, Lendall A. [#3]: ship carpenter; another houseboat resident.

Malmsten, Henry G. [PS/TB]: ship carpenter; broke two ribs when fell to deck from mast—BT 4/15/1899.

Mank, W. [PS/TB]

Marshall, Paul [#2]: ship carpenter; fell 22 feet into hold of vessel at P&S, recovering rapidly—BT 7/24/1905.

Mason, W. [PS/TB]

Mason, W. W.: subcontractor; foreman teamster; mentioned in BT 1/25/1901 in item re: Southard.

Meisner, Calvin L.: steam fitter—BT 10/18/1920.

Miller, Granville [PS/TB]: ship carpenter/planker; one of old men who framed the EDWARD WINSLOW—SB; injured by lightning—BT 7/15/1902; retired from P&S about 1912, obt.—BT 7/23/1917.

Miller, Leander F.: killed by lightning, 7/15/1902, worked at P&S "for several years"—BE 7/16/1902; 77 Lincoln St.

Mitchell, Hans [#2, #3, CAC]: rigger; jammed hand while handling rope—BT 5/15/1911.

Mitchell, William [#3]: millman; "of Brunswick, who has been engineer at P&S"—BT 1/14/1919.

Montgomery, Frank: employed at Percy & Small—*BT* 4/2/1918.

Morey, Edward S. [#3]: joiner.

Morrison, G. [PS/TB]

Moss, A. [PS/TB]

Mulligan, Alexander: ship carpenter; killed when fell from staging on the W. C. CARNEGIE—*BT* 5/24/1900.

Murray, B. [PS/TB]

Murray, Kenneth [#2]: ship carpenter; injured by lightning, 7/15/1902, and later Miller's pallbearer; 454 High St.

Nash, Columbus P.: ship carpenter; dies from injuries received at P&S—*I&E*, 9/12–15/1906; 3 Drummond St.

Neagle, D. [PS/TB]

O'Brien, B. [PS/TB]

Oliver, Alton S. [CAC]: joiner; Winnegance.

Oliver, Ben [JHC/TB]: sparmaker.

Oliver, Bradford: blacksmith; taking vacation before working on Bowker's new schooner—*BT* 4/7/1916.

Oliver, Charles H. [C/S]: foreman caulker; one of the five major subcontractors at P&S; one of two who worked for P&S from 1894–1920; Mechanic St.

Oliver, Harry [SB]: joiner and boatbuilder; 23 Walker St.

?Oliver, John T. [*BT*]: ship carpenter; "worked in every shipyard in Bath," obt.—*BT* 6/17/1904; High and Winnegance.

Oliver, Tylston [CAC]: joiner; son of John T.

Oliver, Willard A. [#3]: caulker; "Bill"—CAC; 12 Goddard St.

Olsen, Theodore [TR]: subcontractor; foreman dubber on the C. C. MENGEL.

Osier, Raleigh [#3, RO]: caulker.

Overlock, G. [PS/TB]

Palmer, Frank [CAC]: foreman rigger; all 41 P&S schooners were rigged by Palmer's crew; one of two subcontractors to work for P&S from 1894–1920.

Parks, Alonzo [C/S]: did some unspecified work on the NOTMAN in addition to framing the CARNEGIE.

Parks, Edward [#3]

Parris, Everett: item reported he was 6 feet 6 inches tall—*BT* 8/9/1900.

Parris, Frank W. [C/S]: sparmaker.

Parson, Henry D. [C/S]: caulker on the NOTMAN.

Pattee, Hiram R. [CAC]: subcontractor; foreman blacksmith; replaced Gibson when he retired.

Patterson, George [SB]: planker; went to Aberdeen, WA, to work at shipyard there—*BT* 5/1/1916; became general foreman of Peninsula Shipbuilding Co.—*BT* 8/27/1917.

Patterson, Harold [WD]

?Percy, Leonard [*I&E*]: ship carpenter; lives near P&S, obt.—*I&E* 9/16/1905; 12 Weeks St.

Perkins, Eugene [CAC]: blacksmith; loses tips of three fingers in cutter—*I&E* 8/29/1908; 14 Robbins St.

Pinder (Pender?), Willis: ship carpenter; an African American from Cambridge, MD, he returned to Bath after a sixteen-year absence to see what was happening. Worked at P&S until weather got cold then returned south. "Well-liked by fellow shipyard workers"—*BT*, 10/15/1901; returned to MD as passenger aboard the GRACE A. MARTIN—*BT* 10/24/1904; still at P&S and returning to MD in fall—*BT* 10/31/1905; reported at P&S again — *BT* 5/8/1908—but lived winters in Dorchester, VA; resumed place at P&S, been there for eight summers—*BT* 5/24/1909.

Pinkham, Elwell [CAC, SB]: night watchman.

Pinkham, Jaruel B. [CAC]: caulker; 389 High St.

Pitman, J. [PS/TB]

Plante, Percy [CAC]: blacksmith.

Plante, Wesley [HP]: worked at shipyard as teenage boy; son of Percy (above).

Potter, H. [PS/TB]

Potter, W. A. [C/S]: subcontractor; shipcarver.

Pottle, F. B. [PS/TB]

Poucette, J. [PS/TB]

Powers, Charles L.: millwright; injured when clothes caught by "jig saw" in mill—*BT* 6/13/1908.

Pratt, Fred [PS/TB]: "lumper"; P&S worker at whose home Fahey died—*I&E* 7/13/1904; 44 Maple St.

Pratt, H. [PS/TB]

Preble, Herbert "Bert" [*]: 177 Middle St.

Pushard, Arthur [CAC]: blacksmith.

Pushard, Charlie [PS/TB, #1, #2, #3, CAC]: caulker, planker; lower Middle St.

Pushard, Maurice (or Morris) [PS/TB, #1, #3]: joiner; lower Middle St.

Reed, Winship [CAC]: outboard joiner.

Rice, James [#1]: 21 Washburn St.

Rideout, Frederick [C/S]: subcontractor; design, lofting, timber surveying; trained under William Pattee; loft on Commercial Street; obt.—BT 2/4/1904.

Rideout, G. [PS/TB]

Right, Holden [JHC/TB]: sparmaker.

Robinson, Hiram (Harry): injured when slipped on log—BT 5/3/1901; 1149 Washington St.

Robinson, James F.: ship carpenter; "had been employed at P&S for many years," obt.—BT 9/3/1913; lower Washington St.

Robson, Thomas [TR]: ship carpenter; English-born son-in-law of James Lord; Middle St.

Rounds, Harold F. (Fred) [#2, CAC]: ship carpenter; injured by fall from staging—BT 7/1/1910.

Royles, Clarence: ". . . is employed with Percy & Small"— BT 11/6/1913.

Sampson, John: injured by lightning—BT 7/15/1902.

Sampson, Willard H. [*]: sparmaker.

Sanford, Alfred [#3]

Sanford, James: ship carpenter; working on the WELLS when son killed aboard the PERCY—BI 8/10/1901; both from Nova Scotia; High St.

Sanford, Morton [PS/TB]: ship carpenter; killed when he fell into the PERCY's hold—BI 8/10/1901; 27 Pleasant St.

Sanford, Wilbur H. [#2]: planker.

Savage, Franklin M. "Buck" [*]: fastener; injured by lightning—BT 7/15/1902; 246 Water St.

Savage, Horace E. [#3]

Scott, Fred [PS/TB]: subcontractor; foreman joiner; boss joiner for P&S from 1894–1918—BT 3/1911 and obt.—3/13/1918; one of Percy & Small's major subcontractors; 300 Washington St.

Scott, William: ship carpenter; fell 30 feet from staging but not seriously injured—BT 12/16/1915.

Seymour, H. [PS/TB]

Shattuck, G. W. [PS/TB]

Sidelinger, Albert: ship carpenter; overcome by heat—BT 9/11/1897; later fell into hold of six-master, no bones broken, seventy years old—BA 9/12/1908;

20 Mechanic St.

Small, Earnest: ship carpenter; received call to West Hampden, ME, Baptist Church—BE 10/23/1901.

Small, Henry W. [PS/TB, #1, #2]: foreman millwright; obt..—BT 11/28/1914; worked P&S 20 years—BI 12/5/1914.

Small, Isaac: ship carpenter; working with Morton Sanford when latter killed; later injured—BT 8/13/1901; Lemont St.

Small, Lemuel C. [C/S]: subcontractor; decorative painter.

Snipe, ? [PS/TB]

Snow, A. [PS/TB]

Sonia, John E. [PS/TB, *, #2]: planker; one of four old men who framed the WINSLOW—SB; mentioned as one of Mitchell's pallbearers; 21 Dummer Street Court.

Soule, Sam [*]

Southard, James: teamster; injured when jammed between two timbers—BT 1/25/1901.

Spicer, Thomas E. [#3]: rigger.

Spinney, James Clifford [#1, #3]: longtime P&S bookkeeper and office manager; assistant superintendent succeeding Eliakim McCabe, who became master builder for Pendleton operation in former Donnell yard.

Spinney, Levi: fastener; injured by lightning bolt that killed Miller—BE 7/16/1902; 177 Middle St.

Spinney, Timothy: "employee of the Percy & Small yard" fractured collar bones and received concussion falling into hold of the CORA F. CRESSY from lower deckbeam—BT 6/17/1912.

?Stearns, Hobart [BT]: teamster; injured by horse while pulling load of sawdust out of P&S; 954 High St.

Stewart, James C. [#3]: ship carpenter.

Still, J. [PS/TB]

Stinson, Harry [PS/TB, C/S]: subcontractor; boatbuilder; built many of the schooner yawl boats; leased P&S the land for storage and office; 266 Washington St.

Stinson, John P. [#1, #2]: beveler; father of Harry.

Stuart, J. C. [PS/TB]

Sturtevant, Fred [CAC]: joiner.

Sullivan, J. H. [PS/TB]

Sylvester, Frank [*]: blacksmith; 23 Cherry St.

Thebeau, Louis B. [#2, SB]: ship carpenter; dies suddenly, "for past nine years employed at P&S," obt.—*BE* 7/16/1902; native of Nova Scotia and father of Eugene Thebeau who was third member of triumvirate to rebuild Bath Iron Works prior to WW II.

Thomas, S. [PS/TB]

Tobey, James: ship carpenter; Captain Percy's father-in-law; fell from staging, no broken bones, sixty-eight years old—*BE* 5/16/1896; died after another fall—*BT* 7/13–14/1897.

Toothaker, Ephraim J.: caulker; killed in accident at P&S aboard the DOROTHY PALMER—*BT* 12/6/1910; 117 Oak St.

Totman, Frank [PS/TB, #2]: teamster; "the teamster"—*BT* 8/16/1900; 74 Western Ave.

Trafton, ? [PS/TB]

Trainor, Archibald [#2]: ship carpenter; 25 Shaw St.

Travers, W. [PS/TB]

Traverse, Stephen W. [PS/TB]: ship's carpenter; foot jammed by timber—*BT* 2/29/1897; 928 High St.

Trott, Edwin [C/S]: subcontractor; decorative painting.

Varner, Charles: blacksmith; hit in eye by hammer—*BT* 11/3/1903.

Varney, Elisha: blacksmith, foreman blacksmith; while working at Reed yard goes to aid of little girl hit by trolley—*BT* 9/18/1900.

Vaughan, Henry: teamster; at scene of lightning strike—*BI* 7/19/1902; obt.—*BT* 3/20/1912; 16 Granite St.

Warner, Harry D. [#1]: 320 Washington St.

Warnes, E. [PS/TB]

Warren, Frank [#3]: painter.

Watson, W. H. [C/S]: subcontractor; ship plumber.

Waugh, George [#1]: 1096 Washington St.

Weber, J. [PS/TB]

Welsh, E. J. [PS/TB]

West, James [PS/TB]: ship carpenter; overcome by heat—*BT* 9/11/1897; 263 Washington St.

White, C. [PS/TB]

White, Fred [RO]: inboard joiner.

White, John S.: caulker; formerly employed by Oliver and Tibbets, obt.—*BT* 11/26/1906.

Wildes, J. [PS/TB]

Williams, Melville C. [PS/TB, *, #2]: ship carpenter; Washington near Hunt.

Wilson, E. [PS/TB]

Woodman, B. [PS/TB]

Worrey, Frank [CAC]: painter.

Wright, Alvin [CAC]: rigger.

Wright, E. [PS/TB]

Wright, Holden [JHC/TB]: sparmaker.

Youland, S. [PS/TB]

Zwicker, Harding [*]

Bibliography

MANUSCRIPT SOURCES

Private Collections

CAPTAINS DOUGLAS K. AND LINDA J. LEE COLLECTION
Newspaper Clipping Files
OAKLEY C. CURTIS Log Books, 14 May 1915–
8 August 1917
Percy & Small Schooner Files
Photograph Files
Plan and Reconstructed Plan Files
Specifications, Schooner #43

CAPTAIN W. J. L. PARKER COLLECTION
Building Cost Estimates and Accounts
Construction Bill Files
Construction Contracts
Earnings Statements: CORA F. CRESSY
Earnings Statements: EDWARD B. WINSLOW
Miscellaneous Papers
Personal Research Files
Plan Files
Photograph Files
Specifications for Schooners

Public Collections
CITY OF BATH
Assessor's Records

MAINE MARITIME MUSEUM
William A. Baker Collection, MS-57
City of Bath Ship Books, MS-46

James Cameron Papers, MS-89
Frederick Drake Papers, MS-197
James Drake Papers (includes Humphreys Survey
Notebooks), MS-8
Mark W. Hennessy Research Papers, MS-53
William F. Palmer Collection, MS-50
Percy & Small Journal, 1894–1908, MS-157
Percy & Small Materials Lists and Memoranda (on
loan from the Small family)
Percy & Small Time Book #5 (23 July 1898–
24 December 1899), SM 44/5
Percy & Small Workmen Interviews (Tapes and
Outline Transcripts)
Sewall Family Papers, MS-22
Small Manuscript Collection (SM)

EDMUND BLUNT LIBRARY, MYSTIC (CONNECTICUT)
SEAPORT MUSEUM
Schooner EDWARD J. LAWRENCE File
Various J. S. Winslow Schooner Earnings, Microfilm
Roll 80

SAGADAHOC COUNTY COURT HOUSE, BATH
Sagadahoc County Probate Court Records
Sagadahoc County Registry of Deeds

BOOKS AND PERIODICALS
Albion, Robert G., et al. *New England and the Sea.*
Middletown, CT: Wesleyan University Press for the
Marine Historical Association, Incorporated, 1972.
Baker, William Avery. *A Maritime History of Bath,*

Maine, and the Kennebec River Region. 2 vols. Bath, ME: Marine Research Society of Bath, 1973.

Brooks, Bryant B. *Memoirs of Bryant B. Brooks.* Glendale, CA: Arthur H. Clark Company, 1939.

Bump, Morrison. "Notes on the Palmer Fleet." Unpublished manuscript.

Bunting, W. H. *A Day's Work: A Sampler of Historic Maine Photographs, 1860–1920, Part I.* Gardiner, ME: Tilbury House, Publishers, 1997.

Chapelle, Howard I. *The History of American Sailing Ships.* New York: W. W. Norton, 1935.

Cochran, Thomas C. and William Miller. *The Age of Enterprise: A Social History of Industrial America.* New York: The MacMillan Company, 1942.

Currier, Isabel. "Captain Harold G. Foss—Master of Sail and Steam." *Down East* (September 1963): 24–28, 48.

_____. "Captain Stinson W. Davis, Maine Master of Sail and Steam." *Down East* (May 1970): 48–50, 55.

Desmond, Charles. *Wooden Shipbuilding.* New York: Rudder Publishing Co., 1919.

Dickman, Francois M. "America's Largest Wooden Vessel: The Six-Masted Schooner Wyoming." *Wyoming Annals* (spring/summer 1994): 38–49.

Duncan, Roger F. *Coastal Maine: A Maritime History.* New York: W. W. Norton, 1992.

Estep, H. Cole. *How Wooden Ships Are Built.* Cleveland, OH: Penton Publishing Co., 1918.

Everson, Jennie G. *Tidewater Ice of the Kennebec River.* Maine Heritage Series No. 1. Freeport, ME: The Bond Wheelright Co. for the Maine State Museum, 1970.

Fairburn, William Armstrong. *Merchant Sail.* Ed. by Ethel M. Ritchie. 6 vols. Center Lovell, ME: Fairburn Marine Educational Foundation, Inc., 1945–1955.

Gardiner, Robert, ed. *The Advent of Steam: The Merchant Steamship Before 1900.* London: Conway Maritime Press Ltd., 1993.

_____, ed. *Cogs, Caravels and Galleons: The Sailing Ship 1000–1650.* London: Conway Maritime Press Ltd., 1994.

_____, ed. *Sail's Last Century: The Merchant Sailing Ship 1830–1930.* London: Conway Maritime Press Ltd., 1993.

Greenhill, Basil. *The Archaeology of the Boat.* Middletown, CT: Wesleyan University Press, 1976.

_____ and Sam Manning. *The Schooner Bertha L. Downs.* London: Conway Maritime Press Ltd., 1995.

Haskell, Loren E. "The Glamorous Six-Masters." *Down East* (April 1965): 20–25.

_____. "The Second Palmer Fleet." *Down East* (May 1968): 26–31, 49ff.

Heffernan, John Paul. "A Winter Voyage on the Six-Master 'Wyoming.'" *Down East* (January 1970): 48–50.

Humiston, Fred. *Blue Water Men—and Women.* Portland, ME: Guy Gannett Publishing Co., 1965.

Hutchins, J. G. B. *The American Maritime Industries and Public Policy, 1789–1914.* Cambridge, MA: Harvard University Press, 1941.

Kaiser, Frederick F. *Built on Honor, Sailed with Skill: The American Coasting Schooner.* Ann Arbor, MI: Sarah Jennings Press, 1989.

_____. "Six-Masted Schooner Began Short New Era for U. S. Sail." *National Fisherman* (August 1978): 46–48.

Laurence, Frederick Sturgis. *Coasting Passage.* 2nd ed. Concord, MA: Charles S. Morgan, 1968.

Lee, Captain Douglas K. "The Reconstruction of Plans for the Five-Masted Schooner CORA F. CRESSY." A paper presented at the Maine Maritime Museum Symposium, Bath, May 1992.

Lipfert, Nathan. "The Shipyard Worker and the Iron Shipyard." *The Log of Mystic Seaport* 35, no. 3 (fall, 1983).

Lyman, John, ed. *Log Chips.* Washington, DC: 1948–59.

Marine Steam. New York: Babcock & Wilcox Company, 1928.

Martin, Kenneth, and Ralph Linwood Snow. *The Pattens of Bath: A Seagoing Dynasty.* Bath, ME: Maine Maritime Museum/Patten Free Library, 1996.

Mead, Janet Cutler. *Bent Sails.* Cincinnati, OH: Mail It, Inc., 1962.

Morgan, Charles S. "Master in Sail & Steam: The Notable Career of One Maine Shipmaster." A paper presented at the Maritime History Symposium at the Maine Maritime Museum, Bath, May 1981.

_____. "New England Coasting Schooners." *The American Neptune* XXIII, no. 1 (January 1963).

Morison, Samuel Eliot. *The Oxford History of the American People.* New York: Oxford University Press, 1965.

Nealey, Robert. "Far Away—and Long Ago." *Down East* (July 1963): 40–43, 47.

Owens, Henry W. *The Edward Clarence Plummer History of Bath.* Bath, ME: The Times Co., 1936.

Parker, Captain W. J. Lewis. *The Great Coal Schooners of New England, 1870–1909.* Mystic, CT: Marine Historical Association, 1948.

_____. "Percy & Small, Shipbuilders and Shipowners, 1894–1920." A paper presented at the Maine Maritime Museum Symposium, Bath, May 1973.

_____. "Problems of Ship Management and Operation 1870–1900." *National Maritime Museum (Greenwich) Maritime Monographs and Reports,* no. 5 (1972): 17–24.

_____. "The Schooner in America." Robert Gardiner, ed. *Sail's Last Century: The Merchant Sailing Ship 1830–1930.* London: Conway Maritime Press Ltd., 1993.

Quinn, William P. *Shipwrecks Around Boston.* Hyannis, MA: Parnassus Imprints, 1996.

Rowe, William Hutchinson. *The Maritime History of Maine: Three Centuries of Shipbuilding and Seafaring.* 1948. Reprinted with new Introduction. Gardiner, ME: Harpswell Press, 1989.

Rowland, John T. *Wind and Salt Spray: The Autobiography of a Sailor.* New York: W.W. Norton, 1965.

Rumsey, Barbara. *Hodgdon Shipbuilding and Mills: A Documentary History of the First Hundred Years, 1816–1916.* East Boothbay, ME: Winnegance House, 1995.

Sands, John, and Ralph L. Snow, eds. *Wooden Shipbuilding and Small Craft Preservation.* Washington, DC: National Trust for Historic Preservation, 1976.

Snow, Ralph Linwood. *The Bath Iron Works: The First Hundred Years.* Bath, ME: Maine Maritime Museum, 1987.

_____. "Oh Shenandoah: Captain James F. Murphy and the Daughter of the Stars." A paper presented at the Maine Maritime Museum Symposium, Bath, May 1993.

_____. "The Restoration of Percy & Small Shipyard: Reasons and Directions." A paper presented at the Maine Maritime Museum Symposium, Bath, May 1973.

Stevens, James P. *Reminiscences of a Boothbay Shipbuilder.* Boothbay, ME: Boothbay Region Historic Society, 1993.

Trowbridge, J. T. *Lawrence's Adventures.* Boston, 1870.

NEWSPAPERS

American Sentinel (Bath)

Bath Anvil

Bath Daily Times

Bath Enterprise

Bath Independent

Bath Sentinel

Boston Globe

Courier-Gazette (Rockland)

Natrona County Tribune (Wyoming)

New York Journal of Commerce and Industry

New York Maritime Register

Philadelphia Press

Portland Express

Portland Press Herald

Zion's Advocate (Portland)

Index

Baltimore & Ohio Railroad 11
Barcelona (SPN) 191
Barge losses 266
Barge/tug competition 258–59, 261, 265
Baring Brothers 18
Barker, Captain James Platt 221
Barlow, Captain George F. 201, 214, 235–36
Barnes, Captain Charles H. 324
Barth, Charles 279–80
Bath (ME) 3, 4, 12, 231, 235, 239, 240, 269
Bath Daily Times 8
Bath Galvanizing Works 44, 164
Bath Iron Works 4, 38, 110, 133, 156, 171, 300, 304
Bath Marine Band 3, 7
Bath Marine Museum 342; *see also:* Maine Maritime Museum and Marine Research Society of Bath
Bay of Biscay 240
B. B. Brooks & Company 228, 231
Bean, Holly M. 74–75, 205
Bean, Robert 205
Beebe, William 307–08
BENJAMIN F. POOLE 37, 214
Bermuda 320
Bernardston (MA) 228
Berry & Richardson shipyard 39
Blackburn, Samuel P. 37
Blaisdell, Daniel Orrin 38, 39–42, 75; *see also:* D. O. Blaisdell shipyard
Block Island (RI) 273
Boca Grande Pass 36
Boggs, Elizabeth T. 308
BOHEMIA 16
Bohndell, Christian Henry 166, 168
Boothbay Harbor (ME) 199
Boston (MA) 11–12, 180, 200, 207, 214, 218, 224, 235–36, 239–40, 242, 252, 255, 261, *262*, 294
Boston Lightship 200–01
Boston & Lockport Block Company 218
Boston & Maine Railroad 268
Boston Naval Shipyard 133, 337–38
Bowdoin College (ME) 304
Bowker, Captain Francis "Biff," quoted: 309–10
Bowker, Frank S. 324
Brava seamen 255

Brazil 286, 293
Bremen (ME) 224
BRINA P. PENDLETON 299
Brisbane (AUS) 271
Broad Sound 201
Brooks, Abby *229, 231*, 231–33
Brooks, Governor Bryant B. 228, *229*, 233, 236, 242
Brooks, John 6, 67, 228–30, *229*, 242
Brooks, John B. "Cadet" 284
Brooks, Lena 6–7, *7*, 228, *229*
Brooks, Mrs. Bryant B. 6, 7, *229*
Brunel, Isambard K. 13
Brunswick (GA) 214, 218, 240, 275
B. R. WOODSIDE 18
Buenos Aires (ARG) 215, 236, 239
Bunker, Captain G. W. 275
Burden, Dr. Charles E. 342
Bureau Veritas 23, 96

C

Cahill, Charles 66, 225
Cahill, Mrs. Osceola 288
Cahill, Osceola "Ocea" 66–68, 225, 228, 239, 242
CAMDEN, SS 4
Cape Canaveral (FL) 317
Cape Charles (VA) 273
Cape Cod (MA) 226, 234–35, 258, 261, 267, 273, 293
Cape Cod Canal 267, 286
Cape Hatteras 95
Cape Henry (VA) 273
Cape Horn 13–14, 16, 170, 272
Cape Polonio (URU) 215
Cape Race (NFD) 192
CARL F. CRESSY (P&S Hull #32) 191–92, 287, *292*, 292–94, 350
Carleton, Clarence 31
Carnegie, William C. 76
Carrabelle (FL) 239
CARRIE A. NORTON 18
Cartagena (SPN) 205
Casco Bay (ME) 240
Casper (WY) 228
Catholic Sea Cadets 311